# Gulliver's Troubles, Or the Setting of American Foreign Policy

# Gulliver's Troubles, Or the Setting of American Foreign Policy

STANLEY HOFFMANN

*A Volume in the Series*
*"The Atlantic Policy Studies"*

Published for the Council on Foreign Relations by

McGRAW-HILL BOOK COMPANY

*New York   Toronto   London   Sydney*

Gulliver's Troubles, Or the Setting
of American Foreign Policy

*Copyright © 1968 by Council on Foreign Relations, Inc.*
All Rights Reserved.
Printed in the United States of America.
This book, or parts thereof, may not be reproduced
in any form without permission of the Proprietor,
Council on Foreign Relations,
58 East 68th Street, New York, New York 10021.

Library of Congress Catalog Card Number: 68-13516
    456789101112131415 VBVB 754321069

29196

*To Inge*

# The Atlantic Policy Studies

The Atlantic Policy Studies is a series of major works on the future of the Atlantic Community. The project was undertaken by the Council on Foreign Relations assisted by a generous grant from the Ford Foundation. Mr. Hoffmann's book, which grew out of a series of lectures delivered at the Council in the spring of 1965, is the ninth to be published in the series. This volume reviews the constraints, particularly the domestic constraints, on United States policy in Atlantic affairs and their significance for future policy.

Undertaken out of a conviction that a re-examination of U. S. relations with and policies toward Western Europe is urgently needed, the Atlantic Policy Studies are an attempt to come to grips with basic questions about the future of America's Atlantic relations.

The studies are policy-oriented, seeking not only to describe and forecast but also to prescribe. Each of the ten studies is the responsibility of its author, but considers its special problems in the light of the general aim of the program as a whole. The program is under the guidance of a Steering Committee, of which Charles M. Spofford is chairman.

The Atlantic Policy Studies are divided into four broad categories, dealing respectively with the broad strategic problems of the Atlantic Alliance; with economic relations among the Atlantic countries and between them and less developed countries; with the external environment of the West; and with Atlantic political relations.

Mr. Hoffmann's book is one of three in the series dealing with political relations among the Atlantic nations. Miriam Camps of Chatham House and the Council on Foreign Relations wrote a volume on the future of European unity, *European Unification in the Sixties: From the Veto to the Crisis,* published in 1966. A third political volume, by the Director of the Atlantic Policy Studies, *The Atlantic Idea and its European Rivals,* published late in 1966, addresses the question of the future shape of political relations among the Atlantic countries.

Two studies of the Atlantic world's external environment have been made: *Alternative to Partition* by Zbigniew K. Brzezinski of Columbia University, published by McGraw-Hill in May 1965, proposed a new American approach to the problems of a divided Europe. A study by Theodore Geiger of the National Planning Association, *The Conflicted Relationship: The West and the Transformation of Asia, Africa, and Latin America,* published in February 1967, examined the nature of the great transition now going on throughout the three continents in which development is hoped for —not always realistically.

Atlantic military problems are considered in their political context in Henry A. Kissinger's *The Troubled Partnership: A Re-appraisal of the Atlantic Alliance,* which McGraw-Hill published in April 1965.

Four studies have been made of the economic issues facing the Atlantic nations. *Atlantic Agricultural Unity: Is It Possible?* by John O. Coppock, was published in 1966. John Pincus's volume, *Trade, Aid and Development: The Rich and Poor Nations,* which discusses the role Atlantic trade and aid can play in the economic growth of the developing countries, was published in January 1967. Bela Balassa's analysis of the effects of various liberalization measures was published in June 1967 under the title, *Trade Liberalization Among Industrial Countries: Objectives and Alternatives.* In a fourth volume dealing essentially with economic issues, Richard N. Cooper of Yale University will examine international financial arrangements and monetary policies among industrialized nations.

HAROLD VAN B. CLEVELAND
Director, Atlantic Policy Studies
Council on Foreign Relations

# Contents

# PART IV.  FOREIGN POLICY REVISITED

# Introduction

In Albert Camus' most striking play, Caligula discovered that however much he wanted the moon, he could not get it; he also discovered that the nihilistic use of absolute power was suicidal. This book will try to determine what the United States, with its enormous power, can attempt and expect to achieve in the Atlantic area, what ends and purposes it is realistic to have in mind, and what means it will be wise to use in order to achieve them. I am interested in establishing what the United States can or cannot do, given the kind of nation it is, in the kind of world we have. Purposes that go against the grain of a nation's deepest beliefs or habits, or against the grain of the world in which it is trying to fulfill such purposes, are not sound. Power at a nation's disposal ought to be used in full awareness of the external conditions that define which uses are productive and which are not, as well as of the domestic predispositions and institutions that channel national energies in certain directions or inhibit the country from applying them in other ways.

The lectures on which this book is based, delivered at the Council on Foreign Relations in April–May 1965, were entitled "Restraints on American Policy." But I realized in the course of later discussions that the word "restraint" or "constraint" was too restrictive and constricting—not only because I was also concerned with analyzing the choices open to American policy, but because one normally associates constraint with external pressure, not with internal reflexes or imperatives or inhibitions. We are not used to calling a person's heredity or temper or habits "restraints" on his personality; indeed, they define his identity. Yet, one's character is at the same time the source of one's acts and the limit of one's possibilities; it explains the courses of action one takes, while excluding others. The term "environment" is better able to designate both the domestic conditions that affect how statesmen move and the external milieu that they try to affect, but it also gives the misleading impression that these conditions and milieu are outside the statesman's mental and operational universe. It does not convey the sense of entanglement I wish to stress, for often both the national and international worlds are to the statesman what Nessus' tunic was to Hercules: the harder he tries to remove them, the more lethal they become. Perhaps the word "setting" communicates no better the idea that the world beyond the statesman's national boundaries and the circumstances within them inescapably condition his acts and shape his choices, but I believe that "setting" is less inappropriate and shall use it here.

The student of foreign policy must avoid two pitfalls. The first one is the unwitting presentation of foreign policy as a kind of residue —what is left after all the external constraints and domestic imperatives have been taken into account. Foreign policy is no more determined by its setting than Supreme Court decisions are dictated by the Constitution: in both cases, the statesmanship lies in discovering what is clearly ruled out, what is possible within the frame of reference, and how that frame can be stretched without damage. The setting is a challenge, not a *diktat,* comparable in this respect to the rules of French classical theater: the playwright's obligation to observe the rules was both a constraint that eliminated certain kinds of actions and a goad to his imagination. However, the rules of drama were clear and unmistakable, whereas the foreign policy setting is controversial and flexible.

The second pitfall is exactly the opposite: mistaking foreign policy for the mere definition of valuable ends and the mere selection of the best means to reach them. A foreign policy setting does not abolish the creativity of statecraft, but creativity does not operate in a vacuum. The statesman is not a Michelangelo who gives to stone or clay whatever shape his vision requires. Yet, in a country with unparalleled power, considerable self-confidence, and a protective tradition which Arnold Wolfers has called the "Anglo-American tradition in foreign affairs"—one that stresses choice and is impatient with necessity—the tendency to make this mistake is almost irresistible. This is what Denis Brogan has called the "illusion of omnipotence." It shares with the illusion of determinism the assumption that making foreign policy is easy. For if it is true that the limits are compelling, clear, and close, then foreign policy is simply what is left after one has taken them all into consideration; and foreign policy is simply a matter of making up one's mind and using one's tools cleverly if "the limits . . . are on a distant and receding horizon; for many practical purposes they are what we think we can accomplish and what we think it is necessary to accomplish at any given time." [1] *O sancta simplicitas!* Even if the outside world were to the statesman exactly as clay or stone is to the sculptor, he still could not choose his aims in complete "freedom," insofar as they would be inspired largely by his own experience, shaped by his values, born of his expectations. It is only if we are aware of how our selection of goals, our vision, reflects our character that we may become truly free. Moreover, the world is never so amenable to our vision, and freedom also depends on the awareness of the relevance or irrelevance of our preferred goals to the world we live in. In foreign policy, too, one cannot master nature if one does not first obey it.

This book, dealing with American foreign policy, argues against the illusion of omnipotence rather than the illusion of determinism. Much of the present crisis of the Atlantic Alliance is due to a tendency of policy-makers to approach the issues somewhat along these lines: "This is the area of our common interests (or, these are the supreme national interests), and we must promote them by active leadership and all means at our disposal." In other words, "This is what we should do, and this is how we ought to do it." The procedure I would recommend is more complex: "Given the interests and aims of our friends and foes, and given our own values and institutions, our own concerns and hopes, what ought we to be doing? And what, in the present circumstances, can we and can we not do?" In other words, "How much freedom of action do we actually have? What is imperative, imposed by our world and our own nature? What is prohibited in this setting? What is desirable and easily obtainable? What is desirable, yet attainable only with skill and some difficulty and only by changing what can be changed?"

Such an approach suggests, first, that the definition of a foreign policy is a much more subtle, difficult, and challenging task than the attitude I paraphrased first would indicate. Indeed, like artistic creation, it should be inspired by the French saying *"on ne s'appuie que sur ce qui résiste."* Second, some of the difficulty and challenge occurs because the limitations imposed by the setting are not all of the same kind: some are intractable, others are only temporary; some can be overcome only at a cost that may well exceed the expected benefits from the change, others must be overcome if the nation is to reach goals that are deemed indispensable. Once again, it is clear that the task is one of painful creation, not mechanical adjustment.

[1] Joseph Jones, *The Fifteen Weeks* (New York: Viking, 1955), p. 262.

For the making of foreign policy is not merely adaptation to the world outside in accordance with one's own nature; as I have written in another context, "the very task of statesmanship consists of selecting the most favorable interpretation of the facts, whenever the lessons they carry are ambiguous; or choosing the most subtle and dignified form of submission, when the lesson is beyond debate; and, most importantly, of trying to change the facts whenever they are intolerable but it is in the nation's interest to transform them." [2]

What makes statecraft exciting to the statesman and fascinating to the scholar is precisely that it consists of assessing, exploiting, and shaping uncertainty: it emanates from a milieu—the domestic society—whose values, political and social institutions, experiences, and patterns of authority are never entirely fixed or coherent, never point in only one direction, and, while ruling out certain choices, leave a considerable margin for maneuver, just as the body of judicial precedents leaves a wide area of choice to the Supreme Court; and statecraft operates in a milieu—the international system—that has repeatedly been defined as an arena of competition for multiple stakes, with uncertain rules which the players (especially the major ones) hammer out by trial and error, and characterized by moves which, however cleverly calculated, are more like wagers than rational adaptations of means to ends. (At worst, they are hair-raising gambles and, at best, inspired stabs in the dark.)

The problem of attaining freedom of action in foreign affairs is complicated not only because the intractability of the setting varies so widely, but also because the factors that affect freedom do so at two different stages—or, to put it another way, there are two different ingredients of freedom of action in foreign policy. The first, and most obvious, is its *indeterminacy*. The questions the statesman must therefore ask before he defines his ends and his means, are: "How much choice do I actually have? How compelling are the foreign and domestic forces I must take into account? What liberty do geography, my neighbors' (or rivals') policies, my resources, the stability and effectiveness of my political system, the morale of my people leave me with?" There are times when the margin is narrowed to a choice among different forms of death—for instance, Poland at the end of August 1939; when the choice is between disaster and response to a challenge—for instance, the United States in the fateful

---

[2] Stanley Hoffmann *et al., In Search of France* (Cambridge, Mass.: Harvard University Press, 1963), Ch. I, "Paradoxes of the French Political Community," p. 74.

winter of 1946–47; and when the margin is much wider—for instance, Hitler's Germany between 1935 and 1939. The second element is just as important but not always so well understood. One danger of using the so-called "decision-making approach" to foreign policy is that, in focusing attention on how the decision is made, one may neglect what happens after the decision has been made. Now decisions are made literally for effect, and they are not like pebbles thrown in a pond, designed to cause a few ripples, after which the water returns to calm. They are, to use a formula of Malraux's, attempts to leave a scar on history. Power is not merely stock that one keeps in storage and does one's loving best to increase; it is a relation; it is the art of moving others. Stock that can be freely accumulated but cannot be used, a decision freely made but without impact —these are symbols of frustration. The freedom the statesman wants is freedom for *effective* action; the decision he wants to make is the decision most likely to affect others (or his own people) in the way he intends; effectiveness is the art of reaching one's goal so that it serves one's interests.

One reason for stressing the importance of these *two* elements is that there are frequent discrepancies or disproportionalities between them. Often, in a setting that considerably narrows the area of choice, in which action is very largely dictated by huge writings on the wall without and by reflexes and impulses within, the statesman finds his greatest opportunity to move others and to shape the world: this, it seems to me, was where Churchill's greatness lay in 1940. At other times, when the indeterminacy is great and the forces within and without are complex and contradictory enough to give the statesman a large loan of freedom, he may nevertheless be unable to do more than scratch the surface of history—either because the world is like a landscape dotted with fences and hedges and woods that stop or slow down the explorer, or else because he does not have the energy and resilience to pursue his course effectively. Thus, when we look at the international system, we must remember that some of its characteristics may impel or rule out certain possibilities, whereas others, not apparently compelling, nevertheless may prove to be powerfully detrimental to the success of the choices made. And, when we look at the internal national situation, we must remember that some of its factors similarly limit choice and others may reduce the effectiveness of the chosen act.

In a way, all the volumes written for the Atlantic Policy Studies of the Council on Foreign Relations deal with the "setting" and the "choices" as I have defined them here. This is particularly true of the works of Henry Kissinger and Zbigniew Brzezinski, who discuss new conditions in the relations between the United States and Western Europe, between the Soviet Union and its East European satellites, and the courses of action open to the United States in its efforts to reshape the Western alliance and promote European unification.[3] This volume, however, differs from the other works in the series. First, I intend to examine the present international system *as a whole,* rather than to concentrate on those segments of the system that make up the Western alliance, or what was once called the Soviet bloc, or the underdeveloped countries. For I remain convinced that the best way to understand any fragment of a "social whole" is to start with an approximation of the whole; less abstractly, that the events which have provoked far-reaching changes within the two camps in the Cold War are of a general and fundamental nature that can best be analyzed at the "systemic" level, to use the scholarly jargon.

Second, I will examine the domestic setting of American policy—American style and America's institutions—in order to see how and to what extent American values, experiences, traditions, government, and bureaucracy affect the area of choice and the effectiveness of decisions. Here, I will deliberately, and insistently, accentuate the negative, precisely because my goal is to show as clearly as possible whatever limits our choices and our effectiveness.

Third, I will return to the international milieu, this time specifically to the Western alliance, and analyze the impact of the present international system on political relations between the United States and its European allies. My discussion of the alternatives available to the United States and of their effectiveness will be less detailed than that of other writers in this series; their primary concern is to make policy recommendations, whereas mine is to demarcate the area of effective choice.

It is in part because other writers in the series have taken up the task of analyzing the Atlantic Alliance in detail that I have preferred to be analytic at a more general level and to review the main policy recommendations rather than propose new ones. But I am willing to recognize that my approach (and its shortcomings) reflect even

---

[3] Henry A. Kissinger, *The Troubled Partnership* (New York: McGraw Hill, 1965) and Zbigniew Brzezinski, *Alternative to Partition* (New York: McGraw Hill, 1965).

more my "internal setting"—my inclinations and experiences. My own interests go in the direction of theory (in the rather loose and modest sense of a network of questions about the principal features of international relations, a systematic effort to understand its determinants and logic) rather than in the direction of policy. One should not expect an apple tree to produce cherries—one should judge it by the quality of its apples. A man without practical experience as a policy-maker or as an adviser to policy-makers is unlikely to contribute much by usurping a role for which he is unqualified; his best chance of being useful lies precisely in the realm of academic analysis. Indeed, the value of prescriptions is not unrelated to the strength of the basic analysis.

Second, there is no doubt that the kind of analysis to be found in these pages reflects something of the author's own background—and that the effect of this background is ambiguous, as much an asset as a liability. There may be an asset in my remoteness from the heady delights and exalting ordeals of statecraft, and in the measure of my detachment from a country that has been mine for less than a third of my life. But distance does not guarantee objectivity, and the drawback is that my own values, intellectual approaches, and prejudices, acquired in a European youth and training, will inevitably color the tone and shape the analysis. Another drawback lies in my training as a political scientist, interested in economic affairs but quite incapable of making any worthwhile contribution in that domain—hence my decision to leave it out altogether. But, as I have said, knowledge is the beginning of freedom: my own awareness of my shortcomings will allow me, I hope, to guard against them, and the reader, thus warned, will be free to accept or reject my assertions.

A first version of this volume was finished in the summer of 1966; an edited and revised version was completed in May 1967; minor changes, designed to take account of subsequent events and of various publications that had not been available to me earlier, were made in September 1967.

I want to express my gratitude to Mr. Harold van B. Cleveland, Director of the Atlantic Policy Studies program, who, with constant generosity and good humor, has encouraged me and trusted me. I want to acknowledge my intellectual debt to my wife, to whose ideas, suggestions and criticisms this manuscript owes a great deal, and to Mrs. Elisabeth Sifton, who has edited it with skill, style, speed, creative thoroughness and wit. And I want to thank the Director and staff of the Center for Advanced Study in the Behavioral Sciences at Stanford, California, who provided a beautiful and peaceful setting for writing this study of a world that is all too often neither.

S. H.

# PART I

# The World Outside

CHAPTER ONE

# The Nature
# of the Problem

## I. The Crisis of Complexity

Official American government statements, authoritative studies, and press comments on Atlantic affairs during the past few years show two recurrent themes. First, there is a serious crisis of the North Atlantic Treaty Organization, which is "flawed by increasingly sharp disputes among the allies," marred by "absence of agreement on major policies." [1] Second, whether in the Atlantic Alliance, or in the United Nations, or even in areas it once took for granted, such as Latin America, the United States finds it difficult to make its policies popular and to induce other governments to share them. However much presidential aspirants and academic writers issue calls for "bold leadership," a "dynamic style" and "fresh ideas," the presidents and their advisers are faced with the burden of having to make a myriad of decisions and with the frustrations of the "outer limits of decision." [2]

Neither complaint is new, neither situation original. The Atlantic Alliance has always been in ferment, not only because of the many challenges to which it has been subjected by its enemies and to which its members have not always responded in full harmony, but also because the initiatives taken by some of its partners have frequently created turmoil and dissent. Americans remember how France let the European Defense Community slowly die of political leukemia, and they now observe how de Gaulle has gradually withdrawn from NATO; they remember the British and French fiasco at Suez; they grumble over the constant need to reassure West Ger-

[1] Theodore C. Sorensen, *Decision-Making in the White House* (New York: Columbia University Press, 1963), Ch. 3.
[2] Same.

many and over the intransigence that used to mark Bonn's policy whenever *détente* was in the air. Europeans remember America's relentless pressure for German rearmament, which disrupted the incipient progress of West European integration; they have been bewildered by frequent changes in its strategic doctrine and estimates, and by contradictions between stated policies, exhortations, and behavior.

Similarly, stringent limits have been placed on American foreign policy throughout the postwar period. The build-up of Western strength has not persuaded the Russians to negotiate broad agreements "registering the existing facts," contrary to Dean Acheson's hopes; [3] America's allies have again and again disregarded its pressures or advice in areas of vital interest to them. The United States has not been in the easiest of positions: it is caught between allies that try to blackmail it out of weakness and allies that flout it because of their pretension to strength; between allies that want to push it to take a "tough" line and allies or friends eager for relaxation; between third parties at odds with one another, none of which it can afford to antagonize; between allies suspicious of any unilateral move it might make toward Moscow and a foe with which common interests have emerged; between colonial powers asking for its support on behalf of an alliance it cannot afford to undermine and anticolonial powers it cannot afford to leave to the exclusive courtship of its rivals. Just as the presidency is the most impressive yet lonely position in the American government, the United States has been in the most powerful yet difficult position in the world.

It is important, however, to recognize when a change of degree becomes a change in kind. Insofar as the Atlantic Alliance is concerned, there is a difference in kind between the earlier troubles and the present disarray: it is the difference between a crisis *in* the Alliance and a crisis *of* the Alliance which puts into question the very future of the Alliance itself. Insofar as America's freedom of action is concerned, there is a difference in kind between the world of the late 1940s and the world today. In record time, there has been a switch from a period in which the United States' margin of indeterminacy was very narrow but its capacity to affect events great, to a period in which the margin seems broader and the capacity less. In 1947–48, the United States had to consider the collapse of British power in the Middle East, the political and economic demise of Europe, the op-

---

[3] See Coral Bell, *Negotiations from Strength* (London: Chatto & Windus, 1962), p. 14.

portunities opened by misery and civil strife for Communist success, and the skill with which Stalin played his cards. It had a simple choice between abdicating from leadership, which would have been a refusal to act as a great power, and deciding to play such a role: "Rarely has freedom been more clearly the recognition of necessity, and statesmanship the imaginative exploitation of necessity." [4] The rescue of Greece and Turkey, the economic restoration of Western Europe, the beginnings of European cooperation, the consolidation of West Germany, the signing of the North Atlantic Treaty, the use of the United Nations as an instrument against North Korean aggression, the launching of foreign-aid programs—these were acts that transformed and defined the international reality. There were failures and frustrations, especially in the Far East; but many argued that they were due, not to the external limits placed on America's power there, but to America's failure to apply its power. Now, the bipolar contest was not its choice, the ideological battles of communism against the West and anticolonial nationalism against Western empires were not its initiatives, the nuclear race was not its preference. But, where power was applied, despite the sharp constraints of a world America had not at all desired, the United States' capacity to affect events was undeniable.

This world imposed an imperative: the resistance to Soviet imperialism. American leaders, scarred or scared by the experience of the 1930s, were moved by the "vital 'myth' " [5] of the Munich analogy to contain "Communist aggression" with militant fervor. What had to be

[4] See my *The State of War* (New York: Frederick A. Praeger, 1965), p. 163. I agree with the idea of Arthur Schlesinger, Jr. (in "Origins of the Cold War," *Foreign Affairs,* October 1967, pp. 22–52) that the Cold War "was the product not of a decision, but of a dilemma," and that today's "revisionists" underestimate the degree to which the Soviet Union, in 1945, was "not a traditional national state." Even apart from its ideological nature, Cold War between the two superpowers would have erupted for traditional power reasons —those of bipolar confrontation. Settlements would have been difficult in any case, but, of course, the ideological nature of the contest ruled them out. To say that the contest was unavoidable short of appeasement by the United States is *not* to see the Cold War "as a pure case of Russian aggression and American response." America's moves were often clumsy and excessive, and the Soviets' policy was a mix of ideological messianism, defensive concerns, national ambitions and flexible prudence. What is clear to this writer is that the Cold War was unavoidable then—which is no reason to condone its earlier excesses or its deadly grip over the different realities of today.

[5] Robert E. Osgood and Robert W. Tucker, *Force, Order, and Justice* (Baltimore: The Johns Hopkins Press, 1967), p. 171.

worked out was the strategy: where to resist and with what means in areas where the threat was already present, and how best to deter it wherever it was absent or only latent. With multiple answers to the many questions raised by this single imperative, America shaped much of the postwar world. Today, the world is both more comfortable and more frustrating, for there is no longer any simple command. The split between Russia and China has deeply affected the nature of Communist imperialism; military technology has created an imperative of its own, which has helped to transform the main enemy in part at least into a reluctant partner. In many areas of the world, the old imperative provides no yardstick for policy, either because it is only slightly relevant, or because it is hard to see in advance how *any* policy will help keep trouble away, or because to shape policy according to its dictates could lead to diametrically opposed policies. In other words, today's world dictates no single imperative to the United States, and it does not suggest so many possibilities that the area of choice is noticeably enlarged. The achievements of recent years do not compare with those of the earlier period. It is as if the clay which statesmen have to shape had suddenly hardened. The demise of President Kennedy's "Grand Design" for a partnership of the United States and a united Europe, the crisis of the West European communities, the restiveness of the OAS, the failure of U.N. members to follow the United States' leadership in the battle over Article 19, the fate of SEATO, the lack of effective allied support and decisive results in Vietnam—all indicate that the connection between will and achievements, between power and deeds, is no longer what it was. The "gap between what he would like and what is possible" that "every president must endure" has widened in international affairs [6] just as it seemed to be narrowing at home.

The literature on current world affairs often tries to ignore these failures—for instance by presenting an imperturbably rosy vision of the future, or by pretending that the so-called "frustrations of impotence" merely reveal "the serenity of power." [7] But for the Candides of Washington, who oscillate between the exhilaration of power and its agonies, Doctor Pangloss, however comforting his philosophy of his-

[6] Sorensen, cited, p. xii.

[7] See, for instance, Professor Walt W. Rostow's lecture at the University of Leeds, February 23, 1967, reprinted in *Department of State Bulletin,* March 27, 1967, pp. 491–504; the quote is from an article by Kenneth N. Waltz, "International Structure, National Force, and the Balance of Power," *Journal of International Affairs,* Vol. XXI, No. 2 (1967), p. 226.

tory or his reading of world politics, is not the safest academic guide
or policy adviser. Or else, the literature tends to attribute these disappointments to one or both of two factors. Perhaps because of a reflex inherited from the days when the evils that disturbed America's
contemplation of its own happy vision were easily identifiable and
hateable human beings like Hitler and Stalin, some people now look
for a similar devil to blame; in the Atlantic Alliance Charles de
Gaulle has thus served as an evil-carrying doll, to be exorcized by
sticking pins into the stuffing. That General de Gaulle—a statesman
with an almost romantic faith in the opportunities for statecraft—
has contributed to America's frustrations is obvious; that General de
Gaulle—a statesman with an almost perfect classical understanding
of the limits on action and of the irresistible streams that drown
whoever pretends to ignore them—is the sole or even main trouble-
maker is just as obviously absurd. Indeed, American officialdom and
semi-officialdom display a slightly paranoid attitude toward France's
leader. If he has as little power as they assert, if his vision is as
anachronistic and unrealistic as they claim, then there is little reason
to lament over the harm he does; at worst, he will be remembered as
a temporary nuisance, but he could hardly have any lasting impact
on world affairs. After him, or even around him, the wreckage will
be removed, the construction resumed. On the other hand, if he is
able to thwart grand designs or destroy irretrievably enterprises
of great value to the West, then he obviously must have power, in
which case the vital question is, where does his power come from? It
is clear that whatever power he has does not extend to all parts of the
world in which things have not gone our way; the power he wields
so skillfully is merely a particular (if acute) case of a general proposition; other leaders have it also.

Another explanation for the United States' problems is sometimes
sought in the domestic conditions that affect the making of American foreign policy: the complexity of the machinery, the implacable
way it ignores long-term considerations and lavishes energy on improvisations. There is some truth here, but once again it is not the
whole answer. For the events of the 1940s show that the American
government is quite capable of formulating daring plans with long-
range perspective and amazingly successful effect; the present period
shows that occasional attempts to revive these plans in new circumstances do not succeed. In other words, the cause for frustration
must also by and large be sought in the world outside.

What has happened is something comparable to the "loss of innocence" which the United States is supposed to have suffered the day the atom bomb was dropped on Hiroshima (assuming that such innocence had managed to survive the era of imperialism, World War I and World War II). I would call it the loss of simplicity. It was fashionable, a few years ago, to write of America's crisis of *perp*lexity; it was actually a crisis of *com*plexity. We have gradually moved away from a scene in black and white to a scene painted in varying shades of gray.

In the years after World War II, the Soviet threat, as we perceived it then (not all of those who now consider that our sense of urgency about this threat was excessive said so at the time), and the collapse of the European powers still responsible for most of the underdeveloped parts of the non-Communist world converged to produce two patterns. First, there was and could be no serious clash between the United States' predominance in the North Atlantic Treaty Organization and the movement toward European unification. Indeed, the latter helped the Alliance, and was not at all a challenge to the United States; had the European unity movement succeeded in producing a European army, this would have been a contribution to America's strategic design. The issues on which the six member nations of the European Economic Community argued and bargained were, so to speak, beneath the waves of international politics. They were concerned with community-building, not power on the world scene. (The latter would come as a consequence of the former, and the former was difficult enough to require full attention.) Second, the political issues on which the members of NATO diverged (and there were many) were also pushed beneath the waves or made irrelevant by storms. Either the dictates of the situation (i.e., the need to face the Soviet threat) obliged the Western leaders to sacrifice to the task of containment the divisive goals whose pursuit would have disrupted the Alliance (e.g., German reunification, a full restoration of Germany's equality, which France opposed, and, to some extent, the *détente* Britain desired); or else, their will and their forces were broken by the violence of the tempest, as in the case of the colonial powers that wanted to preserve their overseas possessions and did not give in gracefully, like Britain, to the tidal wave of modern nationalism. To be sure, America's anticolonialism whipped up the waves, but only a little. The irresistible force was that of anticolonial native nationalism, and, except to some extent at the time of Suez, the Alliance was saved by its members' realization that the inevitable to which they had to yield was at least not the force of the senior ally.

Today, this happy simplicity and this necessary order of priorities have vanished. The fate of the Grand Design proposed by President Kennedy is instructive here. The idea for his Grand Design took into account a change in one of the two basic data of the late 1940s: with the resurgence of Europe, United States dominance in the Alliance could no longer be so great, and the idea of an Atlantic partnership gave evidence that this fact had been recognized, even if the acknowledgement that we needed a more balanced distribution of power was disguised as a demand for a less uneven distribution of the burdens. However, one of the reasons why the Grand Design has not been realized is its basic assumption that the "Atlantic dimension" must remain the common denominator of both the European and American ends of the dumbbell; that even if there is no perceived identity of interests, differences should and could be reconciled through the partners' willingness to give priority to the Alliance. The trouble is that the assumption begs the question; and the question itself—What is the relevance of the Atlantic Alliance to the new world of the late 1960s?—arises because the old answer of the Soviet threat is no longer unanimously considered decisive. As long as it was, the "Atlantic dimension" was essential, even for those who, like the French and the British, never thought that resistance to the Soviet Union entailed the sacrifice of other commitments and never gave up hope for a thaw in the Cold War. Differences existed over the *degree* to which the threat was compelling and over its likely *duration,* but these were subordinated to a joint determination to cope with it. Once the threat is no longer felt by all to be compelling, these long-suppressed disagreements on priorities and long-repressed divergences in time perspectives come to the surface, with drastic effects.

The question that must be asked, and that all the talk about Grand Designs or a renewed Atlantic Alliance avoids, is: Can the divergences still be compressed and confined *within an Atlantic framework?* Are not the difficulties encountered by the United States within NATO due to the fact that, in these new circumstances, none of the partners is either willing or able to give to the Alliance as decisive a priority as before? The disarray in Europe and the deep uncertainty in the United States about where to go and how to move are part of the same problem. Our foreign policy is in crisis, both because it often still applies old precepts to a world to which they are no longer relevant (partly because of their very success), and because it has tried to adjust to this new world in a piecemeal way, which leads to incoherence and contradictions.

## II.   International Relations and International Systems

The North Atlantic Alliance is part of, a force in, and a stake in contemporary international relations. Now international relations, even in the nuclear age, are characterized by three classic features that give the international milieu its distinctiveness and make inapplicable or irrelevant the analytical schemes developed for the study of domestic politics.

First, the international milieu is fragmented; it consists of units each of which effectively places its highest allegiance to itself, or at least considers that the achievement of any higher aim is inseparable from the preservation of its main interests and values, or the promotion of its goals. As a result, international politics is a permanent competition. Second, the groups are unlike in many ways: in population and resources, in internal solidity and external vision, in domestic structure and ideological outlook, in the length, weight, and nature of their historical experiences, and in geographical position. As a result, the competition is fundamentally uncertain. Third, the absence of any temporal power above these competing units leaves them free to resort to force in order to attain objectives which the very intensity of the contest (and the determination of most contestants to frustrate ambitions incompatible with their own) makes inaccessible by peaceful means alone. To sum up: world politics, in comparison to domestic politics, is marked by a prevalence of conflict over cooperation (bearing in mind that many forms of international cooperation are themselves responses to conflict, and that even these suffer the continuation of conflict within them); and conflict always tends to erupt into violence.

But international competition is not a monotonous ballet in which the same steps are performed, nor, despite its uncertainty, is it a purely random game full of sound and fury. There are different diplomatic constellations in time and in space, each one marked by its own rules. It is the task of the student of international affairs to try to distinguish the types of relations that have existed in the international milieu. This task has been undertaken only recently.

For a long time, the study of world politics was somehow subsumed under that of diplomatic history, which emphasizes the analysis of specific events, and that of international law, devoted not to empirical rules *of* behavior but to normative rules *for* behavior. When the study of world politics finally emerged as a branch of political science, first efforts inevitably aimed at examining its permanent features rather than its varying configurations.[8] Only in recent years has the focus shifted from the somewhat doctrinaire discussion of its eternal essence to a systematic analysis of its recurrent facets. The notion that seems most fruitful in this connection is that of the international system.[9] An international system, to use Raymond Aron's definition, is "the ensemble constituted by political units that maintain regular relations with each other and that are all capable of being implicated in a generalized war." [10]

The idea of the international system is based on an analogy with the domestic political system: both "systems" are intellectual constructs—i.e., schemes of analysis—that focus on a number of key factors, based on certain postulates: that the chaos of political data can be ordered, that there are distinguishable patterns of relations among the participants, that it is possible to select the key variables in a nonarbitrary way, and that changes in one of them will have identifiable repercussions on the others. The notion of an international system is a more chancy one than that of a domestic political system, since the scholar's construct risks being more remote from political reality, especially from the reality experienced by the participants. The framework provided in national affairs by the unit's territory and the state's institutions and laws give to the domestic political system a clear existence, obvious boundaries in space, and easily recognizable limits in time. The international system is harder to delimit—in particular, its decentralization makes the statesmen's awareness of its existence rather problematical, and to place its limits in time and space is a largely academic decision based on one's selection of key variables.

[8] This has been the contribution of eminent scholars such as Hans J. Morgenthau and Arnold Wolfers.

[9] For further elaboration of my position, see *The State of War*, Ch. 4. and *Contemporary Theory in International Relations* (Englewood Cliffs, N.J.: Prentice-Hall, 1960). See also Morton Kaplan, *System and Process in International Politics* (New York: John Wiley, 1957), and Ernst B. Haas, *Beyond the Nation-State* (Stanford University Press, 1964).

[10] *Peace and War: A Theory of International Relations* (Richard Howard and Annette Baker Fox, trans.) (New York: Doubleday, 1966), p. 94.

Still, the concept of an international system is of some use as long as one remembers that (1) its proper aim is to help one understand concrete historical realities; (2) the proper way to fulfill this aim is to analyze "not merely the relations among nations, but the relations among abstractions that can be held to summarize the relations among nations"; [11] and (3) its proper use is a descriptive rather than prescriptive one. Nothing is more mistaken than to assume that the international system is a sort of monster with an implacable will of its own, that the variable elements interact so as to determine the outcome, that the participants are dominated by the system in such a way that their moves are either mere responses to its dictates or exercises in irrelevance or self-defeat when they go against the system's logic. For "it is possible neither to predict diplomatic events from the analysis of a typical system, nor to dictate a line of conduct to Princes as a result of the type of system" [12] precisely because the limits are not rigid, because the variables interact in a way that leaves room for exploitation and maneuver, because systems analysis deals with general properties rather than specific events.

The statesman will undoubtedly ask what use the concept is to him if this is the case. The answer is simple: systemic analysis is possible only at a certain level of abstraction, and its usefulness resides in its capacity to indicate the limits of determinism and the areas of effective free action. A politician who violates the basic rules of a political system (for instance, an American presidential candidate who offers "a choice, not an echo") is not *ipso facto* condemned to failure; but awareness of the rules should convince him that the task he has set can be performed only in certain circumstances and against great odds. The main purpose of the somewhat abstract analytical exercise that follows is to throw light on the nature of the reasons for the external restraints on American freedom of action.

Although the study of international systems is still in its infancy, it is already possible to establish a simple typology of interstate systems, which consists of two categories: moderate systems and revolutionary ones. We are, of course, dealing here with ideal-types: no actual international configuration has ever been entirely moderate (insofar as each one ended with either a gradual breakdown or a spectacular crash) or entirely revolutionary (there were always forces that brought back a modicum of moderation). But these ideal-types

[11] Haas, cited, p. 53.
[12] Aron, cited, p. 32.

help us to understand the actual concrete configurations. The criterion I suggest for them is the nature of the objectives pursued and methods used.

The ideal-type of a moderate system is that of the so-called *balance-of-power system,* in which the main components behave so as to curb each other's ambitions and opportunities, to preserve an approximate equilibrium of power between them, and to reduce the level of violence. Among the basic conditions, we find multipolarity (the presence on the stage of more than two big powers) and a code of international legitimacy that has, at a minimum, agreed rules of competition and that originates in the measure of similarity among the regimes. In short, the balance-of-power system must be multipolar and homogeneous.

What interests us here is the position of a major power within such a system (England in the seventeenth century, or Bismarck's Germany). The dynamics of the system seriously restrict such a power, whether by self-restraint, due to the power's intelligent anticipation of unfavorable responses to an adventurous policy, or by the actual reactions of others to such a policy. This is because a lack of restraint would entail high costs; consequently, the operation of the system encourages a balance-of-power *policy,* so that these costs are avoided even if each power's individual goal is anything but the maintenance of the system. As a result, the main units tend to pursue moderate goals with moderate means. Their foreign policies are marked by peaceful methods and their foreign relations by limited wars. On the other hand, subtle advantages in the system compensate for these possible frustrations. First, there is the advantage of hierarchy: a balance-of-power system puts the smaller states under a kind of collective trusteeship of the big powers, which constitute a society divided by conflicting ambitions but having no permanent hostility (so that the recruitment of a following among the smaller states is not necessary for any of them); and the big powers are bound by a kind of complicity, a sense of common interest *qua* big powers. Second, there is the advantage of flexible alignments: in the pursuit of moderate ambitions or in the attempt to frustrate the excessive ambitions of another member of the system, each nation can try to enlist the support of his rivals on, so to speak, a rotating basis; for, thanks to its homogeneity, the balance-of-power system will operate without any consideration given to domestic politics and ideologies. To sum up: when the conditions are ideal, each major power has a considerable margin of indeterminacy, but its capacity for effective action essentially depends on either its willingness to be moderate in order to avoid the penalties of excess, or its ability to exploit the flexibility of alignments so as to prevent its rivals from stopping it.

Similarly, the system as a whole is characterized by a mixture of assets and liabilities. It is fragile, even when all the basic conditions for its successful operation are met, because the basic uncertainty of competition leads to recurrent wars, provoked by the various ambitions of states that exploit their freedom of diplomatic maneuver in order to test and push back the constraints which the mechanism normally imposes. It is also fragile because when big-power ambitions are successfully frustrated, the powers may be led to take action that undermines the system. Yet, the system is moderate (particularly in that it prevents many wars and keeps those which do break out limited) and flexible (in that it is able to survive drastic transformations in the internal characteristics of each national unit as well as considerable redistributions of power among the main units).

There are different types of *revolutionary systems*. All are marked by a wide scope of national objectives, a tyranny of international over domestic politics, the use of immoderate means, a lack of neutrality in regimes, inflexibility of alignments, and both an exaggeration and a subversion of the international hierarchy. One such revolutionary type is that of the bipolar system. Here, each of the two main powers pursues ambitions of a very wide scope with all the means at its disposal; at first glance, therefore, its freedom of choice appears much greater than in a balance-of-power system. But in fact the margin of indeterminacy is narrower, since each rival has little choice but to pursue a policy of hostility toward the other, whereas in balance-of-power systems the major units can choose between (temporary) antagonism and (temporary) amity. Also, this total competition leads to a scramble for allies, which subverts the hierarchy by making each of the two powers dependent to a large extent on the support (or if not support at least neutrality) of third parties. While the lesser states are more open to direct or indirect domination than they are in an effective balancing system, the situation also provides them with blackmailing opportunities absent in balance-of-power systems.

Within these sharp limits, then, the two powers have considerable capacity for effective action, due to their unrestrained might. But it is vertical action, so to speak—they can move toward and among the lesser states (even if the ulterior purpose is to affect the chief rival)—and not the kind of horizontal action (moves toward and among other members of a great-power club) that characterizes balance-of-power systems. The system itself is marked by instability, since both camps try to preserve their internal cohesion in the face of constant hostility and disrupt the cohesion of the rival, and by inflexibility; as a result, a general war brought about by the logic of unrestrained competition and unavoided escalation is a likely end.

In the multipolar case, a great power enjoys the advantage of being, together with its rivals, something like a co-manager of the entire international milieu, so the frustrations born of voluntary or involuntary restraints are compensated by the rewards of high responsibility and low insecurity. In the bipolar case, the great power enjoys within its own camp the mixed blessing of hegemony, but this is offset by the risks of total insecurity. In both cases, the resort to war is an integral part of the system. In the balance-of-power system, the great power needs force to wage "in-system" wars whenever its own ambitions lead it rightly or wrongly to calculate that the benefits of this action will be greater than the costs of its rivals' reaction; it also needs force to wage "pro-system" wars designed to frustrate the ambitions of a rival whose acts threaten to upset the balance of power. In the bipolar system, each great power needs force both to impose its will within its own camp, when challenged, and to confront its enemy should there be a direct test of wills.

Balance-of-power as well as revolutionary systems are ideal-types of diplomatic constellations in which there are at least two rival great powers, and those powers do not overshadow all other actors in size and resources. Still another ideal-type would be that of an imperial system: an empire can be defined as "a state exceeding other states in size, scope, salience, and sense of task." [13] An imperial system is one in which international relations are determined, hierarchically, by the policies of the empire toward its dependent and client states, and

[13] For a stimulating discussion, see George Liska, *Imperial America: The International Politics of Primacy*, Studies in International Affairs No. 2 of the Washington Center of Foreign Policy Research, School of Advanced International Studies, The Johns Hopkins University (Baltimore: The Johns Hopkins Press, 1967); the passage quoted is on p. 9. But some of Liska's criteria of imperial world politics are also characteristic of bipolar systems in which the "poles," without being empires, are hegemonial powers like Athens and Sparta: for instance, the fact that the role and status of other states is defined by their relation to the dominant power(s), and the fact that alliances are instrumentalities of control, as well as of conflict.

also by the occasional challenges to the empire either from rebels inside or from other states or empires outside. The imperial power, while it needs to know and to practice the economy of force, has both a large measure of indeterminacy and a large capacity for effective action. The system's stability depends on the empire's internal capacity to adapt to changing conditions (especially those created by its own expansion) and to channel social change, as well as on its capacity to defeat external challenges at a low level of violence and disruption.

What we must examine now is the present international system. To which ideal-type is it closer? And within it, what is the position of a great power such as the United States?

# CHAPTER TWO

# The International System Today

## I. Revolutionary or Moderate?

At first sight, the international milieu of the 1960s is almost a textbook example of a revolutionary system. If we examine its main *elements,* we find:

(A) Bipolarity, i.e., the existence of the United States and the Soviet Union, whose power far exceeds that of other units and which are sufficiently matched to be placed in the same top league, if one applies to the present system the customary yardstick of power, namely, the capacity to wage war and to inflict damage on an enemy. Whether this yardstick is still decisive in the nuclear age, whether a bipolar structure means an actual dual hegemony in interstate relations, whether indeed the *structure* of the system (i.e., the distribution and hierarchy of power) can be called bipolar, is a matter that will have to be explored later. But we can expect the present international system to be marked, as all previous bipolar systems have been, by a tendency toward instability, due to the dialectic of reciprocal fear, and inflexibility, due to the dialectic of opposed interests.

(B) An unprecedented heterogeneity in the structure of the system. For the first time, the international system covers the whole planet, but it nows includes ingredients of widely different origins and vintage. What Raymond Aron calls the "unity of the diplomatic field" is a fiery unity. Even though the basic unit of modern world politics is the nation-state, this over-all term conceals an extraordinary diversity. For one thing, modern nation-states differ in their degree of integration. Some are states still in search of a nation, marked by serious discontinuities among tribes, ethnic groups, or classes. Others are nations in a formal but not in a substantive sense—i.e., although they have national consciousness, authoritative central power, and social mobility across regional, ethnic, or social lines, there is no consensus on political purposes and institutions. Others are national communities in a substantive sense as well. They also differ in their historical dimensions. Some (well integrated or not) have had an independent existence and an institutional framework for generations or centuries, others are new and ramshackle. Finally, they differ in size, ranging from tiny units that are little more than dots on the map, to traditional territorial states, to what might be called empire-states, huge and often ethnically heterogeneous. Because of this heterogeneity, the distribution of power between and around the United States and the Soviet Union is highly discontinuous and uneven. Consequently the "relation of major tension," the opposition of the two great powers, breeds a permanent danger of conflict through aspiration, expansion or escalation in the various "soft underbellies" that lie between or within the two camps.

(C) Extreme variety in the domestic political systems. Verbal agreement on the two principles of self-determination and self-government conceals fundamental differences over the meaning of democracy, and there are many uncertainties about where the limits of self-determination must be placed and about its relevance in racially or ethnically mixed situations. The variety of regimes is so dazzling that political scientists cannot even begin to agree on classificatory schemes. As for the economic regimes, they range from the most backward societies, where governments have no effective control over economies that are still at subsistence level and/or in foreign hands, to modern societies of mass consumption, heavily regulated by the state. As Henry Kissinger puts it, "When the domestic structures are based on fundamentally different conceptions of what is just, the conduct of international affairs grows more complex. . . . Statesmen can still meet, but their ability to persuade has been reduced for they no longer speak the same language." [1]

(D) Sharp ideological clashes: communism vs. the so-called free world, anticolonial nationalisms of Asia, Africa, and Latin America vs. the West. These are doubly asymmetrical: in each case, one side is heavily ideological and the other rather pragmatic; in each case, the ideological side is on the offensive.

(E) A technological revolution contributes to instability both because it proceeds so fast and because it aggravates the uneven-

[1] "Domestic Structure and Foreign Policy," *Daedalus*, Spring 1966, pp. 503–4.

ness among nations. There is a technological race among the powerful or would-be powerful, and an increasing gap between the "haves" and the "have nots." And there is a race between what might be called the technological factors of equalization (the revolution in communications which makes of the world an echo chamber, spreads information all over the globe and equalizes concern) and the countless disparities and inequalities—military, economic, political, ethnic, ideological—which distort this revolution and often put it at the service of the most powerful and of the most dissatisfied.

If we turn to the *relations* of the units within the system, we can see why such a milieu is likely to be immoderate in ends and means. All the factors mentioned above contribute to the inflation of objectives, to the rise of universal claims. In a bipolar contest, prestige, power and security are rolled into one; moderate compromises are made difficult (because the contest is acted out in apocalyptic fashion, since any local move may affect the entire field, any hole in the tapestry may lead to its total destruction). When this contest is ideological as well, the distinction between a threat to the physical existence of the foe and a threat to his moral integrity becomes blurred. And the unprecedented heterogeneity of states, political regimes, and economic stages creates total insecurity, in which leaders try to consolidate their power by making enormous demands on the outside world.

The immoderation of means is due to the proliferation of conflict situations. A bipolar contest implies the risk of clashes at any point of contact between the two great powers and elsewhere in the search for supporters. And the heterogeneity of the system makes it likely that border clashes between "empire-states," imperial wars of extension and disintegration, and traditional international wars will all occur. The variety of principles of domestic legitimacy invites clashes between rival conceptions and makes it possible to invoke one of the principles as a cover for national ambitions. The unevenness of economic development condemns the poor to do their best to control their resources, and this may be at the expense of the wealthy. Lastly, the ideological substance of the contest leads to generalized intervention in international conflicts and in civil wars. "Total diplomacy" thus requires virtuosity over a range that goes from mere propaganda to the use of force.

This immoderation in ends and means of course results in instability. Both the United States and the Soviet Union, out of reciprocal fear and opposed interests, try to court neutrals, win friends and keep them (hence the proliferation of alliances), and detach the friends of the rival. This need for support from lesser powers (whether for strategic, diplomatic, or symbolic reasons) tends to make the Americans and Russians dependent on their clients; the latter want to safeguard their independence and exploit every possible asset in their position, and this subverts the hierarchy. (The United Nations contributes to this trend.)

One would thus expect each of the "poles" to enjoy a position very close to that which the model of revolutionary systems suggests. One would expect, as a bitter effect of total insecurity, that each would search for at least partial hegemony and full exploitation of its power in order to marshal support, to protect its areas of influence, to stop penetration by the rival, and to penetrate his domain in turn. One would expect that these efforts would lead to a kind of *de facto* partition of the world or to conflagration; at any rate, the likelihood should be a pressuring of all third parties to choose sides— "total diplomacy" in a vertical dimension and ominous deadlock on the horizontal level.

But reality has not gone so far. The present system is also one of relative moderation. Whereas the dynamics have by and large been those of a revolutionary system, the actual results have not differed so much from those of moderate ones. The most important factor here has been moderation in the use of force. The international milieu is saturated with conflicts and violence, and the list of armed conflicts between and within states from 1945 to the Middle Eastern war of 1967 is long and varied. But, on the whole, the use of "brute force" to take and to hold, and the use of force as a means of "coercive violence" to hurt and punish [2] have been kept at low levels and within limits. In the past, multipolarity and homogeneity led to moderation in ends and means; today, relative moderation in means seems to bring back some features of multipolar systems, including some moderation in ends. Demonic or global ends, while maintained intact in proclamations, are pursued only piecemeal. As in the nineteenth century, the great powers have resorted more to threats and confrontations than to war.[3] There is a modicum of flexibility. The system has outlived countless conflicts and confrontations and accommodated drastic changes in the distribution of power; there are some signs of a

[2] A distinction made, with his usual relentless virtuosity, by Thomas C. Schelling, *Arms and Influence* (New Haven: Yale University Press, 1966), Ch. 1.

[3] Robert E. Osgood and Robert W. Tucker, *Force, Order, and Justice* (Baltimore: The Johns Hopkins University Press, 1967), pp. 89–90.

return to flexibility in alignments and to neutral acceptance of a variety of regimes; there has been a beginning of an erosion of ideology. The two main rivals are beginning to temper their hostility not just with prudence but with cooperation: as in balance-of-power systems, the notion of mixed interests of the great powers spreads.

Do these transformations improve the situation of the great power? Do they decrease its insecurity, giving it greater freedom of choice? Do they at the same time preserve the advantage of hegemony? That is, do they unblock the "horizontal" level while maintaining the effectiveness in the vertical dimension?

## II. The Three Levels of the System

We can find the answer by analyzing the present international system as a three-level one. The fundamental level—the foundation—is bipolar. But there are two more levels, which we will call *polycentric* and *multipolar,* corresponding to two trends in present world politics, a dominant one that modifies bipolarity, and a secondary, derivative one that challenges it.

### A. *Muted Bipolarity*

I refer to muted bipolarity in order to suggest, first, that the bipolar level remains; second, that the bipolar conflict has been dampened; and, third, that the two poles have not been willing or able to switch from a full bipolar conflict to a full bipolar partnership.

CAUSES

The dominant modification of bipolarity is caused by the convergence of two separate features in the contemporary system: the consecration of the nation-state, and new conditions in the use of force. Those two features emerged only gradually, during the first decade after World War II. Since 1955, the triumphs of decolonization and the nuclear stalemate between Russia and the United States have brought out fully the meaning of these two new developments in international politics.

Virtually the entire globe is now covered with independent states, most of which are or aspire to be nation-states. Sixty years ago, the international landscape was, in cadastral terms, dominated by the big landlords. Today, it resembles those European countrysides so remarkable to the traveler who observes them from the air, with every piece of land cultivated and marked out, with the fields divided into countless strips. This fragmentation has occurred at a time when all the factors of conflict we mentioned before, as well as developments in military technology, have rendered the notion of the "impermeable territorial state" [4] obsolete. Still, the very existence of more than a hundred sovereign units poses formidable obstacles to open, free, and easy penetration of national borders. A border is like a burglar alarm, in that it has value only if there are *other* factors that deter the burglar, such as policemen, or the burglar's sensitivity to noise, or scruples that a ringing alarm would heighten. This is the case today.

First, there is the *nation's* legitimacy in most parts of the world. (It is tempting yet misleading to analyze international politics at a level so abstract that one forgets what stuff the units of international relations are made of, for their nature shapes their goals and the stakes of the contest.) The collapsing colonial empires learned the hard way what resistance to an irresistible claim for national self-determination entails. A world of nations in which most political leaders are engaged in one way or another in the "social mobilization" of their followers is a world in which even the most ruthlessly brutal and expansionist rulers cannot afford to be *too* crude. For, as Hitler's fate showed, any great power that embarks on a policy of destruction of other nations provokes a decisive countervailing response. A would-be conqueror in a world of non-national states did not worry too much about the attitudes of the conquered; but in a world of nation-states, even the cynic will acknowledge that, however much "world public opinion" may be an empty cliché, a statesman's means must be appropriate to his end when the support of other powers is as stake. The burglar himself must pretend that he respects the jewelers' integrity.

Moreover, the nature of the contest between the United States and the Soviet Union makes of the formally independent nation-state a point of saliency, and a beneficiary of the rivalry. Here again, we are dealing not with *any* bipolar competition but with a *specific* struggle. National self-determination is one of the principles of the United States and one of the cornerstones of its conception of world order. We are thus inclined to use it as a weapon against the Soviet Union; but *ipso facto* we also are obliged to take it into account or be embarrassed when we do not, for we cannot afford to blunt a needed tool. And, whereas Communist ideology devotes little attention to the idea of the independent nation and certainly does not rank it as an integral

---

[4] See John Herz, *International Politics in the Atomic Age* (New York: Columbia University Press, 1959).

part of its creed, it has used the aspirations to national independence as a club against its enemies. Thus, this fundamentally equalitarian kind of legitimacy, which tends to impart to every nation, whatever its size and resources, a right to existence, obliges both powers to define their competition as one for the "voluntary" support (or non-hostility) of other nations, rather than as one for the enslavement of other territories; the rivalry of Athens and Sparta could afford to be blunter. This does not mean that they are devoid of means of influence, but only that the means are altogether changed. The present contest is well described by the familiar vocabulary: each leading power wants "friends," or clients, or "satellites"—terms that maintain a distinction between actual dependence, which is sought, and formal independence, which is preserved.

Lastly, the effect of the United Nations must not be ignored in this connection. On the one hand, membership in the United Nations has become a concrete symbol of national independence, one of the foundation stones of the Charter. On the other hand, the deadlock between Russia and America and the tendency of each to fan the flames of independence for its own purposes have aided in the well-known increase in the power of smaller nations in the General Assembly.

We may well ask how long and how well the distinction between "friends" or "clients" and "servants" would have lasted, how long and how well the fences between the varous plots of land, while frequently crossed or damaged, would have formally persisted if the second great change had not occurred: the appearance of new conditions in the use of force. Here again, we are dealing with an objective and subjective factor. The new attitude toward force reflects both a change of heart and a change in costs.

The change of heart can best be described as a growing sense that resort to force is an illegitimate instrument of national policy. In the West, the horrors of the last world war, the new implications of national legitimacy, the traditional American dislike of the use of force—all explain the thorough discredit of Darwinian theories in whatever form applied to politics. The strength of this feeling is such that even the Communists, in their more pugnacious statements, have adopted it to the point of saying that if or when war comes, it will be due to imperialism's inevitable resort to violence, not to their own preferences.

But even the most sincere repudiation of aggressive war is usually marked by equally sincere qualifications, which pierce the mental barrier to war with holes through which entire armies could pass. Nobody, of course, repudiates defensive war, and in a situation of protracted conflict in which contenders thrust and parry across contested borders and arbitrary partition lines, or around shaky regimes, each belligerent convinces himself that he is on the defensive, or he cleverly tries to put himself there.[5] Nor does the repudiation of violence extend to so-called liberation wars waged on behalf of the sacred principle of self-determination. Here again, one can easily imagine war provoked by diametrically opposed interpretations of "national liberation" and of aggression or defense; consider Hungary in 1956 if the United States had chosen to act, or Cuba in 1961 if the United States had intervened more openly and the Soviet Union reacted more vigorously. No, I would not stress the deterrent power of this subjective change of heart, were it not reinforced and supplemented by more tangible evidence. The reason these wars did not occur is to be found in the realm of fact, not thought.

The evidence is that the costs of using force have become excessive in two kinds of cases. First, if the aim is to subjugate (or to continue to subjugate) a people that is determined to resist and that has the capacity to organize protracted revolutionary warfare (a capacity which tends to entail outside support), the cost in suppressive military measures will probably be so high as to make statesmen prefer the costs of secession. It may be still too early to celebrate the end of conquest: poor but militarily strong nations may still be tempted by the fruits of conquest; a nation stronger than its neighbors and threatened in its very existence by them may still attempt to buy security, or time, through conquest; and developed nations, which know that economic exploitation and territorial sovereignty can be separated, and that the costs of maintaining sovereignty over reluctant foreigners exceed the economic benefits, may still be tempted to conquest for purely strategic reasons, or to subjugate a rebellious partner so as not to lose face. However, the chances of this kind of

---

[5] The Middle East crisis of 1967 is particularly interesting in this respect. As was shown by the failure of the emergency session of the U.N. General Assembly to pass any meaningful resolution, Egypt's acts of May 1967 (whether they were deliberately aimed at provoking a war or merely represented a risky bluff that boomeranged) were judged by a majority of states to have been rash enough to legitimize, or at least to redeem, Israel's resort to preventive war. The Arab argument that Israel's very existence is an act of aggression that deserves and requires violent suppression (assuredly a major exception to the "change of heart" described here) has obviously failed to convince even many of the Arabs' supporters.

conquest being attempted are minimal when the prospects of liquidating the rebel in one fell swoop are also minimal or nil.[6]

Second, and more important, there is blinding evidence that nuclear war is, for antagonists capable of inflicting intolerable devastation on one another, a suicidal policy to follow for any purpose whatsoever. Between the United States and the Soviet Union, the two poles of power, fear of nuclear war inhibits the use of force at any level above that of subversion; United States armed forces have never fought Soviet soldiers. Leaving aside American attempts to "communicate" (with some success) to the enemy the message that limited war is the only practicable alternative to the dilemma of humiliation or holocaust in a "hot" test, the residual uncertainty about employing nuclear weapons has itself effectively prevented any confrontation from becoming "hot." Between each of the two main antagonists and the allies or clients of its rival, the fear of provoking a full-fledged (including possibly nuclear) intervention by the rival, in what has been called war by proxy, has also kept the limits of violence low (although much less so than between America and Russia directly). In conflicts between third parties, or in civil wars in which the chief antagonists are not directly involved, the fear of a general war with unpredictable consequences has often led the United Nations, with the tacit consent of the two superpowers, to request and obtain an early end to violence.

Thus, the effect of nuclear weapons so far has certainly not been to compel nations to renounce force (how could they, given the absence of any compelling supranational authority and the proliferation of conflicts among and within states). Rather, it has compelled them to adhere to a considerable amount of both deterrence and self-deterrence in the use of force, and to make the two chief rivals behave at times exactly like partners in a balance-of-power system— i.e., associates with a common interest in not having world peace upset by lesser powers.[7]

In balance-of-power systems, each major power must curtail its ambitions and moderate its means so as not to bring upon itself a damaging response from its rivals. There are important differences in

---

[6] The preceding remarks apply only to wars of conquest or to attempts to safeguard conquest against rebellion. So-called wars of national liberation in which each side sees itself as a champion of freedom are a different problem.

[7] See my *The State of War*, Ch. 8, and "Nuclear Proliferation and World Politics," in Alastair Buchan, ed., *A World of Nuclear Powers?* (Englewood Cliffs, N.J.: Prentice-Hall, for the American Assembly, 1966).

the system today. The margin of deterrence and self-deterrence has increased enormously. Whereas in the balance-of-power system a state that failed to be deterred by the prospect of a coalition against it paid a relatively small and temporary price for its mistake, the cost of miscalculations today could be final. Then too, the hierarchy of big and small states is more complex today. In fact, the United States and the Soviet Union are in a unique situation, both with regard to one another and with regard to the lesser powers. In order to clarify this situation, we must first look at the modern revolution in the nature of power, and at its effects on the structure of the international system.

### THE TRANSFORMATION OF POWER

The consecration of the nation-state and the new conditions in the use of force have brought about a revolution in the nature of power, which can best be understood if one keeps in mind the fundamental distinction between the *supply,* the *uses,* and the *achievements* of power. The supply of power consists, today as always, of a kind of reservoir of *capabilities.* Some of these are material assets available for the state's international efforts: the state's geographical position and its resources, the manpower potential, and the actual forces at hand (i.e., that part of the potential which is ready for immediate use). The capabilities also include intangible assets such as the ideas and principles symbolized or promoted by the state, or the personality of its leaders. On the other hand, the supply of power also encompasses the state's *capacity for collective action* (i.e., the way the capabilities are being used). This capacity can be inward-looking—the capacity for mobilization, for extracting what is needed for foreign policy from the state's material and spiritual assets—and dependent on the attitude of the people and the aptitude of the state's political and administrative system. It can also be outward-looking —the capacity for enforcement, for applying in the outside world the assets thus mobilized—and dependent on diplomatic skill in peacetime, or strategic skill in wartime, and a combination of both in periods of "neither war nor peace" such as the 1930s or the 1960s.

Statesmen must decide how the power their countries have will be used: nobody ever uses all of the power available all over the map. That is what foreign policy is about: it defines the goals and the means, and these determine in turn how the supply of power will be used.

We can distinguish different *types* of uses. At one end of the spectrum there are coercive uses, intended to affect someone else's will either by denying him some gain or by inflicting some damage on him.[8] There are also uses of power that consist of the giving of rewards, either in return for present or future advantages or in order to prevent hostile acts. At the other end of the spectrum there is the use of power purely and simply to influence other states; this involves neither coercion nor reward. Each kind of use involves a different kind of supply: when a statesman decides on a certain kind of use of power, his decision will have been dictated in part by the international system (which may rule out certain uses), in part by his nation's general policy (which forbids some and requires some), in part by what kind of power is available.

The *degree and form* of the use of power also matter. Coercion can be either total (in unlimited war) or limited; it can be military, economic, psychological, or diplomatic; it can consist of the actual application of force or merely of threat.[9] Rewards can be tangible (e.g., economic) or intangible (e.g., diplomatic); they can be merely promised or actually carried out.

Finally, the type as well as the degree and form of use are ordinarily affected by the difference between peacetime and wartime uses. In wartime, a nation's behavior is likely to be close to the model of pure coercion. In peace, the uses of power are more guarded and involve primarily the forms related to bargaining and the milder forms of coercion.

A state uses its power to achieve certain goals. Without trying to classify these goals (a Sisyphean task), we can suggest a simple classification of what nations can in fact achieve. There are positive achievements—*gains* obtained either at the expense of a foe, by offense or what Schelling calls compellence,[10] or through concessions made, advantages granted, or cooperative acts undertaken by other states. And there are negative achievements—*losses* avoided by denying gains to others either through defense, deterrence, and "repellence" against a foe,[11] or through concessions or adjustments that preclude greater losses.

[8] These coercive uses include both of Schelling's categories (the power to take and hold, the power to hurt and punish). (See above, p. 20.)

[9] Schelling points out that whereas "brute force" to take and hold requires an execution of coercion, the "power to hurt" often consists of mere threats.

[10] Offense is a gain wrested by "the power to take and hold" (brute force), compellence a gain obtained by use of the "power to hurt."

[11] Schelling's "compellence" includes acts aimed at making a foe withdraw from what was his domain, and acts aimed at inducing his withdrawal from one's own domain upon which he had encroached (cf. the difference between

Not every use of power is successful. The use of power will be a failure if the supply was insufficient for the purposes, or if the capacity for collective action, being less impressive than the capabilities, had earned a mediocre reputation that detracted from their strength. The use of power will also be a failure if the supply was badly exploited; that is, if the use selected was badly tailored to the goal or to the nature of the challenge. The calculation of how best to use what kind of power in order to reach one's goals is a subtle, not a simple, a creative, not a mechanical, act. In can be successful even if the supply of power is limited—for instance, when one's aim is precisely to increase one's power so as to give oneself the means to reach further goals; or when one's method is to build up power by installments, replacing what is lacking with someone else's power, which is "borrowed" or used to raise the level of one's own strength. Then too, the international system itself may frustrate the use of power—either when a nation correctly anticipates the adverse reactions of others and decides on a "voluntary" restriction of its power, or when, mistakenly discounting or miscalculating such reactions, its use of power backfires.

In the past, military force was like a reservoir of power, from which states did not draw constantly but from which they could freely draw in case of need.[12] This military power could not be analyzed exclusively in terms of available or ready men and weapons. (Otherwise, England's importance in the early years of this century, for example, would be hard to understand.) There were also such elements as the geographic distribution of military might (which gave Britain a double advantage: a military presence all over the world, quasi-invulnerability at home).

There was never any one-to-one relationship between the supply of military power and a nation's achievements, because the full use of coercive power was rare and other uses of power required different elements. But the reservoir of military power was like a stock of gold underwriting a paper currency. For one thing, the stock was frequently called upon: the moment of truth, in which a nation's genuine "worth on the market" was determined, was the moment of

---

"rollback" and the Cuban missile crisis). I prefer to coin one more word, "repellence," to refer to the latter situation, keeping "compellence" for the former.

[12] For a brilliant discussion, see Michael Howard, "Military Power and International Order," *International Affairs,* July 1964, pp. 397–408.

battle, which could come at any time. The possibility of resort to large-scale violence was ever present.

A great power, then, was a nation with a sufficient supply of military power to permit it to employ not only military means but also mild forms of coercion (as well as the power to reward) in order to deny its foes the goals they sought or obtain whatever gains it wanted. It did not have to use military force at the first provocation, precisely because it was known to have "what it took" at the moment of truth. With softer kinds of power, it could therefore achieve results commensurate with the power it held in reserve.

Today, the most fascinating aspect of the utility of military power is that this once fairly persistent link between military strength and positive achievements has been loosened. The power to coerce has never been so great or so unevenly distributed (the difference between the great powers and the rest of the pack has never been so great), but its nature is now such that its possessor must restrict its uses. The fullest use of nuclear power is in *denial,* but this must consist in threats—in deterrence—and by definition shuns execution. Actual execution has largely been limited to what I have called repellence and has not involved nuclear weapons; even so, the application of military power in order to deny an adversary gains he seeks by nonmilitary means has become extremely delicate. Moreover, when used in order to obtain gains, only very small applications of force have been deemed prudent.

True, as Schelling has stated, the "power to hurt"—the power of coercive violence—has for the first time in history caught up with "brute force" both in quantity and in the sense that, with nuclear weapons, the enemy can be destroyed without having to be disarmed first; "victory is no longer a prerequisite for hurting the enemy." [13] However, the increase in the costs of force affects both forms of coercion. For this "power to inflict pain," which the United States and the Soviet Union indeed possess to an unprecedented degree is, if one examines it closely, very hard to use to its full extent, since it consists in part of threats to resort (for deterrence, "repellence," or compellence) to the very weapons whose brute force prohibits their use. Thus, the "power to hurt" is devalued, just when it has come into its own, precisely by its ultimate dependence on the "power to take and hold," even though its chronological subordination to brute force has ceased.

The result, then, is a devaluation of the standard on which the

[13] Cited, p. 22.

currency of military power is based. The moment of truth is post-poned—not because of prudent adjustments made in favor of the states with superior might by those who would have been their vic-tims, but because of the prudence of the mighty. Yesterday, the mighty did not always want to use all their strength to achieve their goals because they did not have to. Today, they do not want to be-cause of their own imperative of prudence. Since the reasons for restraint have changed, the same kind of behavior—a resort to the softer forms of coercive power—no longer delivers the same results. To be sure, there are replacements of the moment of truth, incessant, varied tests of wills; but the power used in them is only partly military, and that part is small; their resolution is therefore not determined by the antagonists' force ratios. In other words, the dis-proportionality between military power and positive achievements is even greater than before, because military power is used more rarely.

This transformation also affects the geographical component of military might. No corner of the earth is beyond the reach of almost instantaneous destruction. On the other hand, the geographical dis-persion of military forces, which was once primarily an asset (against less well-distributed foes) may become more of a liability, for not only does it increase the scope of what one has to deny one's foe (as it did before), but it can no longer easily serve as a base for forcibly obtaining more. Above all, it exposes a wider front to hos-tile acts by other than forceful methods, against which a widely dis-persed, albeit overwhelming, military power is not easy to use.

This change in the conditions for a full resort to military power re-quires a re-evaluation of all the other uses and supplies of power. Today, since nations can make only limited use of their power to punish, they are led to use more often the milder forms of coercion, the power to reward, and the power to influence—all those forms of power that are not proportional, and are often unrelated, to power as material supply. A nation may, for instance, use the threat to be-come a nuclear power, i.e., it may exploit not its existing capabilities but its latent ones (a future potential which in fact will be more difficult to exploit once it exists); the potential for troublemaking thus becomes a counter for gains, whereas actual capabilities for such troublemaking are essentially a counter for denial. And a na-tion's capacity to use moderate forms of coercion—in subversion, or in rebellion against the armed forces of a foreign power—may be to-tally out of proportion to its power to raise conventional forces and produce modern war matériel. Both the Algerian and Vietnamese wars show that when a greater power's capacity to inflict pain is inhibited by either or both of the two major factors we have discussed —the legitimacy of national self-determination or the increase in the costs of force—this disproportion is largely neutralized.

Nothing in this argument supports the erroneous theory of "military obsolescence." Obviously, even if conquest loses its appeal, there remain countless goals that states could not try to reach, or to prevent each other from reaching, without the possession and the use of force. Obviously, the new conditions for this use affect those who have the greatest supply of force (i.e., the great powers) more than the lesser states, which "do not partake of any nuclear balance of terror." [14] Obviously, when its survival is at stake, a state will tend to behave as states have customarily behaved—by resorting to all-out force. But the novelty lies precisely in the fact that the great powers try not to challenge too rudely each other's survival, nor to let others provoke such a challenge.

In short, the inhibition on a total use of coercive force has led to diversification and repression toward lower levels of violence. This development has also disconnected the once close link between mobilizable military potential and gains, even in the use of coercive power.[15] Inversely, other ingredients of the supply of power—geographical spread (understood as the basis, not for a major coercive effort, but for moderate coercive uses), the possession of scarce resources, intangible assets of human talent, or a superior capacity for mobilization and warfare—are on their own perhaps for the first time, in the sense of being fully exploitable even with no military force. Of course, prestigious and skillful statesmanship may not be a satisfactory substitute for military power, since the latter may still be needed at any time whereas the former is transitory. But the devaluation of the (still present) *ultima ratio* does mean an inflation of the other counters.

[14] Klaus Knorr, *On the Uses of Military Power in the Nuclear Age* (Princeton University Press, 1966), p. 130. Knorr's careful analysis of the uses of military power reaches conclusions similar to my own.

[15] The one glaring exception is the Israeli victory of 1967. But it is due to an extraordinary convergence of favorable circumstances—considerable Arab provocation, widespread sympathies abroad, a decisive superiority if not in capabilities at least in the capacity for collective action, and a technically flawless *fait accompli*. Other states in comparable situations, or eager to change the *status quo* on their behalf, may be tempted to emulate Israel. But not all the circumstances that allowed Israel to win and (by contrast with 1956) to stay in the conquered areas can be reproduced at will.

The increase in the costs of using force has telescoped war and peace in a most peculiar fashion. While the price of all-out war is such that states now behave with a new sense of prudence (which the scholarly emphasis on mixed interests and bargaining reflects), peacetime international relations seem less like peace than ever before. They are like a permanent war waged without the traditional trappings—a vicarious war. Every possible element of usable supply becomes a precious power asset—just as, in wartime, when coal, gas, and electricity are rationed, civilians adjust by using ingenious *ersatz* devices in order to continue moving, feeding, and heating themselves.

With international relations less like a battlefield and more like a chessboard, less like a test of force and more like a bargaining matrix, a particularly important kind of power supply is a state's *position,* whatever its strategic location on the map or its strategic role in a regional or global organization. Once, the peacetime uses of power depended on the possibility of its wartime use; today, it is paradoxically the reverse, and the peacetime uses of power matter most. To some extent, the international scene is now becoming more like domestic politics, where brute force is also (and far more effectively) ruled out.

The traditional analysis of the nature of an international system was largely based on the assimilation of power to the capabilities for full coercive use. But a study of power in international relations that equates power with coercion, and deals with coercion in terms of traditional supply, is obsolete. The new and changed restraints on the military dimension of power, having led to an emancipation and multiplication of other kinds of power, should lead to a much more diversified (and much less assured) analysis. For the new dimensions of power are much less measurable than the traditional ones.

To be sure, one could argue that one of those dimensions is the power to reward, which ought to be measurable and has gained in importance both because of the devaluation of the power to punish and because of the needs of the poorer countries. This power is indeed usable and is most unevenly distributed; were it the only yardstick, the system could be characterized by American predominance rather than by bipolarity. However, here again we must take into account the barrier erected by the nation-states between the uses of another state's power to reward and its achievements; for even a shabby sovereignty limits the leverage a rich nation can exert and the benefits it can derive, in the absence or partial paralysis of coercive power, from aiding an entity that is not a mere colony. More-over, such aid provides the recipient with elements of power that in-crease his capacity to resist his benefactor's will and to play a role of his own on the world stage.

## B. *Polycentrism*

### THE DISTRIBUTION OF POWER

The distribution of power among units is, as we know, of great importance in defining the nature of the system. And a system's moderation or immoderation could, in the past, be measured by ex-amining the goals of the major units. Traditionally, a moderate sys-tem was a homogeneous, multipolar one, the logic of which led to each unit having restraints on both its ends and means; a revolution-ary system was either multipolar (when the great powers had revolu-tionary ends and means) or bipolar. The very reasons given by Ken-neth Waltz for our system's relative stability [16]—the intensity, cer-tainty, and scope of a bipolar contest with, so to speak, no loose ends—are ordinarily reasons for instability and war. Today, for the first time, stability is achieved *despite* revolutionary aims and *despite* apparent bipolarity.

In terms of ultimates, there are today only two poles of power, only two states whose military and economic capabilities permit them to be "present" more or less overtly all over the globe, whose resources as well as policies involve them more or less discreetly in the affairs of all other nations. They exceed all other states in the supply of the power to reward. Only they have full reservoirs of coercive power from which they can draw; only they can destroy one another completely and almost instantly. Only these two states could embroil the world in a general nuclear war; and no important settlements can be reached without their consent.

Now this means that in terms of the capacity to incite a "moment of truth"—i.e., the aptitude to use fully the coercive power for gen-eral war—there is a *latent* bipolar system (latent because of the hes-itancy to use this power). Second, this means that while the weight of the two powers is theoretically preponderant and their voice is es-sential in all matters in which both are involved and power can talk (Germany, disarmament and outer space, Cuba, the Near East, and Southeast Asia), practically, the meaning of this preponderance is

[16] See "The Stability of a Bipolar World," *Daedalus*, Summer 1964, pp. 881–909.

reduced by their competition, and their achievements are essentially negative. Each one is able to prevent the other (as well as, *a fortiori*, all others) from achieving goals sought by force or through diplomacy; each one is therefore likely to preserve his preponderance in areas that are, so to speak, on the firing line—such as the two Germanies, each of whose security and political future depends on the effectiveness of its protector's power. *Denials* prevail, *gains* are few. Due to nuclear weapons, the two "poles" enjoy an exceptionally high negative productivity but suffer from a low positive productivity of power. In their mutual relations, they are frustrated not only, as in past bipolar contests, by their very competition, which prevents a moderated duel from becoming a condominium, but also because they cannot freely resort to coercion in order to force one another into either agreement or submission. In relation to lesser powers, each one is able to use its superiority only when those lesser powers have made the mistake of resorting to large-scale force themselves.

We come thus to the notion of an international system where the bipolarity is a *latent* one of *potential* ultimates. The actual manifestations of these ultimates are moments when everyone's heart misses a beat while the superpowers "confront" one another. No one else much matters then. But these confrontations have been, when direct, nonmilitary. When they are violent, they are so indirect or at such low levels of violence that the final outcome has not been determined by the ratios of the military strength.[17]

As a result, a kind of *de facto polycentrism* occupies the forefront of the stage, in which almost anyone who wants can play. Old-fashioned multipolarity resulted from the distribution of coercive power, but this polycentrism results from the devaluation of coercive power. The "centers" are states many of which lack the traditional ingredients of military might, but which are well supplied in the new factors of power and eager to play the game. Because the fullest use of modern coercive power is for mutual deterrence, these lesser cen-

[17] The mistake made by Kenneth Waltz in his analysis of the international system (see the preceding footnote and footnote 7 in Ch. 1) lies in his failure to distinguish between the supply of power on the one hand, its uses and achievements on the other, and in his analysis of the supply in traditional terms. If the supply of full coercive power were (still) the decisive criterion of the system's structure, Waltz would be right in analyzing the system as bipolar and in charging critics with confusing the structure of the system and relations in the system. But what makes the relations different from those of a typical bipolar system are the diversification of the supply of usable power, and the consecration of the nation-state, i.e., the two features discussed above, which greatly affect even the structure of the system.

ters can push their pawns between the deadlocked giants. Because the new factors of power are complex and varied, their playing has a flexibility that seems to defy analysis.

This is the most novel element of today's international system. As long as international affairs were dominated by a contest between two rivals, either of which was thought ready to use its military power in order to reach its goal, all other participants were reduced to being anxious dependents or frightened spectators, who hoped that their abstention from the game would help them escape the holocaust. Once it became clear that neither of the two rivals wanted to use (or could easily use) precisely that supply of power that made it one of the "superpowers," once it became clear that, being in a bottle, the two scorpions had lost some of their sting, other beasts decided they had their chance.

THE FATE OF THE INTERNATIONAL HIERARCHY

Nuclear bombs have not "equalized" the big and the small. Since there is no "military obsolescence," differences among states in the supply of military power—both in capabilities and in the skill with which they can be used defensively or offensively—continue to matter, even in the intervals between the great confrontations when the bipolar conflict obliterates the polycentric game. So do, of course, differences in economic resources. But if "equalization" is absurd, the coexistence of bipolarity and polycentrism plays havoc with the international hierarchy. For one thing, it moderates the usually exaggerated hierarchy of a purely bipolar system, since the two superpowers restrain themselves from using force to discipline misbehaving partners or ill-behaving neutrals out of fear of how the rival could exploit such a deed in a competition that is necessarily more psychological than military. (The importance of the United Nations in this is not negligible.) For another, the usual possibilities open to small powers in a bipolar system for subversion of the hierarchy are enhanced by the new conditions in the use of force. There are certain new limitations here. Any overt resort to force on their part is likely to recreate a hierarchy at their expense; and, as in any bipolar system, for reasons of history or geography, many of the smaller powers are strategically, politically, or economically utterly dependent on one of the superpowers' protection and aid, and are thus unable to exploit the basic rivalry or challenge the power to which they cling. However, within those limits, there are many new vistas open to middle and even small powers. Let us examine some of them.

In a pure bipolar system, opportunities for the small states are both created and curtailed by the drive of the two great powers for allies and resources. As Thucydides so clearly showed, a small power too close to one of the rivals and beyond the reach of the other's help was in a tragically determined situation. Opportunities existed only in two cases: when a state submitted to inevitable domination but then subtly blackmailed its leader; and when a state was so luckily located in the field of tension that each "pole" would prefer its neutrality to a conflict for its allegiance. Such opportunities were defensive, precarious, and few. As John Burton correctly puts it,[18] they were "part of the strategy of conflict"; today the opportunities are "part of the strategy of avoiding conflict," and they are better.

One reason is that the transformation of power has strengthened the *defensive* position of smaller states. The inhibitions that now restrict the use of force by the two superpowers protect many more of them from the superpowers' military might. And the deadlock of deterrence assures that a superpower will refrain from overtly threatening their integrity, lest the other intervene and start the machine of escalation ticking. Even when the rival superpower is unlikely to help, the smaller nations feel somewhat reassured by their own aura of national legitimacy, which the United Nations reinforces. Moreover, because of the relative security that mutual deterrence gives to the superpowers, these feel less desperately the need for satellites than in past bipolar systems. Also, the compression of the use of force to lower levels and diversion from open coercion serve the smaller nations well, since their capacity to resist at those levels and in those realms is often considerable. Since the basic bipolar contest is not a direct military confrontation, what the smaller powers have to offer (and defend) is likely to be something less than territory and men (diplomatic strength for instance)—i.e., something that it is easier to defend, and whose defense will not inevitably trigger military action on the part of the pressuring superpower. In such a contest, purely diplomatic support may matter more to a superpower than anything more tangible; the weakest of states still has one kind of useful power—the power of its mere existence. These smaller states, whether allies or neutrals, are the real if relatively peaceful battlefields; an uncommitted state that threatens to move toward a superpower's enemy, a minor ally who threatens to obstruct an alliance, are obviously not military threats; their defection would not be a disaster in traditional terms of power. But in the new contest, it is

[18] In a book that reveals a fascinating mixture of insights and wishful thinking: *International Relations* (Cambridge University Press, 1966), p. 115.

the psychological and diplomatic chessboard that matters. In short, by a remarkable paradox, what conditions the defensive power of the small state is *at the same time* the intensity of the contest between the two larger powers, and its predominantly nonmilitary aspect.

This defensive power is largely provided by internal factors: a small state frequently shows a considerable capacity to resist—indeed to integrate and flourish—under threat, and thus disposes of an increased potential to inflict pain should the threat be carried out. Tito benefited from Stalin's pressure; Albania has survived Khrushchev's displeasure, and France has survived America's; and South Africa has not crumbled. Consider in this regard the contrast of the two Cubas. When Cuba became, briefly, a Soviet military base, the potential bipolar system suddenly became actual; in the naked confrontation between the two powers, the United States won, because of its over-all strategic superiority and because it superbly turned the tables. What prevented the confrontation from escalating was, at heart, the fear of nuclear war. Now it is this new, rational recoil before the use of force that explains why, when faced with a hostile Cuba acting *on its own,* the United States has hesitated to apply heavy pressure and why it has failed when it has done so. The Soviet Goliath defied the American Goliath and lost; the Cuban David continues to defy the American Goliath. And the North Vietnamese David has been defying him despite all the bombings.

This example tells us something more. Prevented by the conditions of their rivalry from open coercion, the Soviet Union and the United States, each in its own way, try to find ways to reassert their mastery over the smaller states. The Soviet Union does this by encouraging subversion, but this "indirect aggression" is a form of Russian roulette. Whether Communism will ultimately triumph in the subverted state without the help of the Red Army is a gamble. Unwilling to provide such help, the Soviets have therefore switched more and more from covert coercion to seduction. The United States, interestingly enough, has more often resorted to what could be called conspicuous force (Cuba in 1961, Lebanon in 1956, the Dominican Republic, Vietnam) but it has always done so with inhibitions (both internal and external) that limited its effectiveness. Often, the United States has tried to use the United Nations as an instrument of policy (as in the Congo), but this has obliged the United States to submit to the influence of small states skillfully exploiting the power given them in the voting regulations of the General Assembly.

Second, the transformation of power increases the *offensive* power of smaller states. If they remain nonaligned and act cautiously, they are insured of a modicum of impunity not merely to avoid subservience to the great, but also to realize ambitions of their own. Nations "may now be imperialist on a shoestring." [19] They can exploit their less tangible elements of power, particularly their diplomatic potential in fronts and organizations. They can exploit each rival's interest in keeping them out of the other's orbit in order to get economic aid from both. Moreover, within each camp, the blackmail of weakness is no longer the only form of self-assertion: a restive ally can risk a test of strength (if not of military force).

Thus, the opportunities open to the lesser powers in the present bipolar contest both result from its muffling and contribute to it, for they fill the air with clamors different from the familiar noises of the dominant conflict. These nations enjoy a considerable negative productivity of power—i.e., military safety from the great powers—unless they imprudently overreach the limits of permissible violence, and they can achieve such safety at considerably lower costs than the superpowers, which have to spend astronomical sums on the weaponry, research and development of mutual denials. The lesser powers also have a small but respectable productivity of power, not through overt coercive uses, not in achieving tangible territorial gains, but often, through skillful bargaining, in achieving economic gains and gains in prestige.

We can see, then, why earlier models of international systems have become less than relevant. The bipolar systems of the past led inevitably to war, because the costs of using force were deemed bearable. Today, the rivals tend to move away from the points at which they confront each other directly, to avoid the dilemma of "humiliation or holocaust," and the contest therefore moves toward lower levels and grayer areas—a dilution that gives more of a chance to the smaller states. Multipolar systems of the past, in which rivalries among the strong were similarly muffled and diverted to "frontiers," were marked by a continuing series of moments of truth. In the relations between the weak and the strong, disproportion was more effective; and in the relations among the strong, since there was a greater possibility both of resort to force and of accommodation, the positive productivity of their power was much higher. But such moderate systems came to fiery ends—either when (as before 1914) the conditions for a favorable balance of power deteriorated

[19] Andrew M. Scott, *The Revolution in Statecraft* (New York: Random House, 1965), p. 162.

so badly that the major powers divided into groups between which the fatal process of rigidity and escalation would occur, or when (as in 1792 and in the 1930s) one major power tried to disrupt the balance by forcibly imposing its ideas and ambitions on others. In today's system, both bipolar and polycentric, one major power's capacity to destroy without expecting to be destroyed has vanished.

Another change in the international hierarchy is apparent in the hierarchy of *concerns* of smaller and greater states. The smaller states, feeling stronger in their defenses against threats from the superpowers, are often able and willing to pursue goals beyond mere survival and security. Conversely, the superpowers, encumbered by their nuclear power, must concentrate as never before on the requirements of security and survival. For, while mutual deterrence provides for survival and security at far lower levels of applied coercion than in the past, the energy and resources spent on *avoiding* the application of massive (nuclear) coercion divert the superpowers from other goals. The might of the strong used to be like the commander's statue appearing at the feast of the puny. Today, it is a brooding presence at the meals of the mighty. (These contrasting trends make terrible mischief, of course, in alliances. The small powers take offense at the preoccupation of the mighty patron with his own security and use it as a pretext to pursue their own ambitions.)

Thus, in the present international system, the superpowers suffer from an acute case of what Aron calls the impotence of power.[20] In a pure bipolar system, small states enjoy a kind of vicarious power to coerce and destroy, thanks to their capacity for embroiling larger states in inexpiable rivalries—the kind of power so well described by Thucydides. But in a moment of truth they stood naked before the armed might of the only states that finally mattered. Athens' warning to Melos rang true: the strong do what they can, the weak what they must. Today, by contrast, the great powers' capacity to destroy is to some extent annulled by its very nature. So the strong do what they must (and can do only a little more), the weak do a little better than they must.

THE FATE OF THE NATION-STATE

At the end of World War II, E. H. Carr[21] predicted that we would not see again a world of more than sixty independent sover-

[20] "Macht, power, puissance," in *Archives européennes de Sociologie*, 1964, Vol. V, No. 1, p. 44.
[21] *Nationalism and After* (London: Macmillan, 1945), p. 51.

eign states. We are living in a world with twice that number. John Herz [22] has observed, however, that the territorial state as a unit of defense is obsolete: most units have neither the dimensions nor the capabilities for effective deterrence or defense, and those that do, have means of mutual total destruction. This argument would be decisive only if the threat of war dominated the international system as it did in past revolutionary systems. But today, the fear of wars of conquest has abated, and the fear of total war has lessened. Moreover, the very fact that no state, however powerful, is beyond the reach of nuclear weapons has a paradoxically static effect. For their possessors, atomic weapons "by their power strengthen the sense of sovereignty which their destructive capacity undercuts." [23] Prudent fear of this capacity on the part of those who possess it strengthens the sense of sovereignty of the nuclear have-nots.

What destroyed the city-states was a combination of debilitating fratricidal conflicts and their conquest by empires. What destroyed the small medieval units was the labor of princes who, by cunning and coercion, enlarged their domains and built the modern territorial state. The present international system, as we have analyzed it above, literally blocks those avenues of change. The sanctity of the nation's legitimacy protects it from obliteration via sale or dynastic marriage; the change in the rules of force protects it from obliteration through conquest. Many of the wars that break out take place, in fact, *within* national borders, not against borders, as Evan Luard has put it; [24] the thrust of coercion is to change internal regimes and their foreign allegiances, not to absorb states. The threats against the nation are no longer foreign military powers, then. Some (like subversion or domestic chaos) would not disappear if the nation-state ceased being the basic unit; others (like poverty) can be handled by the efforts of the poor (separately, through cooperation, and through intricate bargaining with the rich) just as well or as badly as by a merger that would be no more than an addition of miseries.[25]

What preserves the nation is simply the absence of any decisive incentive to go "beyond the nation-state." The Cold War at its most

[22] Cited, Ch. 1.

[23] Jean Laloy, "L'évolution de l'Alliance Atlantique," *Preuves*, June 1966, p. 39.

[24] In a book to be published by Little, Brown in 1968.

[25] For further elaboration, see my "Obstinate or Obsolete? The Fate of the Nation-State and the Case of Western Europe," *Daedalus*, Summer 1966, pp. 862–915.

intense produced a bipolar bloc formation in which some scholars saw a beginning of new forms of organization. But the "thaw" in the Cold War has lessened the need to huddle together in a shelter, while the persistence of the rivalry has both perpetuated a sufficient fear of a conflagration to prevent the smaller powers from acting too rashly and continued to be probably the most divisive factor in every regional grouping that might possibly move "beyond the nation-state." In every regional alignment, there is a kind of race between "inward" factors of interdependence and the destructive impact of the "relationship or major tension"; and the alignment tends to split between the members that continue to see the world primarily in terms of the Cold War, and consequently advocate either solidarity with one superpower or self-effacement, and those that see a new opportunity for striking out on their own. (Of course, the superpowers do their best to exacerbate these divisions.)

There *is* one other force that could conceivably persuade a smaller state to commit national hara-kiri: the realization of the limits of its power, and of the greater pull it could have if the unit it ruled were bigger. But here again the international system acts as a conservator of the museum of nations. Many of the new states are not really nations yet; they are unlikely to engage in transnational integration until they have achieved a modicum of national integration. As Rupert Emerson has pointed out,[26] in many parts of the world, to reach the national stage gives a tremendous lift to people's horizons. Even when one is dealing with genuine nation-states, the incentive to melt into bigger units with more power has to be balanced against the fact that forming such units is always troublesome, and likely to remove the energies of the participants from the world scene for quite a while and focus them entirely on the intricacies of building the larger community. The possibilities open to larger units in the present kind of world are not so much greater, nor the opportunities open to existing states so pitiful, as to justify the gamble.

It is important to realize exactly what this survival of the nation-state means. I have suggested elsewhere that a distinction should be made between national consciousness (a state of mind), national situation (a condition), and nationalism (a doctrine or ideology).[27] Not every nation-state in the present system has either the first or the last, but everyone has a national situation: a set of internal fea-

[26] *From Empire to Nation* (Cambridge, Mass.: Harvard University Press, 1962), Ch. XIX.
[27] In "Obstinate or Obsolete?", cited.

tures and a position in the world. The very fact that ours is the first global international system obliges each member to be involved; but each becomes involved according to its own character, sees the world from its own place and in its own time perspective, analyzes events and trends in a way that spells diversity rather than community. The rivalry of the superpowers tends to encourage this kind of separateness—bred not by isolation, but by involvement. Since the countervailing forces are weak, the multiplicity of national situations perpetuates itself even in the absence of strong national consciousness or nationalist leaders.

If one denounces the vicious obsolescence of the nation-state, then, one must be cautious, not only because its obsolescence has still to be demonstrated, but also because its vices may not be what they used to be. Not every national leader puts the nation at the top of his hierarchy of values; even leaders who do are not necessarily nationalists of expansion and aggression. What is happening is more subtle and complex. The form of the nation-state, including its traditional apparatus of legal rights, is preserved, even universalized, yet its substance is transformed. The old boy is still there, but he has lost much of his vigor and bite. The present international system removes simultaneously the incentives to madness and to merger. Nations are economically interdependent enough not to indulge in the kinds of suicidal policies that marked the national responses to the great depression of the 1930s, yet they are not so interdependent as to be forced to break out of their national shells, or able to disrupt the world through isolated acts of autarchy. They are militarily interdependent enough to be well aware of the ever-present peril of annihilation in a world without hiding places. Thus, through the cunning of History (one dare not call it Reason), the kind of world Wilson dreamed about emerges in circumstances that would have given him nightmares. It is under the umbrella of bipolar deterrence that a system of sovereign nations linked by ties of cooperation and reluctant to use large-scale force has come into being. Rapid and expanded communications, the poorer states' often desperate need for help, the richer states' fear of various explosions among the poor— be it the population explosion or famine or revolution, the fierce political struggles that project the superpowers into each other's and everyone else's affairs, the network of institutions which serve as clearinghouses, stakes, or springboards—all of this contributes to the obsolescence of the purely territorial aspects of sovereignty.

The vessel of sovereignty is leaking, but it is being filled by other liquids that infiltrate through the holes. In a world of active transaction flows, the bottle of sovereignty, however pierced, permits each group to try to capture some of the flow and harness it to its own needs. And, in a world of frequent political dependence, the claim of sovereignty permits the dependent to try to dilute dependence. (Here, we must remember that international organizations, far from overcoming the nation-state, help it to defend or promote what is left of its sovereignty against the pressures of external domination.) In other words, in an age of rapid social mobilization, and at a time when no one is ready for or able to manage a centralized world authority, the function of sovereignty may well be to prevent chaos in one essential respect: by giving to the changing, often confused social groups a framework for identity, some protection against the undertow of economic currents, the blind pushes of technology, and the brutal pulls of the mighty.

## C. *The Emergence of Multipolarity*

The survival of the nation-state is not just the by-product of what I have called muted bipolarity, the basis for the polycentric level of international relations. The nation-state can also be the elevator to a multipolar nuclear world. The "nuclear revolution" explains why the bipolar system is now more latent than manifest, and why the world appears polycentric at the same time; but the uncertainty of this revolution explains a secondary trend, which leads to nuclear proliferation. This trend is both a reaction against the fragility of the limits on force, and a consequence of the persistence of force.

For the balance of terror is fragile in two ways. For one thing, it could always collapse—hence the desire of other powers to consolidate it by complicating the would-be aggressor's calculations. Yet, to the degree to which it is stable, it both undermines the nuclear protection of third parties and requires a re-evaluation of non-nuclear force—hence the desire of other powers to plug the nuclear hole and to deter the threat of a return to classical war. On the one hand, the persistence of the trappings of force in an armed world, the mileage its possessors can still get out of it, at least in preventing other states from reaching a desired goal, and on the other, the consequences of the "balance of terror" in lessening the protection of the lesser powers, together incite the states that can afford it to seek power themselves in the traditional way and to try to become nuclear powers. They use the freedom created by the "impotence of power" to build up their own.

At first sight, this appears paradoxical, not only because the costs of acquiring nuclear weapons are high, but because they are compounded by the risks of eventual application. Why invest so much into getting equipment that it is then almost impossible to operate? First, since the two major nuclear powers are capable of annihilating one another, the plausibility of their accepting suicide to protect a lesser power decreases, and the lesser power is tempted to buy an insurance policy of its own. If "peril parity" strengthens mutual nuclear deterrence between the superpowers at the cost of weakening the indirect nuclear deterrence that protects their allies (as well as third parties whose safety is vital to the superpowers), it is the duty of the now less protected state to shore up its position. Second, since, in a polycentric world teeming with sources of conflict, there are acute tensions at the "subsystemic" (i.e., regional) level and since force, while muted, is not banned, one side in an international dispute is sorely tempted to acquire nuclear weapons so as either to deny its opponent any gains, or to do at the local level what "peril parity" precludes at the top—exploit a nuclear monopoly or first-strike advantage for offensive purposes. The only development that would thwart such reasoning would be a joint agreement by the superpowers not only to denounce but also to prevent the proliferation of nuclear weapons by joint measures of disarmament, by joint punitive action, or by joint guarantees to the potential nuclear power or its rival—something the competing superpowers have not been able to devise. Third, this trend toward the proliferation of nuclear weapons is a precaution, indeed a reaction, against polycentrism. The pattern of many new "centers" of power is felt to be fragile, since it results from circumstances that would disappear if the two major powers suddenly moved from deadlock to duel or duopoly; to a middle (or would-be middle) power, it is felt as a nuisance, since it distorts the hierarchy. If polycentrism is unstable and unhealthy, like inflation, then multipolarity, paradoxically enough, is a deflationary remedy.

Thus, the spread of nuclear weapons exploits *and* reacts against the muted bipolar contest and the rise of polycentrism. As long as there is no change in the basic structure of the international milieu, the possession of the *ultima ratio,* nuclear weapons, increases a nation's power of inflicting death and makes it virtually inevitably a party to any settlement of issues in which it has a stake.

The attempt to acquire today weapons that a nation could not easily use and may not want ever to have to use is a way of exploiting the present polycentric system so as to turn latent bipolarity into emergent multipolarity. It expresses the desire to increase the negative productivity of one's power. At present, it is the uncertainty of the balance of terror—the fact that no one knows whether a conventional fuse can be stopped from setting off the nuclear detonator —which keeps the use of force repressed at very low levels. If the balance of terror became much more stable, so that the superpowers' inhibitions against the use of force at higher levels disappeared, then the negative productivity of the power of small states which they owe to the restraints kept on the power of the two poles would decrease, unless they too become nuclear possessors.[28]

The drive toward multipolarity also corresponds to a desire to increase the positive productivity of one's power, by more aggressively exploiting one's new strength or by helping to force the superpowers to make settlements in which their challengers participate.

In the present phase of world politics, the mere threat to become a nuclear power (or a state sharing in the nuclear capabilities of a possessor) or the mere fact that one is known to be capable of becoming one—what might be called the power of holding back—is an asset in the game. While it obviously does not provide a state with all the advantages of being a nuclear power, holding back on the threshold saves the costs and risks of actual nuclear weapons and delivery systems, yet enhances the capacity to extract concessions, guarantees, or support from the superpowers (due to their interest in preventing proliferation) or to prevent issues in which one has a stake from being settled by the superpowers alone. Being on the thin line that separates the polycentric from the multipolar level increases already the productivity of one's power.[29]

What is difficult to know at this stage is whether the emergent multipolar system would be latent, like the present bipolar one, or actual. If it should consolidate the freeze on force—which the stability of the balance of nuclear power on top threatens to crack at the conventional level, and which the uncertainty of this balance threatens to crack at the nuclear level—then the actual system would still be predominantly polycentric. The new nuclear powers would simply share the bittersweet fruits of that impotence of power which now affects mainly two nations. If, on the other hand, the proliferation of nuclear weapons leads to *more* rather than less widespread use of

[28] See General André Beaufre, *Dissuasion et Stratégie* (Paris: Armand Colin, 1965).

[29] West Germany's case is an exception. See below, Part IV.

force, or to a new hierarchy tied more directly to the military component of power, then the new multipolar system would be the actual one. But there are other possibilities, to be discussed in Chapter Ten.

## III. An Imperial System?

The preceding analysis has tried to explain the relative moderation of the international system. Yet another explanation is conceivable, has indeed gained some popularity, and deserves discussion. Some American officials, as well as political scientists, have developed the notion of the United States as the preponderant world power; according to them, the international system is no longer bipolar, but not for the reasons I have suggested. To be sure, there is a latent bipolarity at the "apocalyptic" level of ultimate military might. But what is apocalyptic—like what is exaggerated, according to Talleyrand—does not matter; at the level of manifest international politics, what matters is not polycentrism and the trend toward multipolarity, but "imperial America." This thesis has been accepted by a number of French commentators. But whereas they tend to fear the effects of American world hegemony, the American writers attribute the relative moderation and stability of the international system to America's combination of firmness (in resisting the forces of disruption) and self-restraint.

Powerful arguments can be made for this thesis. First, in terms of "usable" coercive power, the United States not only has provided capabilities for limited war to match those of the U.S.S.R. but also, as already mentioned, has shown a greater willingness to use them—even by attacking the territory of an ally of the Soviet Union, North Vietnam, thus far without incurring Soviet retaliation. American naval and air superiority is unquestioned. American soldiers, military bases, and military advisers can be found in more than forty countries. America's huge power to reward has been used through military assistance and economic aid to three-fifths of the world's nations. The Soviet record, in all these respects, is much less impressive.

Second, if we look not at the uses but at the achievements of power, we find that the United States, through the skillful use of the power to reward and more or less subterranean uses of coercive power (for instance, the power to threaten the end of rewards), has succeeded in preserving or establishing friendly or at least nonhostile regimes in all of Latin America except Cuba, most of Africa, and a great part of Asia, not to mention Western Europe. Moreover, in the great nonviolent confrontations with the Soviet Union—direct ones as in Berlin from 1948 to 1961, or in Cuba in 1962, "by proxy" as in the Middle East in 1967—the United States has prevailed, either (in 1967) because its opponent happened to back the losing side and chose to accept defeat rather than risk escalation, or else (Berlin and Cuba) because American resolve even more than the balance of military forces (unfavorable in Berlin) gave the United States a decisive edge in "the balance of interests as manifested in the relative capacity of opponents to convince each other that they will support their positions with war, if necessary." [30] Third, if, as George Liska has suggested, an imperial power is characterized by the scope of its interests and involvements and by its sense of task, then the United States does indeed wage "the international politics of primacy": for whereas its chief rival assuredly has a sense of universal task, the breakup of its camp and the scope of American success have sharply curtailed its effective involvements.

A case can be made to show that what has muffled the bipolar conflict and reintroduced moderation in ends and means into the system is the assertion of American primacy. Both the early American nuclear monopoly, and later the nuclear stalemate, have encouraged the Communist states to use all forms of power except full coercive power in the pursuit of their goals. This could have led to violent instability, had it not been for America's ability to meet and thwart them at every level, and thus to oblige them to recognize, either in their doctrinal statements or in their actual conduct, the failure or limits of offensive violence. It is America's primacy that has led to the disintegration of the enemy's camp. As for the troubles in its own, they mark both a futile attempt by lesser powers to challenge American preponderance, and the decline of the strategic and economic importance of other areas for the United States. Thus, stability and primacy can be seen as synonymous: like all empires, America is said to have "a great margin for error," to face only "differences in kinds" and timing of success, but not "alternatives that [spell] the difference between conspicuous success and total failure." [31]

In my opinion, the thesis of "Pax Americana" (seen as the nature of the international system, rather than as merely a tendency in American foreign policy) is an optical illusion. What it suffers from is not, as in the case of the bipolar interpretation, a confusion between the

[30] Osgood and Tucker, cited, p. 152.
[31] George Liska, *Imperial America: The International Politics of Primacy* (Baltimore: The Johns Hopkins Press, 1967), pp. 29–30.

military supply on the one hand and the uses and achievements of power on the other, but a confusion between the kinds of purposes for which power is used and between the kinds of achievements of power—gains vs. denials. It neglects the asymmetries between the two great powers: diplomatic-strategic asymmetry (one side is on the ideological and political offensive, the United States is on the defensive), and geographic-strategic asymmetry (the Soviet Union is a land mass, the United States, so to speak, an island-continent).[32]

Thus, what is interpreted as evidence of primacy is merely the success of the United States in *denying* its adversaries either the establishment of bases close to the United States, or the conquest of areas challenged by them, or the dislodgement of Western economic and political influence in areas once controlled by the West but now politically independent, or the establishment of regimes ideologically allied to the main adversaries of the United States. Now, in order to deny such achievements to its foes, the United States has indeed had, first, to show superior resolve so as to make them back down even when the local balance of force was in their favor; second, to maintain naval and air supremacy in order to protect communications with other continents and to be able to strike at enemy forces coming outside of their land mass, and also to spread its own forces and bases abroad, so as to deter piecemeal aggression by assuring American involvement; third, to strive for a strategic superiority in "nonusable" nuclear power, so as to deter eventual nuclear first strikes against America's allies as well as against itself, and to discourage major Communist non-nuclear military attacks by posing a credible threat of an American first strike. In other words, what appears as "primacy" is largely a superiority in the supply and uses of defensive power. Given the nature of the challenges it has faced—either, as in Korea, a massive military aggression, or, as in the Middle East in 1958 or in the Congo since 1960–62, political anarchy exploitable by Communist forces or powers, or, as in Greece in 1947, economic and social chaos, or, as in the Eastern Mediterranean in the spring of 1967, a risk of active Soviet support to its anti-Western Arab friends—it is not surprising that America has had to use its huge economic power to reward and to develop and use (albeit in limited ways) its military power.

A more widespread use of superior or comparable supplies of power is one thing; world primacy is quite another. For if the negative productivity of American power has been high, three sets of factors make

---

[32] For further elaboration, see *The State of War,* p. 165.

it quite different from primacy. First, the celebrated achievements have often been obtained not merely because of the array of American advantages, but also because of independent factors. Those factors: the proliferation of nation-states and nationalisms and the new conditions in the use of force, hinder the U.S.S.R. (and Red China) as offensive powers more than they hinder the United States, yet they also restrict both the uses and the achievements of American power.[33] Second, in the defensive struggle against Moscow and Peking, American power has not always achieved the denials sought. Military force has not proved a panacea, either in Cuba or, so far, in Vietnam, any more than the combination of economic aid and military supplies had proved effective in China in 1949.

Third, the barrier between denials and gains remains. On the one hand, no Communist nation has been decommunized and while the Soviet bloc has cracked, the United States is now faced with two major challengers instead of one. To be sure, the fear of a major military clash with the United States has led the Soviets to dampen revolutionary violence in many parts of the world; but their preference for dealing with governments rather than revolutionaries is not unrelated to their continuing hope of exploiting those governments' own grievances against Western influence. In the non-Communist parts of the world, the United States has won all the major confrontations except Vietnam, thanks to that "favorable balance of interests"; but then, the United States has never chosen to stage a confrontation within the enemy's domain: there was no East-West crisis over Hungary. On the other hand, while the non-Communist nations assisted by the United States have, on the whole, been kept out of communism, they have not *ipso facto* served the other purposes and interests of American foreign policy. The existence in many countries of "American parties," "economic ties converging at the center,"[34] and military programs directed from Washington does not annihilate the assets which the transformations of the map and of power give to the smaller states: nor does this existence provide the United States with effective means of making others do what we would want them to do, or refrain from doing what we dislike.[35]

---

[33] In one instance—the 1967 Middle Eastern crisis—the Soviet defeat was due clearly not so much to America's actions as to the defeat of the Arab "proxies" by a nation endowed with superior national fervor and the willingness to use force.

[34] Liska, cited, p. 24.

[35] For further elaboration, see Ch. 3.

The United States has indubitably contributed to moderating the international system by obliging its enemies to delay and fragment the pursuit of their ends and to restrict the scope of the means they could use with some chance of success. The United States' failure in "containment" would have led either to some desperado American escalation that would have brought World War III, or to the primacy of the U.S.S.R., victorious in its search for positive achievements. But America's own "margin for error," while large, may not be so huge as to keep the system safe from potentially immoderate disruptions. These could be caused either by American mistakes, especially in the use of force in situations where the sword opens wounds but does not heal them, or by too unbroken a series of successes in denial, for the Soviet Union can hardly afford to be rebuffed everywhere without trying to snatch some success of its own even at great risks. Room for error stems less from America's imperial primacy than from the transformations of the map and of force, which leave the great powers more serene about local fiascoes, and seem to provide many powers —not only the United States and the Soviet Union but, say, France in the Algerian drama, or China in its present turmoil—with a comfortable margin for mistakes. Indeed, only the superpowers face the peril of crossing the brink.

Finally, the moderating impact of the United States has merely resulted, first, in keeping the international system latently bipolar in terms of general war or essential settlements, and, second, in allowing the spread of polycentrism and multipolarity. If America were serene in her primacy, and the Soviet Union had resigned itself to it, would each of the superpowers show so much of an interest in the *other's* preponderance within its coalition? [36] If order in an imperial system "rests in the last resort on the widely shared presumption of the ultimately controlling power of the imperial state . . . even if the manifestation of the controlling power is only intermittent," [37] then we are wide of the mark, for the world seems to have at present two "controlling" powers, each in a different sphere, and wide areas in which neither exercises control, although one may try to score some gains at the other's expense, while the other succeeds in denying control to its rival.

Raymond Aron has argued that, for the West, to achieve survival and peace—deterring one's adversaries from destroying the West, making them accept moderate objectives and means—would be tan-

[36] Osgood and Tucker, cited, p. 171.
[37] Liska, cited, p. 37.

tamount to achieving victory.[38] Even if one agreed that victory has been won (a statement that would ignore the uncertainties of the nuclear balance, the risks created by polycentrism, and the perils of multipolarity), one would have to distinguish such a victory from imperial primacy. It may be that, in the nuclear age, only a world empire could assure peace, but the limited "victory" won in the past twenty years leaves the world exposed to major hazards, the great powers embroiled in dizzying dilemmas of control, and the international system in a state that bears little resemblance to past configurations.

[38] See *Peace and War* (New York: Doubleday, 1966), Part II.

# CHAPTER THREE

# *Gulliver in the Chain Gang*

## I.  The Stalemate of the International System

If I had to represent the present international system by any one metaphor, I would say that the system is like a long chain gang. Some of the prisoners are small, two are huge, and several manipulate explosives. Each is a separate personality, but none can do very much with his. Should anyone try to step out of line, he would badly cut his ankles, and, by throwing his fellow prisoners out of line, would risk blowing himself and others up. And so, despite the inequality in weight and muscles and fists, despite the murderous hatreds and jealousies and grievances, they are all tied together, alive but impotent.

It is not a pretty picture, but it is an accurate one. I have once, when analyzing France's traditional society, polity, and authority relations, called it a stalemate society dominated by the fear of and need for authority.[1] The fear of authority dominated, and it led to social and political stalemate; but since the need for authority persisted, there were safety valves (the civil service in normal times and resort to saviors in emergencies). Today's international system is dominated by a fear of force that explains why there are unusual restraints on violence and gives substance to the legitimacy of nationhood. Yet it is also dominated by a need for force, as the most effective or only available way of shaking a status quo that pleases few, and this underlies the nuclear build-up, the large-scale resort to low-level coercion, and the continued legitimacy of revolution and "internal war." It could be called a stalemate system of international relations. In order to assess more closely the nature of this stalemate, I should like to discuss it from two perspectives: the imbalance of national achievements

---

[1] Stanley Hoffmann *et al., In Search of France* (Cambridge, Mass.: Harvard University Press, 1963), Ch. 1, "Paradoxes of the French Political Community."

and the transformation of the nations' stakes. This discussion will, I hope, clarify the meaning and the scope of America's predicament.

## A. *The Imbalance of Achievements*

Never before have international politics been so important to so many states, but never before have they been so frustrating. The various coercive forms of power can be used more successfully than ever to deny to another state forcibly achieved gains. At the atomic level and at levels of conventional power, deterrence does just that for the superpowers and their allies; and limited "repellent" uses of coercion have in many cases succeeded in thwarting attempts to effect gains by force. The factors that inhibit the superpowers' exploitation of their enormous military machines for other purposes *ipso facto* increase the lesser states' capacity to use their own power for denial against the superpowers and their allies. When the eagle's claws are clipped, the dove can save its life. At the level of conventional power, in clashes between those lesser states, the only spectacular case of gains through force is Israel's blitzkrieg of 1967, the product of quite exceptional advantages and circumstances. It is at the subconventional level that force has been most effective in continuing to produce gains, and that the negative use of force—for deterrence or "repellence"—has been least successful. But successful resorts to force in order to make positive gains have occurred mainly in the case of rebellions against foreign rule, by peoples eager to become nation-states. Once statehood is achieved, making gains even by subversion has been less effective.

Thus, the achievement of gains—which is not exactly a minor aspect of foreign policy—can be primarily effected only by more subtle uses of power than the blunt wielding of military might: by threats and rewards, by nonviolent yet deadly techniques of "informal penetration." The effectiveness of such techniques is undoubtedly considerable when backed by a reserve of huge military power and when they can draw upon huge economic resources. Nevertheless, even they are affected by the freeze on military force pure and simple, for in a decentralized international milieu, nations deprived of the easy use of force find it much more difficult to reap gains. Just as the new conditions of force inflate the counters of power, so do they tend to increase the efficiency of defensive uses over offensive uses (even though, as we have seen, they put offensive opportunities into the hands of small states).

We have, fortunately, not reached the ghastly stage where every unit would have its own deterrent, every scorpion its sting—General Gallois' dream and most other people's nightmare. But we are already in some approximation of the "unit veto system," [2] in the sense that all nations find it easier to deter than to advance—and not only in purely military terms. When the actual application of large-scale force tends to be reserved for prevention of forcible changes in the *status quo*—i.e., used as a weapon against, and not, as in the past, for, change—the core of power, the imposition of my will upon yours, is itself corroded. There has never been anything quite like it. If they could limit their ambitions to the disintegration of colonial empires and the loosening of America's alliances, the Soviet Union and Communist China would be pleased. But their ambitions are for a world safe for communism; and the impossibility of carrying revolution at gunpoint (and the desire of newly emancipated peoples for genuine independence rather than new subordination) has made indigenous Communist victories exceptional indeed. When the Communists try to make the wheels of history turn faster, but not by pushing the carriage into a ditch—i.e., by subversion but not aggression—their dilemma is acute. Moderate doses can be neutralized by local antibodies, heavy doses threaten to incite a forcible repelling reaction on the part of the United States, eager to exploit its own military advantages. Yet the American rival itself finds it easier thus to deny its foes the satisfaction of shaping the world to their specifications than to promote its own preferred schemes.

The same pattern can be seen in area after area. De Gaulle blocks Kennedy's Grand Design and Monnet's great design, but his own European Europe is also blocked. Nasser is still in power, but his grandiose plans for a United Arab world never left the blueprint stage and were shattered twice by Israeli force. But Israel's own hopes for direct, peaceful relations with its neighbors have not been fulfilled, for victory could bring territory and breathing spells (and headaches) but little more. Never before has the world seen so many statesmen whose vision is not conservative—revisionists bent on improving their nations' status, reformers concerned to strengthen bonds "beyond the nation-state," and, above all, revolutionaries committed to the spread of their own ideology—yet never before have their disappointments been so great. Each one can defend his faith from the needling or the wrath of others, but he cannot promote it really well. As a result, while the least cosmically ambitious, the revisionists,

[2] Morton Kaplan, *System and Process in International Politics* (New York: John Wiley, 1957), *passim*.

may find satisfactory ways to exploit the limited action available to them, the more messianic are condemned to frustration or to the erosion of their power.

Dreams, then, are the victims of this system. The universal involvement of nations in this now less tense system makes possible the re-emergence of long-submerged issues and divergencies that were necessarily repressed so long as urgent and overriding concerns dominated the world, i.e., either the Cold War or the struggle against colonialism. Now, instead of simple alignments in which divergent perspectives and ultimate goals are subordinated to a common, immediate objective, we find a luxuriant and ebullient growth of subtle and shifting alignments and, in the relations of states, a prevalence of mixed interests over the earlier sharp division between friend and foe. The stability of the nuclear balance of terror returns to the lesser powers, who live in the shelter or the shadow of the two interlocked giants, the luxury of discord and rivalries of their own. Their disputes, unsolved by force but too ardent to be solved by agreement, continue to fester, provoking recurrent tests of wills without decisive outcome: in the Middle East or Cyprus or Kashmir. The present international system, hard on wars, soft on revolutions (so long as they do not partake too visibly of the rivalry between communism and its foes), eats up regimes with appetite but preserves these unhealthy situations, unviable states, and fictional nations. Herculean internal transformations, a world-wide process of development, the breakup of empires, revolutionary conditions, life-and-death rivalries—all these seem by some supreme paradox to result in an international system that moderates them with some impartiality and perpetuates them. Confrontations and crises occur as if to relieve the boredom and to remind the participants how horrible it would be if real international motion became possible again, or how dangerous it would be if the immobilized actors once again extended their clenched fists and claws to their enemies' faces.

The polycentrism of the world today, as we discussed it in Chapter Two, and the predominance of denials over gains permit the argument that the world scene is like a children's play. The nations are children who romp and make mischief on the stage only because their quarrelling parents have retired to the wings; the minute the parents started to fight for real or agreed to discipline the children, the real show would begin. The facts of the matter are that what relegates the parents to the wings is not their fancy but their excess power—or, to put it more accurately, their excess power makes of them overgrown and dangerously rough kids playing among the others. For them, to fight it out would be disastrous, yet reconciliation is likely to occur only when and because some of the real children, having grown big and tough in turn, posed a challenge of their own. Also, some of the urchins do their best to use this freedom not only to emancipate themselves from the parents' tutelage but also to accelerate puberty, so as actually to challenge the parents.

The metaphor has another merit: it reminds us that the weakness of the parents gives strength to the children only *comparatively*. It would be an error to explain the predominance of denials over gains in the international system exclusively in terms of restrictions on the use of force. These restrictions put a kind of ceiling on possible achievements, but there is also a floor, through which some of the smaller nations can fall. Certainly, they enjoy power in a way that was never before useful to or exploitable by minor actors on the world stage, but this is of no use if their domestic situations are so messy that they literally cannot act on the world stage. The chief limit on their effectiveness, the chief obstacle to a total and genuine polycentrism of 120 centers, is not imposed from without by the might of the strong but—and here is a change from the past—it is imposed from within, by the plight of the weak.

The lesson to be learned in the history of Sukarno's confrontation with Malaysia is not that a lesser power's resort to force will not be tolerated by the stronger powers, for the small doses of force used by Indonesia were kept below the threshold where international reactions are triggered. The lesson is that even the more accessible and cheaper games of power cannot be played by a bankrupt. We can read the same lesson in Nkrumah's fall and in Ben Bella's overthrow. As China's cultural revolution confirmed, when the burden of domestic disorder becomes too heavy, attention cannot be properly focused on the absorbing international game of power. Domestic chaos either removes the will to power or makes it impotent. Since many of the would-be centers are in a condition that requires that priority be given to internal emergencies, the gap between aspiration and achievement is immense. And while the inhibitions on the use of force protect the nation-state from the outside, the one factor that often undermines it is not the appeal of transnational togetherness but the threat of internal disintegration, tribal secession, and so on.

The superpowers are like albatrosses and the lesser powers like seagulls. The albatross, as in Baudelaire's poem, has giant (nuclear) wings which hamper its walk; to flap those wings in flight would bring about the blinding flash of Hiroshima. The seagull at least can fly. But it is too light and small to fly far or high. The middle powers—seagulls that try to grow into hawks—are not too large to enjoy the pleasures of flight or short walks, and they can fly faster and higher than ordinary seagulls. Yet, over an ocean where any collision with the albatross spells disaster, no bird can indulge in long-distance flights.

There is yet another reason for the predominance of denials over achievements, and, like the restrictions on force, it affects all nations, albeit unevenly. In every social system, the effectiveness of the "power elite" naturally depends on the structure and dimensions of the system. When the system is too fragmented and too large for the means available to the elite, when much of the territory is beyond the easy reach of the rulers, frustration will be frequent. In today's international system, power is decentralized, the once homogeneous system is broken down into a number of subsystems, the number of actors is large, and the factors determining their policies are innumerable. The capacity of any one state to affect decisively a great variety of other nations is limited, especially if we think once more of gains. Of course, the superpowers' resources allow them to be present in most of the subsystems, whereas lesser states must limit their horizons. But even on an unlimited horizon, the sun of full success may never rise, for the first duty of the great power is to prevent others from moving in the wrong direction. Statecraft is absorbed, once more, by denial. For the United States, the moment of realization can be traced to 1955, when the enlargement of the United Nations changed the pattern of voting in the General Assembly. For India, the prestige it had accumulated when only a few ex-colonies were independent vanished when the number of new (especially African) states in the United Nations rose sharply. For China, the day of disillusionment may well have been the failure of Indonesian revolution.

### B. *The Transformation of the Stakes*

Henry Kissinger has written with eloquence of the clash between the statesman and the prophet. Today's international system is filled with prophets. Whether they can be described as what Kissinger calls the bureaucratic-pragmatic, ideological, or revolutionary-charismatic type,[3] leaders make claims that far exceed the interests of their countries defined in narrow or traditional terms. Yet their chances of achieving what they claim are small. The factors I have analyzed in the previous section explain why the international system forces all

[3] "Domestic Structure and Foreign Policy," *Daedalus,* Spring 1966, p. 514.

leaders to be satisfied with the pursuit of "instrumental values" (i.e., with a pragmatic adjustment of means to intermediate ends) instead of the pursuit of preferred but inaccessible "consummatory values." [4] Why, then, do they persist in the latter? Is it only because of the intensity of the contest?

There is another reason: the change in what is at stake in the international game. International relations used to have clearly visible and measurable pay-offs. Today, the pay-offs are singularly elusive: hence the game's *viscosity*. There is some, indeed considerable, fluidity left—the scene is anything but quiet, and the players' attitudes can hardly be called hieratic—but the results are as we have discussed them. In past international systems, the dominant stakes were those comprised in Arnold Wolfers' notion of goals "pertaining . . . to national possessions . . . the enhancement or the preservation of one or more of the things to which [the nation] attaches values, which are in limited supply and for which the competition is necessarily intense." These "possession goals" were sought through an interplay of force and diplomacy. In revolutionary systems in particular, the chief contenders also played the game of intervention and gave special importance to "milieu goals," which consist of "shaping conditions beyond national boundaries." [5] But this shaping of the milieu was largely a by-product, a kind of inflationary extension, of the pursuit of possession goals; intranational political intervention was the complement of international moves.

Today, the picture is different. The new conditions of the use of force and the legitimacy of the nation-state complicate the competitive pursuit of possession goals. To be sure, they facilitate the *cooperative* pursuit of possession goals. Here, the states best able to benefit are underdeveloped nations that can exploit the rivalry of the superpowers in order to get economic and military aid. Once more, the advantage belongs to smaller or middle states. But on the other hand, the logic of international competition, as we have seen, relentlessly impels states to desire goals that can be achieved only at the expense of others, and the very resilience of the nation-state sharply limits joint ventures. Possession goals remain exceedingly important to many states, especially when their attempts to establish nationhood are closely tied to the possession they covet (Kashmir,

[4] See David Apter, *The Politics of Modernization* (Chicago: University of Chicago Press, 1965), pp. 85 ff.

[5] Arnold Wolfers, *Discord and Collaboration* (Baltimore: The Johns Hopkins Press, 1965), pp. 73 ff.

Indonesia, Middle East), but the price of attaining these goals is often prohibitive.

The same factors explain why traditional international moves have been frustrated. Moving others on the international chessboard becomes inhumanly difficult when force loses its legitimacy and efficacy as an instrument of gains. Therefore, the competition changes focus, and the way to move men's minds is to move the men—i.e., to affect domestic politics.

Moreover, a variety of contests aim to shape the domestic order of the many units in the system, as well as to create a certain type of international order. For many of the new nations in particular, security and material progress depend on the establishment of a certain type of world order and on the existence all around of congenial regimes. Therefore, "consummatory" claims correspond not only to the new rules of the game, but to the state of mind of many of the players.

Thus, for "systemic" as well as for national reasons, the stakes of the international competition have changed in two ways. First, there is the new prevalence of milieu goals over possession goals. States want first of all [6] to shape the domestic "environments" that affect international affairs (for instance, the United States wants to see to the establishment and consolidation of modernizing and moderate regimes in underdeveloped areas, and to obtain an end to Communist proselytism), and then to shape a favorable international milieu (for instance, by measures of arms control, or the promotion of peaceful change—or of violent revolution, or development schemes).

Second, concerning means, there is the new prevalence of what I would call internalized world politics: the migration of force from, say, conquest to subversion and the mutation of war into a legitimate adjunct of revolution are one part of this phenomenon; another part is the resort to a variety of nonviolent techniques of "informal penetration," ranging from cultural programs to economic aid, from military assistance and the training of administrators to the rewarding and financing of friendly or potentially friendly leaders or groups, or to the control of "front" organizations, etc.

These two changes are the inevitable compensation for the inaccessibility of possession goals and the frustrations of international relations. A statesman concerned to use his nation's power produc-

---

[6] I am dealing here with the *gains* they seek, beyond the successful *denial* of their possessions to other states.

tively and positively, who finds that the direct control of events or the influencing of others is prevented, will look for the indirect controls of intervention and define his gains in milieu terms. For the United States, success will be defined as the liberalization of the Soviet Union or the victory of prudent reform in Latin America; for the Soviet Union, success will be defined as the decline of Western influence in underdeveloped countries or of American influence in Europe; for Nasser, success will be defined as a "revolutionary" Middle East.

To be sure, force is widely used on behalf of such goals—for instance, in the form of guerrilla warfare to establish a regime friendly to the Soviet Union or to China, or in the form of Marine or Army landings to protect a pro-American regime from a revolution: the intensity of the competition gives even to intervention in the pursuit of milieu goals a perfectly remarkable fierceness. But this is even more remarkable: since the legitimacy of the nation-state and the new moral and physical conditions for the use of force have put restraints on its use for possession goals, states that do resort to armed coercion, such as the United States in the Dominican Republic or Vietnam, or Egypt in Yemen, are careful to justify their actions with the argument that their arms serve lofty milieu goals and help consolidate authentic but threatened regimes, instead of pursuing selfish aims. Thus, these "unselfish" goals, as stated, still give to force a kind of legitimacy (along with self-defense and self-determination). This may be the tribute of vice to virtue. But the nature of the tribute gives a precious indication of the change in the stakes.

These changes make of international politics a concern, indeed a fascination both more elusive and more continuous, a more generalized and permanent "engagement" for most states. The superpowers' economic and military dependence on the rest of the world may be low, but the shift in the stakes diffuses and perpetuates their involvement; and lesser powers, with limited possession goals, few means, and strings that tie them materially to the larger states, can nevertheless play their own game on the new chessboard.

This shift can also be seen as a drive for restoring mobility to a system otherwise threatened with blockage—and at little cost. To set as a "national goal" the triumph of anticolonial forces all over Africa, or of communism (or democratic pluralism) all over the world, sets up a distant time perspective and conveniently fuzzy criteria of success even when force is used, whereas traditional possession goals had fairly narrow time spans and did not permit leaders to waffle. One either got what one wanted, or one didn't. But with milieu goals, a leader can always declare himself pleased with results (positive or negative) achieved so far; yet by definition the task is never completed—there are always neo-colonialists, neo-imperialists or reactionaries, and new threats to democracy—and consequently one will never be in the embarrassing position of having to invent new goals. Then too, not only does the milieu goal, like a mirage, recede as one moves toward it, but reaching it depends on the co-operation of others, so failure can always be blamed on others; one's own contribution need not be expensive. Similarly, the game of intervention has the excitement of immediate action and that of unending possibilities. Since what is at stake is the influence over forces that one does not totally control (as long as the façade of sovereignty persists), whatever virtuosity one shows, there will always be a need for more. Whereas diplomatic or conventional military defeats are usually unmistakable, defeats in this new kind of game are easy to present as temporary reversals of no great consequence to the nation's vital interests. As one shrewd analyst has put it, such activities allow for easy disengagement after "overcommitment." [7] The more the game entails covert intervention, indeed, the easier the reversals can be concealed.

Thus the two changes in goals and means are correctives, or attempted correctives, to the prevalence of denials over gains. But these *indirect* ways of reaping gains are still far less satisfactory than the old direct ways; today's positive productivity of power remains far more uncertain than the negative productivity. For this attempt to restore mobility to the system cannot really be called successful, precisely because the criteria are so fuzzy and the whole enterprise so unending. There is more movement than motion forward. No state can, by itself, change the international milieu or control the domestic affairs of other nations sufficiently to manage a genuine breakthrough—hence the contrast between frantic movements and slow motion.[8] Yet changes take place, and we have often emphasized their importance. Where, then, do they come from?

They have two sources. One is in the great "confrontations" that now take the place of large-scale war—the situations of acute tension

[7] Andrew M. Scott, *The Revolution in Statecraft* (New York: Random House, 1965), pp. 162 ff.

[8] Here again the Middle Eastern crisis of 1967 is instructive: the "possessions" gained by Israel have primarily a defensive value; but the positive objectives of Israel—i.e., the goals beyond denial—were milieu goals, which have not been achieved.

such as the Korean War, the Berlin crisis, the Cuban missile crisis, Vietnam. These tests of will are the short change of traditional wars. Paradoxically, they are not very productive in helping the contenders reach their possession goals, precisely because denial prevails (by defense, deterrence, or repellence). But they do succeed in transforming the milieu. The Korean War gave teeth to NATO and indirectly disrupted the process of European integration, although it did not give all of Korea to either the North Koreans or the U.N. forces. The Cuban missile crisis did not give the Soviets a base in Cuba or the United States a way of liquidating Castro, but it had enormous repercussions in both "camps"—contributing to the disintegration of the Communist one and straining the Western one, and it changed the climate of United States–Soviet relations, leading to previously blocked agreements. The confrontations are like rocks thrown into a pond: the stones disappear, but the reverberations ruffle the waters all around.

The other great source of change is the domestic one—the ups and downs of internal politics. Internal changes, especially revolutions (such as the Chinese one or Castro's), do what intervention tries to do. They determine the "posture" of the actors, and throw on or off the stage leaders whose goals, claims, and clamors will shape or had shaped the international milieu.

Thus, in the last analysis, violence is still the midwife of international society. Among nations, it tends to become what one might call the *ersatz* of the *Götterdämmerung*. Within nations, it becomes more important than ever, as though everything lost by war had been gained by revolution. Still, in terms of trying to promote change so as to reopen the road to gains and correct the imbalance between gain and denial, this violence does not serve the nations as well as war often used to. For confrontations affect the milieu rather than the possessions, and do so in largely uncontrollable ways. Indeed, the more two powers control their confrontation so as to avoid large-scale war—thus putting to use the negative productivity of their power—the less they are able to manipulate the effects on the milieu itself. And domestic violence, while frequently an object of foreign policy, obeys dynamics of its own.

Although the new stakes may not be an adequate substitute for the old ones, and the new processes of change may be even less under control than the old ones, the pursuit of milieu goals and the internalization of world politics have had two important repercussions in the making of foreign policy. One is that the symbolic dimension of foreign policy has become increasingly important. Traditionally, symbols such as honor, rank, or prestige were a kind of halo around a state's possessions. They were the intangible emanation of the tangible goods enjoyed (or coveted) by the actors. This is not the case today. A large power can have its libraries burned, its officials molested, its businesses expropriated without losing face, and yet "face" and reputation are more than ever essential objects and ingredients of foreign policy. Possession goals cannot easily be sought by traditional coercive means, but they can still be sought by skill and statecraft floating, so to speak, in the air unballasted. Reputation, personal authority, the awe or sympathy created by one's manner and style, the respect accorded to a nation—a whole stock of symbols can be used as counters of power.

And these symbols have a broader function: the more one aims at milieu goals, the more important it is to have the prestige that will encourage others to listen to and follow what one has to say, to imitate what one stands for. When interaction is more intense than ever, yet direct control across borders less frequent, leadership must consist largely of pace-setting, and the pace depends on the face. Yet, *ipso facto,* prestige depends less on actual goods, *paraître* is disconnected with *avoir*. A nation may lose an empire and gain prestige for the way it handled the loss; or it may consolidate an empire by force and lose face for the same reason. When the market for goods becomes sluggish, the market for symbols becomes frantic. Possession goals entail a struggle for the control of scarce goods; milieu goals, a struggle over the shaping of international legitimacy.

In relation to the internalization of world politics, since the overt manipulation of domestic structures is illegitimate, the disguise needed in the relentless pressure on the various polities provides another reason for the inflation of symbols. No nation dares to advocate the overthrow of a regime that is hurtful yet not openly hostile; hence, the appeal for change is made in terms of general values and symbols. No nation dares to ask friendly yet independent regimes to make major political or social changes; hence, the appeal is made in purely technical terms and in broadly symbolic ones.

This symbolic dimension covers not only the formulation of goals, but also the actual content of foreign policies. The distinction between acts and verbal policies is losing its usefulness. It used to be true that great powers could act, whereas the smaller ones could mainly talk. Now, when the most spectacular kind of action— military action—is either very much under controls or displayed primarily for purposes of denial, when the smaller states can act quite effectively either through subversion or diplomatic bargaining, when threats are more frequent and productive than "real" moves and more evenly distributed, the distinction no longer makes much sense. It is rather futile to ask, as a criterion of "seriousness," how many divisions the Pope has at a time when the Emperor can hardly use his divisions or must sink them into a morass opened by guerrillas. For the ratio of purely verbal policies is extraordinarily high today in everyone's foreign policy. The discord between the superpowers, which prevents a final showdown and final settlements, condemns each to a policy of proclamations and declamations for the record. The universal competition for prestige (which can be lost through excess use of force) and the prevalence of wielding influence and using mild forms of coercion put a premium on verbalism. The importance of signals, messages, communications in bargaining situations like today's (marked by mixed interests and limited force) implies that verbal policies are indeed policies and tantamount to acts insofar as they affect an opponent's understanding of a nation's attitude and reactions. What is deterrence if not a nexus of credible threats, i.e., of verbal policies? On issues such as the reunification of Germany, West German ambitions for possession or control of nuclear weapons, France's role in NATO, China's relations with Russia, United States-Chinese relations, the strategic postures of the superpowers, a mixture of "acts" (often within national territory or reserved domain) and verbal policies characterizes the behavior of all the interested parties, big and small. To a large extent, verbal policies are a substitute for acts that would lead to doomsday, just as the proliferation of strategic theorizing in peacetime is a substitute for strategic action that would lead to the holocaust. In both instances, the substitutes communicate more than a state of mind; they indicate a state of will.

One sees then why an author [9] has suggested, albeit mistakenly, that in the analysis of international relations the old "power model" ought to be replaced by a "communications model." The current importance of communications is a direct result of the revolution in the use of power. Affecting others remains the basic stuff of world politics, but the premium is now on indirect psychological ways of affecting others. Communications prosper because they are the new and necessary vessel for the use of power in contemporary circum-

[9] John Burton, *International Relations* (Cambridge University Press, 1966).

stances. And communications and signals will remain essential in the new international system, even if the revolution in the use of power should somehow be reversed, simply because the number of actors in the diplomatic field is so high, relations are so tense, and the kinds of interdependence so varied.

The second effect on foreign policy-making caused by the pursuit of milieu goals and the internalization of world politics is what I would call the inflation of personal skills. The skill of the diplomat, from the statesman at the top to the minor functionary at the bottom, was always vital to foreign policy. But material ingredients of power could go far to compensate for deficiencies in the capacity of enforcement. Now, with the decline of direct and forceful action, and with the decline of the kind of diplomacy based (subtly or not so subtly) on the availability of a highly convincing *ultima ratio,* the two requirements of effectiveness have become the skillful exploitation of the symbolic domain and of the subterranean realm of contemporary world politics. To convince other nations that their national interests must be reinterpreted in the light of higher considerations (be they considerations of international security or of ideology) and to throw support to the right group or prevent the success of the wrong group within the polity of another nation require personal skills almost divorced from material ingredients of power. Of course, "pure brains" (and nothing else) or mere bluff will hardly guarantee success, but sheer mass without brains is of very little use. As the physics of power decline, the psychology of power rises. The present international system increases not only the symbolic component of foreign policy, but also the intelligence function, in all the meanings of that word—the function of comprehending, for analytic and operational purposes, how other minds and societies work; the function of processing and learning from the torrents of information each nation acquires about the acts, intentions, prospects, and uncertainties of others; the function of exploiting this knowledge so as to affect the behavior of others in the desired way, either through a mastery of the communications media, or through mastery of the darker arts of "informal penetration."

In conclusion, then, we might remark on the interplay of opposites—the contradictions, if you like—that make world politics today look like a universal and frustrating exercise in Russian roulette.

First, there is a contradiction between the density (the tightness and interdependence) of the system and its fragmentation. The closeness of the system explains the overarching importance of milieu goals to units whose possession goals would be worthless if the milieu blew up. It also explains the intimacy between domestic and international affairs. Yet this first world-wide international system includes more actors than any previous one and is more heterogeneous. Hence, it is difficult for any one unit to control events beyond its borders, especially in the new conditions of force and of national legitimacy. And although the pinnacle of power (assessed in traditional terms) is occupied by only two states, whose greed for control is voracious, their ability to do so is shaky. Our first paradox follows: there is increasing dependence on the milieu, and decreasing control.

Second, there is a contradiction between the stability or viscosity that results from the prevalence of denials and the difficulty in achieving clear-cut gains, and the instability that results from unpredictable confrontations and revolutions, from the resort of states to a multitude of "inflationary" counters of power (currency unbacked by the gold reserves of traditional military might), and from the increasing importance of that most unsteady factor, personal skill. Hence, a paradox of increasing tactical mobility without strategic breakthrough.

Third, there is the contradiction between the visible aspect of international politics, in which spectacle—that of "postures," statements, visits, and symbolic moves—dominates, and the invisible side—the *sub rosa* activities of subversion and support—in which acts flourish. Hence, a paradox of overt and continuous moves without discernible impact coexisting with discontinuous events without an overt cause.

There are also certain ambiguities. First, there is the question of originality. On the one hand, the pursuit of milieu goals, the internalization of world politics, the legitimacy of the nation, the importance of kinds of power unrelated to military might can hardly be called innovations. On the other hand, there comes a point when changes in degree amount to a change in kind. The sum total of all the transformations we have noted is something original indeed. And there is the question of permanence. To what extent are these transformations merely a temporary convergence of ordinary features of revolutionary systems (which always elevate the importance of milieu goals and intervention in domestic affairs) with a taboo on large-scale force? To what extent will international relations revert to the old model whenever there is a return to genuine moderation—endogenous moderation in the various elements of the system, rather than the exogenous, forced restraint imposed by nuclear weapons —or whenever the taboo collapses, perhaps under the impact of nuclear proliferation? We cannot decide here whether the present gives us a good indication of what the future holds, but it does give us a clear explanation of why being a superpower is a very mixed blessing.

## II. The Servitudes of American Power

The preceding analysis has emphasized the kinds of restraints the international system imposes on its members and particularly on the superpowers. We must now examine more specifically the restraints that operate on the United States. The first, and most general level of analysis here is to compare its present position with the position of a major power in past international systems. The second is to examine the present international system, interpreted as before in abstract terms, as a "network of relationships among relationships." [10] The third is to analyze the actual realities of the present international milieu.

### A. *The United States in the International System*

I have mentioned earlier that the United States appears to embody the disadvantages rather than the advantages of the great power's position in both bipolar and balance-of-power international systems. United States foreign policy suffers from the narrowness of its range of indeterminacy, as in bipolar systems, and from the disadvantages of insecurity, continuing inflexibility, and a modicum of dependence on lesser allies. The insecurity persists because the nuclear stalemate is "delicate" and because its effect on clashes between the superpowers, or between one superpower and allies or associates of the other, at lower levels of violence, is uncertain. By inflexibility, I mean the impossibility of "playing the balance" as Great Britain did in the nineteenth century, compensating in part for the limits on her military resources: aligning in shifting fashion with a number of other powers against whichever is at the moment the greatest threat to stability and even removing oneself from the forefront at relatively peaceful times. The United States cannot practice a game of shifting alliances, despite the Sino-Soviet split, and the competition be-

[10] Ernst B. Haas, *Beyond the Nation-State* (Stanford University Press, 1964), p. 53.

tween the United States and its rivals remains too intense to allow for "disengagement." In other words, the kinds of commitment forced on a great power by a lasting and intense relation of major tension limit its freedom of action by eliminating the "options" one finds in balance-of-power systems.

In exchange for these servitudes, the United States does not have the advantage enjoyed by a great power in past bipolar systems, of being able to coerce by threats or by force dependent smaller states that are unable to appeal to one's rival. Nor does the United States have the advantage of being able to exploit military superiority so as to force its chief rival (or even other bitter foes) to a showdown. In other words, the opportunities for effective action within the narrow limits of indeterminacy are fewer.

That is to say, the United States must quite strictly curtail its goals and its means. Other great powers had to do this in past multipolar systems, but they had the compensatory advantages of indeterminacy: flexibility, relative security, and hierarchy. What makes this curtailment particularly irritating is that, as we have seen, the basic conditions of the present system are revolutionary. To have to restrict one's options and then to have the remaining ones rendered only dubiously effective by the nature of the milieu is annoying when the competition is not so diffuse as in balance-of-power systems, but on the contrary is intensely specific when one starts out with fairly universal claims, and especially when one's supply of power is the greatest in history. Moreover, past multipolar systems gave the great powers not only flexibility, security, and hierarchy, but also various opportunities for aggrandizement in exchange for any restraints. Today, the combination of a bipolar contest and nuclear weapons makes unilateral expansion far more difficult, since it would immediately upset the over-all balance (at least in political terms), and the relative atrophy of force makes such expansion far more laborious.

The fact that the bipolarity of the present system is latent, not actual, provides various *apparent* improvements. There is some increase in the range of indeterminacy. By creating a small measure of security, the nuclear stalemate tends to emancipate each superpower from excessive dependence on its allies, and the allies' emancipation from tutelage, due to the opportunities of the polycentric and multipolar levels, further estranges them from the protecting superpower. The superpowers are now less likely to be dragged into war by their allies and less likely to be stopped from fighting their own wars by allied vetoes. But this gain is limited. Each of the superpowers is caught between a desirable lessening of its burdens because of a tendency of its alliance to disintegrate or crack and its continuing fear of "falling dominoes" should any one of its commitments, present or past, collapse under the enemy's assaults. Moreover, a gain for indeterminacy is not *ipso facto* a gain for effectiveness. Although the United States has a theoretical "option" of disengaging itself from, say, the dangerous activities of its ally France, the intense and lasting "relation of major tension" vis-à-vis the Soviet Union suffices to curtail the effectiveness of this theoretical freedom of action: the annihilation of even a troublesome associate by a foe would remain a highly improper consequence of the United States' taking the new "option." Where it exists, the improved capacity to disengage oneself from one's allies or associates' enterprises entails a loss in one's ability to control their moves (as both the United States and the Soviet Union experienced when they tried to restrain Israel and Egypt, respectively, from going to war in May 1967). And while each superpower, in exchange for this loss, gains a limited amount of freedom not to climb the ladder of escalation in order to redeem its associates' eventual fiascoes, it may still suffer heavily when that fiasco is spectacular and its own passivity conspicuous (as the Soviet Union discovered in the 1967 Middle East crisis). Conversely, although the United States has a theoretical "option" of fighting alone (or almost) in Asia, the new limits on the coercive uses of force restrict the effectiveness of this option.

Another apparent improvement is the reappearance of a characteristic of multipolar systems ordinarily ruled out by bipolarity: the neutralization of certain areas, instead of ruthless competition for every bit and piece of the world. The fear of the consequences of direct clashes and the cost of such confrontations suggest to both rivals that the neutralization of remote areas may be more beneficial than a struggle in which success adds little to one's supply of material power. However, this opportunity for relative disengagement actually restrains the effectiveness of the superpower's use of power. In the present circumstances, a neutralized state will be tempted to act, not as a meek dependent insulated from international politics, but as a player in its own right. In past multipolar systems, the neutralization of a small unit freed the great powers from pressures applied by the small; today, the capacity of the small to defy the great is enhanced. Thus, a gain in flexibility is partly offset by a loss of control. Also, the contest persists, largely in subterranean attempts to control or subvert the "neutral." As we know, foreign attempts to master domestic processes are often harrowing. Again, the advantage in indeterminacy is not a gain in effectiveness.

The United States suffers from the disadvantages that come from each of the "layers" of the present international system, as well as from the interdependence of the three. We have already dwelt on those that result from bipolarity. There is first of all the obligation to use one's power so as to hold one's own in the contest, an obligation that weighs with especial heaviness on the defensive superpower, which must see to it that the progress of its foes is stopped or prevented all over the world while those foes may choose the time, place, and manner of their blows. This naturally limits the positive productivity of its power, for it is difficult to meet the complex requirements of world-wide vigilance and also use one's resources and skills for gains. In particular, one's defensive military power might well be no more than an umbrella under which offensive uses of largely nonmilitary power are possible, yet the energy it takes to hold and deploy the umbrella is missing for those other uses.

Then, in addition to this heavily determined concentration on the various forms of denial, there are several restraints on effectiveness—limits on action against one's adversary, or its consorts, or against uncommitted states, or even against one's own allies. These are caused by the combination of deterrence and self-deterrence, out of fear of provoking a holocaust, or of playing into the enemy's hand, or damaging the milieu, or unfavorably affecting the many domestic polities one tries to impress and to shape.

The polycentric "layer" creates problems of its own. The "untouchable" legitimacy of independent nation-states and the very multiplication of foreign powers with votes in the United Nations, diplomats everywhere, and public pronouncements on all issues complicate one's own diplomatic task. There are certainly possibilities of action, but only at a level of indirection and subtlety that, as we have seen, is not so unevenly distributed among nations as military hardware.

Finally, the development of middle powers, whose ambition to rise above the level of the merely small inevitably conflicts with the superpowers' habit of considering themselves the only legitimate pursuers of world-wide designs, adds a global complexity to the local and regional complications which polycentrism creates. The superpowers are like two giants who try to walk through a crowded room, in which they are not only slowed down by a pack of midgets but pushed aside by men of normal size, and cannot hit back.

The interdependence of the layers introduces a whole network of supplementary handicaps. First, the persistence of the bipolar "relation of major tension" inhibits the reactions of the United States and the Soviet Union against the perils created for them by the behavior of new "centers" and the rise of new "poles." The most effective way to reduce rebellious, restive, or hostile small and even middle powers to their "real" size would be either for the superpowers to start fighting, or for each one to remove support from false friends (especially, in this case, military guarantees) and from neutrals and to crush the hostile powers. But this is precisely what cannot be done. The peril of high tension prevents a full-fledged return to pure bipolarity; yet it also prevents each superpower from cutting off the challengers' noses for fear of spiting its own face. When a nuclear challenger denounces a superpower's nuclear umbrella for being full of holes and starts to make his own small umbrella under the protection of the allegedly torn big umbrella, he knows that the challenged superpower cannot call his bluff by removing the big umbrella, because in doing so he would expose not only his indocile ally but also himself to rain. When, moreover, the challenger insults and (cautiously) attacks the superpower's foe, that injured party must calculate a response with considerable care, lest he provoke the intervention of his chief rival. On the other hand, another effective way for the superpowers to respond to challenges would be to join forces, especially with the aim to end nuclear proliferation. But the intensity of the contest still prevents this. At this point, another factor intervenes.

The second problem raised by the convergence of bipolarity, polycentrism, and multipolarity is that it perpetuates for the superpowers the constraints of bipolarity. This occurs in a variety of ways, which inhibit the superpowers from turning their duel into a duopoly. The need for the superpowers to prevent new or potential nuclear powers from posing a real threat to their forces, the need to preserve the distance between superpowers and challengers leads to a new twist in the arms race between the superpowers themselves: they are now engaged in deploying "light" anti-ballistic-missile systems; an agreement by the superpowers not to deploy ABM is made difficult precisely by the boost such a "duopolistic" agreement would actually give to the nuclear ambitions of third parties.[11] The existence of challengers in each camp does not reduce the superpowers' political dependence on their lesser allies (a characteristic of

---

[11] For a brief discussion, see Alastair Buchan, *War in Modern Society* (London: C. A. Watts & Co., 1966), p. 162.

bipolarity). Indeed, it increases this dependence, for should either superpower disregard the interests of a minor ally for the sake of *rapprochement* with the other, that ally might then be thrown into the arms of the challenger, always ready to exploit tensions within the camp. Moreover, a nation eager to preserve its independence can pursue an ambitious policy without undertaking an alliance with the superpower on whose protection it nevertheless ultimately depends. Why should it submit to the irritations of unequal alliances? Why should it put itself in the position of having either to blackmail out of weakness or irritate its protector by challenges, when it is convinced that the superpower's interest in its security will force that superpower, in a pinch, to defend it anyhow? Compare, for example, relations between India and the United States with the irritated relations America has suffered with Turkey (over Cyprus) and Pakistan (over Kashmir) because of pressures we applied in the name of our alliances with those two countries. In this way, the superpowers suffer from the servitudes of contest yet forego the compensatory advantages (however limited) of "camp" domination. Lastly, attempts at *rapprochement* between the superpowers, which have a joint interest in remedying their plight, are impeded by their inability to impose by noncoercive means agreements affecting the newly emancipated centers and poles of power, and their incapacity to resort jointly to coercive means as long as they are rivals.

The third difficulty is that the muffling of bipolarity obliges the superpowers to encourage some of the very tendencies to emancipation that so adversely affect their freedom of action. Each superpower must try to deny to the rival access to and control over parts of the world where the rival has not yet penetrated or in which an unsettled contest goes on. In other words, each contender must try to increase the cohesion and impermeability of its own camp and build up the resistance of third parties. In the present conditions, the most effective way to do this is not to impose one's own *imperium,* but to build up, to inject self-sustaining strength into one's lesser allies as well as neutrals. Now this is likely to encourage polycentrism and multipolarity, since this aid will provide the recipients with elements of usable power, which they may use in ways highly obnoxious to the benefactor. The greatest beneficiary of United States aid has been France; Jordan has used American arms not in successful self-defense against subversion but in a disastrous war against Israel; Pakistan has used American arms against India; and Indonesia has used Soviet weapons against its own Communists. The superpower cannot fully apply the logic of bipolarity (which involves using all means, including force, to preserve the integrity of one's camp) or the logic of polycentrism and multipolarity (which involves accepting and indeed exploiting shifting alignments). Thus the superpower stands challenged both in its relative impotence—by the new "centers"—and in its power—by the nuclear middle powers, as well as by its rival.

## B. *The United States as a Political Power*

Analysis of the international system has something skeletal about it; we learn nothing about the muscles and blood and nerves. It is therefore necessary to return, so to speak, to the flesh of contemporary world politics. The international system deals with abstractions. Now we must reintroduce the real states, their concrete goals and policies, the real networks of amity and hostility, the specific issues. If the more abstract analysis is useful, as I have claimed, it should have provided us with a kind of schematic explanation of the basic factors—to use a familiar metaphor, a kind of map of the landscape. Now we must move on a landscape that is infinitely more varied than the map, but the map has hopefully made it understandable.

The preceding discussion has focused on the servitudes of United States power, on the restraints that affect its area of choice and the effectiveness of its choices. Here I will focus on the dilemmas of its foreign policy.

We can begin with the most general ones, which are caused by the nature of the challenge the United States faces. In one respect—but in one respect only—this challenge is simple: the United States has no choice but to be a great power on the defensive. By virtue of its power as well as of its values, because of its "possessions" as well as of what it stands for in the international milieu, the United States is the inevitable target of Communist offensives and of the more extreme forms of anti-imperialist revolts. Thus, isolationism is literally ruled out. True, the nuclear revolution provides Fortress America with ample protection against direct attack and also devalues the importance of foreign bases and territorial control in other parts of the world, but the umbrella of nuclear weapons cannot stretch to cover every quarter of the globe against every kind of attack. Still, the United States' over-all power must defend threatened areas outside its territory, because international competition continues to be the traditional one over space, resources, populations, and because, like all revolutionary contests and especially with the prudence induced by nuclear weapons, it is also a struggle for minds and about values.

The balance of nuclear terror modifies, and to some extent super-imposes itself on, the traditional requirements of defensive powers, but it does not substitute for them. And these requirements are complex and often contradictory. First, there is the general problem that a defensive power has to be prepared against a bewildering array of possibilities: subversion and conventional attacks; operations initiated by one or another of its foes, and their exploitation of autonomous troubles; *faits accomplis,* "salami tactics" or deception. At the level of deterrence or "repellence" of large-scale attacks alone, the United States confronts many strategic dilemmas (for instance, the advantages of a "rational" strategy versus those of a strategy that emphasizes the "rationality of irrationality," or the advantages of a strategy that stresses deterrence above all versus those of a strategy for use should deterrence fail).[12] But the United States must be ready at all levels, since stalemate at one level encourages the offensive side to break through at another. And it must take into account the intentions and capabilities of its foes—although intentions are often obscure and hard to infer from acts (witness the diversity of interpretations of what the Soviet Union intended in the Cuban missile crisis), capabilities are hard to assess (witness the "missile gap" scare), and the interplay of intentions and capabilities is uncertain. The defensive great power lives in the famous burrow of Kafka's creepy short story.

Second, there is the complexity that arises because of the modern world's pluralism. The United States must defend its positions and values against threats of differing origin, and in cooperation with very different nations. Even when the United States and its allies define a threat in the same terms, they may disagree on the best strategy for meeting it. The more the threat is decentralized, the lesser the chances for agreement on their "priority." Then too, if one looks not only at allies but at other states, one sees that what may be a menace to the United States may elsewhere well be deemed harmless or insignificant. America's aim to "defend the free world" is by definition a collective problem, yet there is no free-world consensus on diagnosis or on prescription.

Third, there is the complexity that comes from the bewildering ar-

[12] See my *The State of War* (New York: Frederick A. Praeger, 1965), Ch. 8.

ray of possible American responses to the challenges before it. There is permanent tension between the priority given to containment, to the defense of American possessions and the international milieu in general against threats (i.e., to the negative productivity of American power) and a desire to "seize the initiative," to help transform the milieu in a way that will cripple or altogether deter threats, assure the promotion of American ideals, and perhaps make the foes' possessions and postures weaken (i.e., to emphasize the positive productivity of American power). And even within the limits of the containment alternative, there are many possible priorities. Since resources (even American ones) are inevitably limited, should the United States give precedence to the negative productivity of coercion (i.e., to its military capacity of deterrence, defense, and repellence) or to the virtues of political and economic uses of power? Finally, there is the constant problem of geographical discrimination: where should the United States give priority to a wall of containment, where should it give priority to less defensive enterprises, etc.?

In trying to solve these problems, the United States will inevitably run into contradictions. There will be conflicts between possession goals. For instance, the need to defend one area (say, South Vietnam) may necessitate a weakened military and political position in another part of the world (say, Germany). Even more frequently, there will be conflicts between possession and milieu goals. For instance, the desire to minimize damage in a possible large-scale war (that is, to save the international milieu from obliteration) may lead the United States to advocate a strategy that breeds resentment among allies who believe that it will lessen the protection given them insofar as it encourages the common foe to move more aggressively against them. The intention to reach agreements, even with opponents, on restricting the nuclear club, may antagonize allies who are potential nuclear powers; it may require genuine and risky measures of nuclear disarmament in order to convince nuclear have-nots. Strengthening the United Nations as a force for development, peacekeeping, and peaceful change may lead to sharp conflict with allies who have suffered from the United Nations, and may inhibit American freedom of action in a crisis, or American control of the power to reward. Or the determination to insure the military defeat of a foe in a certain area may detract from efforts to give greater and more autonomous economic and political vigor to a larger area; the milieu goal would have been the establishment of a nonhostile yet not necessarily "aligned" group of states healthy enough so that they do not encourage subversion, but the possession goal requires a diversion of efforts and an attempt to line up immediate support even for a very shaky state. Resort to various kinds of intervention, from diplomatic to military, in order to prevent the loss of established positions of influence (for instance, political and economic influence in the Dominican Republic, or economic interests in Latin America generally) may conflict with the milieu goal of moderate reform.

Finally, there are contradictions between milieu goals. One such goal is the establishment, behind the wall of containment, of a prosperous, secure and cooperative segment of world order within the alliances of which the United States is a member. Yet the pursuit of this goal may clash with the pursuit of a *détente* with the Soviet Union, which is considered the precondition to the establishment of any kind of global world order with a universally observed code of behavior. Nor is *détente* necessarily compatible with another goal —the prevention of the proliferation of nuclear weapons, since some non-nuclear states may interpret such a *rapprochement* as a more or less direct threat to their security, and as an indication of the superpowers' intention to disengage from local conflicts. The milieu goal of political stability in all those parts of the world which are susceptible to subversion and extremist revolutions is not always reconcilable with the goal of economic development, even though the latter is a long-term recipe against upheavals.

These complexities and contradictions in American foreign policy can be examined from a different perspective: that of the problems that confront the United States concretely at each of the three levels we distinguished in our more abstract analysis of the international system.

The persistence of a bipolar conflict entails for the United States—

(A) Considerable difficulty in finding areas of explicit agreement with the Soviet Union without giving up principles held important on general grounds (self-determination of peoples, inspection of nuclear-testing sites); or feeding the hostility of China, eager to exploit the theme of a collusion of conservative duopolists; or appearing to sacrifice the interests of allies, who fear the consequences of *détente* for their grievances or for their security (Germany) or for their rank (France, England); or freezing the arms race at a level that would be unacceptable to at least one of the superpowers.

(B) Considerable difficulty in resisting the often conflicting demands of troubled allies. They are eager either to pursue their own course with their own means (France) or to hold onto American ends and means so as to deter an unfavorable *détente* (Germany), but to sanction the first or brush off the second could throw either ally out of the camp or, in the second case, into each other's arms. If both the United States and the Soviet Union should decide to deploy ABM systems around their cities, the United States can expect its allies to request a similar deployment around theirs, while resisting American attempts at preserving control of those defenses.

(C) Considerable difficulty in dealing with the problem of subversion. There is first the problem of protecting American allies and neutral states against Communist penetration or takeover, or against extreme revolutionary movements that are intensely hostile to the United States; this is a matter of deterrence, defense or repellence. Then there is the problem of the overthrow, by subversion, of Communist regimes or regimes that appear to give to Communist forces a privileged stronghold or easy opportunity; this is a matter of offense and "compellence." Now the United States has only a short experience and mixed expertise in those shady realms. Its rivals are masters of ruthless means and the guerrilla's organizational skills. The result is that for offensive purposes the United States may find overt, coercive intervention easier and more effective than covert subversion. But the open use of force against Communist regimes soon reaches a point the United States is unwilling to cross: the level at which the conflict would escalate into a major confrontation with the Soviet Union or China. Then, in the matter of defensive policies, the existence of or potential for Communist agitation in various parts of the world either obliges the United States to support anti-Communist political forces whose myopic policies may actually help Communist infiltration in the long run, or else reduces the margin of action for the kind of democratic, reformist forces which the United States would prefer to encourage but which are caught between two powerful extremes. Also, when Communist elements are obviously in control of the subversive forces or when they are threatening to gain control of allied or neutral countries by subversion, the United States could use its regular forces to deny them victory, but at the cost of devoting an important amount of resources and attention to a negative task, i.e., at the expense of other uses of power and other kinds of achievements.

On the "polycentric" level, America's frustrations come from—

(A) The fact that whereas wars among lesser nations can be handled under existing practices (a tacit agreement of the superpowers, carried out through the United Nations, or United Nations action backed by one superpower without the overt and active opposition of the other), "world policing forces" carefully leave out the United States and U.S.S.R., whose control is at best indirect (the United States is obliged to negotiate a common ground with the lesser powers). On the other hand, violence in human affairs redoubles in the form of civil war or revolution, which international intervention is much less well designed to subdue, as the Congo, Cyprus, and Yemen affairs have shown. Thus, in order to stabilize the international milieu (quite apart from Cold War considerations) and in order to prevent third parties from becoming Cold War arenas, the United States must play at being Sisyphus. It must try to stem avalanches with its mighty shoulders—to shore up regimes against revolutions—but it hesitates to promote revolutions lest they get out of control and benefit Communist or anti-American forces, or to become too committed to shoring up shaky regimes lest their unavoidable collapse bruise America's shoulders.

(B) The fact that various measures of help designed to promote political stability and economic modernization in underdeveloped countries suffer from many uncertainties. Their effectiveness depends on local circumstances often beyond manipulation, their results are often unintended, and their specific forms are often in conflict. Yet these difficulties (and those often added by leaders who are as eager to exploit the anti-American feelings of their people as they are to receive American aid) are not such as to incite the United States to give up the effort, for only the Soviet Union or China would benefit from its withdrawal—or so we fear.

(C) The fact that within its alliances, the United States now pays the price for the successes of its policies. The United States, largely for "bipolar" reasons—that is, in order to prevent Communist advances due to political, economic and social chaos—has strengthened many of its allies. It now finds that the lowering of tension that resulted from the success of this deterrence has incited its allies to challenge their benefactor. Moreover, having acted its hegemonial role in a most unclassical way—as a power that dominates by weight, not will, out of necessity, not choice, because of the situation, not ambition—the United States has made the revolt against its hegemony as easy (and hard to repress) as it appears unfair to Americans. The lesser allies feel free to rebel not only because the penalty for doing so is smaller than at a time of high tension, but also because "peril parity" raises questions about the United States' willingness to risk nuclear extermination for the protection of others.

Understandably, they are cool toward a theory of "limited" war that would be unlimited for them. Thus, the revolt is caused by a feeling of greater over-all security, and by a fear of lesser security should the improbable occur; by the idea that an ally can afford to be difficult, and by the idea that being an ally pays less than it did, since the continuation of the Soviet-American contest assures their protection whether they are allied or not.

Finally, on the level of emergent multipolarity, the United States suffers from three forms of embarrassment.

(A) The challenge within NATO over nuclear programs or demands increases the intractability of the issue of "alliance management," for it exposes the United States to two equally sour alternatives. If it tries to maintain a predominance that is in fact already breached, so as to avoid the hazards that nuclear proliferation within NATO entails for peace and for the American position, the United States actually risks encouraging the breaking up of NATO. But if, in order to preserve NATO, it agrees to give up the claim to central control over nuclear weapons, it encourages a trend that it considers futile and dangerous, and it introduces into the alliance a permanent struggle to prevent the emergent "poles" from implicating the United States in concerns vital to them but not to the United States. Moreover, the challenge of actual or potential nuclear powers considerably limits American freedom of maneuver vis-à-vis the U.S.S.R., since any direct American attempt at a dialogue and entente, for instance, might throw West Germany into France's arms, whereas any attempt to define joint alliance positions toward the Soviet Union runs into divergences among the allies.

(B) A second problem here is to prevent other powers, which are neither adversaries nor allies, from following the atomic pied-pipers. This is almost impossible to do. In order to close the nuclear club to new members, the United States cannot use solitary coercion or joint coercion with the Soviet Union (since neither rival is ready to give priority to a nuclear/non-nuclear division over the present vertical solidarity), nor can it give individual or even joint guarantees at a time when "peril parity" throws doubt on any individual guarantee and competition still rules out joint ones.[13]

(C) A third problem is created by the emergence of China as a

---

[13] For a fuller discussion, see my *The State of War*, Ch. 8, and "Nuclear Proliferation and World Politics," in Alastair Buchan, ed., *A World of Nuclear Powers?* (Englewood Cliffs, N.J.: Prentice-Hall, for The American Assembly, 1966).

nuclear power with a foreign policy that challenges both the United States and the Soviet Union. The United States cannot evade China's challenge, any more than it could decline to pick up Russia's. But the desire of many nations that are America's partners in the conflict with Russia, and of many of the Asian powers potentially threatened by China, to "exploit" the possibilities opened up by the muffling of pure "Cold-War" bipolarity makes them extremely reluctant to join the United States in an anti-Chinese alliance in the Far East. They fear that this might reactivate bipolarity by forcing the Soviet Union to come to the rescue of China, thus plunging the international system into crisis, and clipping the wings of the "centers" and new "poles." Yet they appear to believe that any nation threatened by China would be defended by the United States in any event, perhaps by *both* superpowers.

For the United States, the outcome is a bitter kind of fragmentation of the international system. It must still man the barricades all over the globe, but in increasing isolation. Yet the only alternatives to its "guarding the whole world" seem to be, on the one hand, positive gains for its enemies, and on the other (as in the Middle East crisis of 1967), letting the fate of each segment of the system be determined by the hazards of local confrontations. The rise of China prevents the United States from treating the Soviet Union as the main enemy (although it is still the only other superpower), precisely because the United States cannot act as though the danger came only from actual military capabilities. Nor can the United States deem the Soviet Union as somehow a potential ally, because the ultimate keys of death and "coexistence" are in the hands of the chief rivals only, their rivalry is perpetuated by intractable clashes of power and values, the very limits that the fear of major war and the strength of America's defensive power put on brutal Russian thrusts encourage more subtle and indirect ones, and their ultimate reconciliation is as much hindered as helped by the sudden rise of challengers. The challenge of Red China, especially in the struggle for diplomatic allegiance of the uncommitted and for ideological allegiance of the malcontents in backward areas, condemns the Soviet Union to prudence in *détente:* for if collision with the United States must be avoided, the charge of collusion must be averted too.

Earlier, we discussed in broad terms the kinds of achievements possible for all states in general, and great powers in particular.

Once again, we must look at the specific instance of the United States.

In the first place, we cannot fail to see, as we have already remarked in the preceding chapter, that America's power has a very high negative productivity. Military means—ranging from technical support of friendly governments (Congo, Brazil, Venezuela, Greece) or open intervention against alleged subversion of friendly governments (Lebanon, Dominican Republic) to defense (Korea, South Vietnam), repellence (Cuban missile crisis), and deterrence (Europe, most of Asia)—have been particularly important in keeping Communist power largely within the boundaries it possessed in 1945. The only places in which Communists have wrested control since have been behind the Iron Curtain, and in China, Cuba, and North Vietnam. Thus, it is obvious that military force remains an indispensable part of power, especially for a defensive state. And the prevalence of denials over gains in the present international system favors the United States. Its foes are reduced to putting their hopes in vague milieu changes and in the success of specific revolutions.

We are accustomed to recognizing America's advantages at the conventional military and nuclear levels. But these advantages extend further, to the defensive struggle against Communist subversion. Today, revolutions have little chance of success unless they are supported by foreign arms, or stimulated by a large, determined and widespread section of the population, or staged by forces with a monopoly of arms, i.e., by the military. Revolutions supported by Communist powers (the Soviet Union, China, North Vietnam, or Cuba) run into the formidable capabilities of the United States to deny its opponents the gains they seek—capabilities that can be used either to "take and hold" or to inflict pain. United States "technical aid" to military forces in threatened states or countries likely to be threatened makes subversion much more difficult, and it obliges rebels or potential rebels to disperse their efforts or to look for the kind of outside support that Communist states are uneager to provide, precisely because this would encourage the very confrontations in which the formidable coercive power of the United States could be used most effectively. Thus, in one essential respect, the "internalization" of world politics helps the United States. Since successful revolutions have become far more costly affairs than nineteenth-century *coups d'état,* the defensive side has a great advantage; for the anti-*status-quo* forces, escalation is almost indispensable, but it will bring into play the United States' huge military machine. It is wrong, therefore, to think that the United States is deprived of "denial capacity" against subversion. But it is also wrong to imagine that its uses of military power for this purpose are foolproof, that coercion has a guarantee of effectiveness, a writ of success. As a deterrent of subversion, military support (or support to the military) may well turn out to be a form of *reculer pour mieux sauter*—prolonging the lull, but making for wilder storms. As a defense against and repellent of revolutions, military force is ineffective unless certain political, social, and economic conditions are also met, as the history of Chiang Kai-shek in 1947–49 or of the French or Americans in Indochina amply shows. Indeed, if those conditions are not met, the wielder of military power will discover that if he increases its application on the spot so as to hurt and destroy the enemy, he risks exterminating those whom one allegedly protects. Thus, today's avoidance of a possession loss may lead to serious milieu losses tomorrow which no amount of coercion can prevent. And if one extends the application of force outside the contested territory so as to hurt the enemy's outside bases *in lieu of* destroying him where he is, one may cross over the limits within which force remains useful.

In the second place, the positive productivity of American power is not negligible. The United States has had notable successes in improving the "milieu" behind the barriers of containment. Moreover, there have been gains in the context of "internalized" international politics: the United States has been directly or indirectly involved in the overthrow of regimes that seemed to be on the verge of providing communism with impressive victories; in Guatemala, the United States played a conspicuous role; in the fall of Mossadegh, in the fall of Goulart, in the demise of Sukarno, in the overthrow of Nkrumah, the involvement of the United States was more discreet yet far from nil.

But here I must re-emphasize points I made earlier. The positive productivity of American power (including military power) is limited. The less overt the American intervention and the more tenuous the link between the revolutionaries (or counter-revolutionaries) and the United States, the more lasting the success of offense or compellence will be (the forces that brought it off will appear genuinely national), yet the less easy it will be for the United States to control the consequences. Now, for such indirect productivity to be less uncertain, the United States must be able to affect the processes of change and decision-making in as many countries as possible (instead of relying exclusively on dubious hunches and temporary clients), and it must be able to define its milieu goals clearly enough to know where it wants to go, and skillfully enough to have a chance to bring the indispensable others along.

Whether any one power could accomplish this today is doubtful; the task is too huge. But in the case of the United States, there are unique constraints and imperatives, springing from domestic sources, that make the task especially hard to perform.

# PART II

# America's Style

# CHAPTER FOUR

# The Nature of the Problem

"If the study of national character is an effort to establish a collective personality, the examination of national style seeks to define how that collective personality reacts to and acts upon its environment." [1] The notion of national character has turned out to be of dubious validity, but the notion of a national style holds greater promise. It is, exactly like the concept of an international system, a postulate and a construct. It attempts to establish order in a chaotic mass of features by positing that a nation perceives the world, and its place in it, in a fashion which is never quite that of any other nation, just as no individual ever faces the world like any one else. This way is a procedure of selection, and therefore inevitably one of exclusion, and it is a procedure of distortion, because things that may be important are left out and also because the things selected are refracted through the prism of the nation's or individual's character. A person's style is shaped by his predispositions—by his character and what Pascal called his second nature, his habits and experiences transformed into character.

Like any postulate and construct, the notion of a national style is useful insofar as it creates some verisimilitude of order, but it shares with its subject matter the property of simplifying or distorting a much richer reality. Therefore, critics of the concept are always at liberty to deny that there is such a thing as a national style (or an international system)—although nobody really claims that these are "things." They are intellectual tools, which have a way of creeping back into the analysis even after being thrown out for lack of rigor.

Even if one accepts the concept of a national style as a working hypothesis, difficulties abound. After all, foreign affairs are handled by *limited* groups of people. What Raymond Aron has called "dip-

[1] Walt W. Rostow, in Elting E. Morison, ed., *The American Style* (New York: Harper & Bros., 1958), p. 147.

lomatic-strategic behavior" [2] is the realm of the diplomat and the soldier, with—in the rear, so to speak—limited elites of informed citizens with some experience or expertise. Is it not unfair to attribute to a whole nation traits that characterize only the policy-makers?

And what about the other implicit assumption, that there is *a* style continuing from one generation to the next? Are not the policy-makers divided over time, as well as at any one given point? In the case of the United States, what is there in common to the imperialists and anti-imperialists of the turn of the century, the isolationists and the champions of collective security of the interwar period, the realists aware of the need for and limits on American power and radical activists in search of victory in the postwar period? What unites Theodore Roosevelt and Woodrow Wilson, Cordell Hull and Dean Acheson, Douglas MacArthur and John F. Kennedy?

Third, what about the very notion of a *style?* How do we define the way the policy-makers approach the world: by studying what they actually do, what they intend to do, or what they say they are intending and doing?

Fourth, how can one *isolate* that which is the nation's own way toward the world from that which is merely its response to the world's drives and pressures? In a policy, what, in other words, is it that comes from the nation's own heritage, culture, beliefs, and reflexes, and what is it that constitutes a less individual reaction to a compelling situation? Does the nation's style fluctuate over time because the vicissitudes of the world's history affect it far more than the nation's own ideals or procedures do?

And, finally, is it reasonable to assume that there is anything *unique* about a national style? Is it not made up of features that can be found elsewhere? Also, for every feature found in a "collective personality's" way of behaving, can we not discover the opposite feature?

All these questions and objections justifiably put us on our guard, stressing as they do the limits of usefulness of a partly arbitrary notion. Yet they do not really dispose of the notion itself.[3] For it *is* possible, in every nation, to find common features displayed by policy-makers and interested elites. While it may be somewhat arro-

[2] *Peace and War: A Theory of International Relations* (Richard Howard and Annette Baker Fox, trans.), (New York: Doubleday, 1966), p. 16.

[3] See Herbert J. Spiro, *World Politics: The Global System* (Homewood, Ill.: Dorsey Press, 1966).

gant to call them *a priori* "national" features, this is more accurate in the case of a nation like the United States, in which policy-makers and the relevant elites are not a hereditary caste or clique drawn from a narrow segment of society, and in which the "power elite" and the "people" are bound together not merely by functional ties and relations of command and dependence, but by a truly remarkable tissue of common beliefs and feelings.[4] All we need to know in order to be able to talk about a national style in foreign affairs is that the citizens who come in contact with world politics tend to behave in a certain way. Thus, when we speak of "America" in sweeping terms fit to infuriate social psychologists, we shall be using a short cut; we shall be talking about the beliefs, attitudes, and acts of those Americans who are responsible for and concerned with the nation's foreign affairs.

As for the possibility that each country has a variety of "styles," it would be foolish to deny that anything approaching unanimity ever exists in the ordering of priorities, the formulation of issues, the statement of solutions. But one should not mistake substance for style. A Frenchman of the right and a Frenchman of the left may disagree about every conceivable substantive issue, from the meaning of the French Revolution to the nature of man, and yet they will present their arguments and try to convince their audience in a way that is common to both and not quite like the Englishman's or American's, a manner shaped by education and family customs and based on assumptions about reality, time, or authority that transcend substantive disagreements on issues. The more deeply divided a nation is on substance, the more the notion of style must be restricted to the handful of beliefs, still common to all its citizens, which underlie its acts. (Unless the nation is a mere fiction, a territory with central power but not really a community, there must be some common values, if not about the polity, at least about society.) The notion also applies to the relations of authority and the patterns of behavior that grow from and in turn shape its class structure and political system and that keep the citizens together. The less divided a nation is on substance, the broader the scope of "style": still concerned with patterns of authority and behavior, it now also encompasses a broader range of beliefs and opinions. In other words, what is common to Theodore Roosevelt, Wilson, Hull, Acheson, etc., is not merely the values and biases one may find present in all their

[4] This was the point neglected by C. Wright Mills in *The Power Elite* (New York: Oxford University Press, 1956).

acts, but also the terms in which they phrase their disagreements and the ways in which they play them out.

The problem of whether to use intentions, acts, or words as the indicator of national "style" is not an insoluble one. What statesmen say, they may say for effect and it may be a rationalization; but the choice of what they deem effective and the kind of rationalization they use are significant. If, over time, the choice and the kind tend to be constant among a nation's leaders, then the pattern is part of the national style. If a succession of statesmen present colonial ventures, say, not (or not primarily) as moves for economic gain, strategic advantage, or increase in power, but as dictates of a "civilizing mission" or a "white man's burden," this tells us something about their national style, both because the choice of the themes expresses a judgment about what fits this style and because the themes will in turn affect the nation's way, creating expectations and provoking action. A statesman who acts one way and talks another reveals something of himself, to be sure; but if the way he talks occurred because it corresponded not just to his own nature but to his assessment of his audience's nature and to a belief that his nation's policy would be most effective if presented in that way, then he also reveals something of the nation's style. When statesmen with different personalities and politics speak the same kind of language, we have a clue as to what the national style is. Intentions matter, too, of course, but so do the contradictions between intentions and acts, the gaps between motives and moves, when they form a pattern.

What is action and what is reaction, what is spontaneous reflex and what is rational response to external pressures are never really separable. The making of foreign policy is a learning process, and any learning process modifies beliefs and behavior through the impact of new knowledge. However, the tensions manifest when an individual or nation is forced to absorb and adjust to unwelcome necessities, the joys and hopes (and boasts) displayed when a challenge is precisely of the kind which the person or country is best equipped to handle, the way very different challenges are translated into similar terms and handled as if they were the same—in other words, all the perceptions of and responses to the outside world are very much the "stuff" of the national style. Changes in the outside world may make certain habitual responses impossible and force a radical shift in perceptions, but often the effect of those changes is more to transform the substance than the style of policy. Even when the style changes, what is important is the *way* it changes, what is discarded, what scars and memories are left, and how much time elapses between the advent of the new pressure and the adjustment or the disappearance of the old approach. When there is a pattern of misperceptions (however much they may be straightened out over time), we are in the presence of another clue.

Finally, the problem of the uniqueness of a national style need not detain us long. No single feature is ever unique; to take two different examples, historians have shown that what Richard Hofstadter has so brilliantly called the paranoid style in politics can be studied in the history of the American Populist movement and the recurrent Radical Right, in French Poujadism, and in totalitarian regimes.[5] Political scientists have spoken of an "Anglo-American tradition in foreign affairs" stemming from a common experience of noninvolvement in the quarrels of Continental Europe, and a resultant common conviction that the area of necessity did not eliminate a respectable margin of choice.[6] The uniqueness of a national style is not a discrete feature but the combination of features characteristic of each country; what is unique is each nation's experience. Two nations with similar stylistic features will respond differently to their environment; being situated differently in the world, they will perceive the environment differently, and, coming to the present experience with a different historical stock, their response to it will be shaped by their domestic predispositions and their memories. True, with all nations, values and behavior are marked by contradictions; but each nation is distinguished first by the specific nature of the "polar opposites" in its style, and second by the reason why these contradictions have appeared and persisted.

All these qualifications, as well as the imprecision of the language, obviously make the study of national style thoroughly unscientific. For various reasons, psychologists and social psychologists are concerned more with the aspects of "international behavior" that are reducible to scientific investigation—i.e., easier to isolate and quantify—than with this confusing realm. They have been concerned more with images than with behavior, more with stereotypes and attitudes toward foreigners than with interaction between nationals and outsiders.[7] And political scientists have been concerned more

[5] See Richard Hofstadter, *The Paranoid Style in American Politics and Other Essays* (New York: Alfred A. Knopf, 1965), and Philip Williams, *Crisis and Compromise* (Hamden, Conn.: Archon Books, 1964), p. 169.

[6] See Arnold Wolfers and Laurence Martin, *The Anglo-American Tradition in Foreign Affairs* (New Haven: Yale University Press, 1956), pp. ix-xxvii.

[7] For a good example, see Herbert Kelman, ed., *International Behavior* (New York: The Free Press of Glencoe, 1965).

with either the international contest itself or the formulation of foreign policy than with the style that both preconditions and permeates all the stages of foreign policy. However, one cannot wait until all the tools for research have been forged and the returns are in. What follows will be a set of hypotheses derived from the mind of one observer.

It should be clear at the outset that a nation's style is both a source of strength and a cause of weakness—like an individual's character. This is so not only because certain features are virtues and others are flaws; the same feature may be a factor for effectiveness and a reason for failure, depending on the nature of the challenge or on what is needed at a particular time. Blinders help one to focus and thus make it possible to act, but they also eliminate from the field of vision realities it would have been useful to see, and put up obstacles one could have done without. Therefore, what follows is neither a celebration nor an indictment: it is a statement. Moreover, to state that a certain feature or cluster of features leads occasionally to trouble does not mean that better results would necessarily have been produced by a different style or approach, especially since in an assessment of the final achievement, we must take into account the workings of the international system. What is of interest is the particular kind of trouble due to, or compounded by, one particular style.

Some years ago, in a first stab at this subject, I divided the American style into the three elements of America's experience relevant to foreign policy: [8] the liberal tradition, which shapes expectations of final harmony and explains both the depreciation of coercion and the lapse into "just wars"; a conservatism that is both a way of life (which opens an abyss between the United States and most other nations) and an approach to action, christened by Walt Rostow "the operator's way"; [9] finally, America's unique position in the world before World War II, which left a legacy of impatience and an "illusion of omnipotence." [10] Here, I will proceed in a slightly different way, first by analyzing three components I consider important, and then by looking at the problems that arise from the combination of them. These three components together affect the

[8] In *The State of War* (New York: Frederick A. Praeger, 1965), Ch. 7.

[9] In Morison, ed., cited, pp. 257 ff. Also see W. W. Rostow's *United States in the World Arena* (New York: Harper & Bros., 1960).

[10] D. W. Brogan, *American Aspects* (New York: Harper & Row, 1964), Ch. 2.

way that the United States perceives and acts upon the outside world; in other words, they operate at the two levels I have distinguished in the introduction to this book. First, they restrict the area of choice by closing off certain options, which are not perceived or for the exploitation of which there are no mental and behavioral tools, and also by dictating certain ideas and attitudes whose adequacy is open to doubt. Second, the effectiveness of the policies that are either dictated by those predispositions or freely chosen within the restricted range left available is often crippled. When we turn to the way those predispositions combine, we will deal more specifically with problems of effectiveness.[11]

[11] The discussion that follows does not pretend to provide a complete explanation of the American postwar approach to foreign policy. For instance, the reader will find here no scrutiny of the famous "military-industrial complex." My purpose is not to deny its existence, but to provide some tools for understanding its importance. Capitalism or the drive for profit strike me as less significant an explanation (of a phenomenon that exists also in the Soviet Union and emerges in China) than the nature of the international competition, the basic elements of the American style which give an eminent position and legitimacy to technological anti-communism, and the structure of the institutional system which gives to the so-called complex a multiple access to the centers of power.

CHAPTER FIVE

# The National Style: An Analysis

There are three aspects of America's singularity that are relevant to the study of foreign policy: the nation's past, its principles, and its pragmatism. All three are part of a national experience whose relevance to the outside world is uncertain, because the conditions in which it has taken place have been so different from conditions anywhere else. And yet, Americans have never stopped projecting into their foreign policy the three facets of this experience: its historical component (the lessons learned and the mental habits derived from their country's unique situation); the American way of thinking, of apprehending the world mentally for judgment and for reform (a kind of rationalization of the American experience); and the American way of acting, of apprehending the world instrumentally, which consists of the tools that have made the American experience a success. Many writers have analyzed the origins and main features of these three elements, and I see no need to go over ground that has been so well covered. I will therefore concentrate on features that are directly relevant to foreign affairs, and on the impact that these elements in American life have on United States foreign policy.

## I. America's Past

The legacy of America's past is a heritage of separation—not only a physical separation between the New World and the traditional centers of world politics, but a moral distance, a willed and self-conscious separation of a "segment" divorced from its European background.[1] This segment has quickly and constantly resorted to a celebration of its uniqueness, of the ideals enshrined in its Constitu-

[1] For the notion of the segment, see Louis Hartz *et al., The Founding of New Societies* (New York: Harcourt, Brace, 1964).

94

tion: "We think of ourselves as growing into our skeleton" [2]—as living a purposeful unfolding of the truths brought by the early immigrants and stated by the Founding Fathers, and as embodying what Max Lerner has called the "theory of exceptionalism," "the working hypothesis of an American character and culture which are set up distinctively from others" and particularly from Europe.[3] If it is true that this segment of Europe not only left Europe behind but "slayed the European father," [4] this truth is enormously relevant to our purposes, since the objective of this study is to throw light on America's relations with Europe.

## A. *American Attitudes toward Europe*

My objective is not to review "America and the image of Europe" [5] throughout the life of the American Republic; I shall therefore limit myself to examining what are in fact different layers of contemporary American attitudes toward (and experiences with) Europe. These layers were formed during the years when the historical and physical separation of the United States gave way to its involvement in world affairs (albeit an involvement still marked with the stamp of the past, still seen through the prism of "exceptionalism"). They differ in time as well as in substance, and yet their effects converge in important ways.

The first layer was formed by the men who were young when World War I began. Whether or not they approved of Wilson's crusade, whether they shared his hope for a "concert of power" in which the United States would play its part or whether they embraced the return to isolationism, they had all been brought up in the belief that America's greatest contribution to the world was its own history and progress, and that its very identity had been found and was to persist in opposition to the evils of Europe. The Europe into which the war had plunged them was not so much a "father" or "brother" to defend as a fallen continent to redeem. To these men, Europe was the practitioner (and victim) of Hobbesian power politics, Machiavellian alliances, intrigues, and corruption; it was the prime mover of an imperialism that aimed not at emancipating de-

[2] Daniel J. Boorstin, *The Genius of American Politics* (University of Chicago Press, 1953), p. 16.

[3] Max Lerner, *America as a Civilization* (New York: Simon and Schuster, 1957), p. 66.

[4] Same, p. 23.

[5] See Daniel J. Boorstin's book by that title (New York: Meridian Books, 1960).

pendents but at exploiting them; it was the continent of class distinctions and, all too frequently, of authoritarian or ineffective politics. This was the Europe the emigrants had deserted, the trap against which Washington had warned in the Farewell Address. One finds this idealistic stereotype at the back of Wilson's idea of America's purpose in World War I as much as in the horrified repudiation of Versailles by so many who had supported him. It left behind what it had itself fed on: a legacy of distrust and moral censure.

A second layer was formed by the men who shaped American policy in the days of the New Deal. Concerned with domestic affairs above all (and, in the case of the most ardent New Dealers, concerned to establish that the remedies they prescribed for America's ills were home-grown products and not alien imports), yet aware of the perils that were accumulating overseas, they saw in Europe, at worst, a ghastly mess that threatened to divert America's "giddy minds" into "foreign quarrels," [6] at best, a battlefield between repellent totalitarian regimes and bloodless divided democracies that were unable to get over the depression, produce real leadership, or defend their interests. Again, there was a legacy of impatience, distaste, and reprobation (although for different reasons), with new overtones of dismay and some contempt—overtones that are not difficult to detect in F.D.R.'s own wartime attitudes. As Robert Osgood has pointed out,[7] there was less evangelism and more circumspection than in Wilson's days, but once the United States had entered the war, former interventionists and isolationists alike tended to treat occupied Europe as a stake, to be liberated and put in its place. F.D.R.'s notion of the United States, England, the Soviet Union and China as the "four policemen" for the postwar world and the State Department's corollary concept of the United Nations testify to this attitude.

The third layer was formed by the heroic generation of American foreign policy, the new Founding Fathers, the men of 1947–48, the architects of a policy that the United States must be involved as a world power and must contain the Communist challenge. These men, whose first task it now was not to police the world along with the other big powers, but to save the world in general and Europe in particular from the other superpower, the Soviet Union, saw in Europe something quite new and different—a prostrate victim of a self-

[6] See Charles Beard's pamphlet by that title (New York, 1939).

[7] *Ideals and Self-Interest in America's Foreign Relations* (University of Chicago Press, 1953).

inflicted war, a continent in need, not of redemption or probation, but of treatment, for the rehabilitation of the damned and the cure of the sick. The damned were those who had fought on the wrong side and who now had to be "reconverted" and "forced to be free." [8] The sick were ill both mentally and physically, their lands in ruin and their minds diseased by Communist parties and unions. Europe was also suffering from fragmentation, which threatened to prevent or slow down whatever cure might be applied to the sickness, and which also threatened to reproduce the very discord and hatred that had already engendered two world wars. This time, the Americans' moral condemnation was replaced by compassion, contempt by pity. But there was still impatience—even or especially when this was hidden behind exhortations of patience intended to calm and reassure the Americans themselves and to warn and push the Europeans. There was still more than a trace of suspicion. And there was now a great activist desire to overhaul and to re-educate Europe—not with missionary or crusading zeal, but with the peculiar self-confidence and expert benevolence of men who know their power, trust their techniques, and define their purpose with an exciting sense of concrete jobs to be done rather than articles of faith to be proclaimed. To these men, Europe was a challenging building ground.

Perhaps we can see in the present decade the rudiments of a fourth layer, formed by men who do not share this fascination with Europe, a continent that remains fragmented, appears parochial, refuses to share burdens, yet insists that somehow it is and should remain the center of the stage, the fulcrum of America's concerns. At a time when the main international issues are becoming, first, the growing gap between rich and poor lands, and second, the new Cold War in Asia (so much more difficult to fight than the old Cold War in Europe, given the direct appeal made by the new enemy to the poor), Europe's confused and conflicting claims fall badly on many American policy-makers' ears. Again, they are impatient, exasperated, and slightly contemptuous, showing traces of reprobation. But the sense that earlier generations had, of Europe as the womb of America (so that the one thing they could never feel was indifferent), is beginning to disappear, replaced by a slight degree of boredom.

One important thing about these layers of attitudes and experience is that they suggest a kind of historical curve. The curve is a

[8] See John Montgomery's book by that title (University of Chicago Press, 1957).

swift and somehow disturbing passage from a long period in which "borrowing from Europe" was anathema, in which American initiatives were to be shown as such and not as European transplantations, to a period in which the United States has become an exporter of its virtues and recipes. There is a shift from isolation to the assumption of international leadership, both extremes having in common the intention to avoid the contamination of unhealthy foreign troubles. (One can argue that the return to isolation after involvement—i.e., the repudiation of Wilson—was in part a reaction by men who saw in the kind of involvement implied in the Versailles Treaty and League of Nations not the opportunity to fulfill Wilson's exhilarating vision of leadership for principles and altruism, but a nightmare of contamination by Europeans unwilling to accept so lofty a vision and so disturbing a leadership.)

This is what distinguishes the "uniqueness" of the American experience from the uniqueness of the British. Great Britain too was separate from Continental Europe, but it was not completely insulated. It was a detached yet active participant in the poisons and delights of European history—and it was perceived as such in the United States. Britain did not play the same kind of game as, say, France or Austria (a difference that emerged most clearly at the Congress of Vienna [9]), partly because it was in fact an island and partly because of its internal political evolution; but a game of power Great Britain certainly did play. The world's greatest trading nation, with an empire on which the sun never set, it played the game sometimes as a mere participant, like others, sometimes as a leader—but then as a leader by virtue of its advantageous semi-detachment from the specific quarrels of the others, more than by virtue of superiority in power or domination over others. The mixture of insularity and involvement continues to affect—or should one say to plague?—Britain's perception of its role in the world and relationship to the Continent, just as the United States' switch from isolation to preponderance affects the American approach. But it is not the same mix, it is not the same legacy.

Another important effect of the various layers of American attitudes toward Europe is that together they have left behind a legacy of impatience—in fact, of varieties of impatience. They can perhaps be summarized, unfair as it may sound, as impatience with, and sometimes ignorance of, the intricacy of European history. It is

[9] See Henry A. Kissinger's *A World Restored* (Boston: Houghton Mifflin, 1957).

worth noting that whereas Americans have made serious research efforts to "catch up" in the once neglected areas of the history and society of America's chief rivals and the "third world," Europe is now the underdeveloped area in social science scholarship.

IMPATIENCE WITH EUROPEAN POLITICS

First of all, there is impatience with various political forms associated with Europe's historical experience. One of these is the balance of power. It has recently been rescued by certain scholars, some of European origin, but the rescue is far from complete. The old distrust of this European sport of kings, so strong in Wilson and Hull, was still strong enough after World War II to incite the men defending the creation of NATO to do so without using balance-of-power terms: "The old veteran, balance of power, was given a blue discharge when the United Nations was formed." [10] The tendency to paint collective-security colors on America's alliances reveals the same residue of suspicion. Today, when hope in the United Nations is less fashionable, this old distrust of the balance of power takes on a new form; it is now argued that the United States is the only world power, or else that a bipolar system is more stable than the delicate European balance of power used to be, than a new multipolar world would be. But this conviction, impressively argued by Kenneth Waltz,[11] is perhaps not so new after all. Writing after the San Francisco Conference that established the United Nations, John Fisher had already concluded that a world "organized into two great power systems" would be more stable than a world of several great powers, "all roughly comparable in strength," with its "almost infinite opportunity for intrigue and combination," uneasiness about neighbors, shifting alliances and "dangerous maneuver." [12] European political thinkers have had a way of presenting the balance of power as about as moderate and reasonable an arrangement as one has the right to expect in the international state of nature and as the crowning achievement of a golden age in diplomacy and international law. But there continues to be considerable resistance to this view in the United States. Somehow, the skies of American thinking about the possibilities of world order do not contain this

[10] Charles Burton Marshall in Arnold Wolfers, ed., *Changing East-West Relations and the Unity of the West* (Baltimore: The Johns Hopkins Press, 1964), p. 24.

[11] "The Stability of a Bipolar World," *Daedalus,* Summer 1964, pp. 883–909.

[12] Quoted in Norman Graebner, ed., *Ideas and Diplomacy* (New York: Oxford University Press, 1964), p. 683.

constellation. They spread over either a world without weapons and under law, a world government in which power has been transcended or transferred, or a "world community of nations" safe for diversity under American guidance.

I am not trying to suggest that, in a nuclear age, a return to the tarnished gold of the Concert of Europe is either possible or terribly exciting: I am trying to explain one source of misunderstanding between Americans and Europeans. The latter (particularly the English and French) have a kind of congenital nostalgia for the days of the balance of power, which were their better days, and no particular enthusiasm for the blessings of bipolarity, which marks their decline. Americans are less in favor of a scheme in which they had no part and the breakdowns of which dragged them into two world wars. They tend to attribute evils to the balance of power that ought to be imputed to its decay or collapse, while their European counterparts tend to forget that this fragile balancing system indeed had the almost invariable habit of drifting into decay or exposing itself to collapse.

Another political expression of Europe for which there is little sympathy in the United States is nationalism. American spokesmen frequently single out European nationalism for denunciation as an evil, while they encourage nationalism in other parts of the world and rarely analyze their own form of nationalism. Here, the heritage of the past is particularly worth observing. The United States, having owed its existence to a revolt against a colonial power, has retained sympathy for such revolts and a certain antipathy to the kind of nationalism that often prevails among colonial powers, an implicit distinction being made between the nationalisms of rebellion and the nationalisms of expansion (the latter associated with Europe).

Moreover, it is a fact that the American perception of the United States differs from what Americans think citizens of European nations perceive about *their* countries. As Daniel Boorstin has pointed out, the American Revolution was a "revolution without a dogma," [13] asserting independence simply as a way to preserve and protect certain values and institutions. Not even Seymour Lipset's attempt to analyze the United States as "the first new nation" [14] has succeeded in discovering nationalist dogma as one of the links between America and the new nations of today. To be sure, as he shows, America developed a sense of national identity, forged

[13] *The Genius of American Politics,* pp. 70 ff.
[14] See his book by that title (New York: Basic Books, 1963).

largely by intellectuals behind the protective wall of neutrality. But what we do not find are the two necessary ingredients of dogmatic nationalism as we find them in Europe: on the one hand, what one could call a tribal celebration of one's nation as an end in itself; on the other hand, a conviction that the nation is the highest good and must receive top priority in the conduct of foreign policy. It may well be that these ingredients appear only when national groups define and develop their identity in constant comparison, competition, and conflict with one another. This was not the American case. There was a break with a colonial power, but it was a break within a family, quite different from the anticolonial revolutions of native peoples against their alien masters, and after that break, the Americans were both fortunate and careful not to have major problems of entanglement with foreign rivals. As a result, their own nationalism has always seemed to them either mild and harmless—a happy celebration of emancipation for virtue—or refined and enlightened—a lofty dedication to the promotion of certain ideals of which the American nation is merely the carrier. In many cases, European nationalism has shown the same capacity to clothe the tribal urge in the garb of ideals transcending the nation. But, to Americans at least, the sham was more apparent than in their own case, since the imperialist and balance-of-power politics of European nations exposed more ruthlessly the pretense. Certainly, Americans recognize that in their own history there was a lapse from mildness and an abuse of mission during the period of imperial expansion, but they see their imperialism as limited in time and reluctant at heart, and they find neither redeeming feature in Europe's.

Since the United States tends to exempt itself from the sins of nationalism, to interpet its role in terms that transcend the nation, and to define colonialism or imperialism in the European sense (the formal control of other peoples by a dominating state), it also tends to be shocked and grieved by two kinds of anti-Americanism. One is the anti-Americanism of people in underdeveloped areas who consider the United States as an imperial power. Since nationalism is justified only against colonial masters and the United States is not a colonial master, the reasoning goes, such anti-American outbursts cannot be legitimately nationalist; they are, rather, instances of a kind of xenophobic nationalism of mere destruction and nihilism. That American businesses might appear to others as a symbol of American imperialism makes little sense in this view. For, in the American experience, business is associated with welfare, not with power; and the American belief in the separation of public and private affairs further dissociates the might of private enterprises from the public power of the nation. And yet, the habit of seeing in the performances of private individuals and firms America's very prowess should allow one to understand why others confuse the two spheres.[15] The other kind of anti-Americanism is that of European or Canadian nationalists who see in the United States' "unctuous pleas to rise above petty nationalism" a hypocritical and arrogant manifestation of America's own nationalism, and who consider American appeals to build an international community as a disguised form of expansionism, since the United States may "confidently expect" to dominate such communities, leading "to an extension of the area in which the American writ would in fact run." [16]

This same narrow interpretation of nationalism and colonialism leads the United States to minimize the nationalist appeal of communism in countries and regions that are not at present subject to direct European control—China, Latin America, or South Vietnam since 1954. It also makes Americans underestimate the nationalist component in communism's appeal in Western Europe immediately after World War II, when, to many uninformed Europeans, the Soviet threat seemed distant while the American presence was real. This appeal has dwindled in Europe—not because the Soviet threat has gotten closer, but because non-Communists have revived their nations' pride and fostered a kind of European nationalism—but nothing similar has yet happened in Asia or Latin America.

The United States' impatience with European nationalism has led, lastly, to a misreading of three aspects of Europe's history. First, the continental as well as the imperial rivalries of European nationalism are said to be responsible for the two world wars. Here, we fail to make sufficient discrimination between the part played by nationalism as such—the doctrine or ideology that puts the nation above all —and the effect of a competitive situation in a state of nature that pushes close neighbors into intense conflicts of interest, even when their leaders and their citizens are not moved by nationalist feelings. If we put the spotlight on actual national situations, then the whole world today begins to look very much like Europe of the past; the nationalisms of today may have intensified, colored, altered the stakes

---

[15] On this point, see Jacques Barzun, "The Man in the American Mask," *Foreign Affairs,* April 1965, pp. 426–36.

[16] John Holmes, in Karl A. Cerny and Henry W. Briefs, eds., *NATO in Quest of Cohesion* (New York: Frederick A. Praeger, 1965), p. 296.

and patterns of the international contest, but the fragmentation of the international milieu is, as earlier, the ultimate and fundamental culprit.

Next, Americans tend to overlook the vital importance, in opening the roads to World War I, not of aggressive nationalism but of the frustration of legitimate national aspirations—not the nation-states' expansiveness but the desires of oppressed nationalities to have their own nation-states. This point ought to be kept in mind, even now, when independence seems to have been granted to almost all those who want it; for in many cases, either the state is a mere fiction and the nation still only a potentiality, or the nation-state, while existing formally, is in fact subordinate to a master's rule (as in Eastern Europe) or hemmed in by subtler and less public forms of dependence (as in Latin America and some Asian countries).

Finally, Americans forget that a key factor on the road to World War II was, in fact, the decline of the national spirit in some parts of Western Europe. Of course, nationalism, an ideology, and the national spirit, a feeling of cohesion and a sense of identity, are not the same; yet our reprobation of the former is often sweeping enough to brush away the distinction. This is a serious error. For disaster may come either when nationalism, rampant everywhere, destroys self-restraint everywhere, or when nationalism is exacerbated in one vital and dynamic spot while the national fiber in other vital spots is rotting. Too great and widespread a willingness to risk war on behalf of nationalist ideals (or anything else, indeed) is dangerous; too unequally apportioned a fear of war is also dangerous. There can be no healthy polity, and consequently no chance of reasonable or moderate international relations, without a modicum of national identity. And the drama of community-building "beyond the nation-state" lies in this paradox: no solid community can be created with partners to whom the common enterprise is merely an escape from their respective doubts and dilemmas, concerns and crises; but if each partner possesses or has regained a sense of identity and purpose, the transcendence of their interests and goals in a common task becomes more difficult, especially in the present international system.

SEEING EUROPE AS A WHOLE

A second form of American impatience with Europe shows itself in the tendency to look at Europe as a whole—to see in it a basket of eels, perhaps, but one basket all the same. In the days of the Monroe Doctrine, and much later during the two world wars, there was something massive and global about the way the United States confronted Europe. To Americans, the continent from which the immigrants came looked like a single, if extraordinarily fragmented and perversely complicated, entity. There have been learned attempts at showing that underneath the fratricidal divisions rudiments of a community existed, but these are an outsider's or exile's view.

This has meant, first of all, that Americans have been impatient with the resilience of national calculations in Western Europe; they find them hard to follow, even harder to approve. After all, the entire contemporary record of Europe, as seen from here, is a record of failure: two world wars, the political demise of Europe after World War II, the loss of empire, and, along with it, a tendency (or so it seems to us) to turn inward. Such a record seems to demonstrate beyond reasonable doubt the fiasco of separate computations and the need for collective solutions: what is the alternative but fragmented impotence and conglomerate irrelevance? America's distance, geographical and historical, blurs intra-European barriers or makes them look grotesque. Europeans, however, see their history rather differently; to each his optical illusion. To them, Europe's experience is of the obstinacy of national barriers, and they are ambivalent about their effects. Europeans are humbled by the record of their past; yet they naturally find it painful to read it wholly as a fiasco, to accept the idea that their fate is futility, that all their wars have been fought in vain. Even when they think that the future ought to be entirely different from the past, they still recognize what each national group of Europeans owes to the culture and cast of its own country, and they are fearful of losing that special strength and flavor in a tasteless brew.

Even the best-informed Americans, accustomed to thinking in large, continental terms, find it difficult to realize that Europe's political and social forces are still profoundly different from one nation to the next. Arthur Schlesinger, describing President Kennedy's visit to Europe in June 1963, speaks of the President's goal of promoting a progressive, democratic Europe based on Christian Democracy and Social Democracy.[17] But Europeans, stewed in the pressure cookers of national politics, know that the "progressiveness" of those two movements varies from country to country, remember the fine persistent vigor with which French Social and Christian Democrats waged colonial wars that were anything but progressive, and think of the days when the British Labor Party denounced a Suez

[17] *A Thousand Days: John F. Kennedy in the White House* (Boston: Houghton Mifflin, 1965), Ch. 33.

policy perpetrated by the strange alliance of British Tories and French Socialists.

Europeans are not only Europeans but Englishmen, Frenchmen, Germans, Italians: however gloomy about the past and future, they still have a sense of alternatives. A collective solution to Europe's problems is possible, and it is hoped for by many—but it is not the only possibility. If a collective solution should satisfy the major demands of each nation and maximize the benefits for all, no doubt it will prevail. But if the distribution of benefits is uneven and the conciliation of demands unlikely, national solutions are likely to be preferred. Even within common enterprises, the whole legacy of separate national histories and interests, which entails different priority scales and time perspectives, leads each participant to try to get the collective solutions tinted his own national color.

The United States' impatience with that legacy is the reason for American dismay when European national calculations reappear despite premature announcements of their death, and it also explains the lack of understanding of what I would call the historical revisionism of certain European countries. Americans have sympathy for the kind of revisionism that is largely physical and sentimental—Germany's desire for reunification. But there is less, or none, for the political-symbolic attempts by France and England to appeal to the future against what they feel to be the unjust rigors of the recent past, to work for a future that will repeal those wrongs, and to do so in a way that perpetuates the subtle differences not only between them and the other European powers but also between Paris and London.[18] This kind of revisionism, as well as the rivalry between its two practitioners, annoys the United States which considers it as the desire of obviously outclassed states to return to "rank." Many of the heirs to Europe's tradition of world politics would consider it as a normal quest, while many Americans consider it as a mere residue of the age of fragmentation, a diseased longing for the divagations of power politics that led to the world wars, a contagious breeder of more rivalry and disunity. The unit of calculation is simply not the same. This may explain why de Gaulle's determination to restore "glory and grandeur to a country geographically smaller than Texas"[19] appears less absurd there than here. And this may also explain why the United States' efforts to level out inequalities among

[18] This point is discussed further in Part IV. See below, pp. 401–403.
[19] Theodore C. Sorensen, *Kennedy* (New York: Harper & Row, 1965), p. 562.

the main European powers, on behalf of European reconciliation and unity, strike some of those who would be "levelled down" as a half-arrogant, half-ignorant neglect of all the reasons why differences in states or power are justified—a true definition of equality being the unequal treatment of unequal situations.

This tendency to look at Europe as a whole has a second consequence: the belief in the possibility that the United States can apply to Europe today the recipes of past American history.

Seen as a whole, Europe presents many apparent similarities with the United States: a largely urban population in a predominantly industrial society, similar political and administrative institutions, etc. Hence there is a natural inclination to recommend for Europe what has worked so well here—a large commercial market and a federal political structure—and to treat the Europeans who preach the same sermon not only as heroes but (more perilously) as spokesmen for the inevitable future, and true interests, of Europe. The style of Jean Monnet has, indeed, much in common with that of America—so much so that a brilliant scholar has described it as the emergent style of the new technocratic industrial society: [20] disdain for formal ideologies, but a faith that almost amounts to one; enthusiasm for procedure, if not at the expense of policy outcomes, at least with the implicit conviction that the right kind of procedure cannot fail to produce the right outcome; a tendency, if not to forget about the long range, at least to believe that it is nothing more than the sum total of gradual, step-by-step moves; a double appeal to the idealism of a common task transcending petty interests and to the selfishness of organized interests, to whom profit is guaranteed as an earthly reward; an air of using and increasing power not for the furtherance but for the transcendence of power politics; and a self-sufficient and self-fulfilling dynamism, which substitutes process for policy and finds purpose in progress.

The trouble begins when one looks at the *differences* between American and European history. The American amalgamation began before the various ex-colonies had the chance to crystallize into separate nations. The federal solution was rapidly applied and gradually enforced on units without a past as distinguishable entities; a common market, spread by the sparse flow of immigrants, unfolded over virgin territories. Industrialization grew in the common market

[20] Ernst B. Haas, "Technocracy, Pluralism and the New Europe," in Stephen R. Graubard, ed., *A New Europe?* (Boston: Houghton Mifflin, 1964), pp. 62–88.

of a nationally unified society. The case of postwar Europe is fundamentally different. Although the social systems have become more homogeneous (within and across borders), national structures and casts of mind continue to differ. For centuries, the national societies have been molded by the states. In no case was industrialization the expression only of the private profit motive; in all cases it occurred in a fusion of private drives and public pressures, individual orientations and state directions. The establishment of a single European market would require something for which there was no need on this side of the ocean—literally, a denationalization of national economies. Another gift of the state (especially in this century), the labyrinthine bureaucratic apparatus that captures and keeps citizens in a maze of social services, shows colossal inertia and resistance to change. The mass media remain profoundly national. Lastly, Europeans, faced with well-grounded national situations and accustomed to discrete national calculations, are now obliged to discriminate between two areas whose relative autonomy is as certain as their interdependence: in one area, demands can always be met with bargains and package deals affecting tangible commodities; and in the other area, either your gain is irretrievably my loss, or else neither of us is willing to give up the little we have at present for the promise of "better" or "more" in an uncertain future—the area of wealth and welfare policies versus the area of high politics. Thus the "metaphysic of promise" runs into obstacles which do not exist in the American experience.

AMERICANS AND EUROPEAN HISTORY

Impatience with European political forms and impatience with the fragmentation of Europe converge in a third variety of American impatience with Europe: this is shown in the United States' magisterial way of looking at European history. The intricacies of the balance of power, clashes of national interests and feelings, the traditions of separate national calculations and of identities shaped in opposition to shifting enemies have given to European history not only its complexity and its violence, but also two features that are missing in America's past; a certain jaggedness, and a wealth of experience. The jaggedness is characteristic of Europe's diplomatic history but even more of the domestic records. In contrast, America's historical surface is much smoother. (There is the deep scar of the Civil War, and it is true that for the South the experience was comparable to what the French lived through in the French Revolution or the Germans in the Nazi Revolution, but this is not true for the

North.) As a result of so many social and political battles, Europe does not show what Boorstin has called the "seamlessness of experience" in America. The public and the private, the political and the religious, the "is" and the "ought," felt here as continuous or compatible, are felt to be opposing poles there. And the wealth of Europe's historical experience makes the Continent like a storage room where all kinds of problems, experiments, and paradoxes have been filed away, always ready for consultation or even use. "The liberal tradition" [21] in the United States, where conservatism is the conservation of progress has, in contrast, a kind of happy simplicity that is both a domestic blessing and an obstacle to understanding, a source of inner strength and a mental and emotional impoverishment. The European response to crisis and challenge has been endlessly varied—Europeans are used to ups and downs, twists and turns, good and bad breaks. Consequently, they are skeptical about the possibility of success in applying recipes, abroad or even at home, that worked once in a particular circumstance. They are not so sure that their history has been a success to want to extend its lessons to the universe. But Americans, whose history is a success story, tend to believe that the values that arise from their experience are of universal application, and they are reluctant to recognize that they are tied to the special conditions that made the American success possible.

Of course, to the giant who climbs mountains easily and meets no avalanche, Sisyphus down there with his rock looks a little silly. And so the giant tends to lecture him. In recent years, the lecture has often consisted of reminders to the Europeans of the need to unite—so that the United States, which had to rescue them twice, would not have to do so again; so that the United States, which finds its world responsibilities a heavy and lonely burden, at last would have a partner with a world view; so that the legacy of bitterness left by past intra-European peace treaties, which discriminated among Europeans, would be overcome. The trouble with this lecture is not that it is wrong but that it is counter-productive. First, it detracts from the United States' rather unique approach to postwar Europe. It is one thing to exhort Europeans to unite as a condition for their own greatness; it is quite another to explain to them that the reason they ought to do so is so that you won't have to be bothered. No one doubted that there was self-interest in the Marshall Plan and NATO,

[21] See Louis Hartz' brilliant book by that title (New York: Harcourt, Brace, 1955).

but the emphasis was on their selfless and idealistic aspects, and one can certainly argue that the conception as well as the scope of American assistance went far beyond the narrow requirements of self-interest; the tone of the lecture now makes that self-interest seem more petty and less enlightened. Second, there is, in international relations, what could be called a Rashomon effect: the truth is never quite the same to different people. For many Americans, the truth is that they intervened twice to rescue the world from disasters brought on by European follies. America's wartime European allies, on the other hand, remember that the rescuer came late and perhaps reluctantly, and that it gleaned from its intervention more benefits than the Europeans did. Similarly, occasional American references to the inequalities of Versailles may bring mutterings of anger from those who were the victims of Hitler's clever exploitation of those alleged inequities.

## B. *The United States and History*

The legacy of the American past has implications beyond American-European relations. The United States' long experience in self-reliance has been followed by global entanglements which, while often brilliantly managed, have brought enormous disappointment and frustration. These would have been less if the expectations engendered by America's happy past had been more modest; as they are, they have in turn perpetuated a lingering nostalgia for a past that could not have been more different from the present. This has not paralyzed American foreign policy; it has, however, created a permanent tension between the needs of the external situation and America's inner psychological needs and hopes, and it has shaped the mood and manner in which the United States has picked up the challenge.

One such broad area of tension concerns the United States' relation to history. It might be amusing for amateur explorers of national psyches (there are no others) to establish a typology of national attitudes toward history—ranging, perhaps, from the new nations' often mythical, Rousseauistic sense of a long-buried golden age followed by the long night of corruption that preceded the recent dawn of independence, to the old nations' sense of history as an ocean with a patternless record of storms and lulls. In most cases, history is seen as a struggle—either a succession of mêlées with no final meaning or discernible order, or a slow, painful emancipation from various forms of enslavement to varying degrees of enlightenment. For the philosophers and ideologues who pretend to find a pattern in the record, a meaning in the jumble, history is a bruised witness constantly to be called to the bar; for historical agnostics, history is a burning garment that clings to our skins, a storybook that proves nothing.

The American attitude to history strikes me as quite different, viewing it, as we do, placidly and from a distance. Americans know that they are in it, that the garment burns, but they do not quite realize how impossible it is to shed the garment or wear it without discomfort. The attitude is one of complacency, but the complacency is threatened.

One manifestation of this distance from history is the American tendency to discount the weight of the past. This intellectual act of faith in "modernity" is not merely the mark of a Lockean society raised on Liberalism, for Liberalism and belief in progress are not Siamese twins. It is the sign of a society which reads its own history as a kind of long prologue to the present and future, whose long isolation has meant that the history of others has been learned, rather than experienced; whereas in Europe, every nation's history is so weighty, and so closely interlocked with the history of other nations, that the legacy of monuments and memories is deeply imprinted in everyone's consciousness. It is also the sign of a society whose faith in progress takes on forms unknown elsewhere, looking forward as it does not so much to a gradual (or cataclysmic) improvement and transformation of history—bad parents engendering better children, who in turn will raise even better ones, etc.—as to a shedding of history, a perpetually renewed historical virginity. In contrast with their psychological difficulty in coming to terms with the inhabitants of Latin America—descendants of Europeans the United States had rejected and Indians the United States had destroyed—the enthusiasm shown by many American students for "meeting Africa" may well be due to some affinity of one *tabula rasa* for another.

There is another example of this same inclination to distance oneself from history. I observe with fascination the enthusiasm with which American scholars in the social sciences, particularly in international relations, prefer a deductive method that begins with abstract models and propositions to an inductive method that begins with the raw data of history. The prevalence of mathematical formulation in the realms of uncertainty, the attraction to computerized knowledge and schemes derived from nonhistorical sciences—in domains in which the purpose of science ought to be a systematic understanding of human behavior in history—correspond to other traits of America's style (to which we shall return): history is not easy to experiment with, nonexperimental sciences are not very scientific, therefore the more one can divorce the data from reality the more manageable they become! This mechanical treatment of historical data—as if they were easily separable goods that could be weighed, labeled, and processed—and the focus of comparative studies on abstract "properties" that are supposed to have a dynamism all their own (neglecting the interplay of these properties, or their relations to men and events in the historical matrix of each society) are both manifestations of this same placid distance from history.

America's threatened complacency about history assumes many guises. One, often discussed by writers on American foreign policy, is the presumption of ultimate and stable harmony—a happy blend of liberal and conservative ingredients. Statesmen who view international relations as a permanent test of wills incur reprobation. International stability is the goal or concept toward which innumerable proposals for arms control or world policing measures have striven; indeed, the hygienic notion of a world purged of power politics—or in which the instruments of power are sufficiently blunted for international politics to become like the marginal quarrels, symbolic contests, and incremental compromises of orderly consensual democracies—can be found in the most surprising contexts, such as the sophisticated arms-control discussions of recent years. History is a plain on which the pilgrims of progress move forward; it is not a mountain range with neither summits nor valleys in sight; foreign policy is seen not as a fluid interplay of kaleidoscopic forces and individuals, a continuum of conflicts and crises, but as an activity designed to deter and avert occasional nuisances that might slow down the march, as a series of rescue operations designed to bring the stranded traveler back into the plain; "trouble avoidance" and "crisis coping" define the task; [22] it is a kind of "solutionism" that dies hard.

Obviously, though, this complacency is troubled by the intractability of the issues. And, since "a failure of events to fulfill expectations" is inevitable, Americans, who expect "so much more than what the world could offer," [23] tend to blame the world (i.e., others) rather than their expectations. In particular, a people that

[22] See Senator Henry M. Jackson, ed., *The Secretary of State and the Ambassador* (New York: Frederick A. Praeger, 1964), p. 11.

[23] Daniel J. Boorstin, *The Image* (New York: Atheneum, 1962), p. 4.

has never experienced defeat will be more likely to view the very possibility of even localized defeats as a catastrophe than peoples that are used to alternations of success and failure and whose expectations are more gloomily modest.

This distance from history and complacency about it converge in the frequently expressed conviction that we are on history's side, or vice versa, and our enemies are not. Other nations also tend to believe that they are history's favorites. In America's case, this conviction is remarkable because of the contradiction between the implied determinism—we appear to know what history will condemn to the graveyard and what it will choose for the future—and the irony or wrath that a comparable determinism provokes when expressed by Marxist opponents. Yet, whereas Marxist convictions rest on an analysis (however lopsided and crude) of economic and social processes, and belief in them can thus be called an empirically grounded act of faith, in the American case the empirical grounds are usually of the wishful-thinking variety, and the act of faith is a kind of whistling in the dark.[24]

Another paradox of America's historical experience which affects the United States' relation to other nations is the difficulty in cooperating with other nations as equals. American society was "born free" of the inequalities of feudalism and the hierarchical class consciousness of post-feudal industrial society, yet its encounter with the rest of the world has not been equalitarian. In this respect, the story is virtually the opposite of that of major European countries, which are far less equalitarian at home but of necessity much more so in the society of the European concert.

Here, there are three effects of the American legacy. In the first place, whereas all past great powers (including Russia) have been great powers during periods in which there were no fixed amities or enmities (even the Franco-German antagonism did not become hereditary until 1870!), the United States' involvement in world affairs has always occurred in a revolutionary period of total hostility (although, to be sure, the enemy has not been the same—a point well made, in his speech at American University in June 1963, by President Kennedy). Instead of a succession of limited antagonism

[24] For a recent example, see Walt W. Rostow's lecture on "the great transition" (with its "view of the millennium" of a world community achieved through the building of regionalism and the defeat of aggression) and its acerbic critique by A. Michael Washburn and Willard H. Mitchell, in *Walt W. Rostow, Vietnam, and the Future Tasks of American Foreign Policy* (Policy Memorandum No. 33, Center of International Studies, Princeton University, September 1967).

and limited cooperation, characteristic of moderate periods, the United States has experienced a succession of unlimited enmities. Germany became an ally after having been a hated foe, not because the world contest cooled off but because a "total cold war" against a new foe replaced the total hot war. As antagonism toward the Soviet Union lessens, it is replaced by antagonism toward Red China. In other words, the potential equal was the former enemy, not ally.

Second, those with whom the United States has been friendly have not been its equals: they have been dependents, ranging from Latin America since the eighteenth century, to Britain during World War II—various kinds of dependents, to be sure, from subordinates to clients, but always sufficiently secondary to deprive the United States of the experience of a coalition of equals. The one time the United States was a member in such a coalition, in 1917–19, the experience seemed unbearable; isolation finally prevailed, America went home.

Third, the long tradition of noninvolvement in foreign affairs gave to American diplomacy a certain rigid limitation which the sudden veering to the extreme of total involvement in an unlimited contest did not completely overcome. The American tradition was one of unilateral action (largely by force) and of highly traditional diplomacy—stately representation and observation at the highest levels. The resistance of so many elderly foreign service officers (those who have reached the memoir-writing stage) to the innovations required by the "total diplomacy" of the 1960s—propaganda, economic aid, the Peace Corps, public relations, etc.—is significant. This was not what they were trained for, but this is precisely what a policy of cooperative international involvement entails today.

For these three reasons, the United States suffers a "severance in communications." [25] And a situation in which one must cooperate with others whose relative immunity from or vigorous resistance to pressure may give them a kind of compensatory equality, despite one's own size and predominance, is highly irritating. But to others (especially in Europe), interdependence is the world's oldest story. They have always lived like sardines in a can—and are only too used to having someone behave at times like a shark. To Americans, interdependence is a kind of decline in sovereignty; if sovereignty is "the situation of being in charge of a domain," [26] then interde-

---

[25] J. M. Domenach, "Le modèle américain," *Esprit* (July-August, September, October 1960), pp. 1219–32, 1360–74, 1520–34.

[26] Charles Burton Marshall, *The Exercise of Sovereignty* (Baltimore: The Johns Hopkins Press, 1965), p. 4.

pendence, in which one must suffer interference from others in discharging one's responsibilities, is a fall from Eden. And, hence, Americans tend to believe in all sincerity that, by being interdependent, they contribute to overcoming the nation-state. For other states, interdependence is the norm and does not really affect the core of sovereignty; what affects sovereignty is *dependence* (as Rousseau so well understoood), being subject to the demands and commands of others. To us, sovereignty seems eaten away and diminished by entanglement; to them, it is lost, not in cooperative arrangements, but only through transfers of power.

## II.   America's Principles

America's past has bred expectations and shaped perceptions that can be detrimental to free choice and effective action in foreign affairs. But because America's history has been one of a national "melting pot," and because it has been so blessed with rewards, it has also bred a set of beliefs that together serve to gild the historical lily; moreover, they serve the function or dysfunction of providing norms for evaluation and action.

### A. *Their Nature*

The United States is not an ideological nation, and its policies are not ideological ones, if by ideology one means a body of ideas, emotions, and symbols that aim at presenting a systematic and global vision of the world and its history, that serve as a commitment to, a guide for, and a legitimization of action, and that are institutionalized in an organized political movement. An ideology in this sense is intensely operational, because of its institutional transmission belts, its dynamism, and what I would call its outer-directedness—supposedly putting into the hands of its champions a key or a set of keys with which to unlock doors, a lever with which to move men and mountains. Moreover, it provides categories for the ordering of data, explanations for events and behavior, sometimes projections for illuminating the future.[27]

On the other hand, American principles do not provide the kind

---

[27] For discussion of these points, see Samuel P. Huntington and Zbigniew Brzezinski, *Political Power USA-USSR* (New York: McGraw-Hill, 1964), Ch. 1.

of nonideological guidelines or traditions that some nations preserve in their foreign policy—rules of thumb defining certain objectives, such as the preservation of the balance of power, in the British case, or the so-called tradition of natural borders or of *l'alliance de revers* in the French. What distinguishes American principles about foreign affairs from such guidelines is, in fact, something they share with ideology.

Guidelines are ordinarily conservative, and by that I mean either (*a*) designed to maintain the over-all *status quo* in accordance with the nation's interest, or (*b*) designed to further *revisionist* ambitions within a system of international relations believed to possess a permanent or necessary pattern. Ideologies, insofar as they deal with international affairs,[28] are, typically, revolutionary—whether the revolution consists of pushing the hands of the clock forward or back. The system itself must be burned down, and the ideological nation is deemed the carrier of the torch.

American principles share two features with ideologies: one negative—their supposed transcendence of national interests (i.e., they are not designed primarily to further peculiarly American ambitions or interests, even if their success has that result); the other positive—in that, in foreign affairs, they go beyond the narrow universe of interstate maneuvers, and express general views about man and society.

Yet these principles differ profoundly from ideology. They are not institutionalized: no single party, no committed state machinery is there to carry the torch and burn the nonbelievers. They do not have the cohesion and interrelatedness of ideological dogmas, and normally they do not inspire the same degree of fervor, although it would be imprudent to generalize on this point. Most important, the vision they express is reformist rather than revolutionary, and they are not so historically grounded as ideologies. While the United States hopes to revamp political life along certain lines, while it envisages global change, its purpose is improvement without apocalypse. The American vision lacks the prophecies and "valued revelations" of ideologies and contents itself with embellishments and ameliorations on a basically accepted design, rather than a repudiation of this design altogether. Ideologies are historically rooted—by which I mean not that they correctly interpret historical trends and provide foolproof instruments for action, but simply that they pro-

[28] There are, of course, ideologies concerned exclusively with the domestic order of a society (e.g., Salazar's corporatism).

vide historical explanations as well as ends, means for action along with fuel for faith.

Now it is true that America's principles are, in two respects, deeply historical. For one thing, "the idols Americans worship are . . . the idols of their own culture transposed upon the world scene," [29] the fruits of America's early beliefs and historical experience. But the trouble with this is precisely this inner-directedness, for, as we know, the American scene and the world stage profoundly differ. For another, some of the principles do reflect the United States' more recent foreign-policy experience. But the trouble here is that what ought to be a flexible and conditional guideline becomes a dogma that loses touch with historical realities and complexities.

America's principles fall into two categories: abstract dogmas and moral imperatives, deeply felt and widely shared, setting goals and defining rules for conduct; second, assumptions about behavior that purport to provide methods of action to achieve the stated goals. These imperatives and postulates explain the unique ambiguity of American foreign policy.

They are a source of strength, precisely because they do express intensely cherished beliefs and experiences, because they are so close to the American essence. They give to the United States its evangelical force, its missionary tone. To be sure, for a long time, the notion of the "chosen people" was interpreted as requiring severance from the world, but as soon as that severance became impossible, then action in the international arena was considered justifiable provided its aim was reform through the promotion of these principles. We often hear about the French idea of a *mission civilisatrice* (as a foreign-policy goal it extended only to France's colonies); in the American case, we would have to speak of an emancipating mission—first *from* the outside world, then *of* this world. The deliberate transposition of policies decided on grounds of power or national interest into the language of principle thus corresponds to two characteristic assumptions: that this is the language that best moves the American people because it is its own; and that it is likely to be the most effective abroad. The first assumption reflects an experience, the second only a conviction.

For these principles are also a serious source of weakness in international affairs. They are like bottles thrown upon the wave, flares in the night, calls through the fog, for one never knows whether they will be recognized or heard. Sometimes they are, because they hap-

[20] Max Lerner, cited, p. 920.

pen to fit a given situation. Then the success encourages the United States to try them again and again. Surprise or dismay is the reaction when the bottle is lost, when the flare illuminates no landscape, when the call is answered only by its own echo. For America's principles are disembodied. They are like a wine that intoxicates the vintner, but that all others find lacking in body. They have a considerable *a priori* element, and insofar as their norms are nevertheless grounded in political and social realities, it is only in America's.

Now, both ideologies and guidelines indicate concrete goals, reveal connections, point out relevant sectors for action, designate concrete enemies. This may explain why the revisionist and the revolutionary are often allies, why the *status quo* conservative and the revolutionary may agree on an occasional truce, negotiated at cross-purposes but in the same language of political history. The reformist vision, on the other hand, which often shares lofty universal goals with the revolutionary, is not sufficiently grounded in history to be fully operational, nor is it Machiavellian or flexible enough to provide the kind of management of power relations in which *status quo* conservatives or revisionists excel. Typically, it consists of ends without means—shopping lists without the prices marked—or of oversimplified notions about means. The Declaration of Independence is not a sufficient charter for policy. The Communist Manifesto and the various programs of the Communist party of the Soviet Union have their share of oversimplification, distortion, and illusions; but they also have enough of an analytic method, enough of a grasp of social linkages, enough of a focus on historical trends to be able to correct their own mistakes to a considerable degree.

The United States has been spared the Byzantinism of ideology, but it has not avoided a harmful oscillation from impractical principles and postulates to sophisticated but also inconclusive sociological analyses, which are even less adequate as guides for action than principles or ideologies. Nor has it avoided one of the most paradoxical consequences of the disincarnated nature of principles: the fact that they neither die nor fade away (whereas ideology can be eroded by the routinization of its institutional support, corroded by repeated errors in interpretation and failures in action). Ideological dogma and principles rely on different kinds of faith: one is rousing, demonic, dynamic, activist; the other is simply hope. The first is a high explosive, yet it does not survive repeated failures and turns, then, into cynicism or passive, bitter indifference. But hope springs eternal . . .

### B. *Their Content*

It is possible here to give only a few examples of the kinds of principles to which I refer. Americans are not alone in believing in them; but they are unique in their determination to act according to those principles as if the only lesson derived from sad experiences was that which Orwell's horse in *Animal Farm* always drew from its failures: "I shall work more" and try harder.

In the category of moral imperatives, two deserve brief discussion: the principle of self-determination and the principle according to which no changes in the *status quo* should be perpetrated by force (let us call it the principle of peaceful change). They correspond both to domestic American experiences projected into foreign affairs, and to mummified foreign-policy experiences.

The critique of the notion of self-determination is as old as Wilson's Fourteen Points, and there is no need to repeat the arguments often made about the indeterminacy of self-determination, the problem of national minorities, the contradiction between individual and collective rights.[30] What is relevant to our discussion here is that the principle itself represents an admirable blend of ideals and self-interest—the ideal of freedom shared by most of the Western world, and the self-interest in using as an aim and as a goad to others a political notion which corresponds to the prevailing sense of legitimacy and which contradicts the adversaries' reliance on violent action by minority groups, their preference for coercion over consent, or their engineering of some sort of rudimentary consent. However, even if the nature of the unit in which self-determination is to be granted were always clear, or if the problem were one not of nationhood but of regime, there would still remain two headaches which the United States' dedication to the principle arouse.

First, there is the dubious presumption that a world-wide application of the principle of self-determination will always "come out right"—that no nation will ever vote itself into communism, as the cliché goes. This presumption in turn is based on the postulates that no nation ever willingly turns to dictatorship and that to people intent on national independence, communism everywhere and obviously

[30] See Rupert Emerson, *From Empire to Nation* (Cambridge, Mass.: Harvard University Press, 1962), and *Self-Determination Revisited in the Era of Decolonization* (Harvard Center for International Affairs, Occasional Paper No. 9, December 1964).

will mean subordination to Moscow or Peking. Insofar as all these postulates are open to challenge, blanket support of the principle of self-determination risks a dangerous conflict between the ideal and self-interest. To be sure, one could argue that since the postulates are right in the long run and in most cases in the short run too, a better definition of American interests would permit the acceptance of the principle even where and when its application goes against our immediate interest. But the question whether this is a good argument must be answered case by case and not on the basis of the principle alone. This brings us to the second headache, which is that the principle of self-determination can be worked out only through machinery and institutions; the key question is often not so much whether a people will be able to determine what their government will be but whether it will be provided with the choices and political instruments of choice without which a vote would be a farce. For self-determination, like most ideal values and deities, has to be "mediated." "The people" is a driving force only occasionally; mostly it is a reserve force or a final arbiter. When there are no organized potential winners, where the people is an inchoate mass, or when there is only one organized force, the problem of self-determination is moot.[31]

The principle of peaceful change (which has as its corollary that the United States must support or promote resistance to aggression) presents some of the same profits and problems. Once again, it blends self-interest and ideals. Once again, the main trouble comes in the application. Once again, it may be self-defeating or not operational at all. It may be self-defeating whenever the United States faces a situation in which its interest appears to dictate its crossing a border with forces or by force and without the invitation of the government in power. The argument that a sound definition of America's interest would prohibit any such violation of the principle begs the question. For the competition often dictates its own rules, and there may be an overwhelming need to violate the principle either for "possession" or "milieu" reasons, either to safeguard concrete interests or to uphold a symbolic value such as prestige. To be sure, a casuist can argue that such a move is not aggressive when the purpose is to overthrow a Communist regime itself established by force or to prevent a forcible Communist take-over. But is the regime then

---

[31] Thus, to take the orderly presence of people at the polls as a key criterion of free elections, as was done by various commentators and observers in South Vietnam in September 1967, is a very naive way of assessing self-determination.

installed any less coercive because it was put in by the champion of the free world? Can one equate a regime established by free elections or by popular revolution, which then drifts into communism, with a regime imposed by force? Thus, the principle fosters hypocrisy.

Or the principle of peaceful change may simply be irrelevant. For, as the specialists who wasted their wit and wile trying to define aggression found out, the notion of aggression is applicable only when there is a clear-cut, forcible crossing, by a foreign army, of the border of a well-established state with a government in orderly charge thereof. The very idea of "aggression" corresponds to a neat peacewar dichotomy in international relations and to a situation of domestic stability. Its applicability in an era of "neither peace nor war" is highly dubious—hence the collapse of so many of the rules of international law dealing with civil or interstate war.[32] In the case of protracted conflicts, in which it is almost impossible to find out who struck the first blow, and even more in the case of civil wars fought over shaky regimes, the principle of resistance to aggression tends to become a rationalization  invoked easily by all sides. And the notion of peaceful change in one case frequently conflicts with an absence of any channel for the peaceful redress of grievances or settlement of disputes; in the other it conflicts with a principle which Americans ordinarily cherish, the right to revolution. The reconciliation of that right with the dogma of peaceful change is a formidable task.

In the category of American principles that consists of assumptions (containing implicit goals, just as the dogmas rest on implicit assumptions), a few words can be said about three of them. The first is one that pervades American plans and programs for underdeveloped areas; it is the assumption that the central problem the newly independent nations raise is economic development. This presumes, first, that the behavior of a new nation will be determined largely by the level of its economic development; second, that the domestic regime is to a considerable extent a function of the level of development; third, that action in the economic sector of society will, if correct, produce beneficent results in the other sectors; fourth, that the proper goal of a genuine leader of one of these nations should be the development of his country; fifth, that the proper path to development is that of the large, competitive market and balanced growth characteristic of America's own progress. And the im-

---

[32] See Richard Falk, "Janus Tormented," in James Rosenau, ed., *International Aspects of Civil Strife* (Princeton University Press, 1964), pp. 185–248.

plicit goal in this set of postulates is that the United States ought to concentrate on "help[ing] underdeveloped economies reach a stage of self-sustaining growth." [33] Now this is not a wrong objective; but if the postulates are only partly accurate, concentration on it will not necessarily lead to the expected results, or there may be instances in which it ought to be abandoned.

Obviously, economic development is an urgent necessity, and political leaders who neglect it are not likely to lead for long. But in the world as it is, only rarely do political leaders consider economic development either as the supreme end or as a goal to be achieved apart from many others, some of which might well curtail development in some way, and all of which tend to imbue this abstract goal with the color and flavor of politics. The experience of today's new nations does not differ so much from that of the nations of Western Europe at a comparable stage: their leaders are moved by a formidable array of motives, among which (for reasons already mentioned) the desire to scintillate on the world stage, the drive to consolidate domestic control, the determination to integrate disparate elements of the population or to achieve certain social reforms figure as prominently as development.

This means that economic development is often seen as a means to other ends. Consequently, development aid will often be appreciated only to the extent to which it furthers those other ends; or development will be minimized if, in the leader's hierarchy of ends, those for which economic growth is a prerequisite are low or if those that are highest might be compromised by the acceptance of foreign aid. There is much truth in the argument that the absence of development is an assurance of chaos (the counter-argument that development often leads to dislocation and trouble, while occasionally true, does not dispose of the case).[34] But it may happen that development will lead to a different sort of irresponsibility—that of a complacent, "inward-looking" society that savors its growing prosperity and leaves the worries to others.

Behind this assumption about economic development, then, one finds less an analysis of the world scene than an idealized projection of America's own experience of economic growth which was ac-

[33] This is a constant theme in Dale J. Hekhuis, Charles G. McClintock, and Arthur L. Burns, eds., *International Stability: Military, Economic and Political Dimensions* (New York: John Wiley, 1964).

[34] See Edward Banfield, *America's Foreign Aid Doctrines* (American Enterprise Institute, January 1963).

companied by a large amount of social stability, social progress, and political democracy; the projection of a nation where for a long time statesmen did indeed "concentrate on making progress at home instead of trouble abroad," [35] yet felt no remorse for looking inward, because they found the outside world to be quite ugly. But how can we forget that the United States' resources and social makeup were almost unique; that its institutions preceded and consequently shaped and channeled American economic growth (as shown by the persistent validity of Tocqueville's analysis, written before the age of mass consumption); that American abundance, the consensus of a "liberal society," and the voluntary limitation of objectives abroad spared the United States those painful choices among equally desirable but not simultaneously attainable goals which confront societies less rich in goods but wealthier in conflicting aims; and that the concentration on domestic issues did in fact entail turbulence and some irresponsible negligence abroad, and in any case was made possible by a completely different international system? For the United States also, economic development was a springboard, a means of action, a prerequisite for world power; but due to their prolonged isolation and their dislike of that power, Americans oscillated between the view that the country's business was business and the view that its business was universal emancipation—two beliefs that isolate the process of economic growth from the pattern of foreign affairs.

Another frequent assumption (or set of assumptions) is summed up in the word "consensus." Americans are convinced of what I have elsewhere called the procedural illusion: [36] that consensus is not only possible, as the outcome of mutual adjustments among men of good will, but the best basis on which leaders can make choices. The implicit goal is, of course, the achievement of consensus. What one finds behind this notion is a certain conception of rationality—a faith in the existence of a single kind of rationality, often obscured by prejudices and bad habits, but, like Rousseau's general will, ready to shine when the layers of dust and dirt have been removed. One also finds the cousin concept of ultimate harmony: just as there is a single rationality between competing biases, there is a potential community behind conflicting interests. Since diversity of views does not preclude the triumph of reason and harmony, it is quite true that community and diversity are "gold dust twins." Third, one finds the

---

[35] Schlesinger, cited, p. 567.
[36] "Europe's Identity Crisis," *Daedalus,* Fall 1964, pp. 1274 ff.

implicitly assumed universe of utilitarianism, which defines values in measurable terms and aims at the greatest good of the greatest number.

One consequence of these notions underlying the idea of "consensus" is that they lead to a definition of politics as interpersonal relations. There is an implicit vision of a continuum of small groups and international politics; each larger whole appears reducible, and susceptible, to analysis in terms of a small group of claimants groping toward consensus through what has been called partisan mutual adjustment.[37] Moreover, here as in domestic affairs, the utilitarian faith in rationality and harmony feeds the touching belief that the reasonable, well-meaning individual will always be able to rally doubting Thomases and open-minded opponents to his views, i.e., to move all mountains except those of bad faith and evil—or rather, the assumption that there are no mountains, no unmovable structures: only individual brains and wills.

What appears to this writer as a sin of transposition—from one type of social action to a very different kind of reality—is, once again, a projection of the American experience; it is the "liberal ethos" writ large, it is the liberal society superimposed on a state of nature. For at the back of all this, there is a kind of super-model of a community whose members share fundamental beliefs (including this unconditional faith in a certain procedure of adjustment). They haggle over a little more or a little less in the distribution of goods, but they are agreed on the need to agree, and adjustment is facilitated by a network of rules and conventions. In such a community, all that is at stake are indeed "relatively concrete choices at margins where the values are in effect traded against each other" and where trading is helped by the knowledge that my loss today will be compensated by a gain tomorrow. The only point in common with the international state of nature is the multiplicity of claimants. But national claimants are under no compulsion, mental or physical, to define values in such a way, to bargain only at the margins, or to reach agreement. In the one case, the lack of any dominant power is an incentive to mutual adjustment, in the other it is a handicap. The intelligence of (a certain kind of) democracy is not that of international relations.

What Pascal said of the quest for God applies to the search for

---

[37] See Charles E. Lindblom, *The Intelligence of Democracy* (New York: The Free Press of Glencoe, 1965), Ch. 14.

consensus: "you would not seek me if you had not already found me." Consensus is possible when a sufficient basis for community exists at the start. When there is a fundamental harmony on ends and disagreement is only over means, or when the means are abundant enough to reconcile diverging hierarchies of ends, pluralism is effective and creative; the ultimate consensus exudes from the procedural consensus that framed the debate, and it is likely to be sufficiently clear to incite and to guide action. When there is no pre-established harmony in a world of competing units, each with its own rationality, it takes more than good will and personal relations to establish agreement; the choice is between a verbal consensus that maximizes ambiguity and paralyzes policy, and discord. The United States, especially in its self-idealized version, is to a large extent a Rousseauistic society, moved by a vision of the general will and marked by a strong social pressure toward conformity. But Rousseau, who was a thorough pessimist, never applied the social contract to the international scene.

A third assumption, a corollary of the second, is embodied in the quest for a nonproliferation treaty. Americans appear convinced both that the spread of nuclear weapons exposes mankind to intolerable perils, and that a world-wide consensus against those dangers can and should be enshrined in a treaty. The first assumption is reasonable. The second one is not. The sin of transposition is manifest again. There is no general will of mankind that subordinates the parochial concerns of states to the higher interest of the human race. As Rousseau has pointed out (and as the Briand-Kellogg pact confirmed), what is in the interest of all may be to the advantage of none. In this instance, the fact that once more the interest of all coincides so well with that of the United States (and of the Soviet Union) contributes to the hesitations of other states to consecrate in a legal document the distinction between the nuclear haves and the have-nots. Each one looks at the general perils that threaten all from the viewpoint of the peculiar perils that threaten him; and a common stand cannot emerge easily, between those who would thereby preserve their superiority (and freedom from inspection) and those who would thereby perpetuate their inferiority and alienate their freedom.

### C. *Their Effects in the Formulation of Foreign Policy*

How do these principles narrow the choices and inhibit the effectiveness of American foreign policy? First we must be clear about what the problem is *not,* for this is an area in which there have been many controversies and clichés. The problem is not that of "idealism versus realism" or "moralism versus power." Ideals are a proper and ineradicable part of reality; international politics, like all politics, is a purposive activity; power neither defines ends nor even determines with any surety their nature and limits; and the choices are never between acting morally and acting immorally in a world in which every action has both moral and immoral aspects, every moral issue its ambiguities, and every actor his own code of morality.

Critics of moral concerns in international relations fall into different categories. Some assert that ethical considerations have no place at all in international relations because all uses of power, all collective actions, are evil; or because the proper way to make foreign policy is to determine what is expedient, not what is moral; or because statesmen are prisoners in an inescapable contest that determines their ends and means. Others reformulate the problem in Max Weber's terms. As he saw it, international politics is one of the inexpiable conflicts of values that are the warp and woof of history; the statesman is compelled, by the very necessity of the ethics of responsibility, to uphold the power of his nation as the supreme value; in this task, means repugnant to the ethics of Christian conviction are often indispensable. Others reformulate the problem in Hans Morgenthau's terms of the morality of the national interest.[38]

None of those theories is satisfactory. The blanket denunciation of collective immorality blithely rides over all nuances and differences. The "naturalistic" view[39] of the captive statesman ignores the purposive nature of political action and the possibility of choice. Weber's view is excessively tragic and unduly narrows the range of choice. The notion of the intrinsic morality of the national interest evades the difficult fact that even statesmen who believe in the high moral value of the national interest feel they must justify their policies in the light of standards higher than mere reasons of state. The equation of morality and the national interest gives them no final solace and leads all too easily, not to the diplomacy of moderation and compromise celebrated by its theorists, but to excesses of self-righteousness—sometimes in brute form through the ritualistic justification of any move in terms of the national interest, and sometimes more insidiously, when the crudeness of this ritual persuades some to opt for the more hypocritical disguise of the national interest in su-

[38] *In Defense of the National Interest* (New York: Alfred A. Knopf, 1951).
[39] See Robert W. Tucker's review of Raymond Aron's *Peace and War*, in *World Politics*, January 1965, pp. 310–33.

pranational terms.[40] Sooner or later, then, the national interest itself gets dressed up as something "higher."

Thus the moral problem in foreign policy subsists; idealism cannot be read out of court. The question is whether abstract principles and clumsy assumptions help to solve this problem and are of use to idealism. What is in question is the apt remark of Oliver Wendell Holmes, Jr., that general propositions do not decide concrete cases. It is not that foreign policy is a matter of expediency alone, but that the decision about what is expedient in a given case cannot be made merely on the contemplation of a dogma. America's besetting sin is not moralism or idealism or legalism (it would be easy to demonstrate that American foreign-policy moves are no more moral, display no more fervent idealism, and demonstrate no greater religion of law than the policy of others). It is what I would call form*u*lism or form*a*lism: form*u*lism, because exceedingly complex realities are reduced to the holy simplicity of a hallowed slogan; form*a*lism, because those slogans reveal an insufficient grasp of the political, historical, and social processes that foreign policy must deal with. This emphasis on the complexities infuriates both true believers, whose faith provides them with yardsticks (however crude) and solutions (however crazy), and the pragmatic operators, obliged by the pressure of events to decide about medication or surgery while the scholars discuss the delicate condition of the diseased organs. But a stress on complexity is not an alibi for inaction: it is a warning against the wrong action. It is not a plea for unprincipled behavior: it is a demand for caution amidst the clash of principles and facts.

For all their generosity and appeal, America's principles are misleading. They often make the men who are concerned with foreign policy ask the wrong question, turn to the wrong analysis, and thus in the end provoke the wrong results.

In the first place, the American emphasis on principles brings about a peculiar vicious circle of wrong questions. It makes the formulators of foreign policy decide issues in such a way that the solution will answer the question: "Which dogma, which assumption is relevant here?" When a debate breaks out over the decision, its defenders and its critics find themselves locked in a dialogue of the deaf, irrelevant on both sides. One side's emphasis on motive provokes the other side to apply an equally formal, if different, yardstick. The supporters of the policy assert that it is right because the ultimate aim is good. As de Gaulle has discovered, nothing infuriates American offi-

[40] See, for instance, the prolific writings of Myres McDougal.

cials more than an attack on their motives (for instance, the charge that they act as leaders of great powers have always acted—out of self-interest). In their eyes, "we often make a mess of our acts, we often use means as ugly as our opponents', but we are redeemed because our cause is higher, our heart purer, our intent better." Their opponents reply: "our acts contradict our motives and stand condemned by standards of Christian morality." One side upholds an ethic of intentions, the other an ethic of absolutes; both confuse the ethics of political action with the ethics of conviction, and both project into the international world a view shaped by Christian ethics as applied in a homogeneous society where questions tend to be treated as psychological rather than social.

The trouble with this debate is that it is nonpolitical. In matters political, "ethical judgment . . . is not separable from the historical judgment of the goals of the actors and the consequences of their success or failure." [41] Hence, a nonpolitical exchange over abstract standards does not even illuminate the moral problem. The ethics of political action is neither one of motives nor one of acts judged in isolation; it is an ethic of consequences. What can spoil our best intentions is not merely our use of "wrong" means, but the politically disastrous consequences of our acts (none of which is, necessarily, morally evil on its face). Morally reprehensible but politically effective means have at least the merit of efficiency; the frequent combination of moral ugliness with political stupidity *and* good motives is the penultimate in repulsiveness. To take a stand on intentions alone may require one to argue in effect that the end justifies the means; a guillotine-like judgment of means alone may require one to argue in effect that means can be judged per se in a competitive, often desperate, situation. What is obscured in this debate is that what may justify the means is not the aim but the result.

The American tendency to ask the wrong question has been frequently displayed in recent years; it somehow hovers around the principle of commitment. American policy-makers, in order to appease fears created in Europe by the consequences of the nuclear stalemate and by the lesson the McNamara Doctrine has drawn from it, have argued that no one should doubt America's commitment to defend Western Europe. In Asia, they have explained that the United States' stand in Vietnam was the fulfillment of a pledge, betrayal of which

[41] Raymond Aron, *Peace and War: A Theory of International Relations* (Richard Howard and Annette Baker Fox, trans.), (New York: Doubleday, 1966), p. 605.

would destroy the credibility of the United States everywhere. The result has been to provoke one of those masterly tributes to confusion—a European debate in supercharged terms of trust versus distrust, an Asian (and intra-American) debate in acrimonious terms of pledge versus no pledge (and pledge to whom?). The relevance of any of this to anything is not clear. What is relevant is a set of political considerations. In the case of Europe, what was at stake was not trust but strategy, not the existence of a commitment but its form— i.e., what *exactly* was the United States militarily committed to? What was involved was neither America's motives nor its military capabilities (both excellent), but America's acts and their possible consequences. In the case of Asia, what matters is not whether America's pledge is or was to Diem or to the people of South Vietnam, or whether a pledge should have been given or ever was, for by now, there is little doubt that simply to leave Southeast Asia would affect American foreign policy disastrously. What matters are the consequences of carrying out the pledge, or the various kinds of consequences of carrying out the "commitment" in various kinds of ways. It is not a matter of capacity, as Walter Lippmann suggested, but a matter of price.

Not only the dogmatic American principles but the assumptions too often make for the wrong question being asked. Thus, the American idea of foreign aid as a key that will open the door to economic growth—and thereby also unlock other connected rooms—has detracted from the task of asking in each case whether the aided nation's regime is likely to put aid to good uses, and how this aid will affect the foreign policy of the recipient. Also, will it indeed serve not only the universal, and very general, long-run interest in economic progress, but also the somewhat shorter-term set of American political interests?

In the second place their principles mislead American policymakers because they distort analysis; they breed misperceptions. The principles create a kind of euphoric *self-delusion*—and policy-makers are persuaded that their goal is already a reality or that the various postulates guiding their action are indeed based on reality. Since the United States stands for the self-determination of peoples, it is all too easily assumed that the American presence in Vietnam is a guarantee of the Vietnamese people's self-determination, and that other Asians will surely not view an escalation of the military effort—which turns a war in support of South Vietnam's independence into a different confrontation between American forces and those of the Vietcong or North Vietnam—as similar in any way to situations in which Asians rebelled against European colonialism. Again, since America stands for the self-determination of peoples, the policy-makers fail to realize (until the realities become too blinding to be ignored) that intervention in the name of that principle against revolutionaries who rebelled against a military regime in the Dominican Republic will be analyzed abroad as a rather twisted way of foreclosing the outcome of a struggle for power. Or again, since it is assumed that community and consensus perforce exist within NATO and indeed are the common purpose of the allies, the policy-makers tend to believe that the degree of effective integration, or the amount of meaningful consultation, is far greater than it actually is, and thus to confuse truly supranational integration with integration that is little more than the centralized control by the preponderant ally. To believe that the principle is the reality may also mislead one into confusing an assumption and an aspiration. The other allies are accused of sabotaging Atlantic community policy, but we do not realize that the definition of such a policy had remained a virtuality. As long as the aspiration was unfulfilled, the assumption that this "policy" existed was unjustified; and no one can sabotage what has not yet been established.

America's principles also distort perception and analysis because they *oversimplify* complicated situations. Sometimes, the oversimplification is so great that the application of the principle becomes completely irrelevant, as when the principle of peaceful change and resistance to aggression was applied to a civil war that broke out largely because peaceful change was not possible, and that, given the nature of the international system, inevitably involved foreign powers on both sides. To be sure, the meaning of the United States' use of this principle in a situation like Vietnam is clear: it symbolizes its determination not to permit Communists to take over by force (even the kind of force that is manifested in civil wars) a territory in which the United States has an important interest. What is at stake is, as President Kennedy tried to explain to Premier Khrushchev, opposition to "the entry of additional nations into the Communist camp." [42] Whether this objective is realistic or not is another matter: at least it has the merit of being a political precept, not a formula. But the trouble is that the formula of aggression and peaceful change has focused attention on the wrong elements and thus led to the wrong analysis. Resistance to aggression inevitably makes one think in terms of "holding a line"—yet Vietnam is a situation in which by definition there are no lines. It makes one think primarily in military terms and

[42] Schlesinger, cited, p. 364.

diverts energies from nonmilitary aspects of the war and from its political causes; it leads one to apply methods of military containment
of an external enemy; yet here the problem is to eliminate not only
the forces of but the reason for a large-scale internal rebellion. There
is a comparable irrelevance in the assumption of community and consensus as the foundations of a strong alliance and of interpersonal relations as the basis of consensus.[43] A more accurate analysis would distinguish between different levels of consensus—some firm and broad,
others vague and narrow—between areas of identical interests, areas
of convergent interests (already more fragile), and areas of conflicting ones; it would remember that even in the best of alliances, conflict
continues in the midst of cooperation; it would note that summit
meetings even between the heads of allied governments no more than
solemnize agreement or disagreement or else—as at Nassau—end with
an improvised "consensus" from the implications, ambiguities, and
uncertainties of which it may take years to recover; it would know
that any assimilation of the North Atlantic Treaty to the American
Constitution—two "outward and visible forms of living institutions" [44]
—overlooks the essential difference between domestic community and
international relations.

To return to the principle of resisting changes made in the *status
quo* by force, this dogma also suffers from its incompleteness. For the
guidelines it establishes are too vague to be useful, since they cover
many fundamentally different situations (outright attempts by a foreign power to take over an area by force, as well as so-called "national liberation" situations); inevitably, the Khrushchev-Kennedy
dialogue at Vienna was inconclusive. Another example is seen in the
principle of equality among members of the Atlantic Alliance, which
has led various American statesmen to warn against any discrimination against West Germany. This abstract formula takes into account
only one aspect of reality (West Germany's economic, military and
political importance) and neglects all the reasons why differences in
treatment of the allies may be justified.

Thus, oversimplification can also take the form of superficiality in

[43] Roger Hilsman in *To Move a Nation* (New York: Doubleday, 1967),
pp. 531–32, explains that America's resort to bombing North Vietnam was
partly due to a conviction that the war was going badly in South Vietnam, a
conviction that grew out of our assimilation of the struggle to a military
invasion.

[44] Letter of President Johnson to General de Gaulle, *The New York Times*,
March 25, 1966, quoted by Roger D. Masters, *The Nation Is Burdened* (New
York: Knopf, 1967), pp. 301–2.

analysis. The assumption of the normalcy of consensus has often led American statesmen to offer friendship to foes of the United States on condition that they recognize the universal validity of America's principles. We do not think we are asking a humiliating concession of them: once they have "mended their ways," they will become partners in the task of ordering the world and will see that their interests are better served thereby than by their currently hostile policies. So we suggest the possibilities of fruitful contacts and even cooperative schemes, which we would be ready to initiate if only they behave properly. Mr. Acheson used to have his idea of coexistence; [45] today, we speak of "containing" China without "isolating" her. What is superficial about the analysis shows in our unwillingness to understand why our offer of cooperation or coexistence, our pleas for contact, risk being in vain. It is not because of the moral contrariness of our foes, but because they seek political objectives that we are determined to deny them and because our (to us) reasonable conditions for friendship are for them the death of their political and ideological *raison d'être*. Their isolation results not from a state of mind which it is in our power to change by gestures, but from domestic and foreign political conditions that will be modified only through the rough and gradual process of international confrontations and internal changes.

Similarly, the United States' assumptions about economic development postulate, as we have seen, the interrelation of economy, society, and politics, but the highly complex patterns of relations are not well studied: hence, a kind of elementary Marxism colors America's happy economic determinism.[46] Sometimes, economic development undermines (but does not replace) a fragile or backward political and social system. Sometimes the latter thwarts development, for interposed between the economic sector and the political benefits expected from economic "take-off" are first the screen of a political system that can distort, waste, or misuse foreign aid; second, the screen of a social system that can pervert or skew aid even if the political leadership has good intentions; and third, the screen of an international system that can expose a society to development by the private interests of a major foreign power. The Alliance for Progress,

---

[45] See the statements collected by McGeorge Bundy, *The Pattern of Responsibility* (Boston: Houghton Mifflin, 1952), pp. 31 ff.

[46] For an example see Walt W. Rostow in *The Department of State Bulletin*, LV, No. 1412 (July 18, 1966), 80: "Latin America is moving—country by country, it's moving," etc.

which manifested a more sophisticated understanding of the nature of this problem than previous American aid attempts, nevertheless reflected excessive optimism about the possibilities for its solution in Latin America. A general comprehension of the elements of the problem was not tantamount to a detailed knowledge of the margins of action; although the facile clichés about the determinism of aid gave way to an awareness of the need for the political leverage of social reform, illusions remained about the availability of such leverage and, when available, about its capacity either to induce the necessary changes despite the resistance of oligarchies and suspicious middle classes or to convince private investors not to be frightened off by these changes.

Irrelevance and incompleteness converge in the idea of self-determination, which creates an image of citizens secure in their rights and protected from violence. This image has only a slight relation to situations such as those of Vietnam or the Dominican Republic, in which the outcome of any vote would inevitably and largely be determined by prior political decisions of the United States,[47] just as the fate of Algeria was settled not so much by "Algerian self-determination" as by French pre-determination. In civil wars where a great power is involved, self-determination of the ideal type is impossible. For what is really going on is a tug-of-war between the foreign great power and another political force; the population is not an ultimate arbiter, it is a stake. A popular vote merely ratifies the result of the tug-of-war. If the native "rebels" (often supported from the outside, as in the Congo, Algeria, Vietnam or Yemen) lose the political and military battle, the "self-determination" of the people will mean the triumph of the great power, not because of its stand on principle, but because it has on its side a local, native force of superior appeal and effectiveness. If the great power fails to find such a force, it only has a choice between a protracted conflict and the recognition of political defeat. A protracted war may well be rationalized as a "war for self-determination," but this is to ask the wrong question and focus on the wrong problem, and the great power will only become inextricably involved and increase the peril of escalation. As for political defeat, neither military victory on the ground nor stalemate is a sure remedy against it; if, in order to avoid protracted conflict or escalation, it is finally acknowledged, "self-determination" will merely consecrate the

---

[47] "In the Dominican Republic, people seemed to be pro-government—to support whoever occupied the Palace." John Bartlow Martin, *Overtaken by Events* (New York: Doubleday, 1966), p. 197.

victorious rebellion. When the great power intervenes in order to prevent a violent take-over and succeeds in restoring peace and quiet, the problem of self-determination remains, so to speak, in suspense. If the intervening power invents a political force on its own side, it makes hash of the idea of self-determination and it risks undermining its position; and if it refuses to play favorites among competing groups (none of which considers resort to the ballot-box a final or sacred procedure), then there may well be a seesaw of coups and clashes until force decides the outcome. (Consider the case of the Congo.)

Consequently, there is something misleading about talk of "unconditional negotiations" in case of an internal war. For internal wars are "zero-sum conflicts"; they end either with the extermination of the rebel side, or with a negotiation that constitutes recognition of only one common interest—in the restoration of peace (but not compromise). Thus rebels are unlikely to let themselves be drawn into negotiation unless the main lines of a settlement have already been set. As a result, formal negotiations consecrate one side's resignation to the other's victory, and merely constitute an effort by the loser to extract concessions from the victor in exchange for the opportunity to reap the final fruits of victory in peace rather than blood; or else they are a sham.[48]

Irrelevance and incompleteness also converge in the United States' current drive to conclude a treaty with the Soviet Union on the non-proliferation of nuclear weapons—a goal based on the principle of avoidance of nuclear war, the assumption of a common interest with the Soviet Union in maintaining peace, and the postulate of the perils of nuclear proliferation. That the principle is sound is obvious; that the assumptions are partly correct is also obvious. But the questions remain: To what extent is such a treaty likely to affect the problem?

[48] There is also something misleading about asking Hanoi for reciprocal concessions in exchange for stopping the bombing of North Vietnam. The true stake of the conflict is control of South Vietnam; for Hanoi to "reciprocate" by "stopping infiltration" into the South (as requested in President Johnson's letter to Ho Chi Minh of February 2, 1967) would, first, expose Hanoi to an open-ended blackmail, since the cessation of bombing could be made dependent on "evidence" of ever-increasing North Vietnamese acts of "restraint," and, second, provide the United States with a unilateral advantage on the real battlefield, i.e., the South, where the United States could continue to reinforce its positions (and to pursue the war) while North Vietnam would, so to speak, recede from the struggle. See Theodore Draper, *Abuse of Power* (New York: Viking, 1967), p. 308.

Do superpowers that have no interest in fostering the proliferation of nuclear weapons need to certify on paper that they will refrain from doing what they will avoid doing anyhow? If the real purpose is to discourage non-nuclear states from becoming nuclear powers, should not the emphasis be shifted to an area that has so far been neglected —from a rather redundant promise of abstention to the performance of acts, i.e., to moves that will reassure the nuclear have-nots (cuts in production of fissionable materials, an extended test ban, or joint guarantees, or provisions for enforcement of a ban on nuclear aggression)—instead of suggesting that the main concern of the superpowers is to perpetuate the gap in nuclear technology between them and the non-nuclear states? [49] To be sure, mere stress on nonproliferation drives a wedge between China and Russia; but it also does exactly the same between the United States and some of its allies.

The general proposition: "nuclear war is the supreme enemy," does not determine the concrete cases. The consensus on the former is too vague to allow one to short-circuit the latter. The diplomatic procedure followed has entailed a combination of two flaws. The treaty asks the non-nuclear powers both to recognize inequality *de jure* and to let themselves be treated as a homogeneous mass. What was attempted was a legal short-cut to a political problem. What was needed—and remains needed—is a series of political negotiations, case by case, with those states (not so many) that are capable of becoming nuclear powers, whose access to nuclear weapons would destabilize the international system or one of its regional subsystems (which is not the case of all the potential nuclear powers), and which require different kinds of assurances, guarantees or compensations to be deterred from crossing the threshold. As long as those political deterrents are not provided, either the states concerned will refuse to sign a meaningful treaty, or else they will accept to sign only an emasculated one. When no such compensations can be provided, it may well be wiser to let the states concerned remain at the threshold, instead of forcing them to make a choice they would have preferred to delay, and may come to regret and reverse if the alternative they choose under pressure is that of signing with reluctance. For it is not the signature of the nations that would in no case become nuclear that

---

[49] *S. Res. 179: Nonproliferation of Nuclear Weapons,* Hearings before the Joint Committee on Atomic Energy, 89th Cong., 2d sess., February 23 and March 1 and 7, 1966 (Washington: GPO, 1966), contains striking evidence of the imbalance between a clear official stand against proliferation and very sketchy ideas about assurances to the nuclear have-nots.

matters; it is the behavior of those that have the means and the incentives. In other words, the simple short-cut risks being unproduc-
tive, whereas a complex detour could have been more effective, and
would have created fewer resentments.

This American tendency to ask the wrong question and invoke the
wrong analysis leads U.S. policy-makers, finally, to arrive at the
wrong result because they *reason by analogy*. For reliance on formulas makes one think by analogy—a very dangerous habit which is
aggravated in the American case by the presence in the government
of many lawyers, who are used to reasoning in terms of precedents.
Analogical reasoning singles out, in the two complex events being
compared, features that are common to both, and suggests that since
they were essential in the first case they must be decisive in the second. Unfortunately, the analogy, instead of being a short-cut to a
conclusion, may be a cliché—an escape from instead of an instrument of analysis. Analogical thinking reinforces tendencies already
observed in our discussion of the American attitude to history; in it,
the fondness for using history as a "grabbag from which each advocate pulls out a 'lesson' to prove his point" [50] converges with the
mechanical treatment of historical data.

Two contemporary examples come to mind. The United States has
argued that unless West Germany ceases being "discriminated" against
in the North Atlantic Alliance, its leaders will feel as humiliated as
their counterparts did after the Versailles settlement, and they will be
tempted to seek an independent, nationalist promotion of German interests; this could break the ties that relate West Germany to Western
Europe or those that bind it to the United States, or it could lead to a
new Rapallo. The fear of this possible chain of events rests on a parallel that does not resist a few minutes of analysis. Rapallo was an
agreement between two defeated and revisionist powers with a common grudge against the Western victors; today the main threat to
West Germany's security comes not from the allies discriminating
against it but from the partitioning foe, and this foe is unlikely to give
up East Germany unless it obtains in return guarantees and concessions that most West Germans are quite unwilling to grant (however
piqued some of them might be at Western attitudes toward Germany). Germany's grudge against Versailles was deep and authentic
(which does not mean it was justified); West Germany's resentment
of its unequal treatment in NATO is more an American anticipation

[50] John Fairbank, "How to Deal with the Chinese Revolution," *New York
Review of Books,* February 17, 1966, p. 10.

of a German feeling than a German drive. If a new Rapallo should occur, it will be because of other reasons—not discrimination alone, but the issue of German reunification.[51]

The other example, of far more ominous consequences, concerns the principle of containment, especially as applied in Vietnam. Containment can and should be a political guideline; yet it has tended to become a formula mechanically applied with the help of analogy. Americans are inclined to reason about the containment of China in Asia as if it were the same as the containment of the Soviet Union in Europe, and as if both foes were to be dealt with in the way that ought to have been followed for the containment of Hitler's Germany. Similarities exist—it is certain that appeasement of a totalitarian regime only whets its appetite—but at a level of generality that obfuscates more than it enlightens. There is a difference between military forces of a totalitarian state or its satellites crossing a line, and the help given by such a state to an ally that is intervening in a civil war, and the psychological example and support such a state provides to revolutions in various countries. The same methods of dealing with these acts are not applicable, and neglect of the differences can lead to one of the two results that the United States' containment of the Soviet Union fortunately avoided—failure because the wrong methods were used, or an escalating military confrontation, for which we have found encouragement in Soviet and Chinese restraint; misled by our interpretation of the war in Vietnam in "Korean" terms, we have seen in this restraint a sign of timidity or of impotence, rather than a policy that combines minimal losses for them with ever-increasing entrapment for us. There is a difference between containment with the help and consent of allied powers whose domestic life is marked by fairly stable societies, sophisticated economies, and effective political systems, and containment in ground that is socially and politically porous and that can be made less tricky only by something akin to total take-over. There is a difference between the deliberate sacrifice of an ally to a wolf that was ready to seize the prey (as at Munich), and the resolution of a *civil* war, despite its international implications. There is a difference between a civil war in which the rebel

---

[51] See below, Part IV, Ch. 11 and 12. In any case, after having made West Germany sensitive to the issue of discrimination, the United States itself has shifted gears and pressed West Germany to consecrate and magnify in the nonproliferation treaty the discrimination between herself and the NATO nuclear powers which she had already accepted when she renounced the manufacture of nuclear weapons.

force is dominated by Communists, and a domestic conflict in which the rebels are a non-Communist anti-Western force.[52]

In short, foreign policy, in addition to recognizing similarities, should make the most of differences. Otherwise, analogical thinking leads to the most irritating kind of wonderland, in which a situation is referred to in terms of another, and disembodied formulas lead to a policy with no grip on reality. Analogical thinking produces a shock of nonrecognition, an inability to see new events for what they are, a tendency to reduce them to something reassuringly familiar. When we invoke Munich in order to exorcise appeasement anywhere, we forget that Munich itself was the product of a disastrous example of analogical thinking—the analogy between the pre-World War I concert of great powers (all moderate states), and the big powers of the 1930s, between Bismarckian diplomacy and Hitler's international gangsterism.

## D. *Their Effects on Foreign-Policy Results*

When reality contradicts one's expectations, the outcome is likely to consist of thwarted policies and outraged feelings—in short, frustration. Examples of thwarted U.S. policies abound in recent years. Consider, for example, the slow death of the idea of a multilateral nuclear fleet for NATO (the MLF), an unfortunate idea launched on the assumption of a consensus within the alliance that turned out to be equivocal. A common desire to improve allied participation in the determination of nuclear strategy concealed sharp divergences on the scope and methods of this participation among partners none of which had overwhelming reasons for being happy with the MLF as the United States proposed it. Another example is the unhappy battle over Article 19 of the United Nations Charter—a battle the United States fought for the principle of financial responsibility, on the assumption that a community existed among the majority of U.N. members sufficient to compel into submission the minority that was willing to disregard the stipulations of Article 19. No only did the assumption turn out to be incorrect (as the attitudes of the smaller na-

[52] See Dwight D. Eisenhower, *Waging Peace: 1956–60* (New York, Doubleday, 1965), pp. 274–75. When he decided to send the Marines to Lebanon in July 1958, he made a radio-television address in which he "drew a parallel between the Lebanon stituation and that which had faced us in Greece in 1947," and he also "called attention to the Communist takeover of Czechoslovakia, the Communist conquest of the China mainland in 1949 and their attempts to take over Korea and Indochina, beginning in 1950 [a strange date, in Indochina's case]."

tions revealed and as an analysis of their earlier, fairly consistent reluctance to take sides in big-power contests would have made obvious), but the principle oversimplified the issue, since the United States itself was ready to drop the requirement of compulsory assessments for *future* peacekeeping operations; thus it waged a battle that paralyzed an entire General Assembly session for the retrospective pleasure of punishing *past* delinquency.

Other examples are provided by United States policies in Latin America. In the Dominican intervention, the principles of self-determination and opposition to forcible Communist take-overs left the United States literally in a political vacuum once the primary purpose—stopping the "rebels"—was accomplished. Knowing concretely what it did not want but only abstractly what it wanted (an unforced choice by the Dominican people in and for democracy), the United States found itself upholding by intervention a principle of nonintervention; this (as the Congo experience has shown) prolongs trouble without at all removing the causes that created trouble in the first place. Elsewhere in Latin America, the giving of economic aid to moderate reformist leaders has often ended with the diversion of such aid, for those leaders, in order to stay in power, have had to appease the military forces by satisfying their demand for equipment (sometimes with the additional result of facilitating army coups).

When we turn from America's thwarted policies to its outraged feelings, we can see that the frustrations created by fallible formulas encourage a black-and-white image of the world. Since the assumptions on which the policies were based were believed to be correct and the principles right, fiasco must be attributed to devils. Since the norm is harmony, the postponement of bliss must be due to a villain. The American approach to international relations as an extension of interpersonal relations encourages this tendency; it results in the "paranoid style"—that of the fire-eaters who see "the enemy" as a sort of formidable, cunning, conspiratorial monster and convince themselves that its successes are helped by internal "softness" or "betrayal," and also that of the fire-fighters who are convinced that a friendlier approach would reduce trouble and restore harmony, and who thus blame our own policy-makers as the villains. Once again, there is something unpolitical in the approach, and it substitutes emotion for analysis, which explains why American opinion of foreign countries is subject to such wide swings.

Applying to a rough surface a grid that has no hold may do worse than lead to frustration: it may incite one to level and adjust the ground until the grid will apply. In other words, whereas a normal wrong result is disappointment, the perverse wrong result is a *self-fulfilling prophecy*—"in the beginning, a false definition of the situation evoking a new behavior which makes the originally false conception come true." [53] Unfortunately, however, things are more complex than in this definition, for although the "false conception comes true," the situation remains one for which it is a false conception; consequently, the policy, adapted to the false conception come true, is still inadequate. There was, as Arthur Schlesinger and others have remarked, the danger of self-fulfilling prophecy in the MLF proposal: it could have created the very appetite for nuclear weapons on West Germany's part that was not there, and, if this had been the case, it would not have stilled that appetite.[54] There is such a danger in Latin America: an intervention in the Dominican Republic based on the inadequate assumption of an imminent Communist take-over first led American officials, locally and in Washington, to exaggerate the "evidence" of Communist activities, and may have ultimately increased the chances of a capture of nationalism by Communists or other anti-American extremists in other parts of the continent—chances that cannot always be squashed by dispatching Marines.

The Vietnam tragedy is of the same kind, only at a more cataclysmic level. This may not have been, in the beginning, a test of resistance to Chinese expansionism, given Vietnamese feelings toward China in general and North Vietnam's consistent effort to keep avenues of access open to Moscow in particular. Nor was it a clear case of North Vietnamese aggression against a "neighbor" that "wanted to be left alone." Nor was it a test of the "domino theory," since no other Southeast Asian nation was in any sense similar to South Vietnam—a fragment carved out after a long internal war, contested by a nationalist movement that Communists had captured at an early stage, and ruled by a regime that had succeeded in alienating most of the population.[55] But treatment by analogy has put in motion the infernal machine of the self-fulfilling prophecy: the neighboring countries' "course of independence rests, in large measure, on confidence in American protection." [56] North Vietnamese infiltration has escalated along with American intervention; China's theory of wars of national

---

[53] Robert Merton, *Social Theory and Social Structure* (Chicago: Free Press of Glencoe, 1957), p. 423.

[54] See Schlesinger, cited, p. 873.

[55] Also, as pointed out by Theodore Draper, if Vietnam had been a test of the domino theory, "the inordinate expenditure of men and money on a relatively tiny, marginal outpost of this [Communist] conspiracy would be strategic lunacy." *Abuse of Power*, cited, p. 114.

[56] President Johnson's State of the Union address, January 12, 1966.

liberation has taken Vietnam as its main object lesson. The trouble is, as we saw before, that the problem of "containment" or "drawing the line" differs fundamentally in situations of revolutionary violence from what it is in clear-cut cases of aggression. There is a French character called Gribouille who jumped into a river in order to avoid being dampened by a light rain. In the Dominican case, the Under Secretary of State for Economic Affairs spoke of "international communism" to justify intervention. In the Vietnamese case, American policy is often presented as a way of showing the Chinese that their brand of aggressiveness does not pay, and therefore as indirectly bringing grist to Moscow's anti-China mill. Yet neither Moscow nor Peking can afford to let North Vietnam go down or let the other keep North Vietnam afloat alone, and American policy keeps North Vietnam partly dependent on Peking, and Moscow, of necessity, quite militant. Moreover, even if the United States *could* thwart the ambitions of the Vietcong and of North Vietnam, the effect of this victory on "wars of national liberation" elsewhere would still be different from, say, the impact of the Berlin airlift or the Korean War on the Soviet Union, for "guerrilla wars, after all, are not links of a single chain that can be broken in any one place." [57]

A final result in foreign policy of the various factors we have discussed is brittleness. The tendency to analyze issues in terms of set formulas or analogies instead of tackling them on their merits encourages the continuance of policies long after they have outlived their usefulness, and then a rather abrupt dismissal of them once their counter-productiveness has become damaging (at which point they are replaced with new dogmas that have the same effect); hence, the alternation of rigidity and radical change noted by observers. Often, the very fluidity and complexity of a situation leads to an extra measure of shrillness in the proclamation of a principle, and then that principle becomes a kind of refuge against uncertainty, until a storm blows up the refuge. (The belated discovery of the SEATO agreement as the basis of United States action in Vietnam is an example.)

Similarly, insufficient analysis of the changing political realities of the North Atlantic Alliance prolongs to this day a formal American preponderance that only preserves the illusory postulate of consensus (and also perpetuates a sense of crisis). The rather sudden death of the strategy of massive retaliation, predicated on a postulate of "total

---

[57] Senator Frank Church, "How Many Dominican Republics and Vietnams Can We Take On," *The New York Times Magazine*, November 28, 1965, p. 45.

cold war" with an implacable foe, was proclaimed long after the doctrine had ceased to be tenable in its full force and long after the postulate had ceased to correspond to the new Khrushchevian version of American-Soviet competition. It was replaced with the strategy of flexible response, based on the postulates that the United States' primary interest was in reducing the risk of nuclear war and that Moscow undoubtedly shared this concern, especially after the Cuban crisis. But the Soviet Union had not earlier cared so deeply as to extinguish its thirst for manipulating the peril of nuclear war to its favor, nor, later, so fervently as to deprive it of the urge to exploit Washington's aversion to nuclear war. Thus, in early 1962, American efforts to negotiate with the U.S.S.R. on Berlin [58] had no other results than to create tension between the United States and West Germany. The investment of disproportionate energy in a test-ban treaty and efforts to agree on a nonproliferation treaty as well before the Western house was put in order have had similar results. The same brittleness appeared in the battle over Article 19. As a last example, the United States' policy of nonrecognition and opposition to the seating of Communist China in the United Nations is perhaps the best instance of this ossifying rigidity, so deeply rooted in moral principle, whose consequences on the day it becomes impossible to sustain are unpredictable.

The lessons to be drawn from this analysis are simple. Reliance on forms and formulas impedes rather than helps the three tasks confronting the makers of foreign policy. The first task is to blend aims that are invariably diverse and often contradictory, but "formulism" either neglects or merely juxtaposes conflicting dogmas, or synthesizes several in an exercise of wishful thinking. This problem has often plagued American policy-makers who, in their daily work, operate according to a set of assumptions that are hard to reconcile with, for example, those on which the government's more far-ranging disarmament proposals are based; [59] it could easily plague them again if

[58] Jack M. Schick, "American Diplomacy and the Berlin Negotiations," *Western Political Quarterly,* December 1965, pp. 803–20.

[59] See Arnold Wolfers *et al., The United States in a Disarmed World* (Baltimore: The Johns Hopkins Press, 1966), and the conclusions of Harold K. Jacobson and Eric Stein in *Diplomats, Scientists, and Politicians* (Ann Arbor: University of Michigan Press, 1966), pp. 493–94.

Also, the European policy of the U.S. has been based on the notion that France and West Germany ought to be treated as equals (one more reason for refusing to help France's nuclear program), but the nonproliferation policy of the United States pressures West Germany to resign herself to permanent discrimination between herself and France in the realm of nuclear energy.

the principle of self-determination collided, as it is not impossible in some parts of the world, with the principle according to which there shall be no change in the equilibrium between the Communist camp and the West through an addition of nations to the former; it ought to plague them when they argue that the principles of resistance to subversion and of economic development are fused in the policy of aid to military oligarchies.

The second task is to apportion appropriate means to the various ends. Here, wrong expectations and analogies can easily lead to measures that make it more rather than less difficult to reach the ends. Thus, in the case of Vietnam, one central question, unresolved by all the otherwise seductive arguments about "dominoes," "prestige," "pledges," and "containment," is: Can we win where the focus of the war is (i.e., in South Vietnam); in other words, can there be a military solution for an internal war of this size and, if not, is there a political force capable of depriving the rebellion of its cause?

The final task is to weigh the consequences of one's actions. Here, formulism is particularly dangerous, for it leads one to ask, not: What is the price of what I am doing, or what are the implications of my assumptions? but: What is the likely price of my *not* upholding the principle, of my *failing* to follow my postulates? And the answer is, more likely than not, a dreadful picture of defeats or miseries: the horror of rewarding aggression, the evil of denying aid, the peril of a Communist take-over, the spectacle of falling dominoes, oppression tolerated, Atlantic integration destroyed, feelings of discrimination fed, flames of regressive nationalism fanned, etc. Alas, the dangers denounced in this way are often as likely to flow from our own acts, when we apply the wrong means or use means that undermine the reasons for trying to attain our goal. An Atlantic Alliance based on an American-German axis, forged in order to assure equalitarian integration, would lead to disintegration. A war in Vietnam that settles into a routine of defoliation, bombing, mass "cleaning" of "infested" areas, mass movements of refugees, and the military-political take-over of the war by the United States can easily alienate the sympathy of the people to whose defense the United States is pledged; and it could precipitate other Asians into a frightened neutralism due, not to the sorry sight of Americans "chickening out," but to the searing plight of a territory destroyed in the course, and in the name, of protection.

Thus, there is a great difference between two kinds of norms. There are political objectives that one tries to reach gradually—in relative harmony of ends and means, means and risks—through the processes of politics, the normal patterns of manipulation and force, and sometimes the compromises and shame of an uncertain struggle. On the other hand, there are short-hand forms and formulas, the all too mechanical application of which one hopes will make those political patterns simpler and spare one compromise or shame. The effect of this is comparable to that of the moral absolutism denounced some years ago by Abraham Kaplan, who rightly pointed out that in the realm of politics, principles hurt at least as much as they help: "Too often the statement of the moral problem is mistaken for its solution. The underlying assumption is that we already know all the answers. . . . The abstractness of principles thus makes them as useful politically as they are useless morally." [60] They are morally useless because they are pitched too high to govern moral behavior in political issues, and indeed they are morally dangerous because they put one in the position of a judge who condemns enemies and dissenters and knows what is good for both. (Kaplan mentioned Eisenhower's suspension of oil deliveries to England and France after the Suez crisis, as a way of obliging them to comply with the principle of no-gains-by-force.) And they are politically useful not because they are effective (all too often they are not) but because they are lofty enough to cover almost any kind of action—to serve as wrapping for the best and the worst, the most cunning or clumsiest, the most effective or the most disastrous.

## III.   America's Pragmatism

The preceding sections of this chapter constitute a plea to consider issues in their elements and on their merits—not a plea against ideals or goals but a demand for political goals and operational ideals. This will perhaps appear to the reader as a defense of pragmatism—a most abused word. Yet I shall argue here that a third component of the American style that puts on foreign policy a not always beneficial mark is, precisely, pragmatism—but pragmatism of a special kind.

### A. *Its Nature*

American pragmatism is the triumph of what Max Weber called *Zweckrationalität*. As Abraham Kaplan and Robert Oppenheimer

---

[60] In Elting E. Morison, ed., *The American Style* (New York: Harper & Bros., 1958), p. 45.

have pointed out, it has nothing to do with philosophic pragmatism. Indeed, the latter's "insistence on the instrumentality of ideas for the enrichment of immediate experience," [61] the notion that "the meaning of a more general statement lies in the relatively more concrete and particular statements which follow from it and in which the truth of the general statement is to be determined by testing the truth or falsity of the particulars" [62] would be most helpful in foreign policy. What I have in mind is a pragmatism that is a way of acting, not a mode of thought—a *praxis,* not a philosophy, unless one describes it as an *implicit* philosophy, a pattern of behavior resting on submerged assumptions all of which correspond, once more, to the American experience writ large and projected upon the outside world.

American pragmatism has two essential components. First, there is a quiet conviction that the ends of action are not in doubt: they are prescribed by America's principles or by the "facts of life" (that is, arising from the international system in which the United States must operate). Second, political action is therefore the choice of appropriate means. But here, there are two possible approaches, the truly scientific one and the "scientistic" one. A scientific approach to political problem-solving would insist that in each field of endeavor, the means that fit the nature of the terrain are those that should be selected; in matters political, the choice entails no more certainty, no greater precision, than the realm of politics allows. For there is no guarantee that a certain type of political means will infallibly help one to reach a political end; political action is not an exact science with a readily applicable body of knowledge (indeed, it is far less so than even economic action), and foreign-policy behavior in particular is competitive; i.e., its effects, however cleverly calculated, can still elude one's goal because of the reactions of other competitors. Moreover, political action is action over time, and this added dimension also increases uncertainty, opening a wide field to the interference of unexpected factors and neglected variables and to the contrariness of competitive moves. Also, the political field is a whole, a *Gestalt,* in which the isolation of one sector for the purpose of action is necessarily artificial; the need to take the whole field into account of course increases uncertainty by throwing in more variables and correlations than any mind or computer can process (especially since the way they affect each other in actual interaction is unknown and in all likelihood unknowable). Finally—and especially at a time when it has

[61] In *The American Style,* p. 36.
[62] Same, p. 115.

become more difficult to resort to force, to the traditional if not always convincing way of replacing the uncertainties of an intangible test of will with the brutal certainties of a material test of strength—political action becomes primarily a matter of psychology, and this too multiplies uncertainty. What each participant is after, when he selects his political means toward ends, is a way of affecting others, yet others are affected not only by the means he uses but also by other factors—their own expectations and images of the actor, as well as domestic pressures or concerns. The actor cannot be sure that his move, although he may think it clear enough to dispel any doubts or misapprehensions, will not in reality be discounted because of the superior power of their images, or reduced to and distorted by their expectations.

With this conception of political problem-solving, foreign policy becomes the science of the unscientific, the art of uncertainty—as Charles Burton Marshall puts it,[63] one of the performing arts, with no reality or existence distinct from concrete performance and no operational code based on laws other than either unguiding platitudes or misguiding postulates. If one accepts this notion, then it becomes clear that the permanent, unavoidable danger of international relations is miscalculation; for there is more in the heaven of diplomatic constellations than in any philosophy of decision-making. Recent events have shown this only too well, bringing continued evidence of miscalculation among adversaries. Studies of the Cuban missile crisis [64] have revealed how Khrushchev misread the United States' very clear warnings, probably because he interpreted (to us unambiguous) statements either in light of American domestic politics, which require bravado, especially when the officials actually choose a cautious course, or else in light of past American actions, which may have amounted in his eyes to a meek acceptance of *faits accomplis*. The studies also reveal that American officials refused to believe that the Soviets would actually install offensive missiles in Cuba, since they interpreted uncertain, obscure, or ambiguous evidence in the light of expectations shaped by the prudence of earlier Soviet behavior. Each

[63] Cited, p. 609.
[64] See Arnold H. Horelick and Myron Rush, *Strategic Power and Soviet Foreign Policy* (University of Chicago Press, 1966); Roberta Wohlstetter, "Cuba and Pearl Harbor: Hindsight and Foresight," *Foreign Affairs,* July 1965, pp. 691–707; Klaus Knorr, "Failures in National Intelligence Estimates," *World Politics,* April 1964, pp. 455–67; Elie Abel, *The Cuban Missile Crisis* (Philadelphia: Lippincott, 1966); Roger Hilsman, *To Move a Nation,* cited, Part V.

side, in this psychological play of power with peril, was conditioned to seeing only what suited him.

There is also evidence of miscalculation among allies. In the tangle of the Nassau meeting between Kennedy and Macmillan, the British misjudged the impression received in Washington of their silent response to talk of the projected cancellation of Skybolt. Washington misconstrued Britain's silence, and later misjudged the impact of the Nassau agreement on de Gaulle's stand toward Britain's application to the Common Market. Both the British and the Americans misjudged the effect of the Nassau decisions on de Gaulle's atomic policies in or toward NATO.

It is not enough to argue that in both examples what was displayed was a formidable amount of bungling and that more skillful foreign-policy practitioners would have done better. Even if they were more skillful, there will always come a time or a place or a crisis in which the very nature of the field and the game will produce misinterpretation. When a nation has so much at stake that it sees only what it has to gain from a move if it succeeds, or to lose if it fails to act, it will underemphasize the likelihood of a thwarting response and will not see the effects of possible failure incurred after making the move. No theory of politics, no theory of games, no simulation exercise have yet disposed of this most human of human factors: the incapacity of any nation to put itself fully and permanently in the position and attitude of another. Thus, even if international political contests could be reduced to games with a beginning and an end, if stakes would be susceptible of quantification and precise ordering and remained stable during the game, there would still be one formidable obstacle to certainty and solutions: the irreducible freedom of each player to misread the other player's moves and to misjudge his own.

The alternative approach to the selection of means shows fewer misgivings, almost no fear and trembling before uncertainty. "Scientism" was originally a sociological conception, according to which there are general, operational laws of social development that can be applied; "social engineering" is therefore a possibility. Indeed, the laws of human behavior also indicate the goals toward which mankind should be guided. The pragmatic American mode of action is marked by a certain kind of scientism, by "the engineering approach," a mixture of Cartesianism and positivism. Tocqueville had already noted [65] in American thought and action the Cartesian way of breaking down a complicated problem into simpler elements—an

[65] *Democracy in America*, Vol. II, Part I, Ch. 1.

ideal precondition for analysis but, insofar as solution is concerned, dangerous, as it risks vivisecting the whole by severing the connections between the parts. The positivist element pervades the treatment of each individual part with an eye to obtaining the maximum of certainty. What is reflected here is the "achieving society"—"Ours is a how-to-do-it society, and not a what-to-do society" [66]—a society in which a consensus on social values indicates, with very little dissent, the ends to which individuals ought to aspire. It is a society in which those ends are to a considerable extent economic, i.e., definable in quantitative terms, describable in words suggestive of quantity: maximization, service, productivity. And these economic goals can be achieved by means that have received a double stamp of certainty: a practical stamp, through the tried-and-true social methods people use to reach such goals, and an intellectual stamp, thanks to the increasingly "scientific" turn of economics. (This helps to explain why the depression of 1929 was the deepest moral and social shock since the Civil War.) It is a society in which achievement has meant industrialization, mechanization, the triumph of technology, and the organization of work in the most productive way. Hence, the American approach to action is not merely informed by the economic rationality of means, but inspired by the engineer's model of conduct.

Americans tend to attribute their successful past to their efficient engineering, not realizing how much their engineering is due to the fact that their past provided the conditions for optimal efficiency. The American experience, from the Puritans to the space age, has been primarily one of mastering nature. The kind of contest for the mastery of man characteristic of other societies has not been a permanent or dominant feature in American life (and when it was, it was handled in a different way, to which I shall turn later). There was always enough of a challenge of nature, and of abundance in nature and in man's artifacts, to push the contest for human control to the back of consciousness, to the margins of society. It should be easy to understand that pragmatism, which ought to be a universally valid approach, becomes highly parochial when it is so deeply rooted in a unique experience; and that a method of operation that seems ideally suited to the advanced industrial society now spreading over so much of the world remains largely confined to this particular nation. In America, the liberal society insured what might be called a pure triumph of technology, unencumbered by the political and social

[66] Kenneth Keniston, *The Uncommitted* (New York: Harcourt, Brace, 1965), p. 254.

obstacles that slow its growth or twist its development elsewhere. But the uniqueness of this society makes it difficult to extend American pragmatism to a world in which technology is impure and imperfect. Within America, pragmatism does not usurp or eliminate the normative function—the asking of questions about meaning and ends —since the consensus takes care of that function. Outside America, where there is no consensus, American pragmatism tends either to eliminate the normative function by wrongly assuming that the ends are not in dispute or to usurp it by wrongly assuming that the United States' own dogmas provide the answers to questions about ends.

### B. *Its Consequences: "Skill Thinking"*

What are the main consequences of the engineering approach on American foreign policy? Political issues tend, first, to be fragmented into components each of which will be susceptible to expert techniques and, second, to be reduced to a set of technical problems that will be handled by instruments which are equipped to deal with material obstacles but much less so to cope with social ones. It gives a privileged position to those areas of policy to which "skill thinking" and the "operator's" way apply best—technical assistance, economic policy, but above all military policy. Here is the realm of the technical expert par excellence: modern war, waging it and deterring it, requires precisely the kinds of skills Americans have possessed and developed. Moreover, a global rivalry with an expansionist opponent, and a need for a world-wide strategy that will lock this opponent within his gates, particularly suited a nation whose capacity to produce military machinery and might had been demonstrated decisively in two world wars. What the United States had applied so well to achieve victory in war, it could use equally well to deny the enemy victory in an armed peace.

This is why American foreign policy has so often been virtually absorbed in strategy, or why the term "strategy" itself tended to mean foreign policy. Like America's principles, "skill thinking" was a way of charting a course on a sea of troubles, a way of injecting as much certainty and predictability as possible into the perils of the contest. Since the natural bent corresponded to the national interest, it was possible to indulge in a creative orgy of operational pragmatism, and a formidable concentration and fusion of talents grew up in the realm of strategy. The engineering or instrumental outlook had always been characteristic of *homo oeconomicus* and *homo militaris:* the former concerned with the most profitable or productive use of scarce resources, the latter with the most effective way to reach simple goals; the former impatient of waste, the latter of ambiguity. It now became characteristic of most "defense intellectuals," many of whom came from a background in economics or physics. Their concepts of strategy developed out of economic models and analogies, and notions of marginal utility, opportunity costs, or cost effectiveness have pervaded a field which, like economics, aims at the optimal use of scarce resources. Their language, which has become that of Secretary McNamara, reflects their attempt at giving to the uncertain and nightmarish realities of deterrence in the nuclear age the cool, aseptic air of science, remote from the impurities of politics. Moreover, modern war involves scientists on a huge scale—men also used to rigorous thinking, to handling data so as to establish clear-cut conclusions and calculable correlations. Hence, the introduction into the realm of policy of another group of men impatient with uncertainty and with a built-in fondness for technology "for its own sweet sake," in Oppenheimer's famous words.

The point is not, as some radical critics of the "military-industrial complex" often present it, that the military establishment dominates foreign policy. Especially during the tenure of Secretary McNamara, nothing could be further from the truth. For one thing, the various groups of men involved in deciding on strategy disagree often and heatedly, and each group—whether the scientists or the defense intellectuals or the military officers—have internal fights and dramas.[67] What they have in common is a commitment to a certain way of thinking; the battles and the bitterness among them occur because this way of thinking, concerned with means toward ends and with the introduction of certainty and calculability, perforce encounters innumerable frustrations. For the engineering approach runs into trouble when there are conflicting ends among which priorities must be established before means can be allocated, but which purely objective methods are powerless to rank, or when there are alternative ways to reach a given end, the choice among which depends on extraneous considerations.

Nor is the point that this way of thinking is dangerous in itself. The point is that in applying it to areas that are not susceptible to it, one ends up with the opposite of what one wants: more uncertainty and

[67] See Samuel P. Huntington, *The Common Defense* (New York: Columbia University Press, 1961), and Robert Gilpin, *American Scientists and Nuclear Weapons Policy* (Princeton University Press, 1962).

less control. This is what is dangerous. And the point, as well as the danger, is also that this way of thinking and its misapplication have been shared not merely by military men, scientists, and defense intellectuals, but by other intellectuals, businessmen, and civil servants engaged in policy-making: for we are dealing here with an American trait that stops at no professional boundary.[68] Even within the realm of weapons, it has been pointed out that the techniques of "cost effectiveness analysis" have a low yield when they are applied to the problem of choosing among weapons systems with different outputs. Even within the areas in which "skill thinking" applies, other modes of thought and action are needed. The realms of pure economics, pure strategy, or pure science are almost by definition inhuman, they are realms in which we do not find man as he really is. *Homo oeconomicus* is far more rational than real men are, more capable of ordering his ends, of assigning a numerical value to them, and of avoiding incompatibility in his wishes. The human beings of strategic theory are either, as in the strategy of "absolute war" à la Clausewitz, total enemies bent on mutual destruction or, as in the theory of mixed strategy, careful, detached players of relatively clear-cut, abstract games. The world of the scientist is the world of nature. But unfortunately, all the theories and all the plans have to be applied in a world of human beings, whose rationality is not a central, controlling attribute that allows them to define their behavior and marshal their resources, but a permanently threatened residual category, locked in a fight with passions, ideologies, memories, and ambitions. Even when rationality wins, it is marked by the battles with the forces it had to overcome.

The application of "skill thinking" to matters of complex choices is a cardinal flaw of the American approach, for the techniques implied in it can and often do displace and replace political judgment. The realm of foreign policy is by essence one of complex choices, and here, the engineering approach leads to three types of moves: actions in political isolation, actions in a political vacuum, and the substitution of instruments for policies.

Action taken in political isolation occurs when a pragmatic concentration on the problem at hand makes one treat it as a kind of unique and self-contained case to which lessons derived from comparable experiences do not apply (the reverse of the approaches I have analyzed above). Disembodied principles and analogical thinking, as well as historical distance, encourage an excessively general

[68] For documentation, see Roger Hilsman, cited.

way of looking at problems, whereas the engineering approach results in an excessively particularistic way of handling them. The former fabricate artificial connections, the latter severs real ones. In the case of Vietnam, for example, while emphasis on the principle of resistance to aggression has made American policy-makers neglect the civil-war aspects of the conflict and the specific fact of Communist nationalism there, the "operator's" way of dealing with the "job" of counterinsurgency has led to a neglect of similarities between this war and others of the kind since World War II, such as those fought by the French in Indochina and Algeria.

The second type of inappropriate action includes decisions made in a political vacuum when the policy-maker, in considering the problem at hand, looks only at one set of factors, those susceptible to the engineering approach. Whereas decisions made in political isolation reveal how an excessively specific approach prevented the policy-maker from seeing which political factors were most relevant, here an excessively specialized approach may divert him from political realities altogether. This has often been the case in American foreign aid programs. The assumption that economic aid will benefit all sectors of society covers and justifies a neglect of factors that are not purely economic (economic almost in the sense of "technological") such as the sociological and psychological dimensions of political change and, indeed, economic *development.* Thus, a "pragmatic" foreign leader is defined as one who teaches his nation "the trick of generating sustained and reasonably balanced growth."[69]

The same phenomenon is even more noticeable in the whole area of international security, which after all constitutes the bulk of American foreign policy. Strategy has its own logic, and the effect of giving it priority is to push aside the nonstrategic factors of foreign policy, which, being less reducible to calculation and to certainty, will appear somehow less compelling or less relevant. Fortunately, until now at least, American strategy has remained by and large more in the realm of discourse than in that of application—a tribute to its effectiveness. But when hostilities have actually broken out (Korea and Vietnam) or when the United States faced the difficult problem of whether to become militarily involved or not (Indochina in 1954, Lebanon in 1958), it has been clear that its strategic doctrines, designed to prevent certain kinds of enemy actions, have failed to take into account enemy attempts to advance in ways the doctrines do not

[69] Walt Rostow, *The Department of State Bulletin,* LVI, No. 1448 (March 27, 1967), p. 496.

cover. Even the best strategic doctrine leaves out the political possibilities of being outflanked (indeed it incites the foe to look for them) and, neglecting those risks, prevents the development of what I would call healthy skepticism toward strategic orthodoxies. A strategy designed essentially for the protection of Europe left the way open for the Korean War; a doctrine of "massive retaliation" can hardly be used in a place like Indochina; a doctrine of flexible response geared to conventional war has little relevance to wars of subversion.

The other problem is that the doctrines themselves are usually presented and revised on technical rather than political grounds, often with bewildering consequences. Paradoxically enough, two doctrines as different as John Foster Dulles' "massive retaliation" and Secretary McNamara's "flexible response" have had the same effect of producing a crisis of confidence in the Atlantic Alliance. The former corresponded to a perfectly comprehensible strategic desire to exploit what was left of the United States' capacity to inflict more damage than could be wrought upon it in order to avoid local wars and local stalemates. But it was presented with a kind of self-assurance that made the allies fear that they might be dragged into war against their wishes or interests by a strategy that had many merits but could not afford to fail to deter. The revision of this strategy in 1961, when peril parity made the threat to wage nuclear war a far less credible deterrent, was indeed a strategic necessity. But the new strategy, designed to cope realistically with the case of a failure of nuclear deterrence, was again presented with such assurance that the reaction of the allies was one of horror at the prospect of a conventional war which the United States now seemed ready to fight on their soil. In both cases, the same mistakes were made: instead of stressing the deterrent value of the new strategy, the United States presented it as a recipe for "prevailing" in case of a failure of deterrence. This was the result of a perfectly comprehensible mode of thinking, aimed at devising a strategy capable of both deterring war, by warning the enemy of what would happen if war came, and waging it if in fact war did come. But in both cases, the doctrine was riddled with qualifications, and it had grown largely out of accumulated experiences and reflections, yet both were presented as radically new, without regard for the political fallout of giving this impression of discontinuity.

American doctrines of arms control and disarmament also suffer from the political vacuum in which they are elaborated. The universe to which they apply often seems to have little in common with the real world. It is a universe in which nations are somehow willing to separate weaponry from the political goals to which weapons are normally assigned, and to abandon the opportunities the weapons provide them in return for a somewhat abstract promise of stability and security—as if stability were everyone's normal goal and as if all nations were ready to permit the means of guaranteeing security to get out of their own control, As a result, not only have those plans had limited success in international gatherings, but there has also been trouble in integrating them with the United States' own strategic doctrine.

Not only doctrines but policies have suffered from the habit of plannning strategy in a political vacuum. The crossing of the 38th Parallel in October 1950—a decision dictated by the military opportunities opened after the successful Inchon landing—was accomplished without sufficient consideration taken of the political implications, especially vis-à-vis China. Or consider the cases of the two men who have been Secretaries of State for the longest periods in the postwar era: John Foster Dulles spent a great deal of his time organizing alliances in Southeast Asia and the Middle East, but he never gave due regard to the political, economic, and social underbrush that made those areas such unrewarding terrain. The nature of the threat and the character of the countries and regimes allegedly under threat were not amenable to traditional alliance methods. In emergencies, the United States has usually been reduced to unilateral intervention anyhow; the alignment of allies has had divisive effects (India versus Pakistan); the alliances have diverted attention from the nonmilitary aspects of containment; and pumping military aid into countries with low living standards, a high degree of corruption, and shaky economies has often resulted in financial disorder, waste, increased social injustice, and demoralization. Then, Dean Rusk has deferred repeatedly—on issues such as strategy within the Atlantic Alliance, the problems of Great Britain and the Skybolt missile, or troops in West Germany or Vietnam—to the Secretary of Defense, not out of timidity, but out of his own apparent conviction that the problems were primarily strategic. As a result, in 1966, Secretary McNamara's pressure on West Germany to keep buying American arms in order to help the United States' balance of payments contributed to the fall of Chancellor Erhard and to a crisis in German-American relations.

An excellent example of a policy in which strategic factors are insulated from nonstrategic realities is the United States' policy that it is necessary to encourage the military containment of Communist China. It is true that not every kind of military encroachment by Communist China on a neighboring state can be deterred, or should be repelled, with nuclear weapons; there is strength in the argument that to be credible, nuclear deterrence must be buttressed, as in Europe, by the presence of conventional forces ready to resist aggression. But stationing American troops on the mainland of Asia may well create a different kind of opportunity for China: it may facilitate Chinese Communist subversion, help the Communists to capture nationalist movements, and undermine the societies in which the troops are stationed even as the borders would be sealed off. Here again, political analysis of the threat, and of the kind of threats to which a society is most susceptible, ought to precede and dominate strategic decisions.

In the case of Vietnam, the decision to carry the war to North Vietnam was based on one strategic expectation—that bombing the North would help isolate the South—and on the neglect of three basically political considerations. The first consideration overlooked was that bombing, while weakening the economy and military apparatus in the North, was likely to strengthen Hanoi's political resolve; the second, that the war that had to be won was the very largely psychological, social and political one in the South; and the third, that escalation in the North would be caught in the following dilemma: either it risked remaining inconclusive as long as it stayed below the threshold of a major confrontation with China or the Soviet Union, or else it would reach such proportions as to provoke the conflagration to be avoided. Earlier, the "strategic hamlets" plan had been carried out in such a way that whatever mediocre gain in security for the villagers might have been made was offset by three huge political errors: too many hamlets were "moved bodily to new locations" ("a politically hot potato"); the Diem regime, far from using the scheme "as the means for a revolutionary change in the peasant's lot," used it as a means of political control and repression; and the weapons and techniques employed in the war—often because of the bent toward gadgetry so characteristic of "skill thinking"—"had political disadvantages," to say the least.[70]

Another area of policy in which strategic decisions made in a political vacuum can have disastrous effects concerns military aid, or the

[70] See Roger Hilsman, cited, pp. 430 ff., and especially 440 ff. One could argue that even what Hilsman, throughout his book, calls the political approach to a guerrilla war, as opposed to the military approach that gradually prevailed, suffered from serious political flaws—i.e., the prerequisite to its success was a legitimate and effective government in Saïgon, and trusted local leaders in the villages; such conditions were never realized.

sale of arms, particularly in Latin America or the Middle East. For the perfectly sound strategic considerations that justify the decision —the need to help a given military force equip itself against subversion, or the need to preserve a balance of power between contending forces—are in conflict with the often dangerous political effects of such aid. Military aid can strengthen reactionary regimes or repressive military cliques, and these regimes are more likely to facilitate Communist subversion, or incite disorders which Communists could exploit, or at least delay economic development and social reform. Military aid also encourages local arms races.

Decisions made in political isolation and measures conceived in a political vacuum are sometimes combined. An excellent example of this is provided by the United States' decision to cancel the agreement to provide Great Britain with Skybolt missiles. The decision was reached on technical grounds and announced when it was for budgetary reasons. But insufficient account was taken of the repercussions the decision would have on the various problems of nuclear control and political cooperation within NATO, and no connection was made with Britain's negotiations to enter the European Common Market. If ever there was a case in which the desire for a strategy based on considerations of costs and efficiency led to "hasty improvisation and high-level imprecision" [71] when the decision-makers were faced with the precipitous re-entry of all the political issues they had earlier discarded or ignored, this was it. A second example, involving not an ally but an enemy, is that of the decision to bomb North Vietnam after various Vietcong attacks on United States' military installations in South Vietnam provided an occasion. Punishing the enemy by air attacks seemed the most rational use of resources, but the rationality of the decision cannot be assessed apart from the objective. If the objective was to inflict on the enemy losses that would oblige it to cease supporting the Vietcong and thus open the way to an American victory, the move was no more debatable than the goal of a final American military victory itself. (The scope of the bombings, however, was debatable.) But if the objective was to force North Vietnam to the conference table, to "inflict plain loss of value on the adversary until he began to behave," [72] then it showed singular ignorance of the usual psychological effects of bombing. In either case, there was insufficient political analysis, and there was no clarification of the polit-

[71] Sorensen, cited, p. 568.
[72] Schelling, cited, p. 171.

ical ends. Similarly, the decision to send large numbers of American ground forces to South Vietnam and to resort to large-scale bombing there ignored the Algerian precedent—i.e., the disastrous impact of extensive "seek and destroy" operations on the population whose allegiance is at stake.

In all these instances, the political isolation and vacuum resulted from lack of consideration for foreign, or international, political factors. In many cases, one could argue, the decision was reached on the basis of *domestic* political considerations as well as on purely local or purely strategic grounds. The doctrine of "massive retaliation" was related to a definite policy to keep a ceiling on the defense budgets; the decision on Skybolt had connections with Kennedy's promised tax cut; the decision to bomb North Vietnam was politically easier to reach than the subsequent one to build up American forces in South Vietnam (which proved necessary anyhow). The decision, announced in September 1967, to deploy a light, "Chinese-oriented" ABM system at a time when the United States was trying to negotiate a limitation of the arms race with the Soviet Union, and when the success of the Geneva conference on nonproliferation depended largely on the superpowers' willingness not to increase the gap between them and other states, was taken essentially for domestic reasons: mollifying the opposition with a "small" step in its direction.

The third type of action that manifests the inappropriate application of "skill thinking" to complex issues might be called the technical short cut, the mistaking of an instrument of policy for the policy itself (a tendency well described by McGeorge Bundy).[73] The possession of specialized skills encourages one to develop techniques or "gimmicks" that will solve political problems, but one is then tempted to confuse one's tools and one's goals. For instance, American methods of counterintelligence and training in counterinsurgency treat only the symptoms and not the roots of the disease. It is a short cut, to be sure, but one that is likely to become a self-fulfilling prophecy when the social and political causes of revolutions are neglected or even strengthened by repression. The application of a military grid to a complex political situation is characteristic of many American decisions—such as the landing of Marines in Lebanon in 1958 and in the Dominican Republic in 1965; the decision to rearm Germany in 1950; the attempts under Eisenhower to make Laos into a military ally; and the decision to support the CIA's invasion plan of Cuba in

---

[73] In Arthur Schlesinger, Jr., and Morton White, eds., *Paths of American Thought* (Boston: Houghton Mifflin, 1963), p. 308.

1961. In all those cases, even when some of the objectives were met, considerable damage was inflicted on other political objectives that were somewhat trampled under. Nor should a formula such as federal integration in Europe be permitted to become an unconditional goal: it is an instrument, no better than the ends it allows one to reach; if it cannot attain those ends, or if it detracts from them, it ought to be discarded. The same is true of the nonproliferation treaty.

The decision on a multilateral nuclear force for NATO, to take another example, shows how a strategic instrument was selected on *non*strategic grounds as the best way to reach various goals: a case of perverted instrumentalism, so to speak. There were few military arguments in favor of this technical device; at best, the strategic experts said, it would not be militarily harmful. But it was proposed as the best means by which the NATO issues of nuclear control, West Germany's status, and France's challenge, the issues of European unification and of the nonproliferation of nuclear weapons could all be coped with. It is not surprising that this master key to so many locked doors turned out to be a Gordian knot tying together many strings. The only result of the introduction of the MLF device on a crowded political scene was to add a new divisive issue to all the others. None of the issues the MLF was supposed to solve could, in fact, have been solved by the gimmick itself, except under ideal conditions (such as all the European allies being willing to proceed without France and to accept the idea of West Germany having access to nuclear weapons, and West Germany being willing to accept the MLF as the fulfillment of its nuclear aspirations, etc.)—in which case it would have been unnecessary.

These three forms of inappropriate action have many consequences harmful to American foreign policy. First, they contribute to that peculiar mixture of rigidity and unpredictability which we have already noted as a by-product of American principles. "Skill thinking," geared to efficiency, devoted to the achievement of ends along the straightest and shortest route—as an arrow flies to a target—reinforces the absolutism of principles, leads to the neglect of political innovation, and contributes to the poverty of political analysis. For while the arrow is in flight (to the target, one hopes), any suggestion of a change in direction or alternative is rejected as detrimental, if not impossible. And confidence in the arrow makes one believe that it will hit the target even after it is clear that it has deviated from the true course. Thus, during the long crisis over the European Defense Community, the idea of preparing substitutes in case the

EDC failed was rejected on the ground that any such preparation would compromise the operation's success. Similarly, during the Kennedy administration's effort to get the Trade Expansion Act through Congress, the "purists of the administration opposed an amendment . . . which would have made tariff reduction . . . fully operative even if Britain did not join the Market." [74] It is easy to see the contrast between this single-arrow approach and the many-balls-in-the-air method of men like Bismarck and de Gaulle, jugglers of so many alternatives that the loss of one still leaves them with enough to work with.

On the other hand, when the United States realizes that the arrow will not or has not hit the target, or that the target is moving, or that there really are many targets, or when it tries simultaneously or in short succession to hit different targets, then there are drastic changes or a delirium of experimentation. Theodore Draper's dizzying account of the Santo Domingo affair [75] concludes: "we have successfully disappointed everyone"—as a result of the frenzied and contradictory attempts to improvise a non-Communist, not purely leftist political force—i.e., at doing what had been neglected when the decision was made to intervene *against* something, rather than in favor of a specific group (as opposed to an abstract principle). "Every move was cancelled out by another move" in a "succession of inconsistencies," because the single principle applied, anti-communism, "tells us nothing about whether a cause is worth fighting for," and the usual "skill thinking" found itself with no foothold in the quicksand where the Marines had landed. The rather abrupt shift from the MLF episode (the arrow flying toward the target of tighter Atlantic bonds, despite Soviet objections) to the nonproliferation treaty (the arrow aimed at the target of closer Soviet-American cooperation, despite the misgivings of America's West European allies) has left West Germany's leaders dazed by the inconsistencies of "skill thinking" devoid of political skill.

A second consequence of "skill thinking" is that it promotes a variety of forms of wishful thinking; it creates an illusion of appropriateness.

One form of wishful thinking is the illusion of efficiency; the illusion that simple, measurable solutions are possible when they are nothing of the kind. This trenchant, if sometimes spurious, air of briskness is reflected in the State Department language so amusingly

[74] Schlesinger, cited, p. 847.
[75] "The Dominican Crisis," *Commentary*, December 1965, p. 65.

denounced by Schlesinger [76] and in the linear imagery collected by Michael Donelan; [77] but all the talk of breakthroughs, fall-back positions, lines, dikes, and barricades does a disservice to thought and action. Dean Acheson has been quoted as saying in 1946 that the American approach to foreign problems was to treat them as headaches: "take a powder and they are gone." Today, all too often, the approach is to treat them as military threats: "take gunpowder," perhaps. Because it suggests that many complex goals can be reached by such a means, this approach makes one overconfident of success. This is the converse of the tendency to exaggerate the bad consequences of any course different from that which American dogma dictates. We know now that the analysis that preceded the Bay of Pigs operation assumed more or less explicitly that all would go well; the same could be said of the plans for the MLF, of Washington's assessment of right-wing forces in Laos, and of various phases in the campaign for the EDC. The same can be said of official expectations at various phases of the war in Vietnam—even of the assumption that South Vietnamese ports could handle all the materials sent so efficiently, on so many ships, from the United States. Equally misleading and self-serving was the analysis that preceded the sending of American Marines to Santo Domingo to prevent a Communist takeover, whose imminence was necessary to justify the expedition but whose unreality, discovered later, complicated the task of American policy-making.

The strategic approach also creates the illusion of objectivity and rationality. Those who use it present their conclusions as inevitable, expert deductions from facts, as if foreign affairs were matters in which facts spoke unambiguously and experts left their prejudices in the cloakroom. [78] However, it takes little expertise to show that insofar as military leaders are concerned, their conclusions usually have a built-in conservative bias. Insofar as the scientists are concerned, their frequent reversals of opinion and their choice of arguments in accordance with their predilections, as well as what one student has called their solutionism or their "whole problem" approach, [79] allow one to cast doubts on their objectivity. Insofar as many civilian strat-

---

[76] Cited, pp. 417 ff.

[77] *The Ideas of American Foreign Policy* (London: Chapman and Hall, 1963).

[78] Compare Secretary McNamara's drive for "fact-finding missions" to South Vietnam in 1963 (Hilsman, cited, pp. 501, 507).

[79] Warner Schilling, "Scientists, Foreign Policy and Politics," *American Political Science Review*, LVI, No. 2 (June 1962), pp. 287–300.

egists are concerned, their models and calculations reveal clearly how they project their own mode of thought on the world, and thus how they operate in a mental universe whose rationality is merely their own writ large—where opponents are supposed either to reason like Americans or to be in need of education bringing them to this level; where the scars of historical experience and the fires of national or ideological passion have either disappeared or are treated as impurities.

This illusion of objectivity is dangerous for two reasons. For one, it breeds disappointment, when others obstinately refuse to behave according to prescription, to fight the kind of war or to wage the kind of peace one had outlined for them. For another, it tempts the policy-maker to disguise a change in policy as a response to unanswerable facts, so as to preserve coherence and continuity. The drastic and confusing alterations in American estimates of Soviet military strength and the needs of NATO forces, so well documented by Henry Kissinger, have raised the question whether "estimates guide or follow our strategic policy," [80] for they reveal that under a façade of objectivity and certainty the instrumental approach leaves room for the deliberate manipulation of facts. A strategic design is adopted for a variety of technical and nontechnical reasons, then justified not on intellectual or political grounds, but on factual ones; this is self-defeating, for it suggests, not that the new policy is a response to new facts, but that the new facts are discovered to rationalize the policy change. Another example is found in the contrast between the United States' placid reaction to China's first explosion of a nuclear device in 1964 and the Secretary of Defense's apocalyptic presentation of "facts" to the NATO Council fourteen months later; China's power and policy had not changed, but the American position in Asia and the American attitude to Europe's complacency about Asia had.

Lastly, "skill thinking" creates the illusion of omnicompetence. Problems other nations' leaders would consider insoluble, issues they would leave to the mysterious resources of time, foreign upheavals which they would want to stay away from—these are seen as America's business. The buoyant optimism that worked miracles at home propels Americans abroad, yet the failure of these well-tested tools to do abroad the job they performed at home exposes Americans once again to frustration, especially since their pragmatic ap-

[80] *The Troubled Partnership* (New York: McGraw-Hill, for the Council on Foreign Relations, 1965).

proach often excludes the long-range vision that either would give them greater finesse in the use of those tools or would tell them that they need not and cannot be used.[81]

## C. *Its Consequences: Short-Range Foreign Policies*

The engineering approach of the United States differs from, say, British empiricism in that, while the latter may be the art of "muddling through" the quagmires of the present, the former shows no aversion to forecasting and planning insofar as the problems it purports to solve require this. Nevertheless, America's brand of pragmatism neglects the long range and the middle range in foreign policy. (To this neglect, the institutions of the country contribute signally, as we shall see in Part III.) The explanation of this apparent contradiction is simple: as one keen observer has put it, policy planning in the United States usually means "cleaning up" a mess created by some force, rather than innovating or anticipating. Long-range or middle-range policy requires a careful definition of ends in political, not dogmatic, terms. A way of making policy that concentrates on the means, and that assumes the ends are either dictated by the situation or established by principles gives America's handling of issues an air of inspired breathlessness.

When American policy-makers *are* concerned for the long or middle range, they make "plans" or "designs." The success of the great policies of 1947–48 might seem to demonstrate, in fact, that the American approach is appropriate to long-term planning. But we should remember that when the Marshall Plan was formulated and the negotiations for the North Atlantic Treaty began, there was less of a conviction of building for the long term than a sense of emergency, an intense atmosphere of crisis, in which the best minds were mobilized to respond to what was felt to be an urgent challenge, a clear and present danger. It so happened that the planning that went on was so sound that it turned an immediate response into a solid platform of foreign policy that endured many long years. But we cannot deduce either that there was *a long-term policy,* or that the appropriate response to short-term emergencies *always,* in and of itself, is the best way to handling the middle or long range. For it is now clear that the long-term views of the framers of those measures were far from unified—ranging as they did from Dean Acheson's "robust,

---

[81] One product of "skill thinking" which has fed all these forms of wishful thinking is the deluge of statistics that has come out of the Pentagon during the war in Vietnam concerning both enemy forces and American successes.

straightforward, and hardheaded" [28] notions about the relation of military power to diplomatic effectiveness, to Kennan's emphasis on Soviet internal changes. Also, the terrain was extraordinarily well suited to the grid of operationalism and *Zweckrationalität*. The ends were clear-cut—economic recovery and military protection—and there was a constellation of ideal circumstances that made of the choice of means exactly the kind of affair at which Americans are at their best. The problem was to restore production and increase productivity, not to change an entire economic system, not to overhaul a class structure and political set-up that were leading to economic chaos or preventing economic recovery. In other words, the task was to help others to do what Americans in general know better than anyone else how to do. The second problem was to protect Western Europe from invasion, in other words, to throw the mantle of America's military might over the area at a time when the United States, for all its deficiencies in conventional forces, had a monopoly of nuclear weapons. The societies to be aided were crying for this help, and despite the wounds of the war, despite the domestic tensions that made the need for aid more urgent, they were far enough from actual collapse to provide ideal conditions for U.S. intervention: they were neither reluctant partners nor helpless dependents, but associates in distress. Thus the power relations were those of a wealthy donor to temporary beggars. Being beggars for welfare and security, they would cooperate; being used to self-sufficiency, endowed with machineries of government in tolerable condition, comprised of social groups long used to coexistence if not harmony, in no threat of genuine revolution (even if this did not always appear to be the case at the time), they would enable the United States to lead without having to take over, to concentrate on what it could do best, to unleash its creativity but only in areas where its effectiveness was virtually assured. As a secondary effect, Europe's structures might be changed, but the designs themselves involved no direct action on those structures. Foreign policy was successfully "unchained" [83] because of those exceptional circumstances, and the policy could be presented in terms of a mobilization of all (including allied) talents on a single team.

It is not surprising if people now think of this golden age of American diplomacy with the nostalgia all golden ages distil, and with the desire to revive it. But the conditions cannot be revived. When the problems involve not merely the flow of goods and the reconstruction of defenses against aggression, but also the reform of societies that presently either block the flow of goods or direct it toward certain privileged groups, the consolidation against internal threats of societies that are not real nations under any definition, the reconciliation of states that are convinced that their political objectives are incompatible—when these are the problems, the mechanical resurrection of Marshall Plan language in Latin America, along the Mekong, or even on the two sides of the Oder-Neisse line is of little help. When foreign policy operates in unfavorable conditions, or in conditions in which control is limited, and when it aims to achieve many ends, the use of "plans" launched like military operations is of little use.

Thus, instead of long- or middle-range thinking, American policymakers will resort to using smokescreens that save them from having to work out a policy. One smokescreen substitutes objectives for policy—defines ends but not the combination of ends, means and alternatives that a long-range policy entails. This substitution, together with the frequent definition of ends in terms of ideals rather than as political objectives, gives many discussions of long-range issues an air of wishful unreality in which uncertainty and risks are blandly smothered under clichés. "For some decades," writes President Eisenhower, "our purposes abroad have been the establishment of universal peace with justice, free choice for all peoples, rising levels of human well-being, and the development and maintenance of frank, friendly, and mutually helpful contacts with all nations willing to work for parallel objectives." [84] Here, the liberal vision of harmony and accommodation takes over. Likewise, it shone through the rhetoric of President Kennedy's 1962 speech at the University of California on a pluralist world. It even shines through more recent attempts to define a long-run policy toward Communist China in terms of slogans ("containment without isolation") that reveal an eagerness to disregard political aims and to substitute the slogan for the means. Similarly—this is a less extreme but perhaps more serious example—military plans are drafted which contain general goals but little or no reference to concrete programs whereby these goals can be reached, thus evading the problem of "reconciling the desirable and the possible." Such was the nature of NSC 68—the document that defined American strategy early in 1950—until the Korean War forced the administration to turn from ends to means; [85] such has of-

---

[84] Cited, p. 621.

[85] See Warner Schilling, Paul Hammond, and Glenn Snyder, *Strategy, Politics, and Defense Budgets* (New York: Columbia University Press, 1962), pp. 271 ff.

ten been the nature of NATO plans (the Lisbon goals, the McNamara Doctrine). American thinking about preventing the spread of nuclear weapons has been so vague that the long negotiations in Geneva have raised, one after the other, a series of nightmarish political issues—between the United States and its allies, between the United States and all potential nuclear powers—that had not been either expected or thought through. The issues are so immense and so hard to solve anyhow that a good case could have been made for avoiding to raise them (or to have others raise them) in the first place. For a conference that arouses one trouble after the other may ultimately promote proliferation instead of preventing it.

The second smokescreen is made of political aims, it is true, but instead of considering all the possible means through which they could be reached, the policy-maker concentrates on those to which the United States' brand of pragmatism applies best. The ultimate vision remains almost as hazy as when the international system of the future is described in the language of the Decalogue. Thus, the trouble with Kennedy's vision of Atlantic interdependence was the imprecision about the specific ways in which the lofty aims were to be brought about. What was left out was the blood and nerves of politics: Who will control what and command whom? The notion of an Atlantic partnership was the United States' response to the felt need for a new set of relations to replace those the Marshall Plan had established, but the "not so grand design" [86] had not been thought through. The only means that had been planned were, on the one hand, a unilateral American response to the economic challenge of the EEC (the Trade Expansion Act) and, on the other hand, the MLF. One was merely the prelude to a new partnership in the "common pursuit of economic expansion," the other, in trying to redefine the common pursuit of military defense, ran into the troubles we had discussed earlier; and so the final vision remained (and remains) cloudy. Another example is set by the history of American aid for development. As one student of the issue put it, political development —a long-range goal if there ever was one—is "a purpose, but not a policy," a set of "declarations" that "bear little clear relation to specific aid objectives and programs." Or rather, the "specific objectives and programs" pursued by the "operators" for the promotion of economic aid are the only concrete means that accompany the statements.[87] No wonder that the policy-makers and the operators con-

[86] Schlesinger, cited, Ch. 32.

[87] Robert A. Packenham, "Political Development Doctrines in the American Foreign Aid Program," *World Politics,* January 1966, pp. 210 ff. John Bartlow Martin's book reveals how reliance on a set of abstract goals (polit-

tinue to be confused about the notion of political development.

Nowhere has this deficiency been more serious than in Vietnam. In his report to President Kennedy early in 1963, Roger Hilsman stated that there was "little or no long-range thinking about the kind of country that should come out of a victory and about what we do now to contribute to this longer-range goal." [88] Here, the pragmatic approach meant that fundamental issues—about the country's future as well as about the specific nature of the war, or "whether a Communist take-over could be successfully resisted with any government" [89]—were constantly avoided or pushed back by the priority given to apparently more manageable, narrower, and more technical issues.

Between a nebulous long term and a demanding short term, the short term always wins. The pragmatic approach means, all too often, *priority to what is urgent over what is important.* Events, not policymakers, appear to order the issues. In wartime, the urgency of winning displaces the importance of shaping the postwar world. Thus, decisions made for military reasons, on short-term grounds and in a political vacuum, adversely determine the political conditions, which are left aside, and the political decisions, which are left for later.[90] In peacetime, situations which do not deteriorate, or do so only marginally and insidiously, are not treated because they go unnoticed. Once they have deteriorated, however, they paralyze policy-making, because by that time whatever chance may have existed earlier for a harmonious solution has dissolved in dissent and acrimony; and the only way to solve the difficulty may well be the military one. Again, there is something self-fulfilling about the strategic approach. (A pragmatism that pursues short-term emergencies is like curative, instead of preventive, medicine.) Then, the self-fulfilling policy becomes self-perpetuating. The drastic remedy used so late is very likely to prolong the disease or provoke new troubles; for, almost inevitably, full priority will now be given to military necessities, rather than to the deep causes that had been left unattended and had thus led to the crisis.[91] Even if this does not happen, the moment of crisis is ob-

---

ical democracy and the avoidance of a "Castro/Communist" take-over) and on familiar means (counterinsurgency training and economic aid) failed to save President Bosch's regime.

[88] Hilsman, cited, p. 465.

[89] Robert F. Kennedy, as reported by Hilsman, cited, p. 501.

[90] See the decision to use the atomic bomb against the Japanese without warning—a perfect example of short-term "skill thinking."

[91] See Theodore Draper, "The American Crisis," *Commentary*, January 1967, pp. 27–48.

viously not the best one for even belated consideration of the long-term implications.

There have been innumerable examples of this curse on American policy. In U.S. relations with its European allies, the best are afforded by the Suez crisis and the problem of control over nuclear weapons in NATO. Throughout the summer and early fall of 1956, as a show-down on the issue of the Suez Canal approached, Secretary Dulles did not alter his dilatory tactics. Strong pressure on Egypt at the time of the various summer conferences, however, might have had results, support of Egypt among other nonaligned states being far from unanimous. A statecraft devoted to the prevention of any use of force in the resolution of the crisis should have striven for serious alternatives to the use of force, instead of which Dulles' reluctance to resort even to mild forms of coercion seemed to condemn Great Britain and France to a choice between a desperado use of force and a humiliating resignation to a *fait accompli*. When they chose the former, the United States used the big stick at last—but against Britain, France, and Israel—and it left deep marks.

On the issue of nuclear control in the Alliance, the United States' limited yet farsighted attempts of 1959–60 to anticipate European demands by suggesting schemes for multilateral forces (made at a time when the French nuclear program was not far advanced and West Germany was not yet the stake in a tug-of-war between Washington and Paris) were put on ice by President Kennedy, whose determination to preserve American freedom of action and centralized control in NATO was apparently encouraged by the Europeans' own discord. But in the final analysis, the European discord did not prevent convergent European demands for a greater say in NATO decisions concerning nuclear weapons; it only made the prospects of solution more remote. The schemes for multinational or multilateral forces were therefore revived, not as part of a grand American initiative, but partly to offset the negative results of the improvisation at Nassau, partly as a response to the Gaullist challenge. By 1963, ideas that might have had a chance of success in 1959 were clearly too timid and vague to be of use. (I cannot resist contrasting this delay, which turned political innovation into a mere rearguard action, with the statesmanship of Jean Monnet and Robert Schuman, who, learning the lesson of the fiasco of France's repressive policy toward Germany and anticipating West Germany's recovery, launched their plan for European economic integration at a moment when it seemed like a major creative act.) The memoirs of President Kennedy's aides made it clear that, to a man concerned above all with American relations with the Soviet Union on the one hand and the Third World on the other, the difficulties of NATO were a relatively minor headache; 1961 was dominated by the Berlin crisis and the issue of nuclear testing, 1962 by the campaign for the Trade Expansion Act and then by the missile crisis, after which, as Sorensen put it, everything looked small.[92] In an area where the sum total of grumblings did not amount to a crisis, it seemed easier to wait for England to get into the Common Market so as to "offset the eccentricities of policy in Paris and Bonn," [93] to wait for de Gaulle to disappear from the scene after the settlement in Algeria, and to wait for Adenauer's power to wane in Bonn, than to cope with the Alliance crisis in a way that might detract from other concerns. But when the disarray became a crisis in January, 1963, "crisis-coping" had to be undertaken in confusion, with no adequate preparation, and with dismal results.

There are similar examples of the vices of "crisis-coping" in U.S. policy vis-à-vis Asia and Latin America. The final neutralization of Laos in 1962 was undertaken after the fiasco of an earlier policy had been demonstrated on the battlefield, driving the United States into the corner of the "humiliation-escalation" dilemma, whetting the Pathet Lao's appetite for further gains, and reducing a final political solution to little more than a face-saving device for the United States. Here, at least, the treatment applied to the emergency was not primarily military.[94] But in Vietnam, the slow and often interrupted deterioration of the political and military situation while Diem was in power evidently never became alarming enough to provoke reconsideration of a policy that tied the United States to the support of his government. Only when this regime was finally destroyed and the United States discovered simultaneously the amplitude of the local political vacuum, the seriousness of the military plight, and the impossibility of sticking any longer to what had been a mere "holding operation," only then, in circumstances of acute crisis, was a new policy defined. This time, the repressive approach was chosen, as was almost inevitable, given the slowly growing commitment to South Vietnam, whose abandonment could not be contemplated precisely because it seemed (by contrast with Laos) impossible to find a local

[92] Cited, p. 565.
[93] Schlesinger, cited, p. 845.
[94] See Hilsman, cited, Part IV.

political "third force" acceptable to all sides, if only as a façade behind which the contest could go on. It was too late to do anything but treat a revolutionary war in terms of an over-all military confrontation with implications going far beyond South Vietnam. A small trap had become an almost bottomless pit. In the summer of 1964, U Thant's timid attempt to initiate peace talks got nowhere because the local situation was too bad to allow the United States to negotiate from strength, and because the pressure of events had distracted American attention from the task of thinking through the terms of a possible settlement.[95] Thus do vicious circles set in: in a situation that is politically precarious and militarily difficult, the urgency of day-to-day problems keeps the minds and muscles on the business of mopping up emergencies; instead of middle-range political planning, contingency military planning prevails.

In the Dominican Republic, the United States was taken by surprise by a revolt that its ambassador evidently expected and that was in any case not exactly difficult to predict, given the economic and political predicaments of Donald Reid Cabral's precarious regime. Having acted once in a Dominican emergency to prevent a return of the Trujillos, and having done much to shore up the regime that had ousted Juan Bosch, the United States was nevertheless surprised, and it reacted in the militant fashion so well analyzed by various observers.[96]

Vietnam and the Dominican Republic reveal another danger of policy-making in crises. When the crisis breaks out, "skill thinking" and the need to cope with the urgent issues of the day encourage an initial creeping escalation to a series of mild measures which, it is hoped, will be able to bring the crisis to an end: thus, we sent "advisers" in increasing numbers to Vietnam and walkie-talkies to the hard-pressed Dominican military forces on April 28, 1965. "At each step of the Vietnam conflict, from 1961 onward, 'constructive alternatives' . . . have been rejected as unpalatable; but . . . all such alternatives have become progressively more palatable in retrospect, once the opportunity to choose them has passed us by . . . They were rejected at each stage because the short-term price of doing them

[95] See Philip Geyelin, *Lyndon B. Johnson and the World* (New York: Frederick A. Praeger, 1966), pp. 202 ff.

[96] See Ambassador Martin's judgment on his successor, Ambassador W. Tapley Bennett, who had "stayed strictly out of Dominican politics": "political noninvolvement in such a country is very likely to lead to military intervention—and did." Martin, cited, p. 709.

seemed infinitely higher than the short-term price of not doing them and continuing, instead, on the same course." [97] But when short-term pragmatism once again proves defective, we finally have no resort but to jump into the stormy waters. Belated or misguided small steps lead to a big plunge.

The integration of different objectives into a balanced American foreign policy is often hampered by this tendency to pick up problems in the order of their urgency. President Kennedy, of all the postwar presidents, was most interested in shaking down problems from the files, catching the latent headaches before they started to give pain, watching ashes for a sign of renewed incandescence. Yet even he was obliged by the pressure of crises to follow a zig-zag course that often gave the impression of contradiction or abrupt change. Integration is replaced by oscillation. Events throw up an issue, which is dealt with "on its merits" rather than according to its place in over-all policy. When a temporary solution has been devised or the emergency is over, the issue goes back to sleep, and events throw up another problem, which will be dealt with again in *ad hoc* fashion. The trouble is that sometimes events throw two issues up at the same time, both of them dealt with in a trenchant manner, but also in contradiction.

In Atlantic and European policy, the earliest case of contradiction would be the inauguration of the drive toward German rearmament in the fall of 1950. This was a response to the Korean emergency, which provoked a sudden acceleration of all American military plans. Had the defense of Europe been in desperately bad condition, only American troops could have saved the day, since there were no West German divisions yet. Events proved that the raising of those divisions, so long delayed, was not essential to the protection of the half-continent. However, the issue was treated as if a rapid German military contribution was essential. The result was that a monkey wrench was thrown into European integration—another goal of United States policy but not one with a fire of emergency burning under it. Nasser's nationalization of the Suez Canal six years later created an emergency in which the United States found itself forced to give priority to avoiding a military showdown, which would have done irreparable harm to the reputation of the Western powers in underdeveloped countries. What had to be sacrificed was the trust between the United States and its two principal allies; what had to be subordinated was its insistence on orderly behavior on the part of the new nations.

[97] James C. Thomson (former staff member of the National Security Council), *The New York Times,* June 4, 1967, p. E 13.

Then, six years after Suez, the meeting at Nassau between President Kennedy and Prime Minister Macmillan produced what had been needed in the earlier crisis, i.e., a formula for Anglo-American collaboration. But the formula was devised so much "on its own merits" alone that its substance and presentation conflicted with two of the President's objectives at the time—the entry of Great Britain into the European Common Market and the return of France to NATO's fold—neither of which could be achieved by a plan that emphasized the "special relationship" of the United States with England and England's dependence on the United States. And it also conflicted with another, more permanent aim: to assure the European allies of the United States' reliability in defending interests they consider major. Later, the MLF, one of the by-products of the Nassau agreement, was pressed on the Allies until an emergency forced President Johnson to consider the matter again. Just before Prime Minister Wilson's flight to Washington in December, 1964, President Johnson, taking full cognizance of the issue, decided to let up the pressure; and while thereby avoiding a painful showdown with a British cabinet that was reluctant to get its collective head banged against the multilateral wall, he also postponed a solution to the crisis over nuclear control in NATO.

These specific events are instances of what were in fact fundamental and continuing difficulties in reconciling objectives in the Atlantic area. On the one hand, as Schlesinger and others have pointed out, President Kennedy never reconciled the notion of a partnership of equals in economic affairs with that of an integrated defense under American control and command. The former was a response to the challenge of EEC; the latter, as we have seen, was continued as long as discord did not amount to crisis; and, when the crisis erupted, in January, 1963, it was only superficially revised in the form of the MLF, which the President rightly felt to be "something of a fake." [98] But given France's opposition, and given the technical characteristics of the scheme—i.e., its series of agreements linking European participants to the United States—the MLF could hardly have been considered, except by wishful thinkers or wishful fakers, as something that would lead up to a European defense system capable of being an equal partner to the United States. That is to say, it could hardly have eliminated the contradiction.

On the other hand, the contradiction between this search for a reinforcement of the Atlantic Alliance and the search for a *détente* with the Soviet Union was never fully eliminated. In 1961 the Berlin crisis

[98] Schlesinger, cited, p. 873.

produced a determined American reaction against Soviet pressure; then the Berlin Wall, because it increased fear of war, produced an equally determined American effort to find a diplomatic solution to the "Berlin problem" in direct negotiations with the Soviet Union—without the participation of NATO allies, indeed against the opposition of West Germany and France. In 1963, the possibility of a *détente,* opened up in the aftermath of the Cuban confrontation, led President Kennedy to stress the themes of mutual tolerance and increased understanding in order to revive the test-ban talks; the prospects widened, subsequently, with the test-ban treaty, and he envisaged further steps, even to "drawing" on the "cash he had in the bank in West Germany." [99] But at the same time, the emergency created in the Atlantic Alliance by de Gaulle's challenge of American policies drove the President into a tour of Europe during which his theme rapidly became "the great issue between the free world and the Communist world"—until the two themes openly clashed in West Berlin. Thereafter, in the absence of emergencies, the two goals of agreement on nonproliferation of nuclear weapons with the Soviet Union and of satisfying West Germany's aspirations to a greater role in nuclear strategy or technology have been pursued simultaneously and inconclusively.

Inevitably, a nation with world-wide concerns will have contradictory policies, especially when the international system is so rich in currents and storms. But the effective approach would be like a symphony conductor's coaxing harmony from a variety of musicians who play different instruments and notes. Instead of this, the United States' pragmatic urgency produces a billiards-player's approach: the ball it happens to hit at a given point displaces other balls from positions that should have been preserved or from courses that should have been pursued. The emergency in Vietnam has been allowed to affect the whole balance of American foreign and military policy.[100] Troops have been withdrawn from West Germany, not in accordance with a political design for Europe, but so as to meet the rising needs in the Far East. Relations with the Soviet Union are damaged, relations with Japan strained, American influence in the Atlantic Alliance hurt, Gaullism helped.

America's particular way of handling foreign affairs as a series of

---

[99] Same, p. 904.
[100] See George Kennan's testimony of February 1966 in *Supplemental Foreign Assistance, Fiscal Year, 1966: Vietnam,* Part I, Hearings before the Senate Committee on Foreign Relations, 89th Congress, 2nd sess. (Washington: GPO, 1966), pp. 331–430.

crises also often results in undermining a long-term objective by short-term considerations, which are then all too easily rationalized as being long range. One example—which I know to be debatable and controversial—is that of Vietnam. Here, the long-term objective is (or ought to be) to avert situations that are ripe for the kind of revolutionary warfare which gives native Communists an opportunity to capture control of forces of nationalism or social change (and to foreign Communists the chance to extend their control). Reaching this objective will become impossible if all energies are concentrated on the military front, and if, in the absence of prospects for a "non-aligned" yet non-Communist regime—acceptable to both sides and strong enough to prevent a Communist take-over in a pacified South Vietnam—energies must continue to be focused on the war itself. Another way to describe the long-term objective is to say that the nations of Asia which are still free of Communist encroachment must be made capable of containing local or foreign Communists, with United States help but not through virtual United States take-over (which would give Communists their golden opportunity). Reaching this objective will not be possible if the main emphasis of American support, and of its Asian allies' expectations, is on the military field. True, there has been a belated shift to the "other war"—to economic and social reform in South Vietnam. But experience shows that the more intense the military war, the less practicable the other, especially if the local regime in charge of the latter effort has little expertise and little motivation to wage it. It may be that a search for a regime broad enough to become a "third force" capable of launching such an effort would detract from the war. But this can be turned around: the war detracts from any possible search for an effective local regime and from the necessary improvement of local conditions elsewhere in Asia.

To be sure, present United States' policy in Vietnam is justified in long-range terms of commitment, containment of China, and discouragement of revolutionary wars. But political analysis of the Asian scene fails to assure us that a prolonged military stalemate in Vietnam actually does prevent the social and political fabric from rotting elsewhere; that China's political prospects are dimmed rather than brightened by it; that the United States' Asian allies are likely to prefer such protection (tantamount to physical destruction) to possible agreements with China that might at least save them from such a fate.

The long-term objective, then, would be served only if the American effort in Vietnam were capable of producing a non-Communist regime, freed of Vietcong subversion, and capable of preventing its return. Yet it is too late for a Vietnamese Magsaysay, if one could be found; the reason for the massive military build-up is that sufficient Vietnamese sources of strength have not been found, and the logic of it makes the establishment of a genuine South Vietnamese government impossible. The day can be saved only if the North Vietnamese and the Vietcong are militarily forced to "give up South Vietnam"; but paying the price for this will endanger countless other major American objectives.

Consider also United States policy in the Dominican Republic. The long-range goal—to strengthen Latin American regimes capable of fostering development and social progress, and to prevent the Communists from exploiting injustices and poverty—is more likely to be damaged than salvaged by an intervention that appeared to favor one or another military clique over a movement which President Johnson himself termed a "popular democratic revolution" whose capture (or danger of capture) by Communists was never demonstrated.

A third, no less dangerous example is that of United States policy toward West Germany since 1963. The long-term objective of both American and French foreign policy since 1949 had been to attach West Germany to the West so as to prevent any German "separatism" in the future. West European integration and West Germany's rearmament within the NATO framework were part of that policy. Along with West Germany's renunciation of nuclear weapons, they were supposed to make the eventual reunification of East and West Germany easier and less dangerous. After de Gaulle's challenge of January 1963, even though President Kennedy believed that "competing with him for the allegiance of Germany would only play into de Gaulle's hands," he "began wooing Europeans more assiduously," particularly the West Germans.[101] This response to an emergency was rationalized in long-range terms—the need to attach West Germany firmly to the leading power of the Atlantic Alliance rather than to let it fall into the orbit of a statesman unable or unwilling to provide it with either security or reunification, and the need to keep de Gaulle from disrupting the Alliance altogether. Ties between West Germany and France lapsed into a state of "cordial potentiality" [102] largely as a

---

[101] Sorensen, cited, p. 573.
[102] De Gaulle, press conference, September 9, 1965 (Ambassade de France, Speeches and Press Conferences, No. 228, p. 9).

result of these American efforts, and progress toward West European integration slowed down. Yet the ties between West Germany and the United States, while strengthened, were no more able to provide West Germany with a means to achieve reunification or the kind of reassurance it had been seeking in the matter of nuclear weapons—partly because of the continued disunity in the Alliance, partly because those German objectives are contradictory, partly because, in order to reassure West Germany completely, the United States would have had to do what neither Kennedy nor his successor had wanted to do: raise tensions with the Soviets so as to patch over Western quarrels. Thus, the possibility of West German disenchantment with the United States was added to the reality of loosened ties in Western Europe. When, in 1966, the United States withdrew some troops from West Germany, insisted on German arms purchases, and pushed ahead toward a nonproliferation treaty with the Soviet Union, the ties between West Germany and the United States were indeed strained, largely through the pressure of short-term concerns. The precedent for this mistake was provided by United States policy toward France in World War II: the long-term goal of friendly relations with France was undermined by a policy which, for short-term reasons of debatable value (the possible influence a United States presence could have on Vichy, the difficulty of getting along with de Gaulle, etc.), obstinately refused to recognize political and emotional realities within France.

Finally, concentration on emergencies reinforces the tendency (already noted as a consequence of "skill thinking") to mistake means for ends and to turn the instrument of policy into the policy itself. Any policy geared to the long or middle range must consider and use a variety of instruments: it is inevitably symphonic. Crises have a way of compelling a policy into narrower and tenser paths: it is a solo performance. Now it is not surprising if the soloist hugs his instrument too tightly, but it is dangerous if he forgets the tune he intended to play, or the fact that it was supposed to be only a fragment of a "work in progress." American attachment to certain institutional formulas—military integration in NATO, EDC, an integrated Europe, the MLF—sometimes leads to a neglect of the aims for which the formulas were devised. Like dead stars, the formulas continue to shine—long after it ought to have become clear that the aims could best be reached with other devices. When a crisis breaks out because of a difference of opinion over ultimate goals, Americans will always try to safeguard the means; this saves us, as it were, from having to think through our long-range policy. Our reaction to the NATO crisis provoked by de Gaulle's withdrawal from military integration in March, 1966, is a case in point; in the determination to keep NATO intact, the United States once again concentrated on the instrument, on the symptoms, leaving the goals, the causes, and the future to take care of themselves. Both in the case of EDC and in that of the MLF, the policy-makers had to choose between a crash against a stone wall, and an abrupt and screeching application of the brakes that inflicts quite a jolt on the passengers. Here we find combined the effects of a certain pragmatism and those of "formulism." It is time to examine how the elements of America's way reinforce one another, or conflict with each other.

# CHAPTER SIX

# The Nation's Dilemmas: A Critique

As we have seen, the historical experience of the United States buttresses the nation's principles, and, together with the domestic consensus on those principles, it explains the United States' unique brand of pragmatism. The total result could be termed an unpolitical approach to foreign policy. Distance from history, dogmas instead of guidelines, an engineering technique that works best on technical problems—all combine to depoliticize world affairs. Just as domestic American politics provide no analytical model for the understanding of other political systems, American foreign policy, precisely because it reflects a polity that has no counterpart elsewhere, seems as if it misunderstood the political dimension of world affairs.

This explains why American foreign policy frequently oversimplifies the complexities, conflicts, and crises of other nations, translating them into a more familiar but less relevant language, maintaining a lofty distance from reality, and channeling the energies of its practitioners into rather predictable and narrow paths.

Second, American foreign policy is marked by what might be called over-expectations, or excessive optimism, or one-way contingency planning—planning for only the most favorable alternative, or the one over which one has most control, assuming that all will go well or that the success of what is being undertaken will *ipso facto* take care of all the harrowing problems that gave rise to the policy in the first place. Marshal Foch's famous edict, *"on s'engage et puis on voit,"* corresponds only too well to this procedure.

Third, whatever its fundamental continuity, American foreign policy shows, like a fever chart, the appearance of a jagged line. A national ethos of progress and "built-in obsolescence," a way of acting that constitutes a kind of full-fledged mobilization in response to challenges thrown down by others, a devotion to principles among which (as among Supreme Court precedents) one can select what one needs—all these explain why changes in emphasis are called revolutions, curves are deemed turning points, and mild waves christened brainstorms. Thus, a qualified reaction to ensure that there will be no Korean wars becomes "massive retaliation," a systematic re-evaluation of the consequences of nuclear stalemate becomes the new McNamara Doctrine; greater emphasis on reform in Latin America and a more favorable attitude toward neutralism are presented as almost sensational reversals in policy. Here, as in other respects, American institutions have a share in the responsibility.

A national style that neglects or distorts the political factors different from those of its own experience creates far more trouble than these familiar flaws. The chief problem within the American style is what I would call its dualism, a deep tension between two ways of dealing with political issues, and this, in turn, leads to two other sets of problems.

# I. America's Dualism

## A. *Manifestations*

Perhaps the primary manifestation of American dualism in foreign affairs concerns the "image" the United States likes to present to the other nations of the world. In a world of revolutionary challenges, Americans like to remind themselves and others that the United States was once the "first new nation," the product of a revolution which was the first act of colonial emancipation in history, and also the first in the "age of the democratic revolution." At the same time, the United States likes to emphasize that it stands for order and stability, for private enterprise, sound finances, balanced growth, constitutional procedures, the avoidance of revolution, the prevalence of legality—everything that, to listeners and observers, appears *not* compatible with revolutionary forces, whether of the new nationalism or of communism. Far from competing under a banner that says, "I can understand the former and am far more genuine than the latter," the United States seems to oppose those forces and to defend its privileged position as the well-endowed leader of the industrialized West.

Similarly, the United States likes to appear as the keystone of an arching, world-wide alliance engaged in a protracted conflict, the basic design of which (although variations may well give statesmen kaleidoscopic surprises) is monotonously unchanging—the containment of forces of evil bent on universal conquest and global turmoil.

At the same time, it likes to proclaim the American faith in the Communists' capacity to understand their common interests with the West, and in the prospect of a diverse world in which everyone will have a place in the sun. One side of the argument stresses that *plus ça change, plus c'est la même chose;* the other suggests that *plus c'est la même chose,* the more things will actually change and improve.

The difficulties that come from this perfectly honest habit of dualism are familiar. The "first new nation" has, in some Latin American countries such as Venezuela, backed forces that appeared willing to do battle with traditional oligarchies; but in Brazil the champion of order and stability has supported a regime that, for all its financial orthodoxy, can hardly be called a force of social progress, not to mention rigorous legality. The "first new nation" saw in the Suez crisis the occasion for what one of its leaders called a "declaration of independence from Europe," but that crisis was provoked by an American decision made largely on Cold War considerations (punishing Egypt for dealing with the Soviet Union) and led in time to the United States' reassertion of its role as protector of the Western Alliance (when the Soviet Union resorted to blustering threats against Britain and France).

A second manifestation is a tendency to speak two different languages, neither of which is entirely convincing and which are difficult to reconcile. The first is the language of power. Here, American leaders "talk tough," they ask how many divisions the Pope has, and they explain to the European allies that power cannot really be shared effectively unless all the sharers can unite to reach a scale "commensurate with the requirements" of power, and unless all of them are willing to accept world-wide responsibilities; they warn their enemies that failure to desist from hostile acts will be met by the full weight of American might. The second is the language of community and harmony. There, American leaders protest their sincere dislike of imperialism; they stress that the United States is a disinterested nation that acts out of responsibility, not selfishness, a world power that for the first time in history leads by giving rather than taking; they explain that power is a tragic necessity but that peace, love, reason, bread, and friendship for all are the goals.

Of course, only a symbolic eagle can hold both the arrows and the olive branch easily at the same time. When other nations accuse us of playing a classical game of power politics, we protest, pointing to our community ideals and our aspirations for brotherhood; and we find the use by other nations of pure or traditional power plays to be nefarious and intolerable when they are our foes, disruptive and ana-chronistic when they are our friends. When other nations appeal to our sense of community and our ideal of human harmony, we are apt to point to our special burdens and to require an admission fee to our school.

Then too, a kind of double bookkeeping afflicts each of these languages. In essence, both the language of power and the language of harmony are universal; they can be used by whoever wants to act on the world stage, yet Americans seem to ask for special treatment. Thus, when we speak the language of force, we do not quite avoid implying that although we recognize power as a universal commodity and the necessary, amoral means for all nations, our power is some-how morally superior and deserves a privileged position; that we can trust ourselves but not others; and that others can trust us, but no-body else. Our policy of trying to stop the arms race, which often im-plies that the optimum would be a situation of equality between the opponents, leaves room for various more or less convincing rational-izations of why we should be allowed to maintain military superiority. Tough talk with our allies about power logically ends with an invita-tion to unite so as to be able to share power with us, and to develop their power so as to deserve being our partners. But if allies develop their power independently, we consider that their multiplicity is rea-son for not taking them too seriously. And our exhortation to them to unite does not go so far as to suggest that the resultant "shared pow-er" would ever apply to the realm of nuclear control. We argue that there is no reason why the continental Europeans should trust a Brit-ish nuclear deterrent or why the Germans should feel protected by a French one, but we are confident that the Germans, the French, or the British should have no doubt about the reliability of ours. In dis-cussions with our allies, we hint that their criticisms would be more likely to be taken into account if they supported us in our policies elsewhere, if they defined world responsibility in the same way we do. In debate with our allies as with our opponents, we assume that our strategy is the only rational one, and that their failure to see this is due either to ignorance or to obstreperousness.

There is the same double bookkeeping in our talk about com-munity. We stress reasonableness, the need to behave as equals will-ing to subordinate separate interests to the higher common good. But, at the same time, we suggest that our very disinterestedness and our world-wide responsibilities thrust upon us the role of interpreter and trustee of the common good; we are the only ones who see the whole picture and want nothing for ourselves; the others have a parochial vision. In defining the common good, we also see to it that our peculiar geographical position, or our special position as the most powerful nation on earth, is taken into account (for instance, our limited-war strategy in Europe just happens to correspond with the possibility, enjoyed only by a superpower situated on a separate continent, of waging war while keeping the home territory a sanctuary).

A third and last manifestation of American dualism is in the issue of the use of force. When the United States overtly or covertly resorts to force in the form of repressive moves against a foe, or deterrent build-ups, or advice and training for friendly soldiers of nations threatened from within or without, it does so with a remarkable technical efficiency, or at least self-assurance. It is as if a button had been pushed and a hidden spring of energy had been suddenly released. The strategic design may be confused, the relevance of the act to the objectives may be dubious, and yet there goes into the undertaking not merely a puritan sense of duty but an exuberant (albeit disciplined) sense of mission and aptitude—in a word, a calling—that can be a little overwhelming. What elicits such a response is the American quest for efficiency, the need for technical expertise, the comfort of self-reliance, the nonambiguity of ends, the pleasure of a morally simple and technically apt job done for a good cause. Restraints are often preserved, to be sure, but at the cost of a difficult exercise in self-discipline, for they do not come naturally. They are respected because the international system requires them; our own instinct does not. They are observed because we want to survive, i.e., because we want our foes to observe them too, not because we want to spare our foes. Significantly, the "internalization" of those restraints has consisted in developing ingenious theories which give to the art of proportioning means to ends the reassuring air of a science that can be learned as engineers learn their trade. But when other nations act as we do, often in quite similar circumstances, we frown, grumble, or condemn. The use of force, the threat of force, the preparations to use force by our opponents are evil; military operations or plans made by our friends (except at our request) provoke laments or sermons—war is too risky, the world is too dangerous for this, nothing is worth playing with fire.

## B. *Meanings*

These contradictions require explanation. No light is to be shed on them by talking of hypocrisy or imposture. A hypocrite is a man who deceitfully pretends that he is what he is not; an impostor is a man who tries to pass for what he is not. The charge of hypocrisy, so often made, is a projection of the national style of those who proffer it. Diplomats and observers who come from a tradition of Machiavellian calculations and elaborate self-serving designs tend to interpret all diplomacies in this way, and to see in double standards or in the legions of principles nothing but a reflection of age-old cynicism, a shield behind which it is polite, profitable, and practical to advance. But things here are not so simple; they go deeper. Nor do the tensions I have described come from pretenses. They come from the fact that the nation's values (and leaders) point simultaneously in opposite directions.

There is, in the American style, a tension between the instinct of violence and the drive for harmony. The United States is a nation impatient with, intolerant of, unadjusted and unaccustomed to basic conflicts of ends. (It would be interesting to analyze the intellectual origins of this attitude, for instance in Puritanism. The *Federalist Papers* display the same hostility in their discussion of "factions.") The immigrants that founded and peopled the United States were exiles or refugees from societies where such conflicts were often inexpiable; indeed, these pilgrims and these huddled masses were often the victims of those conflicts. They wanted to build a society of concord and consensus. Moreover, the elements that made America were so diverse that this new Jerusalem could prosper only if the differences were sacrificed on the altar of harmony. Concord required the melting pot; for in any society threatened by deep conflict yet driven toward unity (from above, by charismatic leaders, or below, by popular messianic hopes), unanimity must be created or maintained as the only way of keeping the society together. The impulse of violence and the thrust toward harmony are both escapes from the unbearable reality of inevitable conflict.

When Americans *are* faced with a fundamental conflict of ends, their experience has been to resort to force—considered the most decisive and compelling of all ways to end such conflicts. In using force, they have sought not just the infliction of pain on the enemy, which Schelling rightly sees as a dirty bargaining process, but the elimination of the conflict through the elimination of the foe. "Coercive violence," being a process, requires rules and structures; it is part and parcel of societies to which conflicts of ends are inherent, it is a way not of eliminating the conflict but of managing it. In domestic affairs, the slightly hagiographic readings of American history have over-stressed harmony and community. Violence was used against Indians, Negroes, and among Americans, in a civil war that was the bloodiest conflict of the nineteenth century, and in labor conflicts that were anything but mild. What is unique about American history is not the absence of violence but the absence of permanent conflicts of ends, and the unwillingness to live with such protracted conflicts. As a result, violence plays the role of a great, cleansing purge. (After the Civil War, the issue of the Negro's civil rights remained, but the inexpiable conflict of ends was somehow appeased.) Whenever conflicts of purposes reappear, or when segments of the population feel threatened, the tendency to revert to violence reasserts itself both on the part of the majority and on the part of a minority that often has no other resort. Just as there is little middle ground in the "liberal society" between the nihilistic "alienation of the uncommitted" and the complacency of the great mass, there is little middle ground between the great consensus and violence in dissent. Arthur Schlesinger has written of President Kennedy's awareness "of the fragility of the membranes of civilization, stretched so thin over a nation so disparate in its composition, so tense in its interior relationships, so cunningly enmeshed in underground fears and antagonisms, so entrapped by history in the ethos of violence." [1] On the side of the committed majority, the "paranoid style in American politics," so well analyzed by Richard Hofstadter [2]—the witch hunts and extremism, the beatings and the lynchings—are the marks of a frustration that expresses itself in a kind of blind hitting out at evil rather than a forcing of the victims into "internal emigration" or permanent alignments, as in other societies marked by conflicts of ends. On the side of the dissenters, one small but significant symptom of violence can be seen in the record of assassinations of Presidents of the United States. In Europe, opposition to society or to the dominant politics has a way of being channeled through various institutions and competing ideologies or belief systems. But when there is a "tyranny of the majority," when the only avenues of dissent are narrow, a kind of desperado violence breaks out that expresses not only dissent but also the hopelessness and helplessness of the isolated, rejected, and unharnessed outsider. When a minority group is organized as a political or social

---

[1] *A Thousand Days: John F. Kennedy in the White House* (Boston: Houghton Mifflin, 1965), p. 725.
[2] Richard Hofstadter, *The Paranoid Style in American Politics and Other Essays* (New York: Alfred A. Knopf, 1965).

force, it becomes part of the great consensus and no longer challenges fundamentals. As long as it does, it is condemned to the frustrations of quasi-clandestinity.

The United States' external experience has corroborated this internal one: conflicts of ends between the United States and other nations have again and again led to the simple and drastic test of arms: with Mexico, Spain, in World War I, in World War II. Thus, to use Ernest May's useful term, the resort to force has been the "axiomatic response" [3] of a nation whose initial harmony within and protected insulation without meant that human obstacles or contrarieties were resented as intrusions, like the sudden burst of a nightmare into a dream. Moreover in such conflicts, a long tradition of successes and pride in one's principles and in one's pragmatic skills foster a fierce competitiveness that clamors for nothing less than victory.

Yet at heart, America—proud of its unique harmony, its lack of ideological trenches, its capacity to absorb and fuse diverse experiences and peoples, its repudiation of power politics—dislikes the very violence that is its spontaneous response: horrendous proof of the fragility of the dream it likes to think it lives. Americans believe that violence is evil, perhaps because of their admirable, if slightly startling, conviction that tragic conflicts of ends are not a necessary part of life, and because force gives to clashes that ought not to exist a sharper reality, a kind of gory blessing and christening in blood. The presence of the damned spot makes it impossible to deny the nightmare. The only way of reconciling one's ideal of life to that presence and to that stench is to spread as much incense as possible into the air: if the means are deeply felt to be repulsive, they can be justified only by a holy end. And it is this lingering awareness of the evils of violence that lessens the role of force in American history. So the only excuse for violence is provided by high principles, but these in turn release in full the passion for unbridled violence. In the last analysis, violence is justified by only one ideal, which subsumes all those principles: not merely the final elimination of force from history,[4] but the final ironing out of conflicts of ends.

It is also part of the American experience and ethos to expect harmony as the norm—at the cost, sometimes, of a national repression

[3] "The Nature of Foreign Policy: The Calculated vs. the Axiomatic," *Daedalus,* Fall 1962, pp. 653–67.

[4] On this point, see Robert W. Tucker, *The Just War* (Baltimore: The Johns Hopkins Press, 1960).

of issues on which there is no consensus and no division deep enough to justify violence (civil rights).[5] When the division does go too deep, the will to restore the norm inspires the use of force. The impatience for harmony makes violence a curse and a necessity. It is because of a basic consensus on values and on structures, on institutions and on directions, that American society can afford to display many conflicts (and American social scientists take as a model a group theory that conceives of politics as a contest of interests for the distribution of resources). For those conflicts are channeled, tamed, and ultimately resolved by the basic consensus; they keep the consensus vigorous by nourishing it (and, in the utilitarian universe of group theory, the absence of "conflicts of gods" reduces political contests to a competition of measurable interests, leading to equilibrium). This is the sophisticated translation of a national experience without ideological differences and without profound class differences, in which political parties merely compete for the management of the basic order, and social classes are little more than the shifting products of income differences, having no metaphysical subjective connotations. In such a society, accommodation can be reached by purely technical means—*ad hoc* procedures of arbitration, mediation, compromise. "Reasoning together" is fruitful because the momentary clash on immediate objectives fails to erase a fundamental agreement on assumptions and purposes. The "engineering of consent" is a phrase that could gain currency only in a nation in which consent is a matter of engineering.

In other countries, differences in ideological outlook (which color, magnify, and distort clashes of interests), class oppositions, and the needed accommodations are infinitely more complex, more laborious, more creative. They require the painful consideration and reconsideration of questions that do not have to be asked here, where the answers are known and shared by all. When accommodation succeeds (as it has, on the whole, in Great Britain), the two extremes of force and "consensual engineering" are avoided. When accommodation breaks down, force is the remedy, but, given the nature of the society, it is more a political instrument, less a moral cataclysm; it is recognized as an inevitable last resort rather than a necessary calling. Since harmony was not a norm, violence entails less shame.

If politics, in Bertrand de Jouvenel's phrase, is what remains insoluble, then the United States is an unpolitical nation. Political sys-

[5] See Kenneth Keniston, *The Uncommitted* (New York: Harcourt, Brace 1965), especially pp. 375 ff.

tems avert force through the more or less dirty, more or less civilized bargaining processes of disciplined violence; they aim less to resolve issues than to manage the unsolvable. In the United States, the bargaining processes aim to solve problems; the unsolvable brings forth the flash of force and the exorcising spell.

In foreign policy also, proneness to force and a pining for harmony are the two sides of the same coin. It would be a mistake to identify each side with a particular school of thought; for although force as the reflex of frustration is characteristic of radical nationalists in American history—from the days of the Spanish-American War to the days of Barry Goldwater—the "hawks" are not found in that one sector only. Even among radical internationalists, one may find the desire to brandish the shiny sword for causes supposedly of concern to whole mankind. On issues like Vietnam, or even the elimination of Tshombe's Katanga independence movement, recent memoirs and events show "evidence of a desire by the peace-lovers to show their belief in military solutions, too" [6] (and unconditional surrender was not an invention of radical nationalists). Conversely, the international harmony of good will is not the preserve of the internationalists. But both sides overestimate America's aptitude to influence the world, both "postulate a world responsive to our will." [7]

However, the tension between the two aspects is not easy to resolve. The nasty crack someone made about John Foster Dulles, that he brandished the Bible in one hand and the atomic bomb in the other, has a caricatural value that goes beyond the late Secretary of State. There is always the pole of force and the pole of friendship, the offer of nectar and the threat of napalm—sometimes in alternation, sometimes in startling juxtaposition (as in President Johnson's speech on Vietnam at the Johns Hopkins University in April 1965).

Toward force, even in the nuclear age, the basic attitude is a crusading one. But the crusader must be cautious; there are all those rungs on the ladder of escalation; and he must master the art of climbing without a fall into nuclear hell. The only justification for this disagreeable task is, still, the cause for which he must climb the ladder. Bad conscience, which explains the crusading attitude, now demands self-restraint, which does not come easily but which is rightly seen as the only way to prevent the use of force from abolishing his-

[6] Theodore C. Sorensen, *Kennedy* (New York: Harper & Row, 1965), p. 638.

[7] Charles Burton Marshall, *The Exercise of Sovereignty* (Baltimore: The Johns Hopkins Press, 1965), p. 88.

tory and man, instead of conflicts among men and force in history. Bad conscience thus turns into its opposite—excessively good conscience—by the satisfaction derived from following a clean, cool, cautious, and controlled strategy of limited brute force and graduated infliction of pain. Bad conscience also explains why the crusader must paint a gruesome picture of the enemy that makes him more diabolical, more effective, more powerful, more insidious than he is. For were the foe anything less, the shame of violence could not be removed; yet if the foe is a monster, guilt can be turned into pride. Bad conscience explains why there remains a strong and sincere dislike of the United States' own use of force for "possession goals." Bad conscience explains why there remains a damning dislike of the use of force by others; they usually seek possession goals and are resigned, nay, sometimes even dedicated to, the perpetuation of conflicts of ends in an imperfect world. Bad conscience explains why America trusts only America with force, for what it has faith in is not its sword but its principles, with which the sword is oiled. Overwhelming foes with our power thus becomes the necessary prelude to the healing victory of our vision of harmony. So strong an insistence on central control for nuclear weapons, on undivided commands in military operations cannot be explained by technical reasons alone; the unwillingness to entrust the sword to others has deeper reasons. There is no deceit in the American way of telling other nations, with a straight and suffering face, that they ought to leave to us the horrors and the burdens and the ironies of nuclear responsibility. Nor is there hypocrisy in the shrillness with which we assert, whenever we are locked in battle abroad, that none "of our political or economic interests [is] involved." [8] since indeed "we have few national interests in the narrow sense, outside our own territory." [9]

Beyond the excessively somber universe of force, there is only the excessively light universe of friendship and consensus: a world in which alliances are interpreted as incipient communities, localized rehearsals for a general world order, laboratories of the common good; a world in which personal contacts, functional assistance, cultural exchanges, and increasing cooperation are expected to grow into order and stability; a world in which legal texts are supposed to turn moral aspirations (deemed sacred to all) into the universal rule of law, and

---

[8] Dwight D. Eisenhower, *The White House Years: Mandate for Change* (New York: Doubleday, 1963), p. 364.

[9] George Ball in Karl H. Cerny and Henry W. Briefs, eds., *NATO in Quest of Cohesion* (New York: Frederick A. Praeger, 1963), p. 18.

to exorcise evil practices by calling them illegal; a world that is just an enlarged and idealized version of home.

Those realms—force and friendship—are combined, not in any organic way, but only at the level of disembodied or contradictory principles and at the level of operational pragmatism. "You are advancing in the night bearing torches toward which mankind would be glad to turn, but you leave them enveloped in the fog of a merely experimental approach." [10] Hence the jarring juxtaposition of the Sermon on the Mount and of the variations on Clausewitz.

The same men, with the same good faith, invoke at one moment their experience as members of the beehive of the Atlantic Alliance in the late 1940s, when differences among nations in power or outlook somehow did not matter (with good reason); in the next, their contempt for world public opinion and their conviction that only power matters. At one moment, they explain their deep distrust of other countries' intentions and habits, in the next they proclaim their faith in a universal rule of law. To be sure, there is a kind of reconciliation in their minds, but it is too extreme to be explicit: given American principles, a world in which American power was supreme and unchallenged would be one of harmony, and the rule of American principles backed by American force would be the rule of law. Unfortunately, we are not ready for such a day; and in the meantime the elements coexist as well as they can, which often means not well at all. Thus, in Latin America, the United States simultaneously makes efforts toward development and progress which cannot succeed unless they shake oligarchies and dislodge vested interests, and efforts to prevent subversion and insurgency which consist of rushing to the threatened gates and which therefore strengthen the *status quo*. In Europe, where we stress the virtues of federation, we tend to forget how few federations have been achieved or preserved without the use of force; and, when we insist that our allies must trust us with the supreme burdens of the common defense, we tend to forget that the community of purposes that would allow for such a mandate has not yet been established.

A cynic could argue that a ruthless use of force for purely selfish purposes, but for such purposes only, is in the end more effective than resort to force on behalf of principles that alternately make one go too far for one's own good and make one stop half-way: the Soviet Union in Hungary, the French in Madagascar, gained more than the

[10] Jacques Maritain, *Reflections on America* (New York: Scribner's, 1958), p. 118.

United States in Vietnam or, in all likelihood, the Dominican Republic. The American resort to force, somewhat uninhibited militarily because of the principles that promote it and the pragmatism that propels it, is often inhibited politically both by bad conscience and by the dream of brotherhood: hence a strange pattern, in which the sword is brandished but then once the dragon is wounded or is slain, one is at a loss. In Santo Domingo, the sudden realization that the use of force led down a blind alley and that the juntas or cliques the American intervention was serving were flawed (to use a polite word) led to a startling desire for a "coalition." In Cuba, only the fiasco of the Bay of Pigs saved the United States from the discovery that the replacement of the regime it wanted to destroy would perhaps have created more headaches than the Castro regime itself. In Vietnam, the contrast could not be greater between a spectacular military build-up and a pathetic political timidity which converts daily victories into glowing ashes.

There is another difficulty: both elements of the American dualism are (for different reasons) ill fitted for political realities. The side of force, by virtue of its heaviness, sinks deep into the mud of the road, whereas the millennial side, by virtue of its weightlessness, fails even to make contact. The sword clinks and swishes and cuts; the words dazzle and vanish. The military efforts leave marks, even if the result is not politically effective, even if the consequence is to divert energies in the wrong direction. Assumptions of harmony and consensus all too often have no result at all, except frustration, for efforts toward reform which lack instruments for reform remain in limbo. The pictures of John F. Kennedy will not hang forever in the huts of the Southern Hemisphere [11] if no deeds follow his ringing words. In Europe, calls for harmony leave the main issues in suspense and perpetuate the disarray in NATO; but in the meantime, American preponderance is preserved, and this too feeds that disarray. In Vietnam, the formidable difficulty of making American principles apply to a people apparently devoid of the capacity to govern themselves in any way we would like should American forces be removed, and the formidable difficulty of convincing a beleaguered opponent of a "sincere" desire to restore a dialogue, give the United States' peace proposals and offensives a singular woolliness, but there is nothing fuzzy about the cutting edge of its military operations. In such a quandary, Americans view their militant fist in an apologetic light: what really

[11] George Lodge, "Revolution in Latin America," *Foreign Affairs,* January 1966, p. 174.

matters is the outstretched hand; and it is the contrariness of those who would deny harmony that obliges us to keep using our fist. Others, to whom disharmony is normal and who discount ideals that have no grip but who notice the fist that smashes, respond with regret or rage.

We thus are caught in a vicious circle. The brutality of force, even used for lofty principles, often suffices to corrupt or destroy our goals or to drive them underground. Marines are not the best agents of good neighborly relations; napalm (or the black market and prostitution that a huge military force brings in its wake) is not the surest agent of a dream of "an end to war . . . a world where all are fed and charged with hope." [12] The great society for all mankind must wait until the military costs of the war in Vietnam give way to programs instead of words. But the more unreachable the ends, the greater the "apotheosis of means." As a substitution for the faded vision, we offer what we know best—the by now familiar combination of force and economic aid. (What these really are is a substitute for political experience.) But "situations of strength" do not automatically convert our might into settlements negotiated on our terms, despite our rather mechanical expectations. They do not bring us closer to our vision; and, since only that vision justifies the force, we feel guilty, and we seek to exorcise that guilt with a purely negative incantation—that of anti-Communism. "The escalation of force" requires "an escalation of theory," to bring "the cost and the return into somewhat better balance." [13] It is the evils of communism that force us to use violence, we say; it is the wiles of communism that prevent us from establishing harmony. The concentration of our energies against the foe diverts us from, and gives us an excuse for giving up, trying to break down the deeper obstacles to harmony. When dissent racks our own alliances, we accuse the dissenters of playing into the enemy's hands.

When only the threat of this hydra-like enemy justifies our action, then we must interpret Marshal Lin Piao's celebrated manifesto, *Long Live the Victory of the People's War!*, as a new *Mein Kampf* (rather than as a devious way of telling future liberation movements to rely primarily on themselves). When harmony is the norm, we per-

---

[12] President Johnson, speech at the Johns Hopkins University, April 1965, quoted in Marvin Gettleman, ed., *Vietnam* (Greenwich: Fawcett Publishers, 1965), p. 329.

[13] Theodore Draper, "The American Crisis," *Commentary*, January 1967, p. 41.

force see our foes as monsters, since their hostility is abnormal. A nation that recoils before the moral complexities of most political issues yet finds that it is not always possible to behave according to one's principles in international affairs tends to apply to its necessary acts the cosmetics of a higher cause. But others see through the make-up.

The trouble is that others judge us as we judge them: on acts, not on intentions. Nations always act as they are, rather than as what they think they are; or rather, in the eyes of other nations, our acts define what we are. Power talks loudly, even if the holders of powers speak softly, using loud words only to protest about the agonies of power. However much we may be convinced that we approach other nations as equals and as potential members of a community, they cannot help seeing the enormous reservoir of power behind us. When President Eisenhower tells Latin American students: "We know we make mistakes, but our heart is in the right place," [14] he may think he has straightened out the record, but they care little about the heart and find the mistakes more tangible than the motives. Aware of the frequent discrepancy between acts and intentions, we try to correct the situation by throwing our "sincerity" into the balance (as in our Vietnam "peace offensives"). But we do not sufficiently realize that the only proof of sincerity in international affairs is, as it were, to pay cash—even though we ourselves have a habit of asking for cash, not credit, deeds, not words. Indeed, we fail to realize that since our goals are often beyond reach or without substance, we tend in practice and for the short term to make anticommunism and pro-Americanism the criterion for our choices and substance of our goals—as when officials of the Agency for International Development define political development as "anti-Communist, pro-American political stability," or when our ambassador's advice to President Bosch, whenever the latter was under fire from the Dominican right, was for Bosch to take tough anti-Communist measures.[15]

## II.    Quietism and Activism in American Foreign Policy

The experience of a nation that built its strength through its ability to control nature and eliminate obstacles, principles that appear to have a built-in guarantee of self-evidence and universality, a method

[14] Same, p. 29.

[15] John Bartlow Martin, *Overtaken by Events* (New York: Doubleday, 1966), pp. 471, 562.

at its best in the assembly-line array of technical means—these do not prepare the nation and its statesmen for the complexities of sharing responsibilities and dealing effectively with other countries. The tension between the realms of force and harmony is compounded by a tension between what one might call the two *tempi* of America's foreign relations.

## A. *The Wilsonian Syndrome*

I take Woodrow Wilson as a symbol of a characteristic tendency in the whole nation's approach to foreign affairs. For years, he did his best to keep the United States out of those entanglements President Washington had denounced; America was "too proud to fight"; she was, in one observer's words, "to save the world through what she did at home . . . a model to be emulated rather than a pattern to be imposed." [16] In 1917, Wilson nevertheless decided that the United States must enter the war, or rather—again in characteristically American fashion—he was gradually pushed into it by the combined pressure of foreign misdeeds and the United States' image of itself. Here, indeed, is the thread of continuity: concern for the purity and vigor of the American message. When clouds on the horizon are thick enough to threaten the clear sky of America and obfuscate the world's vision by removing the American "model" from sight, the clouds must be dispersed and the sky made clear all over the globe.

The chief feature of the Wilsonian syndrome is an oscillation from quietism to activism. It is close to the "cycles" described by Dexter Perkins,[17] from phases of withdrawal (or, when complete withdrawal is impossible, priority to domestic concerns) to phases of dynamic, almost messianic romping on the world stage. When complacency brings crisis, quietism breeds activism. But the world resists and resents America's zeal; hence the United States withdraws, disappointed, from the world. The golden mean eludes. Foreigners are never sure whether they are going to be left to thir own devices, with nothing from Washington except the advice to take whatever initiatives may be required, or whether they are going to be told in no uncertain terms what their fate is to be. But the world of international relations is a world of interdependence. Even the United States depends on its dependents. Both quietism and activism are "compen-

[16] Roger H. Brown in Gene Lyons, ed., *America: Purpose and Power* (Chicago: Quadrangle Books, 1965), pp. 19–49.

[17] *The American Approach to Foreign Policy* (Cambridge, Mass.: Harvard University Press, 1952), Ch. 7.

satory assertions of total independence" [18] and, as such, virulent accesses of nostalgia.

Even in the postwar era, which has nailed the United States to the cross of commitment, the quietistic impulse has not disappeared. It is expressed often enough on the left by men who have a lingering nostalgia for isolationist days, when domestic reform could be made the chief political issue, and who look forward to the day when the United States can practice neutralism. It is shared on the right by many who would like the United States to look after its own business behind a nuclear shield, which could be brandished to ward off foes but which would obviate actual entanglements. To some extent, the doctrine of massive retaliation functioned as a shield in this way, for the basic motive behind it was the avoidance of costly limited wars. Dirk Stikker has noted his impression of General Eisenhower's desire to get American boys home from NATO's Europe, as soon as possible after the recovery of Europe.[19] As in the great reversal of 1920, quietism has a way of following the frustrations of overactivism: the Eisenhower-Dulles doctrine of massive retaliation expressed the United States' revulsion over Korea. President Johnson's prolonged retreat from leadership in Europe follows the disappointments of the Grand Design. Even the very activist involvements in South Vietnam and Santo Domingo are accompanied by a desire to create a situation that would make a quietistic disengagement possible. Moreover, overcommitment in one part of the world may well lead, for institutional as well as for psychological reasons, to passivity and "abdication of power" elsewhere.[20]

There is a world of difference between a policy of self-restraint, which aims at influencing men and events and calculates that the best results will be achieved by vigilant unobtrusiveness, and an impulse to get off and get out. The former is a policy; the latter is not. By its weight alone, a great power influences and acts whether it wants to or not; self-restraint may (or may not, depending on circumstances) be the most productive way of keeping control of men and events. But the quietistic impulse simply gives up the attempt to control and stops

---

[18] Keniston, cited, p. 304.

[19] *Men of Responsibility* (New York: Harper & Row, 1965), pp. 303 ff.

[20] For a critique of American "abdication" in the Middle East crisis of 1967, see Theodore Draper, "Israel and World Politics," *Commentary*, August 1967, pp. 41–42. A case could be made to show that in the days that preceded the outbreak of the war on June 5, a stronger American stand against Egypt, backed by *limited* military means, might have made the bloody "third round" between Middle Eastern neighbors unnecessary.

worrying about where things will fall. Self-restraint is a way of collaborating with others, the quietistic impulse is a way of repudiating them. Self-restraint is responsible, withdrawal is neglect. The trouble with quietism is that a superpower cannot afford it, especially if its overactivism has previously deprived its associates of the aptitude to act responsibly.

For it is true that the United States' periods of activism are marked by a kind of missionary busy-ness that makes effective collaboration difficult. Sorensen said of President Kennedy, but it is true of American statecraft as a whole, that "he was at his best when his responsibilities did not have to be shared." [21] To shake itself out of quietism, the United States has to feel that it is in control—whether as dominant head of a coalition, enjoying the privileges of "multilateralizing" its point of view, as in the days of President Truman; or, when others are too reluctant, slow, or divided to follow, through unilateral actions, as was often Dulles' tendency [22] (despite all his pacts), and increasingly President Kennedy's and Johnson's. It is significant that when the United States awoke to the challenge of the postwar world, its program of aid to Greece and Turkey was put "in a world perspective," in the terms of a need to lead the fight against communism all over the globe (despite George Kennan's objections). When the United States intervenes, it is with the belief in the normality of its total leadership. This is true not only of the United States government. American business abroad also can be unsharing in its own way—in the choice of investment, in the organization of management, in the attitude toward local social customs and legislation, or in the distribution of benefits.

Another difficulty is that Americans express their activist selves by a proliferation of interventions and proposals. Just as the American car industry seems unable to let its yearly models alone, even when the changes are perfunctory, American foreign policy in its activist phases assumes that the national interest is involved in every corner of the globe and showers other nations with proposals and blueprints, as if "doing something" were the only logical way of "getting things done." [23]

[21] Cited, p. 563.
[22] See Victor Bator, *Vietnam—A Diplomatic Tragedy* (New York: Oceana, 1965), Ch. 14, on the "elbowing out" of France and Great Britain after Geneva.
[23] Since the fall of 1966, a shower of suggestions has been advanced by American foreign-policy-makers for "building bridges" to the U.S.S.R. and Eastern Europe—a worthy objective but one that could lead to trouble if our

The activist assumption that the United States leads the world is responsible for America's familiar overoptimism—the rosy expectations that make one wonder why, if circumstances are so favorable, there is any need for activism in the first place. External circumstances must yield to American techniques, foreigners (whose cooperation is needed) are seen as part of the team, and hostile foreigners are held susceptible to one's control. Unfortunately, this postulate of control leads all too easily to an erroneous assessment of the resources and trouble-making capacities of a friend or foe, as we have discovered, for instance, in dealing with de Gaulle's foreign policy and with North Vietnam.

## B. *The Failure at Cooperation*

Both features of the Wilsonian syndrome, quietistic and activist, confirm America's lack of experience in cooperating with others. In this respect, an interesting comparison can be made with Communist China. In America's case, there was a switch from isolation to predominance; in China's, a turn from the assumed superiority of the old Empire, heaven's trustee, to the inglorious inferiority of the quasi-colonial days. America's principles all too often express a simple faith in the possibility of reshaping the world in its own image, and the implicit idea that the United States is the "secular arm" of those principles relegates all other nations to the status of aides or obstacles. China sees itself as the only legitimate interpreter of Communist ideology, thus giving a new substance to the old idea of China as a model for others. There is a parallel here: like the ideological tenets of communism, American principles—those of a deeply Christian, liberal society, a kind of synthesis or smorgasbord of Locke, Paine, and Kant—are universal and equalitarian; all the nations of the world are seen capable of living in peace under law in an association of equals devoted to harmony. This mixture of universalism, legalism, and equalitarianism diverts Americans from any suggestion that their attempt to spread the gospel might be imperialistic or self-serving: what is being sought is the common good, in the best interest of all. But the proselytizing contradicts the stated purpose, the method clashes with the intended outcome, for it is the United States that shows the light, and the other nations are in reform school. "Moral pretensions and political parochialism are the two weaknesses of the

---

activist enthusiasm should be either exploited by the U.S.S.R. for its own political purposes, or misconstrued by our allies, always suspicious of direct U.S.-Soviet deals.

life of a messianic nation." [24] Finally, in their foreign relations, China and the United States have comparable difficulties. In China's case, past traditions and new revolutionary requirements combine to encourage reliance on authority, insistence on conformity, and demands for tribute or at least good will from neighboring states. In America's case, the pragmatic approach, which seeks the most efficient solution of problems as they arise by methods corresponding to the American experience, leaves almost no room for cooperation with other states that do not share in the American consensus and that view the world in a different perspective.

The American beliefs, inherited from the past, expressed in principles and manifested in action, that "man should not be hampered by previously set boundaries" or by history, that all men should strive for and can reach consensus, and that "any apparent discrepancy between the ideal and the actuality is essentially immoral" [25] easily led to an activism that others see as imperialistic: for we expect them to join the consensus, we ignore the boundaries and differences between "them" and "us," we prod them out of conviction that we act for their own good, and we do not take resistance gracefully. Yet, our tendency to want them to be either inward-looking so as to concentrate on their "austere" domestic tasks instead of romantic ambitions, or else outward-looking in the sense of helping us with our burdens is not due merely to a very human rationalization and disguise of the will to dominate. It also reflects that lassitude of leadership, that revulsion against perpetual troubles and insurmountable obstacles which underlie American quietism.

This general difficulty the United States has in cooperating with other nations manifests itself in specific obstacles to effectiveness. One such obstacle is raised by our misunderstanding of other nations' reactions to us. John Fairbank has shown, in regard to the policy of "containment of China," how the United States' image of itself as a nation that supports the self-determination of peoples, fights only when forced to, and is untainted by an imperialist past is in conflict with Communist China's image of the United States as a nation that tries to perpetuate the imperialist tradition of victimizing China and to ring it with hostile powers. [26] We see ourselves as having either left

[24] Reinhold Niebuhr and Alan Heimert, *A Nation So Conceived* (New York: Charles Scribner's Sons, 1963), p. 150.

[25] Laurence Wylie, "Youth in France and in the United States," *Daedalus*, Winter 1967, p. 201.

[26] "Why Peking Casts Us as the Villain," *The New York Times Magazine*, May 22, 1966.

China alone or rushed to Asia in order to defend China against Japanese aggression, or Asia against Chinese aggression. China interprets the open-door policy as well as relations with Chiang quite differently. Many observers have remarked that our own image of American capitalism clashes with the image that Asians, Latin Americans, or even Europeans have of the economic and social system of capitalism, which to them has often meant exploitation, the disruption of traditional values and structures, the alienation of large segments of the population, and the sacrifice of social justice or the public good to the interests of a few.

I am not suggesting that a better understanding of these differences would make it easier to eliminate them. But I am suggesting that the systole and diastole of the Wilsonian heart prevent us from taking the true measure of the barrier and that, to be effective, our foreign-policy-makers must not behave so as to confirm the images of America held by those other nations we want to affect.

In the past, we have failed to anticipate their reactions to something that strikes them (but not us) as our double standard. We follow criteria that others see as extraordinarily self-serving but that we see as the necessary and proper outcome of our position. Our condemnation of nationalism when displayed by our allies seems less than candid to those who notice our encouragement to nationalism in the colonial areas and our unwillingness to relinquish control in our conduct of allied policy. In their cold eyes, our reluctance to intervene in Indochina in 1954 contrasts with our pugnacity there in 1965. But to us, the contrast is only apparent, not real; the Vietnamese Communists of 1954 were fighting a national war against a colonial power on whose behalf the United States ought not to have dirtied its hands, whereas in 1965 the same Communists were trying to impose their rule by force on an independent nation that has called for our help. Our condemnation of the Anglo-French "police operation" at Suez is hard for others to reconcile with the Bay of Pigs and the Marine landings at Santo Domingo: in all three cases, there was no request for intervention—far from it! In Egypt, as in Cuba in 1961, the expedition was aimed at a regime that has repeatedly violated international obligations and fostered subversion. But to us, there is all the difference in the world between a return to gunboat diplomacy geared solely to a reassertion of the influence of former colonial powers, and interventions designed to restore or safeguard the principle of free choice, violated or imperiled by Communist or Communist-infiltrated forces. Others may not find much difference between what the French, during the Algerian war, claimed was a right of hot pursuit into Tunisia (much criticized in the United States) and our bombings of North Vietnam; and they may find a contradiction between the deaf ear we turned to French requests (in the name of Atlantic solidarity) for help in Algeria and our appeals to our Atlantic allies for support in Vietnam. But to us, our principles and our position as the only diviner of the common good explain it all.

Not only do we misunderstand how other nations view us, but our evaluation of their policies is often mistaken, sometimes out of ignorance—"only infrequently do Americans really enter the texture of a foreign society" [27]—sometimes out of impatience. We believe that it is only a matter of dispelling prejudice or ignorance before others see things the way things are. And since we believe that everything that ought to be learned can be taught, we instruct others about their interests. Of course, we are often right. We were right when we told the European powers that colonialism was dead, we are right to stress the advantages of a "flexible response," the disadvantages of small nuclear forces, and the perils of nuclear proliferation. We were right to tell Diem to mend his ways, and we are right when we put pressure on the present Saigon regime to effect economic change and political constitutionalism. It would be wonderful if a nation's experience and convictions were transmissible by reasoning, but the only known way of making a nation realize its mistakes is to let it stew in the juice of its errors. The best teacher is experience, people and nations being what they are; and especially when the subject of the course is unpopular, a reasonable lecture will only increase the normal proclivity to obdurateness. Also, persuasive reasoning and self-righteous sermons are different. And nothing is less persuasive than an attempt to show other nations that their policies are too costly, or represent the wrong allocation of resources, for if those policies are based on a more or less desperate conviction of necessity, then considerations of cost-effectiveness are no more decisive than they are, say, in the case of the United States' space program.

When we misunderstand other nations out of impatience, it is because we expect too much from our friends; and when they disappoint us, we go in for wild flings of disillusionment. Love turns to hate, as in the case of our "broken illusions" about a gentle and pli-

---

[27] Edward Stillman and Edmund Pfaff, *Power and Impotence* (New York: Random House, 1966), p. 45.

able China,[28] admiration changes to denigration, as in the case of our response to de Gaulle from 1958 to 1967.

Sometimes our misjudgments are based on gullibility. When others, slyly exploiting our familiar weakness, tell us that they are truly "with us"—that the margin of disagreement is minimal or consists merely of nuances due to different internal priorities—our basic faith in consensus and our concern for the solution of immediate problems often mislead us into taking their words at face value. Thus we accept purely verbal protestations of support as genuine even though they may conceal profound disagreement with our policies or an intention to move quietly away from us. Sometimes, our misjudgment is based on what can only be called arrogance—a belief in our capacity to decide policy for others and a conviction that other nations, however hostile, do not really measure up to us (which impels us either to quietism or to rash activism). Examples are many; viz., when we underestimated Castro's army and overestimated the prospects of a revolt against him in April, 1961; when we consistently understressed the Vietcong's resistance; when we were so surprised by the early Soviet and Chinese nuclear achievements or by the Soviets' establishment of antiballistic missiles around some cities. This arrogance contrasts strangely with our frequent tendency to see our foes as ten feet tall, but the contradiction is inherent in our dualism.

Lastly, we raise a barrier between us and other countries by our very acts. Consider our approach to negotiation with foes. On the one hand, American diplomats resist engaging our foes in active negotiation, since this is not the ordinary way to deal with conflicts of ends and our principles might be corrupted. The United States' long insistence on "negotiating from strength," the belief that agreements actually reached with our foes will probably be either deceptive or worthless reflect more than Cold War realities: they correspond to a conviction that there really is no negotiable middle ground except insofar as requirements of survival are concerned. On the other hand, Americans do attempt to convert their adversaries to harmony: either with a global offer to "reason together" (spoiled, unfortunately, by the hard fact that good will and soft words are no substitute for clear objectives and clever tactics) or with pragmatic attempts at "fractionating" conflicts and issues (which reflect the lawyer's and operator's ways but can be dangerous or end in deadlock). This last technique is perilous to one's own interest when one is dealing with a foe with

---

[28] See A. T. Steele, *The American People and China* (New York: McGraw-Hill, 1966), pp. 57 ff.

long-term designs, who uses a local issue as a pawn on a global chessboard, and who knows how to make extreme demands so as to get half of what he asked for; it ends in failure when we realize what the foe is after but still refuse to deal with the central issues. The method can succeed only when there is no basic conflict of ends and the negotiations are intended merely to settle the details of a previous agreement, or when disagreement over objectives is contained within a framework of common legitimacy and consensus.

In dealing with friends, the trouble is of a different kind: it lies in the sin of condescension. This has been true in allied strategic planning, as it has been in the realm of nuclear control; also, in our handling of the Organization of American States (especially during the Guatemala affair, the Cuban crisis, and the intervention in the Dominican Republic), and in our policies at the United Nations or at the U.N. Conference on Trade and Development concerning capital development funds and the stabilization of commodity prices. We protest that there is far more consultation and cooperation in our alliances than our critics recognize; but what in fact is the case is that we invite other nations to work with us in carrying out our schemes, and we refuse either to endorse proposals that might entangle us in policies we would be unable to determine, or to allow them to share in the determination of our policies. Our control is thus preserved intact, as the Latin Americans have often found in economic conferences, the British in the Skybolt affair. The MLF proposal, which some envisioned as a first step toward European unity in the field of defense, would have left *us* with the decision as to whether, when, and at what a price to relinquish our veto. C. B. Marshall has ironically described American approaches to negotiations as either the intercollegiate debate or the business deal or the Quaker meeting: what they have in common is the absence of any attempt, or need, to bridge fundamental gaps.[29] When we discovered such gaps between us and our allies, as we have repeatedly been forced to by de Gaulle, and as we have belatedly been forced to by their protests over the nonproliferation draft in the winter and spring of 1967, we fall back on the approach to negotiation we exhibit toward our foes, oscillating between self-righteous immobility and marginal or irrelevant offers.[30]

The barriers raised by our actions abroad are perhaps most evident

---

[29] *The Exercise of Sovereignty,* cited, p. 95.

[30] See *The New York Times,* August 28, 1966, p. 20, and Sect. 4, p. E 13, for the tangled story of U.S. reactions to de Gaulle's efforts in favor of a "triumvirate."

in the style of our interventions abroad. The subject is important enough to deserve a special section.

## C. *The United States and Intervention*

Any major power today must be fully informed of and able to influence the domestic affairs of other nations. The "internalization" of war is largely responsible for this; some of the main occasions for international action are provided by domestic upheavals. The difficulty of relying on brute force makes it even more important (hence what I have called the inflation of personal skills). Moreover, decisions on foreign policy properly so-called are shaped by domestic political and social pressures within. Schlesinger called John F. Kennedy the "first American President for whom the whole world was, in a sense, domestic politics." [31] This is now a necessity for any American leader.

The plight of the United States in this regard is particularly acute. For it is the leader of a coalition of autonomous states whose domestic polities preserve a considerable amount of freedom. (To be sure, there are limits to this freedom, especially when the allies are economically or strategically dependent on the United States, but the limits are subtle and shifting.) Moreover, a legacy of insulation from other countries, principles that express genuine opposition to overt interference in the domestic affairs of other countries, and *ad hoc* methods of limited functional scope and short-range value combine to leave the United States without adequate handles. In America's national experience, the polity reflects rather than shapes society, and the function of political parties has been much more restricted than in countries where the parties were the mobilizers and architects of the nation. The government's main function (always challenged, anyway) has been managerial and bureaucratic. Abundant resources and an ethic of service and achievement have made private enterprise tantamount to public welfare. America's principles are those of the limited state, of the self-fulfilling individual, of the bargained harmony. American pragmatism is certainly manipulative, but lacks, by definition, any theory of manipulation. Neither the principled sword nor the arms opened to a world consensus are designed for skillful intervention. Neither the withdrawals of quietism nor the return to activism are modes of skillful intervention.

The sum total is familiar: disembodied optimism. It is reflected in the current enthusiasm in American universities for comparative politics, which shows awareness of the new states and of the need to

[31] Cited, p. 559.

have an impact on them. Optimistically, Americans have contrived a new notion—that of political development—which assumes that in the realm of politics there is order and direction, just as in the realm of economics there is a clear direction, and a set of norms, measurements, and strategies for moving in that direction. This notion rests on the shallowest reading of history and corresponds to a belief that the *cursus honorum* of advancing societies must be that of the United States: the criteria adopted by political scientists are all a transfer of American standards. Yet the variety of those criteria and the disagreement on what political development really is and what strategies could bring it about indicate that the instruments and purposes of international action remain in doubt. Problems of organization and motivation plague the United States in its relations with other countries. Often, Americans assume that what has to be created is the motivation to do what they want done—be it social reform, economic development, military build-ups, etc. But this cannot be accomplished by assuming that all that is needed to create the motivation is techniques. Moreover, the techniques themselves are a matter not of eclectic, *ad hoc* selection of relevant instruments, but of social and political organization. Mix the eggs, add sugar and a drop of liqueur, put into the oven, and forget to turn on the heat—the soufflé won't rise; indeed it will not be a soufflé.

In the kitchen of intervention, Americans are not good cooks. Their normal tendency is to lean on the forces that be. This tendency is inherited from the diplomatic past (whose traditions the Foreign Service conserves), reinforced by principles and bolstered by a pragmatism that likes to deal with what exists rather than to create something better—which might be a *productive* detour but is in fact just considered a detour. And this tendency shows a deep conservative bias. A national experience of constitutional continuity that has instilled in us a nostalgia for tranquility, faith in the highly debatable assumption that a stable polity is a healthy one, skills that are most effective when the social system in which they are applied is uncontested have made of political stability the Grail of American foreign policy. True, this grows out of the liberal tradition, with its recognition of other nations' right to govern themselves as they please, just as the liberal tradition explains why sympathy for the idea of revolution is smothered by an atavistic preference for orderly change—the belief that progress can always be moved through legal channels. Because of this tendency, Americans are usually willing to endorse and work with "orderly" revolutions—revolutions "from the top" or consolidated revolutions of (non-Communist) single-party states. Yet when the forces in control are reactionary or immobilistic oligarchies that profess lip service to private enterprise and anticommunism, the conservative bias serves conservatism.

The result is that American diplomacy is all too often the hostage of local "establishments"; political illusions about the degree of support for United States' policy are engendered by the illusion that, to use one of de Gaulle's more devastating passages, the "people with whom one dines in town" are the whole nation.[32] Obviously, nothing but frustration can result from a reliance on elites whose concern for changes that might undermine their position is limited, or who are unwilling to be convinced by the argument that change is in their interest. Here, the American lack of political analysis, the result of the happy experience of a nation without domestic revolution, is a most serious handicap: in states threatened by class divisions, discontent, and ideological strife, an elite's long-term interest in reforms that would prevent revolution conflicts with its short-term certainty that reforms would dispossess or dislodge it, and this always incites it to opposition, calling the reform an opening wedge of a revolution. Thus, the United States' support of apparently docile establishments is like a kind of ventriloquy in which eventually the voice of the dummy says things quite different from the master. Meanwhile, more genuine voices—those of opposition leaders hostile to the establishments and critical of their docility—are not heard, or they are distrusted, by American diplomats.[33]

Sooner or later, the desire to get things done efficiently, the principles that inspire American policy, the impatience with immobility and the fear that the disintegrating *status quo* might breed violence and disorder bring disenchantment and a shift in behavior. Moreover, when a foreign regime is hostile or impervious to American interests or pressures, the ordinary reliance on officialdom is useless anyhow. The drama then takes the form of a search for better leverage—and reveals a peculiar form of ineptitude: Americans do not know how to work with "effective political organization" [34] where it exists, nor

[32] *Memoirs*, Vol. II: *Unity* (New York: Simon and Schuster, 1959), p. 10.

[33] See John Bartlow Martin, cited, p. 721 on the lack of contacts of the Embassy with the students and labor leaders; his successor, when the rebellion of April 1965 broke out, had obviously lost touch with pro-Bosch officers and politicians.

[34] Samuel P. Huntington, "Political Modernization and Political Decay," *World Politics*, April 1965.

how to set it up where it does not. Instead, they prefer one of three different approaches. The first, which is generous but has a way of evaporating in the air, is the "people-to-people" approach. Instead of or in addition to technicians and diplomats confined within the walls of officialdom, the United States sends lay missionaries to the people. But good will is no substitute for structural reform, and individual achievements have a way of drowning in an ocean of stagnation. What is true of efforts such as the Peace Corps—whose inspiration is not in question, only its efficacy—is also true of all efforts at carrying messages over the heads of governments to the people as a whole, such as President Kennedy did during his trip to Europe in 1963. A second approach consists of relying on the one organization that often appears to be divorced from the staid oligarchies opposed to disorder: the so-called "lesser evil," the army, or at least cliques of the army. But in most cases the army's horror of disorder is stronger than its inclination to reform, and when inner rivalries paralyze or break up the military elite, or when it becomes "a focal point for graft, the principal lever for . . . coups, and a symbol of . . . repression," [35] one has neither reform nor order. A third approach consists of relying purely and simply on docile individuals who assert that the United States' goals are their goals and agree to serve as informants or even agents.[36] But the United States may end up, if not their captive, at least with the blinders that such men wear. Unfortunately, our lack of expertise in the intricate arts of political organization, our fear that in relying on large-scale parties or unions we would foster disorder— i.e., that we would enter the universe of conflicts of ends and move away from the problems of the moment—these fears mean that we abandon the field of genuine manipulation to our opponents, while paradoxically we create an impression of messy manipulation.

There are other features of American intervention that detract from its efficiency, even when the political lever is of good quality. So strong is the conservative bias that even when the normal reliance on established elites is dropped, American intervention will be, so to speak, ashamed of itself. Not only will it hide behind the fig-leaf of alleged noninterference, but it will be emasculated by the piecemeal, technical process by which it is undertaken. Once again, pragmatism

---

[35] Roger Hilsman, *To Move a Nation* (New York: Doubleday, 1967), p. 113, discussing U.S. policy in Laos, 1954–61.

[36] Ambassador Martin had sympathy for and reliance on "Tony Imbert": he (and his friend Luis Amiamia) "would listen to me, at least up to a point, and they respected the power of the United States." Martin, cited, p. 205.

becomes a refuge: expert assistance, administrative advice, and some secret shenanigans express the limit of our daring. Whatever good may come out of such fragmentary measures runs the risk of being submerged in the political and social swamp. Perhaps more important, the *purposes* of the intervention tend to be questionable. Here, the dictates of American dualism may orient action in unsuitable directions. Ignorance and inexperience of political complexities will preserve among foreign-aid experts a "modal tendency" that makes political assistance look bad. American political advisers in countries dependent on or occupied by the United States will be eager to push off what to their hopeful eyes look like temporary obstacles to a return to the norm, i.e., to disengagement. Yet American know-how, the "modal tendency" that makes technological aid look good, incites American officials to favor "global populism" as the reform panacea and private enterprise as the master key to development. And often, of course, intervention is pushed into the narrow but familiar channels of military aid. The private plowshare and the public sword thus become the symbols of both the deficiency and the excess of American intervention.

The American reliance on officialdom (a passive aspect of foreign policy) and search for substitutes (the activist side) have one thing in common: a desire to operate with and through men and forces that belong to the American universe of discourse. It is always the same: a narrow interpretation of diversity, confusion between diversity created by division of labor in one firm and diversity created by a variety of firms; in the final analysis, it is the same conservative bias. Our inability to depend on or help create forces capable of effective mobilization (that is, of change) throws us back on isolated people or groups that are unlikely to challenge the basic order of their society. In Latin America, President Kennedy wanted to break away from the view that a rise in the living standard can only follow an accumulation of wealth to be achieved by a "free system," but success would have required the United States to exploit the prospects for collective change and democratic reform far more systematically and creatively than it did. We lack the experience and the inclination, and our fear of fostering communism interferes with our good intentions.

In the Dominican Republic, American support for President Bosch in 1963 was extraordinarily inconsistent. The Embassy played a very active role in advising him; aid and counterinsurgency programs were promoted; and the Ambassador often lamented about Bosch's excessive caution as a reformer. But he also resented Bosch's failure to take his advice, Bosch's refusal to come to terms with the "real power structure of the Republic"; he fretted about the possibility of land confiscations; and he saw his task as "tying Bosch to the businessmen." [37] The lesson is clear: the purpose of America's activism was the same as that of earlier (and subsequent) reliance on the "real power structure"—political stability—which meant, in 1963, an ambiguous attitude toward social change. Reform was welcomed in theory as a possible contribution to stability, and feared in practice as a possible contribution to the growth of left-wing nationalism. For once, the lever for intervention was an authentic and representative Dominican political force, but the methods of intervention were inadequate and the purposes negative. The prevention of a "Castro-Communist" take-over became the overriding goal, rather than the achievement of a democratic polity or of social change. To be sure, even this kind of intervention contrasted with our quiet support of Reid's oligarchic regime in 1964 and early 1965, which in turn contrasts with our massive intervention during the crisis of 1965. However, one should not exaggerate the differences. If excessive complacency in 1964–65 brought about excessive intervention in April 1965, our half-hearted intervention throughout 1963 had been insufficient to save Bosch; at the end, there was always the oligarchy.

The one kind of successful American intervention is the simple, one-shot affair designed to overthrow a shaky regime that is hostile to us: Mossadegh in Iran in 1953, when the army and court were opposed to him; the Arbenz regime in Guatemala in 1954, when the armed forces refused to fight for him. Unfortunately, what is needed all too often is constructive intervention which orients to long-range objectives rather than to denial. It may well be that we can never achieve this since our sources of information and aptitude to control domestic currents elsewhere are limited. Even the Communists, masters in the art of political infiltration, manipulation, and exploitation, are having their troubles. But the question remains whether it is not better to substitute the alternatives of no responsibility where one can have no impact versus effective cooperation with whoever can be effective, for the alternatives of support to immobile officialdom or

[37] Same, p. 453. The State Department's refusal to "intervene militarily" to save Bosch "unless a Communist take-over were threatened" (same, p. 570) shows clearly the limits of our reformist zeal, and the strength of the conservative bias. Just before the fall of Bosch, the Ambassador had recommended both that the United States support Bosch and that "we immediately begin planning for either a covert power take-over or an overthrow with our tacit consent" (p. 522).

unreliable yet apparently compliant tools versus no support of native forces that are insufficiently "moderate" and pro-American.

Support of a government in power often makes the United States (fairly or unfairly) seem guilty by association. But intervention, while it may be enough to stir up resentment, can be politically too timid, misguided or naïve to prevent the recurrence of the conditions that made it necessary in the first place. It is as self-defeating to rely on dummies in power as it is, in working for change, to rely on the wrong objective, the wrong activity, the wrong group, or the kinds of untrustworthy adventurers whom the CIA occasionally supports precisely because they ask no questions. To be sure, there are situations in which officialdom is unmovable, and the alternative is despicable. But then, the choice ought to be between disengagement from a hopeless situation in cases where no essential American interests would be ruined, and, when the United States must cooperate with the country, a determined effort either to influence the government if it resists reform, or to support it without reservations if it is willing and able to move boldly.

The worst of all is to back away from a government after prolonged but ineffective support, for instance, when one finally realizes that "stability" only bred social discontent, but when one no longer has a chance to disengage safely. This was shown by the situation in Vietnam after the fall of Diem, or in the Dominican Republic at the time of the rebellion of April 1965. Our very reluctance to intervene then inspires what I have called creeping escalation, half-measures that, far from keeping us out of trouble, finally lead to a major crisis.

The world is full of places where America's decision to shore up a rotting *status quo,* or America's failure to back fully an experiment in social change, may ultimately lead to that curative resort to force that is "an admission of political insolvency." [38] The world is also full of places where even total support to a progressive and democratic regime might fail because local opposition is too strong, because overcoming it with American participation would compromise the national authenticity of the regime, or because the United States, lacking experience with or understanding of the processes of radical social transformation, would not know how to use its power effectively. But in all those cases (as well as in the countries where the United States merely buttresses repressive or regressive regimes), American involvement in political failure risks leading to that submersion of the political by the military, "in action if not always in

[38] Theodore Draper, "The American Crisis," cited, p. 28.

intention and thinking," [39] which is likely to be far more damaging to American long-term interests than a deliberate policy of noninvolvement. The latter will at least save one from being not only the target of reprobation but the focus of revolt.

For our behavior creates an impression of arrogance, a sense that the United States has failed to treat others with the necessary dignity and has failed to preserve their self-respect. Our habit of relying on a dubious government, with few questions asked, means that when disenchantment sets in, we will resort to sudden retaliatory or disapproving moves which are humiliating, particularly when the governments in question had originally been encouraged to do what is now condemned, e.g., Phoumi Nosavan in Laos in 1962, or Diem just before his fall.[40] Dirk Stikker makes bitter reference to the American attempt in March 1949 to use denial of Marshall Plan aid as an instrument against Holland's Indonesian policy.[41] Also, if the officialdom runs into trouble, the United States may be forced to intervene openly and brutally (i.e., again in a humiliating way) either to buttress it or to save whatever can be rescued after its fall.

In situations of turmoil, too, the United States' attitude can be equally distressing, giving the impression that all it wants is docility and that it knows better than the people involved what would be good for them—ironical, for a nation that holds high the banner of self-determination. Consider, for example, American policy in Laos before the shaky settlement of 1962, with its hectic boosting of the Royal Lao army, its arming of tribesmen, its creation of a "mass patriotic group," its flood of corrupting commodities, its toppling of governments. Consider also the disturbing similarities between America's foreign policy toward post-Vichy France in World War II and its policy in preparing for the Bay of Pigs invasion. In both cases, the men on whom the United States relied—Giraud and the exiles' brigade—were more docile than they were truly representative of the nation's spirit and better forces. In both cases, the external leaders of the resistance—de Gaulle and Miro Cardona's Cuban Revolutionary Council—were left out of the planning. In both cases, the domestic resistance, whose importance was considerable, was kept at arm's length and treated with some suspicion of its political make-up and objectives. In both cases,

[39] Same, p. 33.

[40] For a comparison of the fall of Batista, Diem, and Reid, see same, p. 35. Both in Laos and in Vietnam, we have had to stop paying our very creatures or protégés in order to try to make them change their ways. Cf. Hilsman, cited, pp. 111–12, 511.

[41] Stikker, cited, pp. 145 ff.

the men concerned were not told the whole truth about the expedition they were being sent on (Giraud had been enticed by a vague promise of being commander-in-chief; the exiles' brigade believed that they would receive full American support). In both cases, undoubtedly, the public, Cuban and French, has not forgotten.

## III.   America's Interpretation of International Relations

Pascal's contrast between *esprit de géométrie* and *esprit de finesse* could not be more apt. A long separation, during which the United States built the most advanced technological society in the world, which it understandably wants to protect and promote; principles with an inflexible air and difficulty in being put into practice; an engineering method that projects the world of science into the affairs of man—all these elements make America's image of the universe geometrical. In discussions among Americans about world order and domestic "development," the word "stability" recurs. We have already noted the linear imagery of "containment." We are familiar with the notion of rows of dominoes. We talk of "nation-building," of edifying world order. We are in a universe of foreign policy the most relevant metaphor for which would be the construction of a house: it is a matter of proper foundations, sound calculations, adequate assemblage; if the architect is good, the contractor efficient, the workers skilled, a stable house will be a happy home; but in a world of storms and earthquakes, vigilance must be maintained lest the whole house fall down. The whole approach reflects the voluntarism of a nation confident in its capacity to master the obstacles if only persistence and coherence are preserved. The question is whether the more relevant metaphor would be that of a flow. The universe of international relations is not an engineer's preserve, it is a Bergsonian drama. The nations are like swimmers caught in waves and eddies (often of their own creation). Persistence and coherence are essential because one would be drowned otherwise. Yet one never swims twice in the same waters, and the statesmen who survive are those who know how to swim with the stream, which waves to ride and which to buck.

Because of a tradition highly influenced by legalistic thinking, the nature of their principles, and their desire for certainty, Americans attach to the formal side of international relations far more importance than citizens of many other nations. Change has to come through, and be guaranteed by, legal provisions rather than by political processes. Those treaties, those procedures, those tangible links are like the walls of the house—insulating protection against the dangers of the outside world. The geometric imagery, the desire to receive a counterproposal for every proposal of one's own made in vain, the new channels or committees for every new difficulty in an alliance—all of this expresses the wish to capture, to domesticate, to solidify, the uncertainties and flow of international events, to erect a barrage against the floods and rising tide. When Senator Fulbright, in pursuit of "old myths and new realities," tries to define a new Atlantic partnership, he calls for new transoceanic contractual links but fails to describe what they should be. It is as if the substance of the agreements, the purposes of the procedures mattered less than their mere existence; the actual shape of the house is less important than that it simply have walls. The trouble is, of course, that the ebb and flow of events, of friendships and enmities, of needs and concerns cannot be curbed; the house one hoped to build is a burrow in the ground, resounding with strange noises, cracks, squeaks, and knocks. Far from imposing form and security on the world, the United States ends up surrounding itself with barriers and dominoes, most of its own making, without the freedom of maneuver that would have permitted it to discriminate between areas of strength and areas of weakness.

If international relations is a Bergsonian universe, then it would be proper to expect substantive change and to discriminate among events: to refuse to buck irresistible trends, channel them in the direction of one's goals, resist events which go against one's interests and are resistible. But the American approach is quite different: it is too static and too frantic. To be sure, the United States' conviction of being on the side of change—indeed, an example and champion of change—is unshakable. But, as Kenneth Keniston has subtly pointed out, the portrayal of change "as inevitable and good" *in toto* on the one hand, and the emphasis on *specific* changes on the other,[42] often mask the depth and disruptiveness, the calamities and capriciousness of change. The kind of change expected by the United States is progress, a continuation (despite occasional halts) of a march forward along the same tracks. This is not the kind of change international affairs provides. But if the future has nothing worse in store for us than the promise of victory for our principles, there is no need for our vision to become less abstract and disembodied. Our vision is static not in the sense of perpetuating the present, but in the sense in which

[42] Cited, p. 210.

a car moving along a road that never passes through new landscapes would be static: by evening, the car might be hundreds of miles from its starting point yet its passengers would not have seen anything new. We see change merely as the ever-expanding application of our principles and methods. Our stoically immobile China policy provides a good example. What used to be our official line on German reunification provided another one: requiring the triumph of the principle of self-determination, which would lead to the extension of West Germany to all of Germany. But today, instead of a reunified Germany as beneficiary of a Western victory in a world in which the United States and the Soviet Union were still leaders of two coalitions, the problem has become how to dissolve the two camps and proceed to a gradual reunification of Europe, which is a more unsettling view. Change often requires modification of our principles and methods: that we, as well as others be changed. Similarly, America's approach to the problems of development is, in a way, static. To be sure, development is the goal, but the tracks on which economic progress is supposed to run are the tracks of stability, and the landscape is supposed to be as flat and as familiar as possible. Our view of change is quantitative, not qualitative.

Behind these examples, there is one vision: the Wilsonian one. It is not flawed by the kind of conservatism that tries to stop time altogether, but it sees in the future merely the growth of what is best in the present. The model is already here, and all that is needed is that reality become more and more like it. A world of self-determined, self-governing nations with mild disputes and nondisruptive internal issues until the end of history, a history kept busy by discrete crises and gradual changes rather than by cataclysms and deep transmutations; such is the vision. It is progressive enough to justify indignation and pain when others accuse the United States of being a conservative force, but it is bland and simple enough to justify American discomfort or anxiety when events do not fit the pattern.

The optimism of this vision does not quite manage to suppress a lingering doubt about the validity of its whole approach to time and events. Because it is too static, because it has too little room for middle-range goals defined in political terms, the United States' approach to international affairs has a way of being unsettled by occurrences which suggest (as they continually do) that the forces of evil are stronger and more cunning, the forces of progress weaker and less active, the forces of surprise and genuine change richer and more imaginative than America had expected. Consequently, we must tinker, to make sure that nothing will prevent our ultimate vision from becoming reality. A vision that looks forward to the dissipation of clouds, but does not tell us much about the way clouds are formed or are actually moving, obliges one to treat every passing mist as a threat of storm that has to be chased away. Only a philosophy of history or a clear-cut vision of the main trends (or a moderate system with well-established rules of the game and players with limited stakes) enable a nation to discriminate between the events that require its intervention and those that do not. But this nation has no clear-cut vision other than its utopia and no philosophy of history other than the static one I have described, and the game is played for the highest stakes ever known, with rules hammered out in trial and error. As a result, it behaves, not like a man secure in his house, or a captain steering a ship through changing weather, but like a beast burrowed in the ground. Its past, its principles, its pragmatism either provide it with or reflect a colossal need for security; hence so many assertions of faith in the direction taken by history. But in the absence of a compass, it is gripped by a fear of insecurity commensurate with its desire for safety, and anti-communism becomes both the expression of that fear and the substitute for a compass.

For a nation so hopeful about the benefits of time, the United States is singularly unwilling to let time operate, to trust "the force of circumstances"; it is as though we knew we were whistling in the dark. A noise hits us from Lebanon: we land Marines; a tremor reaches us from Santo Domingo: we send troops. Russians appear in Conakry or Chinese in Brazzaville: we shudder. The Communists help the rebels in the Congo: we think all is lost. We overestimate the capacity of distant powers to ignite subversive fires. Yet the more we act and overact, the more we endow others with the same capacity to affect events that we attribute to ourselves. And when events show that their capacity is indeed limited, we exaggerate in the opposite direction, seeing in each tactical test a decisive contest that will determine the future. Then, when we have won the test, we proclaim that the fight is all over and primacy safely ours—until the next mishap reveals that we relaxed too soon and revives our frenzy. We become again like a tennis player who rushes to the net in order to stop every ball; instead of playing farther back in the court and letting many of those balls fall as they will outside the court, we try to stop the shots our opponent aims too high over the net, and we exhaust ourselves, letting our vigilance drop after a series of volleys. Mobilized for immediate perils, we do not see that time, the intricacies of a highly differentiated world, and a discriminating dose of intervention would take care of a great deal; as a result, we oscillate between lack of attention to the nonvisible sources of trouble, which will force us to take up arms when the pool of trouble has become a sea, and frantic attention to the visible sources. For we are cued only to certain kinds of trouble, and they elicit almost Pavlovian responses of anguish and action; but the more insidious and long-range troubles which would require action of a very different sort, we fail to heed.

Our past, our principles, and our pragmatism breed not only millennial hopes, but an embattled sense that we are the chosen champion of those hopes—and this buoys and harries us in turn. Little do we realize that the international system of today aids the champion on the defense, insofar as the hedges of diversity exhaust our foes' forces. Maybe what keeps making us frenzied is our dim awareness that this very system, those very hedges, will also prevent us from ever giving to the whole world the shape and color of our own ideal. What the system requires from us, as Kennan once said, is more gardening and less militancy. Yet Armageddon is what we seem to need.

These criticisms will undoubtedly elicit from the reader the reaction: If all this is true, how did the United States achieve so much? To this question, I have two answers. First, my purpose was not to deny the achievements but to describe the peculiarities that mar or limit them. To borrow a nice metaphor from André Gide, I was concerned with the lion's fleas, not with denying that there is a lion under the fleas. The other side of the qualities whose defects I have discussed reveal, after all, America's virtues: from its past, the United States has inherited a remarkable self-confidence; to its principles, it owes a determination to see certain admirable forms of international relations prevail; and its method entails a considerable ability to adapt. The flaws I have described operate not as preventers or saboteurs of adaptation but as delayers or qualifiers. Second, and more important, the United States is now entering a period in which those flaws are more of an obstacle than they were in the past. The American style was admirably suited to the late 1940s and early 1950s—to a world in which there was an apparently monolithic enemy; in which the United States' main allies were at the same time in sufficiently dire straits to permit the United States to exert very strong leadership, and in sufficiently good shape to keep it from taking over; in which the nature of the threat posed by the enemy was the kind to which the United States reacts best by manning defenses, by drawing lines, by using its weight. The question is whether, in the new international system that is emerging, that weight can be substituted for other, subtler forms of power. When our enemies are divided and some of our allies no longer regard them as their foes, the two familiar poles of hostility and "consensus" disappear. When the new fences that protect independence go up, our inability to share responsibility becomes an inability to affect events; and the drawing of lines is no solution when the threat comes, so to speak, from below rather than from the outside. What is required is a capacity to share responsibility, but not with conformists, to whose blackmail of weakness one will have to capitulate, nor with dummies incapable of real effectiveness.

The skills required in the postwar world were largely those the United States possessed, and those skills continue, of course, to be required. But others, of a very different sort, are also needed. The style of the United States has been the substance of American policy, but now another substance is needed. Theodore Draper has written that, in the Dominican crisis, the United States' policy was "marked by such bungling and blundering that only the strongest power in the world could afford them." [43] The question is: How much bungling can this power afford? If the lion cannot afford it, it must bite its fleas.

[43] "The Dominican Crisis," *Commentary,* December 1965, p. 61.

PART III

# America's Political System

# CHAPTER SEVEN

# The Nature of the Problem

Freedom of action in world affairs cannot be discussed with reference only to the international milieu and the national style. One failing of psychologists and social psychologists who write about national beliefs, images, and habits is their neglect of a subject that used to be the political scientists' special domain until many of them deserted it for the supposedly more fertile fields of "political behavior": I mean the *political institutions,* which can do much to magnify and also to correct flaws in national behavior, and through which any major reform must be effected.

This failing is even more regrettable in the analysis of foreign policy than in discussion of domestic economic or social policies. For domestic political action can take many forms other than the action of elected officials or government bureaucrats. There are hundreds of associations and movements, spontaneous or well organized, in which citizens can join together to affect community affairs—to promote as well as to prevent change. Neither the legislature nor the executive nor the police need to be mobilized or concerned. But foreign policy is not made by "the people." Civil-rights movements are capable of preparing, accelerating, and supplementing public policy, but when citizens try to take action beyond national borders, to talk to each other over the heads of their respective governments, the limits of their effectiveness are painfully visible. Despite the hopes of many in a utopian world in which the collaboration of governments would be required and supported by "international public opinion," shaped and made effective by internationales of parties and interest groups, reality is obstinately hostile to the idea. Only when states engage in "community-building" of the West European kind, with supranational institutions, do transnational forces and pressures begin to have a force comparable to the citizenry within a nation. But in the international milieu as a whole, what persists is nationalization of opinion and domestic forces by national governments, instead of internationalization of the governments by world opinion and transnational forces. The focus of decision and the locus of achievement in foreign policy is the political system.

Any political system that is more than a ramshackle construction of a powerful adventurer reflects at least some basic features of the nation's style. Even when it is a dictatorship, the citizens' tolerance of it and their willingness to carry out its policies can often be understood only by reference to national experience, beliefs, and attitudes. These are the reasons why the national style deserves study in itself. Especially when the political system is as stable and legitimate as the United States', a study of "foreign-policy decision-making" abstracted from all the features I have described in Part II would be like a performance of *Hamlet* without the sweet prince. Even when the political system *reflects* basic values, social structure and economic practices (as the American one does) rather than *shapes* them (as the Ancien Régime did in France, say, or as the Soviet regime does today in Russia), the political institutions are vital in their own right. A nation's freedom of choice in foreign policy is crippled if its institutions rule out certain kinds of decisions or, on the contrary, dictate responses required by the system, however damaging they might be to the nation's foreign policy. And a nation's capacity for effective action is damaged if the institutions render consistent and purposeful execution of policies impossible, if other nations know that they can count on domestic discord or bureaucratic confusion to reduce the impact of a policy they dislike.

The importance of political institutions in the making of foreign policy was well demonstrated in the drama of France's decolonization. Certain French traditions, beliefs, and attitudes concerning the empire—the myths of assimilation and integration, the quest for grandeur and universality—made a retreat from empire difficult in any case. However, the real trouble lay not in public opinion, which was divided, confused, and bewildered, but in a political system that ruled out strong leadership. The divided legislature, the paralysis and irresponsibility of short-lived coalition cabinets, the strength of opposition parties that did not accept the rules of the parliamentary system—these created a situation in which power was occupied rather than used by the executive, and in which policy was in the hands of two forces whose willingness to retreat was minimal: the bureaucrats, wedded to routine and the continuation of past practices, and the army, devoted to an imperial mission. Decolonization in other than catastrophic style became possible only after three changes had occurred: the return of General de Gaulle as a kind of Roman dictator; a constitutional change providing him with full executive powers; and a (much more painfully won) political change that consisted in a mixed coaxing and coercing of the army into submission.

There are a number of reasons why a thorough study of the impact of American political institutions on U.S. foreign policy has not been made (it is not my intention to fill the gap, not even in capsule form). For one thing, it would be an almost impossible complex undertaking. The number of government agencies involved is considerable and is growing rapidly; an assessment of their impact would require an army of researchers, interviewers, and archivists. The operations established by the United States in the pursuit of its interests abroad have been so varied and have developed so rapidly and in so many lands that enormous amounts of space can be spent merely in listing them.

Another reason is the persistence of certain assumptions, which go on more or less unchallenged precisely because a reconsideration of their relevance or truth requires such an effort of empirical research. A frequently accepted view is that the American political system is singularly unfitted to the effective pursuit of foreign policy. From Tocqueville to Carl Friedrich and Walter Lippmann,[1] observers have pointed out that the requirements of success in world affairs contradict the inclinations of democracy, especially when those inclinations are unchecked by pre-democratic traditions or institutions, un-self-disciplined and undisciplined by political parties, as in the United States. Secrecy, cold rationality, experience, continuity—the requisites of foreign policy—are antithetical to democratic policy. Critics of American diplomacy have often used the British model as a club with which they thrashed American practices; what they long for is a kind of eclectic synthesis of what James McGregor Burns [2] calls the Madisonian and Jeffersonian theories. The former distrusts the public for its factionalism, inconsistency, shortsightedness, and crudeness and wants the public's desires and impulses filtered and refined through the political system; the latter aims at avoiding

---

[1] See C. J. Friedrich, *Foreign Policy in the Making* (New York: Norton, 1938) and Walter Lippmann, *The Public Philosophy* (Boston: Little, Brown, 1955).

[2] See his *Deadlock of Democracy* (Englewood Cliffs, N.J.: Prentice-Hall, 1963).

fragmentation of power (which Madison provided along with the dilution of the public will) and at promoting effective power through majority rule, i.e., the rule of strong yet moderate parties under firm leadership. This synthesis is supposed to have existed in England, with its career civil service, its tradition of putting foreign affairs above party disputes, and its cabinet system, which guarantees parliamentary support to the prime minister.

In my opinion, and in the opinion of other students of British foreign policy, this deification of the British system is a fine example of mythmaking.[3] Moreover, the sour view of the American system is, even on the face of it, unjustified by events. For here is a network of institutions that the Founding Fathers obviously did not set up to deal with foreign policy as the first priority—a system marked by checks and balances that hardly facilitate prompt, coherent, and persistent action, a system with loose political parties, huge turnover of personnel after each presidential election, and a strong expression of public opinion in frequent elections and in the powerful mass media. Here is a nation whose State Department and Foreign Service remained small and discrete until after World War II. Yet in twenty years, it has provided leadership for the non-Communist world, expanded economic and military assistance, spread its cultural activities, blanketed the world with its armed might as well as its intelligence services—in short, it has carried out tasks that England, a leader in quieter periods or in revolutionary eras when the international system was small and when it had allies its own size, never had to undertake—and it has brought it off on a scale unmatched before by any nation, over a period far shorter than any other nation ever required to switch from isolation to predominance.

*Prima facie* evidence shows that the American system of government has a capacity for adaptation unsuspected or unrecognized by its critics. The presidency has been able to chart a course, to keep the nation on it, to make the necessary adjustments to adversity, and to discriminate among alternatives. Despite the threats and showdowns, there has been neither general war nor ignominious surrender, neither retreat into isolation nor design for world domination. The integration of diplomacy, strategy, and economic policy—which had been blatantly ignored in World War II, when the first was sacrificed to the second, and was unpracticed even in the days before Korea, when the State Department appeared indifferent to the mil-

[3] See Kenneth Waltz, *Foreign Policy and Democratic Politics* (Boston: Little, Brown, 1967).

itary budget [4]—has progressed, despite institutional obstacles and frequently conflicting objectives.

Congress has succeeded, on the whole, in subordinating its basic distrust of the executive (and of the executive agencies' extension of power) to a sense of national necessity and patriotic responsibility—to the point where its function in the shaping of foreign policy is not notably different from the functions of over-all review and piecemeal special pleading performed by parliaments in cabinet systems. Congress is in the temperate zone of surveillance rather than at the poles of shared power or guerrilla-type harassment. There has been nothing like the repudiation of Versailles and the League in the 1920s. Even the Republican onslaught on President Truman's Far Eastern policy now looks like an aberration from the norm.

Finally, the public has proved its aptitude to respond to leadership, to provide the executive with what V. O. Key has called a supportive consensus, a permissive consensus, and a consensus of decision [5]—i.e., to equip the president with a comfortable margin of credit and with freedom of maneuver. To anyone who starts with Tocqueville's assumptions or with Lippmann's straw man, the performance of America's political system is astonishingly good. The flexibility, indeed the hidden resources, of a system built in the fundamentally different universe of the 1780s are nothing short of miraculous.

Miracles can be celebrated, but they are not the subject of this book. My purpose here will not be to stress what precedes, although what follows ought to be read in the light of these remarks. It will be to stress the difficulties and obstacles to free choice and effective action that remain—the black spots that mar the performance.

Two kinds of flaws deserve emphasis: those which provide some residual evidence for the common assumptions I have listed, and those which reflect or reinforce features of the national style analyzed in Part II. These two groups often coincide. The fact that the postulate of democratic inferiority in foreign affairs has not been vindicated does not mean that some of the specific charges are without foundation. Just because the postulate makes one expect to find the scene black, and one finds it merely gray, one is not authorized to proclaim it white. As for the national political system and the national

---

[4] Warner Schilling *et al.*, *Strategy, Politics, and Defense Budgets* (New York: Columbia University Press, 1962).

[5] *Public Opinon and American Democracy* (New York: Alfred A. Knopf, 1961).

style, where they reinforce one another, not only do certain defects, inhibitions, or impulses become magnified, but correction of them becomes much more difficult. A distinguished political scientist has said that "congruence" [6] between the style of authority in society and the style of authority in the political system is a precondition of political stability. Congruence between the national style and the political system, while a guarantee of stability, may also guarantee intractability, inadaptability to external forces or at least adaptation with costly delays and strains. Moreover, the beliefs and practices that a political system enshrines are also the ones most likely to make for difficulties in relations with other nations: they are the ones a nation will most naturally project on others, so to speak, without sufficient concern for their relevance to the issues at hand.

As I remarked previously, no feature taken in isolation is unique. Some of the traits examined here are present in other nations, too, and they will be found to have the same results there. But the coexistence and interaction of the traits is unique; for a student of United States policy, the fact that, say, the fragmentation of executive power into many agencies in another country also results in confusion and rigidity is no consolation. The argument that such or such a leader, such or such a parliament, such or such an elite behaves exactly like ours is really irrelevant. Yet a critique of the foreign-policy consequences of some American institutional features does not imply that the regime of the United States is being judged against some ideal-type of a government that is altogether as democratic and is more effective than ours. No system of government displays all the political virtues simultaneously; one always pays a price for whatever values one chooses to embody in constitutions and institutions. Moreover, the scope and weight of the operations undertaken, the issues confronted, the events faced by the United States are such that even the most ingeniously flexible and efficient institutional system any Solon could conceive would occasionally be caught in deadlock, or slow motion, or confusion, or contradiction.

It is incumbent on critics of the United States to bear in mind that no political system ever had to carry such a load of foreign policy —to be sure, the nation's resources help carry it, but what matters is the capacity to translate resources into action. The critic has the right to say that the load is excessive, but he must recognize (unless he shares a conspiratorial view of history) that in the past twenty

[6] Harry Eckstein, *A Theory of Stable Democracy* (Princeton Center for International Studies, Research Monograph No. 10, 1961).

years the United States has been in the position of a nation on which international burdens accumulate almost by themselves, more than in that of a nation which has deliberately sought them. Whether the United States should continue to carry them all in the new international environment is a major question. But we must assess recent performance against the burdens borne, not against our opinion of what they ought to have been.

The purpose of the following analysis is not to advocate a different set of values, nor is it to engage in retrospective diatribe. It is to make one aware of the price the United States has paid for bearing this burden and upholding these values. None of the flaws denounced here can be remedied easily; the remedies would undoubtedly create other difficulties. In political systems, we are faced not with a choice between realizable ideals and imperfect realities, but with a choice between alternative modes of conduct, each producing its own set of constraints. Total effectiveness on all foreign fronts is a delusion; increased effectiveness might have to be paid by sacrificing domestic values that nobody would want to give up; or increased effectiveness in some part or performance might have to be paid with decreasing effectiveness in others. However, by the same token, it is clear that there is some choice: if the United States decides that the present price is too high, that another alternative is preferable because less costly in foreign-policy terms (and that effectiveness in foreign affairs should be the highest value), or if the United States judges that the new international milieu allows for a reduction in its international obligations, which would help close the gap between performance and promise, then remedial action ought to be undertaken.

Here, once again, an institution or procedure can be both a source of strength and a cause of weakness. An institution that at times imposes a dangerous inhibition on valuable actions which would otherwise have been undertaken, at other times serves as a useful counterbalance to rash impulses or risky moves. A process whose length and complexity diverts attention from foreign affairs, or whose needs make political leaders wage foreign policy in a damagingly flamboyant way, may also often give the nation's acts the internal support and continuity other nations lack. One cannot eliminate the liabilities without destroying the assets. However, the decisive question is: how important is the debit side? If it is very important yet one deems the credit side vital, then knowing the defects should help at least to try to reduce them. If the debit side is important, and the credit side does not apparently justify maintaining the institution or procedure, then (at a cost, no doubt) one should be ready to scrap it.

Thus, the following remarks imply a dissent from two, I believe equally unjustified, attitudes: that which uses the evidence of American adaptability and the unquestionable existence of other defects in other systems to instill complacency about the American performance; and that which laments over the handicaps, the waste, and the rigidities, while remarking that nothing can be done to change them (not infrequent among policy-makers after their withdrawal from the corridors of powers). In social affairs, awareness need not be the prelude to resignation; it can be the prelude to change, just as it can (or ought to) set the limits of what change can accomplish.

The following chapters are not based on expertise and personal experience in American government; they are derived from observation, readings, and conversations with practitioners. They are of necessity fragmentary, yet I have tried to focus on certain key problems. As I did in Part II, I shall first examine the main elements of the system that lead to questionable foreign-policy results, then the problems that result from the interaction of those elements.

# CHAPTER EIGHT

# The Pieces of the Puzzle

He who celebrates in the American presidential system a mechanism that allows for strong leadership, responsibility, and responsiveness to the people, for free scrutiny and challenge by the people's representatives, for a clear-cut confrontation of "options," hence well-informed citizens and well-prepared decisions; and he who denounces the frequent overstatements, clamorous debates, protracted exercises in coordination and half-baked compromises are not so far apart as they seem. They are pointing at two sides of the same coin. In this analysis, I shall leave the celebration to others and shall concentrate on the tension between this presidential system and the requirements of effective foreign policy.

Tension results from the residue of concepts that inspired the United States Constitution and shaped constitutional practices before America's involvement in world affairs. The *Federalist Papers* are marked by a distrust of *all* power: the power of the people, to be sure, but also the power that a "power elite" or ruling class could exert—hence the various checks on and balances of governmental power, and the various filters which are supposed to reduce and purify the impact of the people. Then, especially after Andrew Jackson, the distrust of concentration of power in the hands of a governmental caste continued, but a variety of factors, including an understanding that such concentration can best be checked by the people, led to an increase in the people's role in the political system. The fear of power in Washington persisted while power at the grass roots increased. In this century, contrary to Woodrow Wilson's gloomy predictions, the growth of the presidency has been spectacular enough to create the impression of a total change: the president appears to have both concentrated power around him in Washington and taken it away from the grass roots. But, especially in the formulation and execution of foreign policy, there are traces left of the two traditional trends which made American democracy a people's democracy and which kept it a democracy of power dispersion. Thanks to the growth of the presidency, those traces do not cause fatal damage; but they cannot be ignored, either by the president or in this study.

## I.   The United States as a People's Democracy

What I mean by "people's democracy" has nothing to do with the meaning given the phrase by Communists. Communist states have usurped the title by assertion and reiteration, to the exclusion of any evidence. A genuine people's democracy, however, is a nation in which suffrage is universal, the citizens enjoy a broad range of individual and collective rights, and the institutions are based on consent and operated by men chosen freely among alternative political forces. Such a definition would rule out not only Communist regimes but also non-Communist single-party regimes. There is much truth in the argument that the latter are not necessarily authoritarian, that they can have room for citizens' rights, a basis of consent, and the expression of dissent and formulation of alternatives; and there is some truth also in the argument that political democracy according to my definition is a luxury for many nations. But a revocable democracy in which the basic features of democratic systems are not institutionalized is a problematic democracy; the facts that democracy is a "good thing" and that in some nations one-party rule is also a "good thing" do not warrant tucking the latter under the expanding cover of the former.

In fact, our definition covers very different types of political systems. But it is useful to remember that there are democracies in which the impact of the people is minimized by means of many different techniques and institutions (some of them apparently contradictory). One institution that tends to minimize the people's impact on decision-making is a permanent career bureaucracy. For another, the people's power is reduced whenever the legislature is dominated by a few parties, disciplined and centralized to the point where the representative's first accountability is to his party rather than his constituency. True, the parties themselves will be responsive to popular moods and desires, but the relation between the public and the parties is circular. The people's power is reduced also if the legislature is split among many parties, for the result will be irresponsible, shifting coalitions that leave the voters with much less of a say about the political color of the government than in a two-party cabinet system in which the head of the government is practically chosen by the electorate. However, even in a two-party cabinet system, the "people's will" is a reserve force, a final arbiter between the contending strong parties, rather than a daily inspiration, since, while parliamentary elections determine what party will have the premiership, the premier will be first of all a party leader, and the role of the public or even of the average party member in selecting him is small. In a cabinet system with strong parties, the executive's control over the parliamentary majority assures a great deal of freedom from popular pressure; in a cabinet system with many weak parties, the impotence of executive *and* parliament makes for "political games" from which the people are absent.

To sum up, in these democratic regimes, decisions are made (or avoided) by a governing oligarchy, ultimately but *only* ultimately responsible to the people. The oligarchy consists in the civil service and either the ruling party (or stable coalition of parties) in control of both the legislative and executive branches, as in the "British model," or the parliament, as in France's Third and Fourth Republics.

In a "people's democracy," on the other hand, decision-making is not so sheltered from the public; popular demands and desires are more than a residual element in the political system. This does not mean that the people govern in the fashion of Rousseau's general will, but that the ruling oligarchies, elsewhere like corks sealing off the neck of the democratic bottle, are considerably more porous. There is some irony in the fact that a political system like England's, based on pure majority rule, actually filters out the "general will" more than the system of checks and balances Madison devised precisely in order to dilute and fragment the impact of that will on the polity. But in a cabinet system, majority rule sets up the majority party as the decision-making body, whereas the American system, with its checks and balances, not only fragments governing power, but bathes all the organs of government in a popular tub. This is the outcome of a variety of features: the popular election of the president; the separation of judicial, legislative, and executive powers, which prevents him from exercising over Congress the kind of domination, say, that a British premier enjoys over the House of Commons and makes the president's power over Congress a direct function of his ties with the people; decentralized parties incapable of constituting a genuine oligarchy largely because the governmental separation of powers prevents them from keeping on the executive branch the stranglehold French parliaments once had over the French executive, and amorphous enough to be highly sensitive to shifts in the popular mood; a theory of representation that sees a member of Congress as the delegate of his constituents rather than as a national spokesman (as in the French theory of representation); the very short term of office in the House of Representatives; and the nature of the civil service. In such a system, the powers that might dominate a field of decision are either weak or (in the case of the president) in a state of permanent and necessary dialogue with the public. The public therefore deserves to be treated as one of the forces that affect the definition and execution of foreign policy, since it exerts various influences on the president, and since specific elements of it, as members of the bureaucracy, play a direct and tangible role in policy-making.

## A. *The Public versus the President*

The president, entrusted by the Constitution, by custom, and by necessity with the burden of making and carrying out United States foreign policy, finds himself locked in a tight embrace with the public. A British prime minister or a French premier of the Fourth Republic is (or was) engaged in a dialogue with the legislature, on whose support he depended. In the British case, the prime minister's control of the house turns the performance into something of a monologue (interrupted, while he catches his breath, by the interjections of the Right Honourable members of the opposition). However, behind, before, and after that monologue, a dialogue goes on within his party (primarily among the party's M.P.s), and the prime minister's first duty is to be a skillful leader and faction broker in the party. In this respect, his statecraft will tend to be unspectacular. The attempt of French premiers in the Fourth Republic to converse with parliament usually were doomed, for it was like unarmed, weak-voiced liontamers trying to raise their voices above the lion's roars.

The foreign-policy consequences in those cases have been varied. Occasionally, the British and French executives have been capable of decisive acts of creative statecraft, like the Schuman Plan or the decision to retreat from India. But in the postwar period, the execution of British foreign policy has usually been timid and halfhearted, the French deadlocked and blindly obstinate. In both cases, the position of the premiers ruled out an extended dialogue with the public on foreign-policy issues; in France, any desperado attempt by a premier to light a fire under the frozen body of a deadlocked National Assembly by going directly to the people (as Pierre Mendès-France did in 1954) was likely to be suicidal; the public had no real way of coping, for the benefit of the lion-tamer, with the lions.

In contrast, the American president's first partner is the public. The way for the president to get at Congress (and to get administration bills through Congress)—in addition to arm-twisting, coaxing, patronage, promises, barters, and bargaining, which is necessary but rarely sufficient, since the president does not always have a majority, and the Congress in any case has independent powers—is to appear as the people's trustee. What was a catastrophic tactic for Mendès-France is an indispensable one to an American president, disastrous only if he were to go beyond the mere attempt to mobilize public support so as to get or keep Congress moving, to an attempt at making the public reward or punish individual congressmen on Election Day.

A president has another reason for turning to the public: he must marshal public support to get his policies understood and accepted; in the American system, this is his task, not the parties'. A British prime minister or a premier of the French Fourth Republic, if he had a parliamentary majority, did not have to worry too much about the public, in the former case because the majority party did the job of mobilizing the public for him, in the latter case because the parliamentarians tended to leave the public sulking and to play their games without it. The American president, even if he has a "good" Congress, must himself do the job of securing public assent to his policies.

What are the consequences in *foreign* policy of this exposure of the executive power? We must consider this question in the light of three aspects of the relationship between the president and the electorate: the nature of the president's tenure, the nature of public opinion on matters of foreign policy, and the nature of the president's appeal to the public.

A national ruler, in order to do his job well, needs a certain amount of distance from the public from which he has emerged and which he wants to lead. This distance is abolished and policy-making is inhibited by two circumstances of the *president's tenure* in the office. One, well described by Richard Neustadt in his perceptive post-mortem of President Kennedy's administration, is the difficulties of the four-year cycle, particularly of the first and fourth years.[1]

[1] "Kennedy in the Presidency: A Premature Appraisal," *Political Science Quarterly*, September 1964, pp. 321–34.

The first year of a new administration is a painful period of on-the-job training for a man who, usually, reaches the presidency with two kinds of parochialism. First, he comes out of a "political class" that is probably more peculiarly ethnocentric than any political class in the history of great powers. In all representative systems, the political class consists very largely of provincials or small-town politicians devoid of experience with the outside world. But in nineteenth- and early twentieth-century Britain or France, say, such men were "socialized" and their horizons broadened by a variety of factors: life in the capital, whether London or Paris, and the influence of certain national traditions made the provincials over in a national image. This image was often exceedingly nationalist, yet the length and intensity of the nation's participation in international affairs were such that nationalism meant advocacy of the nation's interests in the international contest; it could never mean priority to domestic concerns or the innocent projection of national experience upon other states. No doubt, the American political class will become like this in the future, but for the time being (especially among senior Congressional leaders), the involvement is too recent and interpreted too much in terms of the Wilsonian syndrome. National traditions are too abstract or self-centered, and Washington is too protective of parochialism, for American political leaders to act with ease on the world stage as soon as they climb on it.[2] Second, the new president has often had less national political experience than a British prime minister, and certainly little experience in the management of national policy machinery. If he was a governor, his executive experience was incommensurably narrower than the one he faces; if he was a senator, he will have expertise on at least some national or international issues but no executive experience. British or French premiers normally reach their positions after some apprenticeship in a cabinet office.

As a result, the new president's first year is often shaky, for it takes time for the president to build a team, put the team to work, get the bureaucracy to respond, get the priorities straight, and understand the mood and moves of other national leaders. It was during the first year of the Truman administration that United States foreign policy drifted—torn between a president with strong impulses but little self-confidence, a Secretary of State with frustrated ambi-

---

[2] De Gaulle is alleged to have remarked, in praise of President Kennedy (a man less representative of America's political class than most presidents) after his assassination: "*C'était un Européen.*"

tions and limited competence, a Secretary of Agriculture with grand visions, equally grand illusions, and no responsibility in foreign affairs. It was during the first year of the Eisenhower administration that Senator McCarthy succeeded in putting his hideous stamp all over the government. And, in 1961, the failure of the Cuban invasion, planned during the previous administration, was a cruel ordeal for a young president who, after the artificial exhilaration of the campaign, had obviously thought that continuity rather than reconsideration was the better part of prudence, and the best response to a very narrow mandate; nor was President Kennedy's early timidity and hesitation over South Vietnam without consequences for the future of United States policy there. In other words, in his first year, the new president is still the product of the public rather than its leader.

At the other end of the presidential cycle, the year of the elections—while certainly not lost for foreign affairs, as the Berlin airlift shows—is nevertheless not the best for carrying out coherent foreign policy, especially in non-crisis areas. Between November 22, 1963, and the campaign of 1964, Kennedy's successor followed a tip-toe policy, tantamount to standstill, in practically every important area, especially Vietnam and Europe.[3] If the election year is also the president's last year in office, than his lame-duck position inevitably puts reservations on his actions. The shy attempts at NATO reform undertaken by Secretary of State Christian Herter in 1960 were pushed halfheartedly not only because the administration itself was far from determined on this policy, but also because it was reluctant to commit the succeeding administration to it. At the end of his cycle, the president tends again to become the public's servant rather than its guide.

The other feature of the president's tenure that affects foreign policy is the election campaign itself. At the beginning and end of the presidential cycle, the president's decline from leadership leaves foreign policy to "the momentum of an unattended bureaucracy." During the campaign, the danger for foreign policy does not lie in its being unattended but in its being attended in rather sorry fashion. Campaign oratory does just that, and foreigners have learned to take it with a grain of salt. Given America's world position and the nature of American aspirations, the candidates have a kind of rivalry in the promotion of lofty ambiguity; both will be for peace, and both

[3] Philip Geyelin, *Lyndon B. Johnson and the World* (New York: Frederick A. Praeger, 1966), p. 142.

will favor a patriotic posture, strength, and opposition to communism.[4] But this competition may incite irresponsibility. On the one hand, the incumbent's desire to preserve peace so as to be able to appear its champion—although not at a cost his rival might successfully attack as exorbitant—can lead at times to excessive caution, to a policy of coasting, in the hopes that this will postpone the reckoning until after the campaign. President Eisenhower and Secretary Dulles' strategy during the Suez crisis cannot be properly understood except in the context of the 1956 campaign, when it was essential for the man who had brought an end to the war in Korea to keep the laurels of peace on his head. In a crisis that was triggered by an American decision dictated by the imperative of anticommunism (the rebuff to Nasser, who had been flirting with the Soviets), the administration's strategy was marked not only by a determination to avoid the use of force but also by a determination to delay or fend off the storm. When the storm finally broke, just before the election, the violent reaction of the United States government to the British-French operation against the Egyptians revealed its intense displeasure at its failure; the American response was also an attempt to capitalize—through energetic recourse to U.N. action and vituperation against its allies' misbehavior—on the role of peacemaker. In 1964, the President also chose to stress his role as a defender of peace against the imprudent jingoism of Senator Barry Goldwater. The cost was a continuing deterioration of the military situation in Vietnam and the postponement of policy-making there, since that could only have meant either an escalation of the war, unwelcome during the campaign, or an attempt to withdraw, easily denounceable as appeasement.

Election campaign contests to appear tough or defiant have led even more often to irresponsibility. When this reached proportions as monumental as it did in 1952, with the Republican promises of "rollback," the damage was obviously limited—according to Talleyrand's dictum that what is exaggerated does not matter. However, the promises were harmful; for far from being a masterpiece of psychological warfare, they scared other nations instead of inspiring them, and they led to gestures (such as the resolution that apparently repudiated the Yalta Agreements in retrospect) that were devoid of effectiveness. When the irresponsibility is, so to speak, mar-

---

[4] Barry Goldwater's failure in the 1964 election was largely due to his failure to preserve such ambiguity and to the "trigger-happiness" he seemed to display in his anticommunism.

ginal, ironically it matters more: where posturing in favor of "liberation" can obviously mean nothing but a choice between world war or stepped-up propaganda, the desire to be "tough" in a less impossibly risky way may commit a candidate far beyond his intentions. Candidate Kennedy's strong attacks on Castro and statements in favor of anti-Castro "fighters for freedom" [5] made eventual disengagement from the incipient Bay of Pigs enterprise rather more difficult. President Johnson's reaction in August 1964 to the incident in the Gulf of Tonkin—including the resolution empowering him to take all necessary action in Vietnam, drafted in the State Department and voted by Congress—while it did not amount to a policy, as we have just seen, was a reflex that helped to orient Vietnam policy in the direction it finally took in 1965.

Both these features of the president's tenure in office make him extremely sensitive to short-term losses or failures. One of the great assets of the American system is that it provides him with a clear four years in which he can work unimpeded: his horizon does not have to be low. But the unwritten rule seems to be to avoid any short-term fiascoes at the end of the cycle. One can recover from a Bay of Pigs in the first year, but a burden such as a deadlocked negotiation at Panmunjom while American casualties rise in Korea, or a collapse of a summit meeting after the U-2 incident, are clear warnings. Fiascoes at the end of a term in office are bad in every political system, but here there is the added impact of it coming every four years at a fixed date.

The pressure the general public exerts on the presidency through these circumstances is not even direct; it is a kind of *ambiance* that affects the president or presidential candidate, not a specific set of public beliefs on foreign-policy issues, but a vague, diffuse state of mind. It is, so to speak, opinion as an undifferentiated force, remarkable both for its insensibility of the outside world (a feature brute opinion exhibits in every country) and for its reflexive response to certain events or issues. For all its indirectness and diffusion, therefore, public opinion conditions the president at times to let foreign policy go by and at times to feed the requisite cues to an otherwise inattentive public.

However, there is such a thing as a *specific public opinion on foreign policy;* this is a force that directly affects the president; he must take it into account before formulating or executing policy. I am

[5] See Arthur M. Schlesinger, Jr., *A Thousand Days: John F. Kennedy in the White House* (Boston: Houghton Mifflin, 1965), pp. 223 ff.

concerned here not with that small section which has been called the attentive public or the even smaller group of opinion-makers (about whom, more later), but with the mass of the public. What makes it important is, as we have seen, the nature of the United States government: elsewhere, the public is like the foundation of a house (essential but, once the house is built, taken for granted, at least until an earthquake hits); in America, the public is like a sea on which various, connected rafts float and try to chart their course. I wonder whether Americans' frequent overestimation of "world public opinion" does not result from an implicit projection of the American system on other nations. But even in the case of the United States, "opinion's" relation to policy is infinitely more complex than in the postulates or clichés of classical liberalism. For it is a fact that opinion does not "dictate" a policy; what V. O. Key calls a consensus of decision is a consensus that "is so closely articulated with governmental action as to appear to be decisive if not directive"; [6] it emerges from a process of discussion and controversy in which the government normally plays a leading role, so that even the most compelling kind of manifestation of opinion is not a spontaneous command that leaves the leader with no choice but to obey. Moreover, this is rare indeed; "supportive" and "permissive" consensus is more frequent. In these respects, opinion turns out not to be a rigid set of limits to governmental action either. For the truth of the matter is that mass opinion is anything but consistent. [7] Inconsistency, used as an argument against the influence of opinion by most elite theorists, turns out to provide its own remedy, since it allows a skillful leader to shape and structure opinion as he sees fit.

On many occasional issues of some importance but small urgency, the American public, like the public in other countries, lacks information and concern and has little more than contradictory feelings, as Bernard C. Cohen has shown in his careful study of peace-making with Japan. [8] On the major, lasting issues of the international competition, the public shows broad support for the main lines of United

[6] *Public Opinion and American Democracy* (New York: Alfred A. Knopf, 1961), p. 35.

[7] For a sophisticated argument that "voters are not fools" see V. O. Key, Jr., *The Responsible Electorate* (Cambridge, Mass.: Harvard University Press, 1966). His demonstration proves the decisive impact of "perceptions and appraisals of policy and performance" on votes. It does not disprove the points presented here.

[8] *The Political Process and Foreign Policy* (Princeton University Press, 1957).

States foreign policy since 1947. In both cases, opinion is not among the imperatives or constraints the government must heed in adopting a specific policy. Thus, President Kennedy could give impetus to a *détente* with the Soviet Union and sign the nuclear test-ban treaty with the enthusiastic support of a public eager to respond both to "Cold War" cues and to "peace" cues (as long as they would not be interpreted as "surrender"). Moreover, when a crisis erupts, the public will tend to rally around the leader and to trust him as the only man with all the facts and the responsibility for all operations— hence, the increase in popularity of presidents in emergencies (even the Bay of Pigs). Whether the emergencies result from foreigners' ventures or our own, all the public seems to want is that the president act. The Kennedy administration, in weighing the alternatives before it during the troubled summer of 1961, had to worry about the Soviet Union and about the European allies, but not about the American public. The Johnson administration, in the summer of 1965 and again in 1966, saw its popularity increase when it stepped up the war in Vietnam.

If all this is true, then why is there a need to consider the public at all as a factor impinging on foreign policy? Because of two closely related categories of cases, in which the permissive can turn into the punishing, the supportive can become angry. These are cases in which the ocean of the public becomes restless and stormy, cases in which fundamental national attitudes are expressed in ways that affect foreign policy deeply and often adversely. The first category embraces what I would call traumatic defeats. As the eulogists of American adaptability have stressed, the American people have been mature enough to understand that the "loss" of China and Castro's turn toward Communism can hardly be blamed on the United States, and also to resign themselves to living with the resultant troubles instead of asking that the events be undone. In other words, the American public has drawn from such shocks neither of the two possible "unilateralist" reactions—retreat into isolation or revenge. This is true, remarkable, and worth noting.

But these cases also reveal what I have called the price of adaptation. For the psycho-political cost of resignation to involvement without a guaranteed success is a kind of malaise. When failure is the outcome, politicians in search of power can turn this malaise against the administration; the rub is not in mass opinion itself but in the interplay of opinion and democratic politics. The result need not even be a public vendetta against officials allegedly responsible for the "disgrace"; it might take the form of intimidation of the officials, of deterrence rather than punishment. President Johnson's reaction in the Dominican crisis of April 1965 may well have been in large part a reflex conditioned by the history of Communist Cuba: he was deterred from a more cautious course by the fear of the political consequences should the Dominican events come to resemble those in Cuba. "For him, it was never necessary to satisfy himself that the revolution was Communist-controlled, or that it would produce another Cuba. The point was that it might." [9] Indeed, the "Cuban syndrome" required that what was first presented as a "mercy mission" be boldly proclaimed a "rebellion-blocking mission." President Kennedy had gotten away with a policy of toleration of Castro, despite Republican criticisms, because of his superb handling of the Cuban missile crisis; but the only lesson drawn by American officials from this episode seemed to be, not that a leader could permit the establishment of a Communist regime in the Caribbean, but that the risk of such a development should not be tolerated again. Similarly, the course followed in Vietnam by Presidents Kennedy and Johnson owes a great deal to the memory of the punishment the public inflicted on the Democratic party after the fall of China.

In the particular drama of Vietnam, not only the fear of the malaise created by resignation to defeat has proved inhibitive. For there exists another kind of malaise, which results from prolonged, uncertain military conflict. What is resented here is not, technically, a defeat; neither in Korea nor in Vietnam have American forces been beaten. In a first approximation of the truth, we might say that what is criticized, by a nation that has never lost a war, is the failure to win. But the situation is more complicated: the unpopularity of these wars may well be due less to the indecisiveness of their outcome than to their protractedness or, even more, to the unsettling contrast between the effort and the results.

If the war is unpopular, this does not mean the public will refuse to support it: in neither the Korean nor the Vietnamese case did a majority of the public favor a pull-out—and, in this respect, the Eisenhower administration may have drawn the wrong conclusion from Korea when it later adopted a strategy that seemed to rule out limited wars. President Johnson may have interpreted the lesson of Korea correctly when he boldly decided to build up American forces in Vietnam so as to hasten the outcome. The important factor, then, is not opposition to the war but the damage to consensus, the split

[9] Geyelin, cited, p. 254.

—even among supporters—between those who favor keeping the war limited and who look forward to an honorable solution, and those whose impatience with the frustrations of limited war make them favor escalation and increased risk-taking. For this split considerably reduces the number of those who actively support the policy, and it increases doubt and anxiety. So long as the situation does not reach the stage of protracted indecisiveness, the inconsistencies of public opinion (on a subject like Vietnam) do not inhibit policy; indeed they allow for flexibility. But once this stage is reached, the same inconsistencies become troublesome. For escalation, in addition to the obstacles it would encounter in the international system, lacks popularity; retreat appears disastrous to citizens and foreigners alike; and continuation (even when a majority prefers it to either escalation or withdrawal) increases domestic tensions and begets a recurrent need for the president to revive his sagging popularity. There is some merit in the argument that in the Korean case the public's displeasure was increased by the administration's uncertainty about its own strategy.[10] However, there, as in Vietnam, the tendency of officials to speak of "victory" revealed not so much a lack of understanding of the political and military goals of limited war, as an instinctive reaction to and understanding of the predispositions of the public, a conviction that the only way of justifying a protracted conflict is to appease the public with the lure of victory. Moreover, as de Gaulle showed in his handling of the Algerian issue, even if the strategic goals are clear (in his case, the limitation of violence, a return to peace, and a settlement reflecting political and military realities), the very nature of a protracted conflict in which the adversaries are far apart obliges one to adjust one's tactics incessantly in order to bring the ordeal to an honorable end. These adjustments, which are often anything but glorious, must, so to speak, be covered up. But the gap between cover and reality, promise and performance, only perpetuates the malaise.

As with the malaise caused by actual or feared defeats, the danger here comes less from the feeling itself than from the exploitation of it. But the peril is even greater here. First, as demonstrated by Richard Hofstadter, crises of doubt, anguish, and unhappiness feed the "paranoid style" that looks for conspiratorial explanations on an apocalyptic scale. Discomfort with the international "posture" of the United States is added to whatever economic tensions, status uncer-

---

[10] Kenneth Waltz, *Foreign Policy and Democratic Politics* (Boston: Little, Brown, 1967), Ch. 10.

tainties, and ideological dissents may exist in the body politic. This naturally provides opposition leaders with an opportunity to whip up storms in the troubled public waters. It is enough for them to point at the mess without having to offer a coherent alternative. The simultaneous presence of a longing for peace and of a drive for "prevailing" enabled the Republicans in 1952 to cash in on both the bellicosity of General MacArthur's champions and the peace charisma of General Eisenhower: a lesson remembered by the Republicans in 1966–67. Furthermore, within the party in power, support for a deadlocked policy also begins to drop, and the administration's options are reduced to stoic perseverance in an unpromising situation or to frantic attempts to please all kinds of critics simultaneously. If the first option wins, as it did in the Korean War, neglect of the people's anxiety imperils foreign policy in the long run, since their malaise may become a storm and the storm a twister. If the second option is preferred, cultivating domestic opinion (i.e., concentrating the administration's energies on taming the gale) may end by paralyzing foreign policy, since there are no clear guidelines about the best way to restore good weather at home *and* put an honorable end to a protracted conflict abroad.

It has been America's good fortune that such protracted conflicts have been few and traumatic losses have been rare. Consequently, the restraining or distorting effect on foreign policy of a brooding or disturbed opinion has not been constant, and, in most circumstances, the president has operated in the more healthy ranges of the permissive or supportive consensus; i.e., he has shaped policy by exploiting currents that do not threaten the ship of state. Thus, the direct weight of public opinion on the president is usually bearable.

The third aspect of the relation between the public and the president concerns the necessity of his *appealing to the public for support of policies* he hopes they will accept. For the public is the normal partner of the president, the kibitzer immediately behind the player in the game of world politics, the frame of reference as well as the final referee. What matters here is the president's own interpretation of what it takes to conquer or seduce his audience; not "brute opinion" but specifically opinion on foreign policy, which he tries to mold.

One important aspect of this problem relates to a basic American attitude I have already discussed: the tendency to stress principles and general propositions. Case-by-case arguments are tiresome, overcomplex, hard to follow, and confusing. They are for experts who provide information and advice. But from the public, the president wants support and trust, and his appeal to it must be broader and more striking, especially if he wants this confidence and approval to be translated into pressure on the legislators. This approach has advantages as well as drawbacks. It is an asset to be able to act with the kind of assurance and pride that comes from knowing that one enjoys the loyalty and the moral involvement of the public. But it is a liability insofar as it obliges one to draw pictures in black and white, to exaggerate the differences with (and among) one's adversaries and the solidarity with (and among) one's friends. It is no coincidence if cabinet diplomacy—of the kind that treats friends as potential rivals, foes as potential allies, and asks of an ambassador who died at a conference what he meant by doing such a thing—developed in countries whose leaders did not have to harangue their public. What American diplomacy gains in domestic solidarity it somewhat loses in smoothness and skill. For the need to keep the spectacle going may commit the president a bit more than is wise—either because the expectations raised cannot be met, or because the need to meet them may prevent him from making distinctions it would have been good to make. This was essentially Kennan's sensible objection to the Truman administration's decision to put aid to Greece and Turkey in a "world perspective" of communism versus democracy, as the only way of selling a major departure in United States policy to a public that had been isolationist not long before and had recently demobilized.[11]

Moreover, when a principle is found not to work or leads to embarrassments or dead-ends, this approach means that the president may have to climb down a high horse only in order to ride another one—to jump from one set of general propositions to another, which may again raise false hopes and lead to an impasse. It is apparently not easy to develop in public the notion (so well worked out in theory by Thomas Schelling) of mixed interests between antagonists. The necessity of carrying the public with one seems to require first a dominant stress on hostility, and later—when the consequences of zero-sum games become too obviously prohibitive and the zone of mutual interests begins to grow—an equally dominant stress on friendship, as in President Kennedy's switch of June 1963 toward

[11] See Joseph Jones, *The Fifteen Weeks* (New York: Viking, 1955), pp. 154–55.

the U.S.S.R., in the speech at American University—a tremendous clash of cymbals and change of signals designed to underwrite a much more modest enterprise, the limited test-ban.

Such a political system dramatizes what others dampen. The need for constant public support also entails a permanent necessity to keep the public's attention, to keep its emotions engaged and its senses aroused. Unfortunately, international politics today offers little tangible substance besides the austere virtues of deterrence. Thus, the public must be satisfied with images instead of substance, with inflated symbols. This frantic quest for imaginary satisfactions appears to be as much a requirement of domestic political life as it is a compensatory by-product in the modern international system. Even "filtered democracies" are run by leaders who want to be re-elected; many nondemocratic regimes are ruled by men whose power has a large component of magic, constantly renewed by popular endorsement. It is particularly characteristic of presidential regimes, viz., the pomp and circumstances of Gaullist diplomacy. What Gabriel Almond some years ago called "moods and cues," [12] what has been termed style or posture, what Daniel Boorstin has so entertainingly denounced as pseudo-events,[13] what I have called "barometrics" (a propos of resolutions in the U.N. General Assembly) prevails.[14] If I may use an undignified metaphor, the makers of policy, in their quest for public support from the spectators beyond the confines of the "policy machine," behave like beasts in a cage throwing bananas and nuts to the gazing public. Very often, the exercise is merely childish and harmless. But it can have drawbacks.

This desire or need to satisfy the public encourages a tendency to sell policy like products, to give policy announcements the slick tone of commercials, to pay more attention to the impact of a "dramatic" move on domestic popularity ratings than to its external effectiveness. It may not be impudent to put President Eisenhower's "Open Skies" proposal in that category, as an example of what happens when psychological warfare seems like the only way of "unfreezing" a stalemated Cold War abroad, and like the best application of Madison Avenue techniques at home. More recently, a foreign economic aid program, remarkable mainly for its switch in functional areas for

[12] *The American People and Foreign Policy* (New York: Harcourt Brace, 1950).

[13] *The Image* (New York: Vintage Books, 1962), pp. 7 ff.

[14] "An Evaluation of the U.N.," *Ohio State Law Journal,* Summer 1961, pp. 472–94.

expenditure, has been presented by the Johnson administration as almost revolutionary because it allegedly puts a new stress on performance by recipient nations to which every administration has already used the same strong, if not always effective, language. In the Vietnam conflict, efforts to promote nonmilitary aspects of the war —be it reform in South Vietnam or peace talks with Hanoi—have been launched with a blinding glare and a deafening din. Regrettably, and inevitably, the emphasis slips from the package to its wrapping. The peace offensive of December 1965 undoubtedly was of value in rallying opinion at home and convincing opinion abroad of the United States' sincere sense of urgency. But the very magnitude of the show detracted from what really mattered: what was in the package? The ultimate test of a policy is whether it works: a policy of force that wins (at a tolerable price, for otherwise it cannot be said to work) impresses more than a peace offensive that fails.

The need to keep opinion alerted fosters a need for inventing something new; as with youth pills, returns diminish, and after the genuine products have been exhausted, imitations take over. But the policy-maker, having fed illusion to the public, then tries to determine whether the public responded to the treatment, and a game of mirrors is on. As in the plays of Jean Genet, sham and reality become inextricably mixed. Public-opinion polls at home and abroad on the United States' conduct of its foreign affairs become the subject of political controversy, and, when the returns are poor, the administration's frequent reaction is to suppress the poll and redouble its efforts to improve the "image."

These bold strokes, flashing images, and striking postures will impair foreign policy to the extent that they run counter to the logic of international affairs, which is not one of grand gestures. But another, even more serious, problem arises. Normally, actors distinguish between their role on stage and their personality off stage. The difference here is great: the danger in this unreal drama is not merely its inappropriateness to foreign policy but also the risk that the actors may become self-intoxicated. The president and his chief advisers (at least those who are in the public light) must lead. A leader who is first of all a mover of opinion, a pied piper of democracy, and not a smoke-filled-room bargainer and machine administrator, cannot lead by rational argument alone. Rational arguments will be used, of course—in more restricted circles, where the leaders meet the "attentive public" and professional "opinion-makers," or in public by the president himself, especially if (as in Kennedy's case) rational discourse is his preferred mode of discussion. But even a Kennedy cannot stick to this mode alone. (Indeed, if he had, I doubt whether he would have become president; note Stevenson's fate.) He must inspire, exhort, sermonize, edify, or warn, resort to pulpitry in general. Although democracy relies on rational authority rather than traditional authority or charisma, presidential democracy in the United States depends on a subtle blend in which the element of incantatory magic is strong: the syncopated and alliterative poetical prose of so many of President Kennedy's addresses, from his Inaugural to some of his speeches in Europe in 1963, represents him as well as the cool, rational speeches on the United States' resumption of nuclear testing or the blockade of Cuba.

There is nothing wrong a priori in this magical appeal, except that a political system in which it prevails inevitably produces leaders devoid of those refinements of cynicism or skepticism which parliamentary regimes often encourage. To be sure, American political leaders need a solid skill in manipulation and horse-trading: they need to be politicians in what might be called the pejorative sense, but good presidents should be more than that. C. Wright Mills' critique of the "higher irresponsibility" of America's power elite failed to understand that the bond between the "mass public" and its leaders, especially its presidents, is solid not because of the public's gullibility or its atomization, not because of the leaders' Machiavellianism and deceit, but because the bond—despite all the cynicism and the disappointments—is something like a bond of faith: there are true believers at both ends. A president may (indeed must) be a master manipulator, geared to the public mood, picking up the sounds and signals of public opinion. And he must also present his decisions in terms that transcend the messy political kitchen. However, perhaps out of a need to compensate for this, the president may use words that soar so high they disappear from sight like a balloon; these are indeed the terms Theodore Sorensen used to describe what happened to President Kennedy's appeal for civil defense during the Berlin crisis, on July 25, 1961: the idea was launched before a policy was defined.[15] The president, as leader of the public, cannot be statesman only; he must have something of a prophet in him. The trouble is that the statesman is often reduced to a bureaucrat, and the prophet is bloated into an illusionist.

[15] Theodore C. Sorensen, *Kennedy* (New York: Harper & Row, 1965), pp. 615–16.

All too often, the rhetoric of presidential leadership is damaging to the policy involved: a pose is struck before its implications are thought through, because it is considered necessary to maintain whatever image or create whatever posture the president thinks advisable at the time; and then the president and the nation find themselves committed by that pose. To announce that the United States acts on behalf of such-and-such a principle, the abandonment of which would be disastrous, makes it much more likely that retreat would indeed bring calamity. If the language is generalized and vague, on the other hand, maneuverability is preserved, as the British have repeatedly shown. But when the vagueness is traceable to a general principle that has not found a level for practical application, rather than to a deliberate self-protecting generality with no "commitment" and no emotional grip, then the statesman risks being the first victim of these verbal, sentimental knots he has fashioned. To change the metaphor, the rhetoric has lifted him to a branch higher than he should dare to sit on and has cut off any easy way to climb down. To break the ties, to climb down anyhow, takes either a thorough-going cynic, which the American political scene at the highest level does not seem to produce, or the self-assurance of a man to whom reason of state and the call of history are sufficient justifications for discarding whatever has ceased to be useful—a de Gaulle in the Algerian drama. Few presidents are so distant from themselves, so capable of seeing themselves impersonally, that they can detach themselves from their own rhetoric. The French Catholic writer Georges Bernanos thought that the only dangerous form of imposture was that of the man who, having begun in falsehood and deceit, ended by sincerely assuming—as his second nature, so to speak—the insincere identity he had deliberately fashioned. If we accept this unorthodox definition, we may say that the president's dialogue with the American public encourages precisely this kind of imposture, except that often there was no insincerity to start with. Insincerity would perhaps be a blessing, for the way a policy was sold would at least be distinguishable from the policy's content. But instead, the medium becomes the message, the style becomes the substance.

## B. *"In-and-Outers" versus Career Civil Servants*

The second aspect of America's "people's democracy" relevant to foreign affairs concerns the civil service, in particular that part of it that deals with international relations. In the United States, the desire to give the public a part in managing public affairs that no oligarchy could usurp has perpetuated a reluctance to entrust the affairs of the nation to a permanent, professional corps of servants of the state. This reluctance, it would seem, stems from a belief that the best way of preserving the notion of a limited government, servant not master of a free society, would be to make the civil service as much as possible an emanation, perpetually renewed, of society. To be sure, a kind of battle goes on between this deep implicit belief that affairs of state should be handled by ordinary citizens because such affairs ought not to be different from those of the nation, and the national respect for expertise and specialization. The second trend has increased the professionalization of the civil service, created a career foreign service, and recently, established "the basis for a genuine career service for American information and cultural representatives." [16] However, the obstacles to an effective foreign policy posed by the personnel involved have not been fully overcome. Both the career civil servants and the temporary recruits from outside the government, Neustadt's "in and outers," [17] have deficiencies; and although the strengths of each are supposed to compensate for the weaknesses of the other, it is also true that their flaws reinforce one another.

The problems of the career civil servants in foreign affairs, ably reviewed by the Committee on Foreign Affairs Personnel [18] (the group of distinguished private citizens set up at the request of Secretary Rusk in 1961 and presided over by former Secretary Herter), can be discussed under three headings: career, training, and recruitment.

The most striking feature of the career problems is an excessive diversity of systems and services, which give to America's foreign-affairs bureaucracy a peculiar fragmentation, complexity, and, frequently, inconsistency or inflexibility. "The Foreign Service of the United States is not the only foreign service," since the Agency for International Development and USIA have distinct foreign services,

[16] Vincent M. Barnett, ed., *The Representation of the United States Abroad* (rev. ed., New York: Frederick A. Praeger, for the American Assembly, 1965), p. 124.

[17] "Shadow and Substance in Politics: White House and Whitehall," *The Public Interest,* Winter 1966, pp. 55–69.

[18] *Personnel for the New Diplomacy,* report of the Committee on Foreign Affairs Personnel (April 1962). The quotations in the following lines come from it.

although not career systems (until the recent decision to establish such a system for USIA). Many of the personnel in the State Department are not under the authority of the Foreign Service Act but under the more rigid Civil Service personnel system. Moreover, other departments and agencies now have their own services abroad. The proposals of the Herter Committee, if enacted, would introduce greater rationality and flexibility into personnel systems, especially by the creation of a "family of compatible systems, reflecting substantial uniformity in personnel policies and coordinated personnel operations." But a better "framework for personnel management" will not suffice to improve matters if success in one's career is the reward for caution or routine, and if the training the personnel receives is poor.

The literature on the training received and transmitted by foreign service officers reveals a debate that is something of a *dialogue de sourds*. On one side, there are critics of the present situation, who deplore the conservatism of the Foreign Service, its resistance to specialization, the discontinuity of its assignments (tours of duty are so brief and assigned with such geographical fancifulness that they also discourage specialization), the slowness of promotions, the poverty of foreign-affairs agencies in area experts, these agencies' frequent ineptitude in "supervisory or managerial responsibilities," the traditional diplomats' proclivities for "ambiguities and blandness," for the "preservation of options" or "semantic compromise," [19] and the smothering of initiatives by the State Department's "pyramidal mass." [20] On the other side, there is a kind of united front of foreign service officers who resent and denounce what they see as the dilution and degrading of their career by the intrusion of men with less expertise and less rigorous training into their elite. The lament against the effects of "Wristonization," [21] statements such as Henry Villard's "like guinea pigs in an incubator, specialists multiply," [22] the shafts aimed at the increase of America's foreign-affairs bureaucracy and at the "busy-body" new activities, pooh-poohed as the application of a

[19] See Thomas L. Hughes, "Relativity in Foreign Policy," *Foreign Affairs*, July 1967, p. 675.

[20] Smith Simpson, *Anatomy of the State Department* (Boston: Houghton Mifflin, 1967), p. 121.

[21] I.e., the integration of civil service staff and reserve personnel into the Foreign Service recommended by the Wriston Committee in 1954 and subsequently carried out. See Ellis Briggs, *Farewell to Foggy Bottom* (New York: McKay, 1964).

[22] *Affairs at State* (New York: Crowell, 1965), p. 33.

businessman's idea of diplomacy or as social engineering on a huge scale [23]—all this indicates the state of mind of a group of men steeped in the traditional concept of diplomacy: restricted, not open; generalists, not specialists; reserved, not activist.

There is undoubtedly a peril, especially in the United States, in inundating foreign-affairs bureaucracies with specialists, be they area experts or technicians of aid or information. George Bernard Shaw has remarked somewhere that a man who is only an expert is often an idiot, and indeed each new field of expertise may be built on assumptions that are as arrogant or shaky as they are untested. But the dirge about the decline of generalists would be more convincing if we could be sure that the kind of "generalism" that pervades the traditional Foreign Service were relevant. The answer to the flaws of expertise cannot be the absence of expertise, the monopoly of foreign affairs by the traditional diplomat who is superficially familiar with the history and customs of many places and socially at home in the salons and offices of many capitals. If the narrow expert is, in a way, an anti-intellectual intellectual who tends to ignore the complex connections of various fields of knowledge, the old-fashioned generalist is often a cultivated anti-intellectual who fails to examine his own assumptions, believes all too blithely in the virtue of mere experience, and mistakes the often uncritical reporting of "facts" for an analysis of events and trends. Neustadt is right in suggesting that whereas one can probably not build up within the State Department all the specialties it needs, "what one does need to build in State is great generalist capability combined with great competence in political analysis." [24] He is right in pointing out that such a combination presupposes an understanding of the difference between diplomacy and politics now that foreign policy extends to the latter. In contrast, yesterday's generalist, who *specialized* in diplomacy, is not only a helpless witness to the "new diplomacy," but is also unable to bring to the new politics of foreign affairs the perceptive judgment that is required; and it is this that leaves the practitioners of the new diplomacy free to indulge in the excesses of their own specializations.

The Herter Committee has recommended the creation of a Na-

[23] John Paton Davies, *Foreign and Other Affairs* (New York: W. W. Norton, 1966), pp. 183 ff.

[24] In Senator Henry M. Jackson, ed., *The National Security Council* (New York: Frederick A. Praeger, 1965), p. 285.

tional Foreign Affairs College for in-service training at an advanced level. Critics of this proposal state that there is no need for such a college, either because the training programs of the existing services already do the job or because the job can best be done by universities outside the government. Neither objection strikes me as valid. The committee minced no words in explaining why the existing training programs (including the Foreign Service Institute's) do not do the job: parochialism and failure to adapt to the "new diplomacy." As for universities and their international relations programs, area institutes, or international affairs centers, they simply cannot offer the needed resources and attention. If they are universities or colleges worthy of the name, their first responsibility will be to scholarly research and to the education of degree candidates. Foreign service personnel will either feel neglected, if no special curriculum is established for them, or be treated with some condescension if it is. This does not mean that the occasional presence of a foreign service officer in an academic community which happens to have an unrivaled program in a given area would not be useful, but the resources of America's educational pluralism do not make it possible to dispense with the special kind of training described in the Herter Committee report. It is illuminating to compare the training received by France's future top foreign service personnel in the Ecole Nationale d'Administration: it differs from academic training in that it emphasizes the management and policy-making aspects of public affairs, and it provides the trainees with experience and knowledge not only in foreign affairs in the traditional sense but also in economic and financial policy.

The real difficulty of the Committee's proposed college is its staffing and organization. The skills of what Neustadt called political analysis are often lacking in the government because they are located in the universities, and even there they are extraordinarily dispersed. The government (by which I mean, here, the permanent bureaucracy) is by and large manned by operators, the universities by analysts; to appoint ex-operators to the universities would not turn them into analysts, to appoint academics to a Foreign Affairs College would not turn them into policy-oriented analysts. One would have to rely, as the report suggested, on "persons who have that rare mixture of high academic standards and rich exposure to the practical world of foreign affairs," [25] i.e., teachers and scholars

[25] Cited, p. 107.

who have served in the government. But they are in short supply—and sometimes they are too wedded to past policy to be open and flexible. However, they have one great merit: they exist.

The final problem is recruitment. The Herter Committee report makes sensible suggestions about the competitive entrance examination into the Foreign Service and about the need for a more systematic search for candidates in the nation's colleges and universities. As the report noted, the failure to canvass graduate schools sufficiently is particularly regrettable. Bright undergraduates recruited into the service may well have had only limited training in international relations, and the present foreign service examination does not test them vigorously enough in this respect, yet it is hard to blame the examiners, given the weaknesses in the teaching of international relations in many colleges. Once in the service, the recruits may not have a sufficient opportunity to deepen their knowledge. However, even a more vigorous canvassing of the graduate schools will be useless unless the young men there are eager to join. It is not malicious to say that their eagerness decreases between college and graduate school as they find out more about the outside world and also about the career—as the drawbacks I have mentioned (particularly slow promotion and fast rotation) become better known, as the appeal of less rigid or splintered careers increases, as the story of foreign service demoralization in the 1950s is studied. A service that suffers in many ways from the handicaps Americans have built against what might be called nonspecialized professions, will not be able to recruit the best available candidates. It may be the time to acknowledge that fear of bureaucratic power that tolerates narrow-minded experts but flinches at the thought of a genuine career foreign service officer has helped to create experts' citadels of small or no public accountability, and has lowered the quality. "Our national weakness . . . is to try to make up by elaborate organization for the defects of the men on the job." [26] In short, an improvement in the quality of the career foreign services supposes nothing less than a radically new understanding of the kind of mind and approach required; these are unlikely to develop unless the colleges, graduate schools, and an eventual National Foreign Affairs College devote more time to the study of international relations and give it more historical depth.

The other side of the coin, the shiny side, consists of the temporary recruits, the delegates from the public—men called either

[26] Don K. Price, in Jackson, cited, p. 249.

into the higher levels of the bureaucracy at home or to represent the United States abroad for a short or long period of service in between private activities. These men compensate for the occasional stuffiness, rigidity, or mediocrity of the permanent personnel; they prevent a deadening coalition of career bureaucrats and "career"-like senators or representatives; [27] they bring in fresh ideas and shake the machinery out of the routine; they innovate and experiment. The advantages of using them in this way are unquestionable: from the viewpoint of the American polity, these men maintain the identification of the citizenry with their political regime—which contrasts so thoroughly with the situation between "us" and "them" in France, for instance, where the bureaucracy is a competent yet insulated elite into which a breath of fresh air is rarely permitted to blow. From the viewpoint of foreign policy, much ridicule has been poured on political appointees whose only ground for becoming ambassadors is the size of their financial contribution to the president's victory or their loyalty to a politician to whom the president owes a debt. But no amount of derision can obscure the benefits derived for American diplomacy by the service of very distinguished men whose expertise and professionalism are scarcely less accomplished, albeit at times less orthodox, than those of the career foreign service officers. Yet there are disadvantages, which deserve being discussed, both because they are often mentioned privately by some of these men after their period of public service is over and because so many people obstinately insist that the system is nothing but advantageous.

A first set of disadvantages concerns the comings and goings of these men, introducing what John Paton Davies, Jr. (a former career diplomat, to be sure) has called a "gypsy encampment atmosphere." [28] As Henry Villard (another retired career diplomat) puts it, "The career man does not abandon his career, but the departure of a politician may occur at any time." [29] These shifts have an effect in the American system somewhat comparable to the frequent changes of ministers in the French Third and Fourth Republics: a combination of administrative discontinuity and overly persisting continuity of policy. In other words, the brittleness of American foreign policy, which I discussed in Part II, has institutional causes

[27] See Neustadt, "Shadow and Substance," cited.
[28] Cited, p. 175.
[29] Cited, p. 84. See also Simpson, cited, pp. 207–8 and 233–34 on the "mystifying round of Presidential appointments" at the top of State and in Asian affairs.

also. The rhythm of the administration is syncopated by personnel changes; with every gust of fresh air, and then with every new cross-current, papers are blown off the table. Then too, the training and "house-breaking" of new appointees often does waste precious time. But policy is rarely deeply altered. The impulse of the new man, whose experience on the job may be limited, will be to apply the principle "First, continue; later, change," and he may never get to the second stage either because he will be domesticated by the permanent staff or because he will have moved elsewhere. Moreover, a practice that is supposed to make for consistency and to correct the appearance of instability—the shuffling of certain key men from one agency to another—does nothing to repair the damage to bureaucratic continuity; it only consolidates and, so to speak, escalates conservatism in policy.

The new men bring to the government all kinds of mental habits and practices, some of which may not be suited to policy-making. What is serious here is not so much what the foreign service officer turned memorialist usually regrets in his settlement of accounts with political appointees—their lack of experience in diplomacy or whatever line of governmental business they have chosen. It is the irrelevance of, or the debatable predispositions created by, the experiences these men have had before. One large group consists of lawyers, businessmen, and military men. The practical experience of lawyers in the handling of disputes and their analytic skill are undoubtedly of the highest use in government, and the same is true of the administrative abilities and organizational skills of businessmen and military leaders. However, in all three cases we are dealing with men whose careers display one of those basic features of the American style we have discussed: they are primarily concerned with the efficiency of means, with instrumental reason, not with the selection of ends, with normative reason; they are experts in the "manipulation of the known" [30] and inexperienced in the anticipation or creation of the new. It is not surprising, as a result, that even able businessmen should at times find it difficult to perform well, even on the score of administrative competence for which they were supposedly most gifted, in government agencies whose disarray was due less to bureaucratic confusion than to confusion about ends or the impossibility of having adequate yardsticks to measure achievements. Moreover, all three types are unprotected against overselling or wishful

[30] Henry Kissinger, "Domestic Structure and Foreign Policy," *Daedalus,* Spring 1966, p. 517.

thinking: lawyers are by profession special pleaders of specific cases, businessmen are salesmen of the products of their skills, military men are servants of their craft. Whatever their assignment in the government, they tend to play their new roles with all-consuming zeal but without regard for perspective: the part devours the whole. Thus, the failure to integrate divergent strands of policy or ends and means has roots in the nature of the personnel also. The in-and-outers' drive to success through activism and the professionals' bent toward success through prudence do not average out: they combine their defects.

Another group, far smaller, consists of intellectuals from universities or research organizations. Their *raison d'être* is (or should be) to be concerned with ends and to hunt after illusions. However, they have other deficiencies. There is no guarantee that they will be administratively skilled: experience in the labyrinth of an academic bureaucracy does not prepare one for the shock of a governmental jungle. There is no guarantee that they will have the necessary sense of power—both the art of fitting means to ends, and skill in the use of the means, without which the translation of ideas into policies cannot occur. Sometimes they have a sense of power, but then try to prove to other members of the policy-making elite who are assumed to have it—career civil servants, soldiers, business executives, etc. —that they can be as tough or as devious as the best or worst: in which case they lose their *raison d'être* and become superfluous, or dangerous. Often, of course, they have pet theories and illusions of their own.

Another set of disadvantages concerns the relations between the temporary and permanent groups. The problem is not the same as that which results from the juxtaposition in Britain, say, of career civil servants and cabinet politicians. The career servants have a kind of elite status and self-assurance that their American counterparts do not possess (a comparison of foreign service officers' memoirs would be instructive); and the politicians, while in a way as temporary as the men brought in from outside the government in an American administration, constitute a political class endowed with a permanence of its own. In the American case, there is not enough of the relation that exists in England: confidence mixed with condescension (of the political leader who makes decisions, for the civil servant who prepares and executes; of the civil servant who shapes decisions and achievements, for the gullible and transient politician), or deference (of the bureaucrat for the elected official, of the politician with no administrative proficiency, for the smooth civil servant).

The presence of men who do not come from the ranks of the foreign service in about one-third of America's ambassadorships and in many positions of responsibility in Washington produces two attitudes that are not ideal for policy-making or the carrying out of policy. One is the exasperation and resentment felt by the "professionals" over the interventions, innovations, intrusions, and experiments of the temporary insiders; the other is general insecurity. Nothing can discourage a bureaucracy as much as the sense that it is so stale that it requires frequent gusts of fresh air. European bureaucratic establishments have frequently suffered from overconfidence, from their annexation, as it were, of the public good; but lack of confidence is not a good thing either. An "in-and-outer" whose initiatives backfire still has a future, even if it is outside the government. A career foreign service officer will tend to avoid initiatives altogether, in countries or over issues where the chances for success are few. The frequent timidity of the bureaucrats—the concealment of doubts about their adequacy behind a façade of routine work—and their occasional sniping at temporary recruits confirm the latter in their conviction that they are indispensable, and in their exasperation at the slowness, the caution, the elaborate rituals of self-protection of the bureaucracy. Nevertheless, their own self-assurance is weak, due to lack of practical experience and knowledge in foreign affairs, and to the presence all around them of the professionals. In the area of foreign-policy-making itself, I would tend to agree not with the Herter Committee's suggestion for an Executive Under Secretary of State, but with its two dissenting members who pleaded for a permanent Under Secretary drawn from the career foreign service.

## II.  Power Dispersed

The popular character of American democracy does not guarantee that the people will be prudently and effectively served, for the public does not always provide enlightened guidance, not do its emissaries in the government always act wisely. But the American system, which can do little to protect the people against itself, tries at least to protect the public against any monopoly of power in Washington. Not only is there to be no ruling oligarchy, but the rulers must be divided up. Power is dispersed. Here again, the results are not always such as to provide the American political system either with the most appropriate restraints on power or with its most efficient use.

The dispersal of power distinguishes the American political system from other democratic regimes in which (although representative government almost always developed as a set of limitations on unchecked executive power) the growth of party government or the reinforcement of executive powers results in a concentration or reconcentration of power in the hands of the executive, as if the people's greatest enemy were not the abuse of power but the paralysis of power (which has indeed proven to be the case in many of Europe's crises of this century). The American system of government, despite its recent and formidable concentration of authority around the presidency, remains institutionally marked by its origins. It is a system built on the open clash of arguments and interests between groups with a broad access to the machinery of government.[31] The whole system of checks and balances that give Congress an independence that parliaments in cabinet regimes have lost (and that the French parliament lost due to its ineffectiveness in past regimes) and the virtual autonomy of so many executive agencies make the problem of concerted action paramount.

There are two views about how such a system works (apart from the much oversimplified view that the growth of the presidency, both through necessity—the external and domestic problems faced by the nation—and by the acts of a number of strong presidents, has actually been such as to overcome the checks and balances). The optimistic view asserts that the American government, while having to pay a certain price in dramatized conflicts, publicized dissent, or superficial confusion for its success, functions extremely well. The process may be bumpy, but the outcome is superlative; indeed, the very turbulence of the process assures that the outcome will be concerted and enlightened action—decisions reached with the consent and participation of all the forces concerned, and decisions that are wiser and sharper because of the clarification of the issues through the process.[32]

A less optimistic view was picturesquely described by Robert Lovett: what the optimists refer to as clarification and searching scrutiny, he labelled the "foul-up factor." [33] To what extent is this gloomier view justified? The former Secretary of Defense was allud-

---

[31] Waltz, cited, p. 9.
[32] Same, pp. 73, 109–10.
[33] In Jackson, cited, p. 78.

ing to maximum fragmentation (in the executive as well as in Congress) combined with enormous growth in the size of the many agencies concerned—"elephantiasis," as George Kennan once suggested.[34]

For clarity of discussion, it will be best to distinguish two areas of "foul-up": executive-legislative relations, and relations within the executive branch itself.

A. *The President versus Congress*

In executive-legislative relations, there was once an almost tragic notion according to which the power of the Senate and the increasing role of the House (due especially to its power of the purse) in foreign affairs would destroy the effectiveness of American foreign policy by forcing the executive branch constantly to choose between bold, usually partisan, action which might invite or incur Congressional retaliation and destruction, and laborious, harassing, and mediocre efforts at bipartisan fence-mending and support-building. This notion has been somewhat invalidated by events. The disaster of the Versailles Treaty and the League of Nations and the drama of the last year of the Truman era (during which, however, the President's foreign policy, outside the Far East, suffered more debate than damage) appear to have been blown out of proportion. Bipartisanship, or what Westerfield labelled extrapartisanship,[35] has triumphed, both in Congress, where most important foreign policies have been approved by the majority of one party and a sizable fraction of the other, and in the executive branch, which (except perhaps under Eisenhower) has used talents drawn from both parties. Since 1965, there has been more talk about the abdication of responsibility by Congress than about its nuisance value or destructive power. And the fiasco of Senator Barry Goldwater's presidential candidacy confirmed the theory according to which, even in loose two-party systems, an opposition party's best chances occur when it offers more a strong echo than a drastic choice. But it would be absurd to pretend that the peculiar structure of the American Congress—the loosely organized parties and mushrooming committees, insusceptible to dissolution—has no repercussions in the making of foreign policy.

[34] Elting E. Morison, ed., *The American Style* (New York: Harper & Bros., 1958), p. 128.

[35] *Foreign Policy and Party Policies* (New Haven: Yale University Press, 1955).

Insofar as Congress fails or has failed to debate major foreign-policy issues, it has renounced a role that the U.S. Constitution obviously allows it; it has deprived the executive branch of the advantage of open disagreements and clarifying confrontations; and it has allowed for a gradual accumulation of errors.[36] These failings may ultimately grow into major embarrassments, and they may also provoke a belated attempt by Congress to re-assume its neglected role, in ways that could be more destructive or at least far less edifying than if it had occurred earlier. This once happened concerning Yalta, and it could happen concerning Vietnam; for inadvertence breeds vendettas.

But this kind of behavior is not unique to the American system. Parliaments in cabinet systems have also oscillated between unquestioning support and retrospective revenge. What concerns us here is how Congress affects policy when it *does* play the role afforded by the system. The functions it has then can be called direction, destruction, delay, and deterrence.

There are only few instances in which Congress has directed the president to follow a course which he was unwilling to adopt. (Of course, the scarcity of broad policy directives does not mean that Congress has refrained from specifically instructing the executive to carry out certain details he would have liked to avoid.) There are a few famous examples in the realm of military policy, especially in the battles provoked by Congressional solicitude for airplanes in the missile age. In foreign affairs, the most celebrated case was that of giving aid to Spain, imposed upon a most reluctant Truman administration by a majority in Congress. But there have been cases in which Congress has pushed the president firmly in directions which he was hesitant to take. During the debate on the Marshall Plan in 1948, Congress considerably strengthened the "federalizing" implications and statements in the draft bill submitted by Secretary of State Marshall,[37] who inclined toward more caution. In 1962, when the Kennedy administration pleaded with Congress over the issue of U.N. bonds, which it wanted to buy, a kind of understanding was reached according to which, in exchange for Congressional acceptance of the purchase of bonds, the administration was forced

---

[36] See Holbert N. Carroll, *The House of Representatives and Foreign Affairs* (rev. ed.; Boston: Little, Brown, 1966), p. 365, on the lack of attention of the House and its committees to Vietnam. See also Senator William J. Fulbright, *The Arrogance of Power* (New York: Vintage Books, 1967), Ch. 2.

[37] Ernst Van der Beugel, *From Marshall Plan to Atlantic Partnership* (New York: Elsevier, 1966), pp. 116 ff.

to take a "hard line" on Article 19—with fateful results in 1964, when Congress "recorded in a 351-0 vote that it was in the American national interest to apply sanctions against recalcitrant U.N. members," [38] but the U.N. General Assembly remained unconvinced. Finally, at the crossroads of military and foreign policy, Congressional pressure has played a decisive role in the process which has led the President to the deployment of a "light" (at least as a first step) ABM system in September 1967.

Only rarely in the postwar period has Congress been truly destructive. But there have been interferences. These are important not because they cripple foreign policy—they do not—and often they provide useful scrutiny, balance, and restraint to executive measures. But they do create an array of problems for the executive branch.

One instance concerns the Joint Committee on Atomic Energy. Endowed with legislative powers that go considerably beyond the usual powers of Congressional committees, it has on occasion blocked avenues the executive wanted to explore in its difficult search for accommodation of the NATO allies' nuclear desiderata. What happened in 1958–59 and again in 1962 to the promise to aid France in developing an atomic submarine, the fate of General Lauris Norstad's suggestion of making NATO a "fourth atomic power," and the fate of the original concept of a multilateral force of nuclear-armed submarines shows that in this area, where it might perhaps have been wise to show some imagination and flexibility, the Joint Committee's more restrictive and conservative policy impaired U.S. policy. (It also led to an unorthodox attempt by the French ambassador to deal directly with the Joint Committee.)

Probably more serious (for the instances of actual interference by the Joint Committee are few) have been actions in Congress concerning foreign aid. Reluctant to alter foreign policy in an emergency or to initiate military policies (except usually to ask for more rather than less or to favor one service over another), Congress has used what is left of its destructive power in the realm of foreign aid. It has used veto power, as it were, either by cutting or rejecting repeated requests for long-term authorization of aid programs, or by refusing to allocate foreign aid to countries found guilty of "misbehaving." It has also attached to the foreign-aid bills all sorts of riders about the allocation of funds, the compensation of nationalized U.S. interests, or the conditions to be met by recipients. In

---

[38] John Stoessinger, *The U.N. and the Superpowers* (New York: Random House, 1965), p. 185.

short, it has interfered with the administrative set-up. While Congress has not destroyed the basic American commitment to foreign aid,[39] Congressional interference has resulted in discouraging the creation of a rationale for aid, as John Montgomery [40] and others have deplored, and in occasional embarrassments, such as those suffered by Ambassador Kennan in Yugoslavia.[41] Congress, in its interference with foreign aid, uses the power of the purse to find a molehill that would compensate for the mountain of defense expenditures. (A similar kind of interference can be seen in Congressman John Rooney's examination of diplomatic and cultural representation abroad.)

The most spectacularly destructive interference was, of course, Senator McCarthy's witch hunt in the State and Defense departments, combined with a widespread attack on the Truman administration's Far East policy. This was less an attempt to influence policies than a retrospective vendetta. And we must bear in mind that only a minority of Congress was involved, although the Congressional system tends to give "exaggerated prominence" to the views of a minority. Nor should we forget that foreign policy was used as a handle (or crowbar) by men looking for a way to return to power after a long period in the wilderness. It is important also to note that this wrecking operation took place at the time of one of those malaises of opinion I discussed previously. (International entanglements, in a world that promises turmoil rather than triumph, could bring this about again.)

The delaying power of Congress is sometimes hard to distinguish from its destructive one. What makes it so important is that it is inseparable from the structure of Congress: it results quite naturally from the number of committees, the leisurely pace of deliberation, the complexity of the budgetary procedure, the frequency of investigations. Dean Acheson and John Foster Dulles have given interesting statistics about the time spent in (and frequency of) their appearances before Congressional bodies—one-sixth of Acheson's time, according to his calculations. [42] All writers on foreign aid have cursed the "fourfold Congressional obstacle course" [43] of authoriza-

[39] Waltz, cited, Ch. 8.

[40] *The Politics of Foreign Aid* (New York: Frederick A. Praeger, for the Council on Foreign Relations, 1962), pp. 201 ff.

[41] See Harry H. Ransom, ed., *American Foreign Policy Reader* (New York: Thomas Y. Crowell, 1965), pp. 587 ff.

[42] *A Citizen Looks at Congress* (New York: Harper, 1957).

[43] Montgomery, cited, p. 234.

tion and appropriation. The impact of such procedures does not *have* to be bad: queries and inquiries expose bad practices and challenge dubious policies. Yet, since the hearings are often repetitive and divagating, precious time is lost for the policy-makers and administrators, who not only have to be present (physically and mentally) but must spend hours or days in preparation for the ordeal. Nobody denies that public accountability and even policy efficiency require Congressional hearings, but the proportion is not right. "Collecting and processing information is a relentless obligation of aid administrators, and one which may override other obligations directly connected with the implementation and success of American policy." [44] Moreover, especially in matters of aid, the foreign impact of a program can be dissipated by the sheer length of time its adoption consumes, not to mention the kinds of questions and answers which Congressional discussion provokes.

The deterrent power of Congress may well be its most dangerous, although (or because) it is the most difficult to document and track down. Deterrence can be as effective in policy-making as it is in international strategy. The inhibition of boldness and the prevention, delay, or diminution of initiative in a new direction (to be distingushed from change that is really "more of the same," from new moves in old directions) is a frequent consequence of the American system. Here, the inherent institutional conservatism of Congress and the strength of conservatives in Congress reinforce one another. Often, decisions are not made and reforms are not introduced because of the fear of a battle over the issue in Congress or because of the fear of the consequences even a victorious battle would have for other parts of the president's program. In this respect, contrary to the optimists' claims, the price of domestic peace or apparent harmony is the dampening of debate, the deadening of policy. Congress reflects some deep-rooted American attitudes and beliefs, even though they inhibit success in foreign affairs, and, like most deliberative bodies, it has an understandable attachment to policies and poses that were successful in an earlier period (what I have elsewhere called its thermos-bottle aspect). Therefore, Congressional support for innovations the present international system may require in the national interest is not automatic: conversion is required. The executive branch does not always feel that the importance of the issue justifies the cost of the effort, or that the results would be proportional to the cost. As a consequence, some desirable innovations

[44] Same, p. 219.

have to be ruled out (after which it is never difficult to find a rationale for routine) and others have to be introduced in tiny doses. It is possible that on general issues of the Cold War—the feasibility of a *détente* with the Soviet Union, bold moves toward it in Europe, or arms-control or disarmament agreements—the conservatism of Congress has coincided with the requirements of a sound foreign policy and actually prevented dangerous experimentation. Whether this will be true in the future remains to be seen. Already the delays in Congress over the Johnson administration's proposal to facilitate East-West trade may well deter the President and his advisers from other sound moves. And even in the past, Congressional conservatism has sometimes inhibited changes that would have been useful. Thus, it has probably played a large role in keeping the President from drastically reorganizing the CIA so as to remove it from political adventures, and from finding better ways of supporting controversial American and foreign organizations which the CIA had been helping. The advantage of covert operations that escaped Congressional scrutiny prevailed over the risk of legislative displeasure, despite the other risk of embarrassment and discomfiture in case of a collapse of secrecy. So great was the fear of the former peril that the latter was discounted. And Congress has deterred any slowing of the arms race.

Evidence of Congressional deterrence is particularly convincing in three more areas. One is American policy toward Communist China,[45] since executive obstinacy on the issue of recognizing China and permitting it United Nations membership is due in no small measure to the fear of Congressional reaction. Another one is American aid policy, since excessive concern of the Congress about "creeping socialism" and its insistence on private enterprise are easier to justify in terms of domestic prudence than in terms of international wisdom (note the Bokaro steel mill episode). American support for Juan Bosch had to be dampened, lest Bosch's program of land expropriations create a "calamitous" reaction in Congress.[46] The limitations in size and coherence of our aid program result, when combined with China policy, in the paradox of insufficient attention being paid to the social and economic fabric of South and Southeast Asia—i.e., to the conditions in which revolutionary warfare might break out

[45] See Schlesinger, cited, p. 479. Also, Roger Hilsman, *To Move a Nation* (New York: Doubleday, 1967), pp. 558–59, concerning China, and pp. 306–7, concerning Outer Mongolia.

[46] John Bartlow Martin, *Overtaken by Events* (New York: Doubleday, 1966), pp. 472–73.

—at the same time that hostility to China persists. These concerns and limitations have been responsible for Congress' long neglect of Latin America until the threat of Castroism put the spotlight on the subcontinent. A third area is, once again, that of atomic energy. In East-West relations, "the frequent hearings of the Joint Committee on Atomic Energy kept before the public the difficulty of controlling underground nuclear explosions, and no doubt this inhibited the executive's freedom." [47] The procedure which gives the Joint Committee the power of legislative veto on executive agreements for sixty days, its right to be "fully and currently informed," and its opposition to any drastic changes in the MacMahon Act may well have inhibited executive initiatives within NATO; certainly President Eisenhower dolefully complained about it.[48] More recently, the opposition of influential members of Congress powerfully contributed to the President's decision not to press the NATO allies on the MLF issue.[49] And the demise of this rather "fake" scheme of nuclear sharing could mean that wiser, more daring and imaginative schemes, requiring greater sacrifices of U.S. sovereignty, would also be "deterred." In all these respects, it is hard to assess exactly, yet impossible to discount, the impact of the "negative consensus" of conservative Republicans and southern Democrats, who owe their power to the seniority system, to the senatorial desire to be patriotic, and to the representatives' obligation to face their constituents every two years.

The difficulty of executive-Congressional relations should not be exaggerated. After all, the major initiatives undertaken by American presidents from the Marshall Plan and NATO to the Alliance for Progress, from the test-ban treaty to the Trade Expansion Act, and more recent decisions of President Johnson were endorsed by Congress. Moves that might have been expected to arouse Congressional ire—the sale of wheat to Russia, or the abandonment of the battle for Article 19 of the U.N. Charter—were endorsed or tolerated without a major row. The number of American military commitments abroad endorsed by the Senate is formidable. Nevertheless, it must be remembered that, just as military deterrence has a component of bluff (or, if one prefers, just as it is a process that occurs in the mind of the deterred), fear of Congressional opposition may be important even it is misplaced. And the only way of dispelling it

[47] Jacobson and Stein, cited, p. 476.
[48] See *The New York Times,* May 22, 1966.
[49] Geyelin, cited, pp. 169–70.

decisively would be to bring each matter to a successful showdown. Also, as I have already suggested, the president can always gain support and minimize the bad effects of Congressional opposition—but at a cost.

The cost is first of all felt in the presentation of measures the administration either must or has chosen to submit to Congress. Observers have noted that it is easier to get Congressional approval if the three following conditions are met or strategies adopted.

1. Produce a sense of crisis. This will give the measure an impressive air of urgency and will facilitate passage by putting on Congress the burden of the effects of inaction or delay. This technique was used by the president in such comparable matters as the 1955 Formosa resolution, the 1957 Middle East resolution (Eisenhower Doctrine), and the 1964 Tonkin Gulf resolution. In all three cases, there were compelling reasons (both domestic and foreign) why the president wanted to receive an endorsement of his foreign policy from Congress: it would free his hands and warn America's enemies. But requesting such a resolution in the first place, in order to make "national unity" clear, only reinforces the frantic nature of the American approach to international affairs.

2. Stress the "vital interest" angle of the proposal. Given the inclination of Congressmen, the kinds of vital interests that impress them tend to concern either security or the health of the American economy. As a result, they merely strengthen two tendencies in the American approach to foreign affairs: the tendency to use the contributions of other nations to the military strength of our alliances as a yardstick for foreign-policy programs (including aid programs); and the tendency to "oversell" by exaggerating foreign dangers, allied contributions, or international prospects. President Kennedy's strategy in waging his fight for the Trade Expansion Act in 1962 presented the bill as a choice between the "beginning of a new chapter in the alliance of free nations—or a threat to the growth of Western unity," and as a measure providing "the unifying intellectual principle of the New Frontier." [50] Since performance does not always follow on promise, a cumulative process is set in motion, and the next time around, the president has to revive expectations with fresh promises. This has all too often happened in aid legislation. Thus, techniques 1 and 2, above, contribute to the atmosphere of high drama and public relations so characteristic of American foreign policy and so often inimical to sound international relations.

[50] Schlesinger, cited, p. 847.

3. This technique, already alluded to, consists simply of anticipating Congressional suspicions or prejudices, particularly in the fields of weapons, aid, or nuclear cooperation, and incorporating them in the proposed bill.

I do not mean to suggest the president can obtain support for his policies only by using such tactics. The well-known histories of the North Atlantic Treaty (growing out of the Vandenberg Resolution), the Japanese Peace Treaty, and the test-ban treaty show that reason without frenzy and persuasion without hucksterism can prevail; and, of course, there are genuine emergencies (the Marshall Plan). However, the less satisfying techniques *are* used, and they fail to accomplish what one might call the political education of Congress, thus contributing to the lag between traditional reflexes and beliefs on the one hand and adaptation to international necessities or exploitation of international opportunities on the other.

The cost which the executive branch has to pay also includes the choices the president must make in his relations with Congress. One set of choices relates to the question of how much time it is advisable for the president to spend "selling" foreign policy to Congress, how much of a priority should be given in executive-legislative relations to foreign-policy issues. The choice must be made in crises and in long-term programs.[51] In the case of crises—whether genuine international shocks of major proportions, smoldering danger points, or incidents that might become emergencies—the choice is between speedy and independent action by the president and a build-up of broad, bipartisan support. The advantage of the latter is obvious: it provides the president with the mandate that he needs to assert his international authority. But the liabilities are real. Whipped into unity by the crisis, Congress may give the president a blank check and thus apparently remove concern about Congressional support for whatever action he takes from his list of worries. Unfortunately, the "immunity from future criticism" [52] he thus obtains, on the cheap, is more tinsel than gold, for this kind of unanimity expresses not so much a genuine consensus as a patriotic emotion, sincere but possibly shallow. Thus, if the administration later takes steps that turn out to be inadequate, Congressmen can always argue that the

[51] For this distinction, see Andrew M. Scott and Raymond H. Dawson, eds., *Readings in the Making of American Foreign Policy* (New York: Macmillan, 1965), pp. 148 ff.

[52] Cecil V. Crabb, *Bipartisan Foreign Policy: Myth or Reality?* (Evanston, Ill.: Row, Peterson, 1957), p. 253.

Congressional mandate must be understood in the light of the circumstances of its adoption; this has been the case with the Tonkin Gulf resolution. And to ask for a mandate is a move that could boomerang: instead of immunity from criticism, the mandate might lead to mutual recrimination, as happened when some senators, annoyed by President Johnson's insistence that our economic aid in Southeast Asia manifests our commitment to the area's security, balked at his attempts to put foreign aid on a long-term basis. Thus Congress remains free to pierce holes in the very "cloak of legitimacy" [53] it has consented or even rushed to drape around the president.

On the other hand, despite a crisis, Congress may be reluctant or slow to grant the president special powers, and the process may tarnish the image of a united government that the executive wanted to create. It took President Eisenhower two months of considerable haggling to get his Middle East resolution approved by both Houses. And in the Indochina crisis of 1954, he had found that Congressional approval for American intervention was hesitant and would only be given after laborious efforts on the part of the executive branch. Also, there is always a risk that in the course of discussion, an amendment will be adopted that will add a mandate the executive does not want and thus cripple flexibility, as Secretary Dulles argued in rejecting the offer of a resolution on Berlin to strengthen his hand in 1959. This explains why presidents have so frequently preferred to act by themselves, reducing Congress' role to consultation with (often meaning simply the giving of information to) important Congressmen: President Truman's decision on Korea and his subsequent decision to send U.S. troops to Europe, Eisenhower's intervention in Lebanon, Kennedy's handling of the Berlin crisis and the two Cuban crises, Johnson's move into Santo Domingo are cases in point. But the danger here is that the unilateral act is a gambler's move. If things go well, no questions will be asked, even if it leaves a lingering resentment. If things go sour, knives will be sharpened and belated vendettas may break out—even when the "list of influentials" [54] had been checked—as President Truman discovered during the Korean stalemate.

As for programs, the president's choice does not have to do with whether to include Congress in the definition of a foreign policy, but with the ranking of priorities, the balance between support for do-

[53] Carroll, cited, p. 364.
[54] Neustadt, "Shadow and Substance," pp. 65 ff.

mestic measures and support for external ones. Any bill the president submits to Congress that is at all controversial and that he wants to have enacted into law will require a considerable effort of lobbying, arm-twisting, flattering, promising, making deals, throwing luncheons, giving briefings. Time is the scarcest commodity in an otherwise affluent society, especially in Washington. When the question of whether to introduce the bill or not is a matter of presidential decision, the president must calculate how the submission of, and pressure for, the bill will affect the rest of his legislative program. It is here that the deterrent effect of Congress is most important: it is easy to list the programs accepted, renewed, or rejected by Congress, but we must also remember the bills that were not submitted, the innovations that were not pushed (for nuclear sharing, extended foreign aid, or new international ventures in capital development, etc.) because a presidential commitment to them would have cost too much in his over-all resources and objectives. Fearful of the political fallout from an anticipatory move, the president finds it easier to wait for a crisis, at which time he will be able either to act alone or to get more cheaply the kind of support he needs. The basic decisions about America's military presence in Europe came, not simultaneously with the ratification of NATO, but after the Korean War.

Another kind of choice relates to the president's international tactics. Should he deal abroad as a free agent? Or should he make no move that would risk being defeated or deflated by Congress? Congressional dragons often provide a convenient excuse not to act for a president who is reluctant to undertake a commitment or who is not sure that the cost of disarming the dragon would be less than the foreign-relations benefits from the policy move. Using Congress as a shield when you want to stand still but not be blamed for it, letting Congressional reluctance tip the scales when your mind finds arguments on both sides of the balance, is a temptation that not every president can resist, nor every secretary of state. A converse tactic consists of arguing for a policy because of alleged Congressional pressure for it or because any other course would incur retaliation from a disappointed Congress.

John Foster Dulles and President Eisenhower used those related tactics several times: the latter tactic in attempting to get EDC ratified, when Mr. Dulles, at Bermuda, stated that Congress would not support NATO unless EDC became a reality; the former method in the Indochina crisis of 1954, in refusing to join the Bagdad Pact, and in the Suez crisis. In the Indochina affair, as the President recognized in his memoirs,[55] the conditions and hesitations of the Congressional leaders he consulted coincided with his own. In the Suez affair, Dulles invoked the Senate Appropriation Committee's opposition to justify cancellation of the Aswan Dam project,[56] and both he and the President explained (or tried to explain) to Prime Minister Eden that they could not secure Congressional authorization for the use of force or "even for the lesser support measures for which you might have to look to us." [57] These may be sound tactics in international affairs and often, of course, the position that Congress takes, which the executive invokes, is a sensible one.

Unfortunately, however, there are two drawbacks. When an administration is divided on an issue and lets the mood of Congress tip the scales, the issue is not settled on its merits, which might indeed have required a move unpopular with Congress and an effort by the executive branch to change its mood. In other words, the tactics described here contribute to inertia or inflexibility. Second, while it is true that the president can use Congress as a shield and a lightning rod, that body can also function as a club or a live wire: by treating Congress in the way I have described, the executive branch in fact increases Congress' veto or deterrent power, and Congressmen may later exploit the tactical importance granted them. On the other hand, when the president makes commitments and uses pressure abroad in support of certain proposals, he may expose his administration to unpleasant surprises if he has not protected its flanks against a Congressional rebellion. Dulles' promise of aid to France's nuclear program, Eisenhower's rather fumbling attempt to negotiate a transfer of a limited number of nuclear weapons to Britain in 1960,[58] are cases in point; one wonders what would happen if American negotiators signed arms-control agreements with the Soviet Union without sufficient concern for Congressional sensitivity in this realm. The golden mean was probably reached in instances like the negotiation of the North Atlantic Treaty and the nuclear test-ban treaty, when the executive branch clearly led, yet was careful to include influential Congressmen in the proceedings. But the golden

[55] Dwight D. Eisenhower, *Mandate for Change* (New York, Doubleday, 1963), Chap. 14.

[56] Dwight D. Eisenhower, *Waging Peace* (New York: Doubleday, 1965), pp. 33 ff.

[57] Same, p. 667.

[58] See H. L. Nieburg, *Nuclear Secrecy and Foreign Policy* (Washington, D.C.: Public Affairs Press, 1964).

mean is not always attainable, and pursuit of it may narrow the range of the administration's enterprises and use up precious resources of time.

I do not mean to suggest by this long list of headaches and handicaps that the peculiar difficulties of the American system could be remedied without other troubles appearing. It is easy to demonstrate that the British governmental system, while it considerably reduces the nuisance power of the legislature and provides the prime minister with greater assurance of support at less cost, nevertheless does not save him from having to plead and calculate in order to gain the support of his cabinet and party. Also, this system often hems in the leadership: an independent president is freer to take initiatives before public and Congressional acquiescence are obtained than a prime minister before his cabinet and party have been won over; and the British process of consensus-building does not take place in the open, despite a clear-cut division between government and opposition.[59] But the American system sometimes combines all kinds of disadvantages. The need for executive-branch authority in international relations, the absence of a well-organized opposition with clear-cut responsibilities, the looseness of the president's own political organization, and the Constitutional separation of powers together make the president even more immune from scrutiny and criticism (at the time when they would be useful, i.e., before fiascoes) than a prime minister would be, and make it impossible for the president to know whether a fiasco will not lead to a vendetta, or for the public to be assured that a fiasco must lead to a reshuffling of the men responsible for it. A president's loss of usefulness, due to imperviousness to mistakes and attrition from legislative harassment, is a possibility, and not a pleasant one.

## B. *The Splintered Executive Branch*

It is possible to argue that, on the whole, difficulties in executive-legislative relations have less detrimental an effect on the making and executing of foreign policy than the splintering of the executive branch itself: a conclusion reached by a high official, who should know.[60] It is here that the combination of fragmentation and size inflicts the gravest damage. Officials who testified before Senator

---

[59] Waltz, cited, Ch. 3.

[60] Roger Smith (pseud.), "Restraints on American Foreign Policy," *Daedalus*, Fall 1962, pp. 505–16.

Henry Jackson's Subcommittee on National Security and International Operations have, with varying degrees of weariness, exasperation, or resignation, listed the drawbacks. "At the heart of a Secretary of State's dilemma is his Department," whose "growth would dismay even Mr. Parkinson," [61] Secretary Rusk said, describing its growth as "layering." He mentioned the fate of the telegram that comes in during the morning with a question to which he knows the answer but which he must route through all the layers nevertheless; the answer will be sent only "a week or ten days later," [62] when every layer will have had the time to "review" and ponder over it. The classic description by Charlton Ogburn, Jr., of the "flow of policy-making in the Department of State" [63] gives only a beginning of the idea. For the difficulty is compounded by the many other departments and agencies in foreign affairs besides the State Department. Loan policies, as John Montgomery has shown, have involved the departments of Agriculture, State, Defense, and Treasury, the Export-Import Bank, the Office of Defense Rehabilitation, the Budget Bureau, and USIA. The many and diverse career systems and the overlapping activities of security agencies are other examples. The Department of Defense has become, in some ways, a second State Department, engaged in negotiations with foreign countries and (through military assistance, "civic action," and counter-insurgency programs) in manipulating foreign societies, often to the dismay of traditional State Department officials who lament their own service's displacement but are reluctant to assert their authority in realms so unfamiliar and unorthodox. A continual reshuffling and reorganization adds to the mess: foreign aid was administered by six successive agencies and ten directors between 1948 and 1966.

Some of the consequences of this state of affairs are particularly serious. One is, paradoxically enough, that key officials are overworked but emphasize the wrong kind of work. Overstaffing and the fragmentation of responsibilities, far from lightening the load for each official, increase it along with its frustrations. Waste is an inevitable by-product, and the form of the waste, just as inevitably, is

[61] Senator Henry M. Jackson, ed., *The Secretary of State and the Ambassador: Jackson Subcommittee Papers on the Conduct of U.S. Foreign Policy* (New York: Frederick A. Praeger, 1964), p. 43.

[62] Same, p. 125.

[63] In "U.S. Foreign Policy: The Formulation and Administration of U.S. Foreign Aid," a study prepared by the Brookings Institution for the Senate Committee on Foreign Relations, 86th Congress, 2d sess., p. 727.

the proliferation of paper-work—too many "pieces of paper" that repeat the same story.[64] What is lost is time to *think:* the men in charge must spend too much energy keeping the machine from breaking down, getting the papers read as well as moving, pushing the "flow" along, and they naturally run the risk of creeping intellectual numbness.

Slowness is another drawback. (President Kennedy's impatience with the delays in the executive bureaucracy has been well documented.) While one can make a case for occasional deliberate slowness when caution is needed, the slowness that comes from routine and organizational handicaps is an indiscriminate habit. A striking example of its possible costs in foreign policy is given in the case of President Kennedy's order to remove American missiles from Turkey in August 1962—an order that had not yet been carried out when the Cuban missile crisis broke out.[65]

A third and most serious flaw is the dilution of authority and responsibility. A writer who is far from hostile to the "new dipomacy" has documented his proposition that the present organization of the executive branch violates all the basic rules of bureaucratic organization: [66] duties are not clearly assigned, the diffusion of authority slackens responsibility, the same job is done by different people, the proportion of staff services to the rest of the personnel is unsound (all three agencies primarily concerned with foreign policy—State, AID, and USIA—have a higher percentage of staff dealing with management than the other agencies), top officials have too many subordinates reporting to them, and comparable activities are dispersed among various agencies.

Many examples of the consequences of this flaw can be given. One is the familiar story of the U-2 fiasco, well analyzed by the same writer. As he points out, at the core of that incident was the failure to coordinate preparation for the Paris summit conference with the collecting of intelligence; i.e., failure to coordinate no less than twelve different agencies. The confusion of responsibility became such that the President had to step in and, in an act of administrative courage and international imprudence, assert his own full responsibility for the incident. Another example is that of the "gap

---

[64] See Schlesinger, cited, Ch. 16.

[65] Elie Abel, *The Missile Crisis* (Philadelphia, Pa.: Lippincott, 1966), pp. 189 ff.

[66] Robert McCamy, *Conduct of the New Diplomacy* (New York: Harper & Row, 1964), Ch. 6.

between purpose and policy" in foreign aid. A careful study has shown that it is due not only to the deeper reasons I discussed in Part Two, but also to the "continuing institutional battle between AID and the Department of State." One agency wants to apply strict economic criteria, the other tends toward "short-term political" ones, and the outcome of the "shouting match" is that the goal of political development is lost.[67] Even top Washington officials often publicly advocate divergent policies. In March-April 1954, when the crisis in Indochina was posing a difficult problem for the administration, Admiral Radford, the Vice President, the Secretary of State, and the President himself differed widely in the belligerency and emphasis of their positions. In the spring of 1966, "every day the United States [was] reported to have a different view [on nuclear sharing and nonproliferation]. It may well be true that it [had]. It depends on what part of this dinosaur you tap." [68]

The dilution of responsibility in Washington is often compounded by a similar one in the field, where the various agencies are all represented, and where, for instance, the Central Intelligence Agency and the embassy often work at cross-purposes. Hence, Washington often gives the impression of being in the same position President Truman uncharitably predicted his successor would find himself in—giving instructions, thinking that the policy is being carried out, and then discovering that little is happening.

All these drawbacks together encourage parochialism and, frequently, lack of imagination (or, more accurately, resistance to political creativity) in foreign policy. Parochialism is the inevitable concomitant of fragmentation: each agency has its own rituals, its own recipes, its own jargon, its own mental habits and defenses against criticism, its own lightning-rod relations with Congressmen or interest groups. "It [ambiguity] encourages departments and agencies to mount their horses and ride off in all directions. It fosters pressure groups and empire building. It creates strong temptations for Indians to act like chiefs—and for chiefs to look for cover. NATO Indians hawk their much loved fetish; U.N. Indians powwow while disarmament Indians smoke their peace pipes; AID Indians sometimes mistake policy for potlatch; and management Indians brandish organ-

[67] Robert Packenham, "Political-Development Doctrines . . . ," *World Politics,* January 1966, pp. 194–235.

[68] Dean Acheson, in Henry M. Jackson, ed., *The Atlantic Alliance: Jackson Subcommittee Hearings and Findings* (New York: Frederick A. Praeger, 1967), p. 97.

ization charts as though they were powerful medicine." [69] As for political creativity, while it is true that the international system itself limits the horizon, there is surely something wrong when an innovation as modest as the test-ban treaty has to be negotiated away from the agencies concerned (except for six top men).[70] Moreover, the bigness and complexity of the "policy machine" foster some kinds of lethal antidotes to parochialism: in order to protect itself from disgrace in case the stand it had taken gets knocked down, a smart agency knows how to "keep the options open," and in order to protect the policy-making process from the rigidities of parochial commitments, the higher policy-makers often appoint "unoriented personalities" whose only commitment is to what a knowledgeable critic has called "relativity," or "perpetually reserving judgment." [71]

To be sure, also, the degree of "routinization" varies from agency to agency. In recent years, the Defense Department has shown a remarkable capacity to innovate. But the example of the Defense Department is misleading. The kind of creativity needed there is the technical, technological sort. The Defense Department's contribution to political innovation is far more questionable—at least to those who have reservations about the diplomatic consequences of the way the McNamara Doctrine was presented, about the pressure put on West Germany to help our balance of payments, and about American policy in Vietnam. Also, the Defense Department's lack of old traditions has given it a considerable edge in mobilizing the talents of scientists or scholars, leaving the State Department all too often deprived of the kind of expertise that would have allowed for a less "geometrical" approach to foreign policy.[72] The linchpin of American foreign policy remains the State Department, and, while Schlesinger's charge that "one almost concluded that the definition of a Foreign Service Officer is a man for whom the risks always outweighed the opportunities" [73] may be unkind and unfair, it is true that the blows suffered by State in the 1950s and the penalty for unconventionality inflicted on many of its best servants left deep marks. Insofar as American foreign policy has to be defined through "negotiations within the government," [74] "serving the machine be-

[69] From the Initial Memorandum, in same, p. 4.
[70] Sorensen, cited, p. 734.
[71] Thomas L. Hughes, cited, p. 674.
[72] Jacobson and Stein, cited, pp. 479 ff.
[73] Schlesinger, cited, p. 414.
[74] Jackson, *The Atlantic Alliance.*

comes a more absorbing occupation than defining its purposes." [75]
Political creativity is the casualty of permanent bargaining.

A final drawback is a more subtle one. Getting a policy adopted
or carried out in the executive branch is a complicated process, both
lateral and hierarchical: the men in a given agency who advocate a
certain policy must acquire the support or neutrality (or, to put it
more bluntly, must convince or neutralize) the other agencies involved (and other agencies are always involved). They must also
obtain the blessings and enlist the leadership of the men with whom
the final decision rests: the president and his immediate subordinates. As a result, in the bureaucratic battle to besiege and beseech
the president, a variant of the oversell, so often encountered already,
puts its stamp on the acts of the "prime movers." They tend, uncon-
sciously in many cases, to interpret frequently ambiguous evidence
in the light of their own desires. Analysis is slanted by an activist
bias, interpretation slips into prescription, data are treated as arguments, preconceptions color reports, and reality is distorted. The
CIA's top officials, in advocating a landing on Cuba in 1961, deliberately neglected intelligence, paradoxically enough for an intelligence
agency, and gave far too optimistic an assessment of the prospects
for success. [76] Similarly, the CIA's presentation during the Dominican crisis of a highly debatable interpretation of events, from which
the conclusion that U.S. intervention was needed to prevent a new
Cuba could not fail to be drawn, raises important questions. [77] But I
am not sure that this failing is peculiar to the CIA. Observers and
participants have noted the State Department's peculiar analyses of
European affairs at various crucial times: the spring and summer of
1954, the fall of 1962, the months of 1964 when a decision on the
MLF was being sought. Not only were the interpretations wrong
(especially in assessing the mood of the French Parliament on EDC,
General de Gaulle's determination and freedom of maneuver in
1962, and British nuclear policies in 1964), but the analysis on
which they were based were tipped in the direction the State Department wanted to go. The same charge can be made against the State
and Defense Departments' assessments of Chinese intervention in
Korea in the fall of 1950, and against the Defense Department's fre-

---

[75] Kissinger, cited, p. 507. See also William Attwood, "Labyrinth in Foggy
Bottom," *The Atlantic Monthly,* February 1967, pp. 45 ff.

[76] See Sorensen, cited, pp. 291 ff., and Schlesinger, cited, Ch. 10.

[77] Theodore Draper, "The Dominican Crisis," *Commentary,* December
1965, pp. 33–68.

quent optimistic assessments of the situation and prospects in South Vietnam, especially from 1960 to 1964. In 1966, the Defense Department and the Arms Control and Disarmament Agency, eager to obtain a nonproliferation treaty, underestimated first the likelihood and later the strength of the objections from potential nuclear powers.

These defects, caused by fragmentation and gigantism in the executive branch, lead into a vicious circle. Officials try to remedy the defects and make the machinery work through procedures of coordination. But coordinating efforts only add to the difficulties by creating new dilemmas. The literature on the making of foreign policy provides a crushingly weighty encyclopedia of the methods and headaches of coordination. It is not possible or necessary to produce a digest of that encyclopedia here; but I should like to analyze the dilemmas.

The fundamental one is clear. If coordination becomes a major preoccupation, its difficulties will complicate the already complex responsibilities of overburdened officials. But if the officials do not treat coordination as a major problem, they run two serious risks. One is that of committing a major blunder because of faulty cooperation among agencies, as in the U-2 affair (which, amazingly enough, occurred in the one administration for which coordination was otherwise a dogma). The other is that of having separate, perhaps even divergent, foreign policies running their courses concurrently. The tendency for this to occur exists already, despite repeated attempts at improving coordination, and will in all likelihood get worse—especially since different agencies have different constituencies, in the public and in a divided Congress, on which they can depend for support for their continuing autonomy. (And the problem of coordination is as serious abroad as in Washington, since the ambassador presides over a mission full of specialists whose first loyalties are often to the services on which their careers depend.) This has evidently often been the case with the CIA's foreign policy operating simultaneously with the State Department's, a situation made possible by its position as an executive agency of the presidency, its considerable amount of money (which allows it to have not only a highly diversified and enormous staff, sometimes even military forces, but also networks of native clients abroad), and the flimsiness of Congressional supervision over it. (The "watchdogs" have shown that they are concerned more with protecting the CIA from Congress than with supervising the CIA.)

What the autonomy of the executive agencies can mean in practice was well demonstrated in the Dominican crisis, where, when violence first erupted, the military attachés evidently acted alone before the diplomats did, where later "one arm of United States policy was working against [Juan] Bosch and one arm was working with him," where later still the State Department tried to promote a coalition regime while the military officers on the spot helped one side against the other.[78] The same problems occurred in Laos during the Eisenhower administration and in the early stages of the Kennedy administration, and in Vietnam during the first months of Ambassador Henry Cabot Lodge's first mission: with the State Department on one side, Defense and CIA on another, no coherent policy could be followed.

Thus coordination is a major concern, yet there is no foolproof method for it, although three are frequently attempted: a coordinating agency with its own staff, an interagency organ, or selected individual coordinators.

The first method, coordination by an agency, raises the troublesome issue of the State Department's role in the making of foreign policy. If we believe that the State Department's adaptation to the "new diplomacy" either is hopeless or will come only slowly, and consider that it is just one agency among others whose right to manage foreign affairs is good, then we must conclude that the job of coordination must be undertaken by an agency at a level higher than State's. This may mean the creation of a new department—comparable to the Defense Department's position vis-à-vis the military services—such as a Department of Foreign Affairs, suggested by the Brookings Institution to provide for "unified direction of the mainstream of foreign policy and operation," [79] and to supervise and direct three component departments: State, Foreign Economic Operations, and Information and Cultural Affairs. Or it may mean, as Governor Rockefeller once suggested and President Eisenhower and Secretary Dulles endorsed, the establishment of a "First Secretary" above the Cabinet, with a staff of his own, in charge of the machinery of coordination.[80] (Given his exalted position, this would undoubtedly result in this machinery becoming a superdepartment.) These proposals have been criticized on a variety of

---

[78] Same, pp. 62 ff.

[79] In "U.S. Foreign Policy," cited, p. 3.

[80] For a discussion, see Don K. Price, ed., *The Secretary of State* (Englewood Cliffs, N.J.: Prentice-Hall, 1960), pp. 185 ff.

counts, the most valid being that the constructions they suggest are too heavy and would add one more formidable layer to the existing ones. If the new layer merely broods above the others (as in the First Secretary proposal), problems of coordination would be complicated, not eased. If the new department actually directs the old ones, yet the latter are still headed by cabinet officers (as in the Brookings suggestion), confusion and dilution of responsibility could persist. True, there is the precedent of the Defense Department, but its job of unification was in fact a long ordeal, and the misgivings raised by its success would probably encourage Congressional opposition to a repetition of the experience.

On the other hand, if we want to try, in what would be a mammoth job of recuperation, to get back into the State Department all the activities relating to foreign affairs that are presently outside its jurisdiction, then we would be internalizing the problem of coordination within the State Department's own structure without solving it. To be able to be the supreme coordinator, the entire department would have to be reorganized, and the Foreign Service rearranged and redefined. Given the diversity of functions that would then be grouped under one roof—a diversity not only of techniques but of goals—the kind of unification achieved in the Defense Department by Secretary McNamara, largely through budgeting techniques based on cost-effectiveness analysis, would be out of the question.

All of these problems explain why the first method of coordination, while the most rational on paper, has never been tried. (There is another reason as well: the problems of coordination involve—perhaps above all else—the cooperation of the agencies in charge of aid, culture, and diplomacy with those in charge of intelligence and defense. No proposal has really addressed itself to this point.)

Hence, greater favor has been shown the second method: coordination by interagency bodies. Here again, there are two versions—more and less heavy. The more heavy type was practiced under President Eisenhower: a mushrooming of committees in the National Security Council "system," which grew exactly like the corpse in Ionesco's nightmarish play. Its procedure of follow-up, debate, and coordination, rather lovingly described by Robert Cutler to Senator Jackson's subcommittee,[81] almost defies analysis. Governor Rockefeller estimated that the number of interdepartmental and interagency committees in the field of international affairs amounted in 1960 to

[81] Jackson, *The National Security Council*, pp. 111 ff.

160.[82] The Operations Coordinating Board had thirty-six working groups. Another student reports that, at one point, forty working groups and committees were in charge of coordinating United States cultural and information activities.[83] To such a machinery, the familiar critique of committees applies—none more devastating than Robert Lovett's reference to them as a "glutinous mass of lonely men" [84]—that they give disproportionate influence to officials who are too low in the hierarchy of their departments to have much sense of responsibility and action, and too parochial or specialized to produce anything like an integrated policy. They are by their very nature not very good at challenging, changing, or transcending their frames of reference; and they tend to treat problems as discrete cases to be analyzed in isolation or through an all too mechanical application of precedents. The papers produced by such committees either reconcile differences on the basis of the lowest common denominator or conceal unreconciled differences under vague formulas—in the best diplomatic tradition, and at the end of a very long process. A recent study of the test-ban negotiations during President Eisenhower's tenure concludes that "the result tended to be a compromise which straddled the issues and occasionally contained contradictory elements . . . one set of obstacles replaced another. . . . Decisions were taken at an extremely slow pace." [85] Mr. Cutler himself, as Executive Secretary of the National Security Council, recognized that to get fresh ideas he had to add *ad hoc* committees to the institutionalized ones. Moreover, the distinction between planning and operations in the NSC system made no sense. This is a considerable price to pay for coordination. But, what is worse, the result is likely to be pseudo-coordination rather than real integration (even at a level of considerable mediocrity). Because the formulas are so bland, so generalized, so easy to interpret in divergent ways, the various services involved remain uncommitted to the outcome, however entangled they may be in the process.

This combination of rigidity in procedure, generality in treatment, and irresponsibility in outcome led President Kennedy to dismantle

---

[82] Same, p. 169.

[83] W. Phillips Davison, *International Political Communication* (New York: Frederick A. Praeger for the Council on Foreign Relations, 1966), pp. 286–88.

[84] Same, p. 87.

[85] Jacobson and Stein, cited, p. 472.

the machinery of the Operations Coordinating Board. But the other kind of interagency formula, which he tended to favor—the task force, put in charge of a concrete problem and geared more directly to crisis and to action—obtained only mixed results. One such body, which has become legendary, was the Executive Committee of the NSC, which debated America's strategy during the Cuban missile crisis. But what made the Executive Committee most remarkable was its exceptional nature as a group not of middle-level representatives but of the highest officials in the United States. The normal task force often had no place in the hierarchy and suffered from a kind of weightlessness that deprived its recommendations, however striking, of the impact one would have wished for them. And the State Department's attitude toward such bodies—"control or divert" [86] —already manifest in the days of OCB, reasserted itself after a few setbacks. As a result, "independent reviews" and "honest appraisals" capable of challenging State Department policies once again became difficult. And, by definition, the task forces, while maintaining flexibility, suffered from the failure to solve coordination problems in situations other than crises.[87]

There remains a third method. When machinery fails, one rediscovers that men make the difference between a good job and a bad job. A decision-making procedure is no substitute for a decision-maker. But the dilemma here is, which decision-maker? At what level? If coordination and decentralization should be sought simultaneously, as a report by Senator Jackson's subcommittee investigating these and related problems has suggested,[88] with an increase in coordinating responsibilities for the desk officers and Assistant Secretaries of State, two difficulties still remain. Will these men have sufficient authority to make the necessary decisions? While there is an analytic difference between policy-making, supposedly at high levels, and its transformation into effective programs, coordination involves a double dose of genuine decision-making, of a kind we might grace with the awkward name of para-policy: the preparation of decisions, which entails choices, and the translation into programs as well as the carrying out of them, which implies directives.

[86] Jackson, *The National Security Council,* p. 47.

[87] It is too early to know whether President Johnson's reorganization, announced in March 1966 and aimed at creating a Senior Interdepartmental Group and Interdepartmental Regional Groups, has been able to discover the golden mean between the top-heavy and the flimsy.

[88] Jackson, *The Secretary of State and the Ambassador,* p. 49.

Second, will there not still remain a need for coordination at a higher level? Joint decisions reached by the officials concerned with the Congo, for instance, or Central Africa, in agencies such as State, Defense, AID, USIA, CIA, and Agriculture, will still have to be co-ordinated with policies concerning other parts of Africa and Western Europe. Decentralized coordination has its limits. If, on the other hand (as the same subcommittee has also suggested [89] and as President Johnson has been inclined to do) the main load is placed at the top—on the Secretary and the Under Secretaries—it over-burdens men whose responsibilities are already crushing, and who, even without it, are already caught between their duties as policy-makers and their administrative tasks.

The gravest consequences raised by the fragmentation of this huge apparatus of the government *and* by the dilemmas of coordination are flaws I have already discussed as problems in the American national style. There inevitably occurs a subtle (or not so subtle) shift from the specific foreign-policy issues to be resolved, to the positions, claims, and perspectives of the participants in the policy machine. The demands of the issue and the merits of alternative choices are subordinated to the demands of the machine and the need to keep it going. Administrative politics replaces foreign policy. As a corollary, the tendency to short-range thinking is reinforced. Time simply cannot be wisely used in such a system; it is miraculous that the wastage is not worse. Time is wasted not just on paperwork and coordination (more paper) but on keeping up with the implacable flow of events. Inevitably, the hierarchy of issues is established by external shocks and necessities rather than by deliberate reflection. The policy-maker is no longer the master of the job, he is driven by events. Importance is defined as and by emergency. Quite apart from the consequences for policy itself, the human toll is considerable.

A third problem is brittleness. When a policy has been selected, it becomes difficult to change since change would require renegotiation within the bureaucracy. This is the reason, for instance, for the frequent rigidity of United States positions on disarmament and arms control or the behavior of the United States delegation in the battle over Article 19. When rigidity leads to failure—but only then—the policy becomes unstuck and sudden reversals become possible.

The difficulties of defining a coherent, integrated policy are compounded by the organization. In the absence of satisfactory coordination, cacophonic pluralism will continue to mar the effectiveness,

[89] Same, p. 14.

not to mention the "image," of America in world affairs. In the spring of 1966, America's response to de Gaulle's announcement that France would withdraw its troops from NATO was extraordinarily feeble, because the various policy-makers in Washington were divided on every conceivable related issue: between those for whom the cultivation of ties between the United States and West Germany came first and those who were eager for arms-control agreements with the Soviet Union; between those for whom the goal of U.S. policy in Western Europe is a partnership of approximate equals and those who believe that bilateral links with privileged allies is less likely to endanger America's predominance in NATO; between those who think that priority must be given to intra-Atlantic ties and those who are for a "policy of movement" toward European reunification. In the absence of any intra-Washington agreement, coherent policy on NATO was obviously impossible: *ad hoc* measures to stop the gap opened by de Gaulle were all that could be agreed on as a single common denominator. During the months that followed, the moves initiated by the Department of Defense, those sponsored by the White House (eager to build bridges to the East), those pushed by the Arms Control and Disarmament Agency, and the various policies advocated within the State Department raised havoc in German-American relations.

Nor will the possible ways in which cacophony could be overcome produce coherent policy. If the president hesitates to intervene, one group of bureaucratic players may still prevail. To change the metaphor, if many cooks prepare different dishes on different stoves, the one who finishes first has the best chance of feeding the hungry customer; when many services support many different policies, the most determined and energetic will probably win. In a contest between several countervailing forces, the alternative to deadlock is breakthrough by one such force. The group that is best at capturing the president's ear (or most eager to act as if it had) has the best chance. This may be better than deadlock. But the rival policies continue underneath, so to speak, and instead of an integrated policy, there is first the determined push of a prevailing group and then a sudden reversal (as in the case of the MLF).

The group that breaks through is usually distinguished more by its will than its wisdom, by its energy than its judgment. Policy by cliques is always a danger; but in a system like ours, the winning clique is likely to be the one that rings the alarm bell of worried activism rather than the one counseling prudence and watchful waiting: viz., Santo Domingo, or the strategy over Article 19 of the U.N. Charter. It is likely to be the one that stresses the things in our unilateral power to do, rather than the one that suggests the difficult and uncertain course of multilateral or bilateral diplomacy, which always seems to leave our policy's fate in other people's hands: viz., the Bay of Pigs, as a method for eliminating the danger of Castroism, or, in the delicate mix of a search for negotiated peace and a quest for a military solution to the Vietnam problem, the way of the former often amounts to little more than a sugar-coating of the latter. The clique that claims to have found a technical solution to political headaches is more likely to prevail than the group that suggests that these headaches ought to be faced frankly and dispelled. Consider the case of the MLF. (Henry Kissinger has written a classic account of this, which ends with his verdict that "one small group in the government . . . acted as a lobby rather than an organ for calmly weighing alternatives."),[90] and the case of the nonproliferation treaty. The lesson is clear but unedifying: the demise of the MLF brought in its wake the decline and dispersion of the State Department "Europeans" who had pushed so hard for their technical short cut; as a result, the balance (or stalemate) between Atlanticists and champions of a *détente* which would have been broken in favor of the former, had the MLF prevailed, was broken in favor of the latter, who were now free to push with equal zeal in the opposite direction—for that other technical short cut, the nonproliferation treaty.

Presidents who are aware of these dangers sometimes try to solve them by methods that contribute to the incoherence. In a desire to restore bureaucratic harmony, the president may settle for a soothing policy of half-measures described as "keeping all options open"—a euphemism for avoiding choice, yet in a way that stacks the cards and insidiously curtails his ultimate freedom of choice. President Kennedy's final decision on the Bay of Pigs, which both accepted the expedition and emasculated it, is a case in point; the course he selected on Vietnam, when pressured by many of his advisers to send troops, was "merely [to] let the decision slide, at the same time ordering the government to set in motion all the preparatory steps for introducing troops." [91] President Johnson's Vietnam policy has been of the same order. It has kept together an administration composed of doves and hawks by means of a subtle blend of measures that are not only

---

[90] *The Troubled Partnership* (New York: McGraw-Hill, for the Council on Foreign Relations, 1966), p. 157.

[91] Hilsman, cited, p. 424.

mutually exclusive, but also too limited to attain any of their conflicting goals yet constantly weighed in favor of escalation. President Johnson's rare decisions on NATO—in December 1964, when Prime Minister Wilson visited him, and in the spring of 1966, when de Gaulle walked out—have also been of this minimal order, avoiding showdowns abroad and within his administration, rather than settling foreign-policy issues and contests of bureaucratic clans. Or else, when the difficulties of coordination are compounded by the seriousness of splits on policy between various agencies or policy-makers, as has often been the case over Vietnam, there is a tendency for the President to leap above the obstacles by reserving the decision to the "innermost circle" in the policy-making process.[92]

Or else, when he realizes the shortcomings of the regular machinery, the president may fall back on flamboyant *ad hoc* devices to restore a sense of unity or correct a faulty course from the outside, so to speak, rather than through internal balancing. These devices also contribute to the characteristic American sense of frenzy and breathless pragmatism in foreign policy; they contribute to the public-relations halo spun around U.S. foreign policy by the president-to-people system. Personal emissaries, special or roving ambassadors, presidential fact-finding missions, vice presidents in orbit are often like meteors: they return all to quickly to the limbo from which they came, never really displacing the constellations, yet adding a fleeting excitement for the star-gazers. Ultimately, coherence can be provided only by the president.

[92] Hilsman, cited, p. 543.

# CHAPTER NINE

# Tying up the Package

In our preceding discussion of the pieces of the puzzle we have remarked constantly on two factors: the dilemmas or drawbacks in the American system reinforce one another (just as the various elements of the American style do); and the more extreme possibilities of deadlock or disaster can be avoided by deliberate action of the president. An effective foreign policy requires that the president not be obsessed by opinion, that the career personnel and temporary recruits in the civil service coexist fruitfully, that Congress be responsible, that the fragmented executive branch be well coordinated. The whole package must be tied together, so that the drawbacks are minimized instead of cumulative. There are so many pulls and pushes that the problem of giving a sense of purpose to the whole and of keeping the machinery of government on course is formidable despite the dominance of the presidency.

Not too surprisingly, however, the ways the package can be tied raise problems of their own. Between the requirements of effectiveness abroad and the requirements of domestic success, there is a permanent tension. This tension will be described in terms of three questions: Who is in charge? How is it done? How is it seen abroad?

## I. The Men

The emergence of the presidency as the focus of pressures and hopes and the center of action, the nature of the governmental bureaucracy, and the need for leadership to override Congressional trench warfare and the fragmentation of the executive branch—all these factors throw an enormous responsibility on the shoulders of the one man who can keep the system in operation, the president. As in any advanced and institutionalized polity, to be sure, the system operates even with a mediocre president—but only as long as he has at least the virtue of selecting capable aides; even then, the machine may perform at less than its optimal level.

Insofar as foreign policy is concerned, the package is such that only the men at the top, the president and the secretary of state, can tie it up. Since World War II, this is indeed where the package has been tied: the "teams" of Truman and Marshall, Truman and Acheson, Eisenhower and Dulles prove it. Yet the price these men paid for success achieved at such an altitude was great, both in organizational and in purely political terms.

## A. *Organizational Choices*

In deciding how to organize their administration of foreign policy, presidents face two kinds of choices. First, should they not only take final responsibility for "tying up the package," but also assume a primary and decisive role in that process; or should they rely for this on their secretary of state, who thus becomes their *alter ego* in all matters pertaining to America's foreign relations? Second, should they advocate a tidy administration and a rigorous, hierarchical organization, or should they be the experimental promoters of organizational pluralism—flexible, competitive, occasionally untidy, yet imaginative? In practice, these two sets of questions are related: to rely primarily on the secretary of state is a way of showing a commitment to "straight lines and tidy boxes"; to retain the primary and decisive role for oneself is easier when one keeps one's subordinates permanently on their toes (and sometimes in confusion), so as to prevent the machine from slowing one down, isolating one, or depriving one of the chance to be a "Great Initiator." Yet for analytical purposes, it may be useful to examine the two questions separately.

On the first issue, the president's reliance on the secretary of state—manifested by Truman, by Eisenhower, and increasingly by Johnson—is likely to be effective only so long as three conditions are met. One is that the president does not disagree so profoundly on important issues with his secretary of state that the country emerges with two policies at the top. President Truman's experience with Secretary of State Byrnes was rather exceptional, but his account of the troubles he had in 1948 imposing his policy on Palestine is most suggestive.[1] Another condition is that the secretary of

[1] See his stern comments in *Memoirs*, Vol. II (New York: Signet Books, 1956), pp. 192 ff.

state be a first-rate administrator and "initiator" within his own department. Otherwise, many of the problems of coordination discussed in the preceding chapter will remain unsettled and unsettling. One of the State Department's problems during the Dulles era was the personal way in which the secretary of state conducted diplomacy: he put his relation with the president far above his relations with the department, and as a result the State Department staff was not always sure of his intentions, when he was abroad or in the air. Moreover, when his illness removed him from the scene, the penalty that had to be paid became obvious. It had been less a matter of confusion than a kind of flattening of the imagination, a dampening of initiative (to which, of course, Dulles' brutal way of insuring the loyalty of his department was not exactly alien). The gap between Dulles' subtle tactical moves or improvisations, at what one could call a level of inspiration, and the routine of a department reduced to being a huge paper-producing contributor to the NSC machinery, with low morale and inadequate guidance, has had lasting and vicious effects.

The third condition (usually met by Secretary Dulles) is that the secretary of state be sufficiently forceful to prevent the displacement of political considerations by purely military ones in the coordination of foreign and defense policies, and to define a foreign policy that is fully integrated not only with the defense establishment but also with "our third Foreign Office," the Treasury. Dean Acheson, certainly an excellent administrator and unlikely to go down in history as a weak secretary of state, nevertheless performed less than perfectly in this respect at crucial moments; the relative indifference of the State Department to the military budget in 1949–50 led to a rude awakening in Korea; in the Korean War, during the fateful period of September–November 1950, he fell into the familiar trap of letting military considerations and prospects determine the nature and the scope of political objectives. As for Secretary Rusk, he has been criticized for "regarding Vietnam as essentially a military problem." [2]

If the president is particularly aware of the importance and difficulty of coordinating State with Defense, Treasury, and all the other agencies with a share in foreign affairs, and if he realizes how hard it is for the secretary of state to be at the same time the chief coordinator, the president's substitute in the making of policy, and the department's administrator, he will decide to take charge himself of the defining and carrying out of the administration's chief policies.

[2] Roger Hilsman, *To Move a Nation* (New York: Doubleday, 1967), p. 421.

Of course, administrative problems then arise concerning relations between the president's Executive Office and the departments and agencies. The dimensions of these problems were revealed in Kennedy's administration even more than in Franklin D. Roosevelt's, which gave a lower priority to foreign affairs. As many obversers have pointed out, it is essential that the president's staff in charge of foreign affairs remain small; the personal assistant's usefulness decreases as his staff increases, and any institutionalization of his job (such as the creation of an Office of National Security Affairs) would add "another echelon, another level for clearances, another level for negotiations."[3] On the other hand, a small staff in the White House, even if it is composed of men who are brilliantly efficient and discreet (as it was under Kennedy), has drawbacks. Even the most gifted group cannot assure that all important matters receive the proper attention (more will be said on this point later). By its very nature, a small staff tends to operate as a kind of court of last resort that selects the most important issues from those the departments push toward the president; it screens what has already been presented, rather than establishing a hierarchy of importance independent of the flow of current business. Of course, on behalf of the president it can initiate, in the sense of bringing to a department's attention the issues that ought to be considered in anticipation, so to speak; but it can do little more.

This situation raises the problem of the relation between the president's staff and the departments. Almost inevitably, however graceful the manners of the officials in both, there will be tension and resentments. The president's staff will be impatient with at least some of the agencies (and the State Department, given its own internal problems, is of course the main candidate for the role of prime target); the Department will regret the intrusions of the president's men, in whom it will see, if not gifted amateurs, then free-wheeling operators whose self-importance is not matched by administrative responsibility. Since a policy does not deserve the name unless and until it is carried out, and since implementation remains the departments' bailiwick, the situation can result in a final failure of the Executive Office's drive for action and in perpetuation of the tension. Schlesinger, describing problems in policy toward Latin America and

[3] Richard Neustadt, in Senator Henry M. Jackson, ed., *The National Security Council: Jackson Subcommittee Papers on Policy-Making at the Presidential Level* (New York: Frederick A. Praeger, 1965), p. 282.

Italy during President Kennedy's administration, gives a wealth of examples.[4]

Lastly, the president's men may suffer at times from the desire, delicately described by one of them while still in office,[5] to project the right image or correct the popular image they think they have. In other words, there is a problem of presidential advisers' insecurity. This insecurity usually displays itself in a search for glamor, or gimmicks, or gestures. Even under President Eisenhower, whose assistants in foreign affairs had to live (perilously) under the watchful eye of Secretary Dulles, cockeyed initiatives were taken by presidential aides in search of positive images.

These defects can be remedied by a president capable of dominating his staff. If his aides are too dependent on the departments' initiatives and implementations, he can try to anticipate events (as Kennedy did when he set up a task force on Iran) and keep the bureaucracy on its toes. He can also curb his aides' penchant for drama. But the problem of the president's relation to the bureaucracy cannot be entirely eliminated. If he takes an initiative that is not properly communicated to the departments, an incident as bizarre as President Kennedy's unexecuted order to remove United States missiles from Turkey, or President Eisenhower's "wrong" invitation to Khrushchev (the conditions he wanted put on the invitation were misunderstood by the State Department) [6] may occur. On the other hand, if he keeps interfering with the hierarchy, trying to shake the machinery into faster responses and fresher ideas, then Bohlen's "candid" answer to Kennedy, when asked what was wrong with the State Department, becomes valid: "You are." [7] For although one can argue strongly on paper that action at and from the center need not mean interference with the line, because such action would be "strategic" instead of tactical, and because command is

---

[4] Arthur M. Schlesinger, Jr., *A Thousand Days: John F. Kennedy in the White House* (Boston: Houghton Mifflin, 1965), pp. 759–60, 868. See also Delesseps Morrison, *Latin American Mission* (New York: Simon and Schuster, 1965), on the tensions over Latin American policy between "activist" White House officials and more skeptical officials in the State Department during the Kennedy administration.

[5] Theodore C. Sorensen, *Decision-Making in the White House* (New York: Columbia University Press, 1963), pp. 57 ff.

[6] Dwight D. Eisenhower, *Waging Peace* (New York: Doubleday, 1965), pp. 4–5 ff.

[7] Schlesinger, cited, p. 431.

not interference, in practice the distinctions are blurred. The issue discussed by Arthur Schlesinger—how can a president insist both that the departments remain free to dissent and that they be committed to his policies—cannot easily be settled. It is interesting to observe the discrepancy between the views of two Harvard colleagues who have been deeply involved in problems of the presidency and foreign affairs: Robert Bowie, who served under Secretary Dulles (and again under Dean Rusk), writing during the Kennedy administration, pleaded that the secretary of state be the president's chief of staff in foreign policy and asked for interagency coordination at agency level. Richard Neustadt, on the other hand, clearly puts his hopes on the president and his staff.[8]

This brings me to the second dilemma, concerning methods of administration. It is easy to see that both the "tidy" and the "pluralist" methods present dangers for sound foreign policy. (Of course, the president may try to follow a middle course, but it is bound to be closer to one or the other extreme. Neustadt has noted that President Truman believed in tidy administration but tended to act more like a pluralist, at least on domestic issues.)[9] The tidier method, which relies on organization charts, has obvious advantages from the somewhat bloodless viewpoint of order but one enormous drawback: given the size of the executive branch, it is stifling. The Eisenhower administration well demonstrated the system's effects. First, the man to whom the President gave the main responsibility was able to carry out foreign policy only by removing his sphere of operations from the formidable coordination procedures established to maintain tidiness. Second, the machinery succeeded in making order prevail at the expense of substance or initiative; disagreements were not so much resolved as smothered; and the result was to shield the President not only from controversy but almost from his own office in the White House. Judicious arbitration replaced political decision-making. Third, when the President or his aides took foreign-policy initiatives, such as the Atoms for Peace plan or the "Open Skies" proposal, as if groping to put some life into a machinery that turned live issues into dead paper, the initiatives remained outside the policy machine, like exclamation marks in the margins of a letter.

An exuberant and deliberate untidiness has drawbacks of its own, however. If the first approach is stifling, the second is messy; if the

---

[8] See Robert Bowie, *Shaping the Future* (New York: Columbia University Press, 1964), Ch. 3, and Neustadt in Jackson, cited, pp. 281 ff.

[9] *Presidential Power* (New York: John Wiley & Sons, 1960), Ch. 7.

first produces the appearance of homogeneity at the cost of vigor, clarity, or substance, the second can result in cacophony, an over-abundance of substantive proposals, and disruptive clear-cut dis-agreements. President Kennedy's appointment of four ex-governors as subordinates of the secretary of state before he had chosen the latter and his fondness for the interplay of conflicting viewpoints en-sured that the only guarantee of consistency and cohesion would be his own perpetual vigilance—a superhuman requirement. Since no president can spend his term in office making decisions at an early point before the disagreement between cliques has broken out into the open and carrying these decisions out personally so that the op-position of viewpoints does not reappear, a kind of pluralism of foreign policies prevailed whenever President Kennedy wanted to "keep his options open" and his policy flexible, as in Atlantic affairs in 1963,[10] or whenever the decisions he reached were essentially tac-tical, as in Vietnam. The confusion that followed his Nassau meeting with Prime Minister Macmillan concerning the agreement they had made, continuing well into the Johnson administration, and the un-derlying uncertainties about U.S. policy in Vietnam, which have plagued his successor, can be traced back in part to his methods of government. In August 1963 a handful of State and Defense Depart-ment officials, who had not consulted their superiors, drafted instruc-tions to the field on the American attitude toward Diem that consti-tuted a reversal of policy, which the President inadvertently en-dorsed only to regret it afterward. This episode is a thought-provoking example of what can happen when motion becomes insep-arable from confusion.[11]

The truth of the matter is that the United States government is too complex and too sprawling, the problems it faces are too difficult for anything like a monolithic policy to emerge. If its policies give the impression of monolithic coherence, they are unlikely to be very good; they may be a set of guidelines and principles more or less covered by (rather than integrated with) a strategic doctrine, but this is not enough to insure flexibility and relevance. If flexibility and specificity are primary concerns, the outcome is more likely to be a pluralistic administration, kept, if not on the same track, at least in the same direction by the president's necessarily discontinuous asser-tions of command. Presidents have tried to find a good intermediate solution. But there is, alas, such a thing as having the worst of all

[10] Schlesinger, cited, pp. 57 ff.
[11] Same, pp. 990 ff.

possible worlds, especially if one takes both organizational dilemmas into account.

It is not inconceivable that a president would want to find a middle ground in both respects: to be his own master in foreign policy without downplaying the secretary of state or setting up a powerful staff of his own; and to have an orderly bureaucracy without excessive loss of initiative and flexibility. The trouble is that a president without a strong staff, or without the willingness to give his aides a strong voice, is at the mercy of his cabinet and at the mercy of short-circuits in coordination. If there is no one to remind him of the relevance of "routine" U-2 flights to a summit conference with the Russian premier, the flights will go on. If the staff is weak or relegated to the background, yet the president insists on primacy and has a not very strong secretary of state, foreign policy may lose the sureness of touch that strong secretaries of state can provide and that strong presidents can develop when they have the required talent and executive assistance.

As for a compromise between the two administrative models, the result could be a strange hybrid: a regime in which the external impression of cohesiveness and tidiness coexists with frequent changes of policy directions, due to the outcomes of clashes among cliques and clan rivalries. In the untidier model, the president ultimately settles the policies after the bureaucratic clashes and rivalries have had their day, keeping himself above the din so as to preserve his role as initiator and arbitrator. But in the hybrid, he would be himself navigating the ship of state by frequent changes of course corresponding to the pressures on him. In one instance, confusion is tempered and interrupted by presidential direction; in the other, the direction itself is confused and tipsy. An analysis of our intervention in the Dominican Republic and of our policy toward Europe since 1963 in the light of these questions is most disturbing.

## B. *Political Choices*

Organizational problems are fierce, insofar as they have political repercussions. But there are fundamental political problems as well in a system that tends to push almost all major political issues up to the presidency. That formidable complex of sprawling institutions, of pressures, checks, and balances which is the United States government is capped by one man. Systems in which the leader of the executive is a member of a coherent political party or the boss of a well-oiled career bureaucracy do not ordinarily romanticize the man at the top unless he is an exceptional and charismatic savior. The American system of government seems unable to prevent a kind of hand-wringing, starry-eyed, and slightly embarrassing deification of the man in the White House, a doleful celebration of his solitude and his burdens. (When things go badly, there is, of course, a tendency to besmirch the fallen idol.) Institutional overcomplexity breeds paralysis, and a compensatory overpersonalization of power. But whether the coexistence of opposites amounts to the *juste milieu* is doubtful. For although it may well be that no organization could possibly be solid and sound enough to cope well with all the problems the United States government faces, "the easy slogan that all the nation ever needs is a good president who will take care of everything" [12] is obviously unsound too. No president, whatever his method of administration or his attitude toward the secretary of state, can work on all fronts at once. His task is too great and the machinery is too cumbersome; he must concentrate on certain key issues. Moreover, any attempt to do a great deal would result in two errors: the machinery would get in the way, either because it ground too slowly or because it suffers from pluralist disorder; and the public's attention (and Congress') would wander, through fatigue and bewilderment. Thus, the president must be selective. His fundamental political problem is the allocation of time.

First, how does he select the issues on which he will concentrate his energies? Obviously, any president worth his salt will try to anticipate at least some events and to set trends in motion or accelerate others: the creation of NATO, Atoms for Peace, the Alliance for Progress, and the test ban are cases in point. However, for reasons in which many factors play a part—such as the machinery's difficulties in planning, the nature of American pragmatism, public or Congressional taboos, America's position in the world as the major *status quo* power fighting a defensive political war against forces of change or in order to gain control of those forces, the international system itself—the selection more often than not is made by the events themselves. The domestic system reinforces the bent toward crisis diplomacy.

When no emergency threatens, the president's time is divided between domestic affairs and the balancing of views and pressures on foreign policy within his administration. When an emergency occurs, the president's chances of getting the machinery going, get-

[12] Robert McCamy, *Conduct of the New Diplomacy* (New York: Harper & Row, 1964), p. 9.

ting public support, and enlisting the cooperation of Congress are at their best. The Marshall Plan, Korea, Quemoy and Matsu, Berlin, the Middle East crises, the Soviet Union's resumption of nuclear testing, Vietnam since the beginning of 1965: these were the events and issues on which presidents have spent most of their foreign-policy time, and on which the man has most thoroughly mobilized the institutions. A good president is one who seizes an emergency as an opportunity. This is what Kennedy did when he turned the Cuban missile crisis into an opportunity to get a nuclear test-ban agreement at last. Presidential initiatives unconnected with crises have a rougher time, for unless events establish a connection between his initiatives and an emergency (for instance, the Korean War gave impetus to the idea of making NATO an integrated organization; the threat of Castro gave a "security" angle to the Alliance for Progress), the presidents risk wasting their efforts, either because they will not have the time to see the matter through, their attention being diverted by emergencies and domestic affairs, or because after an initial shock "foreign policy slip[s] back from men to institutions." [13]

The next question could be phrased, what are the consequences of neglect? The pressure of time leads to the same results as pragmatism. A president's failure or refusal to give high priority to an issue that is not yet an emergency often insures that it will turn into one, and that curative measures at a perilous level will have to be taken where quietly preventive ones might otherwise have been tried. Before June 1950, President Truman did not treat Korea as a very important area. Under President Eisenhower, policy toward Africa was underdeveloped and later had to be improvised in and through the Congo and other crises. The same thing could be said about U.S. policy in Indochina, until the fateful winter of 1954. Under Kennedy, after the Bay of Pigs and the Punta del Este Conference, Cuba was regarded more as a minor nuisance than as a potential arena for a major challenge—an oversight that may have encouraged the Soviet Union to gamble in the summer of 1962. And the issue of the United States' nuclear relations with Western Europe was dealt with only fitfully until the cancellation of the Skybolt missile precipitated a crisis; when the crisis was over, the issue disappeared again from President Kennedy's agenda and later from President Johnson's, except for a brief moment in December, 1964, when Prime Minister Wilson's visit brought it up again. President Johnson's neglect of Europe in 1965 and early 1966, because of Vietnam and despite de

[13] Schlesinger, cited, p. 918.

Gaulle's reiterated threats, allowed the French president to stage his withdrawal from NATO under optimum conditions, and with optimum results.

The confusion in the nuclear policies of NATO reveals another possible consequence of presidential neglect: a costly and confusing conflict of interests, in a policy vacuum, with the most determined group pushing ahead, can go on while and because the president is unaware of the speed and brutality of the push. This was the case in the 1963 campaign for the MLF.

A third effect of insufficient attention being paid a given issue by the president is that it will prolong the policy *status quo* while the situation is gradually eroded by events. To a degree, this is what happened with Cuba at the end of the Batista regime, with the Dominican Republic early in 1965, and with Vietnam policy under Eisenhower and Kennedy. Indeed, President Kennedy's failure to give his full attention to Vietnam really combined all three drawbacks: it prepared for the tragic military escalation that followed while already "fatally narrowing" the choices; it left the suggested alternative policies in a kind of competitive, undecided coexistence; and it perpetuated the Diem regime's *status quo* in South Vietnam which collapsed just before President Kennedy's own death. Kennedy's deliberate postponement (in large part for domestic reasons) of the issues of China's entry into the United Nations and Formosa's fate has had less tragic consequences thus far but may be as serious in the future. And his successor's failure to anticipate before October 1966 the West Europeans' desire (whether Gaullist or not) to alter the Cold War *status quo* in Central Europe has also proved costly, for his new policy came at a time and in a way that upset the West Germans instead of pleasing them.

Another question is how should the president handle the issues to which he has given priority? Most of the important foreign-policy campaigns must be waged on several fronts, and the outcome may depend on what front was given precedence. Thus, even after the president has decided which problem is vital, he must make another set of decisions as to the essential front in the battle over the issue.

There is, in the first place, a tension between the foreign and domestic fronts. Ought the president and secretary of state to decide that their primary constituency is the domestic constituency of Congress and the public, or the foreign one, in particular the United States' allies and the neutrals? Each choice has its dangers. Secretary of State Acheson rather single-mindedly preferred the foreign clientele and alienated the domestic one.[14] Dulles, having learned the lesson, gained Congressional support along with really remarkable unpopularity abroad (with the exception of a few supporters like Chancellor Adenauer).[15] Here again, there is no perfect solution, but the worst is probably to say different things to different publics. Before his secretaryship, Dulles brought it off in his work on the Japanese Peace Treaty, skillfully emphasizing different issues depending on whether he addressed himself to the American public or to foreign audiences. (The latter heard more about substance and politics than about morality and procedure, subjects he liked to stress in talking to American audiences.) [16] The same acrobatics turned out to be less artistic during the Suez crisis, especially the episode of the Users' Association.

What went wrong in the summer of 1956 had a great deal to do with the second problem in choosing fronts: the problem of tension between different elements within the foreign constituency, when the president must choose which to reward or support, which to disappoint. If he chooses not to choose overtly, and to say different things to each, he is juggling with balls that may crash at his feet. The different publics communicate, and what he tells one foreign official is overheard by another, etc. During the Suez crisis, Prime Minister Eden became exasperated with the divergence between what Dulles was apparently telling the Egyptian government in public—i.e., that it had to disgorge what it had swallowed—and what Dulles and Eisenhower told the British both publicly and privately—i.e., that the disgorging should not be sought by force. And anger led Eden to make the fateful moves that brought the crisis to a boil. Similarly, in the days that followed the Nassau meeting, President Kennedy permitted some officials to suggest to France that the part of the Anglo-American agreement that mattered was the one that evidently put France on the same level as England (above the other Europeans); but Under Secretary of State George Ball went to Germany and NATO headquarters to emphasize the MLF component, i.e., the segment that was attractive to the Germans and least acceptable to

[14] See Norman Graebner, ed., *An Uncertain Tradition* (New York: McGraw Hill, 1961), Ch. 14.

[15] See, for instance, Anthony Eden's *Full Circle* (Boston: Houghton Mifflin, 1960) and Dirk Stikker's *Men of Responsibility* (New York: Harper & Row, 1967), *passim*.

[16] Bernard C. Cohen, *The Political Process and Foreign Policy* (Princeton University Press, 1957), pp. 35 ff.

the French.[17] De Gaulle's press conference of January 14, 1963, drew a crashing conclusion from a situation that was probably more mixed up than Machiavellian.

A third aspect of the problem of choosing fronts concerns the efforts to transcend the embarrassment of the choices, to overcome the contradictions inherent in making different speeches to different audiences, through hyperbole, oversell, and advertising. But this is escapism rather than policy.

## II.  The Methods

It would be wrong to suggest that the organizational and political problems I have discussed above are insoluble: they have often been solved. Presidents without skill make a hash of things; skillful presidents minimize the trouble. But even when the dilemmas are handled skillfully, the methods used for "tying the package" create serious problems of their own.

Almost inevitably, given the nature of the American system, America's political predispositions, and America's way of viewing itself as a leader of other nations (rather than as a power standing alone or dominating others), the method used to make American foreign policy effective is consensus-building. On the one hand, the president must try, as we have seen, to get as broad support as possible from the public, Congress, and all the elements of the bureaucracy. This does not mean that he will not act on the world stage until he has coaxed or coerced the pieces into a package acceptable to them, since his constitutional independent power allows him to act first and bargain later. Indeed, action creates a kind of presumption in his favor and often serves as a catalyst or crystallizer of support. However, a kind of covert bargaining, or anticipation of future bargaining, often conditions the action. Since consensus is of the essence, the move will be made not merely to respond to an external need; it will also be calculated to make the subsequent bargaining easier. Making the decision is only the beginning of the policy process, after all. The consensus the president needs must cover the whole process and give legitimacy to the entire course of action. As a result, there is an acute risk of conflict between external requirements of effectiveness and internal requirements of consensus. While

[17] Schlesinger, cited, pp. 865–66.

it is true that "a foreign policy which wrecks [the president's] domestic policy program or undermines his power at home leaves him incapable of conducting any effective foreign policy," [18] a foreign-policy-maker hypnotized by domestic efficiency may well be internationally impotent.

On the other hand, the president aims at obtaining broad support abroad, especially with allies and friendly neutrals. Now, all leading powers are engaged in building up a consensus in their favor abroad. Any regime based on consent, any policy that does not rely on force alone, especially needs to rally consensus around itself. The particular risk an American president runs is that of a conflict between the aim of external support and the tendency to try to reach it by using familiar methods of domestic consensus-building. The effects of the method on the policy are often disastrous.

A. *Domestic Consensus-Building:*
   *The Diversion from Foreign Policy*

If "conservatism is the English metier," [19] consensus-building is the American one. A radical shift in American foreign policy such as that of 1947–48 could occur because the Democratic President was able to carry with him a predominantly Republican Congress. President Eisenhower had the job of incorporating into the consensus, weakened by the Korean War, as many Republicans as he could of those who had remained outside. And President Kennedy, as Schlesinger reports and as is confirmed by his pattern of appointments, "did not perceive himself as a partisan President, nor did he wish the country so to perceive him." [20] Whether or not Schlesinger's analysis of why Kennedy preferred the "politics of consensus" to the "politics of combat" is correct (i.e., because of the president's anguish about the destructive and divisive instincts below the surface of American life), his analysis of Kennedy's behavior is. And President Johnson, of course, has tried to be the man who speaks for the great majority of the people, who listens to all, reasons with all, and strikes the right balance.

Domestic consensus-building raises many problems for foreign

---

[18] Philip Geyelin, *Lyndon B. Johnson and the World* (New York: Frederick A. Praeger, 1966), p. 149.

[19] Waltz, *Foreign Policy and Democratic Politics* (Boston: Little, Brown, 1967), p. 61.

[20] Schlesinger, cited, pp. 723–24.

policy: those which are related to the circumstances in which consensus-building works best, those which result from the process itself, those which pertain to the instruments used by the president to develop and preserve consensus, and those which are connected with the casualties of the process.

THE CIRCUMSTANCES OF CRISIS DIPLOMACY

Consensus-building immeasurably reinforces the tendency in American life toward crisis politics. In domestic affairs, periods of crisis enable a president to mobilize public, Congressional, and bureaucratic support for measures that might have averted the crisis had they been taken earlier but for which there was no support before: viz., the Hundred Days of 1933, the civil-rights advances of 1964–65. The same is true in foreign affairs. Normally, the policy-making process is an ordeal, in which in-fighting often reaches vast proportions. A crisis abroad acts like a truce at home; also, it makes it easier to restrict policy-making to a smaller, inner circle, and thus alleviates the ordeal. To argue that this charge is a truism, since a crisis is nothing but a situation defined as such by the administration, shows more sophistry than sophistication.[21] There is an element of choice in the presentation of an issue as a crisis, and it is possible to argue either that certain issues ought not to have been presented as crises because no vital United States interest was involved (Lebanon, the Dominican Republic, or even Vietnam), or that others were presented as crises for tactical reasons only (the Truman Doctrine). However, an examination of the record shows that more often than not a crisis is, to the policy-makers, not an event of debatable relevance to the U.S. interests which they *choose* to treat as an emergency, but an event believed, rightly or wrongly, to be of indisputable importance, creating a *compelling necessity* for action. The Dominican situation was a crisis not because of the coup (it wasn't the first), or because the president used this coup as a pretext for a policy, but because the president felt under a kind of obligation to act in the way he did. This feeling was created by a complicated set of factors we have examined in previous chapters: the possible consequences of certain events for America's position in the world, American reflexes and predispositions, and the American political process. In other words, there is no point in trying to find a purely objective and rational criterion: a crisis is not any event that threatens the American position, nor is it (usually) an event the administration simply decides to treat

[21] Waltz, cited, p. 108.

as a crisis; a crisis is an event it *sees* as a challenge and feels it must respond to.

This uncomfortable distinction has a discomforting point. If an objective and rational definition of a crisis in American foreign policy were possible, the consequences of the crisis approach would not be so bad. But instead, when a crisis breaks out, a policy is defined and approved to cope with it; when things settle down again, the government's attention moves on to the next crisis, but, since a consensus was presumably established around the first crisis policy, it keeps on running, once set in motion, even if the tracks now pass through a different landscape. So the crisis approach only strengthens the brittleness of American policy, the *ad hoc* character of American pragmatism. (It also helps one understand why the most widespread scholarly approach to the study of foreign policy in America concerns "decision-making," even though it tends, quite wrongly, to analyze policy as a series of discrete decisions, thus artificially breaking up a flow in which the execution of one decision is preparation for the next.) At any moment, American foreign policy can be analyzed as a set of policies that represent more or less protracted brainstorms provoked by crises and piously preserved since, a sedimentation of routinized inspirations. Its jerkiness does not imply discontinuity, since each inspiration keeps running its course. But continuity is achieved mechanically, through bureaucratic persistence rather than through purposeful statecraft. Consequently, the crisis approach to foreign policy breeds new crises: it is a vicious circle.

But how many simultaneous crises can the system tolerate? Consensus-building is frequently such an ordeal that it pushes into the background all the non-crisis strands of policy. What would happen if two major emergencies burst upon the scene simultaneously is more intriguing than reassuring. Vietnam, since late 1965, has dominated public affairs, like a painful corn that hurts so much one feels one's whole body as all toe; thus, no one has paid enough attention to the NATO crisis. Concentration on Vietnam left American diplomacy sluggish and embarrassed in the early phase of the 1967 Middle East crisis: the main idea was to gain time so as to muddle or "worry through," and only the speed and smashing success of Israel's strike saved us from having to face two protracted calamities. The Executive Committee that dealt with Cuba would have been hard pressed to cope with a crisis in Berlin; the various policy-making groups dealing with Berlin have found that theirs was a full-time job.

A third, probably most serious, drawback concerns the kinds of solutions which crises breed and around which consensus forms. Naturally, many crises were solved well. The Truman Doctrine, the Marshall Plan, the handling of the Quemoy-Matsu crises of 1955 and 1958, the decisions made by President Kennedy in Laos and during the Berlin crisis of 1961, the Cuban missile crisis—all these cases show that crises have been well handled and that support in emergencies can, so to speak, be rallied in depth without damaging the foreign policy of the United States. But the coin has a darker side: crisis diplomacy can encourage foreign-policy decisions that are improvised, abrupt, and lacking in candor.

Crisis diplomacy is by and large improvised diplomacy. Improvisations can be brilliant, as President Kennedy's handling of the missile crisis was. Yet without wanting in the least to tarnish his finest hour, I must add that its success was due not only to a fine blend of momentary moderation and ominous menace, but also to the availability of adequate power. Similarly, a less brilliant diplomatic improvisation—over Berlin, in the summer of 1961—led to excellent results because what mattered was less the negotiating "posture" of the United States than military preparation and determination. Unfortunately, not every crisis is one in which force can be a substitute for or corrective to diplomacy. The perfect adequacy of United States military power is a talisman only in direct confrontations with major enemies. It loses its potency in incidents involving friends, or in civil wars; and it is then that crises in which timing is of the essence are diplomatically most dangerous. When the challenge is of the slow-fuse variety—as in the case of the Marshall Plan (Europe's predicament was real but *imminent* collapse was not a consideration)—then there is time for wisdom and efficiency. But when the disaster is imminent or the deadline impending, there may not be time to integrate the different services and their varying frames of analysis before acting. As a result, short-term considerations are likely to triumph, the urgent issues driving out what may well be the important ones in the long run. Policy solutions will be uneasy and unsteady compromises between what the president deems most likely to form a consensus and what the crisis seems to require. This means policy by trial and error, a need to hit again if one misses. This is why we get the disconcerting impression of day-to-day fluctuations, when Washington diversity goes to work in an emergency. Rarely are things quite as remarkably fouled up as they were during the Dominican crisis: the discord of services, cliques and persons along the Potomac, the ups and downs of the Dominican forces in battle, and the rise and fall of personalities on the spot made for a delirious fever chart—only to have the United States adopt, late in July, after countless detours, a procedure which McGeorge Bundy, the President's Special Assistant for National Security Affairs, had already recommended in May and which implicitly repudiated other U.S. efforts to set up a Dominican military junta. But there are many examples. Compare the Nassau meeting and the Cuban missile crisis, two months earlier, for instance. In one case, American military power gave the policy-makers a kind of assurance that seems to have inspired them. In the other, where subtler issues were at stake, where the uncertainties were assuredly not greater, but where the power to shape them seemed more problematical, since the United States had to deal with friends, the sure touch gave way to fumbles.

Even the successful improvisations, in which diplomacy works behind the shield of America's military might, have the limitation that their success does not go beyond the issues and circumstances of the crisis at hand. Sometimes, there is little one could do to prevent a recurrence of the crisis. No magic formula acceptable to both sides and involving no major concessions could have disposed of the Berlin "anomaly" in, say, 1959 and prevented a new crisis in 1961. But emergencies are never the best occasion for dealing with lasting problems. The consensus achieved can be as deceptive as the solution improvised. In the Cuban missile crisis, for example, the President devised a way of throwing the Soviet missiles out of Cuba and he had the chance to put international pressure on Cuba to permit inspection, but the opportunity was not exploited since that problem was only marginal during the crisis—a loss that has often been criticized even by men who supported him at the time. The Quemoy-Matsu emergencies were firmly handled by a technique that played with "the threat that leaves something to chance," but, as Eisenhower himself has said, attempts to get Chiang Kai-shek to evacuate the islands or reduce his forces there failed utterly.[22]

The shortsightedness of this crisis approach, which consensus-building engenders, only adds to the American habit of plunging into an activist phase of foreign policy without adequate preparation. As

[22] Dwight D. Eisenhower, *Mandate for Change* (New York: Doubleday, 1963), p. 574.

one observer of American institutions has put it, the more the president enhances his power so as to be able to deal with crises as the national leader, the greater the gap between his immediate means and his broader ends.[23]

It is not surprising, then, that crisis diplomacy often leads to abrupt decisions where protracted negotiations would have been preferable. The American instinct to "do something" takes over and justifies itself with the notion that the only proper way to handle an emergency is to respond in some striking fashion. Once again, the reflexes of the style and the requisites for consensus converge. Among the examples that come to mind, there is Eisenhower's decision to send Marines to Lebanon when he heard the news of revolution in Iraq—followed a year later by a visit to Washington by the new Premier of Lebanon, "formerly a leader of the rebel forces" against whom the landing had been ordered, who rubbed salt into the wound by saying "with a laugh that it would have been better had the United States held off sending troops but merely sent Mr. Murphy to straighten out the situation." [24] Another example is the decision to land Marines in the Dominican Republic to "protect American lives" but also to prevent an extremely hypothetical Communist take-over of the "popular democratic revolution" there. The idea of orienting the revolution in a positive direction, which would have required a great deal of tact and persistence, was discarded in favor of more spectacular moves.[25] The United States' abrupt suspension of economic aid to both India and Pakistan in the Kashmir war of 1965—a dramatic move that contrasted with the Soviet Union's smoother behavior—ultimately permitted the Soviets to take over a diplomatic role which the United States had thus foreclosed.

Finally, there is one other subtle difficulty with the decisions reached through crisis diplomacy: an administration may be tempted—although, as I have said earlier, this is not the general case—to engineer crises so that it can get things done. This fabrication of an event that is of dubious diplomatic value even when it is authentic accentuates all the defects we have mentioned. This has been especially true with foreign-aid measures, for which the exec-

[23] James MacGregor Burns, *Presidential Government* (Boston: Houghton, Mifflin, 1966), p. 45.

[24] Eisenhower, *Waging Peace*, p. 289.

[25] John Bartlow Martin, *Overtaken by Events* (New York: Doubleday, 1966), p. 705, on Ambassador Bennett's refusal to mediate between the "rebels" and their foes.

utive branch has tried to rally Congress with appeals that "have borne the characteristic odor of crisis," [26] but that have undercut the simultaneous efforts to put aid on a long-term basis. This crisis, or crash, approach has helped to tie the issue of foreign aid to the issue of military security far longer than was necessary or wise. When the "response" to the "crisis" turns out to have been miscalculated, the underlying problem remains: this was the case with the Trade Expansion Act after Great Britain's failure to gain entry into the EEC. And the deceived supporters see to it that consensus will have to be built from the ground up the next time.

## THE PROCESS OF CONSENSUS-BUILDING

The flaws of crisis diplomacy, someone may argue, are justifiable because they are the necessary blemishes marring the best way to build consensus. The trouble is that the process by which the consensus is formed and by which the president rallies the disparate forces whose support he needs has blemishes of its own. The basic one is that the whole process amplifies the shift of emphasis from the merits of the external issue to the requirements of the domestic consensus. Both the implementation of policies and the formulation of new ones are affected. The defect of crisis diplomacy is that crises are better as means to consensus than as ways of waging foreign policy. The defect of the consensus-building process is that the means (consensus-building) toward the end (an effective foreign policy) tends to become an end in itself. And the complexity of the process explains why both students of and participants in the process become so engrossed with it that they often lose sight of its purpose and substance—*policy or decisions*—and see only the communications and strategies involved in the *making* of policy.

In domestic affairs, the dangers of consensus-building are less visible. The parties to a policy dispute, the contenders in a bargaining procedure, the partners to a compromise, are usually not enemies whose whole future is at stake in the conflict, or allies whose long-term goals may well be at odds. A good statesman, especially in American politics, may be broadly "indifferent to policy outcomes," [27] as one observer wrote of Senator Lyndon Johnson. But this is so only if the range of possible outcomes is narrow to start with, if the choice of outcomes creates no ideological drama or insuperable con-

[26] John Montgomery, *The Politics of Foreign Aid* (New York: Frederick A. Praeger, for the Council on Foreign Relations, 1960), p. 207.

[27] Nelson W. Polsby, *Congress and the Presidency* (Englewood Cliffs, N.J.: Prentice-Hall, 1964), p. 45.

flict of vital interests. Then, the mutual adjustment of claims by incremental compromises that entail only limited alterations of the
previous position makes possible both consensus and a satisfactory
outcome. But with consensus-building in foreign policy, there is a
discrepancy between the conditions that make the method useful at
home and the problems to which foreign policy must address itself.

When the issue is so clear-cut and compelling as to require either
imposing the will of the United States on a foe or enlisting the will
and leadership of the United States in an operation with friends
sharing the same goals, then the process of domestic consensus-
building will not inhibit effective policy (at least for a while). In
operations that flow, drive, or rush toward a single undisputed goal,
the process has its virtues: consensus-building is then the most effective lever for moving the public and private resources of the nation
toward that goal. But foreign affairs provide these "ideal" conditions
in only limited numbers. (The great advantage of crises is that they
appear to create such conditions; the great disadvantage of a crisis
approach to foreign affairs is, as we know, that it does not take care
of the sum total of foreign policy, and it does not even assure that
the treatment applied to the emergencies will not raise unmanageable
problems.) When the policy around which support is needed is not a
"crash" policy, and when the solutions devised for an emergency
must be adjusted to a protracted and intractable situation, the ideal
conditions may be nowhere near. Consensus-building is valuable
when a policy aims at a single goal, because the process holds out
the possibility of self-reliance. But when self-reliance is no longer
enough (i.e., when American foreign policy is entangled with its adversaries' moves, or with its allies' own disparate concerns), the requirements for consensus and for foreign policy diverge in two respects: it may be impossible to develop a deep consensus on a policy
that tries to reconcile conflicting external goals (and the ambiguities
of such a consensus will affect the effectiveness and even the substance of the policy); or consensus may deepen around goals that
are counter-productive because they result from unrealistic notions
about what the world should be. In both ways, consensus-building
reinforces the defects of the American style, and particularly of American pragmatism.

The nuclear age condemns all adversaries to "mixed strategies,"
however much our instinct may be for zero-sum games. Domestic
consensus-building for a mixed strategy means the mobilization of

support for a delicate mix of goals. But the less survival appears at stake, and the less the public and political forces resign themselves to such a mix, the less the conflict seems likely to plunge us into holocaust, and the harder it is to convince the public that prudence is indeed required. In the missile crisis, of course, restraint was almost graphically indispensable; the stakes were so high that the imperative necessity of a mix of force and restraint was never in question. But in cases like Korea, Laos, or Vietnam, consensus is hard to form, since there is a group of citizens and politicians that finds in the perils of future escalation good reason for not pursuing what is only a limited stake, and a group that finds in the nature of the confrontation good reason to accept the perils. The policy process tends to be a field of battle in which contending forces compete in order to convince or coerce the president: the stake is the decision, and the method looks like conquest. As in war, the ends justify the means; each group tries to build up its position against others, or to overcome their resistance, by leaks to the press or alliances with well-disposed and well-placed members of Congress.[28] As a result, the president is faced with a difficult set of alternatives. One possibility is to try to form a consensus around a mixed strategy, but it will be extremely shallow; and to keep it from disintegrating, he may have to spend more time cultivating the delicate balance of hopes and fears among his supporters than the difficult equilibrium of his policy. Thus, the consensus will be the negative, the policy a print developed from it. The need for prudence abroad can then become confused with the need for prudence at home; the former requires careful choices—but choices—the latter might lead to the avoidance or postponement of choice and, thereby, to the unsuspected lapse of all one's earlier options—the contrary of true prudence. The shallower the consensus, the greater the diversion from what the external situation requires.

Warner Schilling's analysis of President Truman's decision to go ahead with production of a hydrogen bomb shows how the "minimal character" [29] of the decision assured that all the issues thereby avoided eventually came back to the president. The same "need to avert conflict by avoiding choice" may lead to a deliberate and simultaneous pursuit of policies pointing in opposite directions, thus either preserving or increasing the distance from the goals. For exam-

---

[28] For edifying examples, see Hilsman, cited, pp. 145, 197–98, 508–9.
[29] "The H-Bomb Decision," *Political Science Quarterly*, March 1961, pp. 24–46.

ple, since 1963, American statesmen have simultaneously pursued an agreement with the Soviet Union on the nonproliferation of nuclear weapons and some agreement on nuclear control in NATO. Pursuing these two important goals has kept the domestic boat steady on the subject of Atlantic policy and has been a way of avoiding a hard-headed examination of the issues underlying both. Concerning Vietnam, domestic hawks and doves have been fed with equal care, and a joint commitment to unconditional negotiations and to the military and economic restoration of South Vietnam has postponed the ordeal of choice and the pain of working out the implications of either goal.

Such ambiguity in foreign policy never takes one as far as one hopes; a statesman is never entirely the master of events, so his credit dwindles before his need for it has come to an end. In another respect, it takes one farther than one might have feared, since a series of decisions of "minimal character" may create by accumulation a mortgage that becomes almost impossible to pay off. Flexible formulas such as that of the Tonkin Gulf resolution, or those of the compromises Kennedy worked out over Vietnam, turn out to have a nightmarish cold grip. Since there are no major landmarks on the scene, it is impossible to see where one went "off the track"; there was never a track, only the invisible pattern of evasion.

But that pattern points in one direction—that of what I have called the coercive or repressive approach, for several reasons. In attempting to reach a "mixed" consensus, the president must take into account not only the substance of the various positions advocated in his councils, but also the respective weight and intensity of their defenders. Almost inevitably, this gives a permanent advantage and final bonus to the proponents of a military solution; for their stance is congruent with America's style, they have a network of powerful supporters in the mass media and Congress, and the military are involved in many countries and issues. A president who yields more to this side than to any other will have an easier time; a president who tries to resist will have more trouble getting his consensus; he will have to spend more time disarming resistance and criticism than building a coherent policy.[30] Thus, contrary to the theory of "mutual partisan adjustment," the final outcome may well be far from the best that should

[30] One frequent way of disarming the opposition has repeatedly backfired: the appointment to important positions of men who stand for a policy different from the president's: this attempt to "appease" critics usually gives them a grip on the policy.

have been devised. Moreover, except in emergencies so acute that decisions are taken by a handful of political leaders, the effort to reach an agreement on a mixed strategy requires that agencies and institutions far removed from the "inner circle" be included in the policy process, in order to produce both the right balance and consensus. The larger the circle becomes, the more "incremental" the decision-making process tends to be; but decisions made on a minimal, short-term basis or in a fuzzy way so as to maximize support have, as we know, a way of avoiding the hard, fundamental issues; they let sores fester and situations deteriorate until the only way of handling them becomes the military one.

Now, the president can decide to avoid these perils by developing a strong (although perhaps less balanced) consensus, the firmness of which will save him from having to divert his efforts from the world stage. But this may be counter-productive if there is a gap between the policy around which the consensus can be formed and the needs of the external situation. A strong domestic consensus will reflect the American predisposition to favor a "tough" line toward an adversary. This may be a blessing in a test of wills that is not yet a test of military strength (Berlin, Cuba), but not necessarily in a military confrontation. For in the latter, the tendency for the needle of the public scales to settle near the point of military advice is most dangerous. If "toughness" prevails, it may mean a major conflagration. If the "tough" policy fails or the president has to apply brakes, the malaise of public opinion and the opposition of Congress (which we have discussed earlier) will wreak havoc on it. This happened over Korea; it may happen over Vietnam. Aside from tests—of resolve or of arms—a tough stance risks buying support at home at a heavy cost in international support, from allies or neutrals, or in external efficiency: our policy of not recognizing China and our recent decision to deploy an ABM system against China despite possible repercussions in Moscow or Geneva are cases in point.

The president faces the same alternatives—of a shallow consensus on a mixed strategy or a strong consensus on a "tough" one—in determining American policy toward allies that do not share the same hierarchy of goals and interests. Again, he can seek a consensus on a policy of caution; but the need to keep advisers, "influentials," and segments of public opinion with differing inclinations and prescriptions together may force him into inaction. Both Kennedy's and Johnson's policies on NATO since 1963 have been marked by a kind of agnostic serenity that preserves consensus on myths and memories,

but not on policies. Or the president may let American predispositions define a consensus around a clear-cut policy that differs from
what the allies want or feel able to accept. In the days of the Marshall Plan and the signing of the North Atlantic Treaty, the administration, sensing the mood of Congress and the public, took a stand
for European integration and an integrated defense (requested by
Congress in the 1949 Mutual Defense Assistance Act), despite its
reluctance to press too hard for these goals. To be sure, this contributed to the acceleration of steps toward European integration, but
perhaps not to their durability. And in U.S. relations with underdeveloped countries (specifically in the legislation for the Alliance
for Progress), the "philosophy" around which a domestic consensus
for aid could be built has almost always given a greater role to private investment than is realistic or sound.

### THE INSTRUMENTS OF CONSENSUS-BUILDING

The instruments of consensus-building include all those media and
organizations whose function is to mobilize, behind or around the
government, what have been called the "foreign-policy elites" outside the government—leaders of various interest groups and professional organizations, members of the "attentive public," the clergy,
etc. These include the institutions that are like hinges between the
government and the private citizenry. Richard Rovere's half-face-
tious account of "the American Establishment" had some merit,[31] if
we include in "the Establishment" not only the "New York financial
and legal community," [32] the major foundations, and the Council on
Foreign Relations, but also the high command of labor unions and
business, the most important research centers, and academic consultants and administrators. Also, there are *ad hoc* committees or conferences set up by the government for the purpose of winning citizen
support on a specific issue—particularly one on which a vote in
Congress is necessary and on behalf of which, it is believed, Congress will more easily act if pressure from below is added to exhortations from on high. This technique has been used on foreign aid issues (the Committee for the Marshall Plan in 1947, with Robert
Patterson as chairman, and the 1958 conference on foreign aid attended by "distinguished citizens"), trade (the Committee for National Trade Policy of 1962), and the nuclear test-ban.

[31] See his book, *The American Establishment* (New York: Harcourt Brace,
1962).
[32] Schlesinger, cited, p. 128.

It is my contention that whatever the actual *purpose* of these groups, whatever the intentions of the individuals concerned, they *function* as instruments of the consensus, as relays for administration policy.[33] Some of them appear at first sight to be advisers, active before the decisions are made, not relays of the decisions; they prepare policy rather than spread its gospel. But the distinction is somewhat artificial: there is a policy continuum, and even the advisers can be considered as relays when their contacts with the administration are frequent enough to blur the line between technical advice prior to decision and contribution to consensus-building after it.

Conversely, the mass media are not used merely to announce a policy: in formulating a policy, in making decisions, the administration that needs these relays takes into account what will appeal to them. What makes it possible to deal, say, with both the press and the RAND Corporation is that they both contribute to the legitimizing function. In the American system of government, this function, elsewhere carried out primarily by political parties and by whatever media the government controls, is performed in a far more decentralized way; moreover, the fundamental American conviction that the government is the loyal and enlightened servant of the community makes it easier for members of the community to behave as loyal and enlightened agents of the government.

The advantages these instruments provide are unquestionable. They give roots to American foreign policy. Given the responsibilities and the risks, the complexities and the costs, it is essential for American statesmen to have not only the cooperation of Congress and the freedom of maneuver that a general public consensus affords, but also substantial, informed support in the enlightened and active segments of the population. Now, while the structures of pluralism in America are more dispersed than elsewhere, they are not less effective: the range of levers and buttons an American president must pull and push is greater than, say, in England, and far greater virtuosity is required and more time consumed in doing so. But it is easier for the president to reach men across party lines and beyond

---

[33] This is not, of course, their only function. Another role is that of instruments of discord and contest, during the battle that precedes the achievement of consensus, as discussed above. There, the fact that mass media, advisers, and analysts can be used as strongholds or as reinforcements in the battle for decision tends to inhibit policy-making in the ways described in the previous section—i.e., they tend either to channel the policy into the safe and narrow path of short-term, minimal decisions, or to push it into the familiar and splashy path of "toughness" and activism. Compare Hilsman, cited, pp. 543–44.

the confines of that small section of the population that is highly politicized.

Yet the use of the relays poses problems: American foreign policy inevitably takes on some of their features. They are not mere tools of the president; he must be careful and persistent in resorting to them; they do not merely transmit his policy, they affect it. Thus, for one thing, the use of these relays fosters an atmosphere of public relations in which the emphasis inevitably shifts from substance to setting. Second, because the instruments of consensus-building are media, institutions, and groups that are not deeply implicated in the policy-making process (or men for whom foreign policy is not the main preoccupation, or scholars deprived of "some part of [their] valuable irresponsibility" [34] by their access to confidential information), their use encourages the national style that takes the ends for granted and channels energies toward means. The government has to spend more time in seducing the relays than on the merits of the policy, and the relays are often not qualified or prepared to test those merits. To be sure, consensus develops on administration policy, but the means used to convey that policy muffle, if not smother, it.

Thus, what the policy gains in depth of commitment, it loses in clarity and flexibility. The broad outlines of the policy are always visible and the principles behind it are constantly asserted, but what I would call operational clarity is fuzzed over: for the same measure or program, "sold" to media, agencies, and committees with different orientations, will be presented in a dazzling variety of shimmering lights. In one forum, the focus will be on toughness, self-interest, continuity, or safeguards; in another, it will be on flexibility, altruism, innovation, or daring. The pluralism of a sprawling government is thus compounded by the pluralism of a dispersed Establishment. The policy will sound like a blurred symphony transmitted through speakers each of which picks up only some instruments; it takes an expert standing in a requisite but elusive place to hear the symphony *in toto.*

The loss of flexibility, on the other hand, may seem an unlikely effect, since the more or less deliberate confusion which the multiplication of voices produces ought to make room for maneuver. But this is not in fact what happens. Insofar as consensus is achieved, it results in a complex phenomenon (Tocqueville noticed it and cursed it in his famous reference to the tyranny of the majority) in which dissent is,

[34] William R. Polk, "The Scholar and the Administrator in International Affairs," *Bulletin of the Atomic Scientists,* March 1966, p. 7.

so to speak, domesticated. Dissent is not eliminated—this *is* a free society and on every important issue the national consensus leaves room for critics and rebels. But it is as if the critics and rebels were in a cage, shown to the "conformitarian" majority as evidence of the existence of dissent and of its harmlessness. The reason, and precondition, for such a climate of opinion is the relation of basic trust between the citizenry and its public representatives: a bond that can lead to blindness and blunders. How a free press and free organizations and associations manage, by means of intense discussion, to cement a national orthodoxy so solid that minority opinions appear derisory, is somewhat mysterious, but the phenomenon is powerful enough to make a skeptical observer almost believe in pre-established harmony. Their very success confirms the mistaken belief in the universal efficacy of such methods among all except men of ill will. It is not the machinations and manipulations of the CIA that have provided the cement. It is the pre-existing basic trust that has led so many groups to accept direct or indirect CIA support without feeling in any way constricted by it, and has also led the CIA to support apparently controversial forces without feeling in any way foolhardy. Consensus bred collusion; mutual confidence bred complicity.

But this brings us to the other side of the coin: this trust, so akin to faith, condemns dissenters to the condition of heretics and protects believers from the heresy. A witty, if uncharitable, Frenchman has written that when unanimity reigns, people stop thinking.[35] When quasi-unanimity obtains, fresh thought is neutralized. Here again, there is damage both for the government, because "the tendency of bureaucratic language to create in private the same images presented to the public never should be underrated,"[36] and for the public, because of the dangerous machinery of self-reinforcing self-righteousness, which may allow room for quibbling about means, about degrees of more or less, but none for questioning ends, visions, or analyses. Only when the means clearly and repeatedly fail to meet the ends is the basic framework of policy questioned, and then only in a roundabout way. Because they are so rare, these re-examinations are more painful, acrimonious, and searing than they need to be.

The closeness to official Washington of the nation's leading columnists and reporters, writing for the main newspapers and televi-

[35] J. F. Revel, *The French* (New York: George Braziller, 1965), p. 17.
[36] Neustadt, *Presidential Power*, p. 134.

sion networks, is especially responsible for numbing the mass media's capacity to question and challenge. It is difficult to maintain a balance between being close in order to get information and being distant in order to preserve a critical sense. The former prevails all too easily, by virtue of the rationalization according to which you can only challenge what you know, and because of the irresistible appeal to the ego. Enjoying the confidence of the great usually kills the urge to investigate. Officials disarm these men by giving them the illusion of being admitted to the mysteries of decision-making, and by making them sympathize with their ordeals. A foreigner used to censored papers or state-controlled radio and television is easily awed by all this; whereas overt censorship and control breed cynicism and disbelief, this relationship of free media to officialdom produces a consensus on national conformity of formidable proportions. What overt manipulation and obsequious docility fail to instill is achieved by a mixture of calculated candor in officials and cooperative compassion in the media.

What the mass media fail to do obviously cannot be done by the many institutions and associations that take part in the process of legitimizing policy. They are often not equipped to go beyond questioning details and side aspects. Moreover, their members are often colleagues and friends of the men in power who ask for their support; they are ex-officials themselves, or future officials, and perhaps the government officials calling on them for support are in Washington only in between tours of private duty. The absence of a sharp break between the bureaucracy and the public, the twilight zone of interpenetration, thus also aids the consensus and stifles challenges. A ritual of self-reassurance, a circuitous process of complacency replaces the critical function.

Second, what the consensus gains in scope by use of these relaying instruments, it loses in solidity and sophistication. The gain in scope is of considerable value, since the government can in effect count on a large number of nongovernmental agencies to do part of its job. The important role played by foundations in economic development, by business organizations in management abroad, by labor unions in promoting the union movement elsewhere, etc.; the advice social scientists give on policy problems; the ways foundations encourage research in areas of underdeveloped knowledge that are important for policy; the "cultural representation" of America abroad by artists and professors—all of these constitute a formidable complement to officialdom. When a newspaper columnist stated that without the press (and his newspaper in particular) American ambassadors abroad would not understand American foreign policy, he put an undiplomatic finger on the need the government (the State Department especially) has for such a complement and on the "positive thinking" effect of the relays. As a report pointed out some years ago, these instruments of consensus-building can, for instance, perform a task for which officialdom is ill prepared or ill fitted: "in trying to reach 'next governments,' . . . we have the incomparable asset of our own pluralism," [37] since the existence of "even a fuzzy line between the actions of private persons and those of public officials abroad" [38] makes it possible to marshal the former on behalf of the latter in many subtle ways. But we pay a heavy price for the privilege.

It is a price in solidity, by which I mean a policy's effective integration in the sum total of American foreign policy and its grounding in a reliable analysis of facts of major and lasting significance. Each mass medium or research organization or other "establishment" contributes its limited expertise in the relevant area, but the sum total is not necessarily an integrated whole. An illusion of solidity is created because of the deluge of "facts" provided, which give the policy a magic halo of indisputability. Yet data without connections are dead, and the deluge of data often submerges the officials themselves. The responsibility rests partly with the government: what Henry Kissinger has written of the government's use of the intellectual—whose contribution "to policy is . . . in terms of criteria that he has played a minor role in establishing" [39]—is true of the government's use of other relays too. What it wants is an endorsement of a policy, which is best obtained when focused on specific moves with all the basic premises left out.

Another problem is that the mass media report foreign affairs in a limited and spotty way, reflecting and encouraging oft-denounced basic flaws: [40] problems are rarely treated unless a crisis has erupted, and consequently large parts of the map are inadequately

---

[37] "The Operational Aspects of United States Foreign Policy," a staff study for the Committee on Foreign Relations, U.S. Senate, 86th Cong., 2d Sess. (1960), p. 34.

[38] Same, p. 34.

[39] *The Necessity for Choice*, p. 350.

[40] See Bernard C. Cohen, *The Press and Foreign Policy* (Princeton University Press, 1963), *passim*, and James Reston, "The Press, the President, and Foreign Policy," *Foreign Affairs*, July 1966, pp. 553–73.

represented; in-depth reporting is hardly possible on the small screen and hardly frequent in the daily press.

We also pay a price in sophistication. As relayed through the media and other organizations, policy appears as a series of disconnected steps (held together only by the hallowed principles), and also a series of grand choices between night and day. The symbolic inflation runs amok. Now, sophistication in foreign affairs is impossible when problems are dealt with only in terms of current events, when the colors are heightened, when divergencies are turned into conflicts and conflicts into life-and-death battles, when the "lively, contentious, sensational, dramatic, personalized" [41] dominate, when military data (tangible and spectacular) prevail over all others. But this is what the media encourage. Sophistication is impossible when policy presentations and discussions stress procedures and generalities instead of the hard facts of political life, the issues of substance. (The questions—Who commands? Who wants what?—are hidden at the bottom of all the quarrels among allies as well as between enemies.) But this kind of clarification, this cutting through the maze of irrelevance and the mist of propaganda to the heart of an issue, is singularly missing. To be sure, the "public" character of most of the relay institutions does not allow for it. Yet not only popular journalism but often also private academic research oriented toward policy suffers from weightlessness: it is often too unhistorical, too narrowly focused, or too single-mindedly geared to a specific policy issue to make up in sophistication for the media's immaturity.

In sum, then, what the consensus gains domestically through such instruments, the effectiveness of foreign policy may lose. A public-relations atmosphere may be indispensable for adding a domestic dimension to policy, but it shrinks its foreign dimension, for one thing because it overpersonalizes the problems involved. The tendency to present (and understand) politics in terms of demons and friends, good guys and bad guys, is due in part to the mass media's need for "human-interest" angles and stories, in part to the other relays' greater familiarity with personalities than with issues. For in organizations with no basic conflicts over ends, the normal way to analyze problems is to identify positions with people and to consider the interplay of personal rivalries and personality traits as the web of policy. This of course matches Washington politics, where the rise

[41] Cohen, *The Press and Foreign Policy*, p. 124.

and fall of policies can best be traced through the rise and fall of certain men, yet where the constant quest for popularity or power is often divorced from substantive issues. Indeed, in America's fragmented political system, the broad agreement on ends and the pragmatic nature of the search for means leave personalities as the only exciting part of politics.

The effectiveness of foreign policy shrinks also because the public-relations mood means a triumph of image over substance—sometimes indeed a triumph of fable over fact. Officials tend to "play the press like a piano" [42] (and the other relays too). But in order to play a piano well, one has to practice, and the time spent practicing is not spent perfecting the policy.[43] Even presidents impatient with images and skeptical of popularity become indignant over criticism and involved in the paraphernalia of briefings, leaks, handouts, special appearances, and informal chats. They find it hard to resist using the press or television for special purposes—putting pressure on Congress or on an ally (as Dulles did when he talked of "an agonizing reappraisal" or as Kennedy did when he criticized the Skybolt program before the Nassau meeting and Diem in a press conference). This "management" is successful only if the media are well disposed; thus, their cultivation becomes a permanent necessity, their "helpfulness" a goal and a criterion. Finally, effectiveness suffers because the need to sell a policy may entail calculated, if sometimes confused, attempts at blowing up events so as to provide plausible pretexts for controversial initiatives. Foreign audiences watch the building and the manipulation, and ultimately domestic media discover the distortions and expose the fabrications. This has been a recurrent hazard of American policy in Vietnam.[44]

The mass media and other relays are not really equipped to resist these uses and to challenge their users. They are staffed by managers, organizers, propagandists, operators—not policy-makers, not men whose function is to raise questions about ends or pinpoint differences in values and objectives. (Such men are usually found in universities, but when they come to Washington as consultants, it is within a frame of reference they do not establish; thus, instead of contributing, as intellectuals, to the definition of goals, they merely bring their skills

---

[42] Cohen, *The Press and Foreign Policy,* p. 29.

[43] Reston, cited, pp. 558–59.

[44] See, for instance, in Theodore Draper, *Abuse of Power* (New York: Viking Press, 1967) the story of the "mysterious" 325th North Vietnamese division, pp. 73 ff.

as experts to an evaluation of means.) [45] In other words, since they cannot justify their presence by an over-all competence in foreign policy, since their specialized contribution may be marginal, the only way to prove their importance to themselves and others may be to make as much fuss and splash as possible—to resort to self-advertising. In such a process, everyone risks being at the mercy of everyone else. The journalist in the field, the commentator on the screen, the local citizens' association, and even the research specialist depend for "inside information" on what the officials consent to tell them—at times with appalling results, when that information is inaccurate. The officials, in turn, have to take into constant account the egos and whims of the men in the relays. There is something rotten in the Madison Avenue patina of Pennsylvania Avenue.

### THE CASUALTIES

The methods used for consensus-building make for two casualties in American foreign policy: discretion and imagination.

It is possible to argue that in the present world almost all diplomacy is fishbowl diplomacy, that there are no important "secrets" which leave no traces, and consequently, that the traditional idea of diplomacy as a silken art of carefully concealed designs and understated sentences trailing off into suggestive silence is obsolete. However, in many large areas of foreign policy, discretion is still of the essence: the fine art of supporting certain forces abroad without destroying their usefulness through public embraces, the difficult art of talking (or resuming talks) with an adversary when public contact could prove embarrassing to both sides, the black art of military intervention without splashes or crashes on friendly (or not so friendly) territories. A policy that consists primarily of denials can get by with less discretion than one that wants positive gains. But even there, in order to know what must be thwarted, all kinds of information are needed, not always obtainable in an honest way or in the remotely dishonest way of spies in the sky. And in order to deny gains to one's foes in the gray areas of subversion, since blunt intervention is counterproductive, discretion is indeed the better part of valor. Whoever considers discretion obsolete should recall the Bay of Pigs, the U-2 incident, and Khrushchev's gamble with missiles in Cuba. The fact that it proved impossible in all those cases to keep a secret to

---

[45] See Hans J. Morgenthau, "Truth and Power," *The New Republic*, November 26, 1966.

the end does not mean that undertaking to do so was of no importance. And if a nation derived from that ultimate failure the rule that nothing should be undertaken that will fail if it is not kept secret, it would impose crippling restrictions on its policy. Such a self-denying ordinance would make little sense in a competition with states (hostile or not overtly so) whose capacity for discretion was greater. The need for personal skills in the international contest today is a need for discretion.

In this respect, American diplomacy suffers from self-inflicted wounds. All the elements we have dissected in this and the previous chapter—the fragmentation of power, the role of the public, the proliferation of clans within the government, the process of consensus, the nature of the relays—put a premium on publicity and a curse on discretion. Publicity in carrying out foreign policy has its virtue: the spectacular display of contradictions and conflicts (best exemplified by the Dominican affair) often provokes correction, whereas a blanket of silence and a mask of unruffled complacency would allow for perpetuation of the folly. But when the United States is engaged in an undertaking that requires surprise, or that involves foreigners whose trust is indispensable, the mass media's merciless scratching for inconsistencies, unearthing of rivalries, and revelations of plans, to which officials often willingly contribute, are perfect recipes for failure. We are all familiar with the fact that the Bay of Pigs fiasco was partly due to its high level of noise and visibility: not only had newspapers broken the story, but "the CIA even dictated battle communiqués to a Madison Avenue public relations firm representing the exiles' political front." [46] In 1964, when speed and silence were of the diplomatic and strategic essence, paratroopers' operations designed to save hostages from the Congo rebels in Stanleyville received a press coverage that assured both loss of lives and loss of support in the United Nations. In 1966, a complacent exposition of CIA activities around the world candidly revealed more than any angry exposé had ever raked up [47]—until the exposés of 1967.

Policy-makers thus find themselves on the horns of a dilemma. If they try to maintain secrecy or discretion in a major venture, they risk the possibility that support will be lacking and the consensus will vanish if the enterprise fails. The domestic repercussions of the

[46] Sorensen, cited, p. 302.
[47] *The New York Times,* April 25–29, 1966. See in particular the listing of Congolese politicians allegedly discovered and boosted by the CIA (April 26).

U-2 crisis and the long-term trauma of the Bay of Pigs (after the initial closing of the ranks around a bruised but defiant president) justify the fear of this risk. Another problem is the "loss of credibility" that Ambassador Arthur Goldberg alluded to when the fact that secret peace offers were made in 1964 by North Vietnam and rejected by the administration was revealed. On the other hand, if the government is resigned to publicity and indeed exploits the necessary evil, then all sorts of embarrassments can result: [48] American improvisations may be exposed (as during the last spring of the Indochina war in 1954, and the summer of Suez), and contradictions between statements at home and behavior or policy in the field may lead (as in Santo Domingo or Vietnam) to as much of a "credibility gap" as an unsuccessful attempt at secrecy.

In this dilemma, government officials try to reconcile the need for discretion and the likelihood of publicity. The way to do this is to give discretion a kind of private domain. Instead of being a quality employed (in varying degrees) in *all* dimensions of foreign policy, it is relegated to a reservation: the CIA. All activities that are not the collection of intelligence, the support of friendly or useful organizations at home and abroad, and the mounting of subversive operations overseas are carried out in the full glare of publicity. It is as if fear of oversalting a dinner entrée made one pour a hail of salt on one portion of food and leave the rest unsalted. Naturally, the results are often dreadful and CIA activities or policies are badly integrated with those of other agencies (particularly in Latin America and Southeast Asia). Also, when there is an overriding need for secrecy to cover an undertaking that does not fall within the CIA's domain or whose scope exceeds the CIA's resources, policy-makers must make a heroic effort to restrict participation in the decision-making process to the strict minimum. This can obviously be done successfully, as the Cuban missile crisis showed. But we can hardly generalize from an instance in which secrecy was needed for only a few days. The very intensity of effort needed to deceive those who smelled something strange then suggests that similar success cannot be expected in a situation in which secrecy would be required for longer. And the story of the Bay of Pigs shows that there may sometimes be a price for excluding from the decision-making process officials and experts whose judgment might have redressed the balance.

[48] See Theodore Draper, "The Dominican Crisis," *Commentary*, December 1965, pp. 55–56, on Ambassador John Bartlow Martin's account of his role in the Dominican crisis in *Life*.

Moreover, both the internalization of world politics and American activism drive us into enterprises that are so removed from traditional diplomacy that only the CIA seems able to sponsor them and to save them from the scrutiny of the public and Congress. In addition, almost inevitably, both the desire to save as many enterprises as possible from that merciless scrutiny and the conviction that "problems that did not yield to power alone [49] when power was used too bluntly would yield to power when it is used covertly have provoked an inflation of CIA activities. The CIA's veil of mystery is wrapped around undertakings that would in other countries be deemed normal (if regrettable) and conducted discreetly if not covertly; it is also thrown over operations that would not be tried by other countries, more aware of the futility and dangers of covert action when it is just a display of technical skill divorced from political realities or put at the service of harebrained schemes. An atmosphere (and techniques) of deceit give the CIA operations almost an air of domestic subversion. Thus, once again, the momentum  of unrestrained "pragmatism" has often led to embarrassing fiascoes.

Finally, the combination of the government's general bad conscience about discretion and the CIA's monopoly on secrecy seems to inspire clumsiness in coping with failures. When a secret leaks out, the exposure makes the secret activities look both sinister and silly; moreover, the "cover" has a way of looking as if it had been naive and routine, incapable of deceiving anyone, indeed leading the bloodhounds on the trail of total discovery. The chain reaction provoked by the blatant absurdity of the "cover" story about our U-2 flights over the Soviet Union and the collapse of the one about the air strike which preceded the Bay of Pigs landing suggest two conclusions. One (candidly recognized by Eisenhower) [50] is that a superstitious need to keep one's fingers crossed and the national bent to optimism together divert the government from contemplating the possibility that its plan might go awry (i.e., that a U-2 plane and pilot might fall intact into Soviet hands, that a genuine Cuban defector might land in the United States just as "fake" Cuban pilots chosen by the CIA and pretending to be defectors returned from a bombing mission). The other conclusion is that this neglect creates monumental confusion within the government, with all the agencies that were not fully informed falling over each other in an effort to cover the cover story.

The second prerequisite for effective policy that is harmed by con-

[49] Hilsman, cited, p. 85.
[50] *Waging Peace*, pp. 546–48.

sensus-building is imagination. As Dean Acheson has put it,[51] shaping the future is the central task of a foreign office, and the central task in shaping the future is recognizing problems in time. Practitioners and students of United States foreign policy have tried to cope with this matter by stressing the importance of planning. The argument (which can be found in dozens of works) starts with a sad recognition that the "overpowering present" monopolizes energy, and goes on to recommend better planning, capable of identifying the forces that will form the future and of preparing to deal with them. But this same literature reveals a serious embarrassment about the proper place of planning in the government, indeed (since discussions of administrative organization normally hide concern for a deeper issue) about the very nature of planning.

Many writers have warned against useless planning of the ivory-tower variety, "completely divorced . . . from any operational relationships," [52] which is not "focused rather particularly on a situation or on a developing crisis or any idea on foreign policy," [53] which is "floating in a void" instead of being built "around one or another of [the] streams of action." [54] What is being rejected here is what one might call academic thinking—thinking about foreign affairs that is not directly related to the concerns of foreign-policy-making—and also the vague generalized paper work characteristic of the National Security Council's Planning Board in the Eisenhower days. But in addition to the Charybdis of irrelevance there is the Scylla of overinvolvement in the present: the tendency to immerse planners in operations, partly because able officials are on the planning staffs and are sorely needed in operations when a crisis arises, partly because the planners want to apply their concepts and prove their capacity to act.

Thus, planning should be "action-oriented" yet separate from daily operations. What does this mean? The experts disagree. "The object of planning is not to blueprint future actions. . . . The object is to decide what should be done now in light of the best present estimate of how the future will look. Planners think about the future in order to act wisely in the present." [55] In this conception, planning becomes merely an enlightened way of performing operations: we

---

[51] In Don K. Price, ed., *The Secretary of State* (Englewood Cliffs, N.J.: Prentice Hall, 1960), p. 47.

[52] Herter, in Jackson, ed., *The National Security Council*, p. 153.

[53] Rusk, in same, p. 269.

[54] Same, p. 283.

[55] Jackson, *The Secretary of State and the Ambassador*, p. 10.

are dangerously close to Scylla. Should the planning staff engage in contingency planning, studying the various possible moves for possible crises? Here, as Robert Bowie has pointed out, the relevance may well be illusory, for "experience suggests that such crises are not likely to occur in the manner which can be foreseen concretely enough to make the planning very helpful." [56] Should the planners then develop a framework of policy objectives, help equip the nation for future needs, and coordinate the various programs that carry out our policies? If this is their task, then they are faced with a serious organizational problem.

If we start by assuming that planning must be the preserve of a small group of able people, then we can easily see why they will be thrown from Charybdis to Scylla. If planners are on one side and operators on the other, the planners' work will remain an academic exercise, since responsibility for the programs will be the operators'. Even George Kennan, the first and most prestigious head of the Policy Planning Staff of the State Department, has complained that the concept of containment that evolved in the staff "was never fully understood . . . agreed with or implemented . . . by those who had the power of decision." [57] NSC 68, a document in the writing of which the Policy Planning Staff played a major role, ignored the "reconciliation of the desirable and the possible," and it took the Korean War to give it operational significance. The multilateral nuclear force, advocated by planners for some time, was taken out of the drawer by the operators at a moment when its relevance and virtues were already questionable. Yet these are works that left traces: next to them there are all those "national policy papers" that have turned out to be mere exercises. If, in order to abolish the gap between the planners' promise and the operators' performance, the planners become involved in operations, then Gresham's Law will inevitably operate, since the numbers and responsibilities are on the side of the operators.[58] The small size of the planning body is enough to condemn it to seeing "many interesting problems go by without [its] becoming involved" and to condemn it to the commonplace curse of fragmentation.

[56] In Price, cited, p. 70.
[57] "The Conceptual Element in Recent American Foreign Policy," Lecture at Harvard University, April 19, 1967 (mimeo).
[58] For a good example, see W. W. Rostow, "The Planning of Foreign Policy" in E. A. J. Johnson, ed., *The Dimensions of Diplomacy* (Baltimore: The Johns Hopkins Press, 1964), pp. 49–50.

But to increase the number of planners would not be a solution. As usual, the organizational problem reflects a deeper issue: the nature of "planning" in foreign policy. For what is basically wrong is having the division between planners and performers at all (another American polarity). It divorces inspiration and management and as a result helps to sterilize both. Management without inspiration is deadly; divorced from planning, the making of foreign policy takes on an air of public administration that experienced observers like Roger Hilsman and critics like Henry Kissinger have so often deplored: "substantive problems are transformed into administrative ones." [59] And divorced from daily practice, planning will also be corrupted; in order to escape from the wooliness of purely academic or generalized thinking and to show their relevance to practice, the planners will indulge in displays of various aspects of the American style. The consequences will be either *ad hoc* planning of a specialized nature, designed to define a course of action in response to a discrete and often pressing problem rather than with proper regard to the interdependence of the various problems faced (this appears to have been the case with Vietnam after 1960 and with so-called peaceful engagement with the East in 1966–67); or contingency planning that accentuates the habit of looking at foreign policy in terms of reactions to crises; or direct involvement in operations; or, in order to be "useful," flattery of the "bias against novel conceptions which are difficult to adapt to an administrative mold," by the planner's indulgence in "the temptation to see in the future an updated version of the present" [60] (i.e., by contributing to what I have called the static American notion of change).

The operators' skepticism about planning perpetuates the divorce between plans and operations. As Acheson has noted,[61] their training and life has not prepared them to recognize its usefulness. But the whole bent of American policy-making also perpetuates it: both the crises, which mobilize the operators, and the Penelopean process of consensus-building, which occupies so many officials in between crises, divert the "policy machine" from long-term thinking. As we know, the pragmatism of America's style contributes powerfully to what the habits and needs of the governmental system dictate. Since

[59] See Roger Hilsman, "Intelligence and Policy-Making in Foreign Affairs," *World Politics*, October 1952, pp. 1–25; and Kissinger, *The Necessity of Choice*, p. 344.

[60] Kissinger, "Domestic Structure and Foreign Policy," p. 508.

[61] In Price, cited, p. 48.

something important is thereby lost, one creates a reservation for planning (just as there is one for secrecy). No wonder that this kind of afterthought fails to restore the balance—or that the men in the reservation feel a need to get out.

Nor is it an accident that military planning is frequently more effective than foreign-policy planning. Military planning involves the selection of the best means toward an end, where the ends are predetermined and the adequacy of means to ends is much less uncertain; it is closely related to economic planning. Both economic and military planning lose much of their effectiveness when they aim at the long range, must choose among ends, and take account of the reactions of opponents or of third parties. To be sure, there was the State Department's Policy Planning Staff of 1947 and the brilliant work that went into the Marshall Plan. But, as I have said, the United States' control over events then is not likely to be regained, and the primarily economic nature of those issues explains the skill of the response (some of the most imaginative planners were young economists). Usually, American planning in foreign policy, like all political planning, suffers from our ignorance of the "laws" of development of political systems; from the impossibility of quantifying values; from the fact that the world is a battlefield of ends and gives us no assurance that ours will prevail; from the fact that our evaluation of the adequacy of the means to our ends is crippled by our lack of control over events.

Foreign-policy "planning" is more like gambling than like military staff work. It is not surprising that the conception of foreign-policy planning which suffers from that disease—extrapolation from the military or economic areas—leads to overconcentration on discrete sectors or to elaboration of strategic doctrines reflecting a strangely bloodless universe for which the only valid question is: given certain ends, what are the means of reaching them? The question: given world trends, are those ends at all relevant? is forgotten. Indeed, a mistaken concept of planning will always sacrifice the questioning and redefining of ends. Strategic planning or the elaboration of strategic doctrines takes as its point of departure the ends set by the makers of foreign policy and their analysis of events. When this analysis is not refreshed, when the foreign-policy planning has either soared into irrelevance or fallen into routine, even strategic planners will prescribe for dangers or evils that may no longer be the most likely ones, and draw a blank or a question mark where the more likely threats now occur. Even in 1947–48, planners took insufficient account of Soviet potential military advances and of the problems in Asia, thereby evolving a military doctrine geared only to the restoration of the balance of power in Europe.[62]

The question is not why foreign-policy planning works badly, but *what* is wrong with it. There is nothing surprising in the hostility of foreign service officers to a notion of planning which is unsuited to the nature of what Raymond Aron calls "diplomatic-strategic behavior," and which vacillates between useless platitudes and instant *ad hoc* gimmicks, although their hostility is regrettable insofar as it confirms them in their own brand of pragmatism. It is true that their daily work is so heavy that "time to think about the job" is scarce, but the solution does not consist in the artificial separation of the overwhelmed and of the misplaced. The operators might find the "thundering present" less overwhelming if they conceived of their job more adequately.

In short, the policy-makers must also be the planners. As Roger Hilsman has recognized, long-term planning, "the making of broad strategic choices," and short-range contingency calculations are "at the political heart of policy-making."[63] The "disciplined and intelligent choice of how time is used,"[64] (for which, as Acheson put it, there is indeed no substitute) can only be strengthened by awareness of the whole, concern for the dimension of time, knowledge of history, understanding of the importance of style and proportion.[65] "All these intangibles are negated when problems become isolated cases,"[66] when the daily avalanche of cables and crises reduces Sisyphus to an automaton, when the foreign service officer is convinced that "speculation about what [foreign policy] may be next year is a waste of time."[67] Foreign policy is an art. Art manifests itself in action—in the works of art produced. But they are works of *art* only if they express a vision—and in the arts of politics, there must also be a correspondence between what the vision dictates and what reality allows. "Planning," in a way, is a diversion, as much a "trap for the unwary" as organization and reor-

[62] Schilling *et al.*, cited, pp. 32 ff.
[63] Hilsman, cited, p. 567.
[64] Quoted in Andrew M. Scott and Raymond H. Dawson, eds., *Readings in the Making of American Foreign Policy* (New York: Macmillan, 1965), pp. 294–300.
[65] See Alfred Grosser, "European Perceptions of American Foreign Defense Policies," a memorandum for the RAND Corporation, pp. 20–21.
[66] Kissinger, *The Necessity for Choice*, p. 345.
[67] Quoted in "The Operational Aspects of United States Foreign Policy," p. 63.

ganization. What is needed is imagination: specialized planners are conceivable but a council of "imagineers" is hard to envisage. A National Research Organization, once proposed by Roger Hilman and endorsed by Dean Acheson,[68] could help; since officials will always have to cope with ceremonies and crises, trifles and emergencies, and to deal with the wearying task of coordination and consensus-building, we cannot expect them to keep abreast of everything important, as scholars like to think scholars do. Yet only if the officials are aware of this drawback are they likely to use the services of such an agency. And imagination requires a sense of historic dimensions and political complexities, i.e., all that "muddling through" disdains, and that planning divorced from practice sterilizes. The roots of the problem are not administrative: they are in the training of men, and in the national approach which the training reflects.

## B. *External Consensus-Building: The Projection of Domestic Politics*

To put it bluntly, a prerequisite for effective foreign policy is awareness of the foreignness of other nations, of the fact that they have objectives and concerns, experiences and expectations, reflexes and memories different from our own. Good diplomacy knows not only how to thwart irrevocably hostile designs but also how to accommodate differences.

On the latter score, American diplomacy is definitely weak. Here, the trouble comes from a projection abroad of the methods of consensus-building we have analyzed, in order to form a consensus among our partners over our policies or over joint policies. These methods, which work well for domestic consensus-building, although at the frequent expense of foreign-policy requisites, very often do not and cannot work abroad.

### THE USEFULNESS OF CRISIS DIPLOMACY

We have observed the fruitfulness of crisis diplomacy in building domestic consensus. The use of crises as the occasion for decision and consensus-building abroad it far less productive. Within the United States, where there is a community of values and interests, a crisis eliminates the existing divergences and rallies all citizens around the president. But there rarely is such a community among nations, unless the peril is very sudden and very overwhelming—an eventuality that the nuclear stalemate makes more and more rare.

[68] Price, cited, p. 49.

Indeed, with no compelling threat, a crisis will tend to highlight and intensify international differences. A crisis illuminates the solidarity of a genuine national community; it illuminates the fragmentation of the international state of nature. If an ally is threatened, and we believe that that ally must change its course so as to deflect the storm, our leverage over the ally decreases when the heat is on; consider our experience with Chiang Kai-shek during the crisis over Quemoy and Matsu, or the situation in South Vietnam today. If an ally takes an incautious initiative, we are forced to use high-pressure tactics that widen the rifts, whereas quiet diplomacy before the crisis might have saved his and our face. If a crisis occurs that requires that we form a common front with our allies, previously neglected differences of opinion over what our reaction should be in an emergency may cripple the front's effectiveness and complicate the task of resolving the crisis; consider the Berlin crises of 1959 and 1961, or our difficulties with Latin American nations during the Dominican crisis of 1965. If a civil conflict with international connotations erupts and the United States believes it necessary to intervene, we are likely to find that, once violence has broken out, the local contenders are at such a point of passion and peril that only risky and politically more costly techniques of military intervention are usable; consider what happened in Santo Domingo and Lebanon. If it is a crisis directly between the United States and an ally, resolution of it, after the respective positions have hardened, will be more difficult than if the differences had been dealt with before we came to blows; consider the meeting at Nassau, or our relations with France after the Skybolt affair or since March 1966, or our difficulties with West Germany over the Soviet-American draft on nonproliferation in 1967.

The use of crisis diplomacy for external consensus-building is also dangerous by virtue of the American origin of some of the crises. When the challenge is posed by our adversaries or by countries in which the United States has (or thinks it has) an important interest, the foreign statesmen who must meet the rapier thrusts of our emergency actions may find the experience rough, but they can hardly fail to understand why we are acting, if not always our tactics and motivations. But this is not likely to be the case when the crisis results entirely or partly from American institutional or political necessities. The Skybolt affair was triggered by American budgetary procedures. The British-French-Israeli invasion of Egypt during the Suez crisis was not unrelated to the Americans' unwillingness to put pressure on Nasser and to the desire to preserve the "image" of the peace-saving administration before a presidential election. The crusading vigor of American representatives (from the president on down) in the hours following the invasion, with little consideration for the relation between the use of force and the underlying political issues, was, again, closely tied to the imminent election. And the timing of the peace offensive in Vietnam at the end of 1965 was not unrelated to the procedure of preparing for the new budget and the new session of Congress.

This last example brings us to a final point. As in the domestic context, the temptation to engineer a crisis in order to put pressure on others is sometimes irresistible. Of course, this does not mean fabricating a disaster, but it does mean giving a tremendous sense of urgency and importance to a certain measure or policy whose endorsement by others is deemed indispensable, and whose rejection is presented as an invitation to calamity. But fabricated crises have an innate propensity to backfire when the method is applied internationally: other governments may resent and resist it for excellent reasons of their own, without ever quite endorsing or even understanding the reasons why the United States used such a strategy. To them, with vital interests of their own at stake, there is nothing essential to be gained by accepting the American position, nothing crucial to be lost by rejecting it— and it may be a disaster to give in. Dulles' threat of "agonizing reappraisals" did not convince French parliamentarians hostile to EDC that the only choice could be between the bitter pill of EDC and an end of America's protection; his "threat that leaves something to chance" was not credible enough, and therefore the French National Assembly, in rejecting the treaty, was able to get away with that other Schellingesque technique—the threat to blow one's brains out on someone else's new suit. Dulles' pressing call for "united action" to stop communism in Indochina, at a time when the British cabinet was looking forward to a peaceful settlement in Geneva, his attempted "diplomacy by *fait accompli*" [69] to build a collective-defense system, not only failed to win Eden over but aroused his indignation. The strong pressure that Secretary of Defense McNamara put on European governments in 1962, when he unveiled the new strategy of "flexible response" and the new plans for increased conventional forces and centralized nuclear control, did not lead either to the death of the small deterrents (which he had denounced as dangerous and wasteful), or to a massive build-

[69] Victor Bator, *Vietnam: A Diplomatic Tragedy* (New York: Oceana, 1965), p. 63.

up of ground forces. "A full-scale theoretical onslaught on major programs of close allies impelled these governments to elaborate a doctrine to justify them, which, in turn, could not help but stress conflicting interests with the United States." [70] As Henry Kissinger has so shrewdly put it, what the United States was doing was undermining the domestic position of governments by denouncing their policies as bankrupt.

The domestic manufacture of a sense of crisis hastens the consensus around a policy; the projection of this technique outside hardens conflicts, for it substitutes bombardment for accommodation. "We shall overwhelm" [71]—Dulles's frequent method, and also President Johnson's as he has demonstrated in the Caribbean and in Vietnam —mobilizes internal consensus and external hostility. Arm-twisting takes on a different meaning depending on whether the twisted arm is the willing arm of Congress or an ally's or neutral's.

This neglect of the differences between domestic and foreign policy is compounded by a lack of understanding for the subtlety and complexities of other nations' domestic politics. The strong pressure the United States exerted on behalf of the MLF in 1963–64 displayed exactly this kind of blindness, and in the process provoked a showdown with England, bitterness in France, and considerable malaise in West Germany. To be sure, the pressure was lessened when the president realized the precariousness of the Labor government's majority; yet even here, a dominant factor was the realization that the task of domestic consensus-building in favor of the MLF would be laborious and costly. Meanwhile, West Germany's international position had become dangerously exposed, since our pressure for the MLF had incited the political leaders in Bonn to take a creditors' stand on the scheme, and when the pressure stopped, they were stranded.

THE PROCESS OF INTERNATIONAL CONSENSUS-BUILDING

Nowhere is the adequacy of dealing with international relations in terms of one's domestic experience more serious than in the extension of the American process of consensus-building to alien powers. At home, the president often permits a shallow consensus around generalities to give the "illusion of policy"; [72] or he gets a strong consensus around a policy that is hard to "sell" abroad. In foreign

---

[70] *The Troubled Partnership*, p. 119.
[71] Geyelin, cited, p. 155.
[72] Acheson, quoted in same, p. 133.

policy, at best he must either settle for an illusory consensus or assume a consensus on a purely American position; at worst, the evidence of disagreement is blinding. The process is the same; the result is different. A process that, at home, leads to some agreement (whatever the flaws of the policy based on the consensus) leads abroad either to no consensus or to a prohibitively costly one.

The main manifestation of this problem, among allies, is in "consultation." Consultation is a very narrow and unstable bridge between the shore of *information-giving* among parties that agree and the shore of actual *negotiations* to turn differences into agreement. In domestic American politics, consultation is a privileged method of consensus-building. When all the parties to the consensus—executive agencies and officials, Congress, and the various strata of public opinion—are in general agreement on goals and directions, consultation suffices. One starts with and proceeds on the assumption that the fundamentals are not in question. Nor is there any doubt about who commands; the president's position is not at stake. In relations with foreign powers, neither the agreement on goals and directions nor the agreement on who commands can be taken for granted. "Consultation, therefore, is far from a panacea. It is least effective when it is most needed: where there exist basic differences. . . . It works best in implementing a consensus rather than in creating it." [73]

When the consensus to be implemented is implicitly assumed, the process of consultation turns into mere information-giving. Indeed, our allies all too often protest that they are not consulted but told. Their share in what ought to be a collective decision-making process is limited to participation in briefings and the right to indicate how they plan to carry out their assignments.[74] Some of them are inclined to see in this situation the United States' will to dominate, but actually, it reflects the characteristic application of American working habits to states of differing national situations and objectives.[75]

Frequently, however, it is assumed that the process of consultation can *create* a consensus. Here, we leave the shore of information, al-

[73] Kissinger, *The Troubled Partnership,* p. 227.

[74] See General André Beaufre, in Cerny and Briefs, eds., *Nato in Quest of Cohesion,* p. 49.

[75] See Richard Neustadt's remarks in Henry M. Jackson, ed., *The Atlantic Alliance: Jackson Subcommittee Hearings and Findings* (New York: Frederick A. Praeger, 1967) on how the multiplicity of voices makes consultation difficult, and how the "load" the United States carries makes it more willing to consult about how "middle powers . . . ought to conduct their affairs" than about the conduct of its own.

though we never reach that of true negotiations. For we project into international affairs our domestic experience of consultation, and we equate it with negotiations because there is some bargaining involved. But what we bargain about at home is "incremental," not fundamental. If the consensus has not been forged first and consultation with our allies runs dry, bargaining to forge a consensus will be misleading if we carefully leave out the political sore spots at the heart of the issues. Thus we often believe we have a consensus, and think we have negotiated an agreement, while our allies think the consultation has concerned merely generalities or marginalia. The history of American reactions to de Gaulle's 1958 idea of a three-power directorate for NATO is instructive: we rejected the notion, yet, instead of negotiating over the basic political differences with him, we repeatedly offered limited talks at low levels or on partial subjects—talks between military experts, not political leaders; on strategy, not foreign policy; concerning parts of the world (Africa) where the French had essential interests (which the negotiations would have "internationalized") and we had none. Similarly, in "negotiations" with our allies over the MLF, we left unresolved the key problems of the force's control and political evolution.

In "negotiations" with friends and allies over the nonproliferation treaty, we tended once again to blame their reluctance on ignorance, to mistake briefings for bargaining, and to deal only with their specific and changing objections, not with the submerged and almost instinctive hostility to consecrated discrimination, of which those objections merely represent an emerged part. However successful our efforts to destroy the latter, new objections would still emerge as long as the deeper reasons remain unheeded.

When we are faced with conflicts of ends which consultation cannot resolve, we tend to propose the setting up of a procedure as a substitute solution. Again, this is a projection into international life of domestic habits. Within the United States, when consultation around the president is not enough to resolve genuine clashes of interest, "mutual partisan adjustment" arrives at consensus through the debates and compromises of committee techniques or, far less verbal and more active, through the technical cooperation of the various interests in a joint enterprise. Instead of head-on collisions on substantive issues, we make a productive detour through procedure; instead of a laborious political undertaking, an effective technical construction. In domestic affairs, when men put the maintenance of their community and cooperation above the triumph of their separate views, there is a deep wisdom in these procedural detours and technical deviations: they provide a low-tension and crab-wise way to solve differences—by attrition, so to speak, or by focusing attention not on abstract and hostile positions but on their concrete and more manageable consequences—and they ingeniously minimize and evaporate discord. I have seen this work beautifully in faculty meetings, and it is an ideal method of parliamentary government. But misapplied, in the wrong milieu, it tends to exacerbate rather than assuage, for the procedure or actual common task devised becomes itself an arena of conflict and a stake. This is true not merely in America's experience; the difficulties in European functional integration are of exactly the same order.

In American foreign policy, the prime example is, once again, the issue of nuclear weapons in NATO. The first idea for a truly allied nuclear force was the MLF, a technical diversion. The next was the McNamara Committee that would discuss nuclear strategy. In it, either the basic issues will be thrashed out or it will be one more roundabout attempt to replace negotiation with consultation—in which case the basic issues remain unsolved and the consensus eludes the contenders.

The fallacy of the procedural or technical solution in international affairs is of course even greater when the would-be partners are not allies (sharing a certain language, a ritual, and interests almost sufficient to justify the false assumption of consensus and community), but enemies. Between allies, procedures can at least help turn a weak pre-existing consensus into a strong one. Between adversaries, procedures can only ratify and add detail to previously negotiated agreements on essentials. When the adversary is a Communist statesman, to assume a common interest in good will, a common faith in personal relations and objective discussions is absurd. Negotiation of agreements must itself develop from meetings between high political leaders or from diplomatic exchanges between them— like the negotiations that preceded the nuclear test-ban treaty, rather than the Geneva disarmament conferences. Indeed, between enemies in revolutionary wars, only exchanges (public or secret) between capitals, and not conferences, have a chance of leading to a consensus. Between allies or ordinary adversaries, high-level conferences can bring agreement when there is a will to compromise (although even such conferences usually do little more than elaborate on what had already been decided in diplomatic give-and-take). But in revolutionary wars, to leave basic issues to a summit conference or to a conference of plenipotentiaries is to insure that the conference will not take place (as the French gradually learned in Algeria). The issues, for instance, of the role of the Vietcong at a Vietnam peace conference or during the interim before elections, or the question of who will supervise elections and what groups will be allowed to compete in them must be solved *before* a conference can usefully be held. The refusal of our foes in Vietnam to meet us at a conference unfortunately confirms the American public and the American policy-makers in their error on this point. We draw the erroneous conclusion that their unwillingness proves they ought not to be trusted and that they do not want to listen to reason, instead of the right conclusion that negotiations are valid only when basic trust already exists and all parties define "reason" in the same way. Even a "sincere" offer to negotiate (especially to parties that are unfamiliar with our assumptions) will exacerbate differences by feeding their suspicions and confusing them about our intentions. It may be too much to ask them to entrust their future to our way of solving problems, and to understand that our instinct to shift basic issues off into technical and procedural channels is a way by which we try to simplify a complex decision-making process—entrusting the resolution of political conflict to the scientific precision of a technical device or to the chemical device of a parliamentary procedure.

There is a final reason why a projection of domestic techniques of consensus-building into foreign affairs is detrimental to foreign policy. It lies in the tendency to "use the process of negotiations to make up our own minds." [76] (In defining this, Henry Kissinger alluded to the MLF proposal, launched by officials who had not yet made up their minds about the crucial issues of political control of nuclear weapons in NATO and the future evolution of the fleet.) There is nothing wrong in using negotiations for this purpose when the stakes of the discussions are not of fundamental importance, but in foreign affairs, when the stakes are high, the consequences can be disastrous. Either our confusion will make any genuine consensus impossible, or a consensus will be reached at the cost of considerable losses. These dangers were demonstrated in the difficult bargaining (particularly at the United Nations) that took place after China's entry into the Korean War, when American goals had to be redefined under fire, and also during the Suez crisis in the weeks that followed the nationalization of the Canal, when no consensus emerged, and again in the months after the abortive invasion, when a painful consensus grew

[76] Henry Kissinger, *The Troubled Partnership*, p. 158.

out of the shambles of allied strategy. During negotiations over Berlin in 1959 and 1961, the United States avoided major losses but failed to carry its allies and proposed very risky concessions. Over Vietnam, during the abortive "peace offensive" at the end of 1965 and for many months after, as well as in the troubled spring and summer of Santo Domingo in 1965, our uncertainties were similarly detrimental to the international consensus we were seeking and to our prestige. In the NATO crisis of the spring of 1966, our confusion permitted France to make tactical gains and made possible only the shallowest consensus among the Fourteen. The negotiations over the nonproliferation treaty have combined the two disadvantages: in our discussions with the Soviets in 1966 we reached an agreement on terms that raised havoc in our alliances, and obliged us to try to appease our dissatisfied friends and allies (a spectacle that the Soviets could afford to watch and could not fail to enjoy); in our effort to repair the damage, we then endangered our agreement with the U.S.S.R. and ran into considerable trouble in trying to establish a world-wide consensus. There ought to be some middle ground between the habit of discovering what is on our mind when our nose is to the grindstone, and the routine of policy papers written when no storm threatens and useless when it breaks out.

FOREIGN POWERS AS INSTRUMENTS OF CONSENSUS

At times, we treat foreign powers or groups not just as potential members of a consensus, but as *instruments* comparable to the organizations and media that are used in domestic political life as carriers of the political consensus to the public. To go so far in "approach[ing] international affairs as an extension of the game of national politics" [77] is to carry the sensible notion of the indivisibility of foreign and domestic policy to absurd lengths. For if it is true that you can't "force a foreign policy issue on the American people," [78] *a fortiori* forcing one on foreign people and regimes makes little sense. Relays strengthen consensus at home; the assimilation of foreigners to relays chases consensus away and leaves only puppets and enemies. The American intention is to bring about a consensus in the manner that works in the United States—exploiting the political process in the countries we want to influence—rather than in the manner of traditional diplomacy, by balancing forces and maneuvering events. But, once more, intentions and results clash.

Frequently, foreign policy is pursued before foreign audiences as

[77] Geyelin, cited, p. 141.
[78] Same, p. 149.

if an American election campaign were being waged abroad. Just as administration officials appear at press conferences or on campuses or before civic groups in order to explain the policy of the United States and marshal support for it, American officials engage in similar exercises abroad, with the same public-relations aura. Vice presidential or presidential tours, "peace offensives" that capture headlines, and the like are a major ingredient of American statecraft. To be sure, there are benefits, but the drawbacks often exceed them. Expectations are built up; the credit of good will obtained is exhausted when other nations discover that the exercise had little to do with actual diplomacy and was primarily an attempt to water the putative roots of a foreign consensus on American policy. A triumphant European tour by an American president designed to show that the principal countries of the continent support American concepts and that de Gaulle is the odd man out is unlikely to produce lasting effects unless the solidarity of interests and policies is subsequently demonstrated in action. When the use of foreign instruments entails the further measure of talking "beyond governments to people"—indeed, against those of their leaders who could be charged with "paternalistic authoritarianism" [79]—the technique is hardly conducive to improved relations.

Foreign relations become especially risky when we play this game with foreign leaders and political forces. It is frequently not at all to our or their advantage to endorse them, which will make them appear like puppets or satellites. The picturesque journeys of Chancellor Erhard to Washington or Texas ceased being of use to him or us when the German politicians and public discovered that he came back with happy memories but empty hands. An unsubtle embrace of opposition leaders in a foreign country by the United States, while not sufficient to make them look like equal partners in America's policy process, may be quite enough to make them look like the instruments of America's will. And when the men we bless are national leaders in countries where control of the government is in question—like Prince Boun Oum, or Marshal Ky—we may grievously harm their cause. "That's my boy" is a presidential seal that usually helps candidates in the United States. Abroad, it humiliates, infuriates, or amuses.[80]

[79] Schlesinger, cited, pp. 882–83.

[80] See John Bartlow Martin, *Overtaken by Events*, p. 517, remarking that he did for Bosch "what an aide does for a President or presidential candidate"—i.e., make suggestions for speeches.

Another example is the use of regional or international organizations as instruments of United States policy. For example, we have repeatedly asked the OAS to bail us out of trouble or to give us a certificate of good behavior, and we have repeatedly treated it in rather cavalier fashion.[81] There was great justification for this during the Cuban missile crisis, but less so in the Guatemalan crisis or over the Dominican Republic. Protracted arm-twisting in order to get a two-thirds majority (regardless of the composition of the minority) or a collective peace force exposes American pressure. In January 1966, the United States' abrupt referral of the Vietnam crisis to the U.N. Security Council, simultaneously with the resumption of the bombing of North Vietnam and followed by an almost equally abrupt decision not to press the case in the United Nations (it had become obvious that the nonaligned members, plus a few others, had no intention of serving as mere transmitters of American intentions and hesitations) also drew attention to the misuse of delicate instrumentalities. No international organization ever performs as well in the symphonic consensus as an AFL-CIO congress.

I have said that the domestic use of relays, intended to knit a garment of legitimacy about the government's policy, often requires that changes be minimized so that new policies can be smuggled in under the cloak. Then, on occasion, when the garment has become moth-eaten, exposing the old policy's nakedness, limited innovations are presented as major revolutions so as to provide a new, warm cloak for a shivering policy. The projection into foreign affairs of these methods will, once again, exacerbate the differences among nations. To present a radically new and important policy about which we have not sufficiently consulted or warned our allies—as has often been the case with our strategic doctrines, and as was the case with the nonproliferation treaty—increases their anger at being taken for granted. And our stress on continuity while we are in fact trimming our sails and changing course only increases their suspicions about the wisdom of our policy. The relatively quiet abandonment of the "counterforce" nuclear strategy, the change in the scale of our commitment in Vietnam, fluctuating emphases in our Latin American policy have not consolidated the mythical consensus among our allies or helped our foreign policy.

THE CASUALTY

There is an added danger. Our external projection of consensus-building reduces further our aptitude to cooperate with others whose

[81] See I. L. Claude, "The OAS, the U.N. and the United States," *International Conciliation*, No. 547 (March 1964).

views differ from ours. Our institutional practices aggravate our clumsiness in intervention. Since we naturally discover that our methods work best (or only) with foreigners who are already convinced of our wisdom, awed by our might, or in need of our aid, we may very well end up talking only to the faithful, the converts, and our clients, and neglecting the proud, the suspicious, or the reticent. This problem has been the bane of American information and cultural programs; indeed, the criterion for allocation of funds for such programs seems at times to have been the degree of sympathy and affection for the United States in the country concerned: the safer it was, the more lavish the effort; the greater the need to reach a reluctant public, the smaller the available resources. That such programs are all too often geared more to American than to foreign audiences, and merely used techniques and themes that have been proved successful at home, shows our inclination to ventriloquy.

Thus, in a kind of vicious circle, our projection of methods derived from our domestic political system expresses what I have called American dualism. We do not know how to reach those who are separated from us by profound cleavages—except by force—since our institutional devices are not fitted to, and indeed would be paralyzed by, the existence of such conflicts. We treat those who are or appear closer to us as if friendship and common interests abolished the distance between us, without realizing that this instinctive and sincere response of good will may appear hypocritical, arrogant, overpowering, or irrelevant. Is it a coincidence if a president whose performance as the leader of his nation in crisis was particularly successful, Franklin Roosevelt, performed far less effectively on the world stage, where he displayed so many features of the American style and used so many practices of the American political system?

At home, we often let consensus shape the substance of our policies; consensus becomes the end. Abroad, where consensus—genuine agreement among states with different interests—often should be an end, these methods of ours prevent us from reaching it. Yet we still need a policy, so we follow the one that emerged from the domestic consensus, even if it fails to take into account the views and interests of the partners whose support we tried to rally. When we do reach an international consensus, on an inadequate policy (because we failed to make up our minds about how far it was wise to go and thus let the process of international consensus-building dictate the policy), we resent it and put the blame on the process rather than on ourselves. We end up losing on two counts: the domestic methods of reaching consensus take precedence over the need for an effective foreign policy, and the misuse of those methods abroad either prevents the international consensus that could make the policy effective, or produces one at a less than optimum level, thus encouraging the habit of acting by ourselves.

To be sure, it would be foolish to argue that external consensus should *shape* American foreign policy, especially in relations with our foes. But it is not foolish to argue that in the pursuit of "milieu goals" the ability to marshal the support of all nations (excepting determined adversaries) is essential. Nor is it foolish to argue that the American tendency to act on our own would be less open to criticism if we were not quite so willing to permit the imperatives of our governmental system to define our foreign policy.

## III. The Mirrors

American foreign relations can be impaired not only by the methods we use, but also by the impact of the image we present to the world: not the "fabricated" image on which American officials, from the president to cultural and information officers abroad and down to professionals of make-believe outside the government work so hard, but the "genuine" image of American political behavior, spontaneous and unrehearsed. Still, the word genuine is misleading, for the image which foreigners see is not a true and complete reflection of American realities. They do not see American political life in all its complexities; they see it as it appears in a distorting mirror in which certain kinds of blemishes are magnified, while the better features appear smaller and less attractive than they actually are.

We must ask, of course, why these distortions occur, and there is no simple answer. Partly, it is because the United States is the victim of its own virtues. The restless raking over of dubious coals which is one of the glories of America's mass media and pamphleteers, of its social scientists and civic groups, and the tumultuous publicity with which everything controversial, contentious, or cantankerous is surrounded inevitably produce a Gresham's Law according to which the ugly, nasty, smelly, wicked, and wrong attract more attention than the good and beautiful. Partly, it is because these practices expose something that may exist more in, say, the Soviet Union, but that is so much easier to document here: a gap between principles and performance, an often ironic contradiction between the ideal of which one likes to pose as the champion, and a reality which indicates that there is still a good deal of work to be done at home before one can in good conscience afford the condescending charity of compassion for the foibles and troubles of others.

But can visibility alone account for the fact that American foibles are so often denounced with more vigor and viciousness than Soviet flaws? Are not the gaps between professed goals and actual deeds much greater in the Communists' case—especially since those goals are often pressed upon others with a proselytizing ruthlessness and a gamut of power devices that the United States nowhere near approximates? For two closely connected reasons, the United States is especially on the spot and singled out for its defects. First, it is the most powerful nation on earth; next to its military might and high degree of economic development, the Soviet Union appears only as a challenger. Next to the United States, any rival is an underdog, and in the eyes of other underdogs, an underdog enjoys greater latitude for folly and cruelty than the top dog. Second, the United States is also the champion of a process of development that puts a very high premium on stability, that favors progress but only if it comes in certain "orderly" ways, and that shows what can at best be called mixed feelings toward violence. Inevitably, all those who find the *status quo* unbearable or unfavorable, who have had to do battle in order to establish their place in the sun, view the United States as the champion of Western colonialism, exploitation and oppression; these people are bound to apply a double standard—a rather more lenient one (which does not mean blind or submissive) to the self-proclaimed champions of revolution, drastic change, and emancipation, and a more stringent one to the professor of moderation and maturity.

This is unfair, of course, but it is the price we pay for leadership. Better behavior is always expected from those who believe, or act as if they believed, that their superiority of wealth and might gives them a claim to shape world order. Great Britain learned this lesson during the nineteenth century, when its envious rivals (particularly France and Germany) mercilessly gloated over its weaknesses and pretenses and found in the existence of these blemishes the consolation for their inferiority and a justification for challenge. Knowing the colossus has clay feet warms the soul; soon enough, the eye sees the colossus as all clay. Aliens are less awed by the leading nation's qualities than excited by its defects. Its virtues impress other powers only a little—not enough normally to make them accept its objectives as their own on the mere strength and showing of those virtues. In international affairs, it is not Caesar's wife that must be above suspicion, it is Caesar himself.

What, then, are the habits or problems in American domestic politics that most sharply limit America's credibility and lessen respect for the United States abroad? Two deserve mention. The first one is the American Right, with its vision of history as conspiracy, of international politics as a struggle against an enemy who "is a perfect model of malice" [82] and can be fought effectively only by a force wholly dedicated to victory and to the thorough destruction of all that wily enemy's tricks, tools, and stooges. The United States' position in the world since 1945 has created many occasions for the display and flowering of the paranoid style; even the splintering of the "Sino-Soviet bloc," the fact that polycentrism multiplies the number of autonomous enemies and risks of frustration, and the fact that the international system is one of denials rather than positive achievements encourage the paranoid right wing. To them, the proliferation of Communist parties, the restiveness of our allies, and the carping of neutrals are evidence of the devil's supreme cunning. The tendency to see in this "frustrating situation . . . simply the product of execrable statecraft—not to speak of treason," [83] in every attempt at drastic social change abroad a Communist plot or opportunity, has deep roots (some of which I have discussed in earlier chapters); "but above all, the far right has become a permanent force in the political order because the things upon which it feeds are also permanent." [84]

Why should this phenomenon, which represents only a small fraction of the American people, have any repercussion at all abroad? The answer may lie in the word "respectability." First, not all fractions are equal; any society is hierarchical, and it so happens that the social roots and props of "paranoid" right-wing movements and pseudo-conservative revolts are mostly found in the upper echelons of American society; moreover, these men are not relegated to one limited corner of society. Whatever the shallowness, the spread is wide, certainly wider than left-wing extremism. Here we are dealing with views that have gained credence in business organizations and among veterans, in Congress and in the press, in parties and among

[82] Hofstadter, *The Paranoid Style in American Politics and Other Essays,* cited, p. 31.
[83] Same, p. 131.
[84] Same, p. 140.

certain military leaders. Second, the American political system is such that minority views can easily gain prominence, as Waltz has noted,[85] if and when they gain access to publicity and power by a variety of channels and with an abundance of wealth. A kind of snowballing takes place, or perhaps something like inflation: the combination of visibility, demagogic tactics, access to influence, the means to intimidate, and shrewd overstatement of their representativity (all of which their adversaries feel compelled to refute and counter) can easily mislead foreign observers, since it also misleads Americans.

Finally, whereas the themes of the far left in many cases go against the national grain, those of the far right appeal to a powerful latent strain of America's emotional makeup. The "illusion of omnipotence" and an angry impatience with a world that resists American efforts are characteristic of both; both appeal to those who believe that with the guts to act with driving determination one can transform the world. Yet left-wing naïveté, in a world full of adversaries and threats, is all too easily denounced as stupid and almost treasonous, whereas right-wing boisterousness is easily presented as the logical and courageous pursuit of American governmental policy taken to the final consequences, which the government fails to reach due to its half-heartedness, lack of stamina, and wishy-washiness. The combined effect of America's situation as a world power in the present international system and its own predispositions give to official government policy a slope (gentle, to be sure) toward the right; paradoxically enough, therefore, the right wing benefits in its onslaught on official policies from the fact that it can appear like an exaggeration or cartoon of those policies, whereas the left is seen as a break away from and reaction against them. Hofstadter has shrewdly noted that Kennedy in 1960 and Goldwater in 1964 stressed similar themes, were both vigorously nationalistic, and appealed "to public uneasiness over the indecisiveness of the cold war." [86]

All of this explains why it is easy—not only for foreigners who are eager to ruffle the eagle's feathers but even for those who genuinely regret the spots on the eagle's plumage—to give right-wing views more importance than they deserve, especially since the "zeal and gifts for organization" of right-wingers put them "in a position to make themselves effective far out of proportion to their numbers," [87]

[85] Cited, p. 73.
[86] Cited, p. 131.
[87] Same, p. 138.

as the election of 1964 showed. To receive only 40 per cent of the popular vote is to be crushingly defeated by American standards; but it is a respectable figure by other standards and even a remarkable one in America, if one remembers that the defeated candidate offered "a choice, not an echo" in imprudently strident tones.

The existence of this impact of the right wing, the contribution which the obstinate quest for scapegoats makes to the "incommunicability" of America abroad, should teach all those in the political and communications system who provide loudspeakers for their voices and platforms for their political programs, that they too are responsible for the effect. To let the "free market of ideas" and the free market of votes winnow out the bad seeds from the good herbs is a most democratic thing to do. But there is nothing particularly democratic in making it easy for weeds to proliferate; and while the market goes through its rites, other nations watch with dismay or malicious delight. We are living in a distorting glass house.

The second aspect of American political behavior that lessens respect for the United States is not a specific force but the quality of American political life in general. George Kennan's familiar (but insufficiently heeded) argument that this quality has enormous significance for the effectiveness of foreign policy needs to be taken seriously. It is of universal validity. A nation like China, which wants to spread the gospel of revolution, can do so effectively only if its domestic affairs reveal a capacity to organize, infuse with a sense of common purpose, submit to a common discipline, and move a population of poor and traditionally exploited peasants toward higher levels of wellbeing. A nation like ours that stands for the ideals of the Declaration of Independence and the Bill of Rights, a nation that has staked its prestige and leadership on the wager that liberty and "achievement" in equality are compatible and mutually reinforcing, will make its mark if its own political life shows that the wager is sound. The reasons why political success at home is no guarantee of success abroad, the reasons why America's historical experience is unique and inexportable are resilient and profound. But in the crowded echo-chamber of the present international system, where symbols matter and personal skills take precedence, many nations, like adolescents in the turmoil of growing up, look for models, even if the factors that made the model what it is cannot be copied. Thus, America may never be an adequate model, in the sense in which one might be justified in speaking of a Maoist model of revolution. But America can at least be an example or inspiration, and in a world in which the relative atrophy of force prevents the deliberate imposition of models and examples, international influence depends to quite an extent on the aptitude for this role. This is why, even in foreign policy, the ways in which the slow and complicated American political processes solve such problems as civil rights, the reduction of poverty, the security of employment, the welfare of the sick and the aged, the plight of crowded and ugly cities are so important. When domestic events are the primary fuel of international relations, domestic virtues may well become a prime ingredient of foreign policy.

# PART IV

# Foreign Policy Revisited

# CHAPTER TEN

# *Gulliver Untied*

In the three preceding Parts, I have discussed the restraints and obstacles imposed by the international system and by America's political style and institutions as they affect U.S. foreign policy. I have
tried to show that even some of the developments from which we derive satisfaction, such as the building of alliances or the incipient
*détente* with the Soviet Union, even some of the domestic features of
which we are most proud, such as our concern for moral values in
world affairs, or the involvement of a vast segment of the public in
foreign affairs, create formidable problems that exact a cost. The
problem in the making of foreign policy is to overcome these obstacles and use the strength of the national style and the political
system to reach goals compatible with the international system. The
world of 1947–48 has passed, and the vision with which we met its
challenges and transformed it is now inadequate. A new vision is
needed.

No course of action can be found in which only one's assets are exploited and the liabilities are entirely cast off; each will be a mix,
every move will be a choice among different imperfect mixes. An
effective foreign policy depends on the discovery of the least imperfect one. There are two ways of arriving at a definition of this least
imperfect course of action. Policy-makers can aim at the one that
will give greatest play to the good qualities of the American style
and to the virtues of its institutions and least play to their defects. Or
they can aim at the course of action that will help to move the international system from its present form to one that will be less frustrating for a superpower. There are important differences between the
two approaches. The first assumes that the American style and institutions are "givens," and that the United States must work for the
kind of an international system that will be most receptive to and
congruent with its peculiar strengths. The second assumes that the

*343*

United States is not omnipotent, that it ought not to set as a goal the objectives that are most congruent with the American style and institutions if those objectives are ruled out by the probable evolution of international politics, or if the attempt to reach them would entail (for America and for the world) perils that far exceed the pleasures of pursuing them.

In my opinion, the second formulation is appropriate. The present international system, as we know, is neither as congenial to the American way as the world of 1947–48 nor comfortable for superpowers. We must choose between working for an imperfect system congenial to our style but uncomfortable for superpowers, and striving for an imperfect system in which superpowers would be less tied down, so to speak, but in which we would have to behave in unfamiliar ways. The first would be a sound choice only if we were able to impose it on others, if the evolution of international affairs did not rule out such a system, and if the outcome were a reasonably moderate world order. Should none of this be the case, we would have to settle for the second choice. Reflexes, traditions, habits that are effective only in an international environment which is not now possible would have to be discarded or rendered harmless.

Thus, in defining the opportunities and goals of an effective foreign policy, we cannot merely ask what kind of a world the United States ought to aim for and what the required actions are to create such a world. Many of the goals we would like to reach are unrealistic, given present trends in world affairs. I do not mean to suggest that we cannot affect those trends, but we can affect them only within limits; some desirable worlds are simply not in the cards. We must ask not what the best world is that America ought to work for, but what the best is of the *possible* worlds. The new vision will have to be more modest than the old.

## I. The Future of the International System

In Part I of this book, I analyzed the present international system. On the basis of that analysis, we can imagine a number of theoretical possibilities for the future. Our task consists of ruling out those which appear impossible, *practically,* and of assessing the remaining possibilities. In order to do this we must first assess the United States' basic interests that derive from its position in the international milieu.

## A. *American Interests*

As a superpower and as a nation engaged in a world-wide contest with a number of foes, the United States has vital stakes in the international competition of the nuclear age. There still may be people who believe that the "right" kind of policy—the smashing one of victory or the soothing one of pacifism—could lead to a world so safe and so self-regulating that the United States could return to its own business (whether that is defined as business or as domestic reform), but they hardly deserve much consideration. Commiseration for obsolescence suffices. And the debate over "neo-isolationism" that has begun recently must be seen for what it is: an honest, if heated, disagreement about the most effective form of involvement, in which one group that believes in a maximalist "forward strategy" of world-wide involvement charges the minimalist group with neo-isolationism. This may be sound tactics, but it is certainly not sound analysis. The debate between critics of the "arrogance" of power and moaners about the "agony" of power is not much more enlightening: the mere possession of great power always creates a presumption of arrogance, even when the power is used with restraint and discrimination, while the choosing of a relaxed, prudent, and limited use of power is no less "agonizing" than a constant rushing to the front lines all over the globe.

Like all great powers in past international systems, the United States has an interest in maintaining (or restoring) a certain degree of *hierarchy* in the system. An international milieu in which the "impotence of power" of the leading states decentralizes power so that the puny and the mighty enjoy the same freedom of action (or suffer from the same paralysis); or a milieu in which the power of smaller states can be used more productively than that of the larger units, in which the latter are Gullivers tied while the Lilliputians roam at will—either would be unacceptable, even if the likely result in both cases were not nuclear proliferation. In the long run, inflation breeds an unhealthy separation between responsibilities and capabilities, in world affairs as in economics. None of this tells us anything about the nature of the hierarchy to be established, but it points to an American interest (and to a Soviet interest as well) in seeing to it that the system does not become more radically equalitarian than the present one.

The United States is locked in a competition with foes that, however divided on means they may be, and engaged as they are in a battle for power of their own, nevertheless agree in their desires to eliminate American power, influence, and interests. The United States naturally wants to *thwart* those designs—how effectively and widely this can be done depends, again, on trends in the international system—and the minimum objective must be to prevent the physical expansion of the power of the two main foes, the Soviet Union and China, and to foil military aggression by minor Communist regimes. In an ideal world, the American objective would be defined as preventing the establishment of any hostile regime that was allied to Russia or China, or even as the elimination of all enemies. Obviously, the range between the minimum and the maximum objective is huge, containing, for instance, the entire area of possible expansion of non-Soviet or non-Chinese Communist influence. But the point here is that there is an incompressible minimum. Some say that the forcible extension of Soviet or Chinese control over some parts of the world would not affect the United States' power position at all, but, as I have indicated, I believe this implies much too complacent an assessment of what is at stake.

The existence of nuclear weapons affects both of these U.S. goals as I have defined them. The national interest in "prevailing" in the international contest is doubly qualified. On the one hand, "victory," or even the kind of defense that involves disproportionate risks, becomes more difficult to advocate, and the interest in thwarting the foe must be reconciled with the interest in survival, which is possible only if armed conflict is strictly restrained. On the other hand, nuclear weapons give an additional reason for deterring a foe's expansion when it is attempted with force, since any resort to force is so dangerous. And the interest in creating or maintaining an international hierarchy is accentuated, since a "unit veto system," where even very small states would dispose of extensive means of destruction, would drastically alter the international hierarchy. Many small nuclear forces would be highly vulnerable, and their vulnerability would increase instability; the possession of nuclear weapons by states that were domestically unstable and poor would make the management of power in international affairs a real nightmare, forcing the superpowers back to a recurrent choice between universal policing (at high costs, both for themselves and in terms of a possible collapse of the taboo on nuclear weapons that has so far prevailed) and letting the world disintegrate into a series of jungles.[1]

---

[1] See the remarks by "Erasmus" in "Polycentrism and Proliferation," *Survey,* January 1966, pp. 70–72.

And it would also condemn the superpowers to a permanent arms race so as to preserve or restore the distance between themselves and minor nuclear states.

Nuclear weapons thus introduce another American interest, namely, in the cultivation of *moderation*—the fleeting characteristic of past balance-of-power systems, the threatened characteristic of the present one. Even sweeping ends must be pursued with prudent means. Since such ends always seem to encourage the selection of incautious means, and we cannot be sure that nuclear sanity will prevail, it is necessary for the chief contestants to define their ends so that the competition can remain within bounds—whether this means a gradual erosion of the more ambitious ends, reduced to rationalized rituals, or a postponement of the more dangerous ends into the increasingly problematic future. This moderation must prevail not only in the "relations of major tension," but also in all other interstate relations; there is a compelling interest in providing effective means of peaceful change or effective means of "peacekeeping and peacemaking" when violence breaks out. To be sure, it takes more than one player to impose moderation on a system. It can be argued that the special circumstances that have created the present paradox of an international system that is both revolutionary and restrained will not recur in the future, however hard the United States tries, either because China's militancy will be far greater than that of Russia under Stalin or his successors or because the proliferation of nuclear powers will undermine the restraints observed now. However, Communist China's actual behavior contrasts with militant Chinese pronouncements, and, although an increase in its supply of power may reduce this gap between words and deeds, the risks of militancy will remain high, and wise American policy would aim at increasing the rewards of moderation. As for the dangers of proliferation, which are very serious, they need not make moderation impossible just at the time when they are making it indispensable.

The United States has another vital interest which encompasses and transcends the ones I have already mentioned. The United States needs not only to protect its material possessions, to preserve its security, to safeguard its power and rank, but also to try to establish a *world order* that will accommodate these concerns. Now which, among likely international systems, is most capable of restoring hierarchy, deterring the main foes of the United States and keeping conflicts moderate? In what kind of world can nations define their goals so that they will be reached, cooperatively or competitively, without large-scale violence, and reconciled without excessive frustrations? The unification of the international system, the shrinking of distance through communications, and the nuclear risks make it imperative to think of foreign policy not exclusively in terms of national strategy and piecemeal objectives, but in systemic terms. And the superpowers are still those most capable of shaping the system—but within its limits.

## B. *Unlikely International Systems of the Future*

One possible future international system is a bipolar one, in which the United States and the Soviet Union not only shared the monopoly of the ultimate power of destruction, as they do today, but also could use their power more effectively and obtain positive achievements commensurate with their material capabilities. Such a system would require that the "centers" and "poles" challenging the superpowers were as circumspect in their behavior as they are restricted in their capabilities; that the advantages which the present system provides to defensive and even offensive uses of power by lesser states were reduced; that any smaller nuclear powers "constantly [found] themselves falling behind" [2] the two superpowers and that their acquisition of nuclear weapons had not improved the positive productivity of their power. How could such a pure bipolar system come about? Two possibilities exist theoretically.

The first one is that there would be a return to intense competition between the United States and the Soviet Union—a contest so hot that the original "camps" of the Cold War would be created anew, and nonaligned states, while huddling together to avoid the storm, would find it in their interest to be as invisible as possible. There undeniably exists a kind of nostalgia for such a system among some men for whom the limited *détente* since 1963 is a mere pause, who doubt the finality of the Sino-Russian split, who see the Cold War in Europe as still the most essential reality, the Chinese menace as a diversion, and the underdeveloped countries as nuisances and only secondary theaters of foreign policy. The reasons for their nostalgia are clear: the American political style and system were admirably suited for the Cold War, as the great achievements of the late 1940s testify. But its return strikes me as unlikely and undesirable. It is unlikely because the policies of the superpowers assume its undesirability. Both America and Russia exhibit a moderation that

[2] Waltz, "The Stability of a Bipolar World," *Daedalus,* Summer 1964, p. 898.

rules out a deliberate reversion to a black-and-white world, with each "camp" obliged to subordinate all other concerns to the necessities of security and survival. Their reluctance to build "heavy" ABM systems around their cities is significant. Such systems would allow them to maintain or increase the distance between the superpowers and secondary nuclear states. None of the latter can achieve the "first strike capability" vis-à-vis the superpowers (i.e., the capability to destroy the enemy's nuclear force), which even eludes each superpower vis-à-vis the other; thus, the typical function of a small nuclear force, as against a superpower, is to deter by posing a threat of countercity blows (what de Gaulle has called tearing off an arm). This threat could be eliminated by the superpowers if they deployed these systems around their cities. But they hesitate to do so because, as long as they have not become genuine partners (neither of whom would misinterpret such a deployment by the other as a threat to himself), the placing of heavy antimissile defenses around cities could be a dangerously destabilizing factor. For it would enormously intensify the arms race between them and increase the "delicacy" of the balance of terror by encouraging the power that would be ahead in protecting its cities to take greater risks at lower levels of violence, and by weakening the fear of escalation to the nuclear level which inhibits large-scale resort to conventional force as long as the superpowers fear an intolerable population holocaust. Moreover, even if the superpowers decided, for some unthinkable reason, to revert to the Thucydidean model of pure conflict or if they stumbled into it, their ability to reproduce the holy simplicity of an earlier time is highly questionable. The modifications of bipolarity that have developed in the past few years have eroded those important attributes which Kenneth Waltz ascribed to their rivalry: certainty, world-wide extension, and intensity. Neither power is much interested in recreating conditions in which it might become obvious that the two emperors have, if not no clothes, at least not as many as in the days of the Cold-War alliances (which rash observers had christened new "bloc actors" in world affairs). Yesterday, the corollary of high tension was hegemonial alliances; tomorrow, the penalty of such tension would be a terrible strain on already cracking or cracked alliances. All these points have been confirmed, in 1967, by the crisis in the Middle East.

While contradictory in one respect, the behavior of the two powers challenging the United States and Russia helps to make a return to high tension unlikely. France, capitalizing on the widespread desire for a *détente* between East and West, has nudged the United

States into presenting itself within the North Atlantic Alliance, not only as the guardian of the Allies' security against the common foe, but also as the true champion of the *détente*. Communist China, by savagely attacking the Soviet Union's "collusion" with the United States, partially succeeds in slowing down the *détente,* but also increases Russia's determination not to come in conflict with the United States, since the main beneficiary of the clash would be China.

There is another version of bipolarity: not a struggle for domination but a joint exercise of domination, not a confrontation but a consortium. This too appeals to Americans—to their activist search for community, to the desire for an unfettered projection of American experiences and methods. Moreover, in such a world, hierarchy and moderation would both be assured. It would be an adaptation of the concert of major states as it existed in balance-of-power systems, with its powers of settlement on major issues and its power to discipline lesser nations. The attractiveness of this notion shines behind many American proposals for arms control and for a world-wide reduction of tensions, which combine "skill thinking" and the dream of orderly harmony. There are, however, two reasons why this kind of an international system appears unlikely.

First, as the story of the nonproliferation treaty shows, it would be difficult for the superpowers to bring the condominium into existence. The muting of bipolarity, in the sense of the taming of the bipolar conflict, is one thing; we have seen, in Part I, why it was possible, indeed necessary, for the "enemies" to become mere "adversaries." But the shift from restrained hostility to cooperation, from an adversary relationship to one of co-management is quite another thing. The trouble with the idea of a grand settlement that would liquidate their rivalry is that it is likely to favor one side over the other or to entail costs and risks unacceptable to both. The inhibitions that throttle their competition at the upper levels of violence foster their contest at all other levels. Moreover, the establishment of a duopoly presupposes an ability on the part of America and Russia to subordinate their rivalry to their common interests, to provide other nations with joint guarantees and joint measures of enforcement. But such a game, played by two, has little of the flexibility it would have with four or five: each superpower, torn between its stakes in the rivalry and the lure of the common interest, is like an acrobat who wants to leap from one trapeze to another but fears he will fall the moment he lets go. The recent development of a sense of common interest between the United States and the Soviet Union is not un-connected with the rise of challengers to each, yet these challengers also perpetuate the rivalry. On the one hand, both must preserve a certain minimum of militancy out of fear of disintegration of each camp—a disintegration that is unwelcome as long as each superpower remains unsure about the new friendship of the other and afraid of provoking the enmity of former allies. On the other hand, even the effort to keep ahead of the challengers entails a new arms race between the superpowers, as shown by the ABM deployment. Were their "camps" in good shape, neither the Soviets nor the Americans would be willing and able to push their *rapprochement* too far. The bad shape of the camps inspires in each superpower both impatience with the allies who are deemed responsible, and reluctance to turn too openly the community of interests with the other superpower into an active solidarity, the muted rivalry into an alliance. The problem of joint assurances to potential nuclear powers (especially those that would have to be protected against a challenger and ex-ally of one of the superpowers) brings this into the open. Soviet-American solidarity increases only as each nation's control over its allies decreases. In the early days of the Cold War, they were inca-pable of using jointly their privilege of settling major world issues; soon, they are likely to want to use it, but it will have disap-peared—i.e., in most parts of the world, their writ will no longer run.

In order to maintain their position, they would have to act jointly against troublemakers, especially against states that acquired nuclear weapons. But this policing role would not be an easy one to main-tain. The superpowers could not easily break the nuclear taboo, since that would underline the importance of the weapons, might in-cite more proliferation, and would "restructure the attitudes of na-tional decision-makers" [3] in at worst a disastrous way, and at best a highly unsettling one. Yet more conventional or less drastic forms of pressure (moderate enough to keep the Pandora's box of nuclear vi-olence closed) would be insufficient, hence embarrassing, to the superpowers in a world where the capacity for resistance and denial was more evenly distributed than before, and where superior force or the threat thereof could not prevent many disturbances. Deter-mined efforts to act jointly as "world policemen" would lead to a world order based on force alone—an unhealthy prospect for stabil-

[3] C. E. Zoppo, "Nuclear Technology, Multipolarity and International Sta-bility," *World Politics*, July 1966, p. 603.

ity, since the victims would (as in past balancing systems) spend their time trying to upset the policemen and to exploit disagreements between them. An effort to act jointly on any other basis would lead to something different from bipolarity, for it would oblige the superpowers to be trustees of a world of nations unwilling to have their fate settled without their participation. Furthermore, many of the important tasks now done by international means (such as economic development aid or the propagation of ideologies and regimes or the giving of various kinds of technical advice), which either are completely new or used to be performed by other means, cannot be accomplished in an international hierarchy based on military might. The world today poses problems that can be solved only with a modicum of democracy—i.e., equalization among states. There is a vital paradox here: even a treaty on the nonproliferation of nuclear weapons will be achieved meaningfully only if the non-nuclear powers are "offer[ed] clear evidence that the Soviet Union and the United States are prepared to exercise leadership in the world on a basis of strength other than that inherent in their nuclear capabilities," [4] that is, if the Soviet Union and the United States are willing to reduce the gap in military power between them and other states or to deal with the latter on a basis other than force—which is their distinguishing advantage over them.

Ultimately, the reason why a bipolar future is unlikely has to do with the problem of force. Resort to force remains a *sine qua non* of all nations' foreign policies; however, the new circumstances of international relations—nuclear weapons, the interlocking of domestic and foreign affairs—deprive force of some of its value as the supreme standard. But any version of bipolarity uses force as the yardstick. The resulting confusions were well demonstrated by conflicting statements and policies of President Kennedy, who appeared to have believed in the joint duty of trusteeship of the United States and the Soviet Union on matters of life and death for the planet yet saw the rivalry between them as lasting, and also professed his faith in a world of diversity and national independence.

What, then, is the possible future international system? The dream of an imperial system, the apotheosis of *pax Americana,* stands condemned both for the reasons that doom bipolarity and for the reasons, listed in Chapter 2, which have kept it a dream or a delusion until now. Can we imagine a perpetuation of the present coexistence of bi-

[4] William C. Foster, "New Directions in Arms Control and Disarmament," *Foreign Affairs,* July 1965, p. 597.

polarity, polycentrism, and emergent multipolarity as I described it in Part I? It would be likely, if either of the two following developments took place. One conceivable development is an effective nonproliferation agreement signed by all the nations of the world. That is to say, America and Russia succeed in resolving their differences and show themselves capable of providing the non-nuclear states with the three sets of assurances that seem necessary to get the latter's consent to such an agreement (assurances about the non-nuclear states' right to exploit the peaceful uses of atomic energy without having to depend on the nuclear powers' good will; steps to curtail the development of nuclear weapons by the "nuclear haves"; and credible guarantees against nuclear attack for the "nuclear have nots"); in addition, today's secondary nuclear powers are satisfied with small nuclear forces capable of inflicting limited damage but not widespread destruction. In such a hypothetical system, the layer of "emergent multipolarity" would be frozen, so to speak, and the dynamics of world politics would be the interplay of bipolarity and polycentrism. The other possible development is that nuclear proliferation continues, but the lesser nuclear powers (including the present secondary ones) discover that they cannot hope to develop more than small nuclear forces and that even this gives them no advantage, since the only result is either a surplus of unusable power or, if they apply their military power rashly, a drastic reaction by the superpowers. With this hypothesis, the situation would remain close to what it is today.

In my opinion—and it is no more than that—the perpetuation of the present system in either fashion is not very likely or really desirable for the United States. The present system is stable if by stability we mean moderation, not if we mean longevity, for it corresponds to a transitory situation in which the United States and the Soviet Union are suspended between hostility and cooperation. It is fundamentally unnatural; it has provoked too many frustrations, and it has radically corrupted the international hierarchy, not because of the spread of an "equalizing" miracle weapon (as General Gallois argues), but because of the stalemate between the superpowers. Like inflation, it corresponds to a turbulent passage from one kind of a hierarchy to the next. Either this situation must evolve toward real cooperation, with the superpowers jointly taking responsibility for keeping the world from further nuclear proliferation (and we have just seen why this is unlikely); or else the system must evolve toward a form of multipolarity, with the superpowers pushed into increasing cooperation by the emergence of new poles of power, without whose support no settlements of important problems could be achieved. Otherwise, and meanwhile, there will (at best) be more localized jungles—inconclusive confrontations between powers, great or small, that prove incapable of settling their disputes through war or through agreements. And while such fragmentation of the international system, such a divorce between the over-all balance of nuclear power and regional or partial balances of power may prolong the system's life, the cost of extension may well be excessive fragility. Thus, the widespread interest in moderation works against a perpetuation of the present system.

Already, we can see two factors at work undermining it. First, there is China's drive to become a nuclear power. To be sure, one may believe, or hope, that ABM defenses in both America and Russia will reduce China's deterrent power to nothing and prevent China from pursuing "toward a superior nuclear power a high-risk policy involving a high level of international violence." [5] But in the race between offensive and defensive capabilities, the last word has not been spoken. Of course, one can argue that if China is successful, the only result will be a transformation of what I called the layer of latent bipolarity into one of latent tripolarity, in which the strategies of mutual deterrence would allow for a continuation of manifest polycentrism. But "tripolarity" would undoubtedly differ from the deadlock of bipolarity in that it would restore diplomatic flexibility; in other words, as in past multipolar systems, the superpowers' main diplomatic efforts would be horizontal (i.e., among themselves) rather than vertical (i.e., focused on the protection of their respective camps and on the seduction of the coy). Second, the limits of polycentrism have already appeared quite clearly. The centers' romp on the stage was made possible by the uselessness of much of the two poles' power and also by the competition between them. The more the contest between the United States and the U.S.S.R. is diffused or restrained, the more difficult it is for those new centers of power to extract the concessions from the superpowers which gave them their effective freedom. And too, the multiplication of new centers of power tends to recreate a certain sense of proportion, if not of hierarchy; as we know, not all nations want to romp on the world stage, and not all of those who want to, can. Moreover, the intensity of grievances, ambitions, and rivalries among the "centers" tends to provoke re-

[5] Klaus Knorr, *On the Uses of Military Power in the Nuclear Age* (Princeton: Princeton University Press, 1966), p. 118.

current tests of military force; and despite the limits which the present system imposes on the achievements of force, such tests act as moments of truth, less by fulfilling the dreams and goals of the stronger than by revealing the domestic weakness or bankruptcy of the weaker. Egypt's fate in 1967 confirms Indonesia's experience with Malaysia.

We cannot assume that the spread of nuclear weapons will be easily contained. An agreement signed by the U.S.S.R. and the United States might slow it down, but it is dubious whether it could stop it once and for all. Thus the first hypothesis I mentioned is probably ruled out. And if proliferation continues, the possibility of preserving the present system will be slight. Some of the new middle or smaller "poles" of power may be tempted to exploit their newly acquired advantages in local matters. As I have tried to show in some detail elsewhere, "the reasons for the relative paralysis of power of the Big Two—i.e., the restraints observed by them, may not operate in a multinuclear world, and . . . the fragility of those restraints . . . may lead to a situation in which at least some of the nuclear powers would try to exploit their newly acquired might and either derive gains [i.e., reopen channels for the positive productivity of their power] or produce a narrowing of the gap" [6] between themselves and the superpowers.

Between a minor nuclear pole (even if it does not use its nuclear force) and a non-nuclear "center," the opportunities for the former to reap gains greater than those available to the latter (or at the latter's expense) would disappear only if it were effectively deterred from every kind of "possession move" by the might of the superpowers or an international organization. The fuzziness of mutual deterrence and "the difficulty of establishing successful preventive and repressive mechanisms" in a world of several nuclear powers could weaken the restraints observed so far by middle powers. To an ambitious new nuclear power, the residual threat of total war and destruction might appear more remote and less deterrent than it does now. The uncertainties of the bipolar stalemate explain much of the desire of other countries to acquire nuclear weapons; the uncertainties in having *several* nuclear powers would, by themselves, restore a hierarchy. Even if the new nuclear powers behaved with extreme prudence, their capabilities would suffice to increase fears of insecurity among the presently complacent "centers"; this would contribute to the restoration, between these centers and the new poles, of a

[6] From my essay in Alastair Buchan, ed., *A World of Nuclear Powers* (Englewood Cliffs, N.J.: Prentice-Hall, 1966), pp. 119–20.

hierarchy based not on unused or unusable power, but on the fear of the use of power. The need to deter and repress that use would restore the hierarchy between the new poles and the superpowers.

Even if there were good chances of having the present system linger on, the United States would hardly find it so desirable, for the rival Fausts have no particularly good reason to find it attractive. Certainly it meets the requirements of moderation, and it deters quite effectively the United States' main adversaries. But it can hardly be praised for anything else. It favors the subverters of the hierarchy, the upstarts, and the *déclassés*. It perversely gives some flexibility to challengers and bargainers—in the polycentric and multipolar strata —while keeping the flexibility of the superpowers at a very low point; for them, to stand still is to keep running all the time.

## C. *Toward a Moderate International System*

What is most likely is the emergence of a new type of international system, which I would call "multi-hierarchical." [7] On the one hand, in such a system, as in past multipolar systems, the traditional major power role would be performed by a number of states, not only by the United States and the Soviet Union. On the other hand, the hierarchy would be more complex. First, there would be more ranks. The relatively simple division between the great powers and the others cannot function any more. The distinction between superpowers and middle powers would remain; the two or (perhaps) three states capable of world-wide destruction would play a major role. But international society has gained in scope and complexity, and just as the hierarchy in a modern factory is more complex than the division between *maîtres* and *compagnons* in an old *métier,* there would be new gradations. Second, there would be a set of hierarchies. Force remains the *ultima ratio,* but insofar as it has become largely unusable and inadequate to deal with many issues, it cannot any longer be the sole yardstick. In a world that must solve internationally the problems once tackled either by domestic or private transnational channels, there will be different hierarchies for different tasks, corresponding to different computations of power. Third, the muting of the competition between the Soviet Union and the

[7] The system described here is in many respects similar to the one outlined by Richard N. Rosecrance in "Bipolarity, Multipolarity and the Future," *Journal of Conflict Resolution,* Vol. X, No. 3 (September 1966), pp. 314–27; to the system advocated by Roger D. Masters in *The Nation is Burdened* (New York: Knopf, 1967); and to the system proposed by Ronald Steel in *Pax Americana* (New York: Viking Press, 1967).

United States, the rise of middle powers in various parts of the world, the participation of so many nations, the risk of general destruction through escalation in either extension (number of states involved) or intensity would produce not only a functional diversification of the hierarchy, but also a *regional decentralization* of the international system, i.e., an autonomy of various subsystems under the brooding omnipresence of nuclear deterrence.

This kind of system is the most likely: its rudiments are already with us. The decreasing capacity of lesser allies in each camp, whether they are nuclear powers or not, to trigger the nuclear involvement of Russia or America has begun to fragment the international system.[8] So does those allies' desire to dissociate themselves from more distant ventures—as symbolized by the attitude of most of America's NATO allies toward the war in Vietnam, by the coexistence of stability in Eastern and Western Europe with a war in Asia in which the United States is deeply involved and the Soviet Union moderately committed. Among the nonaligned countries, fragmentation and a tendency to concentrate on regional issues have also affected the earlier notion of a single "Third World." Member states of the European Economic Community, as well as Japan, whose military power is slight, have a considerable supply of economic power and their acts and opinions matter greatly in questions of trade and international payments. Within the United Nations, some small or middle powers with little economic and military might wield great influence in peacekeeping operations and as diplomatic brokers. But the final shape of such a system is unclear: here is where the policies of the superpowers, particularly of the United States, will be important.

Not every multipolar system of the past has been moderate; it is all too easy to imagine a multi-hierarchical system of dizzying instability. Conflicts, of course, will persist. They are likely to be particularly acute in the "Third World," where states with poor resources, or contested borders, or ethnic grievances, have compelling possession goals as well as ambitious milieu goals and the temptation of interfering in each other's often troubled internal affairs. The rivalry of the superpowers and the contest between each of them and China is likely to feed, as well as to feed on, such conflicts. Nuclear proliferation may not provoke a general nuclear war engulfing the planet, although there exists a risk in the "gray areas" at the fringes of each

[8] The Middle East crisis of 1967 has clearly shown that the superpowers' support to their "proxies" falls short even of conventional military involvement.

alliance system, and the new twists of the arms race among the leading nuclear powers may prove dangerously unsettling. But the spread of nuclear weapons could fragment the international system into unstable subsystems, especially in Asia, where the tension between the United States and China could lead to nuclear war, and in areas such as the Middle East. Proliferation may cause the balance of uncertainty to shift, from inciting caution to encouraging rashness and miscalculation.[9] Even if nuclear wars are avoided, a broader resort to conventional force under nuclear umbrellas is possible. If tensions among the nuclear powers end with large-scale resort to force, the restraints on the use of nuclear weapons may collapse; if tensions lead to stalemates of mutual denials, the leading powers will be unable to function as a collective "ruling group"; the hierarchy will once again be subverted and moderation will in the long run also be threatened. Therefore, the prime responsibility of the United States and the Soviet Union lies in making the international system moderate: if they succeed, it will also be hierarchical and will provide possibilities for world order.

For the United States, the advantages of a moderate, multi-hierarchical system are considerable. Since there would be several hierarchies, America's nuclear superiority would ultimately count less —but it is hard to imagine any system where the hierarchy was based entirely on unusable power. Yet, fortunately, the United States is not badly endowed in usable power, military and otherwise, and would not suffer in a system that permitted major states to use (nonnuclear) power more freely than happens today. By restoring an international hierarchy and recreating a society of major states, such a system would also unfreeze some of the power now frustratingly congealed in the superpowers' storerooms. America's position as a world power would be guaranteed; but, because the responsibilities of world order would be shared by more states and also because of regional diversification, the need to agonize and fret about every incident, to behave as if the United States were an unfortunate Atlas holding up the world, would no longer be so great; selectivity would again be possible.

So would flexibility. The various functional hierarchies, the regional decentralization, the existence of a whole group of powers with interests held partly in common and partly in conflict would allow for supple, shifting alignments. The United States would no longer

[9] These points summarize my argument in *A World of Nuclear Powers*, pp. 101–9.

be torn, in each crisis, between the fear of losing face, security, or power by refraining from confrontation or intervention and the fear of a holocaust if it intervenes or meets the challenge. Crises could more easily be localized and disconnected than is possible when every incident has a potential link to the relationship of major tension.

In the past, the trends toward fragmentation in the Soviet bloc and the Western alliance have resulted in an emancipation of the lesser partners from the concerns of the "bloc leaders," but not in a liberation of the latter from the risks involved in the alliances: the decline of the smaller forces' "triggering function" (nuclear or not) has not relieved the superpowers of the necessity to protect their allies (even the challengers). A moderate multi-hierarchy would reduce the great powers' need for clients and servants and make of the relations among major states the main focus of international politics. Of course, the United States (and the Soviet Union) would no longer enjoy the advantages that leading powers have in bipolar systems—the benefits of domination over a certain group of nations. But, as we know, in the present circumstances, enjoyment has changed to annoyance all too often. The fruits of empire have gone sour, and cannot turn sweet again. And it is hopeless to expect a system where the superpowers would combine the advantages of bipolarity and those of balance-of-power systems.

Can a multi-hierarchical system be moderate? That is the vital question. Any conclusion derived from past balance-of-power systems must be revised. There, the capacity to resort to force provided the yardstick of power and the dynamics of mutual adjustment. The exercise of this capacity could in the future lead to calamity. Since deterrence of major aggression committed by a great power now depends on nuclear weapons, the likelihood of limited wars (like those which agitated balance-of-power systems) decreases, for the risk of their escalation to nuclear war would be too great. On the other hand, the possibility that a coalition of powers could stop a non-nuclear move of one or more great powers by non-nuclear means may be less, since not using nuclear weapons and putting restraints on other military means out of fear of escalation may well result in outcomes quite unproportional to the theoretic force ratios; the regional and functional fragmentation would also tend to "demilitarize" and complicate the traditional calculations of power. The very uncertainty of calculations will put the restraints that have developed in the present international system to a severe test, multiply danger points, and disturb the establishment and operation of mechanisms devised to strengthen the remaining incentives to prudence. "The very flexibility of alignment which brought stability to the balance-of-power system could become a serious threat to the maintenance of deterrence." [10]

As I have said, it is imperative that American foreign policy be focused, beyond the hazards of today's confrontations, on the long-range tasks of moderating a system so complex. It is impossible to give here more than a few general directives:

1. Because "the super-powers predominantly fashion the conventions of the international system" and because "their use of military nuclear technology will crucially influence the behavior of nascent nuclear powers," [11] it is essential that the United States continue to resist the challenges of its enemies whenever they try to reap gains by using or threatening to use force across national borders; otherwise, revolutionary ideologies will have little incentive to become at least externally moderate. But the United States must also continue to keep its confrontations at a very low level of violence, lest moderation be doomed.

2. In a world with several nuclear states, a hierarchy too prominently based on the yardstick of military nuclear power could wreck moderation, for it could weaken the superpowers' self-deterrence or mutual deterrence which has thus far kept them from exploiting their nuclear and conventional superiority especially against challenging secondary nuclear powers; also, it would encourage more states to acquire nuclear weapons. (This is why a universal nonproliferation treaty that tends to underline and even increase the advantages enjoyed by the nuclear powers, especially in the realm of the peaceful atom, risks being counterproductive.) Even if moderation prevailed in the resort to force by nuclear states, stability would survive only as long as the minute of truth were postponed and the "gap between supply [of military might] and achievements" [12] continued. The only way to save the international hierarchy *and* moderation in a world where force is not likely to disappear entirely is for the United States to encourage the formation of hierarchies based on non-nuclear power, i.e., hierarchies that would be based on the conventional defense capabilities, the economic potential (including nonmilitary nuclear power), and the diplomatic influence of other nations.

---

[10] Zoppo, cited, p. 601. See also Osgood's cautious conclusions in Robert E. Osgood and Robert W. Tucker, *Force, Order, and Justice* (Baltimore: Johns Hopkins Press, 1967), pp. 176 ff.

[11] Zoppo, cited, p. 602.

[12] *A World of Nuclear Powers,* p. 120.

3. The temptation that middle and small nuclear powers might have to use their nuclear weapons, or that powers well endowed with conventional forces might have to use them in order to make gains, will have to be fought in two ways. They will have to be deterred from, and punished for, resort to force, but in a way that will restore moderation, not encourage escalation. This means, in particular, that nations threatened by a small or middle nuclear power ought to be protected from nuclear blackmail by a nuclear guarantee from the superpowers; but given the limits and uncertainties of such guarantees,[13] protection against non-nuclear attacks and pressures (which are more likely) will have to be insured by the development of the threatened nations' conventional defenses. Also, a moderate international system is one in which "elementary standards of interstate behavior" will have to be observed; for instance, respect for the principle of free passage through international waters, a rule adopted in the interest of all states. Any unilateral violation of such a rule must be resisted, preferably by collective action, world-wide or regional, but, if necessary, by the United States alone—always with the caveat of proportionality, i.e., of employing means that extinguish the fire instead of enlarge it. Thwarting immoderation is not enough; small and middle nuclear powers will have to be rewarded both for having power and for refraining from using it—i.e., they will have to be given a greater role in the management of regional and world affairs.

4. A serious effort will be necessary to decentralize the international system. The superpowers must assure mutual deterrence among themselves and provide a kind of reserve of usable power against lesser delinquents. Deterrence of nuclear war will continue to depend on them, especially on their clear determination to use all methods short of nuclear violence against a lesser power guilty of having broken the taboo on the use of nuclear weapons. Deterrence of other kinds of violence, and the restoration of peace, would have to be assured in priority by regional organizations, in coordination with the United Nations. Such agencies would also be entrusted with the nonmilitary prevention of violence, i.e, with the settlement of disputes. Any other kind of fragmentation of the international system would mean chaos; but so would permanent centralization in the hands of the superpowers. Flexible alignments will increase uncertainty. But rigid universal commitments by the superpowers would be incredible and make the uncertainty even greater. One kind of uncertainty would make the management of crises possible; the other

[13] Osgood and Tucker, cited, pp. 113–15.

would not. It may take time until such organizations are set up. In the meantime, especially in areas that are too deeply divided to provide regional institutions, moderation will depend, first, on the maintenance of regional balances of power, and, second, on the superpowers' willingness to insure the restoration of peace in regional conflicts, either jointly, or at least under the main responsibility of one of them without destructive opposition from the other, and preferably within the framework of the United Nations. But this not a satisfactory solution in the long term.

5. In order to be moderate, the new international system will have to permit a double change in the pursuit of national goals. The pursuit of milieu goals will still be essential—indeed, keeping the milieu moderate through various and diversified arms-control and enforcement measures will be a major concern—but in the future international system, such goals will also have to be more accessible. National power, in its many functional varieties, will have to be geared less to the hectic and frustrating competitive attempts at shaping the milieu in one's own image, less to the paralyzing anguishes of mutual denial, and more to the joint transformation of the milieu. Here again, agencies of international cooperation will be important. On the other hand, nations will also have to be able to pursue possession goals that are accessible without violence. This means that the range of possession goals which can be pursued jointly, according to rules of competition-through-cooperation (rather than competition-in-separate-action), and the range of possession goals which can be reached in separate action but not at the direct expense of other states, must be increased. The whole realm of technology and development offers opportunities which have been curtailed by the concentration on denials.

6. Moderation requires not only the sharpest possible reduction of interstate violence, but also a gradual withdrawal of one state from the manipulation of another's domestic polity. A world in which some leading powers tried to prevent revolutions in other societies and others tried to foment them would be exposed to all the dangers that revolutionary wars create even in today's world. Revolutions are a safety valve of change in an international system in which necessary restraints on force tend to eliminate war (the most effective traditional instrument of change), in which a thwarted revolution would only lead to an uncontrollable explosion, in which new kinds of possession goals and milieu goals create inevitable domestic tensions, and in which the internal conditions of many states will

continue to be turbulent. But universal involvement in revolutions would make moderation impossible. In other words, moderation requires a distinction between the domestic nature of a regime (the choice of which must be free and unfettered) and that regime's external behavior (which will have to respect certain empirical and legal rules).

What I am suggesting here is the possibility of a world in which a *modus vivendi* is gradually established, through formal and informal rules, among the rival superpowers (two or perhaps three). Under the nuclear umbrella and within the secular arms of world order that the superpowers would provide, regional groupings would play a major role, harnessing the energies of the middle powers, helping to contain the ambitions of neighboring superpowers, and coping with regional crises. In such a scheme, no middle power would, as such, have much business keeping peace in distant parts of the world, but a system so delicate would not function unless the middle powers were incited to responsible behavior, and encouraged to play important roles.[14] Conversely, the superpowers would refrain from manipulating regional organizations; for moderation and flexibility would be threatened if they used them as tools for their universal involvement. The superpowers would also "limit their contest for power and influence in the Third World to relatively benign forms of competition," especially through "abstention from intervention."[15]

The notions presented here are at a level of generality that may make them not too useful to policy-makers. General propositions do not settle concrete cases. For instance, it would still be necessary to decide, say, whether one was dealing with a civil war resonant with international echoes or with an international war exploiting domestic turmoil. No general guidelines can ever dispense with the need for sound judgment. But this does not deprive general propositions of meaning. For concrete cases cannot be settled "pragmatically" on their merits without some general categories for identification, analysis, and prescription in the back of the policy-maker's mind. To pretend otherwise only means that one prefers to keep the categories implicit or that one will be guided by unexamined ideas and perhaps irrelevant reflexes. Also, the guidelines I have suggested are deliberately more political (even if they are so at a high level of abstraction) than the forms and formulas provided by the American prin-

---

[14] For some elaboration of points 4, 5, and 6, see my *The State of War* (New York: Frederick A. Praeger, 1965), pp. 154–59 and 247–51.

[15] Osgood and Tucker, cited, p. 169.

ciples I discussed. Indeed, they try to suggest the need for a change in attitudes and expectations as the precondition for policy changes. The objectives that policy-makers set should be selected in conformity with a long-range vision. To act today as if the system I have described has already been achieved would be a monumental error. But to act today *and* tomorrow in a way that exacerbates present frustrations or insures that the future international system will be immoderate is also foolish.

## II. *American Policy*

We should ask three questions about the matters raised in the preceding section. First, what *are* the concrete policy objectives which the United States ought to set in order to bring about this system? Second, what are the methods it should use in this process? Third, are the system, the objectives, and the methods compatible with America's style and political system?

A meaningful discussion covering U.S. foreign-policy objectives in all geographical areas and policy sectors would require many volumes; in the next chapters, I will try to discuss what they ought to be in the Atlantic Alliance. Here, I should like to concentrate briefly on general guidelines, methods, and compatibility with American style and institutions.

### A. *Guidelines*

In striving for the future moderate international system, the United States should develop two qualities in its foreign policy—one of which has been destroyed by the present international system and by America's political style and decision-making processes, the other one ruled out by the projection of our institutional habits into foreign affairs. I am referring, of course, to flexibility and the ability to cooperate with others. Flexibility would permit Gulliver to be untied, and would allow the United States to approach the world's issues and conflicts in a way that would not threaten to blow up the planet. The needed kind of flexibility is very different from America's typical technical versatility; or its political ambivalence (the superficially wise choice of a middle course between unattractive extremes, which really conceals an absence of choice and combines the disadvantages, but not the advantages of those extremes); or the coexistence of policies that point in opposite directions and cancel each other out; or the political vacuum (the absence of a policy, other than ritual incantation, because of an incapacity to produce one except under duress or because of undue attachment to principles of small policy relevance). The kind of flexibility that is needed can, in fact, be provided only by the inevitably painful learning of cooperation with others.

What our policy should be can be described by a series of guidelines about discrimination, diversity, and devolution.

DISCRIMINATION

The competition the United States faces with its Communist foes is waged on a field that includes many very different and formally independent states. "Communism . . . is not an octopus with one head and a dozen arms, but a hydra with one trunk and a dozen heads, each of them ready to bite the other." [16] As a result, our political strategy can afford to be, and indeed must be, highly discriminating. For the United States, given its values and defensive position, to "win" the competition means not to lose it, whereas for its foes, not to win it means to lose it. The United States can be satisfied with a diverse world in which as few states as possible are under the control of its *main* enemies. The control of many states by national Communists would not be a disaster; what has to (and can) be prevented is their control by the Soviet Union or Red China, or their resort to aggression on their own. Even if there were many independent Communist states, all vocally anti-American, dispersing American efforts against them would be a waste of resources, an exaggeration of the degree of harm they could do to us, an underestimation of the detrimental effect fragmentation must have in the Communist world, and a service rendered to the Soviet Union and China, which both would benefit from the dispersal of our efforts and from the leadership opportunity such efforts would provide them. Of course, the control of potentially or presently important nations by Communists, even local ones, would be a calamity because it would raise the number of our main foes; but the way to prevent this happening cannot be military deterrence (external or internal) alone. Instead of acting like a defensive army in classical strategy—ready for a blow anywhere along an interminable front, where the choice of the time and place belongs to the enemy—the United States ought to wage a strategy in depth: it can limit and rank its objectives instead of overexposing itself.

More concretely, this means remembering the internalization of the contest. American strategic power can deter its two major foes

[16] Steel, cited, p. 159.

from large-scale aggression and help to make the costs of more limited aggressions prohibitive. Hence, the chances of a country being taken over by Communists depend primarily on its domestic circumstances. Even the possibility of preventing by military force a Communist take-over through subversion depends to a degree on the political capacity for resistance in the threatened society. No amount of substitution of American power for missing political forces will do.

It also means the United States must remember that an effective foreign policy uses the art of exploiting differences. Any policy that throws together, even if only as a *de facto* condition, the two main adversaries of the United States (China and the Soviet Union); that consolidates the hold the Soviet Union still exerts on its satellites and clients; that makes Communist movements elsewhere more dependent on one or the other of the Big Brothers; or that throws non-Communist opposition movements in non-Communist countries closer to the Communists, is an absurdity. The division of the world into independent nation-states and the internalization of the international contest make for a kind of natural barrier against the domino effect. In a world-wide defensive contest, some defeats are inevitable; but only if we succeed in convincing ourselves and our friends that the fall of one domino brings down the whole row, will the row indeed be threatened with collapse. In a system as complex as this, it is necessary to compartmentalize foreign policy, even while pursuing world-wide objectives—just as on a modern boat, seeping water in one cabin does not mean the whole vessel will sink. One only increases the prestige and effectiveness of one's adversaries by attributing an omnipotent capacity to subvert and start rebellions to them. "Revolutionary wars" come in all sorts and shapes; countries cannot be compared to fireplaces where the wood and the paper are always ready, waiting only for a Communist match to start the fire. Not even the Red Chinese claim that.

Discrimination also means that the United States must set different expectations and objectives in different places. In other words, there must be a range of objectives. To aim for the maximum when it is out of reach may insure the loss of the minimum. Where the threat of military invasion or subversion is great, where the domestic society is reasonably coherent and equipped with fairly reliable institutions but unable to defend itself by its own means alone, where American aid in the defense of that society is welcome, and where the military presence of the United States does not thwart the achievement of other goals desirable from the viewpoint of international moderation—there the maintenance of the American "presence" is a legitimate objective.

Where the society is weak and much of it discontented, and where the chances for orderly reform are slight, the objectives ought to be to keep from turning the United States into a lightning rod. The best prospect for preserving American influence in these circumstances would be to act so as to avoid contributing to a Communist takeover. This means, first, and obviously, avoiding public identification with reactionary groups, military cliques unconcerned with reform, and oligarchies eager to hitch their cause to the wagon of the United States. For these measures force reformers to become extremists and insure that rebellions will take radical and anti-American turns. The best expression of anti-communism is not the promotion of anti-Communist activities, for when the latter merely prop up regimes that add to or perpetuate the attractions of communism, or divert armies from the reforming enterprises that some American scholars keep expecting of them, short-terms gains will lead to long-term losses. Second, however painful this may be to idealistic advocates of democratic revolutions, the United States must not give to the "forces of progress," to moderate reformers and non-Communist left-wing leaders, endorsements so blatant as to expose them to extreme left-wing charges of a "sell-out" or so loud as to embarrass us if their political experiments founder. Third, the United States must tolerate considerable leeway in domestic experimentation on the part of such leaders even if the cost for American private interests is high. We should be able to ride such storms and protect the truly dominant American interest—the avoidance of a victory for extremism aimed at the United States itself. (This is the policy which de Gaulle has followed since 1962 with respect to Algeria.) If the local leaders deliberately use anti-Americanism as the focus of "social mobilization," restraint by the United States will be difficult; yet nothing would better serve the cause of those leaders and of men even more extreme than an unrestrained American reaction. If the hoped-for punching bag turns out to be an eiderdown, the puncher will soon be discouraged. In all these cases, of course, an American military presence could easily be self-defeating—resulting in something that was never possible in Western Europe, the destruction of the very society it is designed to protect, which is too weak for the impact of American methods and standards. Means of protection against external attack must be found that will not lead to internal radicalization.

When local circumstances are such that there is no organized political force capable of giving the country the legitimate and effective government it needs, the chances for a Communist take-over are inevitably enhanced. In that case, the United States' maximum objective—the avoidance of such a take-over—is likely to be unreachable except at a cost that is not worth paying. Instead, an attempt to achieve that objective could produce what Senator Fulbright has called "a kind of 'counter-domino effect,' strengthening the very forces it is meant to contain." [17] But the United States could aim for a restriction on a Communist victory—seeing to it that it was a victory for *indigenous* communism, trusting in the likely impact of national differences between the new Communist regime and Moscow or Peking, especially if the local regime was not dependent on either Big Brother in coming to power. We can find encouragement in recent trends in Rumania and North Korea.

All these suggestions amount to saying: act in such a way as neither to facilitate the capture of nationalist movements by Communists, nor to compromise nationalists by too close an embrace.

DIVERSITY

The underlying assumption is that in order to make the world safe for diversity, diversity must be trusted. And indeed it is true that when nationalists and Communists clash, the former win, either at the Communists' expense or by twisting the Communist movement out of shape. A sound foreign policy would take advantage of our great asset: the desire of practically all nations, especially the new ones, to preserve their independence from outside control.

In most countries, the armed forces are inevitably on the side of national independence; their vigilance, their frequent opposition to civilian regimes that corrupt or waste national resources, and the difficulty of modern *coups d'état* in the face of police and military resistance complicate the Communists' task considerably. The United States has the means to protect against armed attack the nations situated close to the limits of the Chinese and the Russian domain. If some nations are unable to provide by themselves a sound basis against subversion or civil war, it may be in our interest to help establish such a basis; but American involvement is counterproductive if it (more or less inadvertently) crosses the elusive border between the offer to help consolidate national independence and the presumption to guide the assisted nation in directions we believe

[17] "The Two Americas," McMahon lecture at the University of Connecticut, March 22, 1966.

wise to follow. For we then lose the benefits of diversity. At worst, such a transgression turns the United States into the target of local discontents, the scapegoat, the Saint Sebastian for nationalist arrows. Thus, while in many cases local armies are our natural allies, deep involvement with them may buy temporary "order" at the cost of future upheavals. At best, a hand both heavy and inept would deprive the assisted nations of a sense of responsibility and self-respect, burden the adviser with perpetual minors, and condemn tutor and tutee alike to all the frustrations of subtly hierarchical relations.

Trusting diversity means remembering—as England well understood in her days of leadership—that the leader who is primarily concerned with achieving a moderate international system is like a reserve player: he comes in only when it is absolutely necessary, and not before. Turmoil within the polity of a major foe, such as China, is likely to be encouraged by American restraint and lessened by American pugnacity. If experiments in forced industrialization or rural collective action attempted by "revolutionary" regimes succeed, the resultant strengthening of national independence is a barrier to Soviet or Chinese control; if they fail, the help the nation can receive from Moscow or Peking is minor, since it is hard to manipulate domestic polities from abroad; the chances of a more temperate approach in the future therefore improve. Most of the nations whose actual or potential turbulence worries American policy-makers do not see their problems in terms of the "conflict between East and West." (This does not mean that this conflict is irrelevant, as naive observers have sometimes deduced.) Unless we force them to see their problems in such a light—either by doing so ourselves or by falling into the trap laid by our adversaries—they will tend to stay out of the trap, which is in itself a defeat for our foes.

Trusting diversity also means remembering our own handicaps when we use our enormous power. An observer has noted that "one of the most striking effects of advances in transportation and communication upon the conduct of diplomacy is the extent to which the command and control of foreign policy have become increasingly centralized." [18] The result is close to congestion: the geographical scope of foreign affairs has expanded tremendously, and our decision-making process is slow and complex (except in emergencies). As a result, the amount of attention that can be given to each country is small, too small to allow for an effective "command and control" of

[18] Marshall Shulman, *Beyond the Cold War* (New Haven: Yale University Press, 1966), p. 24.

its domestic processes. By a singular paradox, the "internalization" of international politics inevitably means a victory for pluralism. Any one nation's ability to manipulate not merely the diplomats and the diplomatic aspirations of a small elite (as in the past), but also the social, economic, and political forces of an entire country is mediocre. Neither the United States nor the Soviet Union nor China has been doing too well in this regard. Since the primary determinant of foreign policy is often the domestic component—internal needs, values, perceptions and structures—and since full mastery of foreign regimes exceeds the capacity of any nation, attempts at active intervention and deliberate manipulation run heavy risks of backfiring. Although American contacts with Indonesia's army (even while relations with Sukarno were almost suspended) had an indirect impact on the events of 1965, the spectacular reversal in Indonesia owed nothing to direct American intervention. Indeed, it came a year and a half after President Johnson had decided upon a shift in American policy, given up attempts to influence Indonesia's course, and apparently resigned himself to Communist Party preponderance in Djakarta (dominoes notwithstanding).[19]

DEVOLUTION

The preceding suggestions amount to saying: act in such a way as to let other nations follow their own course; see to it that they are not pushed off their course and that they can follow the course they choose, but do not set the course for them, and if they should stumble and fall, you will not be made responsible.

The only risk in trusting diversity is the risk of chaos in a world of sovereign states skidding on separate courses. This is why the notion of diversity has to be qualified by that of devolution. Many nations, new and old, are engaged in a fight for international recognition—through developing resources that will make them powers that matter, through shrill rebellions against the inequities of past domination or unjust treaties, through attacks on international patterns (such as bipolarity) that deprive them of what they deem their legitimate role. All of this could all too easily make them "turn inward," or turn them into trouble-makers. The United States is caught in a dilemma: if it defines the "constructive enterprises in every corner in the world" [20] that it would like others to undertake and prods them

---

[19] See Hilsman, cited, Ch. 27, and Theodore Draper, *Abuse of Power* (New York: Viking, 1967), Ch. VI.

[20] President Johnson, quoted by Walt W. Rostow, in *Department of State Bulletin*, Vol. LX, No. 1412, p. 79.

to start these efforts, it will clash with the profound desire of most peoples for self-determination and self-respect. We need a "rising tide of good sense in the world," [21] but to define it ourselves is nonsense. Yet to leave diversity to itself may breed immoderation and chaos.

The way out of the dilemma is what I would call devolution. More encouragement should be given to existing international and regional agencies and to the creation of new ones. But it is unlikely that regional and international organizations can become anything but debating societies and limited instruments of technical cooperation unless the United States' attitude changes in two respects. One would be toward a greater willingness to give responsibilities to organizations it does not control or over whose decisions it would have no veto. What often slows down the development of such organizations now (for instance, in Asia and Western Europe) is the fear of some members that they will become trapped in a net held by the United States. The other change would have to be toward a greater willingness to let these organizations handle matters that have so far remained under national control and that will remain so unless the United States gives the decisive impetus by transferring control of various programs to them; this would be particularly appropriate in the realm of foreign aid, but also in that of regional security, especially by giving the organizations of which it is a member greater financial resources.

Second, devolution must consist in placing more responsibilities on the middle powers, such as Japan, India, Britain, or France. They want to play a major role; one must see to it that they can, not as powers concerned only with their own security, expansion, and development, but as partial trustees of world order, interested in the safety, growth, and harmony of a larger area. This means encouraging their diplomatic initiatives for peacekeeping or peaceful change, helping them to defend the area or to initiate schemes for economic cooperation, so that they will have the psychological boost of leadership and contribute to international moderation at the same time. What has often slowed down these developments is our fear that their moves would conflict with our interests or position. We do not seem to realize enough where our higher interest lies. We must understand that our distaste, however justified, for strengthening what we see as "parochial" national ambitions and our preference for collective solutions only prevent the emergence of the latter and reinforces national pettiness by frustrating the designs of states to which

[21] Rostow, same.

the only real alternative is not a collective solution but a foreign —often an American—one. To be sure, we have encouraged such designs when they coincided exactly with our concerns. But that is not devolution, it is duplication; and, since it violates the imperatives of diversity, it is no wonder that it repeatedly fails. Another obstacle has been our dismay at their apparent indifference to or withdrawal from "world responsibility," which obliges us to be involved in areas and issues from which they are absent. But it is our very involvement that both provides them with a perfect excuse for turning inward, and elbows them out of playing any role other than that of our junior partners or satellites. The role they ought to play should be theirs, not ours; and our role should be to let them play it.

## B. *Methods*

To follow such precepts, the United States would need to re-examine its foreign-policy tactics and instruments. The experience of recent years shows that there are two precepts of particular importance for our *tactical style,* one positive and one negative.

The positive precept is: act in each area of policy so that, if it becomes impossible to reach the maximum objective, a minimum one can still be reached and the failure to reach the greater is at least not a disaster. Military strategists have devoted a great deal of attention to devising military doctrines for each continent and to keeping "options" open for military action; there has not been anything like it in the diplomatic realm. The need for it may appear obvious, yet it would require a considerable shift in style. It would require, instead of tense concentration on shooting one arrow, the preparation of a quiver of alternatives, so that a failure to hit the target would not leave us bereft of goals to reach and policies to reach them with. It would require an ability to prepare fall-back positions, and to switch softly and swiftly to them if we had to—instead of the jarring oscillation-in-confusion that has marked, say, our intervention in the Dominican Republic or some aspects of our Atlantic diplomacy. Instead of selling or overselling a course of action by describing the benefits that would come from its success, it would require a more understated exercise and toned-down expectations. In an era of compelling necessity and urgency, the more high-strung approach was useful, especially as a mobilizing device; but now it does more harm than good, placing American foreign policy at the mercy of adversaries or challengers or even loyal allies who have it in their power to refuse to go along with our more grandiose schemes. A style of reticence and diffidence is more suitable. When any American initiative is likely to open Pandora's box, no initiative is better than one. When initiatives are needed, a good way of getting more rather than less may well consist of making it known that "less" would *not* be a calamity, and "more" a necessity. A policy of reticence and alternatives does not mean a policy of absence, abstention, or passivity. We have an obvious interest in not waiting until concessions that could have been the subject of bargaining have to be made under duress, in not letting allied or dependent nations fretfully conclude that on issues essential to them we have no policy.

The negative precept is to avoid dead ends and sword thrusts that cut Gordian knots. It is essential that we rid ourselves of the habit of proclaiming that there is no alternative to a given course of action because anything else would be disastrous. We are not the makers of the final outcome; and since we may have to settle (even gratefully) for an alternative, we might as well be careful not to "insult the future," as de Gaulle puts it. Repeatedly—in the cases of EDC, Britain's application for entry into the EEC, the MLF, Article 19 of the U.N. Charter, Vietnam, the nonproliferation treaty—U.S. policy has deliberately placed too many eggs in one basket, not realizing that the United States was not carrying the basket alone and that if the other carriers dropped their handles, the result would be a sorry mess. Only in military strategy does a clear-cut and irreversible commitment have a strong deterrent effect; in politics, it all too often results in a loss of freedom of maneuver. To lock oneself intellectually in a self-made political Maginot line is perverse, when one cannot be sure that one will be able to stay behind it forever. For if the day should come when it is necessary or advantageous to abandon the position, retreat would appear like a major defeat, instead of a clever adjustment or even a foresighted anticipation. Hence, the bankruptcy of policies of nonrecognition and, hence, the risks in wedding one's cause to rigid principles such as allied integration.

On the other hand, it is also imperative to give up the kind of scheme that seems to provide a short-cut solution of several related problems. International problems are rarely susceptible to instant cure by miracle pills. While all the excitement is concentrated on the merits and demerits of the scheme, the issues themselves worsen. And then, when the gimmick fails, we have to do what we should have done in the first place. Attempts to cut Gordian knots only tighten the knots. A distinguished Dutch observer [22] has shown how, in the case of EDC, the United States insisted on relating issues

[22] Ernst van der Beugel, *From Marshall Aid to Atlantic Partnership* (New York: Elsevier Publishing Co., 1966), p. 265.

such as the structure of NATO, European unity, the future of Germany, and relations between Europe and the United States to the fate of EDC. I have said that the same is true of the MLF; it is also somewhat true of the very notion of Atlantic partnership.

In re-examining our *instruments of action,* it becomes clear that some of them should be played down, some revised, and some used more.

I have frequently mentioned the general reasons why it is difficult for any great power to "play domestic politics" abroad despite the central importance of domestic politics in international affairs, and also the particular reasons this is true in the case of the United States. Of course, it is necessary that much be done to improve American understanding of the political reflexes, institutions, and expectations of other nations; but understanding, difficult as it is, is easier than (and different from) manipulation. The latter is particularly arduous for a diplomacy that, inevitably, must deal with officialdom, and leave contacts with the opposition to informal or secret channels. I do not mean to suggest that the United States can or should renounce the black arts of "informal penetration." But for the sake of flexibility and cooperation, the United States must apply those arts with greater restraint. They are to be kept not so much in reserve for an emergency (for then they no longer suffice) as in the background and at the margin. They remain necessary for defensive purposes: to prevent our adversaries from succeeding, by default, in subverting others. But we should be careful not to cross the line that separates denial from attempts to control. It is dangerous to invest too much energy either in supporting foreign politicians whose profession of faith in the United States may be highly interested and who may well be unrepresentative, or in opposing politicians who may indeed sound anti-American, but who might gain strength from America's hostility or who might, once in office, act with more restraint. In the short run, a successful manipulation may sometimes pay off. In the long run, American interest lies in the establishment of self-respecting regimes in countries not under Russian or Chinese control. What matters is the behavior of those countries on the world stage; their good will, cooperation, or moderation is more likely to grow out of mutual respect than to be bought through manipulation.

Another instrument on which less reliance should be put is the military one (both our own and foreign military forces used as instruments of our policy). It is true that force has not lost its usefulness, even if the costs of applying it have risen and the returns from such application have diminished. Indeed, the benefits derived from the skillful deployment of force for denial and deterrence have increased enormously. The need for the United States to protect Southeast Asia and South Asia from Chinese military forces is undeniable; the need for the United States to provide Western Europe with military security is lasting; the interest in giving military forces of certain countries training in counterinsurgency action, and an inclination for so-called civic action, is acceptable; the interest in orienting nations toward the acquisition of conventional rather than nuclear military means is strong. What is in question is the over-all balance: there has been a disproportionate emphasis on the military means, for American military power has been a rather strange Procrustean bed on which American diplomacy has rested for too long and from which it must now arise. Military power goes a long way when one's goal is denial and preservation, but even for denial purposes it is not enough, when the Procrustean bed is set on too creaky and uneven a political floor; and even when denial is achieved, one must then get up and strengthen the area or country saved by one's might. The truth of the maxim attributed to Napoleon—that one can do all sorts of things with bayonets except sit on them—should be obvious.

Help to foreign armies is not defensible when it merely encourages aggressive rashness or boosts the domestic position of the military. A rejected client might acquire his hardware from someone else— from our allies or even our foes. But this does not justify our initiating or adding to a regional arms race, unless there would otherwise be an imbalance such that our contribution would be less dangerous to stability than our abstention (which may be the case in the Arab-Israeli arms race).[23] In the new and unstable countries and in Latin America, the combination of counterinsurgency tips and civic-action kits does not get one very far. For even the most responsible military

---

[23] Of course, an agreement with the Soviet Union to curtail the arms race in the Middle East would be far preferable. But, given the nature of the competition between the superpowers, which inhibits direct clashes and thus fosters indirect contests, such an agreement is unlikely unless both sides conclude that the arms race is capable of embroiling them in a major direct confrontation: this is not, however, the lesson of the 1967 crisis. Moreover, the competition also rules out explicit agreements, which would provoke Chinese charges of collusion and embarrass each side in its relations with its clients. Thus, the best hope is one of a limited arms race, kept within limits by informal agreements and reciprocal signals.

elite remains a military elite and as such is not the ideal instrument for nation-building. It can provide efficiency, a sense of order, a fight against corruption, limited channels of social mobility, a concern for national independence. But rarely does it show an understanding of political institutionalization, of social mobilization for collective action by citizens (not subjects), of the politics of what David Apter calls "reconciliation" and "mobilization"—because of the "curious inability" shown by military oligarchies "to deal with politics." [24] In Asia, military protection could stir up anti-American nationalism, if it should take the form of a large-scale presence of American troops in countries of weak social and political structure. In Europe, the "reconversion" of NATO into a diplomatic institution may well be the only way of preserving it as a military one.

Military alliances are an instrument of action whose usefulness must be reassessed. As we have seen, they have often become headaches for the senior ally. While it is still in his interest to protect allies from military attack and, by committing himself to their integrity, to deter infiltration or subversion, and while it is also in his interest to prevent some of the allies from falling into the arms of a challenger within the camp, the liabilities of alliances in a basically or latently bipolar system are very serious. They expose the senior ally to the "blackmail of weakness" and to the risk of being forced into a conflict by a clumsy or willful ally. The lesser members' fears of being dragged into a conflict by the senior ally or, on the contrary, being left unprotected by him (or being prevented from pursuing their own ambitions in an emergency) often lead them to try to develop independent means of action, over which the senior ally feels he must try to find some control. He must either accept solidarity with lesser partners about which he may have serious reservations or else damage the alliance.

In those circumstances, there is a serious danger of a "systematic overpayment of allies." [25] In order to keep the alliances intact, the United States may give to allies whose loyalty is badly needed or to wavering allies excessive commitments which puts it at their mercy. An enormous amount of foreign and domestic diplomacy is then spent on maintaining the alliances against attacks from allies and critics who find the costs excessive, against attacks from allies and

---

[24] David Apter, *The Politics of Modernization* (Chicago: University of Chicago Press, 1965), p. 25.

[25] William Riker, *The Theory of Political Coalitions* (New Haven: Yale University Press, 1962), Ch. 10.

critics who want to change the terms, etc. The instrument becomes an end and diverts our attention from other ends. Second, when we are allied with a power (like Pakistan) that is hostile to another, non-allied power in whose security we have a major stake, we complicate our relations with both; the alliance thus may restrict our freedom of maneuver because it inhibits our dealings with our partner's adversary; because the adversary may use aid we give it against our ally; and because the latter will in any case turn its grievances against us. Third, a firm alliance with a weak state may commit United States power and prestige to a quagmire. Some alliances are traps. When a potential ally is geographically located and politically equipped in such a way that formal alliance with the United States would attract the very lightning the alliance was supposed to deflect, and would probably require a protracted drain on American resources, neutrality is preferable to alliance. To be sure, neutrality too must be guaranteed and defended, but a weak nation may have a better chance of building up strength if it stays out of formal military alliances and shamelessly leaves the burden of its defense to others (as neutrals have often done). A military alliance could deprive it of any chance of handling its own affairs, and thus run afoul of discrimination, diversity and devolution.

American military protection can be extended in two highly effective forms short of formal alliance. One is a U.S. military presence *outside* the country but deployed so as to be immediately available. The other is a formal military guarantee against attack—this last defined in a more restrictive way than in present alliances. For what we need are *limited* alliances with the leeway both we and our allies need. What is essential is the possibility of access to a threatened area that one wants to defend: the will and the technology of transport are more important than a big network of permanent bases.

One could object that uncertain commitments create the greatest risks of war, that unilateral guarantees or protection without formal guarantees might tempt a would-be aggressor to adventurous probes which a formal alliance would have deterred. But the strains to which formal alliances are subjected can create the same opportunities and calculations. As Thomas Schelling has observed, the idea of commitment and the concern for multiple options clash.[26] If what deters, however, is the certainty not of a particular kind of retaliatory strategy, but of *some* retaliation, guarantees are not necessarily less deterrent than alliances. The weeding out of all uncertainty is a

[26] *Arms and Influence* (New Haven: Yale University Press, 1966), p. 44.

hopeless task, especially in periods of mixed interests; what is needed is the proper balance between commitments and freedom of motion.

One could also argue that there are nations in which only the presence of American forces can effectively deter the enemy, because such presence makes a threat of nuclear retaliation against a major attack credible, makes a non-nuclear defense against a more limited attack possible, poses a deterrent threat of escalation in the second case, and protects the area against pressures, probes and blackmail short of force. But here again, we must weigh the benefits and the disadvantages. The advantages of alliance exceed the disadvantages only if the area is of vital importance as a symbolic stake or because of its resources, and if the presence of American forces does not risk opening internal holes even while plugging all potential holes at the border. West European nations meet both requirements; few others do. Also, there are other ways of manifesting American concern and commitment. Nor should we forget that even alliances that have not entailed our military presence on the ally's soil have produced all the strains and constraints described here. ". . . Strategy at present depends only minimally on the strength of the defense position, but essentially on a *peacetime maneuver,* made before the outbreak of hostilities, which consists in manipulating and enhancing the threat of recourse to nuclear arms. This is basically a psychological maneuver . . ." [27] in which the existence of a defense system with United States forces present can be an additional deterrent but is not an indispensable one. Also, the mobility of forces makes their deployment in other countries prior to emergency strategically less important. Finally, we should remember that against pressures and blackmail, our allies' domestic self-confidence, combined with our external support, is probably the best defense.

In other words, we must not maintain or extend structures that have become unwieldy, nor must we accept the highly debatable thesis that all alliances should be dismantled in the nuclear age (a thesis that would be valid only if its corollary, the thesis of universal graduated deterrence, had been demonstrated). What is needed is the recognition of zones of common interests and zones of tolerable (indeed, necessary) disagreement. In the case of the United States, there is an additional reason for pleading against excessive reliance on alliances; our faith in solidarity, our mythology of community

[27] General André Beaufre, *NATO and Europe* (New York: Alfred A. Knopf, 1966), p. 75.

and common interests, our taking harmony for granted, our tendency to use domestic consensus-building techniques with our allies, the laboriousness of "consultation"—all these features tend to work against the development of fruitful alliances.

These remarks argue not only against the conclusion of formal alliances, but also for the transformation of existing alliances into less ponderous structures. Already, in many respects, the United States and the Soviet Union have started to act as if their alliances imposed no restraints on them—in Vietnam, in the Dominican Republic, and in test-ban and anti-proliferation negotiations. I do not mean to suggest that these are models for the future, only to indicate that the need for unilateral action (wisely or unwisely carried out) does arise, and that the United States and the Soviet Union have begun to emancipate themselves from their alliances, a process for which they have as yet no rational theory. As a result, they both often find themselves in impossibly contradictory situations.

While the usefulness of alliances ought to be reassessed, the use of international and regional organizations ought to be increased. Naturally, we must avoid treating organizations designed to settle conflicts, preserve or restore peace, control arms, promote economic and scientific development, or provide international legitimacy to certain kinds of behavior as if they were alliances. Alliances are devised to cope with "relations of major tension" by protecting or enhancing the interests of one group of contenders. International or regional organizations aim at coping with a variety of issues unrelated to the dominant tensions, removing certain issues from the heat of those tensions, and reducing the heat in partial, defensive, or deterrent fashion. If our goal is a world in which the relations of major tension will themselves be moderate and will not prevent either the cooperation of the main powers in preserving world order or the management of limited crises without too much competition among those powers, then we will have to re-evaluate the international and regional agencies in which we participate. As I suggested above, a "multilateralization" of American techniques and initiatives will be necessary, and we will have to overcome the fear of losing immediate control. This is of special importance in the matter of foreign aid. Such aid is indispensable in a world where development has become a primary concern. But, as we have found, the road that goes from aid to political advantages for the donor of aid (whether he defines them as obtaining internal stability or as gaining the international support of the grantee) is long, uncertain and frustrating.

Those frustrations often incite the donor to seek better results by intervening, which leads to more frustrations.[28] Here, the resort to international and regional agencies could allow the United States to maintain or even increase its contribution to a difficult but necessary task, and save it from illusions and pitfalls. Furthermore, in order that our techniques and initiatives may have a better chance of delivering the benefits of a moderate international system, it will be necessary for American diplomats to devote to the formulation of American proposals and the bargaining over them within these international agencies much of the energy that was consumed in the past in preparing unilateral moves and building a domestic consensus.

## III. The Problem of Style and Institutions

The various precepts I have formulated above, and the possible future international system I have suggested, conflict in obvious ways with the American political style and system. Neither flexibility nor the ability to cooperate with others who differ with us is among our skills. There is little room in the world I have described for either the quietist or the activist facet of the Wilsonian syndrome. We would have to change our legalistic and hectic-static approach to international relations. We would have to curb our desire for a world that reflects America's historical experience and is responsive to our own consensus-building practices. A concern for the long range ought to inform our foreign policy, geared as it now is to crises and crash programs. We would have to realize that moderate international relations are nothing but the protracted management of uncomfortable balances. We would have to learn to trust uncertainty and to manipulate it without the mental and instrumental protections that we have devised to preserve our illusions of objectivity and certainty.

Perhaps the reader, and even more the seasoned policy-maker, will say that this is obviously impossible, that we should not pine for worlds that cannot be, that we should not expect people or nations to jump out of their psychological skins. Am I not exhibiting American over-optimism when I suggest that we could? When George Kennan, in the early days of the Policy Planning Staff, suggested

[28] See William J. Fulbright, *The Arrogance of Power* (New York: Vintage Books, 1967), Ch. 11.

concepts and precepts similar to those I have put forward, they were promptly modified and distorted by the imperatives of our style and system. Surely, our failure to be omnipotent means not merely that we cannot have the world we would like, but also that we cannot change ourselves so as to be on top of the world we will have. What is the point of listing all the things we should do, if they are things we can't do given our nature and habits? If our political style and institutions are what they are, then (whatever a theorist may say about the unlikeliness of international systems that would suit us best or to which we are used) we have no alternative but to strive for a world where we would feel at home. We have enough resources at our disposal to stand a fair chance of success.

The trouble with this argument is that it does overestimate our capacity to shape the world order, and, more important, the capacity of a nation's style and institutions to define foreign-policy goals. Political style and systems by themselves do not set objectives. In foreign affairs, goals are set by a combination of the nation's values, its domestic politics, and the interests it owes to its position in the world. Its way of acting shapes its approach to these ends; as Henry Kissinger has shown, the domestic structure, for instance, "determines the amount of the total social effort devoted to foreign policy, affects the way the actions of other states are interpreted," [29] and conditions the country's assessment of trends. A study of style and institutions tells us what kind of a world we would feel comfortable in, and in what kind of a world we would face serious psychological and structural strains. Whether we can attain the former and avoid the latter is, however, beyond the reach of style and institutions. They do not tell us what we *ought* to do: they tell us how we do things and what things we do best. To set ourselves the goal of forming an international system that would suit our style and institutions assumes that we can freely give the world the shape of our values and that our values could not adjust to a different kind of world. We do justice to ourselves neither when we overestimate our capacity nor when we underestimate our adaptability.

My suggestion is not, therefore, "Let us stop being ourselves" —an obvious absurdity—but "Let us, without ceasing to be ourselves, see how we can adjust to a world that is likely, but must be made desirable." In the first place, the world I have described *would* appeal to many of our qualities and use many of our skills. The redefinition of milieu and possession goals, the formation of functional

[29] "Domestic Structure and Foreign Policy," *Daedalus,* Spring 1966, p. 504.

hierarchies in which material forms of nonmilitary power are essential, great undertakings of science and technology as links among nations and building-blocks for nations—all these would obviously suit not merely our purposes but our predispositions. Our drive for community would also be satisfied in such ventures. The continuing need for deterrence among the superpowers, the role of the United States as a secular arm in reserve for peacekeeping, the vital importance of arranging and maintaining arms control would, so to speak, suit our instinct for force and our moral compulsion to put this instinct at the service of a higher cause. Our strategic skills would not go unemployed. A world in which violence was restrained, social change was supported yet contained within borders, and national independence encouraged and channelled would be close enough to American ideals to permit American political leaders to dress it up in American colors. A world in which considerable self-restraint, especially in the handling of local crises, combined with competitive or cooperative great-power action in major crises would not be wholly alien to the style of the Wilsonian syndrome.

In the second place, we would be relieved of doing much of what, in our present frame of expectations, we have to do yet are not very good at doing. No state, however well-meaning, can "build" another nation, and we are particularly ill-prepared to do so: a transfer of resources is not enough; it may even be detrimental if we also project all our values, institutions and political techniques, and thus either crush our protégé under our weight or condemn our protection to irrelevance. We feel obliged to manipulate the domestic affairs of other nations, but we often lack the political skills because of our "lack [of] historical sense," [30] our reductionism, our way of flattening the politics out of political issues. We are used to responding to crises, but we are not always deft in handling them, doing too much in volume and too little in depth and doing it too late. In our dealings with other nations, we press them too hard and clutch them too close because we feel that the future of the world depends on our harmony. The kind of system I have described would make it unnecessary for us to act as the "only power that has a sense of world responsibility." [31] As "the attempt to play a role simultane-

[30] William R. Polk, "The Scholar and the Administrator in International Affairs," *Bulletin of the Atomic Scientists,* March 1966, p. 6.

[31] Dean Acheson, in Henry M. Jackson, ed., *The Atlantic Alliance: Jackson Subcommittee Hearings and Findings* (New York: Frederick A. Praeger, 1967), p. 101.

ously in every part of the globe seems . . . clearly beyond our psychological resources" [32] (not to mention our machinery of government) and since it is even more clearly beyond those of other nations, their own response to our attempt will only strain our psychological resources even more and add to all the frustrations and excesses I have analyzed earlier. Indeed, even though our present stance expresses our style, it strains our institutions and creates the risk of a reaction from overcommitment and missionary activism to resentful and "inward-looking" quietism. Filling the present gap between us and lesser nations with states and agencies having at least some sense of responsibility would allow us both to sing *our* praises for having raised their sights, and to let the burden of trying to solve the insoluble weigh on all nations.

Third, we have already shown that we can adjust. Inevitably, as in the recent past, there will be malaise, strains, and a tendency to adjust *within* established American patterns. We have already, for instance, adjusted to the need for limiting violence in a nuclear world, but we have done it by turning the art of restraint into a cool science and without removing the coat of moral conviction that appeases our conscience. No national style ever changes by sudden mutation: one changes one's skin without bolting out of it. A great power is a nation that succeeds in adapting its style and institutions to changing patterns of international relations. A nation that cannot do so declines—not just relatively but absolutely, as Spain did from the sixteenth century on, but as France after Napoleon or Japan since 1945 did not. A nation that adjusts does not cease being itself; it merely proves that it can learn from experience. And in the final analysis, experience is the only test. It is experience that gradually teaches us to expect less, to be more flexible, to practice the delicate and annoying craft of coexistence with foes and cooperation with different foreign nations, to manage uncertainty and insecurity. The United States has never been a major power in a moderate system of more than two leading states. Why wonder, then, that we are unadapted to it now? But why doubt that we could adapt to it just as we adapted to the imperatives of the postwar system?

We have learned that in the nuclear age moderation is indispensable and total security and certainty unobtainable. A system of the kind I have described would merely draw the consequences of these lessons and adapt them to an evolution that in any event we cannot

[32] Henry Kissinger, "For a New Atlantic Alliance," *The Reporter*, July 14, 1966, p. 23.

stop and that it is not in our interest to stop. Today, we live with a permanent contradiction between our proclaimed values and intentions (all on the side of true diversity) on the one hand, and our acts (which thwart diversity), our belief that the American experience is of universal relevance, our habits of control on the other. The system I suggest would end the contradiction. And if the cost is to be a modification of our style and political system, let us at least realize that vigilant self-restraint, or restrained involvement, is worth the pride and certainly not beyond our "psychological resources." *

* Although this book does not deal specifically with American policy in Southeast Asia, it may be useful to suggest briefly how the notions developed in this chapter apply to Vietnam. I have expressed my opinion in a letter published by *The New York Times* on May 1, 1966; a year and a half later, I see no reason to revise my arguments, and I therefore quote from this letter here:

"I am struck by the similarities between the Algerian War and our plight in South Vietnam. In both cases a Western power tried to put down a considerable native rebellion by primarily military means. But the heart of the problem was the absence of any solid native political force capable of legitimizing the fight against the rebels and of preventing this fight from looking like the outside power's attempt to preserve its own interests.

"In both cases a massive military build-up by the Western power served only to worsen its political failure by increasing destruction, pulverizing the social and economic structures and aggravating the "foreign" character of the war.

"In both cases belated attempts at social reform foundered on the absence of a legitimate native political force capable of carrying it out and on the contradiction between a huge war effort and externally induced social transformations.

"In both cases the Western country's effort was doomed by the refusal of most local political leaders hostile to the rebels to put their authority at the service of the Western power.

"Differences are more apparent than real. France, a colonial power, was the target of the rebellion from the start. But United States support for Saigon's rulers is finally making it the target of all South Vietnamese nationalists—Communist or not.

"The Algerian National Liberation Front was not Communist. But the Communism of the Vietcong does not make the American predicament different from the French. The means used so far are not any less appropriate to the objectives, nor are America's objectives—to prevent the violent overthrow of South Vietnam's regime and to thwart Red China's theory of national liberation wars—any more realistic.

"For as long as South Vietnam's rulers concern themselves mainly with waging war, they will be too unrepresentative and too arbitrary to be politically effective; and as long as it has no effective government, South Vietnam will be a fiction surviving only by the grace of America's own force. Since—in Gen. Maxwell Taylor's revealing phrase—it is "difficult to plant the corn outside the stockade when the Indians are still around," the only prospect would be a

Sisyphean pursuit of highly resilient Indians, with the whole balance of American foreign policy and military deployments as the main casualties.

"Wars of national liberation could still break out wherever local conditions favor them, and America's concentration on a most elusive military victory in Vietnam would detract attention from the necessary improvement of local conditions elsewhere.

"We have failed to find a political solution to a war which, being predominantly civil, is susceptible of no other solution. What is needed is both the internal resolution of the civil war, and a definition of the external consequences of the domestic settlement. It is in America's most vital interest to allow those South Vietnamese forces which have refused to side with Diem and his military successors to come to the fore at last, so as to try to find a domestic solution to the war without any overt American involvement.

"For our part, we must shift from the unsuccessful manipulation of domestic Vietnamese affairs to the determination of the external conditions, thanks to which a South Vietnam in which the Vietcong would play an important role, or even a reunified Vietnam under Communist rule, would not be a threat to peace in Southeast Asia; i.e., neutralization with various international guarantees under U.N. or Geneva Conference controls.

"Our adversaries have no incentive to negotiate as long as we stick to our stated objectives and hedge about admitting the Vietcong to political power before free elections in all of South Vietnam. For such elections, to be both possible and fair, presuppose a cease-fire, which the Vietcong is unlikely to grant unless it is preceded or accompanied by drastic change in the domestic *status quo*."

To sum up: our military effort has succeeded in preventing the Vietcong from taking over South Vietnam by force. But it could eliminate the Vietcong and its North Vietnamese supporters and guides only at a cost that would be prohibitive for American foreign policy, for the goal of a moderate international system, and for the South Vietnamese people. What is required now is a suspension of the bombing of North Vietnam, in order to make a negotiated solution possible. The success, indeed the possibility of meaningful negotiations depend on our willingness to accept an interim coalition government in Saigon, whose primary objective would be the holding of free elections under international supervision. After a cease-fire and until those elections, each area in the South would remain administered by the side that was in control on the day of the cease-fire. Political parties representing all opinions would be allowed to compete in all areas. Negotiations would take place at different levels. The South Vietnamese (the Vietcong and present Saigon authorities) would negotiate the establishment and the role of the interim regime (and agree that the loser of the elections would not be the victim of political genocide). The United States and North Vietnam would negotiate an agreement on the gradual withdrawal of their forces from South Vietnam. An international conference would negotiate the international status of South Vietnam. The eventual unification of the two Vietnams would be left to the decision of the future South Vietnamese regime, but the international status of South Vietnam would be intangible.

Such terms meet the various requirements set up in this chapter. They do, however, meet important obstacles in America's political style and institutions.

This is precisely where the remarks of this chapter's last section apply: it is the task of America's political leaders to explain that our capacity to shape the world according to our dreams is limited, and to show that a settlement along these lines, while far worse than the victory that we have unrealistically sought, is nevertheless preferable to any other remaining possibility, such as unilateral withdrawal, drastic escalation, or perpetual war. The storms leadership may encounter are a challenge, they cannot be the pretext of an abdication of leadership.

# CHAPTER ELEVEN

# The Atlantic Puzzle

When speaking of the North Atlantic Alliance, we are dealing with an area in which deterrence and denial have been spectacularly successful; in which the positive policies launched behind the protective barrier of NATO (which give to the Alliance a solidity that none of America's other alliances has attained) have also enjoyed considerable success yet demonstrated the limits of great-power influence. In this chapter, I should like to analyze what I consider to be the central difficulties of American policy, i.e., the constraints within which the United States must operate in the Atlantic Alliance (by which I mean not only NATO but also the other agencies that have developed in the area, such as OECD and the various West European organizations). In the next chapter, I will examine the possibilities and prospects.

Over the years there has developed a certain mythology, a certain Atlantic orthodoxy which stresses, on the one hand, the community of values, political institutions, and cultural heritage among members of the Alliance, and, on the other hand, the need for solidarity as the prerequisite for the accomplishment of any of the common tasks facing Alliance members.[1] Such views deserve criticism. For as a description of interstate relations, this exhortatory approach supposes that what has still to be solved, the political problems of cooperation, is already solved, and that what has still to be demonstrated, the need for solidarity, is beyond demonstration. It requires a kind of leap of faith to believe that common values and a broad range of mutual transactions, i.e., characteristics of a transnational *society,* are the determinants of foreign policies, i.e., of inter*state*

---

[1] See, for instance, the statements of Dean Acheson and John J. McCloy to the Senate Subcommittee on National Security and International Operations, April 27 and May 25, 1966, in Henry M. Jackson, ed., *The Atlantic Alliance: Jackson Subcommittee Hearings and Findings* (New York: Frederick A. Praeger, 1967).

relations. In fact, this is a perfectly untenable assumption: while foreign policy is undoubtedly influenced, colored, affected by the characteristic beliefs and activities of the transnational society, the determinants of foreign policies are far more varied and, all too often, divergent. Areas of a shared culture, compatible values, mutually predictable behavior, intense commercial or touristic transactions have often been areas of violent conflict. For they were, and are, divided into different zones of sovereignty, each developing its own national consciousness and looking at the world through the distorting spectacles of its national situation. Between the existing transnational society and the desired interstate community rises the formidable screen created by the wills of governments.

This Atlantic mythology obscures three very important points. First, it obscures the fact that the Atlantic "community" has been a formidably complex international subsystem, a mass of ambiguities in motion, and not some kind of perfect union suddenly threatened by a willful destroyer. Second, since it assumes that the need for solidarity is beyond argument, it also assumes that, no matter what changes occur in the international system, the Atlantic dimension must remain the common denominator and top priority of all the Atlantic allies—which may be right, but which is far from self-evident. Third, it glides rather too easily over the two central issues of international—indeed, of all—politics: What are the purposes for which the activity discussed is to be undertaken, i.e., what do we want to do and why? And who controls, who commands when we define the common interest and plan the activities of the group (also, who benefits from them)? The conditions under which NATO operated until the late 1950s explain these three defects. But the present disarray shows well enough that conditions have changed.

## I. Systems in Crisis

The Alliance has always been a maze of "diplomatic-stategic" activities and never a homogenous bloc or a simple structure. I will consider it here (as I have done elsewhere) as a subsystem or partial international system in which four types of interstate relations can be distinguished—each one being an analytically discrete configuration of purposes and control relationships affecting a distinct range of subjects or group of members.[2] First, there is a layer of separateness, i.e., a configuration in which fifteen nations pursue uncoordinated (or barely coordinated) policies in agencies that are mere discussion forums. This stratum reveals different national situations differently perceived. It covers a very broad range of economic, diplomatic, and even strategic subjects. Thus, while at least a minimum of harmony has been reached concerning the economic and financial concerns discussed within (but not really regulated by) OECD, serious differences with respect to the American balance-of-payments problem and to the international monetary system continue. Separateness has also marked the foreign policies of the allied nations with respect to matters outside the Atlantic area, especially the United Nations, decolonization, the Middle East, and Asian affairs. They have even diverged over policies toward the Soviet Union, especially in three important realms: East-West trade, a broad range of diplomatic issues (Berlin, summit conferences, approaches to German reunification), and military policies. For NATO members quite independently define the size and composition of their military establishments, decide on their financial and military contribution to NATO,[3] set up logistical systems, maintain arms industries, and formulate policies on disarmament and arms control.

Second, there is the stratum of American hegemony, which is strictly limited to a portion (a major portion) of the realm of defense. It includes the integrated commands under predominantly American leadership of the conventional forces assigned to NATO and situated in Europe; while they are theoretically subordinated to NATO's political and military decision-making bodies, practically they are closer to the Pentagon [4] than to the slow and uncertain collective NATO organs. This stratum of American hegemony naturally

---

[2] See my "Discord in Community," in Francis O. Wilcox and H. Field Haviland, Jr., eds., *The Atlantic Community* (New York: Frederick A. Praeger, 1963), pp. 3–31.

[3] With the exception of West Germany, whose entire armed forces are in NATO, and whose Defense Ministry has no control over military operations in peacetime.

[4] And to the White House: note the abrupt removal of General Lauris Norstad as SACEUR in 1963 and the unilateral appointment of General Lemnitzer as his successor. For a detailed analysis of America's role in NATO, see W. T. R. Fox and Annette Baker Fox, *NATO and The Range of American Choice* (New York: Columbia University Press, 1967), especially Ch. 4.

also covers the privileged position of the United States with respect to nuclear weapons and its resulting predominance in defining NATO's strategic doctrine. Moreover, the United States has used its preponderance to get its European allies to buy American arms rather than producing their own.

Third, there is the subsystem of the so-called Six of Western Europe, the members of the European Economic Community, until now concerned only with economic relations and, inevitably, with reshaping economic relations not merely among themselves but also with other Atlantic states, primarily the United States and Britain.

Fourth, there is an emergent or potential stratum, the object of a fierce tug-of-war among Atlantic states: a possible political community of Western Europe, which would entail as yet undefined power relations among its members.

Notice that the word *integration* applied to Atlantic affairs is devilishly misleading, first because, among the fifteen members of NATO, the scope of integration (in the sense of a range of subjects submitted to a central command, whether collective or the command of one member) has been very narrow, excluding, in particular, strategic nuclear forces; second, because the nature of integration is not the same among the NATO members (where it means American command) and among the Common Market members (where it means the Brussels set-up, which combines supranational and intergovernmental decision-making, unanimity and majority rule).

There has always been considerable interaction among those four strata, but the need to distinguish them clearly was less in the days when the second stratum obviously mattered more than the others. When Europe was recovering from the war, and as long as the threat from the East was felt to be compelling, NATO relations were the controlling ones. The sphere of separateness, while often spectacular, was not disruptive; there was little leeway for diplomacy with the East, and elsewhere the great battle of decolonization ended in a gradual victory of the American viewpoint over other policies. Relations in the third stratum, among the EEC members, dealt with issues below the threshold of international visibility; the fiasco of the European Defense Community and the rearmament of Germany in a NATO framework postponed the potentially disruptive issue of a separate European defense enterprise within the trans-Atlantic system. (This same fiasco postponed the emergence of the fourth stratum for a long time.) As a result, it was not unreasonable to assume that, thanks to the military and political stalemate in central Europe, as well as the shedding of colonial distractions, the Atlantic Ocean would eventually become a kind of internal lake of the nations on its shores. And it was reasonable to pass over the issue of control within the Alliance; a common definition of the common interest in security and prosperity underlay both the North Atlantic Treaty and the efforts to achieve European integration. American leadership was accepted either voluntarily or, as in the case of most decolonization troubles, reluctantly; there was no challenge of the prevailing strategic doctrine—that of massive retaliation—or of America's predominance in the Alliance. The benefits of alliance were real for all. In these circumstances, it was easy for American leaders to believe that the third and fourth strata would not cause any major difficulty or clash with the basic political and military assumptions and goals of United States foreign policy. And the United States supported—sometimes loudly, sometimes (after 1955) more tactfully—the process of unification among the Six. Atlantic orthodoxy corresponded to the needs and realities of the bipolar conflict.

Changes since then have affected relations among the Fifteen and among the Six. Both the "partial international system" of the Atlantic Alliance and the subsystem of the Six have been shaken by developments in the world, as well as by measures taken by individual members which those developments made possible.

### A. *Crisis Among the Fifteen*

Among the Fifteen, the stratum of separateness has become disruptive. Once "strength" had been achieved in the second configuration, the stratum of American hegemony, thanks to policies pursued in the first and third strata, the dominant problems became those of "settlement" between the NATO powers and the Soviet Union and issues in other areas of the world on which there were as yet no NATO policies.[5] And in the second stratum, American hegemony was challenged; both the purposes and control of NATO relationships have become the focus of controversy and crisis.

These trends reflect changes in the international system which I described in Part I; they were already visible by 1960. Concerning them, the muting of the bipolar conflict has had three effects. As the problem of West European security became less central, problems

[5] On strength and settlement, see McGeorge Bundy's testimony of June 20, 1966, in *U.S. Policy Toward Europe,* Hearings before Senate Committee on Foreign Relations, 89th Cong., 2d sess., pp. 3–11.

external to NATO's geographical area became more so. The very success of deterrence, and the American success in preserving NATO's integrity during the Berlin crisis, pushed the East-West contest away from Europe, now too risky and too stalemated for effective action. As a result, the ultimate political questions—the fate of Europe itself, the future of Germany, of the Soviet satellites, and of arms control in Europe—never "integrated" and submerged for a decade, came out in the open again. With America's increasing involvement in parts of the world from which European powers had largely withdrawn, there was therefore a host of reasons why the stratum of separate national policies assumed increasing weight. As Alfred Grosser has put it,[6] as long as the greatest danger was in Europe, the United States could equate the "West" and the Atlantic Alliance; if this was not the case, there was no adequate political and military instrument for establishing a common policy course; indeed, the whole notion of a common course had to be re-examined. Furthermore, if the importance of the first stratum increased and if separateness became synonymous with divergence in policy, the problem of control in the second stratum was bound to arise; for American control gave the United States the means to impose its views as the common views and its purposes as the common ones, even outside the geographically and functionally limited realm of this stratum.

Second, the organization and control of European security became a focus of discord. The decline in the credibility of massive retaliation as a deterrent against armed attack and the prevalence of tests of will (as in Berlin) over armed attacks enlarged the sphere of disagreement over purposes among the allies by putting in doubt the relevance of the previous strategic doctrine. American control of NATO defense policies was accepted as long as there was agreement on the basic doctrine; once the doctrine was in jeopardy, there could not fail to be "polycentric" attempts to gain some control in order to make sure that no one member could sacrifice the security of the whole Alliance by being too rash or too cautious.

Third, behind the wall of deterrence, the six Common Market nations of Western Europe gave their own organization a strong impetus, and this success of the Common Market raised questions of purpose and control in European-American relations that had been submerged. Setting the Common Market's external tariff, negotiating

[6] "European Perceptions of American Foreign and Defense Policies" (RAND Corporation Memorandum, December 1965).

on a common agricultural policy among the Six, determining policies toward the non-Communist world—all involved a possible clash with the United States. In other words, the European Economic Community helped to increase the new disruptive significance of the layer of separateness and to change the relations of decentralized control in it, since some subjects would now be dealt with not by fifteen separate states, but by a grouping of six plus the other allies. Moreover, if a fourth configuration was to grow out of the third—if a West European political community appeared with one policy on foreign and military affairs—this would challenge American supremacy in the second stratum of NATO defense affairs.

By 1960, the trend toward multipolarity had also begun to affect all fifteen allies, although less strongly. Great Britain's nuclear program and France's incipient one exacerbated the problems of the second stratum: to what purposes, in the service of what doctrine, would British and French nuclear forces be used? How would American control of the strategic doctrine and of the nuclear capability of the Alliance be affected by programs whose *raisons d'être* were not only to complicate the calculations of an aggressor, but to influence American defense decisions?

A neat theoretical solution of all these issues would have been to recognize that the problems of alliance purpose and alliance control were interrelated, that there was only one satisfactory way to insure shared policies: by recognizing the urgent need for concerted policies on subjects reserved to NATO but outside the realm of military integration (such as the policy toward the U.S.S.R. and Eastern Europe), and on subjects not covered by the North Atlantic Treaty (such as strategy and foreign policy in Asia and Africa); and by setting up a decision-making machinery that would make for joint control. Although it is never easy to pin down the hopes and final aims of Jean Monnet, one can assume that this is close to his ideas, as it is to those outlined by Lord Gladwyn.[7] But this "solution" was never practical for reasons I shall examine here.

In the first place, the same basic trends in the development of the international system that had created the trouble ruled out the solution. The newly muted conditions of the Cold War made a worldwide harmonization of purposes among the Fifteen more difficult. For it decentralized the Soviet-American contest all over the world, moved it away from large-scale military confrontations, and encouraged prudential *rapprochements* between the two countries. This

[7] See *The European Idea* (New York: Frederick A. Praeger, 1966).

placed the United States in a delicate position. Being the one Western power with world-wide commitments and resources to meet them, it was reluctant to have the Atlantic Alliance become an albatross around its neck. It naturally came to want to pursue its own course in two critical realms: "when the U.S. plays on the solitary solidarity of those who have alone the capacity of destroying the world, or on the crowded solidarity of all who have at any time revolted against imperialism, it builds up the world as a court of appeal against 'Atlantica.' " [8] Also, the new ascendancy of the nation-state and the new nuclear powers complicated the reorganization of control in the Alliance. Not only were the Six, for all their success in creating the EEC, nowhere near having institutions able to "speak with one voice," not only was a clear-cut division of responsibility between the United States and Europe impossible as long as Great Britain was not a member of EEC, but also on the crucial issue of control in NATO defense policies it was impossible to envisage a simple "collective" solution. In the realm of economic affairs, an "equal partnership" between the United States and Europe was conceivable, but in military affairs, especially as long as the United States provided the Alliance's nuclear arsenal, a formula of true "sharing" could not be devised. The United States would not want to alienate a freedom of decision that might allow it to avoid all-out nuclear war; those allies who were building nuclear forces of their own in reaction against or as a way of influencing America's nuclear might, would not want to alienate what they were so painfully acquiring. Secretary of State Herter's proposals of 1960 for a NATO-controlled missile force raised the issue of joint control but provided no answers. One could, for the future, conceive of a separate European defense establishment set up with the help of the United States, but this would have to wait until there was a European political entity. It would raise in any case formidable political problems within the United States, it implied a drastic transformation of the American position, and it was of no use in the present.

In the second place, in two important countries—the United States and France—new leaders exploited these international trends so that the theoretical solution became thoroughly utopian. The administration that came to office in the United States in 1961 recognized the nature of the changes in the Alliance, but its response to international problems tended to diffuse and de-fuse the bipolar contest even more, helping thereby to turn Alliance "troubles" into a

[8] Hoffmann in Wilcox and Haviland, eds., *The Atlantic Community*, p. 22.

crisis. On the issue of purposes, President Kennedy's conviction that the superpowers had a responsibility to agree on restraints that would strengthen the precarious recoil from using force, and his efforts to proclaim that the United States was favorable to the revolt against colonialism, indicated clearly that as far as the United States was concerned, the Atlantic dimension was only one among many. The importance of the sphere of separateness was thereby increased. Then, concerning defense affairs in NATO, the administration drastically revised U.S. strategic doctrine so as to take into account the consequences of peril parity between the superpowers. Secretary McNamara's new strategy, decreasing reliance on nuclear weapons for deterrence and increasing pressure on NATO allies for more conventional forces, provided for a "flexible response" in case of war, so that it would be possible to spare the territory or at least the cities of the superpowers. His new strategy took into account the new conditions of the use of force and constituted a major step toward moderating the world contest. But, inevitably, the old inter-Allied agreement on strategic purposes was harmed. A strategy of graduated deterrence was bound to worry Europeans whose first concern was the deterrence of major war in Europe, not the choice of a strategy in case deterrence failed.

On the issue of control, the United States made a determined effort to reassert its command within the Alliance, particularly in the second stratum. The new doctrine, was, in fact, imposed on the other allies, since the United States had the power to apply it despite their reluctance. The United States tightened its control over the deployment of tactical nuclear weapons in Europe, refused to establish strategic delivery systems there, and criticized the growth of national nuclear forces as detrimental to the basic need for centralized control over nuclear weapons.[9] The Nassau agreements, which tied Great Britain's present and future nuclear force to NATO and set in motion the plans to create a multilateral nuclear force under American control, had the same effect: both the manner and the substance of the agreements exacerbated European-American differences and reinforced the desire of continental Europeans to influence American strategy either by having access to American decision-making or by developing their own nuclear forces. The Cuban mis-

---

[9] W. T. R. and Annette Fox, cited, pp. 94 ff., point out that the withdrawal of Jupiter missiles from Turkey and Italy in 1963 decreased those allies' influence and NATO's role in American strategy, now focused on Polaris submarines under direct U.S. control.

sile crisis strikingly revealed the impotence of the allies and the sovereignty of American control.

The American desire for control existed in other policy areas. While the Trade Expansion Act and President Kennedy's call for Atlantic partnership indicated awareness of the need for cooperation in economic affairs—for narrowing the sphere of separateness and providing some joint control—the United States clearly indicated in what direction it wanted Europe to move by advocating Great Britain's entry into the EEC, by inveighing against so-called inward-looking tendencies, and by supporting supranational integration. That is, the United States used its presence in Western Europe to affect the third and fourth strata. As a result, the structure of the Alliance became more complex and more of a stake: the ideal of a future partnership was presented, but it was made clear that its achievement would have to wait until a satisfactory European partner had developed; that, for the time being, the partner-in-the-making would have to stop short of defense; and, while its future defense role was left obscure, that a battle for control over the policies of that partner was already being waged.

A second circumstance that increased the disarray was the coming to power of General de Gaulle. Between the new administration in the United States and the old French leader, the whole complex of Atlantic relationships became a stake in a struggle between two nationalisms. That of the United States, the nationalism of a leading power, naturally was couched in the language of common interests and "enlightened" vision, while that of France, the nationalism of a challenger, appeared more parochial and jingoistic. Kennedy was the champion of muted bipolarity, the advocate of moderation and the spokesman for the idea of shared interests of the United States and the Soviet Union; de Gaulle made himself the champion of multipolarity. Both men had good reasons to dislike the presence on the world stage of new "centers" of power yet each, at times, played on the dissatisfactions of these centers against the superpowers (in de Gaulle's case) or against smallish powers that were trying to inflate themselves into middle powers (in Kennedy's). De Gaulle had started by asking for a NATO triumvirate that would take "joint decisions" on world-wide political and military strategy, including nuclear strategy. He may well have meant his proposal to be rejected so that he could be covered in and justified for doing what he really wanted. At any rate, he was given the excuse he needed to change his tactics. From then on, insofar as the purposes of the Alliance were concerned, de Gaulle tried to limit their range by insisting on

France's right to follow its own policies in every conceivable respect; he used the United States' own insistence on various separate policies as a reason for acting in the same way. Thus, the sphere of separateness became a stratum of acrimony. Moreover, in the second configuration of the Alliance, he openly opposed the new American strategy and upheld the old doctrine of nuclear retaliation. This challenge would have been insignificant if France had had no means of enforcing her preferred strategic course. But it is precisely the battle for control which de Gaulle has waged with the greatest determination.

De Gaulle shook American hegemony in the second stratum by three moves: by pushing France's nuclear program ahead, by keeping it under purely French control (i.e., rejecting the Nassau proposals and the MLF), and finally, in the spring of 1966, by withdrawing French men and matériel from the NATO organization. De Gaulle has also fought for control in the EEC and the potential European political configuration. Here, his strategy has been dual: on the one hand, to prevent the establishment of a supranational community, since he fears that the United States would too easily control such an entity; on the other hand, to convince the other European nations that they should join in the creation of a "European Europe" with its own policies, independent of American control although possibly coordinated in areas of common interest.

To some, de Gaulle's Europe looked like that "second force in the West" which Kennedy's notion of partnership appeared to favor. In reality, there is a world of difference between them. First, there was never any assurance that a "European Europe" and the United States would jointly make policy for the West: a permanent and dominant "Atlantic dimension" is wholly absent from de Gaulle's vision. Second, one must add that de Gaulle never envisaged his Europe as a federation at least in the foreseeable future, even if we accept the view that, for a while at least, De Gaulle did envisage the Alliance as a global partnership. Third, and most important, de Gaulle's challenge of the very legitimacy of American control has resulted not only in French withdrawal from integration as practiced in the second stratum, but also in totally stopping the development of European political integration at the fourth stratum.

## B. *Crisis Among the Six*

West European unification has been the victim of the coexistence of muted bipolarity and emergent multipolarity within the present international system. The movement toward economic integration in the EEC, focusing on concrete issues and relying on bargaining techniques, could hope to avoid taking a political stand on the main questions of purpose and control only so long as issues affecting the superpowers, especially the United States, were not reached. Once these issues were reached, there was bound to be growing misunderstanding between the two kinds of members of the Common Market enterprise. On the one hand, the smaller countries, the defense of which depended on external protection, naturally preferred the efficient protection of a distant and easy-going power to the ineffective protection of distrusted or disliked neighbors. To them, muted bipolarity was ideal: a bipolar international system insured their protection by the United States; a muted contest allowed them not to worry too much about defense. There was also West Germany, the state on which the security problem weighed most heavily. It appreciated the benefits of American protection far above any opportunity for separate action or even collective West European action. To a divided country situated in the central zone of conflict, security was obviously fundamental; paradoxically, dependence not only ensured security to the West Germans but also had been the condition for their impressive recovery of status and power since 1945. Indeed, dependence on the United States meant a march toward equality with other Western powers; separate action would have meant a loss of security and possibly of status; collective West European action was neither immediately conceivable nor acceptable if it was to lead to a decrease in security or to some kind of discrimination at West Germany's expense. What distinguished West Germany from the position of Italy or Belgium was only its appreciation of muted bipolarity: all three relied on United States protection for security, but West Germany saw dangers in the diversion of American interests to other parts of the world, in the American-Soviet *détente,* and in the new American strategy. The German desire for security and hope for reunification through collective Western efforts led to a search for ways to reinforce bipolarity—not the kind of duopoly that would involve a *détente* at Germany's expense, but the kind of tense, if not necessarily hot contest that would preserve America's protection and make its "betrayal" of West German security or reunification interests impossible thanks to the vine-like grip of West German docility.

On the other side, there was France, for which the bipolar world was but a passing necessity, to which dependence meant a tangible net loss from its prewar international position—and thus to be erased as much as Germany's defeat was erased by West Germany's dependence. For France, the period of intense East-West hostility should be followed not by duopoly but by a multipolar international system. For a while, this belief was not much more than an act of faith in the possibility that a European entity could become a force (not a "third force," to be sure) in the West capable of affecting the international system. When nuclear peril parity made it obvious that the bipolar system itself contained, so to speak, the seeds of its own end, the French saw a vindication of their hope.

Thus, the ambiguity of the international system facilitated a split among the Six. To the smaller countries, muted bipolarity meant protection and a chance to play a decent role in the shadow of the protecting giant. To the West Germans, the bipolar conflict meant protection both from the main threat and from themselves and a chance to regain rank as a needed ally. To the French, muted bipolarity was a springboard from which middle powers could leap to a higher rank. As long as the question of what the world would be like "after the confrontation" had been academic, this split had had only few consequences for the European movement. For the development of a European community as a joint undertaking had been possible.[10] The West Germans could view it as an instrument for a return to equality among the dependent powers, and as a way to strengthen Europe without antagonizing the United States, indeed, as a way of enabling Europe to share its burdens. The French, rudely shaken by the Cold War from their earlier dream of a moderate multipolar system in which they could play a balance-of-power game, could view Europe as an instrument for influencing the temporary leader and the temporary adversary in the direction of moderation and a return to balance. But this ambiguity could have been preserved, and the European idea advanced, only if the question of the enterprise's ultimate political direction and control could have been indefinitely postponed.

A second factor which prevented such postponement was the *differing* appeal of a "multipolar" world among the Six—the complicating and age-old breeder of conflict, disparity. In Western Europe, some of the potential candidates for a "multipolar" role have chosen not to play the part. Italy has been absorbed by her own development, satisfied with regaining the influence afforded by a polycentric world and with the protection the bipolar contest pro-

---

[10] See Ernst B. Haas, *The Uniting of Europe* (Stanford University Press, 1959).

vides against communism and against the need for massive rearmament. West Germany, as we have seen, had chosen to minimize her freedom of action, at least until 1966. Only France has resoundingly accepted the role of challenger.

An early and important demonstration of this divergence among the Six was provided in the fateful period following Stalin's death, when the French showed how their orientation could wreck the common effort. As long as it was believed that a major threat from the East dominated international affairs, most French politicians were willing to subordinate their old distrust of Germany to the need for a joint European effort of rearmament. But as soon as events provided an excuse for trying to escape from the bipolar contest, that excuse was seized upon. To France, the bipolar contest had been a straitjacket because it had meant that in the European enterprise France and West Germany were treated as equals. Yet to Frenchmen, there were really two threats to the east of France: the manifest Soviet menace and a latent German one. Hence, many Frenchmen were reluctant to "disappear into Western Europe." France could not balance German power alone, it could never be sure it could control the joint institutions of the Six, and it did not want to consolidate American preponderance as a price for keeping West Germany fully integrated in Western Europe. So, in 1953–54, France alternated between hoping that the behavior of the Soviet Union would make EDC unnecessary and attempting to involve England in the balancing act. When England declined, France rejected EDC, and the substitute—German rearmament in the framework of NATO and WEU—had, in French eyes, the merit of "keeping the future open" by preserving the existence of the French army while avoiding the creation of an independent West German one.

Even more of a demonstration has been provided in recent years. Under de Gaulle, France has vigorously pursued an acrobatic policy designed to break into the ranks of the great powers and to develop a European entity sufficiently strong to "contain" West Germany but not so autonomous as to thwart de Gaulle's design for a "European Europe" or to prevent him from manifesting his independence (and maintaining the difference between France and Germany) in the realm of defense. France's nuclear program, the prime symbol of French determination to give meaning to the concept of the "Big Five," heightens the dilemma that the story of EDC already illustrated. The dilemma is that the French are torn between wanting a West European entity that could be an ally, not a mere dependent, of the United States in matters of defense—i.e., with a defense system allied to the United States instead of integrated in NATO (hence de Gaulle's repeated appeals to the other Five in 1960–62, and to Germany in 1962–63)—and, on the other hand, wanting to be a major power and to keep Germany from this status (hence, after the repudiation of EDC, the memorandum of 1958 for a triumvirate and the development of an atomic force which, being national, cannot, in French doctrine, be integrated). Meanwhile, West Germany, with its security reasonably assured and its restoration to status accomplished, inevitably turned toward the issue of German reunification. Its preference for bipolarity (as defined above) made it shy away from global foreign policy *à la* de Gaulle, since this might antagonize the United States; but the muting of the Cold War and the slowing down of West European integration enabled it to turn its attention to its major unsolved problem. This was bound to revive French misgivings.

Moreover, the movement toward unity among the Six has also been affected by discrepancies between France and Great Britain: another case of the different impact of the appeal to multipolarity. To some extent, the Franco-German *rapprochement* was eased by West Germany's unwillingness to heed this appeal, i.e., to compete with France. But Franco-British relations have been affected by the competition of two former world powers that selected different ways to try to preserve their major role in world affairs. France's nuclear program is a challenge to the Soviet Union and to the United States, and France's ambivalence toward the idea of European integration reflects a conditional attitude—integration is good if it leads to an entity that will emancipate Europe from any bipolar system, bad if it does not and merely chains France to German national desiderata. Great Britain's nuclear program and ambivalence toward European unity have a very different meaning. In effect, Britain has refused to make a clear-cut choice between bipolarity and multipolarity. Proud of its world interests and past importance and wedded to the notion of a moderate system with flexible alignments, yet conscious of the limits of its power, determined to preserve the American presence in Europe in order to contain the Soviet Union, and appreciative of the assets it can derive from close ties with the United States, Britain has tried to have the best of both worlds. Thus, Britain and France drew opposite conclusions from the Suez fiasco. Britain concluded that it should never again challenge American leadership and Commonwealth opinion; France was all the more determined to build a

European entity with policies of its own and to develop her own military capabilities. The British developed a nuclear force (with arguments strikingly similar to those the French used a few years later), but subordinated it to American strategy: it is a "British contribution to the Western deterrent."

The trouble with Britain's diplomatic exercise has been the problem of European unity. In the early days of the European movement, when American predominance was at its peak, Great Britain refused to join the Six because, among other things, this would have implied equality with defeated Germany and with barely rescued France. In order to preserve a "special relationship" of adviser to the United States, Britain thus missed an opportunity to turn the European enterprise into a major power and, in a kind of chain reaction, increased French discomfiture at the thought of cooperating with Germany and without Britain, a rather sudden reversal of French habits and preferences. If lingering nostalgia for great-power status kept Britain away from Europe in the late 1940s and early 1950s, its apparent resignation to bipolarity made de Gaulle keep Britain out of the EEC in 1963. The protracted Brussels negotiations in 1961–62 can be seen as an indirect French attempt to smoke out Britain's position on the problems that obsess de Gaulle —purposes and control. British negotiators skillfully kept it hidden, but their technical skill would have assured success only if the Gaullist Sphinx could have been assuaged without answers. It turned out that he wanted satisfactory replies, and he made up his mind, at the end of 1962, if not to turn the British Oedipus away, at least to warn Macmillan that he was thinking of doing so. The British answer—perhaps inadvertent, but swift at last—was Nassau; in the Sphinx's view, the reply was the wrong one.

Great Britain, to preserve its position and improve its status, used methods that took into account its important and continuing external sources of power: the Commonwealth, its cooperation with the United States in nuclear development, its "special relationship" with the United States. Inevitably, this reduced the degree to which Britain could challenge American leadership and policies and, even more, its enthusiasm for switching from non-European sources of power to still untapped sources of power in Europe. Whether the British correctly estimated the value of those sources is another matter. The fact is that Britain was conditioned by its whole past, domestic and international, to overestimate the former and to doubt the latter. After all, even in the United States the idea of a "three-pillar" Western world had remained alive a long time.[11]

If Britain thus came to a late and half-hearted Europeanism, France's Europeanism was permanent but conditional. France's extra-European sources of power had melted away fast. And France's relations with the "Anglo-Saxons" had left bitter traces, for the prewar reliance on Britain had proved to be disastrous, and since 1940 French interests had not always been well treated by Britain and the United States. Great Britain divested itself of its empire voluntarily and in orderly fashion; France did neither and found in decolonization new reasons, or pretexts, for resentment against the United States. As a result, France's desire for great-power status necessarily had a sharper edge: the distance to be covered was greater, and the spirit was bound to be revisionist rather than accepting of the *status quo*. Moreover, in that undertaking, the only choice was between self-reliance and Europe, as long as Europe offered France a supplement of power and also an avenue to leadership in an anti-bipolar direction (hence the conditional nature of the commitment). Even with a leader less keen on independence than de Gaulle, France's "option" to follow Britain's example was never open. France had no special ties to the United States, had not been one of the wartime Big Three, had not developed a nuclear bomb along with the United States; moreover, there was no place in the lobby of the Department of State for two would-be privileged advisers.

The French decision to keep Britain out of the EEC was due to fear that Britain as a member would push the European entity away from the purposes France wanted to achieve. But France's veto has not brought that entity any closer to those goals; instead, it produced a permanent "crisis of confidence." The other Common Market members, reluctant to let France use the EEC as a means to elevate itself to great-power status, wanted Great Britain as a check on France and as a guarantee against the open challenge to bipolarity that France desired—even if Britain's entry meant a further delay in achieving "supranationality." Since Gaullist policies blocked the development of supranationality anyhow, at least British membership in EEC could have changed its purposes and affected its control. This is precisely what France rejected.

[11] See Ernst Van der Beugel, *From Marshall Aid to Atlantic Partnership* (New York: Elsevier Publishing Co., 1966), pp. 273 ff.

The European movement, then, has suffered from arrested development as a result of these splits. It has been successful, however, in what I called the third stratum of the EEC, where the need to define a common stand vis-à-vis outsiders (e.g., the United States, Britain and the underdeveloped countries) has acted as a catalyst of compromises and solidarity, as proved by the Kennedy Round of tariff-cutting negotiations and by recent developments in international money matters. In this stratum, ambiguity has carried the enterprise forward, since the different nations there can focus on shared institutions, settle for compensated or "synchronized" gains and losses, and agree to complementary calculations. But this is so only because of the instrumental nature of economics, where an agreement on purpose exists (the common purpose is the maximization of wealth and welfare), and where there is an implicit answer to the question: Who commands? It is an answer not in the sense that one nation dictates the details of the bargains, but in the sense that, to be blunt, the most demanding and obdurate nation, i.e., France, exerts in fact the greatest power. But the solidarity of economic variables gives even the most difficult member an incentive to moderate his rule and his benefits, in a realm where self-reliance is no real alternative. Since the common welfare is to be used by separate governments, all the members cooperate in the same ambiguity.

But where high politics are involved, i.e., decisions on what purposes the wealth will be put to, the underlying consensus dissolves, and so does any existing agreement on command and control. Here expectations clash, compromises fail, calculations change nature because they concern not accommodations of tangible interests but clashes of wills. Between the universe of utilitarian morals preached by Jean Monnet ("your interest and mine will both be served by the discovery of a common goal that transcends and fulfills them") and the Brechtian universe of implacable realism epitomized by de Gaulle ("if someone does the stepping, it will be me, and if someone gets stepped on, it will be you") a formidably resilient barrier continues to close the political kingdom to the Common Market.[12] The

---

[12] Needless to say, the sphere of "high politics" is not defined once and for all. The more ambitious and obdurate the nation, the more subjects it will try to put in that sphere (i.e., the sooner problems of economic policy will be considered as belonging in that sphere rather than in the realm of welfare; consider de Gaulle's belief that trade with Eastern Europe is a national, not an EEC, subject). My point, however, is that there is an irreducible minimum realm of high politics—the vital interests of national diplomacy and strategy.

EEC still draws credit from the consensus on economic integration and from the momentum of previous acts of integration. Here the logic of the "spillover" still functions. But as soon as the realm of welfare fades into that of high politics—diplomacy and strategy and long-range planning—discord replaces collaboration, and there even arises the possibility of a "spillback," as EEC's 1965 crisis demonstrated. Thus, the EEC has neither broken through to more significant sectors nor increased the central organs' autonomy from national control. The increase is rejected by de Gaulle, fearful of any encroachments on his freedom to "drink in his own glass" and to "clink glasses all around"; the breakthrough often suggested by him is resisted by those who suspect him of wanting to turn the Community into French foreign policy writ large.

The development of European supranationality has been arrested, for the supranational approach entails faith in a method and is fundamentally nonpolitical. (Reading Monnet's public statements, one is left with a mixture of admiration and bafflement—admiration for the true believer in European unity who is sure that his method can put an end to power conflicts and replace confrontations of wills with a kind of escalation of the common good; bafflement at his avoidance of any mention of political issues, such as the purposes and control of a supranational arrangement, as if the right method and frame of mind could make them go away.) Insofar as the supranational authorities are absorbed in the exhausting task of preparing compromises, weighing compensations, finding the common interest in areas where there is a shared determination to proceed, they receive everyone's tribute; but when they try to go beyond this and increase their autonomy, they are slapped down. Unable to enlarge their bridgehead of autonomous power, they symbolize both the achievements and the limits of West European unity.

Another victim of the Atlantic disarray is the alternative intergovernmental method of achieving unity, favored by de Gaulle. Just as a nation with weak and splintering parties cannot find stability and effective government either in a cabinet system, which requires a coherent majority, or in a presidential system, which requires a modicum of cooperation between the executive and the legislature, a group of nations disagreeing on the fundamental political issues cannot find unity either in the Russian roulette of supranationality, which presumes their willingness to relinquish national control over certain vital matters, or in "organized cooperation," which gets them somewhere only when they agree on goals and priorities. It was the failure of the Six to agree on the scope of the tasks to be performed together (i.e., the issue of defense) and on the scope of the membership (i.e., Great Britain's application) that doomed the Fouchet plan for intergovernmental cooperation in 1962; it was the disagreement over purposes and command that reduced for several years the Franco-German treaty to a state of "potentiality" that was not always even "cordial." Thus, today, there is a West European torso, but no West European head.

## II. Nations in Disarray: Objectives, Visions, and Policies

It is not enough to identify the main reasons for disharmony within the Atlantic Alliance as a whole and in Western Europe in particular. For the nation-state remains indefinitely the center of aspirations and calculations. Only by turning from the level of the Alliance and from the level of the European Economic Community to the national level can we get a sufficiently clear idea of the complexity of the puzzle.

Among NATO members, there are a number of recognized common interests, translated into parallel objectives. (I am speaking here not of interests that states "ought to" have, but of interests that national leaders have explicitly stated.)

1. There is still a shared interest in West European security against the Soviet Union, to be preserved by a strategy of deterrence, in which the United States' nuclear arsenal is recognized by all as determinant.

2. There is an interest in what could be called tying West Germany to its Western allies, so that it will not become an arena of instability exposed to Soviet penetration or exposing its neighbors to the effects of its isolated efforts (whether aggressive or neutralist). This has been understood by all postwar federal chancellors, by all postwar American presidents, and by all the French leaders since 1950, including de Gaulle, whose Foreign Minister has repeatedly said that despite the remoteness of the present Soviet military threat, the Atlantic Alliance is important as "a factor for balance in Europe . . . as long as a new equilibrium has not been established." [13]

3. There is an interest in eliminating what de Gaulle has called

---

[13] Maurice Couve de Murville, Speech to the National Assembly, August 14, 1966 (Ambassade de France, Speeches and Press Conferences, No. 244A).

"the German anomalies, the concern they cause and the suffering they entail." [14] All the allies realize that the main threat to European security and to West Germany's ties to the West results from the facts that Germany is divided into two hostile entities and that Berlin's status is uncertain. The *status quo* in Central Europe is deemed untenable in the long run and risky in the short run.

4. There is an interest in a *détente* with the Soviet Union and its East European satellites, provided that it entails no loss of security and no setback for interests 2 and 3.

5. There is an interest in prosperity and in aiding underdeveloped countries (which will not be examined here).

However, while at the level of general interests and objectives there is relative harmony, there is discordance among the allies at two other levels: the visions, which determine the meaning of the goals and the hierarchy of objectives; the policies, which aim at turning goals and visions into realities. At each level two questions rack the Alliance: "What for?" and "Who rules?"

Only some of the actors have well-worked-out visions; the others' are either implicit or half-baked. Definite visions leave little room for accommodation; the very fuzziness of the others' obscures the nature of the choices that must be made or the implications of the choices already made. There are two sets of oppositions here. There is, to begin with, a clash between bipolar and multipolar visions of the international world. On the whole, the vision of the United States is bipolar, and does not favor the emergence of a European entity whose foreign and military policies would differ greatly from its own. The purpose of NATO must be the world-wide management of the anti-Communist contest if one's version of bipolarity is the old notion of a permanent duel; or it must be the gradual liquidation of the Cold War primarily by a *rapprochement* between the superpowers if one's version of bipolarity is the new notion of a duopoly. The need for a "seamless umbrella of nuclear power" [15] (provided by the United States in the old version, by the superpowers in the new) requires the subordination or reduction of any European military establishment. The multipolar vision also aims at ending the Cold War but looks forward to the emergence of independent powers other than the United States and the Soviet Union; in this respect, de

[14] Press Conference, February 4, 1965. (See Roy Macridis, ed., *De Gaulle, Implacable Ally* [New York: Harper & Row, 1966], p. 194.)

[15] Timothy Stanley, *NATO in Transition* (New York: Frederick A. Praeger, for the Council on Foreign Relations, 1965), p. 127.

Gaulle in his more ambitious moments of anticipating an "imposing confederation of Europe," and Monnet in his more explicit moments of European supranationalism, are not far apart.

The second opposition, related to the first, contrasts an Atlantic vision with a European one. The Atlantic vision, concentrating on the internal relations of the Atlantic world and the partnership between the two "halves" of the Alliance assumes that the Atlantic dimension is the common denominator of all members of NATO. The European vision is concerned primarily with relations between NATO and East Europe; it gives priority to intra-European relations. The Atlantic vision is usually bipolar (but not necessarily so: it is perfectly possible to believe that the pan-European vision cannot be fulfilled for a long time and that the first duty of Western powers is therefore to establish stable and progressive relations in the Atlantic world, yet to want the American and European elements of that world to be of comparable importance). The European vision is anti-bipolar at least insofar as it calls for the extrication of Europe from the clutches of the two giants. It is multipolar whenever the new Europe it hopes for is seen as having a full role in international affairs, not merely as a "backyard of international politics" or as a neutralized buffer.

It is possible, of course, to try to reconcile and pursue simultaneously these two visions. But such a synthesis would be incredibly delicate. The priorities in each are not the same: thus, in the Atlantic vision, the ties between Germany and the West are of greater importance than the "end of the German anomalies"; in the European vision, they must be construed in such a way as not to impede the second aim. And the importance of the United States is not the same; although it can be argued that the very survival of the Atlantic vision now requires priority to intra-European relations, and, on the other hand, that the reunification of Europe cannot be achieved without our participation, our involvement in and relevance to the enterprise may well be less important than it is seen to be in "Atlantica."

Second, at the level of actual foreign policies, the range of disagreements is particularly wide. Leaving aside all the foreign-policy objectives unique to each nation, the ways the allies attempt to reach their *common* objectives are very divergent. Let us consider a few examples. Concerning German reunification, a whole gamut of policies has been suggested (and attempted). There is the policy of facing the Soviet bloc from a "situation of strength." It aims for a reunification of Germany that would be essentially an extension of West Germany eastward (thanks to some debacle in Eastern Europe). This policy, originally Atlantic and bipolar in the days of Dean Acheson, John Foster Dulles, and Konrad Adenauer, has lately been suggested on behalf of a multipolar Atlantic view.[16] Then, there are different versions of a "policy of movement." One is the policy of reconciliation, which prevails today in the United States, France, Britain, and West Germany, and which views actual reunification as possible only at the end of a long process of reassuring Eastern Europe and the Soviet Union about Germany, instead of believing that German reunification must be the condition of reconciliation; this corresponds to a "European" vision. How this policy is pursued still depends on whether the vision is bipolar or not. There is also the policy of taking "little steps" toward reunification, beginning with direct contact with East Germany, which subordinates the restoration of common German institutions to the restoration of links between the two German states. In effect, it tries to correct the unrealistic elements of the other policies, which seem to ignore the problems raised by the existence of East Germany; also, it does not necessarily entail switching from the Atlantic to the European approach.

Or consider the NATO objective of tying West Germany to the West. The policies advocated by member states are not the same if the vision is bipolar in the old sense (in which case ties to the United States will be emphasized), or bipolar in the new, duopolistic sense (in which case there will be less emphasis on the objective itself), or multipolar and Atlantic (in which case ties to Western Europe will be emphasized), or multipolar and European (in which case West European integration will be shaped and presented as a prelude to German reunification). Or take the policy of working toward a *détente* with the Soviet Union: in a bipolar vision, a *détente* is compatible with or even entails extensive agreements between Russia and the United States on arms control and on disengagement, even if they impose restrictions on Europe that are not accepted by the superpowers themselves on their own territories or if they perpetuate the nuclear disparity between the United States and its allies. This is not the case if the vision is multipolar.

I have said that the two critical problems facing NATO member nations are to decide what the Alliance is for, and how it is to be controlled. At the level of visions, the differences over the first problem

---

[16] On the views of Franz-Joseph Strauss, see below, p. 427.

are greater than those over the second, although the two are obviously closely related. At the level of actual foreign policies, the problem of control is central. Indeed, one can argue that the Atlantic Alliance is endangered more by the pursuit of the same objective by allies each of which is trying to control events than by the pursuit of different objectives by allies that avoid challenging one another. If France pursues a goal of neutralization in Vietnam but refrains from challenging American policy there except verbally, the effects are less serious than if, in the pursuit of a policy of reconciliation with Eastern Europe, the United States, France, and Germany each decides that it must take the initiative.

The problem of control has led to two serious clashes among the NATO powers: over who commands, and over who benefits. The issue of command is at the heart of the argument about NATO strategy, since even those who accept the wisdom of the strategy of "flexible response" are concerned to know who is going to be in charge of that response. As for who benefits, the differences of opinion have been apparent with every one of the agreed NATO objectives that I listed. Over West European security, the European allies object to the American strategy of flexible response because it seems, in case of a failure of deterrence, to organize the limitation of damage by concentrating it on Continental Europe, thus benefiting only the United States and the Soviet Union. Over West German ties to the West, there is a clear opposition between the United States and France, at times with West Germany being used by both as a football. In the spring of 1966, for instance, the United States and Great Britain tried to use Franco-German ties (including French troops in Germany) as a way of getting France to accept a NATO situation as close as possible to the allied military integration de Gaulle had just denounced, while the French tried to use those same ties as an arrangement presaging the kind of loose defense system separate from NATO that de Gaulle obviously would like to achieve for Europe as a whole.

Over the "German anomalies," the problem of who benefits has arisen in connection with the issue of initiatives toward reunification. The United States has been torn between the desire to preserve the Four Power rights in this matter (so as to prevent, for instance, West German initiatives that might disrupt either the harmony of the Alliance or the prospects of a Soviet-American *détente* by reviving fears of West German unilateral action, or to prevent West Germany from falling into a Soviet trap of an "all-German" settlement negotiated by the two Germanies) and the fear that whatever we do, the West Germans would resent our initiative in matters of vital concern to them. This accounts for Dean Rusk's controversial statement at the end of 1964, which seemed to push the Germans into the forefront of future negotiations with the Soviets and East Europe on a German settlement. As for the French, their policy has consisted in (1) pointing out to the West Germans the futility of the previous Western policy of "strength," so as to blame Germany's ties with the United States for the immobility; (2) preventing the United States from reaping after 1963 any benefits in terms of prestige or leadership from the new "policy of movement," by advocating such a policy in terms far less inhibited than those used by Americans until October 1966 and by exhorting the West Germans to "start moving" themselves; (3) helping to prevent the West Germans from being the main beneficiaries of the new approach by pursuing a diplomacy of movement more dynamic than theirs.

The same tug of war, finally, has affected the goal of *détente* with the Soviet Union. When, in 1962–63, it looked as if the Americans were willing to pay the price of a *de facto* consolidation of Europe's partition for a *détente,* the French denounced them vigorously for preparing a new Yalta. Later, when American moves to this end slowed down, first because of the entanglement over the MLF, then because of the war in Vietnam, the French became the champions of a *détente,* spoke of "liquidating the cold war," and, since Gaullist policy had led to closer ties between West Germany and the United States, pointed out the main obstacle now was the Washington-Bonn axis. When the new American policy of "peaceful engagement" with the East and the draft of a nonproliferation treaty were announced, late in 1966, the French reverted to their stand of 1962–63. In all three cases, the French were preventing the United States from acting in European affairs without their consent, preventing West Germany from becoming the main herald of a *détente* (the *détente* certainly being a goal of France, but only if France initiated it), and working from the *détente* toward the development of a fully restored Europe—not a consolidation of the *status quo* that would prolong "the two hegemonies," and not a Europe that would pay with its own neutralization for the disengagement of Russia and America.

A survey of national positions provides an almost too perfect demonstration of my argument about the system of universal deadlocks. We can look at the scene as if a drama with five main actors were being played upon it. Not only do their actions conflict and checkmate each other, but each pursues an increasingly acrobatic line, with its own checks and balances.

## A. *The Soviet Union*

Let us begin with the Soviet Union, fear of which brought the Atlantic Alliance into existence. In its European policy, it seems to pursue two basic objectives. The first is its own national security: although the fear of an American attack was never very great, in my opinion, and exploited primarily for political purposes, there is a genuine and understandable fear of Germany. Hence, the Soviet Union opposes any policy that would tend to make Germany (any Germany) a major, independent actor on the European scene. This means that it must oppose the kind of "Atlantic" policy that makes West Germany a privileged ally of the United States. But it also means that the Soviet Union wants to avoid the kind of NATO debacle that would leave West Germany free of outside controls and in possession of the largest conventional army west of the Iron Curtain. For even though, in the West, the possibility of West Germany's independence seems to evoke fear of "another Rapallo," *thus far* at least the Soviet Union appears to understand that West Germany would be lured into a Rapallo-like policy only if the Soviets delivered in exchange what they alone have the power to deliver— East Germany. And this they have not contemplated doing. A reunified Germany, however friendly to the Soviet Union, would be (even without nuclear weapons) a major military and economic power, a new and unpredictable element that could threaten the security of its neighbors. The Soviets would certainly not want to repeat the experience they had with Red China. Also, the process and outcome of German reunification would seriously damage the second pillar of Soviet policy: the preservation of Soviet control in what is left of the "Soviet camp" in Europe.

If security were the only Soviet goal, security arrangements *not* implying the presence of Communist governments and Soviet forces in Eastern Europe could be imagined. But the "Europeanization" of the Soviet Union (under pressure from China) has made control in Eastern Europe a vital aim in itself. Control is necessary for reasons of ideology and power. Ideological cohesion enhances and facilitates Soviet power, and Soviet power sustains ideological cohesion. The Soviet Union, in its effort to maintain Russian leadership of the Communist movement, simply cannot afford a break-up of its "empire," although the need for support and the "economy of force" both argue in favor of liberalization—of turning the empire into a hegemonial alliance. East Germany is a key factor in this respect: as the second industrial power in the Soviet camp, in which the Soviets have made a tremendous political investment (in contrast to what they did in their occupation zone of Austria before 1955), it has become their symbol of that camp. Moreover, it is the linchpin of the Eastern bloc since the need to maintain a Soviet military presence along the German Iron Curtain, in a state that would in all likelihood be in serious trouble without Soviet support, in turn justifies the presence of Soviet forces elsewhere in Eastern Europe. This is why the Soviet Union persists in taking a stand on German reunification that amounts purely and simply to getting the West to recognize the permanence of Germany's partition and the legitimacy of the East German state.

Because of all these factors, the Soviet Union must adopt a highly ambiguous attitude toward NATO. On the one hand, it has an interest in weakening NATO and exploiting divisions within it—in part because a strong and unified NATO under American leadership would oblige Russia to increase military expenditures, would give West Germany dangerous weight, would preclude Western recognition of the *status quo* in central Europe, and would seem to bear out China's arguments about the inefficiency and timidity of Soviet policy. On the other hand, the Soviet Union has no interest in a collapse of NATO, particularly in a prompt exodus of American forces from Western Europe. For the persistence of NATO provides the Soviet Union with a reason for maintaining its forces in Eastern Europe: a withdrawal of the American forces under NATO command from Europe would not facilitate a Soviet "conquest" of Western Europe (since the main obstacle to this is the United States' nuclear deterrent), but it would leave the Soviet Union as a hegemonial power controlling increasingly restive nationalities, and it would increase the "German uncertainties." Of course, since fear of West German revanchism has become the cement of the Warsaw Pact,[17] it could be said that a West Germany unchecked by NATO would cement it even more. But insofar as the fear is genuine, the NATO check on West Germany is genuinely appreciated as a source of security; and insofar as what is really feared is West Germany's influence on the true possessor of power, the United States, a West Ger-

[17] See *The Warsaw Pact,* Study by the Subcommittee on National Security and International Operations (Washington: GPO, 1966).

many deprived of the means and will to revanche would no longer be a cement. For the Soviet Union, ideally there should be enough of a reason to wave the anti-German flag to keep the "Soviet camp" united, but not so much of a dissolution of the "American camp" as to necessitate a redoubled effort to preserve the Soviet one. In other words, the best West Germany is one that appears potentially dangerous but is in fact contained, especially by an American presence (and/or by international procedures jointly dominated by the superpowers). A strong, unified NATO is unlikely to recognize the Soviet-favored *status quo;* a NATO debacle would threaten it. The best NATO is one that is fairly strong but troubled, providing opportunities to exploit the differences so that, one by one, its members could be persuaded to recognize the Soviet *status quo.* And, for the Soviet Union, the ideal German situation would also be the one most likely to lead to a permanently strained NATO.

There is an interesting melange of symmetry and asymmetry in the Soviet and the American situation vis-à-vis Europe. There is symmetry in that both superpowers view it as an arena essential to their national security, in the use of security fears as a bond between the superpower and "its" German state, in the way those bonds have become the keystones of the two alliances, in superpower control over the alliances, and in the division of each alliance between those who hug the leader and those whose "separatist" national interests come first. But there is asymmetry insofar as in the West the cement is provided by the fear of the Soviet Union, in the East (particularly in Poland) by fear more of West Germany than of the United States. There is also asymmetry in the capacity of members to leave the military alliance (nobody in the East has gone as far as France) and in the diplomatic position of the two Germanies—Bonn is showing a greater aptitude for autonomous action than has Pankow. For there is asymmetry insofar as the maintenance of control (especially over East Germany) is a necessity for the Soviet Union, whereas for the United States, one could argue that a privileged United States–West Germany alliance and the preservation of America's predominance within NATO are not *necessary* goals.

Thus, whereas the present situation in NATO serves Soviet interests well and might help it to achieve the aim of having the West recognize the *status quo* in Europe, the Western hope to end the "German anomalies" appears out of reach so long as the Soviet concern for control is paramount. Only when, for extra-European reasons, the Soviet Union needs an *entente* with the West so badly that it will willingly give up control, or when, for reasons having to do with the political evolution of the East European nations and domestic Soviet affairs, the costs of physical control become prohibitive and the need for ideological control wanes, then and only then will an end to the "German anomalies" be possible. It is a long perspective. It tells us something about what we should avoid in order to keep it open, but it tells us little about what terms the Soviet Union is most likely to accept in the future and about what the Western powers can do in order to make the perspective less theoretical.

## B. *France*

The first question we must answer in discussing French policy is whether de Gaulle's diplomacy is representative of the nation's views. There is no point in denying that the style of de Gaulle's foreign policy is entirely his own; that his concern for independence as a goal in itself distinguishes him from his predecessors of both the Fourth and the Third Republics; that his willingness to risk apparent isolation is unique; that his somewhat Bismarckian skill in simultaneously travelling on a number of apparently divergent roads is unlikely to be emulated by less gifted or less passionately concerned successors. Nevertheless, there *is* a remarkable continuity of vision and objectives in postwar French foreign policy. The main difference between the General and the premiers in the interval between the two de Gaulle regimes is that they—being less daring and obliged to act like corks floating on the surface of stormy domestic waters, rather than like captains in control of their vessel—sought to reach French goals in cooperation with other nations and to bend these cooperative efforts toward their objectives. The General, suspicious of cooperation as a goal *per se* and remembering how easily it can become a subordination to other nations' consent, has sought to make international cooperation conditional upon its serving French national goals. The gap is not large between them: the men of the Fourth Republic were reluctant to let cooperative schemes divert them from their goals (the history of the Fourth Republic is not the story of French subservience to the United States; this is a Gaullist myth); and the General, even in his most outrageously unilateral moments, has always acted in such a way as to drag along (sooner or later) the cooperative schemes he believes useful for France. For de Gaulle believes that the choice is not between acting alone and acting together, as his critics charge, but between acting alone and being *in*active together. He hopes that acting alone now will hasten cooperative action in the right direction (the idea that he thinks France alone can change the course of history and reach her goals is an anti-Gaullist myth).

Moreover, whereas there is one genuine difference in approach—over policies toward European integration—the importance of this difference should not be exaggerated. The non-Gaullists have apparently embraced European integration as an end in itself; but, while Jean Lecanuet's Europeanism looks unconditional, François Mitterrand's is not, for he (like many other French left-wing leaders, including Gaston Defferre) seems to assume that if only France were more pro-European, the other Five would give to the common enterprise the purposes of French foreign policy. Meanwhile, General de Gaulle has made several moves that would be extremely difficult for any successor to cancel, even though his French opponents have denounced them for their inopportunity, costs, or risks. Among these moves, there is the construction of a nuclear deterrent. The two non-Communist oppositions have both attacked it, one (Lecanuet) for its being national, arguing for a "Europeanization" of the deterrent rather than for its abandonment, and the other (Mitterrand) saying that it should be dropped in exchange for world-wide disarmament and arbitration of disputes; both are reminiscent of the Labour Party's position before it returned to power in Great Britain in 1964. Another move that will be hard to reverse is de Gaulle's decision to withdraw French troops from NATO's integrated structure. Here too, however drastic or expensive, the move corresponded to a widely supported French objective, and to reverse it without sufficient compensations would be considered a national disgrace. A third irreversible move, paradoxically enough, has been France's effort to tighten the net of West European economic integration. Whether in 1965 de Gaulle really believed that he could take France out of the EEC if the other Five insisted on more supranationality, and was deterred from playing Samson by the voters' reaction in the presidential election in December; or whether (as I believe) he was merely playing poker—believing that since the interest in preserving the Community was mutual, nobody would really call his bluff lest he carried out this threat, and thus using the advantage of a greater reputation for recklessness—we may never know. We know, however, the result of his gamble: an agreement on agriculture (and decision-making procedures) on his terms.

There is another phenomenon that contributes to what I would call Gaullist irreversibility. The single-minded determination with which de Gaulle has pursued his policies despite criticism from abroad and at home has resulted in a kind of "trickling down" of Gaullism among French elites. A recent study [18] has found that they share de Gaulle's "self-assertive nationalism" even if they do not all respond to the trumpet calls that accompany it, or even if they see less of a contrast than he does between it and various curtailments of sovereignty. What is striking is a fairly even distribution of this nationalism among the various social groups that make up the elites. Pride in the national effort; a conviction that the United States' protection of Europe is lasting but that France's relations with the United States must be revised to give France great-power status again; belief in the disappearance of bipolarity and the advantages of this demise; priority given to European integration or a West European-British *entente* over Atlantic relationships; a certain indifference to the "Atlantic" dimension of Europe; a belief that the purpose of European unity is to gain power, and a determination to use it to challenge American supremacy; a special concern for two "non-Atlantic" orientations (relations with underdeveloped countries and, especially, relations with Eastern Europe aimed at a reunification of the continent) —these are the views expressed by the French elites. They confirm the opinion that opposition to de Gaulle's regime can be consistent with full acceptance of his major goals, nor was there anything in the last presidential and legislative elections to alter this opinion. Lecanuet, the only leader whose opinions could be called orthodox Atlantic in the *French* context (that is, who believed in the idea of an "equal partnership" between the United States and Europe and was suitably ambiguous on the issue of bipolarity versus multipolarity), received only one-sixth of the votes on the first ballot in December 1965. Moreover, much of his strength came from his exploitation in rural areas of farmers' discontent with the Common Market crisis, which has since been resolved, if not to the satisfaction of most French peasants, at least in such a way that their discontent can now only be turned in an *anti*-European direction: for they can no longer blame their plight on the absence of a common European policy.

There is another reason why Gaullist policies will outlive the General. Old Atlantic orthodoxy has no chance of providing French political forces with a common denominator, even with the Gaullists in a minority opposition, and even if the French fail to notice the waning of orthodoxy in the United States itself. Lecanuet's friends

[18] See the study by Karl W. Deutsch *et al.*, *France, Germany and the Western Alliance* (New York: Charles Scribner's Sons, 1967).

might be tempted to espouse such orthodoxy, but that group is far too small to govern alone and would have to share power. Here, two possibilities arise. One is an anti-Gaullist parliamentary alliance with the much more important non-Communist left. But this left, rather unsettled in its foreign-policy views, leans increasingly away from the Atlantic orientation, both because many of its leaders (like Mitterrand and Defferre) are closer to de Gaulle (except in their evaluation of European integration) than to Lecanuet, and because of a strong desire and electoral need not to cut itself off from the Communist party. Another possibility is a right-wing alliance between Lecanuet, the independents of Giscard d'Estaing (who compete for the same supporters), and the more conservative elements of the Gaullist party. Here again, the outcome would not be so far removed from de Gaulle's position.

It is therefore necessary to look realistically at what is unchangeable and what is still "open" in French foreign policy. The determination to dismantle "the two hegemonies" is fixed and immovable. As a result, the French want the American guarantee of West European security to be maintained as long as there is a threat from the East, however remote, but in such a way as to insure the maximum of deterrence and to avoid the prospect of a so-called limited war in Europe. That is to say, they believe there must be autonomous means in Europe of affecting NATO strategy. Also, they want gradually to remove the predominance of each superpower in "its" half of Europe (which is one reason why France refuses to recognize East Germany), to liquidate the Cold War, and to allow the European nations to play a greater role in international affairs. Third, they are determined not to accept, as a price for the end of the Cold War, a perpetual neutralization of or discrimination against Europe, through schemes that would impose restrictions or unreciprocated controls on the continent as a whole. Fourth, they are determined not to be dragged into a general conflict by the moves of the United States or the Soviet Union in other parts of the world.

Another fixed determination is to keep any Germany from filling the vacuum between the slowly retreating American and Russian "hegemonies." In part, this is due to a conviction that if West Germany tries to play a major role, either the Soviet Union or the United States or both will have a pretext to preserve their domination, on the grounds that only they can resist or restrain the rise of Germany. In part, it results from a more parochial but no less essential desire to avoid a return to a disastrous past. Consequently,

France encourages West German hopes for reunification as part of the drive against the *status quo* in Europe, and because as long as such hopes exist, West Germany will be more willing to accept various limitations as the price for reunification. (Keeping these hopes alive is another reason for the steadfast French refusal to recognize East Germany.) Hence, the French want to prevent West Germany from "directly or indirectly" gaining a nuclear arsenal; for by perpetuating the division of Europe, this would also prolong the hegemonies and, if Germany somehow eventually reunified, make it the arbiter of the continent. Also, the French insist that West Germany accept the Oder-Neisse line, for the continuing doubt over borders gives the Soviet Union an excuse for its presence in Eastern Europe and delays European reunification, whereas an eventually reunified non-nuclear Germany without territorial claims would be a less formidable power. Third, the French are determined to tie West Germany solidly to Western Europe, so as to decrease Soviet fears of West German independence, to increase Western Europe's attractiveness vis-à-vis Eastern Europe, and to prevent West Germany from becoming the West European anchor of an American presence that would in turn justify the Soviet *imperium* in the East. Thus, the final vision is that of a reunification of Europe and Germany, prepared by a general and gradual *rapprochement* and made inevitable and acceptable to the Soviet Union—inevitable because of the mutual attraction of the two halves of the Continent, acceptable because of the limits on Germany and the emancipation of Western Europe from the United States.

Ever since World War I, the drama of French foreign policy has been in the realm of means. And de Gaulle's own greatest problem is whether the means he has selected have brought France any closer to the goals I have described. His emphasis has been on national grandeur and traditional balance-of-power techniques: the main beneficiary of the ebb of Russian and American hegemonies is supposed to be France; the "vacuum" is to be filled by a pan-European system that would *not* be supranational; the containment of Germany is to be assured chiefly by France and the Soviet Union, the two main powers of the Continent; the withdrawal of Soviet troops from Eastern Europe along with that of American troops in the West is to be made possible by the integration of West Germany in a West European defense system devoid of aggressive intentions toward the East, then by the inclusion of that system in the pan-European one; and Germany would be rewarded with reunification for acceptance of all other restrictions. But could such an acrobatic scheme succeed? In a vaguely confederated Europe of states, even a militarily and geographically restricted and politically decentralized Germany could be a factor of instability: as one commentator has put it ironically, to contain Germany, the physical presence of American and Soviet troops is a safer prescription.[19] Even if such a "German peril" appears unlikely, the Gaullist scheme could only be carried out through the most extravagant subtlety, the most artful mix of threats and blandishments. To reassure the Soviet Union of German and American intentions, to include the Soviets in a system for containing Germany, and yet to get them out of Eastern Europe; to reassure the Germans on the Russians, to make them partners in West European prosperity and, by providing them with a hope for reunification, in the revision of the *status quo*, yet to maintain German inferiority in over-all status and military sovereignty; to preserve the American guarantee against eventual Soviet aggression in Western Europe (and, presumably, over the whole continent once Europe is unified) while getting the United States to relinquish its privileged position in exchange for the dismantling of the Soviet Union's domain; to build a West European entity strong enough to contain West Germany but not so strong as to imprison France and force her to give up control of her nuclear force, allied to the United States but not so dependent as to deprive it of freedom of movement toward the East, powerful enough to defend Western Europe under America's nuclear guarantee after the departure of United States troops but not so dependent on German might as to frighten Eastern Europe into Soviet arms—all this requires a great symphonic talent, and much more.

In every respect, the performance of the symphony depends on the players' willingness to respond to the conductor. The question arises whether de Gaulle's determination to be conductor of an orchestra in which he is not exactly the biggest star does not prevent any performance at all. His only chance of succeeding in the eastern half of his design lies with the convergence of two sets of events: one set being strong pressures on the Soviet Union, within Russia and East Europe or from Asia (although, as we have indicated, if the pressure from China is mainly ideological, it only makes Soviet control of Eastern Europe more indispensable; if the pressure should become more physical, priorities could change); the other being a

---

[19] Pierre Hassner, "L'Europe entre le statu quo et l'anarchie," *Preuves*, No. 191, January 1967, p. 35.

Gaullist success in obtaining in Western Europe arrangements likely to attract East Europe away from the Soviet Union yet acceptable to the Russians. In order to arrive at such a solution, de Gaulle needs in particular the cooperation of the United States and West Germany. Instead, he has infuriated the United States by insisting on divorcing the North Atlantic *Alliance* from the North Atlantic Treaty *Organization,* and arguing that the indivisibility of West European defense (breached by his secession) obliges the United States to protect even a rebellious France. He has lost sympathies in (while teaching a dangerous lesson to) West Germany by implying that integration in NATO, unacceptable for France, is still essential for West Germany, yet denouncing the West Germans for their subordination to the United States *and* implicitly counting on German-American ties to safeguard the American nuclear guarantee! [20]

De Gaulle's opponents and critics have argued that, far from dismantling the hegemonies, he has helped to consolidate them. His unilateral acts against NATO have tightened the United States' hold over the other members; and, first by strengthening the bonds between West Germany and the United States, later (when those bonds began to weaken) by giving West Germany an incentive to take initiatives by itself, he has made East Germans, Poles, and Czechs cling even closer to the Soviet Union. His overt hostility to German-American ties, to German nuclear ambitions, to a supranational Europe in which Germany and France would be weighted equally and which, he fears, the United States would dominate, have weakened the hold of the "European idea" on West Germany's imagination and set the stage for precisely the kind of West German independence that could best consolidate the East while disintegrating the West. There is no West European political and military entity; on the contrary, there is a fragile coexistence of NATO, in which America's predominance is unimpaired and the voice of West Germany is louder, and of a France precariously tied to NATO in general and West Germany in particular. France does not fill the vacuum between the superpowers. On the contrary, there is, according to some, a weakening of the Atlantic Alliance without any corresponding crisis in the East, or, according to others, a kind of perpetuation of both blocs (at a lower level of hostility and with increasing interpenetration), except only for the flight of two swallows from the nests—Paris and Bucharest—and they are too weak to mean that the spring of unification has arrived.

[20] Bundy, cited, pp. 3–11.

De Gaulle's conviction that in any event nations always follow their interests and that any construct which one does not control is a trap may well be no more than a self-fulfilling prophecy. Yet his own critique of his adversaries' view is not easily refuted. The drama of means versus ends is theirs as much as his. The critics say that a France "going it alone" has a vision but no means to realize it, and that attempts to realize it by maneuvers alone only delay its achievement. De Gaulle argues that the means his critics advocate would not serve the vision and would in fact prevent France from acting independently to achieve it; that the only means which can help France are means under her controls; that until further notice, a European entity of the kind his critics demand, whether supranational (and therefore unlikely to include Britain) or with Britain (and therefore unlikely to be supranational), would not be an instrument of French foreign policy, only an instrument for American-inspired Delilahs to cut off the hair of the French Samson. To believe that the creation of a West European structure would produce a sudden mutation in national foreign policies is indeed naive; thus far, there has been so wide a gap among the Six as to rule out even a consensus on calling defense a subject of common concern. Building a European "integrated" defense system that denies West Germany access to nuclear control is like squaring the circle: the only realities are either domination by one partner (the nuclear one) under the pretext of integration (a solution as unwelcome to West Germany in the West European context as it is to France in NATO) or else a nonintegrated, cooperative arrangement whose conclusion depends on the partners' willingness to conclude it.

Thus, in the French polity, a debate goes on not about goals but about means, and about their relative appropriateness. This is where some flexibility continues to be felt. General de Gaulle's position is: given the present states of mind, all France can do is: (1) set directions; (2) through a combination of unilateral acts, bilateral contacts, and patience, contribute to and wait for a situation in which the other players (without which she cannot get what she wants) will find it in their interest to act the way he hopes; (3) during this long and difficult period, preserve (or avoid the destruction of) those instruments of cooperation that France will need as supplements of her own insufficient power, whatever spectacular acts he may have to take alone; (4) never allow these instruments to obstruct action. De Gaulle's critics believe that a more enthusiastic attitude on his part toward the instruments of international cooperation would hasten the day when the other European powers see things in the

French way. Too much emphasis on unilateral thrusts and bilateral talks only puts off that day by hardening the resistance of those whose support is needed.

The focus of the debate is on Western Europe. It involves differing assessments of the possibilities open to states like France in the present international system. De Gaulle, whose view of international affairs resembles Hobbes' notion of the state of nature, considers that the risks of delay through independent action are less than those of defeat through collective snares. Since states act according to their interests, their resentment of unilateral moves is unlikely to lead them to behave irrationally anyhow. Collective instruments are merely arenas and stakes. The power of other states can best be contained, not through confused "organic" agglomerations that pretend to transcend the issues, but from the outside through ever-shifting combinations of power. De Gaulle's critics, whose views are more idealistic, consider the risk of dilution through collective action less than the risk of sterility through unilateral moves. If they came to power, or if de Gaulle's successors are Gaullists less impervious than he to attacks from the opposition, they would put more emphasis on Western Europe as an instrument to achieve French goals. They would rely on a West European security system (rather than on the French force alone) as the means to make possible both security in alliance with the United States, and the dismantling of the American military hegemony. They would redouble the efforts to extend integration to more sectors, so as to provide West Germany with an alternative to independent nationalism, to compensate for the sacrifices Bonn will be asked to make with respect to borders and nuclear weapons, and to reassure East Europe and the Soviet Union about Germany. They might make a new attempt to get Britain to join the French undertaking. However, the long years of Gaullism, so debatable in their immediate results, may prove to be the necessary prelude to that second phase in the Gaullist vision—the phase that France by herself could not bring about nor de Gaulle's methods promote, but whose chance of being realized would have been even slighter had he never articulated the vision and given France the sense of purpose and the insufficient yet necessary means he has provided.

## C. *West Germany*

As many observers have pointed out, the contrast between West Germany and France could not be more striking. A study of West German elites, undertaken at the same time as that of the French elites discussed above, revealed that for all the increased friendliness, there had been little increase in mutual trust. Whereas the French believe in the advent and beneficence of multipolarity, West Germans believed in the persistence and advantages of bipolarity (seen as a contest) and in a continued Soviet threat. Instead of national self-assertiveness, there was an overwhelming recognition of the need for allies; instead of hostility toward the United States, there was a feeling of dependence and a desire for solidarity; and, although there was still considerable enthusiasm and hope for European integration (more hope than in France), there was also a determination to give priority to Atlantic ties over European ones and not to let the latter weaken the former. Whereas the French are very ambivalent about sacrifices of sovereignty, the West Germans are not and appear quite willing to accept a permanent obligation not to develop a West German nuclear force. So strong were the feelings of dependence on the United States that many of them agreed to the MLF, not out of spontaneous enthusiasm for a scheme allegedly invented to anticipate their claims, but out of docility. Although there have been major changes of policy, reflecting new attitudes, one fundamental difference with France remains. French attitudes express a high degree of self-confidence (whether the French endorse self-reliance, or show faith in their capacity to influence the regional or international organizations through which they think French policy ought to proceed). West German attitudes remain marked by the deep insecurity of a country whose sovereignty, borders, and former capital city are all in doubt, whose national identity has been shattered by the Nazi experience, the ordeal of defeat, and the trauma of partition.

Under Chancellor Erhard, West German policies conflicted with France's at every important point. If French foreign policy was determined to shake off the "two hegemonies," German foreign policy clung to the conviction that only American leadership of NATO could bring about the decline of the other hegemony. At the service of a multipolar vision and in an attempt to demonstrate that interests and means need not be too closely correlated, French foreign policy tried to be global, despite France's limited means outside Europe. West Germany, on the contrary, acted as if the Soviet-American conflict in Europe remained at the heart of world politics; German policy outside of Europe consisted of only two things—active trade, and political moves dictated by the necessities of the European Cold War (the Hallstein Doctrine, which excluded diplomatic relations with governments that recognize East Germany).

France and West Germany both shared the allied objective of strengthening the ties that bind the new Germany to the West. But the only common denominator of France's *"Europe européenne"* and Erhard's Atlantic Europe was an economically integrated Western Europe. And indeed, there was a kind of tacit agreement to leave the task of European integration unfinished. The Germans, despite occasional attempted *relances,* certain of foundering on Dutch opposition, were not eager to tighten bonds that would complicate their relations with the United States; and the French, of course, were not eager for the opposite reason. As a result, the one solid, common enterprise that was most firmly in French and German hands had been downgraded; for both nations, "Europeanism" was conditional, subordinated to other goals. The Franco-German treaty, which de Gaulle envisaged as the motor of the Six (and as a substitute for it if need be), met the same fate as another treaty de Gaulle once signed—the Soviet-French treaty of 1944. In each case, an agreement to promote coordinated policies toward common goals was deprived of meaning by the lack of consensus preceding its enactment.

During Erhard's chancellorship, there was also considerable friction between France and West Germany over the allied objective of "ending the German anomalies." Granted that German reunification must be sought diplomatically, not by force, two questions arose: *To* whom should one address one's efforts? *With* whom should they be undertaken? On the first question, as we have observed before, there was confusion in West Germany. The old, "tough" line—reunification when Jericho's walls collapse—implied that the interlocutor would be the Soviet Union. The policy inaugurated by Gerhard Schröder shifted the scene to Eastern Europe (exclusive of East Germany). Since 1965, the French invited their neighbors to abandon the first line and pursue the second with greater vigor. As to the second question, the French knew what they did not want: they did not want the Germans to handle the issue alone, and they did not want the United States to play a decisive role. So they clung to the notion that the formal negotiating procedure is a Four Power responsibility, and they combined this with the idea that, "the German problem being the European one," [21] the substantive issue must be worked out by the Europeans themselves.[22] The Erhard government, on the other hand, was convinced that West Germans cannot walk

[21] De Gaulle, in Macridis, cited, p. 191.
[22] See the communiqué issued after de Gaulle's visit to Moscow, June 1966 (Ambassade de France, Release No. 943, June 30, 1966).

alone on the long road to reunification, and that they must walk hand in hand with the United States, the only state capable of giving the Soviet Union the right kind of inducement to relinquish East Germany, a development upon which German reunification depends. Europe divorced from the United States would be too weak to bring the Soviet Union to the point where it would regard withdrawal from East Germany as expedient, and in no position to persuade the Soviet Union and Eastern Europe that the cost of withdrawal was low (since a reunified Germany integrated in Europe, and possibly able to dominate it without any check by the United States, would be dangerous to the Soviet bloc). Also, by holding America's hand, West Germany aimed at forcing America to keep holding the German hand too, for West Germans have an interest in not letting the superpowers deal with the "German problem" over their heads. Ever since 1961, German foreign policy has been haunted by the fear that the Soviet-American *détente* would develop into a kind of duopoly that would perpetuate the division of Europe and of Germany.

In short, France and West Germany were on a kind of collision course. One student of French and German affairs has observed that French and German elites consider that their nations have more ties with Britain and America, respectively, than with each other; [23] consequently, the weakening of French ties to the United States did indeed weaken Franco-German bonds. However, West Germany by mid-1966 came to a crisis in its own relations with the United States.

These relations had been at their best in the days of John Foster Dulles when security was the absolute priority; allied policy on reunification was one of maximum demands yet minimum expectations; and West European integration (not yet seen as potentially conflicting with German-American ties) provided for high expectations and concrete results. In the process, West Germany's climb out of the abyss toward respectability and rank was achieved. After January 1963, the United States used West Germany as a roadblock against Gaullist France; and West Germany, while somewhat enjoying its new privileged position in the Alliance insofar as this allowed it to resist French pressures, nevertheless fretted about the damage this did to West European unity and feared that its wager on German-American solidarity would not be won after all.

Meanwhile, the issue of reunification, far from fading, took on a

[23] Karl Deutsch, *Arms Control and the Atlantic Alliance* (New York: John Wiley, 1967).

new importance. West Germany's "turn to the East," while approved by the United States, did not require a primary reliance on America. To be effective, it was up to West Germany to move, since the United States was not the power most capable of "delivering the goods" or of getting them delivered.

Simultaneously, strains appeared in German-American ties in three areas of policy. In the joint objective of attaching West Germany to the West, the United States had waged a gallant battle to prevent discrimination against West Germany within NATO. But just when General de Gaulle's exit from the military organization of the Alliance underlined that discrimination, the United States ended efforts to create an allied nuclear force and simultaneously put pressure on West Germany to help America out of its balance-of-payments difficulties by making heavy purchases of American arms, thus putting a price tag on protection. This introduced another strain, in the realm of security, especially as America's preoccupation with Vietnam indicated a shift in priorities; the United States unilaterally decided to withdraw some of its NATO-assigned forces from West Germany and send them to the Far East and gave the impression that further, more drastic reductions might follow unless German offset payments persisted. Lastly, in the area of the Soviet-American *détente*, the Geneva negotiations on a nonproliferation treaty, dominated by the search for a formula acceptable to the Soviet Union and excluding West Germany from the control of nuclear weapons, revived some German fears of 1961–63 of an American-Soviet agreement at West Germany's expense. Thus, by the summer of 1966, West Germany's foreign policy appeared bankrupt—there was no Atlantic partnership, no West European momentum, no reunification of Germany.

Precisely because of these perils, some West Germans advocated a kind of *politique de rechange*. Apparently convinced that dependence on the United States, far from unblocking the road to reunification, in fact, consolidated the European *status quo*, Franz-Josef Strauss, with Adenauer's support, suggested that the Federal Republic give priority to the construction of a West European entity that would be committed to an independent policy, would organize its own defense, and could change the *status quo* through its own weight and sense of purpose.[24] As a reassurance against and partial escape from the frustrations of 1965–66 the idea had merit. But it

[24] See Franz-Josef Strauss, *The Grand Design* (New York: Frederick A. Praeger, 1966).

was a minority view, and, most important, there was an inherent difficulty in Strauss' scheme. "Gaullist" enough in his rather modest ideas about the first stage of a European defense community (in the sense that he accepted continuing restrictions on West Germany's atomic potential), he was at odds with the French in the crucial matter of Eastern Europe. To de Gaulle, a Western *Europe des Etats* is really an instrument for and prelude to the "great Europe" that will stretch "from the Atlantic to the Urals"; to Strauss, the West European entity is an instrument for the realization of the dream of German unification, period.[25] He understands that German unity and a drastic transformation of the East European *status quo* are related. Yet, to him, the latter means not just a loosening of ties to the Soviet Union, but a "dismantling of these Communist regimes," [26] not an entry into a "vast confederation" but a buffer zone. De Gaulle is in this respect closer to Schröder and Brandt—they want above all to reassure Eastern Europe and the U.S.S.R.—while Strauss clings to the "walls of Jericho" approach, sees the Soviet Union as a permanent enemy and Eastern Europe as a *cordon sanitaire.* It is hard to imagine France (not to mention Britain) playing its part in Strauss' Don Quixote . . .

The new policy adopted by the coalition government of Chancellor Kurt Kiesinger takes a big step in de Gaulle's direction. There is less talk of an Atlantic community or partnership beyond alliance, less priority to the alliance with the United States, more stress on the Franco-German alliance. Dissatisfaction with American policies in the realms of security and nonproliferation is open. The policy of "building bridges" in Eastern Europe goes beyond the former policy of movement in a number of ways: the repudiation of the Munich agreement is firmer, the continued refusal to recognize the Oder-Neisse line no longer implies a claim on the "third Germany," the drive for diplomatic relations with East European states is more active, the existence (although not the legitimacy) of another German political authority in Pankow is acknowledged, the continued claim to be the sole representative of the German people is softened both by this acknowledgment and by the return to diplomatic relations with states that recognize East Germany. Thus both France and West Germany now clearly follow policies that aim at reunification through

---

[25] See especially his rather disingenuous remarks about the Oder-Neisse problem, which would, along with all border problems, lose its importance in a post-national Europe. Same, p. 45.

[26] Same, p. 18.

*détente,* instead of making of steps toward reunification a prerequisite to a *détente.* And both countries object to any *détente* that would consecrate the partition of Europe and Germany. American approval of the new West German policies is welcome, but there is some suspicion in Bonn, if not of its sincerity, at least of its consistency, and Bonn's perspective is now far more "German" than "Atlantic."

The new German foreign policy continues to differ from France's in various areas, for the differences in the national situations of the two states persist, and the more the new government emphasizes initiatives of its own, the more some of those differences are likely to emerge. Moreover, the situation of West Germany precludes as clear a break with American policies as France's situation allows.

Thus, both countries have the special aim of achieving a "rise in rank," a restoration of their status. But in the French case, this means a drive to great-power status, a rejection of demands that France make greater sacrifices of sovereignty than those made by Britain (and sometimes even a rejection of those too), a determination to be treated as one of the Big Five—i.e., to preserve a margin between the victors in World War II and the losers. In West Germany's case, however, since that state's situation, needs, and past preclude any pretension to great-power rank, the drive for status has meant an additional reason for endorsing schemes (such as the EEC or the MLF) in which equality with the middle powers of the Atlantic Alliance is assured. It still means a reluctance to accept restrictions that are not imposed on other Continental European powers, especially not on France (for instance, the nonproliferation treaty). Neither power's struggle for status can ever be completed, and a subtle tug-of-war between them goes on.

Another shared objective is security. The agreement on the maintenance of French troops in West Germany symbolizes it. But here again, past divergences are not likely to vanish; even though recent German disappointments with American policy have restored a kind of Franco-German solidarity based on estrangement from the United States, each country views this estrangement in a different light— France has wanted it, West Germany has not. West Germany's overriding concern has been the Soviet threat which continues to be felt, if less than in the early 1960s. In German eyes, this threat can be deterred only by the United States—hence West Germany's determination to keep the United States vitally involved in the security of Western Europe, even at considerable financial cost (yesterday, in terms of military equipment, and today in terms of helping the dollar) and material cost (in terms of manpower). France's concern with the threat of the Soviet Union has subsided, and even at its highest it never overshadowed the residual fear of a German military revival. Moreover, for the French, security must be achieved by emancipation from both the Soviet threat and the American predominance—hence French policies quite cynically based on the need for American protection yet using the security it provides to lighten the burden of American preponderance and prevent the United States from insisting on a form of German rearmament that France considers dangerous. West Germany's priorities make its foreign office jittery about anything that might be interpreted as a decrease in the United States' "intent to protect" (viz., in the past, the famous, innumerable "pledging sessions," and in the present, West German dismay at the prospects of an American-Soviet *entente* behind the European backs). France's priorities have made its chief of state so certain of America's "obligation to protect" that he feels he can multiply vexations and challenges without weakening French security. Until recently, every French challenge made the Germans hang on to the United States even more tightly, while the very tightness of West Germany's embrace reassured de Gaulle about his capacity to strike a new blow without risking an American recoil from Europe. American moves have helped to cool West German ardors, but the concern for American protection continues.

The two allies, as Alfred Grosser has pointed out,[27] differ not only over the "diplomacy" of protection (on how to behave so as to benefit from the United States' might) but also on the "strategy" of protection (on how to make sure that it will be used to defend Europe). Both countries think in terms more of deterrence than of defense. This is why both are reluctant to endorse Secretary McNamara's strategy of flexible response, although the French push their distrust to vociferous opposition, trying to make the strategy unworkable, and the Germans damp down their misgivings and make only gentle attempts to get the strategy revised. Yet the French—carrying out the logic of their strategic doctrine which puts all their eggs in the basket of nuclear deterrence, the logic of their opposition to the most tangible forms of the American presence, and the logic of their determination to reach great-power status without sharing it with West Germany—have tried to develop a nuclear force whose deterrent value would lie in its potential role as a trigger of America's nuclear deterrent. The West Germans, for whom the nuclear road is blocked, and who would like to exploit for deterrent purposes the element which the American doctrine itself stresses —conventional forces—have insisted on a massive U.S. presence in Europe as the best tripwire against a war. Realizing that nuclear deterrence loses its credibility when it becomes clear that execution of the threat of nuclear reprisals would bring about reciprocal annihilation, they are rightly skeptical about the triggering value of the French force. But the French argue that America's doctrine aims at safeguarding the "sanctuaries" of the superpowers as long as possible; therefore they doubt that the mere presence of American troops would suffice to guarantee the kind of escalation whose prospect would deter a determined adversary. As a result, the French are relatively indifferent to the withdrawal of American troops from West Germany and to American arguments about the ease with which they could be reintroduced in case of need; to the West Germans, the same doubt about the willingness of a superpower to risk suicide for an ally entails a serious crisis of confidence, once it becomes clear that the tripwire that would have forced the United States to meet its commitment might no longer exist.

Franco-German divergencies also persist over the common objective of Soviet-Western *détente,* which at first glance implies a very broad range of agreement between Paris and Bonn. One would think they would agree that any *détente* which recognized the European *status quo* would be a diplomatic disaster. And indeed, this shared view explains both the fleeting Bonn-Paris axis of 1961–62, when negotiations between Washington and Moscow seemed possible, and the shared hostility to disengagement schemes divorced from political settlements. But the French and German ambivalences toward a Soviet-American *détente* are not exactly the same. The French are resigned to the idea of a Washington-Moscow agreement that would close the nuclear club as it is now and rule out German access to nuclear weapons, seeing this as a possible contribution to pan-European reconciliation. Nor does de Gaulle, skeptical about collective control of nuclear weapons, worry much about a treaty ban on a West European force (other than the force of a fully federal, and hence very unlikely, Europe). The nonproliferation treaty, by sharpening the line between nuclear and non-nuclear powers, improves France's position vis-à-vis West Germany, especially as France does not intend to sign the treaty. The West Germans, on the other hand, view the possibility of a nonproliferation agreement as a discriminatory freezing of the *status quo* at their expense, and as a threat to their security if it were a prelude to a further American retreat from reliance on nuclear weapons. Also, to the French, any agreement with Russia negotiated primarily by the United States (except perhaps in the matter of nonproliferation of nuclear weapons) threatens their multipolar vision and tends to take the matter of "containing" Germany out of the European perspective they prefer. To the West Germans, that European perspective is too much like a more or less friendly encirclement, and the only kind of Washington-Moscow dialogue they think is bad is one that preserves their inferiority and division. France too wants Germany united, but not too equal.

Nevertheless, the biggest problems raised by the new West German foreign policy are not such differences with French or American policy, but its chances of success, and the consequences of eventual failure. As long as a declaratory policy of "walls of Jericho" was followed, few expected prompt success: it was a stoic waiting game. The old policy was abandoned for its unproductivity. There is a new emphasis on results. But whereas disillusionment with the old formula has not destroyed West Germany's ties to its allies, disillusionment with the new "turn to the East" could.

The new policy is ambiguous on a central point: East Germany. The earlier version of "bridge-building" to the East, under Schröder, tried to isolate the Pankow regime; and reunification through *détente* also implied the ultimate demise of the Communist government and state. The advocates of contacts with East Germany, however, point to the need to avoid further estrangement between the two halves of Germany, to the importance of promoting liberalization within the eastern half now while leaving the legal formula of eventual reunification until later. In the present West German government, there is some uncertainty about where the new policy will lead. The search for contacts has been intensified, not only for the reasons just mentioned, but also because of West Germany's desire to improve relations with Eastern Europe. For if some East European states persist in rejecting links with Bonn as long as West Germany refuses to deal with East Germany, then the goal of reunification through bridge-building will remain unachieved. A policy of contacts, however, can lead either to the reunification of two gradually reconnected German states (if Pankow is caught in a net that forces it to look more and more westward) or to permanent partition (if the East German leaders, with East European backing, cleverly exploit the West German thirst for contacts and, for instance, make each step of theirs toward liberalization depend on a West German step toward recognition). There is, therefore, a fundamental but inevitable ambiguity in the West German government's policy: on the one hand, its very goal and momentum drive it toward a kind of escalation of direct communications with Pankow, which cannot help but undermine its claim to being the sole spokesman of the German people; on the other hand, precisely because of the goal of reunification, West Germany cannot come too close to a real recognition of a regime that deems Germany's partition final. Some months ago All-German Affairs Minister Wehner hinted at the possibility of official dealings with Pankow if East Germany followed an Austrian or even a Titoist line; this clearly pointed out Bonn's dilemma—contacts might succeed in changing East Germany's policies, but the price of such success could be perpetuated partition.

Ambiguity has its uses. It permits limited contacts with East Germany and some East European states, as well as the goal of reunification. It creates strains between East European states eager to deal with Bonn despite Pankow's objections and East European states that follow a hard line; it exploits possible differences within East Germany between more and less intransigent factions, and, by its very moderation, it may encourage those forces in East Germany that are afraid neither of liberalization nor of contacts. Yet it has its drawbacks, too. West Germany's uncertainties give the U.S.S.R. and Eastern Europe additional rationalizations of the *status quo.* The chances of early success of the new policy are in any case not good, given the persistent policy of the Soviet Union; and the Soviets, in order to preserve the *status quo,* exploit with dexterity—and with no fear of apparent inconsistency—all the weaknesses in the West German position. Thus, Bonn's new policy, while it stirs up the Soviets, East Europeans, and East Germans, also creates opportunities for Moscow, Pankow, and Warsaw to create temptations and tensions within the West German body politic.

If West Germany is eager for a true European reconciliation, why does it not accept the existence of two Germanies and the Oder-Neisse line? As long as West Germany wants to revise the *status quo,* why should it be allowed to have the benefits of a *détente?* The more the West Germans appear to seek to detach some satellites from the Soviet Union, the more the Soviet Union will try to hold on to the others and deny West Germany access to a *détente;* the more the West Germans seek a *détente,* the more the Soviets insist that such a *détente* must preserve the *status quo.* Yesterday, Bonn was cursed for refusing to admit that Pankow existed. Now that Pankow's existence is acknowledged, although not recognized, Bonn is cursed for pretending to be the only valid German state and to speak for all Germans. West Germany is blamed for being the spearhead of a military organization against which Eastern Europe must be protected, and also for objecting to the thinning out of NATO's forces. And West Germany also gets blamed for its independent initiatives and positions: distance from the United States is interpreted (now that American involvement in European affairs is less intense, and the American-Soviet *rapprochement* on nuclear issues more obvious) as evidence of revanchism; West Germany's diplomatic offensive in Eastern Europe is denounced as a dangerous ruse, West German objections to the nonproliferation treaty are listed as evidence of German nuclear ambitions. Thus the West Germans are damned by the Soviet Union both when they are too close to the United States and when they are not.

If West Germany's aim is a gradual reunification through reassuring Eastern Europe and the Soviet Union about its intentions, and through a kind of gradual "subversion" of East Germany, then its new policy is probably too subtly balanced to succeed. It adheres closely to the United States as the leader of a competitive system but is restive toward the United States as a co-leader of a bipolar consortium; it is hesitant on border issues and (understandably) unwilling to give clear priority to the "human issue" over the political issue of reunification in its dealings with East Germany. Thus, it is incapable of disarming the suspicions of the Poles and Czechs and the hostility of the Soviets. Nor is it sufficiently tied to France in a West European structure to give the Poles and Czechs reason to heed French arguments about West Germany's good will.

There is a risk of failure in any "policy of movement"—the brutal failure of continued tense relations with Russia, Poland, and East Germany, the lesser (but no less frustrating) failure of better relations that merely consecrate the division of Europe at a lower level of hostility. What matters is the effects of frustration. The danger of West Germany's new line is that failure in this first attempt to develop an autonomous foreign policy might lead not to German aggressiveness, as some fear, since West Germany's national situation and freedom of maneuver are fundamentally different from imperial Germany's or the Third Reich's, but to a major crisis in West Germany's relations with its allies, with major consequences on the domestic polity. For of all the nations that, in the frustrating international system of today, do not have the means to enforce their foreign policy, West Germany is most likely to be troubled by failure, precisely because its national identity is in doubt. Indeed, the more it tries to move on the world stage, the more problematic that identity becomes. Given France's eagerness for good relations with the Soviet Union and restraints on Germany, and given an American policy that tends to change the nature of America's presence in Europe and to consecrate the *status quo* in at least some respects, West Germany, treated as and having behaved as a dependent for so many years, might be persuaded to blame the failure not on an impossible situation but on allies that failed to keep their promises. The conclusion might be, not that one ought to return to the older, sterile policy, nor that the same policy should be pursued in a better collective framework, but that it failed because West Germany had not been independent enough—because it had been too timid, too respectful of the Atlantic Alliance, and too subservient to both the United States and France (countries whose real enthusiasm for German unity is questionable, whose capacity to achieve the goal of European reunification is dubious, and whose aggressively independent approaches to Moscow should be emulated).

It would be easy for some West Germans to accuse the authors of this failed policy of having unilaterally given up something for nothing; the government could not deny the charge without playing into the hands of the Soviet Union, which accuses it of deceit already. And its nationalistic opponents could then demand a policy of "sacred egoism," neglecting the differences between West Germany's situation and France's (which has no territorial grievances), yet drawing on the examples of France, Britain, and the United States. West Germany's present foreign policy is still pursued within the framework of alliance. But the bonds with Paris have been loosened, at least emotionally, and the bonds with Washington are strained. Failure might push a future West German regime farther along the road where the present government takes its first steps. All that it practices now is some autonomy without detachment; the next step could be detachment. There is a paradox here: the new West German policy (approved by Washington and Paris) gives Bonn a greater role in trying to solve the "German problem," and thus puts Bonn in the front lines facing Pankow and Moscow; yet Paris and Washington's very blessing could make Bonn turn against them rather than against Pankow and Moscow in case of failure. Indeed, even if the West German public and elites should resign themselves without pain to continuing partition, and be satisfied, in their *Ostpolitik,* with liberalization in East Germany and better relations with some East European states, there could still be serious trouble between Bonn and its Western allies. For West Germany would undoubtedly object to restrictions and discriminatory measures that it had tolerated within the Atlantic Alliance as long as there was hope for reunification, and because they were supposed to help put an end to partition. Self-pity, a German trait, could breed chauvinism.

For almost twenty years, West Germany has been anchored in the West. Disillusionment with that anchorage has begun, yet an unanchored Germany means trouble for the Continent and for itself, since its only possibility would then be to make deals with the Soviet Union, any of which would be disastrous for the alliance. One such deal might be West Germany's agreement to recognition of East Germany as the prerequisite to elusive further steps toward reunification. This would be ideal for the Soviet Union, of course, consolidating its control in Pankow, preserving the *status quo* in Eastern Europe, keeping West Germany in the company of allies that restrained it yet making Bonn deeply resentful of those allies. Present Soviet policy seems to have precisely this aim.

There are rather more nightmarish alternatives which, for all their popularity in Britain, have been rejected by many Western statesmen and by most West German politicians—i.e., reunification by means of an agreement with the Soviet Union, in exchange for some kind of neutralization. Of course, the saving factors that have ruled this out include not only West Germany's commitment to NATO but also the Soviet Union's commitment to East Germany and its fear of any dynamic independent Germany, reunited or not. At present, the Soviet Union can have its cake and eat it too, in a way: it can preserve control in Eastern Europe and enjoy the spectacle of West Germany getting annoyed at France, the United States, and Great Britain in turn. So there is no reason for the Soviet Union to play the role of tempter, and that is why Soviet or Soviet-backed proposals for disengagement in Central Europe have aimed at consolidating German partition, not at ending it, and why they have not been pressed hard. If, however, the costs of maintaining control over Eastern Europe increased, because of restlessness there or because of added burdens in Asia, and if West German dissatisfaction with the West also increased, the situation would be different. West Germany might be tempted to follow what could be called the French precedent, and the Soviet imperative of controlling Eastern Europe would become a lesser thing than the opportunity to break up the Atlantic Alliance. We can imagine two situations in which this might occur.

The most extreme possibility is that conditions would deteriorate to such a degree in Eastern Europe that Russia would find it advantageous to permit Germany to be reunited, outside of the Atlantic Alliance. To be sure, the might of even a "neutralized" reunited Germany would make the Soviets hesitate, and the conditions they imposed might be too high for the West Germans. But the sheer disruptive power of the idea itself might make it worth trying. The moment may come when the Soviet Union feels itself at a balance point between strength and weakness—strong enough not to fear the military power of a non-nuclear, satisfied Germany, weak enough to want to relinquish the burden of physical control over East Germany (shrewdly counting on the sheer mass of a reunited Germany to keep the rest of Eastern Europe in Soviet arms). And this moment of balance may also come to West Germany: feeling secure enough against Soviet aggression (in the belief that the United States could not tolerate it any more than America can tolerate a Chinese attack on nonaligned India), and disappointed enough by the forms and effects of U.S. protection, West Germany might be willing to exchange formal ties to the West for reunification. Such a deal would consolidate rather than liquidate Soviet hegemony outside of East Germany, disrupt Western Europe, and destroy all dreams of a "European Europe" or of an Atlantic partnership. However, as sober an analyst as Robert Osgood has remarked that "an inherently powerful, though formally neutralized Germany might well be a disturbing influence in Europe" and "create a far more fluid and unstable political balance in Europe than the division of Germany permits." [28] There is good reason to believe that unless the pressures on the Soviet Union become extreme indeed, the Kremlin will always prefer the division of Germany to such instability.

The second situation the West must beware of is if fear of West Germany lessens in Eastern Europe, depriving the Warsaw Pact of some of its impetus, and West German faith in the allies' capacity to provide for eventual German unity also lessens. For then the Soviet Union might try to tempt West Germany into what would be, in effect, a disguised recognition of the East European *status quo* and a disruption of the West European one; West Germany, disappointed with its allies, might be lured out of the Alliance, in exchange for some vague offer of German confederation (indeed, the Soviets might suggest that the recognition of East Germany be a first step toward a confederal arrangement).

To sum up, then, the current foreign policy of West Germany ex-

[28] *NATO: The Entangling Alliance* (University of Chicago Press, 1962) p. 328.

poses it to possible future blandishments of the Soviet Union. A prolongation of the inherently unstable *status quo* may create conditions in which West German dissatisfaction would incite the Soviet Union to help weaken or destroy the Western Alliance and restore its position in Eastern Europe. Only the Soviet Union can "solve" the German problem, and the Western problem is how to obtain from the Soviet Union a favorable solution. But West Germany's excessive reliance on the United States yesterday and its growing self-reliance today mean, paradoxically enough, possibly excessive dependence on the Soviet Union tomorrow. We must therefore conclude that it is imperative either that the wager of West Germany—i.e., its trust in the fruitfulness of initiatives within the framework of an alliance led by the United States—be won, or that another policy be devised, more productive than the present one and less dangerous than the alternatives discussed above.

## D. *Great Britain*

For some years, a neutralized Germany has had special appeal in Great Britain, where disengagement schemes were popular in the 1950s and early 1960s. Franz-Josef Strauss even professes to have found in Britain's 1964 proposal for an Atlantic Nuclear Force (Prime Minister Wilson's answer to the MLF, intended to help kill the MLF rather than take its place) a "far-reaching political objective: . . . the de-nuclearization of Central Europe. This could have provided the introduction of a preliminary phase of the idea, favoured by Socialists of various shades and various nationalities, of the neutralization of the Central European area." [29]

Thus far, our analysis of the puzzle of NATO has had little to say about Great Britain. And this is, indeed, one of the main points of the story. Some countries have played a major role in the Atlantic crisis by their choices and obstructions, like the United States and France; others, like West Germany, by their needs; Britain has affected events by its absence. This may be a harsh judgment, especially since at two points the British tried to change course and boldly chose to try for entry into the European Common Market and since Britain has tried to affect events by making positive moves to end the Cold War. But at least the first opting for Europe was done in a way that almost ensured defeat, and the moves in the Cold War have had, in the words of one very pro-British French observer,

[29] Strauss, cited, p. 54.

"almost no" effect.[30] France's drama is the discrepancy between a broad vision and limited means. West Germany's problem is the relation of means selected to the end pursued. Great Britain's enigma lies in the deficiency of the vision.

If there is a thread of continuity in British postwar foreign policy, it is in the dual determination to accept the bipolar world and protect Britain's position as the United States' first lieutenant. If France and West Germany are revisionist powers—one seeks a grand revision of the international system as a whole, the other hopes for a revision of its position within an accepted system—Britain has behaved as a *status quo* power. This has led to a permanent misunderstanding both with France and with Germany: with France, for the reasons I have mentioned when discussing the crisis among the Six;[31] with West Germany, because of a wholly different set of priorities. To West Germany, security has come first, nondiscrimination, reunification, and West European integration close thereafter (the order has varied over time), and the search for *détente* undoubtedly last and primarily as a step toward German reunification. For the British, security is certainly a major concern, but they have not felt the hot breath of the Soviet Union across an arbitrary partition line, nor do they have the contradictory French fears of German militarism and of Russians "two Tour de France laps" away from their borders. Hence the British support for NATO rivals West Germany's, but the British also have far greater sympathy for the strategy of flexible response. Moreover, in the area of security, the goal of "status protection" has meant that Britain's nuclear autonomy differentiates it both from West Germany, entirely dependent on the United States for nuclear protection, and from France, whose quest for great-power status led it to refuse to do anything like Britain's assigning its nuclear force to NATO.

But the main difference between the British and German priorities is over the importance and nature of the *détente*. For a variety of reasons, Britain decided that in the search for a *détente* lay the best opportunities to exercise international influence. A *détente* would alleviate Britain's security needs and costs and bring about a more moderate system of international politics, in which middle powers could be more significant and autonomous than in the Manichean Cold-War universe. Moreover, the senior ally and leader of the Western camp, manning the barricades of containment, would prob-

[30] André Fontaine in *Le Monde,* May 1966.
[31] See above, pp. 401–3.

ably have to stress maximum resistance to and intransigence toward the adversary; it was in Britain's interest to be the cool and composed counselor, never losing sight of the long-range goal of moderation. In the present, a muted bipolar conflict was Britain's best option; the goal for the future was to be, so to speak, a muffled duopoly, in which Britain would remain at the side of one of the duopolists and a hyphen between the two.

This priority given to the *détente* would in any case have led to tension with West Germany, but the scope of those tensions and the development of trouble with France, as well, are due to specific British policies advocated in the quest and shaped in part by Britain's peculiar vision, in part by the goal of "rank defense." The British vision of a moderate bipolar world was inspired by British diplomacy's apparently insurmountable memories and traditions of balance-of-power periods, when moderation meant buffer zones, neutralized areas, limited wars, and when military confrontations along fortified lines meant maximum danger. Another tradition contributed to this vision and served the aim of "rank defense": distrust of Continental groupings. Thus rank defense meant a determination, at first, not to "merge with Europe," and later (when Europe became more attractive) to serve as a privileged link between the Europeans and the United States: reasons enough for difficulty with France.

Basically, British policy was to seek *détente* without any sort of autonomous European grouping filling the vacuum between the two giants. England never wanted to join either the Coal and Steel Community or EDC; no British Cabinet has wanted the Western European Union (WEU) to be anything more than a device for giving West Germany's integration into NATO a European color. Both in the proposal for an ANF and in the Geneva discussions on nonproliferation of nuclear weapons, Britain has objected to any "European clause" that might have left the way clear for a purely European nuclear deterrent. With regard to Central Europe, British plans have oscillated between recognizing the *status quo* (at least *de facto*), but rendering it less dangerous by measures of arms control and nuclear-free zones on both sides of the Iron Curtain, and reunifying and neutralizing Germany. Hence, Britain has come into conflict with France *and* West Germany, for Britain's position entailed: (1) concerning security, something different from the forward strategy desired by the West Germans and, at least for a while, approved even by Gaullist France; (2) concerning the reunification of Germany and Europe, a scheme unacceptable to West Germany because in its more moderate form it divorced military considerations from a political settlement, or, in its Gaitskellian version, because it implied that German reunification required the end of West Germany's presence in NATO; and unacceptable to France because in one way or another it consolidated the hold of the "two hegemonies" over their respective parts of Europe; (3) concerning ties between West Germany and the West, a position that treated them as less important than military measures designed to reduce the tension along the Iron Curtain, and agreements designed to divide sharply the nuclear powers from the non-nuclear states.

Since 1961, significant changes in Britain's position have brought it closer to West Germany. There has been less emphasis on disengagement, more on maintaining NATO; on Central Europe, British policy is now very close to the policy of "building bridges." The main reasons for those changes seem to be the British desire to move closer to Europe, which precludes treating the German problem as detachable, so to speak, and a growing realization of the danger of breaking ties between West Germany and the West, endangered by Franco-German estrangement in 1963–66.

By treating West Germany like a responsible power, rather than a subject on probation and an object of negotiation—as it did in the Adenauer years—Britain has made a major adjustment. But there are still areas of suspicion between the two states; Britain's financial and strategic treatment of the problem raised by the cost of maintaining an army in West Germany has done harm to British-German relations in the delicate realm of security. And Britain's concern for achieving a *détente* remains vastly different from West Germany's: for West Germany, it is a means to achieve German reunification; for Britain, it is an end which reunification would perfect but which is worth pursuing for itself. This concern for *détente* continues to combine with the British desire to maintain status in such a way as to entail a willingness to make concessions to the Soviet Union on the subject of West Germany's claims to military nuclear partnership or peaceful nuclear development, or on the subject of a European nuclear force. In West Germany, these concessions are considered discriminatory.

In contrast, the gap remains immense between France and England. At present, both give considerable importance to the *détente*, but in the British case, this is done within a bipolar framework (hence the emphasis on tying West Germany solidly to NATO); in the French case, the *détente* is among other things a means to end the Soviet and American hold on Europe. One tries to reach *détente* through the orderly process of negotiations between camps, with a view to a joint settlement; the other aims at the same end through a disintegration of the camps. Both undoubtedly agree that in the ultimate settlement Germany must be firmly related to a network of friendly states; for the British, this would be provided by NATO, and for the French, by Continental powers.

There are a number of important questions that present British policy does not answer. One question, implicit in Britain's position, is the same as in Germany's: What would be the consequences of a failure to achieve German reunification in the chosen way and framework? It is possible that, with their national aspirations frustrated, the West Germans might turn against the Western allies, especially if Britain's approach to security and the *détente* could be made partly responsible for the fiasco, and if—as British policy seems to imply—within NATO there are subtle discriminatory elements, such as those concerning nuclear matters.

Another question concerns England more directly. More than twenty years after World War II, it is becoming obvious that British foreign policy does not give Britain a role in world affairs commensurate with its continuing potential. For practical purposes, the battle of status has not really been won. Commonwealth difficulties; the United States' increasing reluctance to attach much meaning to the "special relationship"; the risks and costs of maintaining British power, particularly its military presence, "east of Suez" (where "getting the British to hang on . . . was a very difficult task" for U.S. diplomacy);[32] Britain's economic difficulties in reaching "solvent growth"[33]—all these factors, already clear to Prime Minister Macmillan in 1961 and much more obvious today, suggest that British foreign policy has led down a blind alley. In NATO, England is placed uneasily between the United States, the recognized preponderant power, and West Germany, with its uncomfortably compelling fears and needs; in the world, it is caught between reluctance to play a world role, if that means being a junior partner to the United States, and nostalgia for British greatness; in world finance, it suffers from the weakness of the pound yet clings to the sterling's role as a reserve currency; at home, it depends on American finance to support

[32] Christian Herter's testimony to the Subcommittee on National Security, 89th Cong., 2d sess., May 5, 1966, in Jackson, ed., *The Atlantic Alliance*, cited, p. 44.

[33] Bundy testimony, cited, p. 4.

the pound and is hard-pressed by American commercial competition. A policy of keeping all options open has narrowed them all and narrowed Britain's role. Britain's new approach to the Common Market shows little willingness to resolve these ambiguities. The military and diplomatic dimensions of a European entity remain fuzzy, in Britain's vision—or dubious, if one takes seriously some of the implications of the nonproliferation treaty; and Britain's offer to build up European technology is no substitute for a political vision. Britain justifies its claim to a margin of nuclear autonomy by its responsibilities east of Suez, not by the prospects of a uniting Europe, even though it is hard to see how Britain's force could be used in the Far East independently of America's, and even though Britain's role there keeps declining.

To anyone who can read, the choice is clear: either a role increasingly subordinated to the United States, or else a European role. But France's obstacle to British entry into Europe is still there. And when General de Gaulle disappears from the scene, his successor is also likely to ask for clear evidence of Britain's willingness not merely to accept the Treaty of Rome but to engage in the common policies of a "European Europe," e.g., to accomplish the "profound economic and political transformation" requested by de Gaulle. Once again, we end on a note of uncertainty.

## E. *The United States*

Nobody concerned with truth would deny that the American preponderance in NATO has been "situational" rather than deliberate. But there is such a thing as involuntary hegemony. This always produces what the French economist François Perroux calls "domination effects." Those who rebel against a power's involuntary hegemony attribute motives and plans to that power which it never had, thus enflaming passions at the very moment the critics are trying to be dispassionate and power-computing. Those who accept the hegemony also behave as if there were a will at work, interpreting suggestions and preferences in this light, refraining from moves they think might upset the power. In such a situation, awareness is the first of duties for the hegemonial state. For whether it intends to or not, its very position amounts to a policy, even when there are no clear directives and no clear sense of purpose.

Since the middle of 1963, there has been no coherent American policy in the Alliance. There have been a number of policies, some of them pursuing goals that have become axiomatic yet are sorely in need of re-examination, some of them merely reacting to new circumstances or crises without any long-term design. As a result, the United States has suffered from two kinds of difficulties. In part because of the kind of failure to consult and negotiate with its allies which I have analyzed in Chapter 9, American policies have clashed repeatedly with the policies of West European nations, and thus brought about strains and mutual irritation instead of the desired consensus. Moreover, there have been constant contradictions between American objectives; the simultaneous pursuit of divergent objectives, bad timing, and lack of coordination of American moves have added to those strains and reduced the effectiveness of the Alliance as a whole and of specific American policies.

American policy in Europe has been concerned, first, with the organization of a common defense system against the Soviet Union. The goal of security has obviously been achieved, and there is enough of a relation between the organization of the Alliance and this achievement to justify the horror of American leaders at de Gaulle's "resignation" from the "volunteer fire department" [34] of NATO. But there have been bad consequences too. For one, American strategic doctrine has provoked serious inter-allied tensions over two major issues. On the one hand, what Schelling has called the "massive conventional defense hypothesis" has bred suspicions about American strategy in case of a Soviet attack and diverted attention from more relevant problems, like the "serious and more plausible contingency in which something less than instant nuclear war would be the appropriate response," [35] or the prevention and control of crises that could but do not immediately involve the use of force. On the other hand, a doctrine of flexible response that leaves the use of nuclear weapons unclear yet keeps them under American control has, after 1961, diverted the allies' attention to the almost insoluble problem of nuclear sharing, away from the fundamental issues of political cooperation and coordination that should determine resort to such weapons. In the future, new tensions could arise over the ABM issue. For if the superpowers deploy ABM defenses over their territories, leaving Europe uncovered, America's allies would have an increased fear of being dragged into a general war by a now better protected, hence possibly less cautious senior

---

[34] Acheson, same, p. 15.

[35] Schelling testimony, Subcommttee on National Security, 89th Cong., 2d sess., May 19, 1966, in Jackson, ed., *The Atlantic Alliance,* cited, p. 98.

partner; and they "may again be concerned lest Europe became a battleground for the nuclear giants." [36]

Second, American strategic doctrine has itself been undermined by the sudden priority given to goals other than common security. The combination of balance-of-payments difficulties and Vietnam has set in motion a process of gradual withdrawal of American troops. Despite attempts at arguing that this does not in any way affect the capacity of the United States to provide for a conventional defense of the Continent, thanks to new redeployment possibilities, a thinning out of American troops could affect the security of the area in a variety of ways. The doctrine attributed a high deterrent value to the presence of conventional forces on the Continent; their removal changes the picture. As long as the American army is present, any move by the Soviet Union or its allies would put on it "the onus of making the fateful move that will oblige [the United States] to resort to a perhaps fatal response." [37] If these forces have to be reintroduced into the area, then the initiative passes into Soviet hands: it is they who can put on *us* this onus through their move. Even more emphatically, the doctrine asserted that the presence of large conventional forces would allow for a non-nuclear defense if deterrence fails, at least for a while. But, in a large-scale attack, a plan to return American troops to Europe "would be useless . . . if only because the required airfields would probably be unavailable": the dreaded nuclear response would have to come much earlier than is said to be the case in the McNamara Doctrine. And in a small incident, an American decision to send troops back "would necessarily make a large crisis out of a small one." [38] This undermining of an American doctrine unpopular on the Continent does not reassure all Europeans; for insofar as the McNamara Doctrine was unpopular because it gave the United States alone the freedom to choose, so to speak *ad hoc,* the proper strategic course of action in a crisis, a trend that enlarges this freedom cannot be expected to restore confidence. It increases the uncertainties of American protection.

Third, the military setup of what I have called the second configuration of the Atlantic Alliance (the United States' military hege-

---

[36] J. I. Coffey, "The Anti-Ballistic Missile Debate," *Foreign Affairs,* (April 1967), p. 411.

[37] See *The State of War,* cited, p. 237.

[38] *The Atlantic Alliance: Unfinished Business,* Study by the Subcommittee on National Security and International Operations, 90th Cong., 1st sess., p. 6.

mony) conflicts with the American objective of helping to build a West European entity—an objective which the very trend discussed in the previous paragraph makes more imperative. For since 1955 most West Europeans have been actively discouraged from giving the embryonic united Europe a military dimension; in conventional defense matters, the NATO commands (under predominantly American control) and the strong ties between United States and West German armament industries and military forces have left the WEU in a backwater and deprived Western Europe of a sense of collective responsibility.

To American policy-makers, West European integration has been an essential objective. West European unity, like the common defense system, was supposed to provide a framework for West Germany's integration in the West. There was no contradiction between West European and West German integration in the economic realm, but there was a potential contradiction in the realm of "high politics," in diplomacy and defense. To believe that European integration and NATO were compatible, either one had to believe in pre-established Atlantic harmony, or one had to assume that European policies would not challenge Atlantic policies; in other words, the keystone of the arch was the United States. For many years the United States acted as if it did indeed believe that there was no conflict between EEC and NATO. And some have argued that the support it gave to European integration efforts were unwise precisely because the expectations of harmony were so rash; the United States, they say, ought to have supported the Free Trade Area and other organizations less likely to conflict with basic American objectives.[39] But American preference for the Six was justified not only by a hazardous belief in harmony, but also by a generous sympathy for the kind of revolution in intra-European relations that Monnet represented; the "expansive logic of integration" was considered the safest way to bind West Germany to Europe and to turn an area of turmoil into a zone of peace and prosperity.

Rather than question the aims or wisdom of this policy, I would shift the grounds of the criticism and ask whether the effect of the policy was beneficial. It seems clear that the policy has in fact been divisive. If one opposes a federated Western Europe (or even a European entity including Britain) as a potential handicap for the United States, one would say that these divisive effects have been fortunate; but it is also true that, having prevented the emergence of

[39] See Van der Beugel, cited, pp. 358 ff.

a hostile or difficult Western Europe, the policy has *not* thereby facilitated the construction of an Atlantic Community.

How can a foreign policy intended to unite Western Europe have had divisive effects? In part, the very gentleness with which the United States exercises its predominance explains it. Since it restricted itself to functional areas in which European states had become impotent or dependent, the United States left them remarkably important areas for possible independent action. Consequently, even though the United States encouraged West European moves toward unity, the implacable logic of diversity took over in the realm of free determination left to each nation. Instead of coming together as docile clients or as rebellious protégés of the United States, they behaved as independent nations with conflicting calculations and intentions, whose discord over relations with the United States was likely to block or slow down unity sooner or later. In part, the divisive effects of United States policy are due not to the limited scope of American supremacy but to the ways it has been exerted in its chosen sphere. There has been a conflict between America's drive for West European integration, and its desire for control manifest both in the attempt to limit the scope of integration and in the attempt to keep the entity's policies close to its own. I see no reason to modify an analysis I wrote in 1964 of this phenomenon, and I quote it here verbatim:

America's relationship to Europe has been and remains dual. On the one hand it is the relation of the leader in a hegemonial alliance to the lesser states. . . . On the other hand there is a relation of adviser to client: the United States has supported the kind of supranational integration that Monnet advocates. . . .

The combination of these two relations has inhibited in three ways the emergence of a new European sense of identity. First, America's relationship of domination has undermined the policy promoted in its capacity as an adviser. For it is of the essence of any relationship of dependence, be it a hegemonial alliance or a genuine empire, not only that the leader be convinced of the broader gauge of his concerns and of his superior understanding of his dependents' true interests, but also that he succeed in so convincing many of the dependents. Through his wealth, his better expertise, his network of official and semi-official organizations (which in the American case involves the formidable establishment of foundations and centers and councils), the leader is able to develop a perfectly honest and respectable clientele of "friends" who see their nations' interest in exactly the same light and from the same perspective as he. Now, this would not be *necessarily* an obstacle to European unification. But it is *necessarily* an obstacle to the appearance of a united European entity capable of acting in any way but that of a junior partner in the American firm. And it *happens* to be an obstacle to any unification in this particular instance, for two reasons: in matters of diplomacy and strategy the United States has continued to deal with the separate nations of Europe (both a case of responsibility without fault—since the Europeans have not united in those realms—and a self-perpetuating process); moreover, next to the clientele of convinced carriers of America's message, there is a gang of rebellious European urchins who see no point at all in European unity unless it results not in a European echo of American policy but in a European policy (whether it agrees with America's or not being secondary to its being made by Europeans in Europe). Thus domination here is in itself divisive.

Secondly, America's advice and promotion of supranationality have also had divisive and delaying effects on Europe's search for a new mission. Inevitably, people resentful of dependence were bound to be suspicious of any scheme of uniting so ardently embraced by the leader: Europeans especially expect no state ever to act selflessly; and Americans tend to be seen as far more cunning and scheming than a careful examination of their policies warrants. This suspicion could not but be strengthened by the fact that the procedure supported by the United States might be legitimately thought of as damaging to European interests if applied prematurely in the sensitive areas of military and foreign policy. Not only the Gaullists happen to note that enthusiasm for such procedures is greatest among those European statesmen for whom dependence on the United States has become a dogma, among those leaders who see in supranationality a cushion to protect them from the direct influence and impact of their more powerful European partners,* and among civil servants and economists with little understanding of the complexities of strategy and diplomacy.

Finally, America's impact on Europe has been inhibiting because of the ways in which the United States reacted when it discovered—in the areas of tariffs, agriculture, and strategy—that European unification could lead to conflict, not harmony, in the Atlantic world. American reactions have been fourfold. First, there have been offers of "partnership," but so vague and so circumscribed (since they exclude the military realm) as to disconcert America's friends and to feed fuel to America's critics. Second, there has been a reassertion of policies designed to consolidate America's domination, even at the cost of undermining the drive toward unification among the Six. The two best examples here are the wooing of West Germany by the United States in economic and military areas, and promotion by the United States of the MLF. . . . The third

---

* This role of a cushion between larger and smaller European states is played within NATO by the United States itself.

United States reaction has consisted of veiled threats of return to isolationism and unilateral self-protecting or retaliatory action should the Europeans continue to mistake prosperity for power and to harm United States interests. These threats are divisive and regressive because they are used in Europe both by America's friends and by America's critics. The former mention them as reasons why Europeans should be cautious if not docile, and willing to sacrifice some of their ambitions to the overarching need for United States military protection. The latter see in such American arguments merely a form of blackmail that ought to incite all true Europeans to a concerted effort for emancipation.

The final United States reaction, which somehow embraces all the previous ones, consists of stating that as long as Europeans remain divided it is indeed impossible for the United States to share control and to limit its freedom of action. . . . What could be a goad to unity and identity actually turns into a roadblock, for often in the same breath it is suggested that even were a single voice to emerge, there would be no promise in it for the Europeans. It is asserted either that even though united, Europe would not have sufficient power to go beyond words toward a world role—an argument hardly calculated to discourage those Europeans who put reliance on the United States above unity—or that the only united Europe with which genuine "sharing" could take place would be both fully integrated *and* docile—again an argument hardly calculated to push Europeans into self-reliant unity, since full integration is not soon a likely prospect, and docility not a very exalting one. And so among the European recipients of such warnings and promises, the fight continues between those who are hungry for the carrot and those who are angry at the stick.[40]

If anything, the situation has deteriorated since 1964. For while American professions of faith in the *right* kind of Europe have persisted, on a note of growing wistfulness, they have been accompanied by more acts designed to block the emergence of a *wrong* kind of Europe; these two aspects of policy toward Europe meet to prevent the development of any realistic Europe at all, outside the economic realm. On the one hand, encouraged perhaps by Washington's continuing support for Monnet's Europe, the Hallstein Commission's effort in the spring of 1965 to smuggle more supranationality for the EEC into the agreement on an agricultural policy led to the biggest crisis in the Community's history and, ultimately, to a quaint sort of compromise—imperturbably listing on paper the divergent and irreconcilable interpretations of the EEC Treaty, one after the other, which for practical purposes amounts to a setback for the Commis-

[40] "Europe's Identity Crisis," *Daedalus,* Fall 1964, pp. 1279–82.

sion and a watering down of the treaty provisions. On the other hand, until the summer of 1966 the United States successfully used its leverage in West Germany against de Gaulle's concept of Europe. With Chancellor Erhard approving American policy in Vietnam, with German officials placing huge weapons orders in the United States in order to seal the American-German military relationship, the Franco-German treaty was emptied of most of its substance and reduced to a solemn agreement for cultural and youth exchanges that would have occurred anyway. The promise of political cooperation gave way to the performance of mutual blackmail.

Despite—or perhaps because of—the new French-West German *rapprochement,* it is difficult to see what kind of building blocks are left for America's hoped-for united Europe. The United States' preferred policies are obviously unworkable: the concept of a loyal European partner in an Atlantic arrangement is blocked by France. Americans themselves have had second thoughts about a united Europe that might conflict with the United States; they have given little official encouragement to the idea of possible European autonomy in defense matters, except in the very long (and hypothetical) run; and in mobilizing opposition to de Gaulle's Europe, they have leaned heavily on men interested less in a pro-Atlantic Europe and more in an Atlantic Community protected against any European separatism however potential—men who today behave as orphans of American leadership. The paradoxical result is that the "Monnet forces" have been caught between the iron logic of Gaullist nationalism and the aspirations of the Atlanticists. Yet the United States can hardly satisfy the latter: Atlanticists in America and Europe have demanded an Atlantic Community that would require its members to relinquish national sovereignty to a degree far in excess of what either the State Department or the Pentagon or Congress has been willing to contemplate; and in Europe, the aspiration to autonomy, if not independence, seems to survive even the present disarray.

Moreover, just as the notion of indivisible American-European security against attack has been used against proposals for a distinct West European defense, so is the notion of indispensable protection against nuclear dissemination used to prevent a European nuclear force—at least as long as there is no West European federation. (And the proposed subordination of Euratom to the International Atomic Energy Agency also downgrades the West European experiment.) At present, the reality is quite simply a multitude of bilateral relations, all going in different directions.

As the prospects for West European integration dimmed and Gaullist moves against NATO multiplied, American concern with tying West Germany to the West became a drive to tie the Federal Republic directly to the United States. This interfered not only with the movement for West European unity, but also with other American objectives, such as a *rapprochement* with the Soviet Union in matters of arms control, and the Vietnam priority. And it is for this reason that German-American relations have been strained since the summer of 1966, when West German political elites began to feel that the senior ally to which they had been so attached was backing away.

American policy to "end the German anomalies" has changed, but even as it adapted itself to the new temper in Europe—even as it gave up the old "walls of Jericho" approach and endorsed "building bridges" in Eastern Europe—it was fraught with contradiction. And indeed, on this matter the United States is in a particularly difficult position. Its position as a senior partner to West Germany in the quest for reunification is considered necessary for many reasons: to reassure Russia and East Europe that Germany will be kept in check; to keep West Germans from becoming disillusioned and tempted into a bitter resignation to the *status quo;* and to allow for better terms in the end than British, French, and Russians, say, might agree to. Yet throughout the years of the Erhard government, German-American ties made reunification impossible, for reasons we examined earlier. To encourage active bridge-building toward reunification, as President Johnson did in his speech of October 7, 1966, is reasonable as an alternative to a dead policy. But the new policy is a gamble. To prod West Germany almost without warning, as the speech did, is dangerous insofar as it encourages illusions about the chances of the gamble, and makes it possible for West Germans, should the gamble fail, to blame Washington for having boosted such illusions *and* for not having done enough to make the wager pay off.

For with the passing of the Erhard government and the new cooler climate of West German-American relations, a very different contradiction has developed—this time, between reunification and the American objective of a *détente* with the Soviet Union. This contradiction had already emerged in the Kennedy administration; then, the President tried in vain to convince Chancellor Adenauer to join in a policy of East-West *détente;* Adenauer refused, less because of concern for the fate of German unity in such a *détente* than out of a general suspicion of Soviet aims. Today, Bonn is far more eager for a *détente,* but also more actively concerned with reunification. And there are great problems for American policy in keeping the former goal from obliterating the latter. The United States has oscillated between unilateral acts to open up a dialogue with the Soviet Union (this was particularly the case in the Kennedy administration and during the Geneva disarmament discussions) and a belief that a *détente* must be sought collectively by the Atlantic Alliance so that it will lead to the reunification of the continent and of Germany. On the surface, there is no necessary conflict between these two approaches. In his speech of October 7, 1966, President Johnson presented them simultaneously, without the slightest hint of any difficulty. And yet, unilateral moves on our part could damage relations with West Germany if they consolidated the European *status quo.* They will please West Germany only if we succeed in convincing Russia that, for the sake of a *détente,* the two superpowers should take steps together to achieve German unity. But of course the Russians have no reason to agree, especially since refusal is not sufficient to kill our interest in having moderately good relations with them or our desire for a nonproliferation treaty. (Indeed, as the United States finds itself more deeply engaged in the Far East, its interest in keeping the European front quiet increases and its desire to reach agreements with Russia despite Vietnam increases also.)

The nonproliferation treaty is particularly resented in West Germany, because it seems to establish a kind of supreme nuclear council above the non-nuclear states—giving higher status to a common interest of the superpowers than to interests allegedly common to a superpower and its non-nuclear ally—and because it consolidates the Soviets' position in Europe; for through the IAEA inspection mechanism the Soviets (or their allies) could penetrate West Germany, so to speak, without any reciprocity. The American way of looking at problems discretely makes U.S. policy-makers almost unable to perceive how this treaty can have anything to do with German reunification: in a continent reassured of Germany's non-nuclear status, they say, would not "the wounds in Europe which now cut East from West and brother from brother" heal faster? [41] But the tension remains: to achieve the reunification of Germany (and Europe), the West must see Russia as both a partner *and* an adversary—a partner, since the goal presupposes a *détente* and Soviet consent; a foe, since it requires that Russia give up a persistent policy of partition. But we treat the

[41] President Johnson's speech, *The New York Times,* October 8, 1966, p. 12.

Soviet Union primarily as a partner in our search for a *détente*. It is true that it would be dangerous for the United States, as leader of the Alliance, to make all its efforts on behalf of a collective policy of building bridges for reunification, because the Soviets could make those bridges depend at least on our tacit acceptance of the *status quo,* while some allies (such as West Germany) could veto some bridges (such as the nonproliferation agreement). Yet to pursue *détente* whatever its consequences on alliance solidarity and on "the German anomalies," is also dangerous. Too fervent a search for a *détente* rewards the Soviet Union for keeping the Continent divided; it affects security insofar as American forces withdraw without any parallel Soviet moves; it provides a new reason for keeping Western Europe from becoming a military entity. (The old objection was the need for centralized NATO or American control, the new obstacle is the nonproliferation treaty which sharply separates the nuclear from the non-nuclear states.)

This brief review of United States policy reveals what can only be called its sterility. It is sterile because, while it still provides for West European security, it cannot find a solution satisfactory to all NATO members in the matter of nuclear control. Any scheme favorable to West Germany upsets the other allies and threatens the *détente,* yet any scheme that accommodates allied fears and Soviet and East European misgivings leaves West Germany in an awkward position. Nor can it bring about the West European entity that could help to transform the security system into a politically less strained and less costly one. Nor is it likely to result in German and European reunification. Nor does it contribute much to a Soviet-American *détente* on terms acceptable to all of America's allies. All it does is to perpetuate a *status quo* that France rejects and West Germany resents, expose the United States to many challenges and constraints, oblige the Americans to spend their time thinking of ways to prevent the European allies from being lured by possible Soviet offers or being shocked into imitating de Gaulle, and create the possibility of a gradual thinning out of America's presence in a West Europe incapable of providing an effective substitute, for the sole advantage of the Soviet Union. It is as if years of activism, first successful but later ineffective, had ended in familiar fashion—by a return to quietism, partly deliberate, partly the accidental product of the contradictions I have discussed. Once again, our capacity to cooperate with our allies depends on our ability to repudiate the Wilsonian syndrome and to overcome the shortcomings of our style.

## III. What Next?

In 1963, I stated that "within the limits imposed by alliance and relatively good manners," the United States and France were playing a game of "chicken." "However, precisely because enormous interests are at stake, immobility is the least likely outcome. Having checkmated each other, the players will have to choose between switching from denial to punishment or working toward compromises." [42] Since then, the good manners have deteriorated, and the players have chosen to switch to punishment. I argued then that this would be in nobody's interest, that "both the United States and France must see that in their attempt to get the Europe they want, they risk damaging the Europe they have." Events have (as usual) invalidated an "either-or" analysis. Each side has actually damaged "the Europe it had," not so much deliberately as in reaction to events (the imprudence of the Commission's proposals in the spring of 1965, in France's case; the need to react to de Gaulle's initiatives since January 1963, in America's). Each one believed that such damage was less nefarious than (and necessary to prevent) the Europe wanted by the other. One reason that they believed this was a conviction, so far vindicated, that the damage being done to the potential political unity of Europe would not too grievously affect Western Europe's economic integration. The EEC is solid enough to allow each of the antagonists to believe that its version of Europe would ultimately prevail, and that it is both possible and advantageous to preserve EEC as a springboard for a future triumph. Moreover, in the aftermath of the Cuban crisis, with the Soviet Union having difficulties of its own in Eastern Europe (and Asia), the delicate coexistence of continuing (if diluted) integration in the third stratum of the Atlantic Alliance, the Europe of the Six, and relative disintegration everywhere else did not in fact benefit the Communists. A common awareness of the continued, if residual, threat from the East has in effect limited the game of "chicken": France insists it remains in the Alliance and the United States refrains from measures of "extreme punishment." What is so annoying to American policy-makers is the cleverness of de Gaulle's game: he exploits the weaknesses of America's position in the knowledge that the United States cannot quite retaliate in kind. An isolationist reaction would go against the United

[42] "Discord in Community," in Wilcox and Haviland, cited, p. 26.

States' security interests and vindicate de Gaulle's expressed misgivings about America's lack of true concern for Europe's interests. A more effective kind of reaction—stealing de Gaulle's thunder by following the policies and strategy he advocates—is impossible for internal, institutional reasons or because it is deemed not in America's interest. Yet de Gaulle also knows that France and the United States share a range of common interests and that his own independent diplomacy (and strategic force) is made possible by and is inextricably interdependent with America's strategic protection of Europe. Hence a good deal of prudence in his own moves, *and* the expectation of *de facto* accommodation. Thus, he expects to gain both from his challenge and from his (residual) loyalty.[43]

However, the present situation is very dangerous. In the first place, it contains a peril of further fragmentation. In my earlier analysis, I pointed out that "continuing divisions among the Europeans facilitate America's task." However, this is not longer accurate: continuing division now results in a kind of separatist disease that may be contagious. Even if the Gaullist postulate of rational state behavior is correct, even if, for instance, the West German government understands that security and German reunification rule out the freedom of maneuver that France enjoys, it is far from certain that it will tolerate forever the kind of discrimination between West Germany and France which resulted from France's departure from NATO's military organization. If West German security fears decrease, or if, on the contrary, security fears should be increased by some partial American withdrawal or by Soviet-American deals which Bonn deems discriminatory, *and* if reunification fails to come about, discrimination will be even more intolerable. By treating NATO as a kind of self-service restaurant where customers can choose certain items and decline to take others, de Gaulle created a dangerous precedent. The United States has denounced it indignantly, and followed it imperturbably. Rational behavior and sound calculations, moreover, are not certain. It is possible to imagine that West Germans may one day fail to understand that what is bad for their neighbors or for the United States is good for them or vice-versa, or

---

[43] For instance, he bases his *force de frappe* on the notion that the credibility of the United States deterrent has declined. Yet he expects the United States to keep its commitment to its allies, thus arguing that America's *own* argument, according to which his withdrawal from NATO takes us back to 1913 or 1938, amounts to questioning, not his actions, but the validity of America's own guarantee!

that the American public will be swept by frustration and disappointment into taking steps as rationally debatable as, say, the return to isolation in 1919. (After all, with an exuberant economy, an invulnerable strategic force, increased means of inter-continental transportation, and greater attention for Asia, they might be lured into thinking that retreat from an unmanageable Europe is all the Europeans deserve, and not really against American interests.)

In the second place, the *status quo* is unhealthy in itself: all bilateral Western ties have been strained in recent years, the continuing existence of two hostile German states in the heart of Europe and the continuing subjection of nations in Eastern Europe cannot but create dangers. To believe that this situation can be pushed aside by a collective will-not-to-notice (what one writer calls "the reverse [of] Gambetta's famous statement *parlons-en toujours, n'y pensons jamais*") [44] or that it can be regularized without basic changes or resulting turbulence, as contacts multiply and fresh air circulates, is to believe in an illusion. For contacts and fresh air are by themselves portents of change and antidotes to resignation. The only question is whether the changes will be well managed or disruptive: the achievement of a moderate international system does not pass through the *status quo*. In an unorganized Europe, the coexistence of two German states, one of which remains controlled by Moscow while American presence in the other declines, would be full of dangers; the persistence of the "two hegemonies" so as to avoid those dangers provides no long-term solution and multiplies short-term strains. The situation described in this chapter with respect to Western Europe and the United States, the present relations between the Soviet Union and its clients, and the present relations between the two Europes are devoid of permanence. They can last, but not forever. Their passing may be gradual, but it cannot be avoided. If a solution to the European and German problems is impossible in the present international system, this means that a solution requires a different system.

Moreover, to borrow Marxist vocabulary, all the contradictions of the alliance are exacerbated in the present situation. On one side, the United States would like gradually to consolidate a *détente* with the Soviet Union and to help Germany along the road to reunification. The two concerns conflict. Moreover, to combat the Gaullist challenge, it must stress the continuation of the Soviet peril and maintain

[44] Josef Korbel, "Changes in Eastern Europe and Opportunities for American Policy," *World Politics,* July 1966, p. 756.

its effort to keep a check on West Germany, thus feeding Soviet arguments about "the NATO bloc" and the West German peril and legitimizing Soviet preponderance in Eastern Europe. America's military role on the Continent, with a military strategy and certain military policies that do not delight all Europeans (withdrawal of American forces from Europe, forced purchases of United States war matériel, an ABM network for America, and nonproliferation measures for others) also exacerbates intra-Alliance difficulties.

On the other side, de Gaulle, who would like an ultimate withdrawal of the two "hegemonies" and a European settlement, has, by pulling France out of NATO's military structure, made an American "disengagement" more rather than less difficult: since France's real estate is now unavailable, whatever territory remains for NATO is even more precious; and by appearing to remove himself from the collective containment of Germany, he raises that very fear of West Germany that keeps Eastern Europe safely in the Soviets' arms. In order to prevent the nightmare of a Soviet-German *rapprochement,* he moves himself closer to the Soviet Union, but both the continuing ties between West Germany and the United States, and West Germany's recent attempt at raising its voice on the European scene give the Soviet Union pretexts not to follow de Gaulle on the road to European reunification. In order to prevent the dreaded collusion between Washington and Moscow, he strikes at NATO, thus diverting the United States from developing a coherent policy toward the Soviet bloc; he flies to Moscow even though his own negotiating power with Russia has been crippled by the refusal of other West Europeans to associate themselves with him and, probably quite deliberately, thereby makes the neutralization of Germany under the supervision of the two superpowers more difficult, since a defense of Western Europe without Germany and France is inconceivable. But he makes no better solution any easier. His insistent support of the Oder-Neisse line, however justified, increases rather than reduces Bonn's timidity on this score; his consistent support of Bonn's refusal to recognize Pankow confirms Poland's distrust of any German reunification. His call for an end to America's hegemony stirs security fears in Bonn, and his call for an end to Soviet hegemony creates security anxieties in Warsaw. It is as if de Gaulle deliberately wanted to exacerbate deadlocks and contradictions to prove that there is no other road than the one he obstinately wants all to travel; that short of their doing what he wants, his partners-and-adversaries can only prolong the division of Europe, sow suspicion, and reap rebellion;

that the United States and the Soviet Union are locked in a vicious circle in which each one uses the existence and policies of the other as a pretext for prolonging a sterile hegemony. Given the insufficiency of France's means and the absence of available supplements to them, de Gaulle's moves have a certain devilish necessity of their own. Yet one would hope for something less sardonically indifferent to risks, less serenely self-confident about the ability to avoid creating damaging secondary effects and to control unintended consequences. At present, the United States guarantees West Germany against the Soviet Union and Europe against Germany; France tries to pose as a rival in both respects; yet the only results are a preservation of mutual fears and the continuing division of the continent.

CHAPTER TWELVE

# U.S. Policy and the Atlantic Alliance: Closed Doors and Open Roads

We now come to the most delicate part of our task: defining the limits and possibilities of American policy in the Atlantic area. It was necessary to lay out the pieces of the puzzle first, because only a fairly full description of the present confusion can indicate the scope of the difficulties which face United States policy-makers, and because American foreign policy must either move within the limits set by the policies of the various nations or move those limits in directions acceptable to these states.

The problem for the United States is not only to develop middle-range goals, but to have a vision that will inspire those goals and affect the choice of the means used on their behalf. The vision of 1947–48 is no longer valid, in part because it does not correspond to the world of 1967, in part because it has done all that could be expected of it, in part because it was never realistic to expect that the establishment of a situation of strength in the West—a defensive undertaking—would dramatically improve our bargaining position toward the Soviets, while leaving the relations among the Western allies unchanged.

The situation of the United States has deteriorated with respect to its purposes in the Atlantic Alliance. The "Atlantic dimension" has been outflanked by the intensified conflict in Asia and the problem of Eastern Europe. The limits of the Alliance's range of common purposes have thus become serious liabilities. Organizations that focused on defense *against* the Soviet Union and on coordination of economic policies *within* the Atlantic area could not fail to be affected by the eruption of a serious defense problem against forces on the other side of the world and by the emergence of prospects of settlement with the adversary, prospects that could not appear as long as security from this adversary was the main concern. As a result, the ratio of unilateral to multilateral action has shifted to the disadvantage of the United States. When the common danger in the East loomed large, and European nations were faced by the pressing need to reconstruct their own countries and decolonize overseas, the United States could count on support from its allies in the realm of greatest urgency and could dissociate itself from them in other realms. Today, the shoe is on the other foot: the European allies are reluctant to support the United States in the realm of intense conflict, the Far East; while in Europe the gradual emergence of the problem of "peaceful engagement" in Eastern Europe over the problem of defense brings with it a confusion of expectations and approaches.

The United States is also in a poor position to reassert its authority as a leader. It finds it difficult to exploit its overwhelming superiority in power so as to extend or reassert its control where it is challenged, and prevent centrifugal developments. For, especially when the sense of threat has subsided, it is unable to blackmail its restive partners by threatening to withdraw the mantle of protection, since such a move would be disastrous if it encouraged Soviet probes in Western Europe or incited the allies to compensate for the loss by independent means. It is this lack of bargaining advantage that de Gaulle has exploited in such an irritatingly cool fashion. The other great use of power that a leader of a coalition can employ—the power to reward good behavior—has also been crippled. For the decline of the sense of threat (by contrast with 1951) makes the Europeans unwilling to increase their own military efforts or accept American controls in exchange for American commitments; also, the economic rebirth of Europe makes Europeans much less susceptible to American advice than in the early days of the Marshall Plan; finally, the rewards which some Europeans want the United States cannot provide, such as France's demand for a dismantling of American control, and the West Germans' for reunification.

Consequently, in the Atlantic Alliance, the ratio of power supply to use of power and the ratio of supply to achievement are unbalanced; achievements are stringently constrained, and they depend to a considerable extent on intangible components of power (a leader's prestige and vision, the skill of his diplomacy) and derive from its subtler uses (cunning rather than coercion, bargaining rather than bludgeoning).

The United States must therefore deal with new circumstances: it must shift from engineering to gardening, from the comforts of calculable control to the risks of Russian roulette. It must accept the right of its allies not to consider themselves involved in areas in which the United States acts unilaterally toward purposes that are not common. It must limit unilateral action within NATO—the constant temptation—to those shrinking areas over which it has *full* control, i.e., control not only over the instruments of policy (for instance, nuclear weapons), but also over the consequences of the decision about them. When actions affect other nations whose policies in turn affect us, we must coordinate our moves toward carefully defined joint purposes. The possibility of presenting oneself as the self-evident universal spokesman for the common good hardly exists, for the common good is no longer self-evident insofar as ends are concerned, and even then there are legitimate differences over means. Nor is it possible for the leader of an alliance made up of nations that have retained or regained effective means of autonomous action, to assume that it is a single territory for which a rational policy can be defined from the viewpoint of the whole.

The questions facing NATO today are: (1) whether its members can agree on a policy in the "new" area of potential hot war, i.e., with China; (2) how to define the terms of practical settlement of the original Cold War; and (3) how to cope with the pressures that the success of containment of Soviet communism and the decentralization of the Communist threat have created in the West. A number of plans have been proposed to solve these problems, which I shall review in the first part of the chapter. In analyzing policy perspectives, I must make clear that I have made a blend of "ought" and "can." In the present situation, several proposed alternatives seem to me unrealistic because the chances of realizing them are almost nil, or because the advantages expected from them are so small. My critique of these schemes, and my choice of another, are based on a combination of value preferences and assessment of probabilities; inevitably, the latter are influenced by the former, but they have, I think, sufficient basis in fact to serve as a check against the purely *a priori* preferences I may have in my more unguarded moments.

# I. Detours and Dead Ends

## A. *Atlantic Partnership*

The highest authority, the President of the United States, has put forward the idea of an Atlantic partnership. And many high officials continue to hold to the "sweeping goal" of "necessary partnership" between the United States and a united Western Europe. It is essentially an updating of the old vision, which tries to solve the third of the problems I have listed by projecting into the future the main efforts undertaken in the days of 1947–48, but it devotes little explicit attention to the first and second problems. As such, it is simply inadequate to the present situation.

In the first place, the vision of partnership contemplates a special kind of European partner—an integrated Western Europe, not a "Europe of national states." From the viewpoint of the allied goals analyzed in the preceding chapter, "a prosperous, politically stable, and unified West Europe" [1] appears best to many American policymakers. But there is reason to suspect that the kind of integration they believe can alone meet the conditions for "equal partnership" is unlikely to emerge. If it should, the partner's policies might not satisfy American expectations. In other words, the integrated Western Europe that is required is neither likely nor necessarily congruent with the partnership notion. The dilemma could be described in another way: if the United States actively pushes toward the desired outcome, it will probably fail; if it is more reserved and leaves the job to the West Europeans, the results probably will not please Americans. In both cases, there is no getting around the French obstacle. As long as de Gaulle is there, the French will not favor supranational integration. His successor may be readier for it than he, but with a vision not so different from his, and hence quite different from that of the Atlantic partner the United States conceives of. Let us analyze these points in more detail.

American support for European integration has been helpful in the realm of economic affairs. But, as we have seen, it has inhibited development in the decisive area of political integration. West Europeans who believe unreservedly in the American notion of Atlantic partnership take heart in American encouragement, but those who suspect the United States of wanting Europe unified so as better to control it—a standard Gaullist argument, based on the conviction that political integration would breed confusion and paralysis—and even many who want Europe united in a self-respecting West European entity capable of influencing and sharing power with the United States, are hostile to American pressure. Thus, despite the argument that some American advocates of the MLF produced, according to

[1] Robert Schaetzel, "The Necessary Partnership," *Foreign Affairs,* April 1966, p. 431.

which the MLF was to be the embryo of a future European force, a man as well disposed toward European integration and the notion of equal partnership as Gaston Defferre unequivocally rejected the MLF. The lesson is clear. American efforts in this field, far from unifying Europe, only fragment the Alliance and Western Europe. Nor can the United States' support for European political integration be easily reconciled with its support of Britain's entry into Europe. Britain was encouraged in the hope that its membership in Europe would make European policies more compatible with ours, thus facilitating partnership; but Britain's known unwillingness to accept supranational federalism would have undermined the basic rationale of American policy—that partnership is possible only with a partner speaking with one voice.

Let us assume that the United States, realizing these difficulties, leaves the development of European integration to European leaders (as has been the case in the three years from 1965 through 1967). Let us also assume that Britain will be not only admitted but also willing to let the rather unwieldy European Communities move toward federalism, thanks to the need and pressure for increasing parliamentary control and the impossibility of effectively doing business intergovernmentally (an assumption that postulates a complete reversal of postwar British foreign policy). Would the outcome be likely to reward American expectations? Americans expect a partner who may well be difficult, since "a degree of European nationalism is . . . inevitable," [2] but they also expect that it will cooperate with the United States, whose own responsiveness to the European stimulus would lead to results that "enhance the general interest." This federated European entity, well disposed toward partnership with the United States, is an extraordinarily optimistic model, and it ignores the history of the past twenty years. Even when Europeans felt threatened by the Soviet Union, they were unable to unite effectively in defense and foreign-policy realms. Facing their common situation with different pasts, perspectives, and interests, they preferred the mixture of discordance and action in the Atlantic framework to tight European integration; independent moves and common action in an organization led by the United States were recourses against the perils of excessive European togetherness. Idealists of European integration keep saying that many problems—like the residues of Franco-German hostility, or European defense—would have been solved had Western Europe united; but I would say rather that those

[2] Same, p. 438.

problems were precisely the obstacles to unification. If the past is any indication, the path to the future, should we leave it to be blazed by European leaders, will be rocky.

Let us assume, however, that the path will indeed be traveled. Two models of a federal Europe have been offered, other than the optimistic one described above. There is, first of all, de Gaulle's gloomy model of pseudo-federation, where the conflicts of national interests would render supranational institutions a mere façade behind which the various governments continued to pull in different directions. "Collective" institutions would inject one more superfluous yet irritating focus of discord and stake for control. The outcome would be a kind of collective irresponsibility—something like France's Fourth Republic writ large, with parliamentarians split along national as well as party lines, civil servants trying to make policy in the vacuum created by the conflicts among politicians, and political leaders trying to reconcile their responsibilities to their countries with their European functions. The picture may appear overly sinister: after all, this is not what has happened in the existing European Communities. Yet, we must remember that there are vast differences between policy-making in the realm covered by the present Communities and policy-making in defense and diplomacy; even in the former, supranationality has been reduced as the scope of concerned interests rose and the connections with "high politics" became clearer. Even if strategy and foreign policy were as amenable to complex and skillful compromise schemes devised by supranational experts as, say, agriculture or trade is, the time spent working out those schemes and getting them endorsed by national officials would still be enormous. The laborious preparations of a common agricultural policy, of the Kennedy Round and of a joint position on international money matters have shown that the European voice can be "highly uncertain and frequently inaudible" [3]—or at least slow in making itself heard.

One may wonder whether such a "partner" would be very helpful to the United States. It has sometimes been suggested that it would be helpful precisely because it would have so much trouble getting organized that it could hardly find time to bother the United States: "caught up in . . . the sheer magnitude and novelty of the task of

[3] Christian Herter, in Henry M. Jackson, ed., *The Atlantic Alliance: Jackson Subcommittee Hearings and Findings* (New York: Frederick A. Praeger, 1967), p. 107.

unifying Europe . . . [European governments] will be less inclined, at least in the short run . . . to give an equal priority to
urgent international problems." [4] This is a very curious argument;
it confirms Gaullist suspicions that the United States views the
travail of European integration as a diversion and an emasculation,
it contradicts the key argument that only a united Europe could
be mobilized for common "outward-looking" efforts and share
American burdens, and it assumes that it is in the United States'
interest to have a partner preoccupied by the emotions of "introspec-
tive egocentricity." Many Frenchmen, Englishmen, and Germans are
now preoccupied with the whole range of issues that could be termed
the foreign relations of Europe; in my opinion, a verification of this
gloomy model would only demoralize the Alliance further and, far
from providing the United States with a responsible associate, would
encourage instability and irresponsibility.

A more reassuring model is Jean Monnet's real federation. According to this scheme, the new institutional method, far from leading
to complications and dilution of responsibility, will permanently
alter relations among nations and men, making them accept and
apply the same rules, and thus change their behavior. "This is the
process of civilization itself." [5] It is an inspiring vision. Unfortunately, it is nonpolitical (and in this is characteristic of the men
around Monnet). Nothing is said about *what* the rules would be or
*how* the behavior would change: it is all process and not policy, all
style and not substance, all method and not message. Yet, no more
here than in the mass media is the medium the message. Consequently, two major questions remain unanswered—the questions,
precisely, of purpose and control, of "identity" and management.
Action and power: this is what politics is about. There is good reason to believe that any European entity that is to be a going concern, not merely a façade, will be forged, not so much in association
with, as in differentiation from the United States—exactly as occurred in the economic realm with the EEC. For it is always in reaction to one's closest tutor, not to an increasingly less relevant foe,
that one develops one's character. As for control, it may be worth
while to reflect on the dominance in the Communities of French civil

[4] Schaetzel, cited, p. 428.
[5] Jean Monnet, quoted in "Problems and Trends in Atlantic Partnership," a
staff study for the Senate Committee on Foreign Relations, 87th Cong., 2d
sess. (Washington: GPO, 1962).

servants and French conceptions, whenever the French have been able to make French interests coincide with the definition of a common European interest.

Perhaps, when and if Great Britain becomes a member, British civil servants will be able to wrest leadership from the French and shape a less "separatist" notion of the common interest. In my opinion, however, they will first have to overcome the handicap of delayed entry, and they will probably be able to overcome the French contingent and conceptions only if they too define common West European policies in terms of what is, fundamentally, a preferential conception. As part of a Europe in process of unification, Britain might move much closer to France in a joint effort to contain West German dynamism and the dynamism of American industry. Its latent tendencies favoring neutralization of central Europe could hardly be expected to flourish: increasing Europe's role in the world would become Britain's legitimate concern, and this might well endanger, not enhance, America's West German position or America's duopolistic tendencies.

Thus, Monnet's model of a future Europe challenges the American conception of partnership even more than do the Gaullist predictions of doom. Moreover, as others have pointed out,[6] a partnership composed of two forces of comparable strength risks breaking down, if the two partners are equally obdurate, or even merely if the lure of separate purposes proves overwhelming. To sum up: among West Europeans, where vital interests are at stake, institutional arrangements may be of little help in defining joint policies; in this case, the present disarray will not be removed; but if institutions have the impact celebrated by Monnet, the joint policies are likely to disturb rather than delight American officials.

Here we reach the second, and major, weakness of the American dream of partnership. The reason a truly federal European partner would be capable of destroying, not fulfilling it, lies in the American notion of partnership itself. As one of its advocates has shrewdly remarked, "partnership," while "a sweeping concept," is "a confining word." In fact, its formula is too restrictive in matters of control as well as purpose. Its advocates speak of two powers working "in close cooperation and on equal terms," [7] yet the terms are not really equal, and the cooperation is limiting.

[6] Ernst Van der Beugel, *From Marshall Aid to Atlantic Partnership* (New York: Elsevier, 1966), p. 406.

[7] Schaetzel, cited, p. 428.

On the subject of control, we may need a bit more than the "three minutes of serious study" that, in the contemptuous words of the French Foreign Minister,[8] would reveal the emptiness of "ready-made formulas." Certainly, in the realm of trade, the Trade Expansion Act did introduce a policy of "equal partnership," and the potential European partner did succeed in defining a European position for the Kennedy Round of tariff negotiations, despite the differences between members in sympathy with and members opposed to American notions of disparities, free trade, etc. But the lesson of that experience (and of a recent, similar one in the international monetary field) is two-edged: since the competition from the Common Market evoked an American response in an area in which the logic of interdependence operates, Europeans might well conclude that the way to wrest advantages from the United States in the future is, again, to advance a common policy challenging the United States —but this time leading not to reciprocation but to conflict, since the subject matter would be high politics. For in this realm, the United States' will to equality is open to question, as can be demonstrated by analyzing American attitudes on two important issues: (1) *When* are we willing to establish partnership? (2) *What* is it that we want to share with our partner?

On the first question, it has been said that true sharing should be postponed until Europe has become a power comparable to that of the United States in resources *and* political organization. "The United States, carrying a large share of the burdens and the costs, cannot realistically share responsibility for policy decisions with reluctant junior associates."[9] This argument, of dubious value, has the effect (whether intended or not) of postponing partnership *sine die;* the days when Europe's power will be "commensurate with our own" in every important respect, particularly in nuclear might, are far off. Indeed, the argument is more a rationale against sharing than an encouragement to Europe to unify. Advocates of Atlantic partnership suggest that the time has not come to ask the key question: Who decides when the time has come for equal association? And, in more candid moments, they say that it is up to the nation endowed by events with "vast world responsibility" to be the judge. Here, they are speaking from a fundamentally "bipolar" position. As long as there are many lesser allies, it is impossible to share, given the disparities in power. As long as the putative European partner is in

[8] Couve de Murville, Speech to the National Assembly, April 14, 1966.
[9] Schaetzel, cited, p. 426.

the (expected) throes of unification, it will be too self-centered to be interested in or capable of sharing. One asks for European unity so as to be able, at last, to share the agony of power. But the arrogance of power shapes the conception of the task.

I may be accused of "deliberate distortion" [10] in making these points, which happens when people who study implications and outcomes are criticized by people who look only at intentions. Let us, then, be fair and assume that the intention is to prod the Europeans into unification by offering them the prospect of sharing power with the United States. This in itself is questionable partly because the reasoning is faulty and partly because it is undiplomatic. As observers have pointed out, even if the argument were true, it could not fail to antagonize "lesser" powers which learn from it in no uncertain terms that they really do not much matter: Canada, Mexico, Japan, among others. This is not the way to prod anyone, singly or collectively, into "partnership." The consequences of its tactlessness would be less regrettable, if the reasoning behind it were true—if states with vast resources were always willing and able to be responsible powers and if states with limited resources could never play more than "supporting roles." The fact is that a great power can choose to be absent from the scene (as the United States was in the interwar period, with abysmal effects for the international system) or reckless, i.e., not exactly the wise older partner with whom a maturing clerk would be eager to be associated. And while to be a smaller state means, now as always, a limited role, smaller states nevertheless enjoy substantial advantages, due to the decentralization of usable supplies of power and new opportunities for them to obstruct the moves of larger states; and the limits on the larger states are real enough to incite modesty.

In addition, being neither tactful nor accurate, this kind of argument actually incites the European nations to pursue their own interests separately: rather than becoming dependent both on each other and on the United States' subsequent sovereign decision to share power with them, why not use whatever independence the system affords to build up one's own power and show the Americans that one can do without them? As Alfred Grosser has often remarked,[11] there is an inconsistency in American arguments: if there is a one-to-one re-

---

[10] Timothy Stanley, *NATO in Transition*, cited, p. 266.

[11] See, for instance, "Aspects des débats entre Occidentaux," Bulletin SEDEIS, No. 910, February 10, 1965, supplement on "Le grand débat nucleaire." p. 34.

lation between material power and leadership, one encourages French and British resistance to schemes for a European supranationality in which France's and Britain's influence would be watered down; since the United States will not share power with smaller partners, why should France or England dilute their own power? If, on the other hand, the case for European integration rests on the argument that power can be magnified and world responsibility best exercised by overcoming national rivalries and the parochialism of the nation-state, why not go all the way to an *Atlantic* federation, in which the weight of the United States would also be diluted? The American argument, however one looks at it, does imply a special, privileged position for the United States.

Such a position corresponds to present realities, but its perpetuation is not a good formula for the Alliance. One shares by sharing, not by promising a share; the United States would more successfully encourage Europeans by showing that it was willing to share now, even though the process of European unification is not yet finished, than by saying, in fine pragmatic fashion, that the decision on what is to be shared must be left for the day when there is a partner with whom to share something. To this argument, one can fairly say that as long as there is no "European partner," the United States' sharing of power would risk increasing the national power of the individual European states, accentuating diversity rather than unity. But, as I will suggest later, this is not *necessarily* so. And even if the only alternatives were no sharing until unity and sharing with still un-united nations, choice of the former is self-defeating, psychologically and politically, in a world where there is some equalization of power and also impatience with the hegemonial *status quo*. For if it should lead to European nationalism, that nationalism would tend to be rebellious, not docile; no nation likes to receive as a reward for good behavior something that it considers its due: the pleasure is in the taking, not in the receiving (no mean factor in de Gaulle's choice of tactics). And if it did not, it would still be an incentive to act separately; in the eyes of at least some European leaders, the true alternatives are not between dependence and joint sharing, but between dependence (single or collective) and a modicum of independence (if not collective, then single). In the past, the United States' reluctance to share power in the realms of defense and diplomacy with its "supporting" allies resulted in separate efforts by some West European states to develop forces or policies of their own. Disparities of power bred further disparities, not shared uniformity. As a result, today, the development of a European entity is blocked by two obstacles rather than one—by American reluctance and by the national calculations and actions it provoked.

True encouragement toward integration would require the drawing up of a specific program and calendar of sharing: this has never been done. What is being done now, in the so-called McNamara Committee of NATO that deals with nuclear strategy, does not go very far: in nuclear affairs, the allies are more interested in deciding on joint guidelines about the use of nuclear weapons than in gaining "a greater sense of intimacy with American . . . planning and . . . strategy"; also, as Schelling has suggested, we may have very little to tell them. Once more, our national style and our own institutional methods limit our effectiveness. Nor would European integration be helped in the least by a nonproliferation treaty that allowed only the nuclear force of a truly federal Europe.

The preceding discussion does not exhaust the problem, for the chronological difficulties are not the only ones. It is far from clear that we are willing to share with *any* European associate endowed with power "commensurate with our own" and speaking with one voice. Are we willing to share with any kind of European partner, or only with one who would be "committed to the same values and objectives as all Americans"? If the European partner-to-be gives priority to separate European interests, the United States could still refuse to share power with it by arguing about the partner's "reluctance." The criterion in fact appears to be "willingness to accept world responsibility." And since each power may have its own view about what constitutes world responsibility, we are led to believe either that disagreement will lead to deadlock (hence no sharing) or that sharing will depend on a common definition acceptable to the United States.

American supporters of European supranational integration often appear to have assumed that a united Europe would not clash with American policy on any important points. Yet, the writers (here and in Europe) most convinced of the need for firm American leadership and most suspicious of an unguided West Europe's capacity for rectitude are also the most dubious about preordained harmony between the two partners. They make it clear that not all possible Europes would be worthy of the honor of partnership. One author excommunicates, for instance, any Europe that would jeopardize the United States' interest in European security [12] (and, given the rest

[12] Stanley, *NATO in Transition*, cited, p. 75.

of his argument, one wonders whether this means a Europe that disagrees with the strategy of controlled counterforce), seek to become a third force, or turn inward—quite a number of possibilities. Another one (Dutch) would like the United States to make it clear that only an Atlantic-minded, economically liberal, federal Europe, limited in strategy and diplomacy, would be qualified.[13] (One wonders whether there would be any point in christening subordination "partnership".) American officials have been less explicitly restrictive, but they always express the assumption that a "true" united (and federalized) Europe will recognize that its basic interests converge with those of the United States: the right partner is the one who has "a will . . . to share, and this includes a willingness to provide resources to make that sharing effective," [14] "a united Europe able and prepared to collaborate with us." [15] This begs the question of who decides on the degree of ability and the meaning of collaboration, although it suggests, since what is at stake is the sharing of something that was entirely ours, that *we* will. And we call for a Europe with "a world view," yet we have never refrained from calling de Gaulle's vision "inward-looking," even though he is the one European statesman with a world view, albeit a debatable one. Shall we, then, decide what the world is?

That this is not an unfair assessment is shown by an examination of the second issue about control—*what* is to be shared. Here we find an interesting discrepancy: we have been more explicit about sharing burdens than about sharing privileges. We have made it clear that we want to be helped in our balance-of-payments troubles, that we expect a unified Europe to contribute more than before to the common defense in terms of expenditures, military service, and manpower. We have made it clear that we expect Europe to have a greater sense of responsibility, to participate more in aiding the undeveloped countries of the Southern Hemisphere, and to take a liberal position in the Kennedy Round. In other words, evincing attitudes that we derive from our own values and politics, we start by assuming a consensus on what the burdens are, we proceed to redistribute them in a more equitable manner, and we argue that there can be "no representation without taxation." Yet there is little concern

[13] Van der Beugel, *cited,* p. 402.
[14] George Ball, "U.S. Policy Toward NATO," in Karl Cerny and C. W. Briefs, eds., *NATO in Quest of Cohesion* (New York: Frederick A. Praeger, 1965), p. 18.
[15] Schaetzel, cited, p. 433.

for the other side of the coin: among states, consensus must be hammered out, and there can be no "taxation" without a previous agreement on the purposes for which one is to be taxed and represented.

On the other hand, we are vague about the sharing of decisions. The stuffy phrase "world responsibility" lumps together decisions and burdens. Are we actually willing to share decision-making in areas where we have so far decided alone—strategic doctrines, the stationing and use of nuclear weapons and anti-missiles, the allocation of foreign aid, arms control, our moves in Asia? All one finds in official statements is the bland assertion of a "willingness to share." The French say that you can't catch flies with vinegar. One doesn't encourage Europe to move toward integration with a carrot that consists of a request to bear burdens but conceals everything concrete about power. This would be an incentive only if our European allies feared that we would take revenge by reducing our burdens and leaving them with the consequences if they failed us. The trouble is that in most cases we cling to our burdens, out of pride and out of our fear of the consequences of relinquishing them. If we want a responsible partner, we can't set a model of irresponsibility. Yet the contrast between our words and our acts is great: we did not even consult, we merely informed our allies of our moves in the Middle East crisis of 1958, of our resolve over Quemoy and Matsu, of our choice in the Cuban missile crisis, of our decision to start deploying an ABM system. Of course, we feel that we have to act alone because years of dependence have badly prepared our partners to meet our challenge: again, however, our arguments would make sense only if we established in common, not only a calendar, but structures in which they could operate as our partners before they are fully merged, and in which they could do more than bear our burdens. Moreover, should Europe eventually unite, we would be exposed to heavy pressure for a genuine division of control—the very thing we are reluctant to concede.

Our shallowness about "sharing" is shown by the story of the MLF. The MLF was proposed as a "pragmatic first step" toward partnership and as a response to European pressure, like the Trade Expansion Act. However, the discussions were not even held within the multilateral framework of NATO, whose organs were merely briefed. Moreover, the variations among American government officials as to whether or not the fleet would be the embryo of a defense force for a united Europe; the general pragmatic excuse "that since the MLF [did] not yet exist the issue of nuclear control need not be faced until later"; [16] the unlikeliness of either Congress or the Defense Department consenting to share control of nuclear weapons with allies whose strategic doctrine might differ from ours—all this made the notion of a "first step" highly dubious. As for the idea that the MLF was a response to European developments, it was something of a fabrication: Europeans want "nuclear partnership, not patronage" [17] and are more interested in the decisions concerning the huge American nuclear arsenal than in a collective force representing a tiny fraction of it, and notable primarily for the abundance of safety catches: the United States could have blocked the use of the MLF, while the Europeans could neither block the use of SAC when the United States wanted to use it, nor of course force the use of SAC when the United States did not want to use it. Nor is it surprising that despite all the provisions for American controls in the MLF, it disturbed the more control-conscious Americans in Congress and in the Pentagon, for if the MLF had been created, it carried in it the risk that the allies, realizing that they shared only our expenses, would put irresistible pressure on us to give them the control of weapons already in their custody. We asserted our willingness "to envisage a 'European clause' in any plan that may eventually emerge," but the way we defined "the intent of the clause" indicated a frown rather than a smile or a gleam in the eye. "If at some juncture in the future a united Europe should come into being, able to make the most fundamental decisions of peace and war, then whatever we agreed to now should be subject to review and renegotiation in the light of these fundamental changes." [18] This was hardly a commitment. Indeed, the next move we took was to negotiate, not a "sharing" arrangement with our partners, but a nonproliferation draft with our adversary which eliminated not only any "sharing" but also any European nuclear force other than a federal one.

Of course, there is an easy answer: it is too early to talk seriously about remote possibilities. However, our refusal to talk makes the possibilities even more remote. Whether intentionally or not, there is an unfortunate similarity here with the French position. Neither the

---

[16] Henry Kissinger, *The Troubled Partnership* (New York: McGraw-Hill, for the Council on Foreign Relations, 1966), p. 144. On the briefing of NATO organs, see W. T. R. Fox and Annette Baker Fox, *NATO and The Range of American Choice* (New York: Columbia University Press, 1967), pp. 170–79.

[17] Franz-Josef Strauss, *The Grand Design* (New York: Frederick A. Praeger, 1966), p. 64.

[18] Schaetzel, cited, p. 432.

United States nor France really favors the idea of a Europe that would present nuclear claims, and both argue that the absence of a "European defense policy" makes the discussion of a nuclear strategy for a united Europe academic. And in both cases the argument drawn from the nonexistence of a united Europe militates against its creation.

The sharing of command is difficult for the commander, unless he shares it with partners totally in agreement with him—in which case the operation is more like a division of labor than like a pooling of sovereignty. The sharing of burdens is unpopular with the partners, unless they are convinced that they are the main beneficiaries.

The depressing conclusion—that a vision of the future which has blind spots in the most important places is politically irrelevant—is confirmed if we examine the last great flaw in the American idea of Atlantic partnership: the question of its purpose. Here again, the fundamentally bipolar nature of the partnership idea gives us the key. That idea is unsatisfactory for reorganizing the Alliance not only because of what it does (or does not do) about control, but also because it has little to say about the purposes of the arrangements and little to propose about the other great problems: "decentralization" of the Communist threat and the gradual settlement of the original Cold War in Europe.

On the intra-Atlantic purposes of the Alliance, the notion of partnership begs the question, exactly as it did in the matter of control. As a result, for instance, the allies argue *ad nauseam* over the control of nuclear weapons, yet avoid the one fundamental subject that is jointly manageable: the purpose to which such weapons, or the threat to resort to them, could be used. It is difficult to see how a decision to use nuclear weapons can be "collectivized" or "shared," but it is difficult not to see that the core of the trouble lies in the lack of agreement on crisis management and strategy. Without such an agreement, any procedure for joint decisions and weighted voting would become paralyzing. With such an agreement, the actual control of the final decisions would be easier to manage. Yet our opposition to "combined planning with other major nations as a matter of principle" [19] prevents this agreement.

As for solving the problems of the new Cold War in Asia and helping to settle the old one in Europe, Atlantic partnership implies a certain kind of confinement. It suggests the "Atlantic dimension" as the foundation for both pillars of the Alliance. But, while the At-

[19] *The New York Times*, August 28, 1966, p. 20.

lantic dimension was a common denominator of allied interests in the original Cold War, it is not *ipso facto* a common denominator now in the rest of the world (nor has it ever been); and relevant as it undoubtedly is to relations with the Soviet Union and Eastern Europe, it offers no guidelines (except a useful but vague precept of solidarity) for the allies' policies there.

Extra-European policies have never been an arena for "partnership" or even pre-partnership. When the Atlantic area was the heart of the confrontation between East and West and storms broke out in Asia, the Middle East, the Congo, or Latin America, the United States acted either as a power with world responsibilities or as a power with a special position in the Third World. Necessities of world affairs and of domestic politics ruled out any kind of subordination of American policy to purely Atlantic concerns.

In the Atlantic area, there was a broad consensus on the nature of the Soviet threat and on the basic instruments that would be used against it. But there is no such consensus at a world-wide level, and even where there exists something like agreement—on the dangers of Chinese expansionism, for instance—there are overwhelming differences on methods and instruments. Therefore the first question is whether allied harmonization of global policies is so essential as to justify a major American effort to extend the future partnership to what is now, more than ever, in the realm of discrete national policies. The United States would certainly like a universal partnership in which the partner approves America's course of action and plays a considerable part in carrying out the responsibilities now burdening the United States. But if the partner should refuse to call them his own, or should consider American policies mistaken, is it likely that the United States would let itself be immobilized by the Atlantic straitjacket?

The problem of purpose thus brings us back to the central point of control: Who defines the common interest? In the absence of a pre-established consensus, who gives substance to the Atlantic mission? If it is the United States, its chances of being followed are nil. Yet the chances of the United States submitting its policies abroad (especially those that could lead to the use of nuclear weapons) to an inter-allied body are also nil. In the present state of affairs, a consensus on purposes in Asia, Africa, or Latin America appears out of the question, because either it can be reached only on terms unacceptable to the United States, or, in fact, no one wants to alienate his freedom.

As for the third NATO problem, of how to resolve the aftermath of the East-West confrontation in Europe, Atlantic partnership again provides no compass. As theorists of Atlantic partnership have made clear, it is a conception based, if not—as Brzezinski suggests —implicitly "on the notion of continued European partition," [20] at least on the notion that such a partition will last long enough (and the costs of ending it are sufficiently high) to justify giving priority to Atlantic solidarity. The vision, to use our earlier terms, is both bipolar and Atlantic. This does not mean that relations with the Soviet Union and Eastern Europe are neglected, only that changes in those relations are seen as a by-product of intra-Atlantic and intra-Communist developments rather than as a major goal of Alliance policies, or else they are considered of special and primary concern to the United States as leader of the Alliance. In other words, the "Atlantic dimension" can be used either to justify a demand that the West Europeans concentrate on their own integration, or to defend our right, as guardian of Atlantic interests, to deal directly with the Soviet Union on behalf of the common cause. Once more, one may argue that this is merely a consequence of the lamentable absence of a European partner. But it is hard to overlook the likelihood, should Europe unite, of its objecting to a continuation of that dialogue.

If Atlantic partnership does indeed mean that intra-Atlantic links come first and that the policies of NATO members toward the East must be as one, we are bound to conclude again that the chances of seeing this come about in reality are nil. Has France at any time really given top priority to Atlantic ties? Certainly, European affairs, colonial action, and independent French policies have received top priority or shared top billing with Atlantic affairs. When, as in 1961–62, de Gaulle along with Adenauer championed the cause of intransigence toward the East, he did so primarily as a tactic to prevent the United States from settling Europe's fate "behind the backs of the Europeans." Great Britain's consistent and loyal Atlanticism has never prevented the British government from advocating an approach to the Soviet Union that France and West Germany disliked and the United States government distrusted. West Germany's past Atlanticism cannot be doubted, yet the contradictions between the demands of Atlantic orthodoxy and German interests have recently become more acute. As for the United States, it has never let concern for Atlantic solidarity stop it from direct dealings with the Soviet Union, whenever what it considered as the higher interests of mankind (i.e., its view of the Atlantic nations' own higher interests) were concerned. Notions have functions as well as purposes. Thus far, the notion of Atlantic partnership has functioned to brake whatever activities the United States considers separatist. As I argued some years ago, "the United States uses the Atlantic notion as a way of harnessing the Europeans, whose activities . . . threaten to disrupt the charmed circle of Atlantic orthodoxy. The United States does not refrain from warning the Europeans about the aid and comfort such conduct brings to the common enemy" [21] yet has never hesitated to get out of the circle itself. Since allied purposes differ, the United States objects to "sharing" whenever it would restrain the United States from doing things it wants to do (for instance, in Asia) or force the United States to do things it does not want to do (for instance, in order to deter, or fight, a war in Europe).

Now one could argue that the future need not be the same as the past, that the Atlantic dimension should become central where it failed to in the past. But a slogan is not a policy. The real problem is to define common policies and, in case no agreement on them is forthcoming, to ask whether an agreement to disagree, a resignation to diversity, is necessarily worse than a hypocritical consensus on a platitude or a forced agreement to a "common policy" that is nothing more than the preferred course of the most powerful ally. For if the latter alternative were chosen and failed, there would be no "fallback" positions, only a collective Western fiasco. Also, the kind of diversity that lets the allies try different approaches to third parties and set different examples is more in the Alliance's interest than any forced or cramped unity—especially when the problems to be faced are not soluble by general mobilization. It was good that the United States dissociated itself from colonialist enterprises despite the screaming of those in Western Europe who interpreted this as a violation of Atlantic solidarity. It may not be bad for European countries to compete with the United States in Latin America and thus to give future Latin American leaders a possible alternative to Castro or dependence on the United States. It may not be bad for Arab nationalists to find some sympathy (and moderating advice) in Paris or London, instead of being caught between the devious friendship of Moscow and what they deem the antipathy of Washington. And the Western disarray may not necessarily be bad in the Far East. Solidarity is imperative only when the road followed in concert is good. In Europe,

---

[21] "Discord in Community," in Francis O. Wilcox and H. Field Haviland, eds., *The Atlantic Community* (New York: Frederick A. Praeger, 1964), p. 22.

too rigid an application of the Atlantic dogma might restrict Ameri-· can policy in deleterious ways. The United States might find its free- dom of movement vis-à-vis the Soviet Union curtailed, it might find itself obliged to maintain forces in Europe longer or withdraw forces from Europe sooner than necessary, and it would risk having to take sides in all the squabbles that might develop within the West Euro- pean entity or between this entity and the rest of Europe.

Because of its vagueness at crucial points and because of the un- tenable consequences to which it would lead (more easily than to the glowing ones its proponents expect), Atlantic partnership strikes me as thoroughly improbable.

## B. *The Wilsonian Syndrome in Action*

If Atlantic partnership is a vision without adequate substance, the search for appropriate policies must continue. In the present litera- ture, we find two proposals which offer, in many important respects, antithetical suggestions and which can be grouped together because they express in important and subtle ways the Wilsonian syndrome. They correspond to the "all or nothing" tendency still manifest in United States foreign policy, to the habit of oscillating between the polar opposites of excessive involvement and excessive disinvolve- ment. Excessive involvement shows traces of the sense of omnipo- tence; disinvolvement shows impatience with a world too complex for easy control. But there is impatience also in the former case—a belief that only American activism can overcome the frustrations of such a world; and there is, even in the latter case, a residue of faith in omnipotence—a quaint conviction that one can shape the world one wishes through one's very disengagement from it. Both are forms of immodesty. And both are unpolitical to a degree, in the sense that, much as they try to clarify goals and means, to set a hier- archy of purposes and to suggest steps toward them, they leave cru- cial political areas in the dark. The idea of Atlantic partnership does not provide for the very reorganization of intra-Atlantic relations it aimed at, partly because of its inadequate recognition of the impor- tance of extra-Atlantic problems. The two schemes I shall consider now, while concentrating more realistically on these problems, and shifting from an Atlantic to a European perspective, fail to deal adequately with intra-Atlantic affairs.

I will deal first with the suggestions for a certain kind of *disin-*

*volvement.* The various suggestions in fact do not constitute a wholly coherent ensemble. Popular in Britain eight or ten years ago, they have been taken up in the United States by Ronald Steel [22] and by Richard Barnet and Marcus Raskin,[23] years after the famous Reith lectures of George Kennan. They also seem to inspire, in a way that is not always clear or coherent, those officials of the Kennedy and Johnson administrations who have given priority to *détente* and arms-control agreements with the Soviet Union, and many of the politicians who favor large troop withdrawals from Western Europe.

These schemes are all based on the perfectly sound notion that "the old assumptions which once seemed eternal . . . have now become . . . threadbare." [24] The center of international relations is no longer in the European Cold War, and the old Cold-War antagonism between the United States and Soviet Union is *passé.* What is essential is a resolution of that antagonism which will release American energies from what these writers (or officials) tend to call the European trap. The mood is one of disillusionment with the exercise of power. The world is too complex for mastery by any one state, the greatest threats to peace come from the lack of national self-restraint, the only result of the American and Soviet exercises of power has been the rise of power challenges in their camps. Since "the little world of the Atlantic Community [puts] an unworkable and intolerable chain upon American interests," [25] since "the pledge the U.S. has given to make American society a hostage for the safety of Europe" [26] has engaged the United States in a costly arms race with disastrous effects on American society, it is high time to switch to what should matter now—a transformation of American society that will make it more relevant to the problems of the revolutionary societies, an improvement of world order unobsessed by anti-communism and aimed at freeing mankind from economic want, a dismantling of the formidable arsenal of violence. One recognizes some of Kennan's familiar tones, and also themes as old as that kind of Liberalism which thinks of power as evil, sees it as a "yoke," and defines national greatness exclusively in terms of domestic behavior.

Even at this most general level, there is something inadequate. In

[22] *The End of Alliance* (New York: Viking Press, 1964).
[23] *After Twenty Years* (New York: Random House, 1965).
[24] Steel, cited, p. 19.
[25] Same, p. 139.
[26] Barnet and Raskin, cited, p. 76.

Steel's case, there is no vision of international affairs beyond a Soviet Union-United States settlement that, rather than amounting to a duopoly, would amount to their joint resignation to the decline of their influence, a recognition of their common interest in a truce which would allow them to mend their fences in true humility. In the Barnet-Raskin case, there is a vision, but it assumes a kind of mutation of world politics: there will be a modicum of disarmament and arms control with international policing, a world community concerned primarily with economic development and mobilized by transnational private groups and international organizations. That these are desirable ingredients of a moderate system of world order cannot be denied. But what are the political dynamics of the system, the political relationships among the states? In both cases, we find occasion for misgivings in the illusion about how much choice a nation has, in fact, to withdraw from the game of power. The writers sound as if the United States, having made the wrong choice, can easily disentangle itself from the results of its previous moves, and can all by itself switch from one type of "game"—that of weapons, alliances, and calculations of power—to another, primarily humanitarian one. Also, there is a tone of resentment concerning America's European allies, as if they were responsible for the "trap." Impatience with nations to which one is committed, whose behavior entangles one in situations where the costs or risks outweigh the benefits, is a familiar feeling; it overwhelmed the French conservatives in the days of appeasement, for instance, and often made them more anti-Czech than anti-Nazi.

When we move from the general vision to the more concrete objectives and policies, these misgivings are confirmed. The tendency to wish away the entrapments of power is revealed in the way the authors derive, from the correct premise of a need for change in American-Soviet relations, the objective and policy of an American-Soviet "deal"; they neglect the continuing elements of competition between the two states and the fact that challenges to each superpower, as well as their fear of accelerating their alliances' disintegration, prohibit any such arrangement. It is as if awareness of and consternation about the pressures which NATO puts on the United States leads them to advocate a daring deal that will repudiate those pressures and a divorce from NATO that will be by way of retribution on the nations responsible for such pressures. The tendency to resent the United States' allies is particularly strong in the case of West Germany, seen as the biggest obstacle to Soviet-American *en-*

*tente.* These writers therefore propose a scheme whereby foreign troops would withdraw from East and West Germany, both of which would accept definite limitations on its armaments. The two Germanies would then gradually work out their reunification. The two superpowers would disengage from Europe. The United States would "give up weapons aimed at the Soviet Union in return for Soviet weapons aimed at Europe"; [27] France could keep a minimal nuclear force. Disarmament and arms-control provisions would be submitted to international verification and inspection, and there would be an "arrangement for European security, guaranteed jointly by the United States and the Soviet Union and the nations of Europe themselves." [28]

Multiple objections arise. (They can also be brought against the nonproliferation treaty, which raises most of these issues in paler colors and fragmentary fashion). First, assuming that both America and Russia find this scheme to their advantage, there is a question of feasibility. It is hard to imagine West Germany accepting the restrictions suggested here in exchange for a mere promise of reunification and a vague collective-security arrangement. It is hard to imagine France consenting to a scheme that would very likely exacerbate its residual fear of the Soviet Union and its latent fear of an unchecked Germany. And given the total improbability of West Germany and France subscribing willingly to this arrangement, the superpowers would have to impose it themselves (a strange way of practicing disengagement). The likelihood of this occurring would depend on whether they really found the scheme entirely beneficial, whether they were ready to accept risks or losses on behalf of a joint decision on the overriding importance of their *détente,* or whether each had decided that probable gains at the expense of the other exceeded the probable losses for itself. This likelihood is very small indeed.

We must, in the second place, turn to the question of the desirability of this plan. Just as there is today a difference between a trend toward a reduction of tensions that springs from basic factors in the international system (the muting of bipolarity) and a drive toward a *détente* that would amplify the trend and enclose it in symbolic or artificial agreements that risk becoming ends in themselves, there is considerable difference between a gradual process in which, due to internal alliance pressures and pressures from outside the European arena (i.e., Asia), the superpowers would resort to parallel

[27] Same, p. 150.
[28] Same, p. 167.

and gradual disengagement (troop withdrawals), and a deliberate decision to accelerate a process that neither, thus far, appears to long for. The authors argue, however, that such a decision would be in the superpowers' interests. For the United States, there is an interest in turning away from "neurotic confrontations" and in downgrading "the importance of weaponry in political relationships" [29] (a dubious argument, since "weaponry" is a major American asset). For the Soviet Union, there is an interest in curbing German rearmament in exchange for a withdrawal from East Germany (again a dubious argument, since, on the one hand, there are presently other checks on German rearmament so that the Soviets are under no compulsion to pay a price to obtain this, and, on the other, a neutralization of Germany really acceptable to the Soviet Union would have to promise a reduction of Germany's conventional forces as well).

Actually, the scheme is risky for both superpowers. Far from cancelling each other out, the risks tends to reinforce each other, making the scheme unlikely to be desirable simultaneously to the United States and the Soviet Union.

For the Soviet Union, there is the risk of disintegration of both its ideological and its power position in Eastern Europe if Soviet troops withdrew (especially if a severely restricted Germany would cease to push East Europe toward the Soviet magnet). This risk would be worth running only if the Soviets desperately needed an *entente* with the West, which is certainly not the case now, or if the gains from the scheme were large and assured. (But then, why should America give its consent?)

For the United States, the scheme is even more ambiguous. It is impossible to believe that the opportunities for political maneuvering would not be exploited by the Soviet Union, or that *any* grand scheme could turn a *détente* into a true *entente*. Given this condition, the scheme may well serve Soviet interests far more than it endangers them. It is far from certain that a Soviet troop withdrawal from Eastern Europe would necessarily bring about the collapse of the national Communist regimes, which have their own instruments of coercion. The end of the Soviet *imperium* would not be assured. The least dangerous result would be that the withdrawal fostered instability in Central Europe and thus pushed West Germany to the forefront of diplomatic initiatives. The most dangerous would be that all of the West's interests were harmed. And, for three reasons, the former could lead to the latter.

[29] Same, p. 134.

First, as long as hostility between the Soviet Union and the United States persists, concern for Western security must persist also, and the notion of a collective agreement is merely an escape from the unpleasant terrain of strategy to the happy wonderland of legal constructs. Unless the superpowers disarm much more than the writers suggest, and unless a reunited Germany becomes a very powerful military nation (hardly an acceptable proposition for the Russians), the Soviet Union would still threaten a Western Europe left with a very low level of defense. (And American willingness to risk nuclear destruction for its defense would be less than it is today, when the United States has forces in Europe.) The security problem can be discounted only if one envisions general disarmament and world policing, which is not a likely prospect, or an organized and coherent European defense system, which is precisely what Barnet and Raskin brush aside.

Second, the scheme involves a certain breaking of ties between West Germany and its Atlantic allies. The United States would "go home," the West European enterprise would remain in its state of arrested development, prevented by Germany's special status and by the military strictures of the scheme from becoming a genuine entity in the realm of high politics.

Third, while perhaps a dubious case could be made for this if the scheme seriously enabled us to end "the German anomalies," on the contrary there is no guarantee that the Soviet Union would actually permit the two Germanies to be reunited. Indeed, the authors suggest Western recognition of East Germany as a first step! And even if this did, as the authors hope, lead to a final reunification, it is hard to imagine it happening peacefully except on terms extremely favorable to the Soviet Union—and it is possible to imagine it happening in a convulsion (such as the collapse of East Germany) that would expose Europe's disorganization, dependence on outside influences, and openness to Soviet penetration. The picture of the European system that the writers draw bears an alarming resemblance to the one the Soviet Union keeps dangling before German eyes, which I have earlier called a nightmare.

Thus, as long as each of the superpowers finds the strains in its own alliance manageable and the gains from such a scheme uncertain (or the risks entailed by it real), the scheme clashes with the logic of uncertainty in international relations, with the reluctance of states to abandon the certainty of what they have for the uncertainty of what they might get. It is difficult to envisage circumstances in which the strains in the Warsaw Pact were so serious that it would be to the advantage of the Atlantic allies to agree with the Soviet Union on such a scheme. But it is easy to imagine circumstances in which the strains in NATO were acute enough to make the scheme beneficial to Russia, although why the United States would want to negotiate an arrangement that might estrange West Germany *ad majorem gloriam sovieticam* or that would be considered a calamity if West Germany negotiated it behind Washington's back, is not clear. But the verdict is clear: from Washington's viewpoint, the design paradoxically implies an alienation of both West Germany and France in exchange for a highly dubious set of promises from the Soviet Union.

If we turn now to the three policies we have said are crucial to NATO in the future, we find the design faulty on all counts. In the matter of defining a common policy for new areas of international politics, it has nothing to offer except a plea for modesty (which is sound), domestic progress, economic development, and arms control. In the matter of settling the original Cold War, the scheme is too apolitical: the political questions of Central Europe and of Europe's future are either evaded or treated exclusively in military terms. Neither Steel nor Barnet and Raskin offer a genuine formula for German and European unification. Steel proposes to leave reunification to West European-Soviet relations; the latter vaguely speak of satisfying Germany "if the possibility of reunificaton is opened up." [30] Steel, at least, believes that what makes American disengagement both necessary and harmless is the growth of a power nucleus in West Europe around the Paris-Bonn axis. We know what happened there between 1963 and 1966. The Barnet-Raskin thesis opposes a "strong independent Europe," for the authors fear "economic and military rivalry between America and Europe." [31] The outcome is a fragmented Europe, whose eastern half might or might not be under remote Soviet control and whose internal peace would be guaranteed by the superpowers. This is indeed a power vacuum, and one that is hardly designed to attract the United States (not to mention Western Europe!). The Soviet Union would, through the self-perpetuating need to keep Germany restrained, or the manipulation of the dialogue between the two Germanies, or the enforcement of arms-control agreements, have constant opportunities to fish in troubled waters; the United States would have none of the assets of alliance but all the harrowing burdens of a guaranteeing power. It is

[30] Same, p. 113.
[31] Same, p. 167.

a recipe for trouble, for it combines *de facto* recognition of the division of Europe (pleasing only to the Soviets) with a teasing hope for future improvements (tantalizing to the Germans). Far from producing a genuine "disengagement of the great powers from the German issue," it would help preserve Russia's hold, weaken America's, and, given the Continent's lack of cohesion, require the continuation of both. The scheme nevertheless appeals to some American officials because of its ambiguity: it misleadingly promises disengagement, and it also aims at preventing the emergence in Europe of a power bloc that could rival the superpowers. But by the same token, West Europeans are far less attracted by a conception that would in fact keep them submitted to outside controls and exposed to Soviet intrusions, militarily dependent yet without influence on us.

It is not surprising that there is nothing here to inspire the proper reorganization of NATO, since the scheme proposes to abolish it. The question of the Alliance's purposes is obviated, and the question of control is answered in the paradoxical way I have just described.

This kind of proposal exhibits many of the features of American political style and predilections I analyzed in Part II. Here is the tendency to have faith in technical (i.e., military) solutions for basically political problems; distress with "mixed" situations (hence the desire to disband NATO, once the allies are no longer entirely responsive, and to turn the Soviet Union into a partner as soon as it ceases being an all-out foe); hostility to balance-of-power systems (hence the paradox that the plan favors a retreat from world leadership yet advocates a power vacuum under bipolar guarantee rather than the organization of an additional center of power); distrust of Europe; and an alternately static and frantic sense of time, neglecting evolutionary trends in Europe, envisaging a kind of perfected return to the days of the wartime Grand Alliance, and seeing nothing but disaster in any other course.

I want next to examine the seductive, brilliantly argued, and superficially persuasive policy proposed by Zbigniew Brzezinski "for a broader conception of America's role in Europe." [32] Moving from a disinvolvement that turns out to be elusive, we are confronted here with an *overinvolvement* that turns out to be less promising than it seems.

Brzezinski does not deal with the problem of relations between the United States and its European allies over extra-European affairs. He concentrates on the problem that was neglected in the

[32] This is the subtitle of his book (cited).

original vision of Atlantic partnership—what might be called the post-Acheson and Dulles problem: how to resolve the original Cold War. He understands that one of the main reasons for the troubles afflicting the pseudo-partnership that is NATO is the difference in perspective between European and American members. The Europeans are more concerned with the division of the Continent; the Americans have oscillated between a hard line which perpetuates the division, however much it aims at ending it by getting the foe out, and direct contacts with the adversary, which threaten to consecrate it. Brzezinski's great contribution is to make it clear that there is no future for America's "relevance to Europe" unless the United States adjusts to the new consensus of the Europeans. "The Atlantic idea alone is not an adequate response." [33] Instead, the author proposes a plan for America's "peaceful engagement in Europe's future." The goal should be, as President Kennedy wanted it, not confrontation but cooperation, aimed at restoring and multiplying contacts between the two halves of Europe, at producing "a gradual but qualitative change in the relationship between both Russia and East Europe and the West." [34] Only this can bring about German reunification (and we must make it do so). Brzezinski recommends a variety of policies to this end, including the isolation of East Germany, the acceptance of border and military restrictions by a reunited Germany, and the offer of a new Marshall Plan for the development of Europe.

Let us consider Brzezinski's proposals from the angle of the two questions that I said were paramount: the question of purposes and the question of command. His scheme is so well presented and tactically so skillful that only a precise discussion of these two questions can bring its weaknesses to the surface. The purpose of Brzezinski's proposals is clear: a gradual reunification of Europe, by the catching of East European fish into the net woven by NATO (sufficiently international to "provide a framework for restoring the East European nations to independence without . . . stimulating narrow nationalism"), [35] and by an increasing "re-Europeanization" of the Soviet Union, leading it to consent to the emancipation of the former satellites. He asserts that there are trends that might produce a Soviet willingness to give up control; his proposals would both take advantage of these trends and make the loss acceptable to the Russians.

However, there is considerable ambiguity or obscurity on some

[33] Same, p. 174.
[34] Same, p. 137.
[35] Same, p. 133.

essential points in Brzezinski's presentation. He proposes a maintenance of Western military strength, a slow sterilization of East Germany leading to its death, an end of the Soviet grip on Eastern Europe. It looks a little like "a blueprint for Soviet surrender," [36] which may explain its attractiveness to men like Dean Acheson, who have become aware of the limitations of "situations of strength" when they do not bring about a settlement, but find it hard to conceive of settlements in other than overwhelmingly favorable terms for us.

If this were the whole picture, it would of course be most desirable, but still one must ask about its feasibility. Even if having ideological control over Eastern Europe were less important to a less dogmatic and more nationalist Russia, the need to preserve its *power* position vis-à-vis the United States *and* China (i.e., something more than security on Russia's western front) would continue. And why the Soviet Union would permit the East Europeans to become seduced by Marshall Plans any more than it did in 1947 if the West preserves the present Atlantic relationships; why the satellites themselves would take West German reassurances at face value, turn away from East Germany and prefer a unified Germany to a divided one is not clear. At any rate, the picture is that of the (peaceful) victory of one alliance over and at the expense of the other.

But there is more in the picture. The author emphasizes that Russia must be drawn into the design, not only East Europe. Otherwise the "tiger of nationalism" would disrupt not only the "Soviet-dominated world" but all of Europe. One cannot fail to be struck by the absence of any discussion of the nature of the relations to be encouraged between Eastern Europe and the Soviet Union. Brzezinski hints that he favors a continuation of NATO and the Warsaw Pact; he hints at the need for Americans and Russians to be present at all European conferences of heads of government, so as "to maintain a political balance" [37] and avoid breaking East European–Soviet and West European–American relations. He suggests that Soviet security needs in East Europe would be served by states that "came to resemble Finland." [38] This throws a different light on the scheme. Brzezinski appears to believe that this in fact would give the Soviet Union a stronger position in Eastern Europe. The Soviet Union would

---

[36] Edgar J. Furniss, Jr., review of Brzezinski's book in *Journal of Conflict Resolution*, December 1965, p. 536.

[37] Brzezinski, cited, p. 167.

[38] Same, p. 48.

remain preponderant in East Europe at the cost of accepting a return to more moderate and cooperative politics and consenting to the ultimate liquidation of East Germany. This would make the scheme attractive for the United States, and from the Soviet Union's point of view it becomes less sinister. Does it become thereby more feasible? The problem of feasibility cannot be answered without an analysis of the issue of control. Brzezinski's plan, while "European," is still essentially bipolar, as in the case of Atlantic partnership, as in the case of American-Soviet disinvolvement. The difference from Atlantic partnership lies in this fact: Brzezinski understands that bipolarity will not continue unless the United States, instead of ignoring European aspirations, appears to embrace them. And where disinvolvement amounted to a kind of restricted duopoly functioning in effect to the Soviet Union's advantage, Brzezinski's peaceful involvement amounts to a pervasive duopoly clearly to the advantage of the United States. With great vigor, Brzezinski shows why West European initiatives to tear down the Iron Curtain are likely to be unsuccessful—de Gaulle is too isolated and weak, West Germany too hesitant and confused. But he derives a far from self-evident conclusion from this: he proposes a joint Western strategy under American initiative and leadership designed to prevent the disintegration of NATO due to Gaullist blows or the dangers of "a purely bilateral German-American relationship." Brzezinski's answers to problems of control seem to be: Who commands? The United States. Who benefits? The United States, preserving and expanding its leadership; West Europe, fulfilling its dreams of reunification; East Europe, returning to its ties with the West. At this point, doubts about the scheme's practicability abound.

In the first place, it is still not clear why Russia should play its hand in the way Brzezinski so elaborately describes. The trends he describes exist, but the terms he proposes to the Soviet Union are unlikely to be accepted. To be sure, there are strong pressures against the *status quo* in East Europe, but are they so strong that because of them the Soviet Union would pay to preserve its position in East Europe with the sacrifice of East Germany, the opening up of the area to Western influences and investments, eventually even the replacement of "Communist power elites" by non-Communist ones, while NATO, on the other side of the dismantled Iron Curtain, finds new vitality under American leadership? This is a dangerous underestimation of the hold the Soviet Union still has and will have on East Europe *as long as* it is faced with a would-be monolithic At-

lantic Alliance. The Soviet Union's refusal to do its part in dismantling the *status quo* breeds tensions in the East, but the prolongation
of the *status quo* engenders troubles in the West also, between the
United States and its allies. While both superpowers have an interest
in overcoming these headaches, the Soviet Union is unlikely to be so
generous as to help the United States by acceding to a scheme that
would remove many of America's problems while multiplying Russia's. The Soviet position, like part of Brzezinski's, is that a *détente*
must come from an *entente* between the blocs, not from their disintegration; but the Russians have in mind a consolidation of the
*status quo,* i.e., a further weakening of NATO; he has in mind a
weakening of the Soviet position.

In the second place, the moves that Brzezinski suggests the West
make are also unlikely to reach their objectives. East European nations, tempted by the opportunities for contacts with Western states,
would hardly be in a position to let themselves be caught collectively
in the Western net. Moreover, the fundamental unlikeliness of the
scheme makes a West European consensus behind it improbable.
West Germany, aware of the difficulty of making the Russian raven
drop the East German cheese, despite the tactics suggested by the
policy-planning fox, finds it hard to resist the temptation of multiplying "little steps" that knock the "isolation of East Germany" out of
the scheme. Also, despite Brzezinski's plea, West Germany may be
reluctant to reassure the Soviet Union as to its pacific intentions
quite as much as he would like. For if the Soviets should hold out
against a scheme that, as we just saw, is pretty risky for them, West
Germany may not be able to take its concessions back the day a
deal less favorable to the West would come into discussion—i.e., the
Soviets might refuse the bait, and the Germans be caught. France,
with or without de Gaulle, is unlikely to play a minor part in a firm
whose director makes it clear that he intends to keep his job. Events
in 1966 have shown a trend: the more France's dissidence rocks
NATO, and the more the division of Germany produces West German impatience with a leader (the United States) unable or not
eager to deliver the goods, the more the whole scheme will be in
jeopardy, for the West Europeans will be tempted to continue in the
same general direction but, so to speak, under new management. Finally, even the likelihood of the United States playing the part of director is open to question. The United States cannot make the "vast
design" of European reunification its only or even necessarily its first
policy purpose. Between this goal, the security of Western Europe,

and the drive for agreements with the Soviet Union, a very delicate balance must be maintained. The United States has not succeeded in this in recent years. It is hard to imagine that its future diplomacy will display all the required skills. Also, there are domestic obstacles. The ability to carry out a concerted foreign policy with discrimination, finesse, and patience is not the greatest American gift, and Congress' reluctance to engage dynamically in "bridge-building" with countries that are still Communist and whose emancipation remains unsure is well known. Here is the ultimate source of embarrassment: if the United States government trumpets loudly its expectations of East European "defection" and Soviet losses in order to mobilize domestic support, the diplomatic possibilities shrink as the domestic ones expand; if instead it plays a supporting rather than a leading role in Brzezinski's drama, this may improve the chances for success but it will also change the outcome.

Another reason why Brzezinski's scheme is unconvincing, for all its attractiveness, is that it provides no satisfactory answer to the third of the problems faced by the Alliance, the reorganization of Atlantic relationships. What he shows, in the most illuminating way, no writer on the future of the Alliance can ignore: that the solution to this problem will itself be shaped by the answer to the problem of East-West relations in Europe. Atlantic affairs are no longer determined exclusively or predominantly by the combination of one external issue only—the Soviet threat—and internal issues of the Atlantic Alliance. It is because he ignores this, for instance, that Timothy Stanley's book, while valuable for its presentation of the continuing security issues in NATO, is on the whole a historical curiosity. It is because Brzezinski proclaims this that his volume is influential and indispensable. However, part of the answer to the problem that concerns him—relations with the East—itself in turn depends on intra-Atlantic affairs; neglect of the latter factor explains in part the weaknesses of Brzezinski's analysis of East-West relations in Europe.

The word "neglect" is perhaps inaccurate. There is, in the strategy described and in his analysis of the current scene, an implicit judgment which must be brought out. Brzezinski notices a trend toward national reassertion, reflecting "the renewed vitality of nation-states" [39] in both halves of Europe. He is rightly convinced that the nations between the Atlantic and the Urals cannot by themselves reunite the Continent; also, he thinks that their own dispersed efforts

[39] Same, p. 75.

would only lead to instability and (especially in the East) to a revival of intra-European antagonisms. He seems to believe that the
only way to arrive at the right kind of Europe is for the West to proceed, not toward a "European Europe" *à la* de Gaulle but toward "a
future cooperative community involving eventually four major units,
America and Russia as the peripheral participants, and West Europe
and East Europe as the two halves of the inner core." [40] Since this
is still a distant goal, since East Europe would hardly be a really autonomous power bloc (if we accept the less anti-Soviet version of his
design), and since the whole enterprise would be led by the United
States, relations between the United States and Western Europe
would remain unequal.

One may say that nothing in the scheme precludes a West European entity along supranational or confederal lines, associated in
some way to the United States, but a study of Brzezinski's book reveals that what he believes is needed is not merely American association with Western Europe but the United States' active presence
and participation. (His strictures against de Gaulle are based on the
erroneous assumption that the General's desire to break what he
calls the American hegemony amounts to a determination to break
all ties to America; Brzezinski calls his own scheme American association with Europe; actually, de Gaulle objects to preponderance,
not association, and Brzezinski is not after association, but after preponderance.) There is no analysis of what a West European entity
could do politically; his discussion is almost entirely in terms of "the
West" in general, under American leadership; Western Europe is
mentioned only in the form of the Common Market supposed to
help in the strategy of seduction of Eastern Europe (although, significantly, OECD is more important here). Also, Brzezinski believes
that five of the six West European powers continue to be attached to
American protection, that the West German concern for a "continued and stable United States presence in Central Europe" [41] is a
*sine qua non* of West German security and policy, that the other
West European states prefer dependence on the United States to a
West European entity dominated either by a Franco-German axis or
by Bonn alone. This is a correct diagnosis. But other factors are also
relevant, and have affected that "United States presence" and West
German-American relations. Moreover, a scheme that perpetuates
the present relationships is not likely to produce the results he wants.

[40] Same, p. 175.
[41] Same, p. 113.

The disarray among the NATO members makes it difficult even to launch the scheme; also, this disarray itself already reflects a failure of the relationships to produce the results he expects from their continuation.

Even if one assumed that the difficulties of the present situation were overcome, it is hard to believe that Brzezinski's scheme would deliver the expected goods. Here is where the inadequacy of his treatment of intra-Atlantic affairs accounts for flaws in his East-West plan. To put it bluntly, a plan for the reunification of Europe led by the United States suffers from a fundamental contradiction. Either it will not attain its goal, and thus will exacerbate the tensions already present in the Alliance; or it will, but with the United States paying a much higher price. The crises in Franco-American and Franco-German relations owed some of their seriousness to France's determination to prove the sterility of the Washington-Bonn alliance with respect to European reunification. And the clouds that drift across American-German skies reflect West Germany's nagging suspicion that the United States is either not interested in, incapable of, or unwilling to carry out Brzezinski's plan, or else will ask too high a price.

In short, the central weakness of Brzezinski's plan is the same as that of United States foreign policy in Europe in 1964–65, even though he wanted to go beyond it. His scheme is based on the assumption of a close American-German link. Of course, there is awareness of the danger of a purely "defensive" and "bilateral" relation—hence the attempt to make it seem less bilateral by branching Great Britain onto the circuit, and less defensive by giving it the purpose of German and European reunification. By isolating France, by putting Britain and West Germany on the same footing, he and the American policy-makers of 1964–65 believed that they would avert German resentment at being treated as "unequal" by France and Britain. By establishing through these bonds a joint "posture of confidence and openness in . . . dealings with Eastern Europe" [42] in order to end "the division of Germany and the gap between the peoples of Eastern and Western Europe," [43] he hoped to avoid German recriminations that NATO is indifferent to the great unsolved German issue.

[42] McGeorge Bundy "U.S. Policy Toward Europe," in *Hearings before the Committee on Foreign Relations,* U.S. Senate, 89th Cong., 2d sess. (Washington: GPO, 1966), p. 9.

[43] Dean Acheson, in Jackson, cited, p. 80.

However, as events have shown even while Brzezinski's scheme was being endorsed by President Johnson, there are two very different ways of trying to carry it out, each one may lead to a dead end, and there is an added danger when the choice between them is not clearly made. It is not enough to set a process in motion: one has to know what kind of outcome one wants. In its approach to the East, the United States can try to keep West Germany as its privileged ally, as it was in the days of Chancellor Erhard; but the only results will be to give the Soviet Union an excuse to maintain its East European *imperium* and oppose German reunification, and to make West European integration more difficult by increasing French separatism, British suspicions, and the discomfort of the other West Europeans. Alternatively, the United States may choose to approach the Soviet Union directly, to take the West German link for granted, and to negotiate a *détente* without major concern either for West Germany's security and status fears or for the fact that not every *détente* assures European and German reunification and the end of Soviet control. The most likely results then would be a *de facto* consolidation of Germany's partition; new obstacles to West European integration (if the Soviet price for a *détente* should be, for instance, the thwarting of a West European defense organization and nuclear technology); and serious troubles between the United States on the one hand and France and West Germany on the other. Since the summer of 1966, American policy has moved in the second direction, partly by choice (because of the urgency given to "bridge-building" and a nonproliferation treaty), partly as a result of *ad hoc* decisions about American troops in Germany—a choice and a set of decisions largely dictated by Vietnam. This has combined the flaws of premature disinvolvement and those of obstinate overinvolvement. It has induced in West Germany the temptation to draw closer to the French design —to switch from the idea of reunification under American protection to that of reunification at the expense of the "two hegemonies"—and a desire for more independence in foreign policy. The Soviet Union is unlikely to give Eastern Europe either as a gift to Western Europe dominated by the "Bonn-Washington axis," or as its contribution to a bilateral deal with the United States acting as the self-proclaimed trustee of Western Europe.

A proposal for the future that can be carried out in thoroughly divergent ways and that, if carried out, would exacerbate existing troubles is undesirable, even if some of its objectives are praiseworthy. The analysis we have made of this particular scheme teaches certain lessons. First, there are limits to the possibilities: overinvolvement may make it more, not less, difficult to reach certain goals, either if it obliged the United States to give to West Germany (the partner whose interest in the scheme is greatest, and which has no chance of satisfaction unless it accepts certain limitations) a power and a hold that would offset these restraints and *ipso facto* impair the success of the whole effort, or else if the United States' drive for peaceful engagement in Europe, in its eagerness to multiply links with the East, sacrificed the very interests of its allies that it aims at promoting. Here as elsewhere, more is less. Second, the three problems of the Atlantic Alliance must be analyzed interdependently; any scheme that focuses on one of them and deals with the other two by implication only will probably be unsatisfactory. Third, the prescription must face the difficulties squarely and stress the unavoidable choices. There is a danger in being too clever by half—in promising at the same time European reunification and a continuing duopoly, American leadership and Soviet cooperation, the preservation of Atlantic partnership and the reintegration of Russia and Eastern Europe into the world community, Germany as the anchor of the American commitment and as a nation to be contained in the new European order. While such a scheme has advantages for all, it risks multiplying the frustrations of everyone. If the emperor insists on a wardrobe with clothes of every style, he may end up wearing no clothes at all.

None of the three schemes discussed is satisfactory and they are hardly compatible. Yet present American policy in Europe borrows a strand from each. From Brzezinski's, it borrows the concern for European reunification. But this concern has few practical consequences, for it is neutralized by the two other strands. One is the old line, frequently reiterated yet fading, according to which the Soviet threat remains the cement of an Atlantic Alliance that must stay united (as in the days when bipolarity meant a deadly duel) and should evolve only in the direction of a future partnership. The other strand, less clearly presented by officials yet increasingly influential, subordinates the solidarity of the Alliance to the joint interests of the superpowers in managing world order: in this new line, bipolarity is not merely a muted contest, it points toward duopoly. The contradictions between these strands are glossed over: one can argue that a *détente* is the precondition to reunification, that nuclear stability, nonproliferation, a strategy that shies away from the immediate resort to nuclear weapons are in the interest of all the allies. But such reconciliation is purely verbal. It conceals a refusal to establish priorities, or reveals unawareness of the need for them. Because they are bipolar, neither the new nor the old line can contribute much to European reunification. (The old line dismisses *détente,* the second demands it so much that it risks settling for the *status quo.*) Both, in fact, leave Western Europe disunited. And the present combination of the three strands produces this paradox: West Germany is told that German and European reunification is the Alliance's new primary concern, yet Bonn is exposed both to discrimination within the Alliance (due to the new line) and to a possible frustration of its hopes for unity (due to the implications of both the new and the old), and finally it is left to itself in a politically unorganized Western Europe.

## II. An Alternative: Cooperation with a Uniting Europe

The complexity of the interests involved in the Atlantic Alliance, the members' different hierarchies of goals, their intractable policies or policies that can be changed only with difficulty—all these explain the troubles of American officials and limit the range of desirable and practical plans. The time for grand schemes is over; we are moving out of "our architectural period in Europe" [44] into the "Age of Maneuver," [45] and it calls for more finesse than geometry. But we still need a vision.

The vision that is suggested here I have called a policy of cooperation with a uniting Europe, or a policy of limited engagement in European unification—"limited" in contrast to parts of Brzezinski's plan and the Atlantic partnership idea; "engagement" in contrast to the rather misleading theories of disinvolvement.

Let me recapitulate that I have in mind an international system that will be stabilized at the global level by mutual deterrence between today's or tomorrow's superpowers. Under the nuclear umbrella, a certain amount of decentralization should allow for the management of most crises at a regional level, and the number of major participants in world politics will be greater than two. To the United States, relative moderation and a regained flexibility will be the chief virtues. The practice of flexibility and true cooperation with other nations will be the United States' main problems.

Insofar as the Atlantic Alliance is concerned, the implications

[44] Schelling, cited, p. 96.
[45] Riker, *The Theory of Political Conditions* (New Haven: Yale University Press, 1962), p. 229.

would be as follows. The United States would recognize that the Alliance can be of little help in relieving the United States of its "burdens" outside Europe. The dream of a partnership of world-wide scope must be abandoned as neither feasible nor even desirable. The common purposes will be restricted to the "old" Cold War in Europe and its settlement. For the rest, there will be separateness, ranging from convergence (international trade and finance, one hopes) to divergence (in Asia, one fears). In Europe, we must, as all now recognize, revive the Alliance's sense of purpose by making it, in Senator Church's words, less of a fort and more of a forum [46] aimed at the gradual reunification of Europe. It is necessary to provide for a reunification that will be neither a barely disguised Soviet or American victory (the former is as unwelcome as the latter is unlikely) nor a badly disguised duopoly, which would be unacceptable to the Continental nations as a possible prolongation of the *status quo* leading to "intolerable tension." [47] The United States must therefore actively encourage the creation of a European entity (starting with but not limited to Western Europe) that will give the Continent its only chance of emancipation from "the two hegemonies," the United States its best chance of ultimately reducing its burdens without increasing its risks, and to both their best chance of reaching an acceptable solution of the German problem (either through eventual reunification, or through the establishment of a climate and framework in which prolonged partition would become bearable to West Germany). What is required is American involvement toward self-denial.

This policy would suggest the following answers to the three basic problems of the Alliance: (1) on policies in the "new Cold War," resignation to diversity; (2) on the terms of settlement of the old Cold War, a gradual working out of a European reunification settlement in the creation of a European "pole" of power; and (3) on coping with the new pressures in the West, a gradual reorganization of the Atlantic Alliance that will permit sharing of the United States' European privileges and responsibilities with a developing European entity with military and diplomatic powers that will attract the East Europeans and be acceptable to the Russians. Thus, the variety of political, economic, and military policies toward Eastern Europe and

---

[46] *Europe Today,* a report to the Senate Committee on Foreign Relations, May 1966 (Washington: GPO, 1966).

[47] Herman Kahn and William Pfaff, "Our Alternatives in Europe," *Foreign Affairs,* July 1966, p. 599.

the Soviet Union that are now in the realm of separate national policies would be transferred into the second stratum of interstate relations in the Atlantic world, now the realm of American hegemony,
in exchange for which the allies would agree to replace American
hegemony with a genuine partnership, without waiting for the ideal
partner. The associates would be the United States and a developing
West European entity, an enlarged version of our present third
stratum and the long delayed fourth. In the long run, this conception answers what I have called the two basic questions of politics.
On the question "what are our purposes?" the answer would be a
coherent and secure European Europe stretching from the Atlantic
Ocean to the eastern border of Poland.[48] On the question "who controls?," the question of command, the answer would be an association
of major powers in a "multi-hierarchical" world.

### A. *Why?*

Before I go into details, I would like to spell out the basic considerations that inspire these views.

A first, negative consideration is the unproductivity of the present
framework. Any policy which gives priority to the settlement of intra-
Alliance problems is sterile, because only some of the differences
among the allies are due to intra-Alliance considerations, and even
the latter in the final analysis are differences over what could be
called the foreign policy of the Alliance. If policy is confined to the
Atlantic area, attention will be focused on the inevitable inequality
among the allies or on the difficulties of gaining access to the deci-

---

[48] Not "to the Urals." This Gaullist phrase is attractive to many Europeans, since it reminds them of schoolroom maps of Europe; it is probably
also meant to be attractive to the Russians, reminding them of their European
interests and France's concern that the Soviet Union contribute to keeping
Germany in check. But it is hard to imagine seriously a partition of the Soviet
Union, and the entry of a superpower like Russia into a European entity
would obviously unbalance the whole scheme. The political significance of the
phrase is that it implies that the future of Europe will require a European
*prise de conscience* by Russia, which will convince it that it need not exercise
domination, in exchange for a *prise de conscience* by the United States of its
own non-European essence; that is, for the establishment of a "European
Europe," the Soviets ought to get out because, contrary to what they thought,
they *are* a European power, not a universal power and foreign conqueror; and
the United States ought to relinquish its grip because it is not a European
power. The withdrawal of one hegemony is to be justified by *rapprochement*
and cooperation between the ex-threatener and ex-victims; the withdrawal of the
other is to be justified by a lesser need for protection.

sion-making process of the leader; the development of an "equal partner" will be delayed by some of the members' reluctance to have their horizons and their tasks confined by the walls of the Atlantic compound and by the United States' reluctance to risk having them fly from it; and Soviet sirens will keep offering various Europeans (the French or the Germans) enticing advantages if only these Europeans would untie themselves from the Atlantic mast. We have reached a stage where the internal reorganization of NATO must be commanded by a vision of its purposes. The alternative is piecemeal decay, *ad hoc* disintegration.

There is a kernel of truth in the vision of Atlantic partnership: it is the need for association between the United States and Europe. But a solution that puts this first, calls for "sharing" without asking what the responsibilities to be shared are for, or what the consequences on the members' foreign policies would be, and finally pushes sharing into a fuzzy future, just won't do. The Alliance is condemned to what the French call a *fuite en avant*. An intelligent student of the Alliance [49] has shown that in its first phase, there was an attempt to change the structure of the Atlantic system by creating a West European entity; in a second stage, when the development of this entity raised all the crucial issues of its relations with the United States, there was an "Atlantic phase" marked by the tensions we have described; and now we are entering a phase in which "structural change," a new definition of intra-Atlantic relations, implies "system expansion," or system change. The kind of pseudo-centralized world-wide alliance that would mean either deadlock or the permanent need to choose favorites is, as Kissinger has rightly said,[50] far worse than an alliance that survives because its members agree to go their separate ways in non-Alliance realms. Where divorce is not possible or desirable, i.e., within the European area itself, the solution of institutional problems lies in the harmonization of objectives, not in organizational gimmicks that are supposed to transcend the issue but that leave unchanged a *status quo* characterized by unsatisfactory control and discord on aims.

A second consideration is, as I have said before, the interdependence of the three problems. An Atlantic partnership united in its world-wide purposes is an inadequate idea not only because the chances of an agreement on these purposes are nil, but also because

[49] Karl Kaiser, "The US and the EEC in the Atlantic System" *Journal of Common Market Studies,* Vol. V (June 1967), pp. 388–425.
[50] Kissinger, cited pp. 232–33.

the likelihood that it could satisfactorily solve the second problem, that of the European settlement, is nil too. Europe would remain divided, since it is hard to imagine the Soviet Union relinquishing its hold on Eastern Europe under those circumstances: the Soviet Union would use the United States' continuing leadership of an alliance in which Germany was a major partner as a second reason for clinging to the *status quo;* and any formal settlement favorable to the West between the Soviet Union and an Atlantic bloc would be open to Chinese charges of collusion and defeatism. The Soviet Union is of course willing to settle for the *status quo,* but preferably not with the Atlantic Alliance as a whole: with the United States, as long as such a settlement drives a wedge between the United States and West Germany; with West Germany, if there should already be discord between it and its Western allies; anyhow, the Alliance collectively is unlikely to consecrate the *status quo.*

On the other hand, if the Alliance gives priority to the second problem, then the other two begin to look different. If the major purpose is a reunification of Europe in agreement with the Soviet Union, then it follows that the partnership established between the United States and the West Europeans will have to be one which incites the Soviet Union to make such an agreement. While it is true that the road to reunification passes, not past the crumbling walls of Jericho but through a gradual *détente,* the latter could easily lure the Atlantic Alliance away from the ultimate goal, *unless* the partnership is of the right kind, not a permanent monolith controlled by Washington in alliance with Bonn (this is what Brzezinski fails to appreciate), or a fragmented coalition racked by competitive independent approaches to Moscow. It also follows that the long-term perspective would be in fact a *détente* between the superpowers. By enabling the United States to reduce its burdens in Europe, by opening up avenues of tacit collaboration between the superpowers in other parts of the world, i.e., by bringing the international system closer to moderation, *détente* might reduce the need for the United States to "share its burdens" with Europe. Instead of a scheme that emphasizes some sharing of power at the top of a single firm, a joint enterprise intended to establish an entity with its own domain appears wiser. A European organization with its own rights and responsibilities, which will not have to beg to enter the domain of the United States, would have fewer reasons for anti-Americanism or misgivings about being dragged into America's extra-European involvements. For if there is some loosening of ties between this entity and the United States outside Europe, the problem of joint control will be less acute. It is more promising to link the irritating issue of intra-Atlantic organization, which has a way of bringing national desires for status and autonomy (and fears of discrimination) to the fore, with an "outward-looking" policy for a new, non-Atlantic European entity. Moreover, if intra-Atlantic relations are reorganized according to the dictates of such a policy, even the failure to achieve early European reunification or the failure to reunite the two Germanies would be less disruptive than in the present condition of the Alliance, for the loosening of bonds between the United States and its allies would neither give the advantage to the Soviet Union, nor lead to an "untying" of West Germany that would also play into Soviet hands.

A third consideration is that the concept suggested here has the advantage of taking the long range into account. In the short run, as we have seen, the interests of the various countries concerned diverge and clash. A short-run settlement in Europe will be most likely to consolidate the *status quo*. The long-term goal, the kind of world order that can accommodate differences and provide for security, flexibility, and assent, requires a lasting and subtle exercise which (by contrast with grand schemes of a more short-range or illusory nature) cannot be described in advance in all its details. The best way to ease the present disarray is, I must emphasize, an evolutional solution. Here, we can borrow a leaf from the European movement. What the European movement exploited most skillfully was the dimension of the future, of projections or *projets*. Governments have accepted uncertain or dubious compromises because of a conviction that the half-measure of today prepared a better future for tomorrow, that the purpose of the enterprise was not merely quantitatively to redistribute the various nations' assets and liabilities, but to produce qualitative changes whose ultimate virtues justified present concessions or compromises. This is not a method that can be applied everywhere, as I have indicated, for it works only if there is at least a vague consensus on goals and direction at the outset.

The first task of statesmanship, therefore, is to propose a goal and a direction that represent a kind of common denominator, in this sense: that whereas each of the parties involved might prefer a different outcome, the goal would still provide sufficient satisfactions for each and be acceptable to all, each nation's sacrifices being justified by the advantages of the global outcome and compensated by the sacrifices of others. The Soviet Union would gradually forego its control in Eastern Europe but would "gain" in exchange the decrease of the American role in Europe and institutionalized guarantees against any dangers from a reunited Germany. The West Germans would accept restrictions on their borders and military capabilities and a loosening of their ties to the United States but would increase their chances of regaining their national unity and gain an important role in uniting Europe. The French would understand that a vision without instruments remains a dream, and would abandon their heady emphasis on independence for the construction of a confederal Europe consonant with the Gaullist vision. The British would give up the vestiges of the Commonwealth, the burdens of the sterling area, and the fading and costly special relationship with the United States (west and east of Suez) for the reality of European development. The United States would lose its privileged position in Europe and gain in exchange the Soviet Union's return to moderation, the establishment of a European entity, and greater freedom to think and act about extra-European tasks. For these things to come about, there is no doubt that time is of the essence. At present, there is not sufficient pressure from any quarter to incite Russia to go beyond a "relaxation of tensions" to the actual relinquishment of power. The problem consists of building up the right kind of pressures and the right kind of incentives.

It is necessary now to examine the more specifically political considerations that have inspired these suggestions. First of all, they are based on my interpretation of what is in the United States' interest and what lies within its capabilities. It might be argued that it is not in the American interest to be involved in an alliance whose purpose becomes a settlement that decreases American influence in Europe. But this can be refuted by two sets of arguments. First, there are no acceptable alternatives. The continuing presence in Europe of the United States, incapable (because of its special bond with West Germany or because of its drive for a bilateral *détente* with the Soviet Union) of helping to bring about reunification, but insisting on a nuclear defense strategy suspected by Europeans and on a "sharing" of burdens felt by them to be less and less necessary, will produce maximum disruption. A policy that aims at, or results in, continuing preponderance at the cost of continuing partition of the Continent condemns itself to an ugly death. Brzezinski's proposal for a policy combining preponderance and reunification strikes me as a fiction. An early United States withdrawal from Europe would consolidate the *status quo* by removing any incentive for the Soviet Union to tolerate the reunification of Germany. It would leave the nations of a disorganized Western Europe militarily, politically, and psychologically face to face with the Soviet Union and its allies, and thus expose the United States both to a loss of influence and to unpleasant surprises. The second refutation is that the policy suggested here envisions the Alliance not as a kind of sacred cow, an intangible valued for itself, but as a method that the United States can use toward certain goals; similarly, the American military presence in Europe is viewed as an instrument to achieve certain ends that correspond to America's essential interests, not as an end in itself.

Our primary purpose in Europe has been and still is to prevent Western Europe's occupation or subjugation by the Soviet Union. Occupation is certainly ruled out by American military presence, but Russia could exploit the disarray produced by continuing partition. Atlantic cooperation toward a European defense organization and toward a settlement reunifying Europe, giving an explicit guarantee that the United States would move against invaders, and removing Soviet troops and nuclear weapons from Eastern Europe, is consonant with American interests. American troops in Europe are still necessary because "the means of reaching agreement require the presence of the United States . . . but the presence of American troops would become negotiable and their withdrawal might become a part of the agreement." [51] Here as elsewhere, it is essential to separate short-term needs from long-range goals, to prevent the short term from becoming an end in itself, and to adapt it to the end suggested by the long-range vision.

Another basic American interest could be called the establishment of a harmonious Europe. This was, indeed, the driving motive behind the Alliance itself, and the Alliance became the holy shrine of American foreign policy not only because it symbolized the new American involvement in world affairs and the new American leadership, but also because it tried to be a "security community," [52] a zone of internal peace and cooperation, a kind of Wilsonian bridgehead toward a world order different from the cold and cynical balancing calculations of the past. This was also the motive behind United States support for West European integration. In both cases, the central problem was to find a proper place for Germany. A harmonious Europe could only be one that was not dominated by a hegemonic or revanchist Germany, one in which Germany would be

---

[51] Pierre Hassner and John Newhouse, *Diplomacy in the West: Out of Paradox* (New York: Twentieth Century Fund, May 1966), p. 53.

[52] See Karl Deutsch *et al., Political Community and the North Atlantic Area* (Princeton University Press, 1957).

tied to its neighbors. This American interest, which remains central, explains the reluctance to "share" with states whose unification is slowed down or blocked, whose divergences seem to perpetuate the "atavistic" balance-of-power past which is so unpopular in the United States. It justifies Brzezinski's concern for multilateral structures that would prevent trans-European linkages from leading to an orgy of nationalist revivals.

But what we must examine carefully is how this American interest can best be served today. In earlier days, when the Soviet menace was primary, America's interest in a harmonious Europe was inevitably focused on the Atlantic Alliance and the emergent Community of the Six. Today, a harmonious Europe means a gradually reuniting Europe. In the early 1950s, while German reunification was always of concern to West Germany, it did not receive top priority in Adenauer's foreign policy; and the allies had much to gain, in fact, from Germany's partition. For the French, it removed the "German threat"; for the British, it decreased Germany's competitive potential; for the United States, it allowed for West German rearmament. Now, however, the French cannot avoid acknowledging the need to reunite Germany in the process of restoring European independence; the United States realizes that in the long run West Europe's and West Germany's friendship depends on helping European and German reunification, which would, furthermore, decrease Soviet influence. This does not mean that the purely West European enterprise is *passé*—far from it; indeed, it is more important than ever, but its perspective has changed.

Yet the advantages of a harmonious Europe can obviously be purchased only at the cost of a certain American withdrawal. Would not such a retreat be self-defeating? Would not the outcome be the chaotic Europe of nation-states in which old antagonisms could repeat their disastrous course, a reunited Germany could again be a source of instability, and opportunities would arise for perpetual Soviet interference? These are legitimate misgivings. However, what they suggest is not that we should maintain the increasingly untenable *status quo,* but that we need a European settlement in which the virtues we expected from the "Atlantic community" and from a united Western Europe would be cultivated in a different framework. America's interest lies in the creation of a system that would have the advantages of multipolarity without the irresponsibilities and perils of mere polycentrism. By itself, staying in Europe becomes counter-productive; "getting out" is conceivable only if there is a solid, stable, and balanced European structure; creating such a structure requires a drastic change of American policy. America's interest in a harmonious Europe demands a continuing association between the United States and Europe, but presence and association, "partnership" and cooperation, integrated alliance and guarantee are not synonymous terms. Our role in Europe will be "broader," as Brzezinski argues, since it will aim at European reunification and organization, but it will also be more modest.

If we do indeed promote a "European Europe," will we perhaps get Frankenstein instead of Galatea? Of course, there will be no preordained harmony. In some areas we will have to allow a divorce, because a partial divorce will be the only way of preserving a partial association. But in Europe, our and Western Europe's interests will be safely and overwhelmingly mutual. Western Europe will need us for security reasons (and the prospects of even a united Europe capable of dispensing with our nuclear guarantee are remote), even if our ground forces are gradually removed. If the present *status quo* persists, each of the West European countries might be tempted separately to make agreements with Russia, but a uniting Western Europe's only interest in an agreement would be for the purpose of reunifying and stabilizing Europe. A Franco-Soviet agreement more or less aimed at keeping a pro-American West Germany divided from East Germany, or a West German-Soviet agreement at NATO's expense, would badly damage our interest in a harmonious Europe. But an agreement on reunifying Europe between the Soviet Union and a Western Europe associated with us would serve this interest; and the West Europeans' interest in making this agreement requires our association.

Moreover, we cannot talk as if American interests in Europe existed in isolation, for the United States has global interests. The rise of China has already resulted in a displacement of attention from Europe, and this in the future will necessitate greater ardor in the drive to moderate the original Cold War. A *détente* with the Soviet Union and the progress of European unification should facilitate the shift of our attention. Although the Soviet Union must be cautious about "colluding" with the "capitalist foe," it will gradually become more obvious to Russia, as to us, that it has a joint interest with us in restraining China—and a European settlement is a prerequisite. In turn, this presupposes a settlement of the German problem acceptable to all, including the Germans. While the "European" solution outlined here has no appeal to the Soviets so far, it could have one in the future. And it could serve as a more general model for the

United States, in its contest with the main Communist powers outside Europe. The Russian-Chinese rivalry obliges the Soviet Union to pose as the champion of anti-American "liberation" in the underdeveloped areas. In these circumstances, it will rapidly become in our interest not to man the front lines everywhere, but to help to build up other centers of power. In Asia, we are bound to find it unprofitable to try to contain China with primarily American forces, and self-defeating to try to do so with a coalition of pro-American, but weak and dependent Asian states; yet it is in our interest to develop the autonomy of states such as India and Japan that could best affect China by the right mixture of power (for containment) and contacts (for a return to moderate relations).

If, in Europe, the United States' job is to change the *status quo* without creating a vacuum, we must shift the spotlight to the central issue in the evolution of the Alliance, namely, Germany, not France. France, of course, has become an obstacle in a variety of ways. It was France that pulled out of the integrated military structure. Yet the danger lies not in this move itself but in the possibility that others will follow the French example. As long as France acts alone, its acts simply underline the existence of dissent from the defense strategy for Europe that was chosen and controlled by the United States, a determination to move toward the dismantling of "blocs" in order to reunify Europe, a drive to dissociate itself from American policies abroad. The dissociation is more annoying than hurtful, and may prove beneficial in the long run. The dissent, by itself, will not tempt the Soviets into military ventures. The determination could be called disastrous only if one believed either that a settlement can best be negotiated by cohesive blocs (but the more "cohesive" the bloc, the less likely a change in the *status quo*) or that France's solo performance suffices to put the Eastern "camp" in a much better position (but this "camp" has its Rumanian dissent and its own tensions). It is France that has diluted the power of European supranationality and slowed down the construction of a political Europe. But supranationality could not cope with the present "unintegrated" issues among the Six, and the French would be the first to press for common policies if their partners accepted the vision of a "European Europe." Moreover, if the ultimate purpose is a European entity open to Eastern Europe, institutional flexibility is an asset. Again, the real peril lies in the repercussions of French action (or inaction) on West Germany's position and behavior. If it is true, as one commentator has written, that "Moscow is likely to confine its serious negotiations to those parties from whom it has something to fear and to whom it has something to offer," [53] then a Franco-Russian *rapprochement* is not dangerous; but the possibility of a Soviet appeal to a disenchanted West Germany subsists, and once more it is not so much the French move as the French example that is dangerous.

Since it has proved difficult to punish France for bad behavior, the United States has tried for a while to reward West Germany for good behavior. But West German access to nuclear weapons has been blocked, and the only truly important "rewards" are not in American hands: German reunification depends on the Soviet Union, integration into Western Europe on France. There is only the elusive quest for "Atlantic integration," for improved consultation, for more and better committees, but this does nothing to eliminate or reconcile the divergences on policy.

In exchange for maintaining the American presence in West Germany, the United States has asked for more "burden sharing." The result has been a basically unhealthy "special relationship" between the two countries. On the German side, this relationship has perpetuated a mentality in which a mixture of dependence and distrust, docility and doubts, delusions and dilemmas prohibits national self-respect. West Germany, the economic "giant" of Western Europe, has been in the psychological position of an overly dependent child, perpetually in need of reassurance from his loving parent, and perpetually threatened by feelings of despondency when the parent neglects him or shows any impatience or makes any demands. The best antidote to the arrogance that Germany betrayed between the wars is not submissiveness. And the antidote to the old pretenses to hegemony is not illusions, carefully encouraged by the United States, about the ultimate benefits of West Germany's foreign policy, and rudely applied pressures to choose among antagonistic allies and alternative courses of action. Disappointed docility breeds only resentful recrimination.

The relationship has been equally unhealthy on the American side, where it shows a peculiar mix of favoritism and fear, protection and repulsion. On the one hand, we argue that it is essential to avoid putting West Germany on the kind of probation to which the Versailles settlement had relegated the whole nation after World War I; on the other, we fail to pay sufficient attention to the susceptibility of a state that feels so dependent on others. We pay homage to the new Germany's maturity and to its contributions to

[53] Hassner and Newhouse, cited, p. 60.

NATO; but we fail to consult with it in areas it considers important, or we treat it as a client. We sometimes handle the Germans with as much care as if they were a package of explosives—i.e., with extraordinary precautions, but as an object—and sometimes with no care at all, and we are surprised at their resentment. The central German problem thus becomes the pervasive German obsession; the crucial importance of Germany as a stake in the rivalries between camps and between allies becomes confused either with the idea of giving West Germany a privileged position in the Alliance, or with the vain hope of reaching some agreement with the Soviet Union that will somehow make the German problem disappear.

West Germany cannot and should not any longer be treated merely as a stake, used by the United States as a bulwark against France, by the French as a lever against the United States, by both as a card to play in Moscow, submitted to the repeated shocks of French unilateral acts, American unilateral withdrawals, British unilateral statements on arms control and troops, changes in strategy or dictates on weapons procurement, Soviet-American deals or drafts. And West Germany must realize that its best chance of being accepted by all as a genuine actor is to face realistically the interrelated problems that in the past it has failed to relate. If reunification is the goal, the hope of gaining Soviet and East European concessions by threatening to join multilateral nuclear forces was vain, for "the German potential nuclear capability is a bargaining power of negative value." [54] (One American official was even blunter: "there is no bargain here.") [55] Too close a tie with the United States is self-defeating, too hesitant a policy on frontiers is a mistake. The prospects of maximum discomfort for West Germany lie in trans-Atlantic links that would prolong psychological dependence, make for periodic crises of German suspiciousness and United States impatience (especially as extra-European strains on the United States increase), undermine relations with France and facilitate a Franco-Soviet *rapprochement* without in the least contributing to reunification. The prospects of maximum comfort lie in incorporating West Germany in a complex Continental framework in which there would be security from the start and unity at the end, in exchange for restrictions which would at least serve their purpose. What is intolerable in the long run is the present coexistence of discrimination and national division in a fragmented Western Europe; but the ending of

---

[54] Schelling, cited, p. 100.
[55] Bundy, cited, p. 6.

discrimination would in no way promote the end of partition. Within a sterile Western Alliance, Germany's special brand of integration would soon be felt as discriminatory. If, furthermore, out of lassitude, West Germany gave East Germany *de facto* recognition, this would only consolidate the Soviet position; West Germany would then reject the discrimination it had accepted so long as it had hoped that this would contribute to reunification. The best method of preventing the Soviets from trying to lure West Germany out of the West is to strengthen the links between Germany and Western Europe; they are more likely to be productive than the old American-West German link, or than the more autonomous West German policy of today. But the new links must point to the new direction.

Why should it be in West Germany's interest to accept a policy favoring a "European Europe" which would eliminate from Europe the one power that provides it with security and sees in German reunification no threat to its own position? First, because in the long run, any security arrangement that consists of a NATO army which is manned predominantly by Americans and Germans will lead to trouble. If the United States should gradually withdraw, West German "integration" would lapse, and Germany's division be confirmed, along with Soviet opportunities either for debauching the suddenly more independent Germany, or for playing on the misgivings of West Germany's neighbors; if the American presence and command persist, the failure to reunify Germany will lead to increasing West German restiveness, and Soviet opportunities. Second, recent West German disappointments with American policy have broken the spell that a bipolar system had for so long exerted on Bonn: if the duel of the superpowers is over and the duopoly is resented and feared, then Bonn must turn to a different conception of the international system. To a nation of West Germany's resources, mere polycentrism has not enough to offer. Yet Bonn by itself, concerned with reunification and militarily restricted, cannot play the French game of trying to be a pole in a multipolar world without exposing itself and the West to the disastrous alternatives analyzed in Chapter 11. Therefore, the best choice would be to join in the attempt to make of a West European entity one of the poles in a system of the kind I described.

Three, there is no question of "pushing out" the United States until and unless reunification and a new European security system are achieved. French statements about the need to preserve the Alliance and to have American participation in the final settlement of the German problem must be taken seriously. Once again, only an evolutionary approach offers an answer. Only the gradual elaboration of a European defense system in association with the United States will prevent the disenchantment of West Germany with its allies, without giving Bonn so important a voice as to preclude reunification. If reunification does not materialize, the development of a West European entity in which West Germany would be an active but not a dominant part would at least give greater strength to the pro-Western trends in Eastern Europe, and help create in East Germany "conditons that [would] make reunification superfluous or at least its absence tolerable." [56]

Another political consideration favoring this general approach of cooperating with a uniting Europe concerns the development of a European entity. Europe strikes me as the only potential solution of the problems examined here. Europe is the only forum in which it would be possible to have German unity *and* ties between Germany and its neighbors that would make such unity acceptable to them; from which each superpower could withdraw without defeat or imprudence; for which states such as France, England, and Germany would make certain sacrifices of sovereignty and around which they could reconcile their interests. France and West Germany do have a joint concern in preventing a superpowers' deal that would preserve the division or neutralize the Continent; Britain and France share a concern for containing and channeling German energies, especially as West Germany's psychological dependence on the United States wanes; West Germany and Britain have a desire to maintain close relations with the United States; France and, increasingly, Britain and West Germany want such relations to become less unequal. What is needed is a West European partner of the United States, but not a dependent in the plush Atlantic cage; in any event, he is looking toward his East European brother in the other, barren cage. What is needed is a gradual disengagement of the cages' keepers—joint devolution, not joint abdication; not an *entente* between blocs or a disintegration of the blocs, but a replacement of them by a European organization. Moreover, as moderation progresses in Soviet-American relations, the advantages of "polycentrism" in Europe recede. The importance of technological and economic power as one yardstick of the international hierarchy, the desire to prevent the superpowers from either imposing unsatisfactory settlements on the Continent or from

[56] Theo Sommer, "Bonn Changes Course," *Foreign Affairs,* April 1967, p. 491.

letting their continued rivalry impede a settlement, will instill in the middle powers a desire to combine forces and to shed the complacency of mutual denials. What has been called "Europe à la carte" —via *ad hoc* bilateral links—will not suffice, and would condemn the West Europeans to "cumulative underdevelopment," politically and technologically.

This "reconciliation around Europe" will not occur until and unless Washington first accepts the notion of a "European Europe," with a political, military, and economic role of its own in association, but not in exclusive partnership, with the United States, and then encourages its allies to move in that direction. If the United States insists on an "Atlantic Europe" or on the intangibility of NATO, Great Britain will once again be kept out, Franco-German differences will prevent advance, America's frayed ties with Britain and strained ties with West Germany will be unproductively maintained. The best way for the United States to maintain close links with a West European entity is to facilitate the entry into the European communities of its most constant ally, Great Britain, and resolutely to endorse the idea of a more autonomous Europe that will give to West Germany an opportunity to affect rather than block common policies. In other words, the best way to deprive the Gaullist vision of its anti-American edge is to support it; to oppose it sharpens its edge and provides no viable substitute. France, opposed to an Atlantic vision, blocks all European efforts inspired by it, yet keeps alive the European entity that grinds out common West European policies. West Germany, thus far reluctant to accept fully the French vision, nevertheless preserves links with France and protects the Communities of the Six.

There is, therefore, still a focus for reconciliation if the United States actively works for it. Recent events have shown that Pygmalion's statue, while showing signs of life, will not move unless Pygmalion encourages it to do so. Encouragement means something quite different from the dubious promise of equal partnership; it will be necessary to strengthen a uniting Europe by giving it jobs to do, even before it becomes anything like a federal state. It is not enough for the United States to stop acting (often unintentionally) in a way that makes a united Europe impossible—for instance, by insisting that Great Britain remain "East of Suez," where it can be no more than a supplement to American forces, or by considering unacceptable a political organization of Europe that would be in the beginning purely intergovernmental, or by making more difficult a joint

West European effort to develop the peaceful uses of atomic energy. And if the United States waits for initiatives from its allies (as during the pre-Nassau and post-MLF phases of the discussions over control of nuclear weapons), nothing will happen. In the absence of American initiatives, the European powers that want to stay close to the United States will refrain from moves it might not appreciate, and those that want to transform the Alliance's *status quo* will feel that solitary defiance and joint passivity are the only alternatives. It is a vicious circle. Only the United States, only the leader, can break it for the purpose of drastically changing the conditions of his leadership in all realms, including the military.

The instruments exist to accomplish this. A student of political unification [57] has observed that, to NATO members other than the United States, the United States was an "external elite" in the late 1940s, when Europe was economically and militarily dependent on it. Since then, some "internalization" has taken place—"the process in which control of a system is taken over by member-elites." But the process has been uneven: it has varied from sector to sector, being strongest in the economic realm, very limited in the military one; it has also varied from country to country, with West Germany much more "integrated" than either Great Britain or France, and Britain more than France. And this unevenness has naturally bedevilled international relations. Not only has the Europe of the Six remained a rump, functionally and geographically, but the "internalized" functions have often reverted to individual states; this has meant a perpetuation of concerns about national status, etc. We need to reverse these trends: "internalization" must proceed in the sectors that have thus far been controlled by the "external elite," but in such a way as to benefit West Europe as a whole. Three instruments can be used: in the economic realm, the Communities of the Six, to which other states can apply; in the military realm, the Western European Union, which could be revived, expanded and coordinated with the Communities; in the political realm, the Franco-German treaty, which provides a framework that can be filled out (and combined with WEU). The more such institutions are allowed to function, the more attractive they will be to East Europe, especially if their relations with the United States are rapidly transformed. And while the states of East Europe could not be expected to join these agencies, connections could gradually be established

[57] Amitai Etzioni, *Political Unification* (New York: Holt, Rinehart & Winston, 1965), Chs. 2 and 7.

through functional arrangements, or through a presently drowsy organization that could be awakened, the Economic Commission for Europe which has West *and* East European members.

A sense of common, if limited, purpose could thus be restored in an alliance that currently suffers from intellectual anemia. The United States would promote the gradual emancipation of its dependents, as well as collaborate with its defiers—promote emancipation and foster cooperation for responsibility. The European allies would be challenged by the idea of their autonomy, and this would cure them of the need always to define their individual positions with reference to the United States.

This idyllic picture can legitimately be attacked. First, everything I have said is based on the assumption that all the West European nations would be willing to build an entity capable of making its contribution to solving the problems of Europe. If there is no such willingness, if certain states, such as France, prefer "free hands" and others prefer Atlantic solutions, then the whole scheme collapses. However, as I have tried to show, the other approaches are sterile: Atlantic schemes offer no solutions; for France to play "the role of Europe" alone is frustrating, since lack of support condemns the French to perpetual diplomatic brinksmanship. Were cooperative policies possible, it is hard to believe that the French would insist on the privilege of lonely acrobatics. What is involved here, as always in politics, is a matter of will. Even to de Gaulle, the emphasis on the national mission is not just a method of rallying support, but also a consolation and fallback when other nations refuse to follow. When there seemed to be some willingness to follow (in 1961–62), even *his* tone was more warmly European. As for the other European nations, if they lack the will, they too must face the vicious circle of dependence, division, and discontent. Every one of them, and not just France, must come to understand that the advantages of cooperation justify a break with habits or traditions that prevent a consensus on European purposes. For instance, even while waiting for the door to open, Britain's position in the world monetary system, its agricultural policies, its opposition to a European defense system, and its positions east of Suez will have to be modified to make its entry into the European Communities possible, but a refusal to pay this price would not give it a better role in world affairs.

A second objection is that a common will, a consensus on goal and direction, would still tell us very little about the structure of the European entity; and yet the structure matters, if one is arguing for a gradual transfer of American responsibilities to it and indeed ultimately for joint superpower devolution to it. Why should the United States encourage the establishment of a mere conglomeration of nation-states? Is there not a conflict between "two fundamental concepts of international politics and order"—between the idea of unity arising from "the growing interdependence of societies," "the steady drawing together of peoples and governments for functional purposes based on common interests transcending old quarrels," and the notion of compromises to be worked out, through diplomacy among independent states, on the ends and means of national purposes? One concept points to a devaluation of national borders and national sovereignty, the other to a restored concert of nations, a new balance of power. The second concept is undoubtedly unattractive, but the first, while attractive, suffers from weaknesses analyzed elsewhere— i.e., the limits of functional method when it is applied to the vital interests of states in the realm of high politics. If the development of Europe had to be accomplished by either an undesirable or an unlikely scheme, my argument would be pretty weak. What is, however, both beneficial *and* possible is a growing reconciliation between the two concepts.

We cannot expect the old game of power to disappear and to be replaced by functional adjustment of conflicts over vital interests or by national willingness to submit to majority votes or supranational decisions; and certainly we do not want a "restoration" of the Europe of the nineteenth century or the interwar period. Indeed, reality is likely to exclude both these possibilities. Sovereignty refuses to die, independence and freedom from foreign domination are precious, the forms of statehood survive—but the context and the substance change. In other parts of the world, where national independence is a recent political phenomenon, borders are often artificial, and the only profound experience is that of imperial domination, the claims of sovereignty still breed violent interstate conflicts. As for Europe, while there are many contested frontiers in the East, and while the experience of foreign domination there preserves nationalist resentments or prepares nationalist revivals, the lessons of pre-1939 fratricidal interstate conflicts are unlikely to be forgotten; and the desire to have a peaceful zone moderates the claims to national independence in Western Europe. The one major obstacle is Germany: it remains a potential source of conflict, and Bonn's enthusiasm for a West European federation has subsided, now that West Germany has recuperated most of its sovereignty, regained status, and achieved prosperity through other means. Yet it is precisely the problem of Germany's division that cannot be solved in a context of undiluted sovereignty. Moreover, protection against Soviet designs and American technological predominance can be provided only if European nations transcend the traditional limits of sovereignty.

In the Europe of the Six, the tight functional net of economic and commercial relations, while it fails to "spill over" into the realm of high politics, constitutes a safety net that limits the meaning and consequences of diplomatic and strategic solo acrobatics. The development of internal resources is becoming the great concern of each nation (as a means if not as an end), and in Western Europe this cannot be envisaged except in association with other nations. Even at the present stage, the Common Market brakes France's drive toward independence and provides it with a beachhead toward its vision of a "European Europe"; it has braked West Germany's tendency to rely too heavily on the United States, and brakes West German temptations of autonomy; it cushions West Germany against potential Soviet attempts to lure it away from the West. In such circumstances (especially if East Europeans can gradually be attracted into the net, and even if diplomatic and commercial approaches to the East for a while remain in the realm of national rather than Community diplomacy), the new concert of nations will be very different from the old one: the new conditions on the use of force, and the spread of functional links between not only individuals across borders (as before 1914) but governments, make the idea of a "return to 1913" a perfect absurdity. (De Gaulle's brusqueness can be explained in part by his awareness of the limits within which national independence can be displayed. Since these limits restrict the scope for acrobatics, histrionics on the trapeze are justified only by a desire to demonstrate a nation's continued daring, inventiveness, and capacity for "prowess," and by a knowledge of the limited risks— i.e., by a psychological reaction against the net and by a political calculation of its usefulness.) If this analysis is correct, then the institutional form and face of the European enterprise will matter less than the capacity to arrive at common policies and to multiply links between the states, whatever the formal amount of sovereignty still at their disposal, for its exercise will be pooled.

A final objection is that the Soviet Union would have no more reason to tolerate German reunification in a "European" context (especially if Europe's political organization is loose) than it has had to favor this reunification for the benefit of the Atlantic Alliance. Recent events point to a thinning out of American forces in the Western half of Europe. Why should the Soviets, then, accept the Gaullist idea of a withdrawal of both "hegemonies"? Why not wait until Soviet persistence and tensions in the West lead Bonn to resign itself to the *status quo?* The answer is, first, that the Western interest is to reverse or stop this trend. Second, German and European reunification may well depend on the Soviets' resolve, but this resolve can be affected by pressures within Eastern Europe, in Asia, and in Russia itself—by a change in the costs of control. Third, a "European Europe" provides the best opportunity not only for exploiting such a change if it arises, but also for contributing to it and for making the costs of relinquishing control appear less heavy than those of preserving control.

## B. *How?*

For the *middle range,* two familiar precepts must be observed. First, it is dangerous to act in the present as if the desired future had already arrived. This means that even though the outcome ought to be a replacement of the present rival Warsaw Pact and North Atlantic Treaty with a European organization, and a withdrawal of American and Russian forces from the Continent, any premature withdrawal in the West could make the goal unreachable by weakening Western Europe and consolidating the Soviet Union's position (a point often made by critics of de Gaulle, who do not realize that he thinks that the United States will not withdraw prematurely, given its interest in European security). It also means that in the organization of European defense it will not be possible to act as if there existed already a West European Defense Community capable of organizing a European nuclear force; the error of EDC ought not to be repeated. It means, finally, that since the vision is a long-term one, we cannot subordinate to a still distant common future the construction of a West European entity; it will, of necessity, be unfinished and open, yet it will be indispensable as a matrix in the freer half of Europe and as a sun around which the former satellites of the Soviet Union in the other half may gradually revolve. In this regard, there is one important difference between the two halves of Europe: in the Western half, there is the possibility of building an entity that can, even before reunification, try to move things closer to what they ought to be after reunification; it can therefore attract the East European states that would, otherwise, have no alternatives but perpetual subservience to the Soviet Union or an anarchic return to nationalism.

A second precept completes and corrects the first; while it is necessary to separate the short term and the long term, decisions made in the short term should take into account and contribute to the designs of the long term. Otherwise, short-term decisions tend to be "pragmatic" responses to the accidents and incidents of the day, and, instead of imaginative measures informed by a sense of direction, there will be conservative measures designed either to save as much as can be saved of the *status quo* when it is challenged (as by de Gaulle's moves of 1966), or to give in to new demands in a minimal or grudging fashion. International organizations, especially when they are weighty and large, develop a cumbersome momentum, or adaptive inertia. When they suffer a hard knock that should force some rethinking, they tend to absorb the shock; when pressures compel reform, organizational procedures drown the reform in a sea of committees. Also, if this precept is not observed, short-term policies will consist of unrelated decisions and be paralyzed by contradictions among them. In the Atlantic area, for instance, experts have argued fruitlessly whether to give priority to negotiation of a Soviet-American *détente* (especially arms-control agreements) over a reorganization of the Alliance, or to start with the Alliance and then be in a stronger position to face the Soviet Union. The effect has been, at times, to stall both the reorganization and the *détente,* and at other times to exacerbate the contradiction between a decaying Alliance and the drive for a *détente.* A long-term plan incorporating the notion of synchronism (which has proved useful in Brussels among the Six) would eliminate such a conflict: the Alliance would be reorganized in the general perspective of future East-West relations, and the *détente* could thus be approached more constructively. Institutional reform must be seen as a set of means toward ends.

The area in which the application of these two precepts is most delicate is the military one. The first precept makes it imperative to continue to have a security system for Western Europe that, given the mediocre state of the Europeans' own military forces and German security fears, entails the presence of American nuclear weapons and some American forces on the Continent. No "denuclearization" is worthwhile so long as the basic political issues are unsettled; the threat of war does not come from the presence of nuclear weapons in Europe. Those weapons are necessary as a deterrent: as long as Soviet MRBMs threaten Western Europe, Western Europe must have the means of a nuclear response, and its deterrent value is of course much greater if it is in Europe itself. Moreover, denuclearization or a premature withdrawal of United States forces would contradict the second precept, either by helping to consolidate the division of Europe or by making possible a reunification that would damage Germany's links with Western Europe and leave Europe at the mercy of the Soviet Union. The second precept makes it imperative to devise the security system so as to facilitate the passage from the present stage of an "integrated" Alliance dominated by the United States to the final stage of a European entity guaranteed by the United States and the Soviet Union.

These needs can be reconciled but only through a transformation of NATO. Fifteen or eighteen years ago, NATO was hailed by the West Europeans (including the British) as the way of integrating and implicating the United States in Western Europe's defense. The imperative of defense remains, but the priorities have changed, and the structure of NATO must be adapted to the new realities and to the new objectives. Otherwise, an institution that was progressive in the 1950s could become a liability in the 1970s. The present, shaky coexistence of an organization of fourteen powers still dominated by the United States, whose nuclear weapons are not "integrated" and whose partners have misgivings about NATO's strategic doctrine and about its decision-making process, with a semi-dissident France, signatory of the Treaty but unintegrated in the military organization, must not continue.

It would be a mistake to deal with this unsatisfactory present in a regressive way. It would have been absurd, for instance, to try to "punish" France, even for the worthy purpose of deterring potential West German resentment of the United States, for making possible a imitators. To have done so would have only increased the risk of Paris-Moscow "encirclement" of Bonn.[58] It would have increased the alienation between France and West Germany, made the latter ever more dependent on the United States, and moved France closer to Russia. And it would have made the defense of Europe more difficult by eliminating the possibility of NATO's using French "real estate" on "cooperative," if not "integrated," terms. But once again, fortunately, the desirable and the possible have coincided: the wish for harmony expressed by some of the allies, West Germany's desire not to compromise its links with France, the agreement to have

[58] See Kahn and Pfaff, cited, pp. 587–89.

French troops remain in West Germany, and various military considerations all pointed to a *modus vivendi* that safeguards us from such perils.

It would also be a mistake to try to deal with the tensions created by the issue of nuclear weapons in NATO by means of another multilateral gimmick. It would raise once again in sharply focused fashion all the fears of discrimination and concerns about status (especially among the British and the Germans, particularly when there is an independent French force outside): for it is in so-called "hardware solutions" that all such fears become obsessive and such concerns turn sour. Moreover, no collective force, be it the MLF or the tactical nuclear force General Norstad has suggested,[59] would really allow the European allies to veto or control the use of the main arsenal of American nuclear weapons. Indeed, European allies could not even trigger off the nuclear weapons of the collective force if there is an American veto (as in the MLF), or if, although use of the weapons was determined by a majority vote, they remained under national custody and no member of the minority could be compelled to release them (as in General Norstad's plan). At the same time, an MLF would make relations with the East more difficult.

Lastly, we must not insist that Atlantic interdependence means that "neither America nor Europe can be engaged in major hostilities anywhere in the world without the other one also being potentially involved." [60] It is difficult to see how, at present, our allies in Western Europe could involve us in a war in Europe through their activities in non-European areas (and given our first precept, we need not worry yet about future possibilities), but it is easy to see how they could be the victims of an escalation of *our* non-European commitments; Berlin is still a hostage. Consequently, to insist on a strict reading of Article 5 of the North Atlantic Treaty will only increase the Gaullist temptation to independence and encourage our allies to make reservations on their commitments like the one de Gaulle proclaimed when he referred to his willingness to stand by NATO in the event of "unprovoked" aggression. The best way of saving the automaticity of NATO defense in a purely European crisis is not to press for such automaticity in a crisis brought about by our extra-European involvements.

[59] See his testimony in Jackson, cited, pp. 127.
[60] Stanley, cited, p. 126.

For a progressive transformation of the Alliance is essential, progressive in the sense of gradual and in the sense of moving toward the ultimate goal of turning the "integrated" alliance under United States leadership into an alliance between the United States (and Canada) and a West European military organization, an alliance whose very structure would point toward and facilitate the advent of a general organization for a reunified Europe. If one needs a slogan, it could be: from hegemony, to alliance, to guarantee.

The first set of measures to achieve this concerns the present Alliance: its second stratum, that of defense, must be carefully preserved, yet reorganized. The need for American nuclear and conventional forces on the Continent persists (the latter in order to cope with "conventional pressures" and crisis contingencies and to give more credibility to the nuclear deterrent). But the number of American conventional forces could be reduced, by common agreement, as long as their withdrawal did not create a vacuum. The present integrated commands would be dissolved, the commander-in-chief in Europe would be a European; the weapons of the European forces would no longer be provided mainly by the United States; the Alliance's decision-making process would be shared; there would be, in peacetime, a degree of national reassertion, and, in wartime, independent national nuclear forces.

If the notion of integration in the allied defense structure is gradually replaced by that of cooperation, the French could return to the Alliance's military organization without appearing to renege on their original withdrawal. De Gaulle's decision to withdraw was based on two kinds of arguments. One was symbolic: NATO, in his eyes, summed up the old Cold War that he insists on liquidating—hence *his* slogan, "from *détente,* to entente, to cooperation." The establishment in the Alliance of a West European defense organization allied to the United States yet serving a distinct West European foreign policy would not jeopardize his objective. The other arguments were military: (1) The fact that Great Britain and the United States both had national, nonintegrated nuclear-weapons forces and integrated NATO commands to which only their expeditionary forces in Europe were assigned put them in a privileged position vis-à-vis the Continental allies, which merely provided their forces to a NATO command structure that depended on American nuclear weapons under American control and that applied strategic directives from Washington. (2) Integration meant the imposition by the United States of a strategic doctrine that exposed Europe instead of protecting it. (3) Integration allowed the United States to implicate *ipso facto* the forces of its European allies, if American operations outside of Europe should provoke a war that escalated and extended to Europe. An examination of the reality behind these arguments leads one to conclude that France's withdrawal from the integrated structure of NATO and the expulsion of United States forces in France have more nuisance value than destructive impact, and more symbolic meaning than nuisance value. In peacetime, the role of the integrated NATO commands is very limited. The acrid debate between the French, denouncing integration as if it had meant total subordination, and the Americans, accusing the French of sabotaging a coherent defense of Europe, is an exchange of highly dubious arguments. Even the forces assigned to the NATO integrated commands (except for West Germany's) are under national command in peacetime. So the first of France's arguments is questionable. But the second and third are strong, for there is no doubt that the integrated commands are dominated by the United States. The real thrust of France's action thus concerns the Alliance's strategy and decision-making processes: de Gaulle's moves are a protest against a state of affairs in which the senior ally monopolizes crucial decisions within the NATO domain and disposes of means that could implicate the allies in his affairs outside it.

Now a flexible interpretation of Article 5, as I have suggested, would be a step toward the kind of future in which all the allies would reserve their freedom to act alone outside of Europe, and the freedom of the European partners not to be dragged into a war in Europe by the extra-European ventures of the United States. This requires a joint definition of the emergencies that all members agree to consider as armed attacks on, or crises for, them. Such contingency planning would be far better than the present situation, in which, in some emergencies, the Alliance could be wrecked either by a unilateral American decision to implicate all the members, or by a sudden decision of some of them to reserve their freedom—something which (except in the West German case) "integration" is not extensive enough to rule out.

A gradual dissolution of the integrated commands would be a disaster only if the result were a return to full national autonomy. But if it is linked to an improvement of NATO's doctrines and decision-making processes and to the establishment of a European system, there would be no cause for laments. What is essential is agreement on reactions to crises, and on command and operations in wartime. If that agreement exists and if a European organization develops, there would be no inconvenience in having national forces on national soil under national command in peacetime. The prerequisites for the agreement on crises, command and operations are—inevitably—a reconciliation on purposes and a reform of the command machinery in the Alliance.

There is a need for a strategic doctrine acceptable to all. Grounds for the necessary reconciliation exist. The French themselves recognize that, while their small nuclear force is intended to restore the credibility of the deterrent threat that is weakened by the superpowers' stalemate, to be plausible at all the threat can be used only for clearly vital interests and in cooperation with the United States. Especially as long as the deployment of a light ABM network in the Soviet Union weakens the threat of secondary nuclear powers, in the race between offensive and defensive weapons, the French force (or the British one) by itself cannot even provide its nation, much less all of Western Europe, with a sufficient guarantee. However, the Americans must recognize that the relevance of the McNamara Doctrine (finally endorsed in a formal way by the Fourteen as it was becoming obsolete!) has been impaired by a whole series of conditions which limit the "flexibility" of the "response" and tend to rule out a conventional war in Europe: the existence of France's uncoordinated independent nuclear force, the shrinking (through the French defection) of the territory on which a "flexible response" could be executed, the European allies' failure to augment their conventional forces assigned to NATO, the likelihood of increasing British and American troops cuts, the continuing deterrent effect of a "small risk of total destruction," the difficulty of following a counterforce strategy against an increasingly invulnerable enemy nuclear force.

A reconciliation could be achieved on the following terms: First, the Americans would acknowledge the psychological clumsiness of the strategy of flexible response. Second, the French would acknowledge the absurdity of putting all eggs in the basket of strategic nuclear deterrence, and the absurdity of arguing that only the certainty of the enemy's being destroyed will deter him. If the nuclear stalemate has indeed made the United States' nuclear force less likely to deter the Soviet Union, it is hard to see how the French alone could deter a superpower that is capable of destroying France entirely, especially since, as the French admit, their force could at best inflict only partial destruction. Third, the allies would study the cases in which the use of conventional forces would be the appropriate response, i.e., limited attacks which could be met at lower levels than those observed by American and British troops in a perspective of "massive defense against massive attack." [61] Fourth, the allies would acknowledge that "nuclear war—if it should occur—will come only at the end of a long diplomatic process. . . . It seems contradictory to try to integrate nuclear strategy while leaving the process of diplomacy which precedes it bilateral." [62] Fifth, NATO's strategic doctrine must cover the whole of the process that could lead to war. For military planning by military commanders, many of whom can do no more than suggest variations on American designs, only encourages a fatal indifference on the part of European governments.[63] The doctrine must define the circumstances in which certain military measures would be taken and those in which nuclear weapons should be used or in which the threat of their use should be made. This kind of agreement on the manipulation of the nuclear threat in peacetime crises is, as we know, even more important than an agreement on the resort to nuclear weapons in wartime, because crises precede and are more likely than war, and Europeans are above all concerned with averting war.

Such an agreement requires coordination at a high level. The NATO Council would be in charge of negotiating this agreement and of coordinating allied foreign policies in European affairs. Under the Council, NATO's military committee would be in charge of detailed strategic planning, and there could be a special committee for crisis prevention and management, as General André Beaufre has suggested. The nuclear weapons themselves would remain under national control, because there is no real middle ground between national control and the centralized control which the United States has been trying to arrange but which its allies resent or reject, and also because the drawbacks of national control would be alleviated by the coordination of the national nuclear forces according to a common doctrine and directives.

These provisions may nevertheless appear to many as too flexible, too permissive and uncertain to provide for effective security. But those who complain that this loose arrangement would bring us back to the 1930s or to 1913 should remember that the infernal machine

---

[61] Shelling, *op cit.,* p. 98.

[62] Henry Kissinger, "For a New Atlantic Alliance," *The Reporter,* July 14, 1966, p. 22.

[63] See the remarks by Secretary McNamara in Jackson, cited, pp. 249–50.

was set off in the summer of 1914 by the rigidity of existing alliances, not by their looseness, and that Hitler's war would not have been avoided by an "integrated" Franco-British defense structure. Also, the reorganization of the Alliance suggested here plays down those issues which in the recent past seemed most intractable. Perhaps it can be said that the suggested formula has some disadvantages for security, in comparison with the original North Atlantic Treaty; but today, in comparison with 1949, the main sword and shield of the West is still the American nuclear force, the concern for security is less acute, the concern for other goals is more intense, and pursuit of them would be facilitated by the proposed changes.

The second set of measures concerns the establishment of a West European defense system that could be associated with that of the United States. General André Beaufre's scheme indicates the general outlines of what I have in mind.[64] There would be a European organization with its own military committee and council, and with a minimum of "integration" for wartime purposes, in the form of European commands with the right to dispose of the French and British nuclear forces in wartime, and with American members in charge of American nuclear weapons and forces in Europe. There would also be a degree of standardization and specialization of European weapons production. (Until now, the strong links between the American armaments industries on one side and British and German armed forces on the other have prevented anything like a standardization of NATO armaments, prevented a "common market of armaments" for Western Europe, and increased the dependence of vital industrial sectors in Europe on American technology.) [65] West Germans would not have a finger on the nuclear trigger, but they would participate in all military and political decisions; and the logistical integration of forces would insure that, even if there was a peacetime "independent German Army," it would hardly be capable of launching operations on its own. Britain's nuclear ties would be with Europe.

As General Beaufre points out, such arrangements can be made without having to wait until Western Europe is a single entity with a single, strong voice. Indeed, the military realm is the one in which so-called "sharing" or, as I prefer to call it, devolution can begin at

[64] *NATO and Europe* (New York: Alfred A. Knopf, 1966).
[65] See the remarks by General Paul Stehlin in Edgar Furniss, ed., *The Western Alliance, its Status and Prospects* (Ohio State University Press, 1965), pp. 81 ff.

once. The rather loose structure of the WEU can serve as a womb. As the European organization becomes more coherent, as its members become more self-confident, as they discover—through the exercise of responsibility—the need for conventional forces to make the nuclear deterrent credible in major emergencies and unnecessary in small ones, as they accordingly reorganize their defense systems, a thinning out of United States troops could proceed. Although the presence of some American forces would be necessary as a bargaining point as long as Soviet troops stay in Eastern Europe, the Atlantic Alliance would be gradually moving toward the stage of a unilateral United States guarantee for Western Europe.

To American readers, this undoubtedly suggests a loss of American influence in Europe. But it points toward a reasonable combination of security and progress of the right kind: while providing for a common strategy, it reduces the burdens now borne by the United States in a way that frees American resources and attention for other theaters, promotes West European cooperation, and points toward the final pan-European objective. It might be said that the American preference for integration in NATO is due not only to security concerns, but also to the desire to maintain a certain degree of control over the Alliance and get a reward for the sacrifices it requires, using the military structure as a means for political purposes, as Russia does in the Warsaw Pact. The answer to this is that in the long run the maintenance of the *status quo* in NATO merely preserves American responsibilities while adding to the difficulties between restive Europeans and harassed Americans. There are times when great powers discover, in relations with allies, that cooperation with a minimum of autonomy works better than subordination. Today, we ourselves need to disentangle so that we can cope with entanglements elsewhere. And the Europeans have no interest in playing their cards so imprudently as to risk, in a pinch, being left unprotected: the triggering function of small national deterrents exists only where coordination does. No nation without major ambitions or territorial grievances would incur even a small risk of total destruction, on the wager that it could force its senior ally's hand over an issue that ally is reluctant to call his own. West Germany has grievances but would have no nuclear force.

Another objection concerns France. The French show no particular desire to coordinate anything, or to agree in advance on wartime commands and operations, or to set up new European military institutions. On the latter point, the obstacle lies primarily in their allies' refusal to let defense matters be discussed outside the NATO perimeter; on the first two points, the French attitude (which, with stubborn good sense, subordinates military considerations to political objectives) follows from a refusal to subscribe to purposes and controls that contradict French policy. Once again, a change of over-all vision and policy commands all the rest.

What I am suggesting, then, is simply the gradual transformation of an alliance whose central purpose was the defense of West Europe against the Soviet Union, and whose additional purpose became the setting up of a framework within which West Germany could be rearmed, into an alliance whose central purpose would be the establishment of a West European entity both secure and capable of contributing to the reunification of Europe. If this is the aim, one can understand why a certain relaxation of peacetime integration can be allowed and why the *encadrement* of Germany would change form. The participation in a European defense organization of a West Germany without national nuclear weapons would establish links that could justify a relaxing of West German subordination—especially as West German "integration" in NATO becomes more problematic anyhow, now that NATO ceases being "a dominating, all-pervading feature of everyday life" and "is not seriously expected to produce answers to even its own problems." [66]

Also, a defense organization of the type described would avoid raising at a premature stage the issue of a "European nuclear force," while making possible the assignment of the British and French nuclear forces to a European command in wartime and the technological cooperation indispensable for the survival of the British and French deterrents. The door should remain open to a true European force once political unity had sufficiently progressed. It would indeed be "rash . . . to smash that dream," [67] since killing it would only increase European resentment and perpetuate dependence. In the negotiations for a nonproliferation treaty, the Soviet Union, already sure of the demise of any Atlantic nuclear force, has sought to rule out any European nuclear force as well, except that of a very distant federal European state. Britain and, more reluctantly, the United States, have agreed to this. To be sure, a nonproliferation treaty signed by the superpowers and the nuclear have-nots would slow down proliferation. But the problems of guaranteeing the non-nuclear nations against attack by nuclear powers, of providing the non-nuclear

---

[66] Sommer, cited, pp. 484–85.
[67] Bundy, cited, p. 10.

nations with nonmilitary nuclear technology, and of organizing inspection are difficult enough to justify skepticism about the treaty's capacity to end the spread of nuclear weapons altogether. Precisely because *any* European force is a distant possibility, and because it is, to put it mildly, unlikely that a West European organization that includes Britain and France would ever set up a nuclear force that could fall under the control of West Germany, it would be a mistake to "smash the dream" for the sake of Soviet assent to so dubious a treaty. To do so would probably not prevent West European cooperation, but it would make Britain's entry into the Communities more difficult, it would impede the progress of West European military cooperation beyond traditional intergovernmental arrangements, and it would increase tensions among West European nations by submitting some (the non-nuclear ones) to outside inspection while exempting others. Although a middle ground between a purely intergovernmental arrangement (assigning the national nuclear forces of Britain and France to a European command in wartime) and a purely federal one is hard to define, for it would raise all the issues of majority vote and "fingers on the trigger" that helped kill the MLF or the Norstad proposal, the progress of political unity in Western Europe may reach a pre-federal stage where such a middle ground could be found and such issues be resolved. The concession to the Soviet Union implied in the nonproliferation treaty cannot be defended as part of an over-all political strategy aimed at facilitating reunification and at giving West Germany reasonable assurances of security and technological development. Indeed, it exposes West Germany to a humiliating dilemma: if Bonn swallows its objections, partition is confirmed, inequality vis-à-vis Britain and France increased. If Bonn protests, it feeds Soviet and East European hostility.

We must turn now to what can be called the foreign policy of the Alliance. The final purpose is to establish a "stable and balanced" Europe, from the Atlantic to the Bug—the present Polish-Russian border. It is true that neither the United States nor West Europeans alone can reach the goal. Washington acting alone can bring about *de facto* recognition of the Continent's division. The West Europeans alone *"ne font pas le poids"* in Moscow. Thus, as Brzezinski, Hassner, and Aron [68] show, concerted action is needed in the short run. But for the allies to have a good chance of reaching the long-run objective, there must be a transformation of the ties between the

United States and Western Europe, without which present ties between the Soviet Union and Eastern Europe will persist and the German problem will continue to be a source of instability.

"The German problem is, indeed, *the* European problem." [69] What is required in the short term (which in fact threatens to be quite long) is a strategy aimed at persuading the Soviet Union and East Europe to accept the vision described here as in their own interest. We are unlikely to convince the Soviets that German reunification is in their interest by inviting them to keep their troops in the Eastern provinces of a reuniting Germany whose Western provinces were part of NATO. The individual dissidence of France in the West, of Rumania in the East, the individual initiatives of the new West German government have so far failed to pry the other East European states loose from the Soviet Union. The Soviets are likely to consider giving up East Germany only if an alternative to the *status quo,* involving no "German threat" or advantages for the United States over the Soviet Union, increases East European discontent over the prolonged Soviet military presence and the separation from the West. What the West needs is a complex but coherent policy. Let us again deal with the "don'ts" and the "dos."

Three kinds of "don'ts" are important. In the first place, we must avoid policies that appear to give *de facto* recognition to the division of Europe and *de jure* recognition to East Germany. This means that the United States must avoid proposals to the Soviet Union (especially about arms control) that assume the untouchability of the political *status quo;* on the other hand, the United States and Western Europe (other than West Germany) should, if not "continue their diplomatic and economic isolation of the East German regime," [70] at least be careful not to develop any more contacts with Pankow than Bonn itself establishes.

In the second place, we must not leave West Germany exposed as an isolated spearhead of the West. There are obvious dangers in leaving West Germany and East Germany politically face to face—East Germany is, after all, a puppet on a string. It is true, as Karl Kaiser has eloquently shown, that a policy of contacts with East Germany is useful for humane purposes and to prevent further estrangement between the two Germanies during the long interim be-

[69] De Gaulle, quoted in Roy Macridis, ed., p. 191.
[70] Karl Kaiser, "Germany at the Crossroads," in Henry Kissinger, ed., *In Search of Germany* (Cambridge, Mass.: Harvard University Press, forthcoming).

fore reunification; trade with East Germany provides Bonn with leverage on Pankow and with a means of safeguarding West Berlin. But it is also true that the improvement of conditions in East Germany may help to consolidate the Pankow regime, "thus make unification more remote except on East German terms," decrease the Soviet Union's "moral cost . . . of maintaining the division of Germany," and provide East Germany with incentives "to seek to weaken the Federal Republic" [71] by gaining political concessions from Bonn (at the expense of West Germany's Western links) in exchange for further liberalization. That is, the Soviet Union might use East Germany as a lever to pry West Germany loose from the West, or as a tool to sharpen the division of Europe. Consequently, while Brzezinski's policy of total isolation of East Germany is unworkable, for the reasons Kaiser and All-German Affairs Minister Wehner give, Kaiser's own suggestion of "rechannelling East Germany's relations with the Western world through the Federal Republic" might be risky. Therefore, West Germany's allies should not let Bonn act in such a way that, through the policy of contacts, the solution of what is "the European problem" becomes a purely German affair. This is the Soviet position, and it is in the most essential interest of all Western allies (including West Germany) that the solution of the German problem remain at least a Four Power responsibility. Difficult as it may be in practice, a line must be maintained between the kind of recognition of East Germany that would be a prelude to and prerequisite for reunification (for instance, mixed commissions preparing the return to common institutions), and the kind of recognition that would amount to a West German stroll following the pied piper of Pankow.

In the third place, since the ultimate objective is the reunification of Europe, not only Germany, and since the various East European allies of the Soviet Union are neither organized in a grouping all their own, nor capable of moving collectively toward the West even if they wanted to, a monolithic Western approach would backfire. Here again, *le mieux est l'ennemi du bien.* It is wiser to approach these countries separately rather than offering a grand plan to all of them. (Also any such plan would raise the one issue that should be played down, that of East Germany's status.) And they themselves ought to be able to approach different sources in the West. This does not mean that Brzezinski's arguments for promoting multilateral ties are invalid, only that the immediate and direct encouragement of

[71] Kissinger, *The Troubled Partnership*, pp. 213–14.

multilateralism in the East is unprofitable, and that the goal requires a large degree of flexibility.

All these things to avoid are, of course, less important than the things we must do. The nature of the concrete measures that could hasten the coming of a reunited Europe is well known; they have been, on the whole, well covered by Brzezinski. West Germany must recognize the Oder-Neisse line as the eastern border of a united Germany; nonrecognition offers no bargaining position whatsoever but makes Poland cling to Moscow. The Hallstein Doctrine should be abandoned with respect to East Europe, so as to facilitate diplomatic and cultural contacts. A policy of expanded trade and credits would be beneficial. And so on.

Rather than repeat these familiar and convincing arguments, I would like to concentrate on two other issues. The first is how Western action should be organized. Coordination ought to mean a certain division of labor. It is, of course, impossible and unnecessary to dissuade Bonn from talking, from time to time, to Moscow; but it is in no Western power's interest to encourage such contacts. Bonn's area of activities should rather be East Germany, within the limits analyzed above, and Eastern Europe. The nations not so long ago attacked or subjugated by Hitler must be reassured. Their governments (many of which, today, combine a minimum of liberalization with loyalty to Moscow, whatever their misgivings about the degree of Soviet predominance in the Warsaw Pact) must be convinced that neither their nations nor they would be endangered by increased contacts with the West and a withdrawal of Soviet might. So long as the notion of a "European Europe" seems to imply the risk of a Europe dominated by Germany, most of Eastern Europe will gravitate toward Moscow. West German willingness to assure Eastern Europe that it had abandoned its old territorial claims, its dreams of domination or predominant political influence, and any new dreams of military might is essential.

The United States, on the other hand, should be more active in Moscow. For it is the United States that can best negotiate the parallel or symmetrical withdrawals of the superpowers from the Continent. The United States also has a dual role to play in East Europe: diplomatically, we should help to convince the East European leaders that, West Germany not being dangerous, the presence of Soviet troops is unnecessary, and we should remind them of American willingness to agree to a joint withdrawal; economically, we should expand our trade along the lines already suggested by President Johnson. But the main role in East Europe is to be played by the West Europeans. Only they—through contacts, conferences, cultural exchanges, credits, trade—can gradually persuade the East Europeans that the advantages of a "return to Europe" by far exceed the risks, that participation in a continental entity under no one nation's domination is preferable to the perpetuation of the postwar schism, that the reunification of Germany within such an entity offers more chances of peace than a prolonged partition, which slows down economic progress in East Europe and maintains the Soviet military presence. This does not mean that Western Europe should not talk to Moscow too. After all, Soviet security concerns amply justify efforts by France and Britain to show that a European organization would be defensive and capable of containing German military might. Since the final settlement will require both the American and the Soviet guarantee, Western Europe will have to take an active part in the arduous transformation of the other security pact: the Warsaw alliance. For West German reassurances will not suffice, as long as they remain unilateral and uninstitutionalized. If West Germany acts either as part of a strong NATO led by the United States, or as part of an Alliance in disarray, those reassurances will not be taken seriously. Only if West Germany acts as part of a West European organization does it have a chance of success.

My second point concerns more especially the role of Western Europe in this long enterprise. Whatever West European diplomatic and defense entity emerges, it will undoubtedly not assume all the attributes of national sovereignty right away. Still, it will be important to keep the members' separate approaches coordinated, to develop in Western Europe a model and magnet for the East European states, and to convince them and the Soviet Union of the value of the undertaking. Even the best of NATOs will never convince Moscow to dissolve the Warsaw Pact, but the emergence in Western Europe of an organization in which German energies were released without endangering anyone, whose military and foreign policies aimed at establishing a balanced and peaceful world order, whose economic policies aimed at shared expansion without disrupting world trade patterns, is likely to be a powerful force for change—capable, at best, of leading to German unity and East Europe's entry into the organization, or, at least, of associating East Europe with it and of making bearable the coexistence of West Germany with a liberalized East German state that was no longer merely a Soviet satellite. For in the context of a reuniting or reunited Europe, the partition of Germany would be less explosive; yet only a West European entity can bring about that context. The great idealistic idea of Jean Monnet to establish a zone of peace in Western Europe would be put at the service of political goals and worked out, as it must be, through the usual processes of "power politics." Otherwise, it will remain in the outer space of impractical dreams. A West European entity deprived of foreign policy and strategy, as it is now, exerts only a limited appeal and preserves only too well each government's right to approach Eastern Europe and the Soviet Union as it sees fit. Since the EEC never burgeoned even into an *"Europe des Etats,"* each member is free to claim that approaches to the East (including commercial ones) are in the realm of national sovereignty. A full-fledged West European federation is neither conceivable in the near future nor likely to have too much appeal, since it would probably be absorbed by problems of internal organization and much more difficult to "open to the East." Something different is needed, more flexible (again) so as to be effective.

Thus we come to the last of the short-term problems: the organization of such an entity. I cannot emphasize often enough that institutional engineering (a favorite pastime of lawyers) is less important than, and is determined by, prior agreement on goals and directions. Often, statesmen travel the same road, but their goals are far apart, and fellow-traveling does not allow for any common enterprise, only for trading goods and services. Often, the goals are the same, but the statesmen cannot agree on the road, for (here control is decisive) each one wants to command and to benefit, or fears that in a common enterprise he will have to leave the leadership and advantages to others. Without the agreement on goals and directions, international institutions at best provide a framework for intergovernmental exchanges of ideas and cooperative arrangements; at worst, they wither on the vine or obstruct (the Council of Europe and SEATO prove the point). This does not mean that such institutions are useless—OECD is certainly valuable. But if the goal is more than functional cooperation—an entity whose central institutions (supranational or not) would be endowed with some authority—then the consensus to which I have referred is a prerequisite. On the basis of it, the common institutions can, over time, strengthen their authority and define in greater detail the policies to be followed. But it is a slow process, in which the participants are always on the verge of sliding back to mere cooperation or open discord.

Let us sum up the argument: the Atlantic Alliance, by itself, provides no vision. The vision that I deem desirable is that of European reunification. This requires in the first phase the development of a West European entity; but, in turn, its members must agree on the vision and on the direction of common effort. The West European entity that is required must include France, West Germany, and England. A community without England, while capable of grinding out economic agreements, is politically and militarily paralyzed by Franco-German divergences, by Holland's insistence on British participation, by Italy's misgivings about France and Germany. The idea, expressed by some, of a European organization built around Germany and England but excluding France, lacks realism, in part because the defense of Western Europe without France is unimaginable, in part because France's associates in the Common Market (including West Germany) are eager to keep their ties with France and to use the existing Communities as a springboard. However, a West European entity with France, Britain and West Germany will itself become a possibility only if the three countries have come to share the same general vision.

Should this happen, it would be futile, however, to expect total harmony, any more than within the economic Communities. Even if a consensus on goal and direction has been reached, each state will still have its own special concerns. Great Britain will undoubtedly keep at least a corner of an eye east (and south) of Suez, with more than nostalgic references to the need for maintaining her physical presence in parts of the world otherwise left to the rivalries of the giants. West Germany, no doubt, will see in the emancipation of Eastern Europe more a means to a national end than a goal, whereas for France the perspective will be different (and Britain, traditionally rather tepid toward East European commitments, may be more indifferent than either). This is why it is vain to expect supranational institutions to grow fast. If anything, they would complicate matters. Even when there is a broad consensus, each state, on matters involving vital concerns, is likely to want the common policy to reflect its own views; one should expect hard bargaining at every stage along the road.

And it would be a mistake to expect too much too soon. An early federation is not in the cards. A confederation will (however much one tries to hide that sobering truth) have to look in the beginning very much like the Fouchet Plan of 1962. Experience shows that while even this kind of scheme is too great a step without a prior consensus, anything *more* supranational is too great a step even when there is a prior consensus. Obviously, "integration through technocracy" has its limits: functionally, it is hard to extend the Brussels procedures to diplomacy and strategy; politically, there is the problem of responsibility, and the latter cannot be solved by parliamentarianism. Not even within nations are parliaments the dynamos of foreign and military policy—indeed, they usually become the hot plates of parochialism. The diversity of political factions in Western Europe would make a prevalence of transnational party alignments over national ones unlikely, and majority votes based on national conglomerations would not exactly consolidate the union. Moreover, a parliamentary Western Europe would have little appeal to the regimes in the East. This does not mean that the parliamentary supervision of executive organs need not be organized and strengthened, only that one should not ask the brakes or transmission to be the motor. The motor will have to be a council of ministers, and a unanimity rule will probably have to be followed—*de jure* or *de facto*—at least in the beginning. Of course, institutions "governed" by such councils, yet weightless and ineffective, abound. But my point is that they can give substance to a *prior* consensus, while without the consensus, they mean nothing. In intergovernmental organizations including widely different states and endowed with important responsibilities, the principle of unanimity is often a handicap; but in a growing community based on a political consensus, the principle of unanimity is initially a condition for and guarantee of balanced growth.

The risk of splintering and discord would persist. But as the experience of the Common Market shows, the way to minimize this is, not to create more agencies with legal powers, but to find ways of appealing to the members' interests. This does indeed mean power politics, but power politics with a difference. Even if there are still threats and blackmails, in all likelihood there will not be force. Moreover, especially if one begins with simple institutional formulas, and even if one member is more able than others to impose or "sell" its views, the danger of naked hegemony is nil. (In our charges against de Gaulle's *Europe des Etats,* which we accuse him of wanting to "dominate," we have confused leadership and hegemony.) But without leadership, international organization can make no progress, and, in the realms that concern us here, it will have to be the leadership of statesmen, not civil servants.

Turning now to the *long range* (and assuming that our design has been successful in the middle range), the final aim—in a world where nothing is final—would be a reunited Europe's "organized cooperation" along confederal lines, concerned not merely with collective security but with foreign affairs and at least the realm of welfare. The integrity of this confederation would be guaranteed by both the United States and the Soviet Union. The two alliances of today, which would have been progressively transformed during the previous phase, would be discarded. Instead of the old Soviet idea of a non-aggression agreement between NATO and the Warsaw Pact, there would be a single pact—by and for the Europeans—and two unilateral guarantees by the two former protectors and rivals.

Of course, the withdrawal of American and Soviet forces will amount to a partial "denuclearization" of the Continent, and the nuclear stalemate may continue to cast doubts over the United States' willingness to deter a Soviet invasion of, probe into, or pressure on Europe by the threat of nuclear weapons (and the withdrawal of U.S. ground forces may impair the credibility of the American nuclear guarantee even more). It will therefore be necessary that the European entity dispose of sufficient nuclear means—the coordinated national forces of France and Britain or a more federal formula—to restore the plausibility of nuclear deterrence. Yet it is hard to imagine that the Soviet Union would consent to the deployment of tactical (or, *a fortiori*, strategic) nuclear weapons in Eastern Europe. It is difficult enough to envisage a contraction of Soviet power; what the Russians might deem a renunciation of their national security is inconceivable. However, the development of technology or arms-control agreements (with the European entity as a participant, not an object) in the long interim period may help to solve a problem that can at present only be raised. By then, the idea of nuclear-free zones in Eastern Europe and in a zone of the Soviet Union east of Poland may be acceptable.

As to whether the states of Eastern Europe would participate as separate units in the European organization or as members of a regional grouping comparable to a West European one (making Europe the union of two communities), whether indeed they would be able to participate fully—this will depend on events in Eastern Europe that no one can predict. What matters, once again, is not the detailed institutional formula; it is the idea of a body that will bind together states that will find in such bonds opportunities rather than sacrifices. The hope is that the West European entity will provide, in its defense and political organization, a framework sufficiently flexible for other states to join it, and the example of a "security community" that solves disputes peacefully and provides for organs to implement common policies.

## C. *A Final Plea*

I have explained why I believe some of the recently proposed schemes for the future of Europe cannot solve the problems to which they addressed themselves. Is there any more reason to believe that what I have suggested here would have a chance to get off the ground? Why should members of the Atlantic Alliance suddenly show an aptitude for cooperation which has been conspicuously absent and which, if present, would have averted the present disarray? After all, one has, especially in Washington, grown accustomed to a *status quo* that is not so bad: it has allowed for West Europe's recovery, for a modicum of liberalization and emancipation in the East; it has preserved Europe from an American-Soviet war and from nationalist explosions. In Western Europe, there are powerful forces militating against the emergence of the kind of entity I have called for. The European nations, with well-established governments, different pasts, and different situations, find the international system an incentive to separatism without heavy risks; and of course the two superpowers have, in each half of Europe, contributed to making the logic of diversity prevail. Moreover, why should the Soviets let themselves be pushed out of an area they have done their best to consolidate?

First, there is a reason for believing that the goals and directions outlined here would stand a fair chance of providing a kind of common denominator for the Atlantic allies. Their story is one to which the titles of two novels by Balzac could be given—*Les Occasions manquées* and *Les Illusions perdues*. It is a story of bad timing, of nations never in the same phase at the same time, missing appointments or coming to the rendezvous after those they were supposed to meet had already left. Each one of the allies is approaching the end of the road, and now the best future for each lies in a common road. In an international system of built-in frustration, the logic of diversity prevails, but if a system of positive achievements is wanted, diversity will have to be tamed and energies pooled. I have tried to show what the dead ends are that each will soon come to, and the reasons why the common road I suggested could provide all travelers with an opportunity to achieve at last what the logic of diversity has kept beyond their grasp. Since in international politics that logic is hard to destroy, what I have suggested here preserves, both within the common enterprise and outside its limits, a vast range for diversity. But a balance must be struck. In today's system, one thing possessed appears to each worth more than two things promised. But meager possessions—or the avoidance of dispossession—will not satisfy forever, and at that point one thing acquired (in common) will appear as valuable as any thing possessed (alone).

Second, if, as I believe, only the organization of a "European Europe" in the West can significantly contribute to ultimate European reunification, it will obviously take a long while before the required consensus in Western Europe is reached and the entity to be built on it is launched. If the "seduction of Eastern Europe" depends not only on the attractiveness of the alternative offered by the West, but also on the recognition by East European and Soviet leaders that the regimes established under Soviet domination will not be swept away by a withdrawal of Soviet force and a lifting of the Iron Curtain, obviously much internal liberalization will have to precede the reunification of the Continent. There will have to be considerable ideological erosion in the Soviet Union, and strong domestic and extra-European incentives for the Soviet Union to break habits, to budge from positions and slogans, to bear the pain of an "agonizing reappraisal." But my point is that this erosion is already in progress, the incentives exist, and the scheme suggested could give the right impetus to more progress—especially if the United States and its allies put their statecraft at the service of such a scheme.

Third, even if the gradual *détente,* while leading to closer contacts between the two halves of Europe, fails to bring about the departure of Soviet troops from East Europe, the return of the East European nations to the "European Europe" constructed in the West and the reunion of the two Germanies, the scheme would still be worth trying. Not only would it expose and spotlight Soviet hegemony, increase East European impatience with Soviet domination, and raise the costs of Soviet control, it would also give to Western Europe and to its relations with the United States the kind of shape that would help Americans and West Europeans bear the strains of partial frustration—something which the present Alliance does not. West Germany—no longer constrained and ordered about by its quarrelling allies, secure without either dependence or overexposure, participating in basic political and military decisions, and above all engaged in a collective enterprise that would exceed the confines of a common market—would find in a failure to regain unity less reason to resent its allies, and fewer incentives to succumb to disruptive Soviet lures or to engage in spiteful and reassertive nationalism. While I do not believe that in the long run the prolonged division of Europe is really likely without acute tension, the degree at which the tension became intolerable depends entirely on the political context. And the context advocated here would be the one most capable of making the tension manageable. Within the limits set by international trends, there is room for such a thing as vision, will, or statecraft. Nations can live mediocre lives without vision, and the "incremental" adjustment of the *status quo* can prevail over imaginative statecraft. But there is little to be said for perpetuating the frustrations analyzed in this book.

Even if the European Europe remained truncated, the scheme I have outlined would meet the conditions for a return to a moderate international system. Western Europe would be linked with the United States in such a way as to assure the deterrence of aggression from the East, and to "repel" at a relatively low level of violence attacks other than an (unlikely) overwhelming one. The European entity would contribute to what I have called the functional diversification of power—a hierarchy that would not have nuclear weapons or even military power in general as its only yardstick. The scheme suggested takes account of the fact that the purpose of the enterprise is a return to a moderate system in which the use of force, especially nuclear force, would not be the constant theme of international politics. We need a world order in which (paradoxically) the existence of nuclear deterrence will make the acquisition of nuclear weapons less rather than more attractive to states. If this is so, the kinds of arrangements suggested here should help. The place of the European entity in the international hierarchy would be determined not just by its nuclear arsenal, but by its conventional capabilities, its economic and technological resources, its personal skills, etc.

In this European entity, the middle nuclear powers, France and Great Britain, would find occasion for leadership, reward for responsibility, opportunities to act as co-managers of the international system, instead of the solitary rebellion and increasingly ineffective conformism respectively practiced until now. And the European security system would cope with crises within the Continent and help solve disputes among members. Especially in the middle range, diplomatic skills as well as economic resources would be geared to the transformation of the European milieu—i.e., to the goal of reunification—and to possession goals, such as increasing the well-being of the participants and unity for Germany. (This is of special importance at a time when, as Britain well knows and France fears, technological advances in the United States not only produce a "brain drain" but threaten the very existence of certain branches of European industry.) Finally, the condition for harmony and growth of the whole enterprise would be gradual disengagement of the United States and the Soviet Union from the domestic politics of Europe, and the capacity of the Europeans themselves to build an organization with a diversity of national regimes.

The ideas described here obviously make considerable demands of the United States. Instead of pursuing a universal partnership that depends on the emergence of a single European voice, yet hesitating if the voice does not echo America's, the United States would encourage a European entity with which diplomatic and strategic policy over Europe would be shared. The United States would not wait for a United States of Europe, or expect total agreement, or worry if the European alllies concentrated on the reshaping of Europe, or object if their policies in Africa, Asia, and Latin America diverged from the United States'. Instead of expecting priority to be given to the affairs of the "inner sea" of the Atlantic, the United States would accept priority for European reunification. West European unity would be seen as a means to the Continent's full reunification, rather than to the intra-Atlantic partnership. The United States would continue to rely on West Germany but encourage it to give priority to ties with European powers, and to accept a vision of the future that cuts the umbilical cord between the United States and postwar Europe. The United States would shift from asking Europe to share American burdens to sharing the burden of promoting European reunification. Such altruism may appear exorbitant, since the direct beneficiary would be Europe and little direct European solidarity with the United States can be expected in other parts of the world. But it would be justified both because it would ultimately relieve the United States of some of its burdens, and because it would help to establish the kind of world order that is in America's highest interest.

Obviously, all these tasks require skills that have not always shone through American undertakings. The United States cannot do more and do it well. It should do less. In terms of American political culture and style, what has been suggested here requires resignation to less than total solidarity and a "community of fate" with our allies, something in between total leadership and abstention, between monopoly and abdication, a more relaxed approach to time—less frenzy about diversity, and fewer illusions about the speed with which communities can be built. In terms of the American political system, what is required is a capacity to anticipate emergencies, to engage in long-term action, to weave together different strands of policy, to negotiate with other nations without pushing them too hard or expecting the outcome to be their bowing to our wisdom.

It is difficult, but there would be many advantages. Between the nightmare of a centralized NATO plagued by deadlock, dissidence, and evasion, and the chaos of pure bilateralism, room must be found for the kind of scheme that would minimize restraints and restore movement. To preserve the United States' freedom of action without attempting to limit that of other nations; to preserve our relevance to Europe without involving us so deeply as to make both the unity of Western Europe and the reunification of the continent impossible; to preserve the Atlantic Alliance in a still fundamentally bipolar world, but to prepare for a reasonable change of the international system by creating the conditions for a European entity; to accept the inevitable emancipation from the *status quo,* while minimizing the risks; letting go as a form of leadership, using our power so as to minimize the "impotence of power"—this is my proposal and my plea.

\* \* \*

This book has been a long exploration of labyrinths. An international system that encourages diversity but frustrates national dreams, that gives all nations a place in the sun, but no place to go; that showers superpowers with might, but threatens their lives if they throw it around; a national style and political system that reveal a wealth of experiences, beliefs and methods of almost unlimited success within the nation yet of severely restricted effectiveness abroad; an alliance whose early triumphs led to disarray and whose early promise has gone sour—in every case, the road we travelled in order to explore the landscape ended in an impasse. A breakthrough is necessary, and can succeed only if it is global, if it is inspired by a coherent vision, if it exploits existing trends so as to get the international system out of the rut and away from threatening chasms, if it appeals to virtues that our political style and system possess, so as to adapt to the new circumstances our qualities suddenly deprived of their charms, and to discard earlier strengths now turned into weaknesses.

There is a way out of the labyrinth—toward a world that would impede any desire to return to isolation, and check our urge to be the schoolmaster of the world. But it takes a huge effort of political imagination, self-control and self-restraint, the right mixture of vigilance and nonchalance (so as to take neither our friends nor our foes for granted), enough confidence in our own abilities and in those of others to realize that total involvement is not the only form of responsibility, the only alternative to a deluded and dated insulation.

It is a new challenge, the challenge of flexibility and restraint. Is it so different from our customary crusades, our messianic missions, and our pragmatic plans that we shall fail to meet it?

# Index

# COUNCIL ON FOREIGN RELATIONS

*Officers and Directors*

## PUBLICATIONS

FOREIGN AFFAIRS (quarterly), edited by Hamilton Fish Armstrong.

THE UNITED STATES IN WORLD AFFAIRS (annual). Volumes for 1931, 1932 and 1933, by Walter Lippmann and William O. Scroggs; for 1934–1935, 1936, 1937, 1938, 1939 and 1940, by Whitney H. Shepardson and William O. Scroggs; for 1945–1947, 1947–1948 and 1948–1949, by John C. Campbell; for 1949, 1950, 1951, 1952, 1953 and 1954, by Richard P. Stebbins; for 1955, by Hollis W. Barber; for 1956, 1957, 1958, 1959, 1960, 1961, 1962 and 1963, by Richard P. Stebbins; for 1964, by Jules Davids; for 1965 and 1966 by Richard P. Stebbins.

DOCUMENTS ON AMERICAN FOREIGN RELATIONS (annual). Volume for 1952 edited by Clarence W. Baier and Richard P. Stebbins; for 1953 and 1954 edited by Peter V. Curl; for 1955, 1956, 1957, 1958 and 1959 edited by Paul E. Zinner; for 1960, 1961, 1962 and 1963 edited by Richard P. Stebbins; for 1964 by Jules Davids; for 1965 and 1966 by Richard P. Stebbins.

POLITICAL HANDBOOK AND ATLAS OF THE WORLD (annual), edited by Walter H. Mallory.

THE INSECURITY OF NATIONS, by Charles Yost (1968).

U.S. POLICY AND THE SECURITY OF ASIA, by Fred Greene (1968).

NEGOTIATING WITH THE CHINESE COMMUNISTS: The United States Experience, 1953–1967, by Kenneth Young (1968).

AFRICAN ECONOMIC DEVELOPMENT (rev. ed.), by William Hance (1967).

FROM ATLANTIC TO PACIFIC: A New Interocean Canal, by Immanuel Klette (1967).

TITO'S SEPARATE ROAD: America and Yugoslavia in World Politics, by John C. Campbell (1967).

U.S. TRADE POLICY: New Legislation for the Next Round, by John W. Evans (1967).

TRADE LIBERALIZATION AMONG INDUSTRIAL COUNTRIES: Objectives and Alternatives, by Bela Balassa (1967).

THE CHINESE PEOPLE'S LIBERATION ARMY, by Brig. General Samuel B. Griffith II, U.S.M.C. (ret.) (1967).

THE ARTILLERY OF THE PRESS: Its Influence on American Foreign Policy, by James Reston (1967).

ATLANTIC ECONOMIC COOPERATION: The Case of the O.E.C.D., by Henry G. Aubrey (1967).

TRADE, AID AND DEVELOPMENT: The Rich and Poor Nations, by John Pincus (1967).

BETWEEN TWO WORLDS: Policy, Press and Public Opinion on Asian-American Relations, by John Hohenberg (1967).

THE CONFLICTED RELATIONSHIP: The West and the Transformation of Asia, Africa and Latin America, by Theodore Geiger (1966).

THE ATLANTIC IDEA AND ITS EUROPEAN RIVALS, by H. van B. Cleveland (1966).

EUROPEAN UNIFICATION IN THE SIXTIES: From the Veto to the Crisis, by Miriam Camps (1966).

THE UNITED STATES AND CHINA IN WORLD AFFAIRS, by Robert Blum, edited by A. Doak Barnett (1966).

THE FUTURE OF THE OVERSEAS CHINESE IN SOUTHEAST ASIA, by Lea A. Williams (1966).

THE CONSCIENCE OF THE RICH NATIONS: The Development Assistance Committee and the Common Aid Effort, by Seymour J. Rubin (1966).

ATLANTIC AGRICULTURAL UNITY: Is it Possible?, by John O. Coppock (1966).

TEST BAN AND DISARMAMENT: The Path of Negotiation, by Arthur H. Dean (1966).

COMMUNIST CHINA'S ECONOMIC GROWTH AND FOREIGN TRADE, by Alexander Eckstein (1966).

POLICIES TOWARD CHINA: Views from Six Continents, edited by A. M. Halpern (1966).

THE AMERICAN PEOPLE AND CHINA, by A. T. Steele (1966).

INTERNATIONAL POLITICAL COMMUNICATION, by W. Phillips Davidson (1965).

MONETARY REFORM FOR THE WORLD ECONOMY, by Robert V. Roosa (1965).

AFRICAN BATTLELINE: American Policy Choices in Southern Africa, by Waldemar A. Nielsen (1965).

NATO IN TRANSITION: The Future of the Atlantic Alliance, by Timothy W. Stanley (1965).

ALTERNATIVE TO PARTITION: For a Broader Conception of America's Role in Europe, by Zbigniew Brzezinski (1965).

THE TROUBLED PARTNERSHIP: A Re-Appraisal of the Atlantic Alliance, by Henry A. Kissinger (1965).

REMNANTS OF EMPIRE: The United Nations and the End of Colonialism, by David W. Wainhouse (1965).

THE EUROPEAN COMMUNITY AND AMERICAN TRADE: A Study in Atlantic Economics and Policy, by Randall Hinshaw (1964).

THE FOURTH DIMENSION OF FOREIGN POLICY: Educational and Cultural Affairs, by Phillip H. Coombs (1964).

AMERICAN AGENCIES INTERESTED IN INTERNATIONAL AFFAIRS (Fifth Edition), compiled by Donald Wasson (1964).

JAPAN AND THE UNITED STATES IN WORLD TRADE, by Warren S. Hunsberger (1964).

FOREIGN AFFAIRS BIBLIOGRAPHY, 1952–1962, by Henry L. Roberts (1964).

THE DOLLAR IN WORLD AFFAIRS: An Essay in International Financial Policy, by Henry G. Aubrey (1964).

ON DEALING WITH THE COMMUNIST WORLD, by George F. Kennan (1964).

FOREIGN AID AND FOREIGN POLICY, by Edward S. Mason (1964).

THE SCIENTIFIC REVOLUTION AND WORLD POLITICS, by Caryl P. Haskins (1964).

AFRICA: A Foreign Affairs Reader, edited by Philip W. Quigg (1964).

THE PHILIPPINES AND THE UNITED STATES: Problems of Partnership, by George E. Taylor (1964).

SOUTHEAST ASIA IN UNITED STATES POLICY, by Russell H. Fifield (1963).

UNESCO: ASSESSMENT AND PROMISE, by George N. Shuster (1963).

THE PEACEFUL ATOM IN FOREIGN POLICY, by Arnold Kramish (1963).

THE ARABS AND THE WORLD: Nasser's Arab Nationalist Policy, by Charles D. Cremeans (1963).

TOWARD AN ATLANTIC COMMUNITY, by Christian A. Herter (1963).

THE SOVIET UNION, 1922–1962: A Foreign Affairs Reader, edited by Philip E. Mosely (1963).

THE POLITICS OF FOREIGN AID: American Experience in Southeast Asia, by John D. Montgomery (1962).

SPEARHEADS OF DEMOCRACY: Labor in the Developing Countries, by George C. Lodge (1962).

LATIN AMERICA: Diplomacy and Reality, by Adolf A. Berle (1962).

THE ORGANIZATION OF AMERICAN STATES AND THE HEMISPHERE CRISIS, by John C. Dreier (1962).

THE UNITED NATIONS: Structure for Peace, by Ernest A. Gross (1962).

The Long Polar Watch: Canada and the Defense of North America, by Melvin Conant (1962).

Arms and Politics in Latin America (Revised Edition), by Edwin Lieuwen (1961).

The Future of Underdeveloped Countries: Political Implications of Economic Development (Revised Edition), by Eugene Staley (1961).

Spain and Defense of the West: Ally and Liability, by Arthur P. Whitaker (1961).

Social Change in Latin America Today: Its Implications for United States Policy, by Richard N. Adams, John P. Gillin, Allan R. Holmberg, Oscar Lewis, Richard W. Patch, and Charles W. Wagley (1961).

Foreign Policy: The Next Phase: The 1960s (Revised Edition), by Thomas K. Finletter (1960).

Defense of the Middle East: Problems of American Policy (Revised Edition), by John C. Campbell (1960).

Communist China and Asia: Challenge to American Policy, by A. Doak Barnett (1960).

France, Troubled Ally: De Gaulle's Heritage and Prospects, by Edgar S. Furniss, Jr. (1960).

The Schuman Plan: A Study in Economic Cooperation 1950–1959, by William Diebold, Jr. (1959).

Soviet Economic Aid: The New Aid and Trade Policy in Underdeveloped Countries, by Joseph S. Berliner (1958).

NATO and The Future of Europe, by Ben T. Moore (1958).

India and America: A Study of Their Relations, by Phillips Talbot and S. L. Poplai (1958).

Nuclear Weapons and Foreign Policy, by Henry A. Kissinger (1957).

Moscow-Peking Axis: Strength and Strains, by Howard I. Boorman, Alexander Eckstein, Philip E. Mosely, and Benjamin Schwartz (1957).

Russia and America: Dangers and Prospects, by Henry L. Roberts (1956).